As the novel shall reveal, its protagonist has gotten about. Just in work experience, my spirit glided through delivering food, being a deli clerk, an office employee, and at 18 out to sea as a mariner, then soldiering for four years, on to accounting work, then being an auditor, an accountant, and even an English teacher. Through it all, it is my love for music, literature, history, good movies and friendly people which has never terminated. For my happy heart refuses to surrender. Having lived both in Italy and the US, it is the latter which has given me much and taught me plenty, although at times it seems right to question some of our initiatives. Do join me on this wonderful ride as there is never a dull moment and so many incredible tales.

Guy

TAIKI BANSEI

AUSTIN MACAULEY PUBLISHERS
LONDON * CAMBRIDGE * NEW YORK * SHARJAH

Copyright © Guy 2025

All rights reserved. No part of this publication may be reproduced, distributed, or transmitted in any form or by any means, including photocopying, recording, or other electronic or mechanical methods, without the prior written permission of the publisher, except in the case of brief quotations embodied in critical reviews and certain other non-commercial uses permitted by copyright law. For permission requests, write to the publisher.

Any person who commits any unauthorized act in relation to this publication may be liable to criminal prosecution and civil claims for damages.

All of the events in this memoir are true to the best of author's memory. The views expressed in this memoir are solely those of the author.

Ordering Information
Quantity sales: Special discounts are available on quantity purchases by corporations, associations, and others. For details, contact the publisher at the address below.

Publisher's Cataloging-in-Publication data
Guy
Taiki Bansei

ISBN 9798895430941 (Paperback)
ISBN 9798895430958 (Hardback)
ISBN 9798895430965 (ePub e-book)

Library of Congress Control Number: 2025904643

www.austinmacauley.com/us

First Published 2025
Austin Macauley Publishers LLC
40 Wall Street, 33rd Floor, Suite 3302
New York, NY 10005
USA

mail-usa@austinmacauley.com
+1 (646) 5125767

I would like to strongly thank all the workers at Austin Macauley Publishers who have been truly helpful, courteous, and most of all, so understanding. They have made my initiative to publish my book a truly gracious and wonderful experience.

One Late Evening Not So Long Ago...

An awful explosion rocked my head! My sleepy eyes were now fully open contemplating the darkness and roaring commotion around me. I was relieved to discover the howling winds and severe thunder were at some distance and not dancing in my skull.

All those natural forces had just disrupted a most peculiar dream. Off in the distance stood two identical contestants bearing my exact image. But I sensed they were not me as neither one seemed familiar. Their true identities loomed far beyond their shadows. My goodness, they were entrenched in a verbal war, fiercely debating my character and generating such an intriguing sight. Then it finally hit me! In front of me stood the symbols of tragedy and comedy—Melpomene and, to her right, Thalia.

Their presence was bold, confident, and agile. Both had been begging my approval and acceptance in claiming the inherent privilege to present and represent my life story. This seemed rather harmless, so I blessed their initiative. Unfortunately, it was my failure to choose one over the other which had caused their altercation.

Thalia had proposed to use humor and merriment throughout the unfolding tale. She insisted such elements were key to compel an enveloping satire for the audience's pleasure. Fun and hilarity would ultimately deliver the essence of my personal journey and leave all amused rather than bemused. Melpomene would not have any of it. She claimed that while music and joy were humanity's breath of fresh air, its release merely prompted the heart to smooth out life's rough edges. To tarnish such circumstances with comedy would ultimately deceive our soul's natural path and weaken its fabric. Thus, "the heart softens and ultimately distorts the spirit's set course," so she claimed.

Melpomene began to insist life was tragic, but Thalia categorized tragedy as just a brief intermission on our long journey. Melpomene now even praised the art of war. It was deceitful, horrific, and destructive, yes, but the sole remedy to obliterate stalled inherited cultures and their archaic philosophy. Thalia laughed loudly reminding her opponent that it was peace not war which brought harmony and conjured gradual progress while shedding the obsolete in a silent flair.

I stood by helplessly as they continued to battle. My participation seemed irrelevant, although its outcome was heavily centered on my very existence. And it had now apparently been put on hold.

Soon, while viewing all this bickering from afar, a strong feeling of consternation captured my tired eyes, and any attempt to pursue the outcome began to fail. Weariness censored my eyelids and flung me back into a light slumber, but my ears somehow managed to perk up. They refused to miss the finale, and as the duo's blurred image remained slightly in focus, a small bird could now be heard whistling a subtle tune. Such was the melody from nearby. "Life's scars are merely a vestige of the hardships endured." Well, this certainly made sense and required little contemplation. However, almost immediately, a soothing flute replaced the bird's song with "But if you wear your scars well, no one will ever notice them."

Part 1

Chapter 1

I was born by chance, yet I am still here to talk about it. My birth date is December 7, 1953, and my arrival came about at George Elliot Hospital in Nuneaton, which is somewhere east of Birmingham, in England. Destiny would soon reveal that I was born to move. As a matter of fact, it was not long before my departure ensued and so began my odyssey across the face of the earth.

My folks were Italian immigrants who met in a pub. My father was from the southern part of Italy, and his wife from the northeastern part. What brought them together will always remain a mystery. It seems that Dad pawned himself off as an English gentleman that evening, and Mom was mesmerized with everything about him. From what I witnessed as a child and pieced together as an adult, they never got along well, or as one of my relatives so boldly explained some years ago, unless they were in bed. I trust that their marriage came about to accommodate my unwanted arrival.

My father worked as a collier in the mines near Leicester, and my mother was a nanny for a rich family. My mom's dad sent her to work at a young age, and she had been taken in by a well-to-do family who ultimately moved to England. They pursued their interests with her in tow. After the duo's encounter, they saw each other on weekends, then lived together once married yet both struggled in their relationship. My Sicilian father demanded swift obedience and a serious outlook, but his carefree wife loved to joke and entertain those around her. My father threw in the towel when I was a mere three months old.

It was impossible for my mother to make ends meet. But even more disheartening and unthinkable was the idea of returning to her tiny hometown as a married woman with a child but no husband. So, after a bit of investigative work, she discovered my dad's whereabouts. He had returned to his home in the city of Palermo. Soon, we were on a train to become a family unit again, or at least try.

The trip we set out on was a pretty long journey. We left Leicester for Birmingham and then it was on to London where we then crossed the Channel into Paris, France. From there we proceeded to Milano and down the Italian coastline to the tip of Calabria. After crossing over on the ferry to Messina, we finally arrived in Palermo. Mom must have been exhausted! I can't remember if I was too.

My father was shocked and perhaps somewhat devastated by our arrival. Giving this relationship another try might have been part of our agenda, but probably not his. Nevertheless, once explanations came forth, it was my paternal grandmother, Nonna Vincenza, who welcomed us with open arms. It was decided that we would stay.

My Sicilian grandparents had six children. My dad was the oldest at twenty-five, followed by four brothers who were just a few years apart and a sister not quite ten years old. Their house was small, with one large bedroom, and accommodations for the men were situated in the dining/living room area. The bathroom was actually located in the kitchen. Oh, and in the evening, once the day's tailoring work terminated, the dining/living room was strictly reserved for the men to eat. If I am not mistaken the women ate in the tiny kitchen.

What happened next remains a mystery. I have been told different versions over the years. My father could not find steady work, my mom felt rather useless at home, and soon relationships soured all around. After a couple of weeks of this, for some reason, my mother left on her own and returned to her hometown in Northern Italy. Mom had always insisted she was sent away without me, but my Sicilian clan told a different story.

Nevertheless, soon after my mother's departure, I fell terribly ill, and she was sent for via a telegram. A few days later, she arrived but did not stay. My father, mother and I found ourselves on the road, finally a somewhat united family, and we were heading, of all places, to my mother's tiny hometown, Barazzetto.

When this trip ended, a brief but pleasant stay ensued. Life in Northern Italy would be a very joyous affair, although my instincts tended to side with the idea that things could still be somewhat shaky. Intuitively, something warned me that movement would constitute a major part of my personal life's journey.

Now, just so you know, Barazzetto lies east of the city of Udine and south of the lovely town of San Daniele, now famous for its prosciutto and white wines. Today, it remains an itty-bitty town, only now with an ever-shrinking population whose livelihood continues to depend on the vast surrounding farmlands or the nearby city of Udine for work. Oh well, this rural village became my lovely, cozy home for a few years, and it fostered a very happy upbringing.

In those days, most of Europe's economy was not faring so well. Italy was no exception. The devastation of the Second World War had pretty much been cleared away, but the makings of a thriving industrial system were not yet fully in place. To some extent, the urban communities fared better than the agricultural towns, for in the latter area most young people were and had been abandoning their towns for the large cities or simply immigrating abroad.

My folks were in the middle of this predicament. They were also clueless as to what came next regarding their livelihood and their future. Both had good intentions, yet they found it difficult to throw themselves into the scheme of things in the little town of Barazzetto. It was not long before my dad left, and my mom, being pregnant again, was forced to stay put.

By today's standards, our circumstances would not be considered so unusual. However, in those days, especially in Italy, most people frowned upon such untraditional and disruptive ways. It would not be wrong to assume that our family was probably the topic of conversation for miles around.

As in Palermo, the family situation here was also a bit tight. My northern grandparents had six children too. There were four girls and two boys, of which my mom was the second born. Upon our arrival, only the two youngest family members were still present as the others had long ago immigrated to Switzerland.

My grandfather was retired. He had been a carabiniere, and although he enjoyed a decent pension, the man struggled to make ends meet. He provided for his two children and his wife but was also forced to take in my maternal great-grandmother, and now my mother and me. His budget might have been stretched to the limit, yet the farms rendered well, and from what I recall there was always an abundance of delicious food on our dining table.

January 26, 1954, brought a new addition to our family. My brother, Pieri Adriano Di Stefano, was born right there at our home. It was common back then for a midwife to attend to the birth of a child, and my brother was the third person born in that house. So Pieri, named after one of Mom's brothers who had died in childhood, soon became Piero, and it seemed like this family unit was very much at home in our little town. Although a bit tight, for a while everything held steady.

Time rolled by nicely, and Piero and I had become the town's two little darlings. Our neighbors would often take us out on their wagons as they headed to the fields to begin their workday. Everyone was extremely kind to us, and we certainly felt like we were in good hands. Eventually, our Aunt Maria began to include me in all her undertakings. My brother had already attached himself to our grandmother, and they were inseparable.

There is one peculiar detail regarding Piero which needs to be mentioned. From day one until the two of us left our tiny town, my brother was forever crying. My days began with me singing and feeling most happy, whereas he would join me in offering such bitter and painful blues. And no one could ever figure out just exactly what was ailing the lad that led to his constant weeping.

One day, our mom left for Switzerland being assured of finding work. She was actually joining her eldest sister. Of course, we two little ones were now in the custody of our grandparents with our Aunt Maria taking on a greater role as our chaperon. Sometimes we kids were part of a larger group as some of the nearby children were often in the area behind our house.

Our grandfather, Zamparo, was rather tall, and to me, he appeared a giant of a man. He was tough, could easily throw a fit, shout and rant with anyone and everyone, and would not back off. This might have been due to his drinking, which in those days in our little town was a normal everyday affair for most men. Yet with us kids, he remained very affectionate, and I don't recall him ever scolding us.

The man was also the family cook, and a damn good one. Our grandmother preferred to be in the fields rather than at home as kitchen work was the last thing on her mind. Upon entering our front door after a full morning outdoors, there was always an incredible aroma of delicious food wafting throughout the house. Our meals consisted not only of great food but a joyful time together.

Life in our hamlet was just great! We all had very little but loved what we had. Today, one would think our lifestyle rather primitive. There were no vehicles, and everyone got about on foot or bicycle. Folks who were a bit well-off had a scooter, maybe a motorcycle, but no one had a telephone, and the only person who had a television was the priest. Refrigerators, washing machines, and gas ovens were still years away. Please don't ask me what we took to the outhouse because toilet paper was a luxury yet to be discovered.

If you needed water, you went to the well, which was nearby. Everyone washed themselves as best as they could. We two kids received a royal bath twice a year. This ritual was accomplished in a large iron tub which was dragged out and placed in the back of our house. A fire was lit underneath it, and when it seemed the water was just right, we were dunked in and then back out, soaped up, and dunked back in and out again as often as necessary.

Life was simple and the town celebrated its simplicity through the daily grapevine. Everybody knew everyone's business and made it their business to analyze, review, and punctuate every little detail. There were no secrets. But then that is how the town's affairs got ironed out in our friendly little hamlet.

One day, my brother and I experienced one of life's little jolts. It came in the form of an intrusion as we were heading to the sandbox in our kindergarten. Suddenly, a stranger, a very elegant man, picked us up and lifted us both up into his arms. He was all smiles and took us home. The man was tall, a bit stout, very bald, and very handsome. He appeared so happy. This was our father.

The next day, our mom arrived from Switzerland. Our parents were reunited and must have tried to make a go of things, but it just wasn't meant to be. A few weeks later, we four were on the road.

What had gone wrong? It seemed our father was easily agitated. Too often he and our mother had their fair share of verbal fallouts. One day, for whatever reason, things turned ugly as Dad lost his cool and hit Mom. Our grandfather, who was not a person to be taken lightly, got word of it and ordered us all out.

Well, we again boarded a train but with one more member. We headed south to Palermo. Our stay there was a very brief one. A few days after our arrival, we two kids and our mother were back on a train now heading up north to her town. We briefly stopped in the city of Padova, where some of our northern relatives lived, but then resumed our journey home.

We were back! It seemed only right, and the townsfolks also agreed, for in our time with them, my brother and I had become almost like their children. Our mom may have stayed for a few weeks, but she eventually entrusted us to her parents and returned to work in Switzerland.

Chapter 2

One day, I had been invited to ride out to the fields with our neighbors. While heading toward the front door, talking endlessly as usual, I was looking behind me and waving goodbye to my grandparents. My grandfather had left a pail of scalding hot water with cow feed by the front door. Having not properly considered my surroundings, I tripped over it and fell.

My right arm went right into the pail. The screams must have taken the roof off the top of the house. In a flash, my aunt jumped on the family bike and rode off to find the mailman. He was the only person for miles around who had a scooter. Eventually, he arrived and threw me in the back of his vehicle. Off we went to the local doctor in the nearby town of Coseano. I can still recall the doctor pulling skin away as my throbbing arm ached terribly, with me cursing my bloody head off non-stop.

Outside of a few injuries and some occasional minor inconvenience, life for my brother and I was a playful narrative. For the most part, our days were full of fun. Piero now cried a bit less, and we still had very good food, a supportive family, and many simple farmers who cherished us immensely. As most folks knew, our parents became practically nonexistent. Mom did not visit us, nor did she write, and neither did our father, who now worked in America, but at least he sometimes sent a parcel full of nice things like toys, clothes, and anything else he thought could be useful.

My brother and I would refer to our grandmother as mom. She responded like a real mom, always pitching from her heart, and so it became natural for us to think of her as our mother. Perhaps our lives had begun on shaky grounds, but our foundation as young children had settled down gracefully and was surely bound to improve.

Therefore, it was a big surprise when our Sicilian grandfather arrived to take us away. It was grandfather Zamparo who had written to our dad's family in Palermo pleading for a bit of financial help. Maybe the two of us had become somewhat of a burden, and in his last letter to our dad's folks he had basically penned an ultimatum. Either someone sends some money for these kids or come and retrieve them. I have been told that he regretted his rash decision for the rest of his life.

And so, in May of 1958, Piero and I boarded a train again. This time with our paternal grandfather, Giuliano. The man seemed cheerful, yes, but we two kids remained a bit apprehensive. Truth be told, we were scared out of our wits. Our destination was Sicily, the very place we had briefly visited not so long ago, and we would now remain there permanently.

So here we were on another long enduring ride. Ours was an itinerary of "here today, gone tomorrow." We sensed a change coming, but we could not fathom the complete transformation we would soon encounter. It now meant facing a foreign and incomprehensible world. And yet, we two little innocent Friulan children became a couple of Sicilian rascals in no time at all.

Now before continuing, please allow me to introduce a snippet of Italian culture. Every region in Italy has its own dialect, which is practically its own language. Within the country's various regions, the dialects prevailed over the national language, and each one slightly changes a bit from town to town or city to city. It is the core of what makes Italy a country with such different people.

In Barazzetto, we spoke the Friulano dialect. Italian is the national language, but back then, you discovered this only when you started school. The uniqueness of this multi-language culture is that not only do people speak differently, although in close proximity to each other, but they also eat differently, think differently, act differently, and are very quick to point out that difference.

Piero and I were two model Friulan kids. We were well versed in our dialect—Italian or Sicilian were foreign tongues. We loved our local food, and it was polenta, not bread, and red wine which were the daily staple with every meal. Water was something you occasionally used to wash yourself with. We were part of our town's daily activities and much loved and cared for and always spent our entire days outdoors with our neighbors.

I mention this so you may grasp the impact we felt when forced to evacuate our joyous digs. The New World we soon encountered sort of numbed us. I was not yet five, and my brother lagged a year behind me. And with our arrival in Palermo, we immediately stumbled into our first adversity. My brother and I stood in the living room with my dad's immediate family staring down at us. Everyone was present minus our dad and his brother Roberto, who was also in the U.S. We were terribly frightened and slightly frozen in the moment. The spell was soon broken when my brother threw a crying fit and began demanding "aghe".

No one had a clue what this meant. Various attempts were made to shut him up. They offered him cookies, bread, dates, and even tried reasoning with him, but all to no avail. This went on for the longest time until I found the courage to head into the kitchen area and pointed to the faucet. Finally, the poor soul was given a glass of "acqua", and so he rested his case.

Now I can assure you that we were both welcomed and nicely accommodated by our new family. Yet there was an overwhelming silence about us which seemed odd, and I strangely sensed that the homey farmland life we had left behind simply did not exist in our new home. But of course, small children are resilient, and so we managed to get on with things.

The house we lived in had a huge backyard that had been transformed into a stable for the city's horse and buggy service. Every evening the individual owners arrived and went through the process of separating animal from cart and placing the buggy in the designated area.

Those horses faced a wall that had a long curved, concrete shelf where their feed went. In the morning, the process was reversed as driver and horse set out for the area by the train station to assist any newcomers needing to get about. Piero had analyzed the horse feed and discovered it was very tasty. They were sweet but a bit tough to chew, yet they became our favorite snack and we always ate them during our frequent days spent in that yard.

Scattered throughout that area were chickens and baby chicks, and we also had a small goat. My brother and I fell in love with our Uncle Luca's dog, a huge German Shepard. The animal immediately took a liking to us, and we would spend hours brushing him and letting him lick us to death. Our uncle was a hunter and spent most weekends in the mountains, and when he returned from an excursion, he usually had a rabbit or two and various types of birds. There was always a small barbecue in the backyard.

The indoor accommodation had not changed. However, the main and only bedroom had now been slightly altered to accommodate us two. Our grandparents were in their king-size bed in the middle of the room, and there were two single beds on each side propped up against the walls. One bed belonged to Aunt Felicia, the other one was all ours. We slept in the same bed facing opposite directions, which meant Piero's feet were in my face and he had mine to contend with. A bit annoying, yes, but who were we to complain?

You may not believe this, but we soon forgot Barazzetto. The two of us hardly had any recollection of our loving grandparents, our wonderful aunt, and those caring neighbors. And gone with them was our Friulan dialect. This came about so quickly because there was no relationship between the two families and means of communication were barren here too. Our past was a world far behind us, and it hardly left a trace of its origins.

We two kids were immediately indoctrinated into the family ritual. Our Sicilian grandmother was a strict disciplinarian. It was her religion. I must now reveal an incredible and horrendous fact but allow me to emphasize something. Never have I held a grudge or any bad feelings toward the woman. By the way, she lived to the ripe age of ninety-four, and may God bless her little heart wherever she may be!

Nonna Vincenza believed beatings were good for you. All her children, except Roberto, had been severely hit any time they stepped out of line, or whenever she deemed it necessary, which was too often. This was simply a prescribed medicine she administered punctually and skillfully, and we newcomers were certainly no exception to her cure-all regimen.

Just what did her compact therapy consist of? There were no limits to her antics. She attacked violently and continued until she had completely exhausted her enraged madness. It always began with stinging slaps to the face and head, pinching our arms, pulling our hair, and kicking. We would always get thrown to the floor where she got on top of us and continued in an even greater frenzy.

We were also bitten sometimes. And if there was a belt nearby, it obviously offered more efficiency with less effort. Until her anger terminated, there was no letting up, and it did not matter how much we screamed, shouted, and begged for mercy. There was no finale until the very end, which was never brief. Oh, let me not forget to mention that no one ever dared to intervene.

Today, such a barbaric act would be shut down immediately. Nevertheless, in our household, this was the standard procedure to set right from wrong. My poor brother who looks so much like our mother, a person not particularly seen well in our new dwellings, got hit more often and perhaps even more fiercely.

Sometimes our grandmother felt a need to ensure a proper balance. She did not want to give the impression of favoritism. So, although I might not have done anything wrong at that moment, surely there were a few instances she had overlooked. This certainly justified setting the record straight and evening the score, and therefore a proper beating for me was in the making. This is how our new household cleaned its laundry. Such was life in the big city, and we remained part of it until our departure a few years later.

Chapter 3

Our grandfather was a barber by profession and a chatterbox by nature. He was well-liked by all he came in contact with, and the list was rather long. He seemed to have a kind word for everyone and spent plenty of time analyzing whatever topic was in discussion. When not busy attending to his customers, he enjoyed doing crossword puzzles.

I sometimes dropped by his place, and he would take a run to the nearby coffee shop for an espresso. If he could not get away, I went to order his coffee, and very quickly a delivery boy would arrive with a tray and a cup of espresso covered by a saucer. Grandfather Giuliano would send it down so quickly and always belted out a loud groan of satisfaction.

He was very kind and had taken an immediate liking to me. I suspect it was not just because I was the first grandson to carry his name. His shop was less than a quarter mile from where we lived. Across the street from the shop there was a large garden which he cultivated with much love and care. There were fruit trees, different flowers, and rows of vegetables. He tended to everything there as if they were his little children.

What I still remember is the tender juicy red tomatoes, which were so delicious. Also, the pleasant fragrance of basil grabbed my attention, and my grandfather encouraged me to eat it raw, insisting it was good for me. Yet, the most exciting thing there was lifting a wooden board which allowed water to then flow through various ditches to irrigate everything. Soaking my feet in it was one of my favorite treats.

Uncle Roberto, the second brother in line, had moved to the U.S. to join our dad. He was often mentioned, particularly how he had worked his fingers to the bone sewing and mending clothes alongside his mother. Work came mostly from small family-owned firms which needed clothing perfectly stitched and that is what they got. From hearsay, it seemed like the duo worked and sang together in perfect harmony.

With his departure, the other three brothers enjoyed a bit more space when the living room was converted back to a bedroom late in the evening. Soon Uncle Andrea, the youngest but tallest of the bunch, was called into military service and was gone. Now the remaining two uncles had even more legroom for themselves.

Uncle Luca soon came into his own. He transformed our backyard into a shop. The city cemetery was close by, and the dying business had never been better. The horses and buggies got replaced by lots of marble and machines of all kinds. In no time at all, there was a thin veil of white dust everywhere, a daily humming of tools, and customers coming and going. Of course, this was a minor inconvenience considering how quickly the business took off and continued to grow.

Uncle Nicola opened a printing press business in the city center. He once took me to work with him, and the sound of those machines rattling away and spitting out little cards, notes, and other paper items did not impress me very much. It was after taking me to the nearby coffee shop where the rich aroma hit my nostrils and brought me to life. The first café-latte, outside of our home, satisfied my taste buds so wonderfully that returning to that loud war room no longer bothered me so much.

Our aunt was the youngest member of our new family. She pretty much kept to herself and was very strongly taken in by her religion. Her nose was always buried in the Bible, at times for entire days. Eventually, through minor efforts and a little persuasion, she brought religion into my life. I was quickly converted and became a strong believer myself. I must admit, however, it was something which did not last very long.

I have very little recollection of Uncle Andrea. He entered the military, and once discharged and back home, he found work with the phone company. Our aforementioned grandmother, on the other hand, made a strong impact on us two kids. She was a short wiry woman with nerves of steel, quick as a cat, and had the inner energy of an erupting volcano. Always clad in black, she offered a solemn and serious side of herself. Yet on some occasions, she did smile and enjoyed a fun moment, as long as it was just a moment.

One peculiar detail regarding her disciplinary code of ethics bears mentioning. At the end of any beating session, no matter how severe the lesson meted out, and most were triple A quality, she always embraced and kissed us. This would bring us out of our state of shock and back to some level of normalcy. She would remind us, in case we had forgotten, that the beatings had been for our own good. We certainly accepted this at face value and were more than happy to just move on.

Our grandmother's immediate family lived close by and consisted of her mother, a brother and sister. We hardly ever saw any of them. Our great-grandmother appeared ancient and had difficulty making use of her senses. Sometimes we two boys stopped by her house, and she appeared taken in with us. She would hug us and insist on stating we were fine children.

Nadia, our grandmother's sister, was a spinster and took care of her mother. There was also Benevento, who was our grandmother's only brother, and the man was pure seriousness incarnate. He was married to a very quiet woman, had a very quiet daughter our age, and they all lived quietly close by. This is as much as I recall regarding the outer family nucleus.

My grandfather's family was practically nonexistent. With the exception of a brother who once visited from Livorno, we knew nothing about any of them. Oh well, this was the Di Stefano household, and we two resided in its bosom. Life in the town of Barazzetto was like one big family, whereas in Palermo, we practiced complete independence. We were a unit unto ourselves and never had company or visitors call on us. No one ever came by to celebrate a holiday or simply pay a visit. As a matter of fact, I do not remember ever celebrating much of anything.

Moving on! Another issue that plagued us two newcomers was the absence, or so it appeared, of the opposite sex. In Palermo, I quickly noticed that girls were nowhere to be seen. It was customary back then and a strict rule for them to leave the home only with their immediate family members or relatives, but never alone or with friends. They obviously seldom got out. Their existence was discovered upon starting elementary school, but we only got a glimpse of the opposite sex when they headed home after school, well chaperoned, of course.

Our school was partitioned with boys on the east side of the building and girls on the west. No one ever considered crossing that line for it was a serious offense, quite sacrilegious perhaps. We boys did not show much interest in them or ever made them the topic of our conversations. No, sir, it was almost as if they lived on a planet of their own.

While walking home or going to school, we caught sight of some girls. Almost all of them covered their head and face with a handkerchief. Just like when they were in church. It was as if they were not allowed to reveal too much of themselves. At first, this seemed a most sinister thing to us two newbies, but it soon no longer appeared so odd, for we simply got about and accepted our new environment.

A few years flew by quickly. Piero and I were now quite at home in our new digs. We spent a lot of time in the backyard, which was busy producing tombstones and mausoleums, but we found a bit of room to play in. All about us were pieces of scrap material of some sort, and although our uncle was reluctant to have us there, we kept busy with the items therein. One of our first works of art was a pair of wooden swords, which made us feel artistically accomplished.

A worker for our uncle had given us a few pieces of wood he had trimmed down. One was thin and long, and so we cut it into two pieces. Using sandpaper, we smoothed out the edges and then chiseled down a point. We carved out a fine handle on the opposite end, and to add a worthy touch, we topped the handle by nailing a flat piece of wood to create a cross-like finish.

Our new weapons kept us busy most of the day. However, once we tired of being pirates, we would run off to raid the fruit trees nearby. They were not far from our house and stood behind a tall wall which separated the hospital grounds from the main street. The wall went all the way up to the cemetery area by my grandfather's shop, but we had discovered a spot where an abandoned iron gate, which had once been the main entrance to the hospital, was located.

Climbing the gate was easy. It gave us access to a few fig trees loaded with ripe, white figs. My, there is nothing more delicious than a fig ready to plop from its branch. It is sweet and light and the perfect fruit to eat right there on the spot. The only slight drawback was walking away with such sticky hands.

Often, after dining off these treats, we would quickly shut down our operations there and head off in the opposite direction. Near our grandfather's shop was a railroad crossing, and along the railroad tracks were an infinite number of bushes full of blackberries. They were so easy to pick, and when ripe, they were just as tasty and addictive as those figs. We would pick and eat berries till our hearts were content and headed home a bit full, bearing sticky red hands and purple lips. It was a mystery to us two how our grandmother always knew what we had been up to.

Chapter 4

It was the early 1960s, and mom and dad came for a brief visit but not together. They had never parted amicably, even when they last separated, nor had they agreed on how to provide for our welfare or who would take care of us. We were now with our dad's folks having been brought there on a spur of the moment decision.

My recollection of mom's visit is not so great, but she did come with our Aunt Maria. I do remember sitting on the couch between them and hugging my aunt while barely speaking to my mother. This may have been due to her long absence, or simply because of the unpleasant things which were now being said about her when her name came up. At times, Piero and I believed she had abandoned and completely forgotten us.

Our dad arrived a few months later. He came with so many nice things, especially clothes from America. There were t-shirts with strange names stamped on them, like Yankees, and even one with a picture of a reindeer called Bambi frolicking in the grass. There were also shoes, pants, shirts, bathing suits, not to mention some very delicious chocolate which was immediately confiscated and regularly rationed out by our very diligent grandmother. Our dad seemed very generous and loving toward us.

My father was up early and had a habit of disappearing and returning punctually for lunch. Sometimes he arrived holding a fairly flat rectangular green paper package that contained fresh cannoli. What joy this unexpected gesture was to us two kids, and these considerate treats reminded us that life in Palermo had much improved from those first few dark days just after arriving.

One afternoon, my father took me to an amusement park. Coincidentally, we ran into a beautiful woman, or perhaps they had planned to meet. I was still a child, but my superior instincts sensed something was up, for their happy smiles and roving eyes said it all. I cowered behind my dad and began insisting we leave immediately. I even started calling the young lady "tinta", which is Sicilian for "evil" or "wicked." She, of course, smiled at me and tried to caress my head, but there was a look in her eyes that appeared to be holding back a few poisoned arrows ready to be launched my way.

My dad paid little attention to me. His eyes were all over the attractive woman, and they spoke volumes. Well, so much for trying to do the right thing, and at such an early age. It was a few days after this incident that our father simply vanished as he left for the U.S., and we would not see him again until we two joined him some years later.

Chapter 5

At school, I was a dunce. My days were spent daydreaming and envisioning being with a beautiful woman who smothered me in love. When not being devotedly loved, then Giuliano was leading men in battle and had no fear whatsoever. And as far as my scholastic interests went, they were practically nonexistent, unless the topic was history.

That subject always brought me back to life. The descriptions of Greece and Rome, which were my main staple in class, were the only things which kept me awake. As soon as the subject changed, my mind flew off somewhere and never returned unless the teacher called on me, which not only startled me some but also slightly annoyed me a bit.

Sometimes the teacher would march down to my desk, ruler in hand, and very calmly try to instill a sense of responsibility in me. He would accuse me of being evasive and just plain rude. Considering the beatings at home, this trivial punishment seemed amateurish. Nevertheless, it was only right to feign a bit of painful discomfort. After all, a little respect goes a long way.

Besides history, there was only one other thing I truly enjoyed—the school snack. Breakfast at home was simply a cup of café-latte, and so it was a long day to lunch. My stomach was much relieved when an assistant teacher arrived around ten thirty, pushing a small cart loaded with sandwiches. It was full of baguettes, cut into small pieces and filled with chocolate, marmalade, or canned tuna.

It was a pleasant sight, for sure, but there was never enough food to feed the entire class. We were divided into two groups, and we could only eat on alternate days. My favorite treat was the tuna sandwich, dripping in olive oil. It was so delicious. And then came the one with chocolate, whereas marmalade did not quite meet my fancy. Although you would never have guessed it from the way I scarfed down anything in front of me.

School days were Monday through Saturday, but at least they let us out at twelve. My brother and I would head home for lunch. After that, both of us were pretty much on our own to go out to play. However, being the oldest kid, I bore some responsibility for there were several daily chores that awaited me. My first and primary task was getting lunch to my grandfather.

Our grandmother would cover a pasta bowl containing that day's specialty with a regular flat dish. The entire contraption was wrapped in a large cloth napkin and tied with a bow on top. I simply took hold of this portable meal and ran off to his shop. The man was always glad to see me until he had looked at the contents in the pasta dish. Then came the usual remark, "This again." I quietly waited for him to scarf down the unwanted contents and would then head home with neatly wrapped empty dishes. Occasionally, there was a bit of extra change for me for my diligent service.

The next errand was not a high priority on my agenda. About four in the afternoon, it was on to a small, old, stinky barn close to my grandfather's shop to get our daily dosage of fresh milk. Being inundated with cow dung, the stench of that place was fierce, and it also seemed like all the flies and insects in the city dwelled within those confines. As a rather picky and clean-cut kid, stepping inside that shithole was never an easy task. At times, I even tried holding my breath once inside, but this never worked. A few seconds later I was forced to come up for air. Filthy and nasty air. Well, it seemed to me the faster I got out of there, the better off I was.

This chore once got me into some serious trouble. Nonna Vincenza would always hand me an empty wine bottle which had been thoroughly washed and rinsed. It came with me and was eventually handed to the milk lady, a short plump woman who smelled no better than her surroundings. She would stick that bottle under the cow, do some quick massaging, and presto, she would hand it back full of milk.

On my way home, it was sometimes impossible to bypass the area where my friends were playing soccer. How could one pass up an invitation to compete? So, unfortunately, I would forget that my grandmother was anxiously awaiting my return to boil that milk. She, of course, did not. These incidents did not happen frequently, but one fine day, she put an end to my insubordination.

Before leaving home and heading off to the barn, she ordered me to strip down to my underwear. Yes, my entire body was now covered only by my underwear, and an empty bottle was in my hand. Why, she even took my shoes away so I would definitely get the message. Her strategy was to get me home in a heartbeat. And believe me, it certainly worked.

The kid in me was totally mortified. I cried desperately all the way to that stinky farm and back. My agony was so great that the overwhelming stench from cows, cow owner, and cow crap never penetrated my nostrils. Sure enough, on the way there and back home, people on the street began to stare at me. A few kids pointed, laughed, and immediately spread the word. A few others had some unkind things to say about me.

It was not a pretty sight, to say the least. Being a sensitive and proud little boy, this disgraceful spectacle not only pierced my heart, but it also isolated me for days. I did not venture outdoors after school for quite some time. Playing soccer was certainly on hold.

Time heals all wounds, and I soon forgot the unusual and cruel punishment, but as a precaution, it seemed wise to anticipate my grandmother's tactics. It was better to think ahead and prepare for the unpredictable as that tough old woman had plenty of tricks up her sleeve, and I for one would unfortunately see a few more.

Oh, by the way, my last daily chore occurred in the early evenings. It was buying a precious commodity, our daily bread. Around six or thereabout, I returned home from the bakery holding a large brown paper package neatly tied with thin string. Believe me, there is nothing tastier than fresh Sicilian bread. It was impossible to not put the package up to my nose to let the fragrance warm my heart. Then once home, it was my duty to beg for a tiny piece. Now had I worked in that bakery, for sure the owner would have seen little or no profits.

Chapter 6

Our neighborhood was located on a busy street. We lived close to the main entrance to the hospital and not far from the cemetery. Cars were plentiful and there was much traffic. Sometimes in the late afternoon, it got terribly noisy but for different reasons. A local street vendor would invade our area proudly yelling at the top of his lungs, "Cacoccioli, cacoccioli, pigliatevi sti cacoccioli!"

It almost sounded like a call to prayers coming from a minaret. Instead, he was peddling artichokes and inciting the local populace to come get them. We hardly ever indulged in this sort of food as our grandmother saw to all our culinary needs. And while our meals were nicely organized and well-prepared, lunch was not something to write home about. At noon every day, there was a dish of pasta and a pitcher of water on the table.

My grandmother was a wizard at preparing the perfect condiment for each pasta dish. There was pasta with zucchini, marinara sauce, meat sauce, peas, ricotta, garlic and olive oil, sardines, and anything else she got her hands on. Dinner consisted of fresh bread, olives, and maybe some cheese or sliced boiled ham. There was always a huge bowl of salad, which we ate last. Occasionally, Uncle Luca brought home some thin steaks which were grilled in the backyard over wood trimmings. Sausage was a rare but tasty treat prepared in a tomato sauce that got scooped up with that fresh crispy bread.

Every Friday, we ate fish, as required by our Catholic faith. Various types of fish garnered our dinner table in abundance on this day. My favorite one was a thin burger-like fried concoction made from tiny baby fish the size of toothpicks. And when we had tuna or sword fish, something called "a cippuddata" would be sprinkled over it. This required some onion slices slightly sautéed and then topped with a pinch of white vinegar, creating a sweet and sour taste. Nothing ever remained in anyone's dish. In those days, and in our dwelling, it would have created quite a stir.

We only drank water from the faucet. Soda was not yet popular, but one evening, our grandfather came home with a soda kit. It was an empty liter glass bottle with a special cap attached, and there were two small vials and a colorful small packet. He poured in the liquid from the vials and the powder from the packet, added water, and then shook the bottle rigorously. We loved this new sinister novelty called soda, and for some reason, we only drank orange-flavor soda and never tried the others, but no one ever complained.

Our grandfather religiously allowed himself a glass of red wine with dinner. In summer, when peaches were abundant, he would slice one up and casually drown the pieces in the wine before consuming them. It was a personal dessert and the last part of the meal which he seemed to cherish wholeheartedly.

While eating dinner, the man always got a brief grilling from his wife. It was usually over some issue or another. To me it seemed that Nonna Vincenza enjoyed being a bit hostile with the tired but rather happy soul. Of course, I had innocently assumed this was the natural state of affairs between husband and wife, but it would be many years later that my grandmother's somewhat hostile reasoning came to light. It was over a family secret that everyone knew but never spoke about.

The incident had occurred during the Second World War. Italy was getting battered from the Allied bombing campaign. Both the U.S. and England pounded most large Italian cities almost daily, and it was in the middle of this madness that our grandfather did the unthinkable—he abandoned his family and ran off with another woman. Consequently, our dad, still a young teenager, became the head of the family. One evening, he miraculously saved everyone. As the sound of planes flying overhead planted fear in mother and children, and the destruction caused by exploding bombs nearby seemed to edge closer and closer, the new man of the house intuitively sensed danger.

He plead with his mother for them to leave the house and seek shelter in the countryside. His insistence angered her, and she slapped his face to quiet him, but, suddenly, as she paced back and forth with her daughter Felicia in her arms, while the other four children were hiding behind a couch, my father snatched the baby out of her hands and took off running like the very devil.

His mother immediately ran after him, and the others followed her. And run they did. My father did not stop or slow down until he and his followers eventually found themselves in the fields on the edge of the city's borders in a wooded area. They did not return home until the following day, and very little of the house was left standing.

And just so you know, the merciless bombardment was just as devastating as the famine which everyone faced. Our dad, who had now inherited his father's role as the neighborhood barber, also became the provider of food. Funds were never sufficient to feed seven people, and so the young lad had no choice but to improvise to make ends meet. He and his best friend began stealing anything and everything which could bring in some cash to purchase food.

Eventually, our grandfather's escapade terminated. Believe it or not, the man found the courage to return home. He must have faced a lot of despairing and bitter eyes, and without a doubt, I am quite sure our grandmother never forgave him. Something tells me that our dad never accepted the idea that this man, whose role he had gallantly taken up, was so easily allowed back into the family fold.

Chapter 7

Uncle Luca had become an excellent mason but also a bit of an architect. He had found his true passion in this trade, and his shop, the backyard of our house, was supplying the city cemetery with headstones, tombstones and eventually even some unique mausoleums. He would spend hours cutting marble alongside his men and took such pride in the finished product. At times, he would even make something useful for our house.

Our uncle always showed such generous and kind concern for my brother and me. He often took us out, and how can I ever forget my first hunting trip? Facing a very quiet and dark world at about 5:00 a.m. was not exactly my cup of tea back then, but having no choice in the matter, I was up and ready to go. The intent was to get to the mountains early and leave before the sun would slow us down and render life miserable.

Once there, my dilemma was in keeping up with the man. He did not walk but simply glided over some rough, rocky terrain which was tough for me to tackle. Keeping up was rather impossible, and at some point, I must have just given up. Yet my uncle kept moving, and the hunter had a great day. We returned home with dozens of birds. One had adorable dark and yellow-colored feathers, and as it was in perfect condition, it was sent to be stuffed the very next day.

On another occasion, Uncle Luca took us to a soccer match. The game was fun to play, but seeing it done by professionals was a totally wild and somewhat worrying experience. That day we three witnessed our home team, Palermo, bring the city a bit of glory. Almost immediately, once we sat on the concrete seats, seeing and hearing the local fans go into such an uncontrollable state of delirium was a bit shocking. It sounded like that continuous uproar, bellowing throughout the entire stadium, only died down when the final whistle was blown.

I sat there a bit on edge, perhaps even slightly concerned. The constant choral chanting, loud whistling, and enthusiastic cursing were just too much to hear. Of course, being no angel, a fair share of insults and curse words were part of my vocabulary, but here the anger was expressed with such a wild frenzy, which was rather bizarre and was totally incomprehensible to me. How was it possible that everyone around me knew the referee's mother, and could she possibly have entertained that many people?

Chapter 8

We two brothers had been inseparable from day one. Piero's day one of course. Yet, after becoming quite at home in Palermo, we slowly began to part ways. It is hard to say just why. Anyhow, I began to spend more time with my own friends. On one occasion, there were five of us in our favorite place, the hospital grounds.

Truth be told, that area was supposedly off-limits to us. However, once we discovered we could sneak in through a gap in the iron bar fence right across the street from my grandfather's shop, it was impossible to keep us out. Just why we chose to play in this grassy area behind some of the hospital buildings, well, who can say.

And one thing which truly fascinated us kids always occurred on Wednesdays. One of the buildings housed the hospital's incinerator, and as the trash was religiously burned that day, we could hear these popping sounds which sounded like gun-shots. It was light bulbs which had been discarded with the overall waste, or so we were told. Consequently, on that day, we never missed the pop entertainment.

It was on a Thursday that we were playing a game of tag. Suddenly, those explosive sounds occurred quite unexpectedly. Our curiosity demanded an immediate inspection, and to our surprise, there was no trash being burned anywhere. This was a puzzling narrative we four kids could not explain, and no matter how much we argued, no one's theory satisfied anyone. Soon, we decided to call it quits and parted ways.

Two of us headed toward the iron bar fence. The other kids would walk on the hospital grounds and exit through the main gate as they lived close to that area. Once through the fence, my intention was to stop at my grandfather's shop for a small chat. While squeezing myself through the bars, a gruesome scene stood out. A few feet away, a man was lying in the middle of the street with a large pool of blood around his head. His bicycle laid by him, and his sunglasses were next to his face. This frightened me, which is why I tried my best to not look in that direction.

Just as strange was the fact that the area all around me was like a ghost town. Every store had closed, and every store owner had simply vanished. I eventually discovered that my grandfather had taken himself to the main hospital building to cater to those patients who could not make it to his shop. Something he continued doing for years to come. And it was the courageous plump milk lady who took some action as she lived next to her barn. She walked over to where the man lay to cover him with a bed-sheet and then retreated to her digs.

I bolted home. Once at my uncle's shop, there was an ongoing discussion between several workers regarding the incident. The victim was the guard at the cemetery and apparently was on his way home for lunch. He was on the opposite side of the road in front of my grandfather's shop when a car had pulled up alongside him. It stopped, and someone got out from the back, aimed a shotgun, and fired.

The incident led to all the stores being evacuated. It was a respected old code that you did not talk to the police. One of my uncle's workers was referring to something as "la vendetta," a killing to avenge some incident. Some months back, it was the guard who had shot and killed a young lad in the cemetery grounds late at night. He had been caught stealing, or so the guard claimed. It would be many years later before I finally found out the real story. For now, it was time to return to playing.

Chapter 9

City life suited me well. When not in school or playing with my friends or with Piero, I would run errands to earn a few coins. If my uncle or his workers needed cigarettes, it was my pleasure to run to the tobacco shop and purchase a pack or even individual ones when they were low on funds. Yes, you could simply buy cigarettes in any quantity, and no one thought much about it.

The shop-owner would open a pack, unless one was already open, place the loose cigarettes in a small sheet of newspaper, and then seal it up properly. There were no questions asked. He knew me to be an honest kid, and there was a trust system which served everyone well and rendered life easy and convenient all around. I took hold of my merchandise, and my legs carried me back to my customers pronto.

Upon returning to the shop, I confronted an area full of street vendors practicing their art. These folks were operating push-carts full of fruits and vegetables or other items. They worked the morning shift and were usually done by one. Everyone's task consisted of first yelling to the masses indoors to inform them of their sales. The interested clientele, all busy housewives and some elderly widows, would come to their balconies. If in need of something, they lowered a small light round wicker basket.

All transactions were agreed upon verbally and loudly before the basket was sent down. After the usual friendly bargaining, cash was provided in the basket, and then the merchandise and any change due went up to the satisfaction of the folks on the receiving end. If there was an issue which needed to be ironed out regarding a past purchase, this had already been attended to, and it probably led to a discount, and so less money being lowered; that is, if the customer had insisted enough.

On some occasions, my uncle's workers would let me accompany them to the cemetery. A couple of guys pulled a low but large cart loaded with heavy marble slabs. All the necessary tools were in buckets and neatly stacked on that cart. Once at the site, all those items from the buckets were used to create what would ultimately become a decorative tombstone, a personal small temple beautifying the premises, the sacred resting grounds of someone's lost ones.

While watching those workers make everything come together, it touched me intimately to recognize that this was art in the making. My uncle would soon arrive to oversee the entire process. At times, he participated if necessary. I would not leave until the final touch was added, no matter how long it took. Once finished, the workers and I would eventually ride the cart back as the road leading to the cemetery was all downhill.

It would be sacrilegious to not mention the gentleman known as "il professore". Literally translated it means "the professor," and maybe he slightly resembled one, as he was an elderly white-haired and bespectacled man who appeared the picture of serenity. Now, this genius, who came to work at my uncle's shop twice a week, could take a piece of stone and make it come alive. His final products looked like something destined for a museum, and he never seemed to tire, even after several days, of perfecting what appeared like his personal toy.

His angels were not just angelic. They seemed ready to step out to save all humanity. The Madonna-like statues appeared to be a unique class of women onto themselves. And please forgive me if you consider this blasphemous, or plain filthy, but they radiated the same glow of beauty as that woman I very often thought of in my classroom.

In my eyes, that sculptor was simply a genius. For hours, he chiseled away and would sometimes stop to light a cigarette, place it on his lips, and never touch it again. That's right. Somehow, he could inhale and exhale while delicately and slowly carving and smoothing out an area on the stone. The ash would continue to get longer and eventually dropped to the ground. He kept to his trade on that stone, as if nothing at all were attached to his lips.

This was an incredible feat, a sort of miracle. And something within little old me persisted in claiming he certainly deserved some kind of award, like maybe a Nobel Prize or something similar. After all, those whose hands are busy decorating life while not even thinking about themselves deserve some kind of recognition.

Chapter 10

There was a candy store not too far from where we lived. It sat in the middle of a roundabout right in front of the hospital's main entrance. It appeared a bit isolated, and it was not such a fancy shop, but my feet carried me there often to try to win a raffled toy.

You had to be careful when crossing the street to get to it. The wild and reckless drivers not only had no respect for traffic laws, assuming they knew them, but also dictated who moved, how quickly, and when. Pedestrians enjoyed only one right of way, choosing the right moment to dash across the street and hope to make it.

My objective? To win a most enchanting plastic toy—a blue stagecoach. It had four white horses pulling it and two cowboys mounted on top, one holding the reins, the other a shotgun. Oh, how many coins were spent there on that eluding but much desired coach. Once again, having come into some change, I had run off, for walking was not my cup of tea. Actually, my task was to get to the bakery first and buy bread, yet some inner impulse had decided to give my hands a chance to win that sacred gift.

While running across the street a car hit me. I soon came to and looked up, and there was a circle of faces staring down at me. Everyone looked terrified. I was too, but for a completely different reason. Now please do not laugh, but I must descend from the line of the great Odysseus. In less than a second, a plan was formulated and pushed me into action. If I could get to the bread store and back home before news of my misfortune arrived, I was probably safe, and maybe, just maybe, nothing would happen to me.

I jumped up and bolted like a rabbit! Believe me, the folks around me must have been shocked watching a departed one sprint off like nothing had happened. In no time at all, the baker handed me the neatly tied package of bread, allowing me to dash off again like a madman. It was my positive energy which sped me homeward, all along hoping my plan would work. It was not to be. Once close to our dwellings, there was my grandmother standing by the front entrance, waiting for me.

The moment the woman spotted me she made an unpleasant and rather ugly gesture. She put her hand in her mouth and insinuated biting down on it. For you non-Sicilians, this simply meant I was a dead man—I mean kid. That is why yours truly stopped running, started crying, and slowed down to almost a crawl, which might have angered her even more. Knowing what was in store for me had me shaking like a leaf, and tears were racing down my face. There was nothing left to do but enter and face my execution. Once inside, all hell broke loose.

Chapter 11

Piero and I had been in Palermo for several years at this point. We were now steeped in Sicilian culture. We both spoke the Sicilian dialect like true natives, enjoyed the delicious southern cuisine and the culinary street food, and we had obviously developed a local outlook, especially regarding members of the opposite sex.

For as long as anyone could remember, it was the male members of the family who provided for their loved ones. The idea of women going to work was simply not accepted. Please understand, this is not to say women were not employed at jobs. They were now beginning to join the workforce, but old ideas are hard to change, and for some reason, it just did not seem right. As a matter of fact, it was strongly frowned upon.

There were other issues just as provocative for us male members of the human species, including a woman's attire being indicative of her character. The more of her body a female showed, the less pure she was deemed to be. It had been so for ages, and it was inconceivable to think this point of view was somehow wrong.

One of the girls in our neighborhood was often seen walking with her mother. She was never completely veiled. That is, wearing a handkerchief to cover her hair and the sides of her face. It was a custom that was losing importance, but my few friends found it not only wrong, but totally unacceptable. Some of their friends, the more radical element, had labeled her "una puttana."

To me, she seemed quite pretty but a bit too tall to be my dream girl, yet sometimes, my inquisitive mind wondered if she could possibly be the one. The very one whose daily entry into my daydreams kept me hoping such a person existed, and that one day we would casually meet. After all, my school curriculum had not changed one iota.

Oh well, it was in this time, and while bragging about a lucky goal I had scored the day before, when Piero appeared. He informed me we needed to get home quickly because our mother had just arrived. Don't ask me why, but neither of us felt a need to rush as our mom had become someone from our past, and her rightful title had been given to our grandmother.

Anyhow, parked in front of our house was a new spotless convertible. As we usually entered through the back door, we were forced to cross the shop, and immediately we both sensed the workers looking at us a bit suspiciously. They were whispering among themselves, and they appeared a bit disgusted with us. One of them continued to stare at us.

Inside the house, we found Uncle Luca and Roberto, who had recently returned from America. They were in the living room, and on the larger of the two couches was our mother with another woman. Our grandmother and aunt were in the kitchen. However, Nonna Vincenza instantly joined us taking hold of our hands and guiding us into the living room, acting like one of the three wise men come bearing gifts.

Now our mother is a tall woman and so was her friend, but what immediately stood out was the modern clothing they both wore—short skirts and tight blouses. Their well-stocked chests and long, finely curved, and shapely legs stood out quite a bit, to say the least. The scene among the workers in the yard now made sense, making me feel even more put out than before, and it was quite tough going over to kiss our mother.

We two kids, the center of discussion, were made to sit next to the two women. We both remained at a loss as to what to do. A few words came out slowly from both parties, our mother and our uncles. After a while it felt like time stood still, but then some talk began again, and wouldn't you know it—the unthinkable, according to us two witnesses, was being boldly discussed.

Uncle Roberto, who seemed a bit put out, had raised his voice. He stated most emphatically, "We have no money to give you. But these are your children, and if you want them, we can prepare their things in a few seconds." It was like a slap in the face. This tune completely shocked me and put me on the verge of tears. Was it possible that we were being offered up in a bargaining session?

Before their conference terminated, my legs carried me away. There was only one person who could save us, and so once at my grandfather's shop, my tears poured out uncontrollably. Then, like a skilled lawyer, my pleading with the barber in front of me demanded he intervene on our behalf. After all, we two just wanted to stay put, and then even more tears came.

My grandfather took me in his arms and patted me on the head as he spoke softly. He smiled and assured me we would never leave. So, we two remained in the barber shop until closing time, and he chatted away with me, for few customers were to be seen. He was quite an entertainer. We walked home hand in hand that evening, me feeling very safe and quite relieved.

Chapter 12

History was being made in the Di Stefano household. Although I am uncertain which event occurred first, at some point, Uncle Andrea returned from the military and reclaimed his portion of the living room. Uncle Nicola married his girlfriend, Lisa, leaving the returning family member some leg room, but not as much as probably desired.

Well, uncles came and went, and the living/dining room accommodations were a bit tight. Uncle Roberto was still among us, so there were three people sharing the living room. And after many years of the demanding daily tailor operations conducted there, such work had ceased a few months back, along with our grandmother's constant singing, but just the same, she still provided all our clothes when necessary, and they were very fine ones at that.

If a bit of proof is required, the day of my Holy Communion is a qualifying event. Everything we kids wore, except our shoes and underwear, was provided gratis via our grandmother's dedication and hard work. We certainly appreciated the woman's devotion to usher rough disciplinary skills always at hand or on standby which were not so much liked.

By the way, our aunt deserves a few kind words. She was a bit reserved but most pleasant for sure, and she always bore a sweet smile for us two kids. You already know she was super religious, and she had begun to encourage me to read the Bible, which for a while I did. And yet for some reason, there were so many issues which slightly baffled me.

One very puzzling topic lay with the creation story. My aunt had properly explained it to me, but why it took seven days to bring about the universe seemed bizarre. It could have been accomplished in just a few seconds. Was there some long thought-out process accompanying the actual work performed? Even more perplexing was the idea of a powerful and divine entity, the one true God, somehow getting tired and having to rest. This confused me, and the more explanations provided, the more my faith began to dissipate.

Everyone wanted me to stop questioning things, but that was my nature, so this was not easily accomplished. One afternoon, after a game or two of fuss ball, a conversation with the owner of the premises ensued, and upon confiding in him that the idea of an entire race coming from two people seemed impossible, the man stared at me. He and a few other kids my age observed me rather curiously. I asked if someone had not broken some moral laws regarding our ancestor's genealogy and followed up with a problem regarding Cain and Abel, as to who made it with whom in those first few years and sent us humans on our way.

From the looks of the kids standing next to me and the owner offering ideas which satisfied everyone but me, it seemed wise to just stop. Maybe it was I who simply could not grasp the obvious. Well, my decision to speak less on religion matters kept me in good standing at the billiards room and at home with my aunt. Upon arriving there that afternoon, my favorite snack was being prepared.

Our grandmother would cut a small piece of bread in half sideways. She then brushed it with olive oil and a bit of lemon juice and finally topped it with a light sprinkle of sugar. It was pure heaven to both of us kids! And once I finished that treat, it was time to step outside and see what was going on in the world of tombstone making. But the phone rang, and our grandmother was not a phone person, so up to my ear came the handset.

A very pleasant woman's voice spoke to me as if we were best friends, but she refused to identify herself; however, she continued to converse with me. The mystery speaker chatted in a slow, friendly, and happy voice. She insisted I wait in front of our house, for she would soon come by. It was a bit mysterious, this undertaking, but as a curious kid and having to step outdoors just a few feet, I took myself to the designated spot hoping all went according to plan.

Time passed and seemed to drag on, but no one came. Just when I thought it had been a ruse, something very unusual occurred. The city bus was passing, and it was right in front of me when a toy came flying out of one of the center windows. It practically landed right at my feet.

Truth be told, these are the sort of miracles I can relate to. Like manna from heaven, if you may. Perhaps doubting my own faith was not a good thing, for here was an inflated plastic monkey, the size of a football, with a cute round nose and a gigantic smile. It made me feel so good inside, but it soon had me wondering if this could possibly be from that mysterious woman on the phone.

I reentered the house and consulted Aunt Felicia and Uncle Andrea who had just arrived. Both were a bit perplexed hearing me out and had no explanation to offer. They did congratulate me on having lucked out in receiving such a lovely present. Oh well, that very evening around our dinner table, my saga was disclosed and analyzed by almost everyone, yet no one had an explanation.

It was soon put to rest because the TV was now on, and my grandfather needed to follow the evening news. Life always came to a complete standstill once the triumphal music which introduced the evening and only news began. There were only two channels. Color TV was unheard of, and I was told all broadcasting terminated at 11:00 p.m., a time when my body was dead to the world around it.

If not mistaken, our favorite weekly series was *Perry Mason*, followed by *Bonanza*. American programs were our favorite shows, as the stories seemed so cleverly produced and the actors very talented. But one day, Uncle Roberto ruined a bit of my fun as he said something peculiar. He insisted that everything always looks good from far away, even America, especially on TV.

Oh well, the very morning following receipt of that wonderful gift, I was well rested and wide awake at school. As usual, concentrating on class material was no easy task, and today, that gentle, pleasant voice rang in my ears constantly. To my delight, later on that afternoon, there was another phone call, and my anonymous friend asked how the monkey was doing.

Just what was going on? This time, we spoke a bit longer, and I revealed a tad about my lack of school progress and numerated the daily chorus which awaited me once home. It was the start of a friendly and warm relationship. That charming voice belonged to Uncle Andrea's fiancé Anna, whose relationship had not yet been announced at home. We would soon meet, and she treated me with such love and affection that visiting her at her nearby home became something I truly looked forward to.

Chapter 13

There are times when my recollection of the past is far from perfect. For some incidents would get mentioned, and my brother insisted that my version of the facts was slightly off. Still, I remained convinced we had been to the beach with our grandparents and our aunt. Just how we got there remains a mystery to me.

Once we arrived, our aunt and us two kids took turns changing into our bathing suits in a wooden booth. Our grandparents remained fully dressed. Our grandmother was in black, of course, and sat about working on a sweater while her husband completed crossword puzzles. Soon enough, we three bathers dashed off into the seawater, and although it was a bit cold, it did not prevent my brother and I from splashing each other, jumping around excitedly, and acting wild.

Our aunt exited, leaving us close to the shoreline. We enjoyed playing out our wildest fantasies, and absolutely nothing could have dragged us out of that water. It felt like in no time at all our aunt called us to exit for lunch. We had been in the water for some time, and our lips were blue, and we were both slightly shivering, yet we refused to budge.

Suddenly, our grandmother approached the water. She got our attention by making a gesture with her hands, and we were at her side in less than a few seconds. Nonna Vincenza's expression said it all, yet she simply informed us of how she had worked all morning in preparing our lunch, which was "orecchietti con ragu." This, of course, made us stand up and take notice. Plus, we were both grateful she had not jumped into action.

We sat on a large old towel. Knowing the nature of our meal, expectations all around were rather high. As our grandma uncovered the huge bowl, everyone's eyes popped wide open. Ants, lots of them, had invaded the large dish and were busy doing what ants do best—taking over the premises they occupy. Oh well, so much for any kind of lunch. It had most certainly been a fine outing that day, except for the theft of our lunch.

Once again it was summertime, and our Sicilian climate, hot and dry, was sort of calling out to us kids. Yet no family plans to visit the beach were forthcoming. So, Piero and I decided to take matters into our own hands and consulted a couple of friends in our neighborhood. Now let me first clarify the facts. We two kids did the unthinkable. It was rash, dangerous, and unforgivable, if you may, for much depends on who tells the story. We certainly pulled off a risky caper. Truth be told, we miscalculated the severity of our undertaking. After all, I was eight years old, and my brother was still a year behind me.

We huddled with two kids our age and came up with a plan. It was decided we would visit Virgi Beach the following day. That morning, my brother slyly retrieved our bathing suits from the closet, and then we individually sneaked into the bathroom to put them on. Somehow, we retrieved some towels and managed to exit the house without any of this being noticed. A sheer miracle!

Once a small distance from home, nothing else mattered. We simply forgot lunch, which would punctually be served at twelve; my grandfather's meal, which depended on my delivery services, or even worse, the concern and hysteria which would certainly ensue once our plan of action was discovered.

Our friends waited for us at the bus stop. In no time at all we arrived at the beach, just like sailors docking at their favorite port, all smiles and full of ambition. But reality had opposition in store for us as we discovered that the beaches were private and required a steep entry fee. Here was an obstacle no one had anticipated, and being super short of funds, we began to consider if a safe passage at no cost was possible.

All our hopes began to sink as we started walking away from the entrance. There was a wall which separated us from the beach area, and it ran down the street quite a way. We walked next to it, and at some point, the wall curved and ran down to where the sea met the sand. It seemed impossible to get inside until we noticed another man-made barrier to keep out trespassers. Where the wall ended, a barbed wire fence began and extended out into the sea for about ten yards. It did seem a bit difficult to get around but not impossible, and no one was guarding that area.

We devised a simple strategy. We had found our beach, we just needed to get through the back door. It was decided we would slip into the water and once it got too deep, we would carefully hang on to the wire fence. This, of course, would happen after we first prepared for the trespassing. I wrapped the towel around my neck and having tied my sandals together and holding them with my teeth, I soon used my shorts and T-shirt as gloves to protect my hands.

Everyone moved slowly, following my lead. It was crucial to grasp the barbed wire fence carefully, avoiding cutting ourselves, but we all slightly pricked our fingers at some point. The sandy floor descended slowly as we continued, but we proceeded onward while strongly clinging to that fence, which was our lifeline. It was a lucky thing that the lifeguard station was quite a way off, so no one ever noticed us. Perhaps everyone assumed one would be mad to attempt such a daring feat.

Soon, we were on the other side of the fence and continued clinging to it until we reached the shore. Almost immediately, the masses of bathers at some distance came into view, some in the water and many other people on the sand. Once we were safely on shore, we neared the distant crowds which appeared to be absorbed in thrilling excitement, but of course we kept a bit of distance, for if found out, we assumed we would get turned in.

We began jumping up and down in that lovely seawater. Each one of us wanted to impress the others, having completely forgotten the world around us, for here were four free and rambunctious little kids who had only one agenda—having fun. That water baptized our imagination as we played for hours on end, and the very sun itself seemed to fuel our immense energy.

My, how time slipped away. It was now late afternoon and time to head back home. We exited the main gate, like good customers, and soon our laughing and bragging was endemic. While awaiting a bus, we continuously revisited our small vacation and the wonderful moments we had just experienced. Then it happened! A firm grip was felt on the back of my neck, and the word, "MASCARATU" was strongly proclaimed.

It was one of my uncle's workers. Good heavens, the two missing Di Stefanos, wanted dead or alive, had just been apprehended. We were roughly thrown into the back of our Uncle Luca's car. He was yelling at us most viciously. We never even got the chance to thank our companions for the enjoyable outing. Immediately, once inside the car, a devastating silence now engulfed us as the automobile sped away, leaving our baffled friends far behind.

You cannot imagine the pandemonium which broke out at home. Our grandmother had declared a state of emergency once it was apparent that we were missing. At noon, while our lunch meal sat on the dining table, a search party had scouted the neighborhood, but we were nowhere to be found. Our aunt and grandmother then did some investigating and deduced that missing bathing suits could only mean a trip to the sea. So, Uncle Luca was assigned the task of finding us and bringing us in.

Inside that car, the glory of the day became the horror of the imminent future. We trembled, having now understood the severity of our crime, and the inevitable punishment awaiting us. Our complete silence and apparent fear were testimony to our guilt. There would be no trial, no possibility to plead for leniency or clemency, and no chance of seeking asylum. Shortly, we would be massacred. And believe me, we most certainly were.

Chapter 14

Uncle Nicola became a father. His beautiful little son was also named—can you guess? Giuliano, of course. This was practically a sacred tradition and one my grandfather considered the holiest of holy, although he was not a very religious man. Now there were three of us bearing that name, and when baby Giuliano was among us, in his mom's arms, our grandfather beamed with joy.

My brother and I were most affectionate with the little one. We always smothered him with kisses as our aunt slightly held him out to us, and the boy seemed overjoyed. It was during her visits that we would witness my aunt breast-feeding her little one. Aunt Lisa would get a small blanket to cover the ritual being performed, and yet it was almost impossible to not see this huge breast that just popped out.

My, how that serene baby fiercely attached himself to her bosom. You would think he had never been fed. And while watching this scene, as natural and normal as it is, it always made me feel a bit conspicuous as to the true nature of those enormous things. Oh well, like always, my interest would quickly vanish, and so, turning on my inner engine it was time to run off.

I would usually go visit Uncle Andrea's fiancé. We were now so well acquainted, and she lived across the street from the bakery where my last daily chore took me. Her building was new and so was everything inside her family's super large apartment. She always welcomed me most happily and would soon treat me to a snack.

Anna enjoyed reading to me. This often had me demanding some explanations, especially regarding matters of the heart. My future aunt never shied away from delicately tackling the issue at hand, which made her notice just how very shy I was. One afternoon, I was even given a royal bath. It was not so much a necessity which landed me in that fancy bathtub, surrounded by shining colorful tiles, but simply an irresistible urge to be treated to some soapy hot bath-water. And my, it smelled so divine. For a few minutes, a sense of importance took over me.

I believe having mentioned Uncle Roberto had been back among us for some time. He often swore he would never return to America. Life there was tough, and nothing was ever accomplished easily. Plus, he claimed he always felt lonely, overworked, and found it impossible to fit in with the Americans. Outside of a few Sicilian immigrants he was acquainted with where he lived, the man barely knew anyone else besides our dad. Yet, he would sometimes recall something which had deeply impressed him, and so he would happily display a very satisfied look, which made you wonder if he was perhaps deceiving himself a bit regarding not going back.

Aunt Felicia, always lovely and serene, one day did the unthinkable. She simply disappeared but had left a note. And no, she had not gone to the beach. She was not yet eighteen years old, but being terribly convinced of her faith and future, she joined a convent to become a nun. This unexpected move did not sit well with anyone. Her act of insubordination could not be accepted, and just like the campaign against my brother and I for our impromptu beach trip, a war council was convened, which immediately decided that all necessary means would be used to bring her back home.

If I recall correctly, she may have been away for several weeks. Our grandmother was truly devastated and appeared to be so sad. She had stopped singing and looked totally lifeless as she unhappily and barely attended to her daily chores, which were always carried out with much anxiety and love. It was almost as if something vital had been taken from her and getting on with life seemed impossible.

But the Di Stefanos prevailed. Our aunt soon returned home. They had hired a lawyer who threatened to expose the convent for influencing a minor or some such nonsense. Soon enough, our lovely aunt was back among us. However, this deed could simply not be overlooked. Her audacity and lack of consideration toward her loved ones was a most serious offense. And the girl had desecrated the imperative among the family rules—upsetting Nonna Vincenza.

It was at the very moment of her entrance, that our grandmother sprang into action. The woman could not control her fury. My brother and I quickly took refuge in the bathroom, still in the kitchen area, and we both quietly held our breath and silently prayed like devoted monks that we would somehow be overlooked and not be dragged into the fray. From what we heard; it sounded like the pain of souls in hell being burned alive.

We feared the probable. For lately, we had not been hit, but neither had we been responsible for any household insubordination. Nevertheless, it was possible that our grandmother could suddenly remember some past minor deed, which had gone unpunished, and that would be the end of us. We remained in that stinky room silent to the core, hoping not to be discovered, but if found, we prayed that our neutrality would be recognized and perhaps even respected. You never knew what was possible with our overly rambunctious grandmother who was presently on the warpath.

Chapter 15

We had been in Palermo for what felt like ages. Our first day had been a frightening experience, mostly because we were among strangers who spoke a foreign tongue, and no one appeared too cheerful. But there we were, two small children who were sort of getting tossed about and being handed off like a football. Our resistance held—adapting to the changes, eventually fitting in, and nowadays feeling quite at home.

It was 1963, and life was actually very good! Our Sicilian family cared for us and cherished our safety and well-being. Of course, considering the beatings we sometimes got, this at times seemed a tad disputable, but in the scheme of things, it was a sort of familiar family recipe for discipline. All in all, we were in good hands. It seemed like behind it all was life itself, making our unique experience part of its destined journey.

Why, even Italy had been completely transformed. Bicycles had been replaced by motor scooters and motorcycles by cars. The streets were inundated with them, and everyone was in a hurry to get somewhere. The chaotic commotion of street vendors seemed to have intensified, and new stores and buildings were sprouting up all around us. For the most part, people lived well, except that they would never admit it.

There was also a growing trend for modern American music. Especially something called rock and roll, which was slowly starting to take the country by storm. On TV there was a curiosity, a certain cocky personality, swinging and swaying his way through songs, and this was Adriano Celentano. To me, it all seemed very strange, the music and the man, and my grandmother had labeled him "un gran cretino."

Well, our country, whose modern foundation had been mostly established during the Fascist period, was now enjoying a healthy bout of sound economics. Everyone was somehow reaping the benefits of hard work and the dynamics of an enduring business spirit. Our family was a classic example of this, as all were now working, except us two kids and our grandmother. Although we did not have much, we lived well.

It was in the middle of this exciting period that a friend of our dad paid us a visit. He had just arrived from New York City and was in Palermo visiting family and friends. The man was among us, pontificating about the greatness of America right there in our living room. From what we heard, it seemed like everything there was big, including cars and houses, highways, buildings, stadiums, steaks, why, even people. And of course, let's not forget the Big Apple itself, where he lived among many other Sicilians immigrants.

Piero and I were quite speechless and certainly taken in. Once this stranger informed us about our new mother's pound cake—obviously, our dad had remarried—well, let's just say we were quite ready to pack our bags, ourselves, and leave with him.

Apparently, our dad had started life anew in the U.S. He now lived in the Bronx, had married an American woman, and was in the process of sending for us. Of course, we two felt right at home in Palermo. Life was now so good. Plus, we had a mother, for we had been calling Nonna Vincenza mom for years. Was it possible we would have a new mother to contend with? Change can sometime work wonders. After all, who could say, maybe this woman would be our final mom.

On August 26, 1963, my brother and I boarded an Alitalia flight from Palermo to Rome and then on to New York City. Uncle Luca and our grandfather took us to the airport. With us came a bouquet of roses which had come right out of my grandfather's garden and were destined for our new mom.

We were both excited and a bit scared. Anxiety took hold of me on that flight while I tried not to worry about life in this new country. After all, we had seen it on TV many times, and it always looked fine. Surely there were many wonderful things we would soon enjoy. Still, a brief overwhelming feeling of fear seized me, but fortunately it vanished quickly.

Our plane landed on a Friday afternoon. Neither of us have ever forgotten the sight of one of the first passengers to reach the bottom of the ladder on the runway. He literally got down on his hands and knees and kissed the ground. We both assumed he was happy to be in America. While perhaps true, such a gesture today would not sit well with both the airline and the pilots' unions, as it would perhaps insinuate the traveler had had a horrible flight.

We then boarded a large bus and headed toward the airport building. On the terrace of that building were hundreds of people waiving and shouting out names. It looked and sounded like total chaos, yet Piero did not seem at all fazed by any of this. Yours truly, however, was uncomfortable. Once inside the building, the customs agents confiscated our lovely roses. Not knowing a word of English, we could not fully grasp why until we met our father and his new wife and ran the circumstances past them.

Our dad and our new mom were both overcome with joy as we hugged and kissed all around. The two of us wanted to say so many things, and we certainly did. Our father listened, smiled, and took quick intervals to translate to his wife. Everything was just great until we arrived at the parking lot, and our grand expectations of the New World slightly collapsed.

We would be riding home in a tiny car, a Corvair. This was utterly shocking! My brother was quick to point out that even Uncle Luca's car was bigger than this one. It was not a good way to start the first day of our sojourn with our new family. Oh well, there were many more surprises in store for us. But at that very moment, there was a feeling of joy in our hearts and a wonderful sense of hope—an aspiration that maybe, just maybe, we were finally home.

Part 2

Chapter 16

We resided at 1405 Rosedale Avenue in the Bronx which sits near the Cross-Bronx Expressway. To us, the building we lived in looked ancient, even though it was only built in the 1920s. Everything about it was just plain ugly. It had a light brownish color that made it seem antiquated and rather worn out, and the façade looked plain dirty.

Even more baffling for us two were these strange and rather sad-looking balconies. They looked like worn-out iron teeth bearing rusty stairs which led to the apartment above and below. Just what could this mean? Believe me, we two Italian kids were totally clueless. It was eventually explained to us that these were fire escape type balconies, as fires were a constant threat, and were only used as a means out of the apartment if necessary.

We had never seen a fire or heard of there being one anywhere. In Palermo, the fire station was close to our home, but those fire trucks hardly ever went anywhere. So, this was modern America? On TV it had looked very different, and we had even daydreamed of its towering buildings as majestic and reaching up to the sky and beyond. Ours, and those not far off, were only five stories tall, which was not so impressive being similar to those near our old dwelling, except in Palermo the buildings were not so gloomy.

Some things, however, were very good. There was a bedroom just for us with two single beds, and if you consider we no longer had each other's feet to contend with, this was a grand improvement. Plus, there was new furniture to accommodate our clothes, certainly an upgrade, and even a walk-in closet, which was a novelty for us two, one we very much liked even though it simply looked like a tiny bare room.

In a short time, we discovered the empty green lot right across the street from our building. It was only a few weeks later when we got somewhat acquainted with it, spending some time there once home from school.

Our new mother was an American whose folks were of Calabrese origin. Calabria is the southernmost region on the Italian peninsula. Much to our surprise, this mom spoke no Italian, never mind Sicilian. She only knew a few words of Calabrese, which was just as foreign to us as the English we now had to master.

It was the next morning when we confronted our first dilemma. Breakfast in our previous home was simply a cup of cafe latte. Much to our surprise we were given milk in a glass, and it was cold, which seemed odd, but even more baffling, there was no coffee for us. And there were rolls, which one ate after spreading butter on them. Why, we had never even seen butter, and Piero even frowned on the strange black seeds on top of those rolls.

Our faces must have given us away. Our dad was not happy with our opening performance that morning. However, having probably anticipated as much, he decided to cater to our dietary needs for a few days. That very afternoon, much to our surprise, the man came home with mortadella, salami, olives, cheese, Italian bread, and other things we very much appreciated. Nevertheless, my brother and I certainly understood this gesture was simply a temporary accommodation.

On Sunday morning we were given the house rules. We were to be at the dinner table every day at exactly noon and at five o'clock, and not a minute later. Our hands would be clean, slippers on our feet, and we were not allowed to talk unless spoken to. There would be a can of soda to share with our dinner meal. Also, and most importantly, we would eat everything on our plate, and brush our teeth after each meal.

Once supper terminated, we could watch TV until nine o'clock, and then off to bed. We bowed or perhaps saluted and understood the importance of adhering to the new rules in order to remain within the boundaries of our new gig. These instructions, solidly outlined, seemed almost like personal commandments, yet more regulatory than heavenly. And fortunately, the word "thou" was not invoked.

Later that day, we were christened with new names. I became Julian and my brother Peter, and those names have remained ever since. My new name, according to our father, was regal, as if to insinuate that I should feel proud. As for my brother, well, remember he was born Pieri, became Piero, and so still carried the name of a famous apostle, now in English, and it all seemed just fine to us two, but then came something totally unexpected. We were handed a book called, *L'Inglese in Tre Mesi*. That is, "English in Three Months". The man of the house informed us that he would now only address us in our new language, and that we should immediately put the book to good use. Well, three months seemed somewhat plausible, and we saw no reason not to get going once we retreated to our room.

It was the next announcement which startled us both. Dad informed us that if anyone inquired about our mother in Italy, we were to say that she was dead. And so, without further ado, as it would have been unthinkable and dangerous to question this order, we buried her right then and there.

Peter and I faithfully accepted all our commandments. We had new names, had been provided with the house rules, assigned a scholastic initiative, and even adjusted our family heritage. What we could not fathom was how all this began a process, one which would entirely obliterate our past. And although its magic soon worked very well, many years later it would come back to haunt us.

Chapter 17

It was a week after our arrival when we headed off to St. Anthony's Catholic Elementary School. As our dad always had our best interest at heart, he and our new mom had decided we should attend a private school. This would ensure we were in a safe environment, well taken care of, and receive a great education.

Our mom accompanied us on the first day, and she was waiting in the afternoon to bring us home. It was a brief but rather sore walk to school for I anticipated not being able to grasp what to us seemed like a very strange and incomprehensible language. My biggest fear was being made fun of or simply being looked down upon just like we had recently experienced with a few of the kids in our neighborhood.

We walked on Rosedale Avenue and turned right on Mansion Street, and presto, we then stood in front of St. Anthony Church. Once handed over to one of a few nuns standing by, we were placed into our groups according to our grade. To say I was terrified is a mild way of putting it. Perhaps we both looked great in our school uniforms, but we were sweating profusely. Our folks were launching us into the canyon of scholastic enlightenment, something we had both managed to avoid for years. Absolutely nothing would be easy that day. Not only could we not communicate with anyone, but we were also clueless as to what was going on around us.

My most horrific shock was realizing the school had put me back two years in grade. It was explained to me that evening at home that the administration did not consider me ready to tackle the fifth grade. First of all, I did not speak the language, and the scholastic standards here were considered superior to where we came from. Dad even suggested the students in the higher grade were probably too mature and perhaps not so gentle with a foreigner.

It seemed a bit unfair. Here I was ready to give it my best, but my way forward would begin with me taking two giant steps backward, whereas Peter got off to a proper start, placed where he belonged in third grade. So that morning, once our mother departed, we were immediately separated as he went into 3B, and 3A was my lot.

My teacher, Sister Gabriel was an elderly nun. She was slim and wiry and exuded a rather serious air quite akin to a certain grandmother of mine. The nun spoke at length, and at some point, everyone opened their books. It was here that I took a deep breath and raised my hand. Once she gave me my cue, I stated the facts as I saw them. My statement was, "Io non parlo Inglese."

Those words had a magic effect on everyone. Suddenly all eyes were on me. Some smiled, others stared, and a few appeared slightly confused. Yet Sister Gabriel seemed unfazed and quickly provided a solution. One of my classmates was moved next to me, as he had obviously claimed he knew some Italian, but the accommodation ended that very day. We had trouble communicating. I knew Sicilian and Italian but could not understand most of what he said, and our teacher had caught on immediately.

My day could not be over fast enough. At times, while looking around the room, memories of my wonderful home in Sicily came to me. Yet, my resolve to get through the day held fast, and there was something which had quickly caught my attention. A few of my classmates were very pretty, especially Laura.

At exactly three o'clock that afternoon our mom met us right where she had left us. As we headed back to our sad dwellings, we two students debated the day's curriculum, and there was one major item which was not only discussed but also rated. It was lunch. To us it seemed like the most disgusting thing in the world, and we wondered how the other kids ate it so contentedly. Which is why once within the confines of our apartment we pleaded for food. We used whatever knowledge gained that day, or accumulated over the week—new words and gestures, to get fed. If we understood correctly, our mom was asking about the school lunch, and we both immediately stated, "Bad, very bad", which actually got a small chuckle out of her. Please forgive my repetitious nature. You know that on our lovely island of Sicily we ate fresh food, which was delicious. In Palermo, our minds may not have been scholastically nurtured, but our stomachs had always been treated like royalty. Now, at the school cafeteria we were dealt a severe blow. The food was just awful and what little got chewed and went down wanted to come right back up.

Almost everything on our plate came out of a can. No seasoning of any kind was added to make it a bit more appetizing, as if such a thing were possible. The mashed potatoes tasted like glue, and the peas and carrots had no taste whatsoever and even smelled funny. A few days later, they dared serve spaghetti, which, incredible but true, also came out of a can. Now just what kind of a country was this?

Plus, to add fuel to the fire, the table monitor was out to crucify me. He insisted everything on the plate had to be eaten. If not, he would call one of the roaming nuns. Well, a report was in the making for Sister Gabriel, but I held my ground that day. The following day was no better. A truly disgusting meal forced me to comply or starve. So, I closed my eyes, and prayed silently, being in a Catholic environment it seemed only proper, and rather painfully, the foreign fodder in front of me was sent down the hatch.

Chapter 18

There were several groups of folks who spent time in front of our building. A crowd of kids about our age gathered there and played games in the afternoon and throughout the early evening hours. Some older teenagers made their appearance in the latter part of the evenings. In those first few days, Peter and I tried to join in with the former crowd but found it impossible to communicate with anyone.

The older evening crowd appeared somewhat whacky. My brother and I would watch them from our bedroom window as they always sat on the cars parked in front of the building. They were a bit wild, and they were forever listening to loud music. Occasionally, a car owner would confront them to get them off his car. They then simply moved on to the car parked next to that one and carried on like before, no matter how many times they had to migrate.

Now those cars were stupendous! Here was modern art at its finest. There were fancy Thunderbirds, long elegant Chevies, colorful Studebakers with slim fins, Oldsmobiles, Pontiacs, huge station wagons that could probably accommodate two-medium size families and many other impressive models which were kept in excellent shape. All those automobiles appeared quite robust and built to last. Occasionally, the rowdy teens would test them by standing on the bumpers, sometimes dancing a brief jig, and jumping off when they were through. We two foreigners were truly dumbfounded as we stared and had to wonder if these people were not completely insane.

In the mid-court area of our building, some elderly women briefly loitered there. They usually arrived in the afternoon, chatted briefly, and returned in the evening to enjoy the cool summer breeze. They brought their beach chairs and made themselves right at home there. In those days, no one had air-conditioning, and TVs were still mostly black and white and not overly addictive. The ladies religiously descended around eight in the evening to catch up on previous matters not fully resolved.

Sometimes, those crazy teenagers got out of hand. One evening, they had an egg fight and accidentally hit an older woman who was taking it all in. She was certainly displeased with their extravagant behavior. One of the ladies, not the victim but a friend, and someone who would not be silenced, got up and had a word or two with the rambunctious teens. Eventually, she returned to her chair to complain about the lack of respect from young people nowadays.

Nevertheless, life in our courtyard and the surrounding area was sort of a family affair. To some extent, everyone knew who everyone else was, and this provided a sense of comfort and safety. Overall, ours was considered a great neighborhood. It was clean, safe, and at times it even provided a bit of excitement. To Peter and me, it was somewhat peculiar, and yet it set the stage for our arrival, and we were most certainly impressed on discovering how the local natives made the best of it all in our brief summer days of 1963.

Chapter 19

As luck would have it, yours truly fell madly in love with the most beautiful girl in the world. Incredible, but it occurred right there on Rosedale Avenue, in the Bronx. Her name was Frances. She was slim with long light brown hair, a beautiful face, and a smile that penetrated every inch of my soul. Of course, little old me was quite useless, being a shy idiot and lacking any courage in such matters. Nevertheless, she became a permanent fixture imprinted in my mind and practically never left me.

Had I finally met the beauty who had serenaded my school dreams in Palermo? Yes. One would think of me as being super thrilled. Not so: her very presence truly pierced my heart a bit as she had a faithful companion named Teddy, and they were inseparable. Watching them enjoying their time together was a nightmare for all I could do was view from a distance, and, at times, I simply wished I were dead.

There were, however, some perks to our new neighborhood. It was comprised of many stores. There was a pharmacy on the corner where we lived. Someone once remarked it had been there for ages. Next to the pharmacy stood a laundromat, run by a Chinese family, and they too looked like they had been there for a long time. At the very end of the block was a grocery store, which came in handy when you ran out of something and getting to the supermarket was not possible.

Most importantly, somewhere between the laundromat and grocery store was Nick's candy store. Nick was a rather swell guy. He was friendly with everyone, and he had immediately taken a liking to us two kids from Italy. His store had a long counter, and there were round stools where you either accommodated yourself and enjoyed a treat or you simply sat for a minute, decided what to buy, got it and then moved on.

Candy was practically nonexistent where we came from, unless it was All Saints Day which provided plenty of marzipan candy in the shape of fruit. But that was it. In our new environment, candy was even sold in school. It was a bit shocking when in the latter part of the afternoon, Sister Gabriel would set up shop at her desk and sell different candy bars which seemed to be in big demand. However, we two newbies were simply not interested and never cared to even try anything.

But Nick's store had a different appeal. There were many new and even strange treats, and some could be bought with a few pennies. Well, if not a few pennies, certainly a nickel or a few nickels. You had a choice of pretzels, bags of potato chips, ice-cream, and many delicious drinks from the soda fountain. My favorite was a concoction of chocolate syrup, a dash of milk, and seltzer water. My goodness how a glass of this went down so quickly, tasted so heavenly, and just made me feel happy all over.

By the way, we finally tried Coca-Cola. It was so gassy and much too bubbly. One peculiar thing we discovered was that it also had a medicinal use.

If someone suffered from a terrible cold, they could go to Nick's and buy Coca-Cola syrup. Some people said it was the best remedy for several ailments. It was not unusual back in those days to see someone walking home with a glass full of this thick, brown liquid. Then you knew why a family member had not been seen around for a while.

Peter and I soon became serious customers once introduced to Nick's. Our only problem was not being able to compete with our few friends. That was because our father gave us a quarter each as a weekly allowance, which, if spent prudently, but very prudently, at times got us by for a few days.

As things stood, all our friends would spend that much in one sitting. So, we had to often fake it and show no interest in being as extravagant as they. We would figure out what to buy daily with the week's allowance and stuck to it. Unfortunately, sometimes we would splurge, so then we were forced to avoid the candy store for a while. It was never an easy thing managing our tiny budget.

One day, our next-door neighbor Robert, a kid our age, gave us some incredible news. He insisted that if we brought empty Coca-Cola bottles to Nick's, we could get money for them. Peter and I were a bit suspicious! How was this possible? We were sure he was putting us on, but later that day, our mom confirmed the fact. My goodness what a wonderful country this was after all. We certainly recognized a good thing when it came our way.

The very next day, we took to the streets searching for these prized items. We discovered the best place to conduct business was at a nearby construction site. There, tossed about almost everywhere, were tons of bottles and all for the taking. It seemed like an incredible finding, and so we got to work, having decided to take our enterprise seriously.

We managed to get an empty fruit box from the grocery store. The two of us immediately began to work in earnest collecting bottles from that site. Sometimes they needed a little washing as bits of plaster covered them, which forced us to expand our operations and make some trips to a nearby park. The water fountain there gave our products a clean and acceptable look.

In no time at all, we had it down to a science. As a matter of fact, once Robert caught on, he decided to join us. Things were certainly going very well, and the three of us believed we were on the verge of striking it rich. But no, sir. A week later, the foreman at the construction site warned us to get off the premises and stay off as we could get seriously hurt. The huge guy was very matter-of-fact which forced us to immediately comply.

Oh well, we dumped our box and gave up working for a living. Returning to our old ways was no easy task, yet we did. Nevertheless, we had both learned a rather valuable lesson which would stay with us forever—find a need, and then simply roll up your sleeves.

Although my entrepreneurial aspirations had been squashed, my academic life was soaring. It is difficult to state how it happened, but the dunce in me became a scholar. That is right, you have heard correctly. And why the big change? Maybe it was the presence of my father. Instilled in me was a certain dose of fear due to a few negative incidents from years back which had left their impact.

Anyhow, I now paid attention in class. My schoolbooks were used properly when doing homework in the evenings, and it wasn't so bad after all. My photographic memory made it so easy to retain information from those books, and, of course, it was American history which truly fascinated me. Why, the stories of Davy Crockett, Sam Houston, Jim Bowie, and other great American heroes became my idols, and I truly enjoyed expanding my knowledge of their incredible feats.

Life on the rugged frontier or any place Americans ventured into was all that mattered. What held me captive was the courage and tenacity of these rough characters who had now taken center stage in my favorite scholastic subject. They feared absolutely nothing and had, therefore, gained the fame and glory I believed they deserved.

My need to expand on that subject is what brought me to the local library. Whereas I would replenish my new love with different books, Peter had absolutely no interest in them and never came with me. He would soon have problems with his teacher, which reminds me of a small incident that left a sour taste in my mouth for a while to come.

As my brother's progress in school was not faring well, Dad declared it crucial that he start applying himself properly. I was given a direct order. Bring Peter to the library on my next trip. It was imperative that he came home with a book or two. A few days later, my brother and I headed to the library, and once inside, my browsing, reading, and skimming pages of different books that interested me kept me busy. Unfortunately, I never took time to try and enhance my brother's literary career. Peter must have felt like a fish out of water as he sat there staring off into outer space.

Suddenly, we realized it was time to run home or risk breaking the daily curfew. Having already picked up several books for myself, I simply grabbed a book off the shelf for my brother, and handed it to him, doubting he would look at it. That evening, the man of the house followed up with an inspection. Unfortunately, the book for Peter was written in Spanish. Dad exploded like Vesuvius, and there was now an instant uproar throughout the entire premises. Not sure if the severity of that crime led to some sort of punishment, but perhaps somehow, miraculously, it did not.

Such was life in the New World for us two. Our lives were very organized and supervised. Once home from school, we changed into regular clothes and ran off to play, usually in the empty lot across the street. At exactly five o'clock, we sat at the dinner table in complete silence. We were well-groomed, as per house rules, and it was forbidden for us two to talk freely, but we could be interrogated about the day's activities. We certainly knew better than to share any negative news. When asked for info, we briefly highlighted the positive and buried the rest. You could say we were applying our own code of silence. Sicily was far away, no longer in our hearts, yet our roots had not fully vanished.

Chapter 20

Months rolled by quickly, and we were soon at year's end. Unlike in Palermo, November 1, All Saints Day, had come and gone, but without any celebration attached to it. When Christmas had arrived, we were not expecting anything. In Palermo, it was only in the last years before our departure that a Christmas tree adorned the house, but that was basically it.

That morning, once up, our dad invited us to step into the living room. My goodness, we could not believe our eyes! The entire room was packed with toys. Why, there were so many things everywhere, it was hard to see the floor carpet! What caught our attention immediately was a huge racing track with two cars ready to go, which immediately sprung us into action.

The many presents were unwrapped, the donors, although not present, were thanked while we exclaimed our overwhelming joy. It was our mom's family members and relatives who had made the super huge contribution. What a truly splendid morning! Our new home had felt like a real home for some time now, and much like the place we had always longed for, where at the center of everything is the love and care any child longs for. But even a more beautiful gift was in store for us. Soon there would be a new family member as our mother was now in the final stage of her pregnancy.

Something both warm and joyous was brewing inside us new American kids. Perhaps this is the happiest we had ever been for a long time. Our dad had somehow established a new family and given us new identities, and we slowly began to have a different outlook on things. Unconsciously, we were also bolting the door to our past. In retrospect, the year 1963 was exciting and eventful for us as so much had occurred in our lives, and not just because we had landed on U.S. soil before the Beatles.

Richard, who we also referred to as Ricky, was born on January 6. A few days later, Peter and I were playing in the lot across the street when quite unexpectedly we spotted our dad's car parked in front of our building. We flew home in a flash. The excitement of anticipating our brother's arrival was very hard to contain.

Our mom was all smiles and happy to see us. She invited us into their bedroom where a crib had been set up the week prior. There was Richard, his pink baby face both beautiful and serene. He was sleeping and displayed such a peaceful look. What an incredibly special moment we enjoyed in seeing this little angel among us and feeling so much love for him.

Our dad was rather picky about us being in his bedroom. Therefore, the visit was cut short, allowing us to return downstairs with extra time to play. Truth be told, if we could have had our way, we would have been by that crib every single moment. As a matter of fact, once back, we immediately went to have another look at him. The baby gave us such a unique and special joy. All we wanted was to be close by and kiss those delicious baby cheeks.

Now back in school, everything proceeded on an upbeat scale, at least for me. My studies were good, history remained at the top of my list, but art, specifically design, was a disaster. I could not even draw a simple flower and watching most students creating something out of nothing while making it look so easy was somewhat very frustrating.

Fortunately, our music teacher, Ms. Morales, rescued me from my lack of artistic talent. Once a week, along with almost everyone, we happily belted out tunes from the Halls of Montezuma to the shores of Tripoli. It all came out so spontaneously and joyfully, for my tenor voice thundered loudly along with that of others. And the fact that I was two years behind no longer entered my mind as my time in school was quite good.

Unfortunately, Peter was not doing well at all. His teacher's reports were negative, and occasionally Dad became somewhat angry and even hit my brother out of sheer frustration. Perhaps he believed this would somehow bring about a change in him. It became difficult to watch the beatings while standing by helplessly, perhaps my anger not showing, yet my resentment toward Dad began to slowly grow.

At the end of the first school year our parents were advised to send Peter to a public school. So that year he did not return to St. Anthony's but began attending P-S-47, where, unfortunately, his problems intensified and eventually led to more serious concerns.

Chapter 21

Our next-door neighbor Robert had become good friends with Peter and me. After school hours we often played in the lot across the street from our building. One day he shared some peculiar news with us. He would ask his mom if we could join his family that coming weekend to their huge home in upstate New York.

An attractive woman came over that evening. Surprisingly, our father happily approved of our weekend outing. It seemed incredible! What good luck! It was the first time we believed ourselves to be free at last. Between house rules and the lack of freedom of speech, what a sour lifestyle plagued us once home. We simply longed to be like the other kids; for the most part, nobody we knew ever ran home at five, and when my school friends discovered our strict rituals just to eat dinner, they laughed in total disbelief. All Peter and I wanted was just to be like the other kids.

On a Friday afternoon, we three kids were laughing and carrying on as Robert's dad drove a huge station wagon. The chap was not so talkative, but we two guests soon went into overdrive, reciting bits and pieces of our amazing past history. Of course, the excessive measures of our upbringing were left out so as not to startle anyone, and our three hosts appeared fully pleased in listening as we yakked away freely with much gusto.

We arrived in a valley setting close to a small town. It brought to mind a forest scene from my reading "The Last of the Mohicans". Surrounding us was so much green beauty, which was quite a novelty for us two, and I felt slightly intoxicated, or perhaps totally mesmerized. The woods we settled into happily accommodated us, but the following afternoon we kids got into a small scrape while getting about in that attractive forest land.

None of us were much experienced in fighting. Robert appeared a truly docile boy, and once it was apparent things were turning bad, I was slightly concerned. We were in the vicinity of the local school, and it being Saturday it was closed. About four or five kids were on their bicycles, and they decided to play a game using us as their targets. While riding past us, they would kick us, and they kicked rather hard, making it perfectly clear they were challenging us to do something.

The bunch continued having their fun as they met no resistance. Perhaps, they also assumed this was a natural sport which they could enjoy effortlessly. We, on the receiving end were scared, and we simply continued on our way hoping their fun would soon end, but destiny had other plans in store for us. While they continued kicking us, suddenly, out of nowhere, Peter lunged at one of them and sent him flying off his bike. He hit the ground rather hard. Well, so much for keeping the peace. As you can imagine, all hell broke loose!

We three spun on our heels and ran like the wind. The angry mob of kids were coming after us on their bikes at full speed. They must have been foaming at the mouth while yelling out what was in store for us. It was a frightening scene, to say the least, but fortunately, we were close to a very narrow path in the woods which thankfully impeded their pursuit. We returned home without a fight and laid low until our departure back to the Bronx.

Apart from this, it was a wonderful weekend! We enjoyed a tasty barbecue, and even tried joining our hosts in singing songs unfamiliar to us two as Robert's dad strummed an acoustic guitar. Soon enough, my brother and I became a hilarious show, for we continued to talk our heads off. We had found the perfect stage, and having been deprived at home, our speech perk was not to be denied. Robert's folks, much to their surprise, discovered how the more we spoke the funnier we got.

Unfortunately, it felt like much too soon we were heading back to the Bronx. Our folks got a very positive report card, which truly pleased them both. Naturally, we resumed that same strict spartan lifestyle forced on us, and for a moment, it almost felt like we had left Disneyland to return to a monastery.

We continued our close friendship with Robert. However, before the year ended, he informed us that his family would soon leave the Bronx as his parents were now separating, and Robert and mom were moving to her home state in Florida.

Chapter 22

Although Peter was no longer in St. Anthony's, he still spent time with his old schoolmates. Once home from school, he would head off to Noble Avenue, which runs parallel to Rosedale Avenue, and spend the afternoon with the kids he was close to, especially Sarah. The two had truly bonded in class and were happily sharing their love for games, sports, and just being together.

I had taken up residence elsewhere on my own. It was a small side street which was practically void of traffic as my roller skates were my new challenge. During one of the daily outings there, a guy named Jose introduced himself. He lived nearby and had caught my attention one afternoon. We began talking, and our friendship grew quickly, for he also was an immigrant in a new land. Jose was from Puerto Rico and quite happy to know someone who came from Italy. This was the first true friendship I developed in our neighborhood.

Occasionally, he invited me to his house. He always prattled on about the importance of hospitality, good friendship, and strong family ties, and he once insisted such things were lacking here in the U.S.

There was always Latino music playing loudly at his place as both he and his older brother seemed to live off it. To me, the living room walls appeared to tremble some as Jose attempted to indoctrinate me to this music, but all to no avail. As a matter of fact, one afternoon, he informed me that two musicians living in my building played with Tito Puente's band, which led me to ask just who was this Tito Puente, only to discover we had been listening to his music for the past hour.

Oh well, such were the few modifications to our lives in the Bronx. We two kids now separated after getting home from school, arriving from different directions, only to regroup in the bathroom before rushing to the dinner table. Absolutely nothing had changed at home regarding wearing slippers indoors, unwashed hands or not being on time, and if you slipped up, you were in a world of trouble. Forgetting the golden rule of silence would bring on a look from our father which immediately silenced you.

Sometimes Peter would slip up. Wanting to joke around, he would say something funny quite unexpectedly. It not only brought an immediate reprimand from the man of the house, but also a few unkind words from his wife. Plus, at almost every meal, my brother would roll up a piece of his paper napkin into a tiny pin-sized roll that looked like a toothpick. This led our mother stating to our dad, "Look Adrian, he likes to make little things. That's because he has a small brain."

Such words stung. Fortunately, Richard's presence gave us the warmth and joy we needed, and once off to our room, the unnecessary jabs coming our way were tossed aside. Now I must mention that our mom's family and relatives were super nice to us. For whenever at their place, they seemed extra gentle and gracious with us two, but even more so with Richard, who was an adorable little boy. And on some occasions, if Dad was not present or just not looking, our grandma would casually slip Peter and I a few coins.

Aunt Mia was our mother's younger and only sister. What a truly charming person she was. That woman always made coming together a special time for everyone. Her every word had a positive and rich tone for she enjoyed chatting and had much to say. The family, which consisted of her husband and their kids John and Sophia, lived in Smithtown on Long Island in a lovely house with a huge backyard. At times we five spent our weekends with them.

Our mom's relatives were many. They always appeared in a festive mood no matter what the occasion. Whenever with them, Peter and I were simply impressed seeing such a large crowd of people eating, drinking, and carrying on in such a happy fashion. Sometimes you even heard some of the craziest stories which soon had everyone in stiches. Why, even our dad, usually so serious, would manage to get into the swing of things and let go a bit, but just a bit.

We had first met everyone a week after arriving in the U.S. It was at an anniversary party in an Italian restaurant, and it was packed. Of course, not being accustomed to such gatherings, my brother and I felt a bit out of place, even afraid. For it was not only our mood suffering but our arms, too, as the previous day, we had gotten some required vaccine shots and they were effectively in full swing.

Soon enough, we were among these folks on various occasions. If it was a holiday and being celebrated at someone's home, it appeared like a cooking contest. For almost everyone brought some holiday treat and would claim to have perfected that dish, consequently providing everyone the best food possible. We tasted lots of appetizers, especially various pies, with meat or cheese or both, and I so much loved the ricotta pie which mother always managed to bring home, and it became an after-school snack.

Eating at these parties was an all-day-affair. One which usually began sometime around two p.m. and would finish any time in the latter part of late afternoon. And it was the size of the portions which at first startled Peter and me. Back in Palermo, having more food than necessary at any meal was considered sacrilegious. And just as sinful would have been the idea of giving away food not eaten. Whereas here, these rituals were part of the course as everyone had prepared and brought tons of food to share to their heart's delight.

All kids sat at a separate table. It allowed us a bit of privacy which meant we could cautiously goof off. Nevertheless, it was still necessary to remain somewhat inconspicuous, but maybe it was understood that sitting still for such long hours was quite challenging for kids our age.

Well, these gatherings full of abundant tasty food and heartfelt laughter soon grew on us two. Not only because we happily participated, but because what truly captured our hearts was the lively, carefree, and jolly environment, along with a rather contagious festive mood. Perhaps our personalities were neatly being sown into the fabric of a new lifestyle, one which entailed a rather spontaneous, innocent, and a somewhat loud and cheerful attitude.

Soon another celebration was upon us—Richard's first birthday. We were at home, and our grandparents, and Aunt Mia with her husband and kids came. It was a small but fun party, and everyone present was so very attached to our delightful brother. That beautiful boy was the perfect picture of serenity and happiness, a child who never carried on unnecessarily. And overall, he was simply just a good kid, and his warm smile would immediately grab your heart. We soon called him Ricky.

That Ricky was our stepbrother was something which never occurred to Peter and me. And folks unfamiliar with our family background would have never suspected we were not natural brothers. On this very special day, we all felt the magic of the moment. Eventually, everyone gathered around the kitchen table to sing his birthday song, and we were all so very happy. I truly believed ours was a unique and everlasting bond and was convinced it would last forever.

Chapter 23

Sometimes our dad spoke badly about the U.S., especially if the topic was WWII. I once witnessed a verbal shouting match between him and his wife's cousins, and my father claimed that Americans were the real Nazis—violent and ignorant, as they had no clue what they had done to the civilian populations in Europe and Japan.

Such statements embarrassed me. My, how I wanted to hide. However, it was only a few years later when the man changed his tune, and he began to proudly claim that America was a great country. There were jobs plentiful. Plus, the possibility to improve your lot was accessible to all. If someone wanted to work, they certainly could. Even the least skilled moron could get rich. Americans were certainly a nice bunch of folks.

Our dad was now doing quite well in his new environment. Not long ago, he had arrived as a sailor on an Italian merchant ship, and once it docked in Brooklyn, he made his way ashore and quietly disappeared. It may have been his plan all along. The man then went on to labor in restaurants, bars, and was now putting in a serious daily performance in construction. His knowledge of English was very good, but his pronunciation was less than perfect. Yet he managed to charm the woman who soon married him, and it was with her help that he became a U.S. citizen. So, Adriano Di Stefano became Adrian.

Now our Adrian was simply a perfectionist and very proud of it. No matter how complex or menial a task, nothing short of applying heart and soul and rendering a perfect outcome was acceptable. Unfortunately, he was soon laid off due to a downturn in the world of construction, but he soon found work driving a taxi. Sometimes we did not see him for entire days and certainly missed him. For he may have been this gigantic figure always towering over our every move, but we loved him just the same, not so much the old-fashioned foreign ways which he swore by. Dad changed work again and began making plastic slip-covers for couches, sofas, and armchairs. Although employed by someone, his new job allowed him flexibility in setting his own hours, and he was soon moonlighting as much as possible. He proudly proclaimed that the money was good.

The man did not have many friends. Yet, those allowed into his domain were friends for life. If you were in, you had earned his absolute devotion, but if someone betrayed his trust, they were out for good as forgiveness was just not part of his repertoire. Besides, he always seemed okay with small periods of isolation.

Someone very close to Dad was from Palermo, Nino La Casa. The two spent their Sunday mornings at a coffee shop called Iacuzzu. What a name, ha? It was located somewhere on Arthur Avenue, and Peter and I had been there on a couple of occasions after we had arrived. Within or outside the coffee shop, all were in small groups divided by ethnicity. For Sicilians, Neapolitans, Calabrese, and others had only one thing in common—they dressed impeccably sharp as perfectly tailored suits exulted their appearance to the status of the rich and famous while they appeared to be practicing a social ritual in venting or bragging about their latest escapades in the new land.

Dad's only American friend was John Cariaccio. They had bonded strongly on the construction site years back. Apparently, early one morning, Dad misunderstood John's quip. He then said, "I beg your pardon, John." His buddy shot back, "Look, Joe, this is America. We don't beg." Thus began their friendship for life, lasting even after our dad had severed all ties with his American-Italian friends.

We kids were of a different breed as we always enjoyed our time together, no matter what. Ricky was our little hero. Peter and I relished spending time with him. We took him out whenever possible. In spring and fall, we would go to the park to play, and when not there, we stayed in the area close to the building. Our mom was not always so keen on our ventures, but if she was plenty busy, she accepted our initiative to bring Ricky with us.

One winter day, the unthinkable came about. Peter had discovered a perfect place to go sleigh riding. It was a steep hill adjacent to the entrance road to the Bruckner Expressway. Of course, we made sure no cars were in our proximity before launching ourselves downhill. Plus, we were both cautious by steering our snow vehicle far from that road. Nevertheless, once our mother got wind of us taking our little brother there, she immediately terminated our outings. She also promised and complied to not mention it to our father.

One day, a severe cold had me home in bed, and our dad had left me his transistor radio. This is when I discovered the Beatles. There was a song being replayed continuously, and it captivated me as I heard such a pleasant tune, plus a few cheerful notes. Thus began my love affair with this band's music and its four musicians. Very soon we three brothers loved everything they did. That year, a phonograph player was given as a Christmas present, and we soon had plenty of their music.

Well, we actually first inherited our mom's collection of music. It was mostly recordings from the 1940s and 50s, and they came on large-sized vinyl records, called 78s, referring to their rpm. Our favorite tune was "Yakety Yak," a fast-swinging cheerful song which soon had us singing wildly, while Peter devised some crazy dance moves. But it was the records called 45s, which our dad occasionally brought home for us that were the best. This was the case with the Beatles' "Ticket to Ride". Peter agreed the song had an electrifying beat and was well crafted, and the lyrics were so easy to grasp and sing along to. That music would be our main staple of entertainment as we enjoyed blasting it away in our room.

At times, our bedroom would become our safe-haven. Much too often the mood at the dinner table was not so cheerful, perhaps even a bit toxic, if you may. So, once we retreated to what had become our personal karaoke club, a mike being the only thing missing, we usually sang away for dear life. Our music sustained our cheerfulness, and the Beatles' tunes were musical poems dipped in a magical happy tempo. We three bonded most happily, coming alive with each song we took on.

Ricky started going to a Head Start program in 1967. My, how he loved his school and all his teachers. Back home he would happily share his stories, all peppered with little details about some things which he found funny. We also learned about the various activities he participated in and how much he enjoyed everything.

His teachers were impressed with his keen interest in learning and how well he could express himself for a child his age. They were also taken in by his manners and kind approach toward the other kids. And once he was better acquainted with them all, he would mention Peter and I in almost all his conversations. He seemed to have made heroes out of us.

It was so unexpected when tragedy struck. We celebrated Easter Sunday at our aunt's house in Long Island. What a gorgeous day it was, and one which went by without any scrapes. After a truly wonderful meal, we spent some time hunting for Easter eggs behind the house. For sure, Richard had certainly eaten his fair share of eggs.

The following day, our brother complained of a severe stomachache. No one thought much of it. He stayed home from school and was in bed all day. He fared no better the following day, and while Peter and I went about with our daily schedule, our mother became concerned. She soon consulted a friend in the building, Leslie, via telephone. It was she who advised her to immediately call a doctor who made house calls.

I have never forgotten that man's expression while examining Richard. It was late afternoon when a slim and well-dressed gentleman arrived. Perhaps he was from India, or so it sounded from his voice, and he certainly appeared reserved in his manner. The moment he touched my brother's stomach and saw his painful reaction, the doctor immediately instructed our mother to call an ambulance.

Peter and I remained with our next-door neighbors, a Cuban family. Our mother and Richard were taken to Jacobi Hospital, while we passed time with these very nice folks whom we hardly knew. They had always appeared so kind and ready to share a few words whenever we ran into them. We were now being treated like royalty, yet it was hard to talk much for there was a lingering painful feeling that something terrible had just occurred.

We ate together and eventually moved to the living room to watch TV. Our parents arrived home late that evening and informed everyone that Richard had been operated on. His left kidney had been removed. Once in our apartment, our mother broke down and cried uncontrollably while our dad sat alone in the living room lost in his thoughts. Peter and I retreated to our room and although sharing their pain we remained unaware of our brother's true illness.

The next day, once home from school, we both stayed put. Life at the dinner table became super dismal for several days. We would eventually find out that Ricky had cancer. He came home after an extensive stay at Jacobi Hospital and recovered nicely, but his struggle with his health would continue.

Chapter 24

Summer arrived early that year. It was very hot. We often spent our Saturdays at Jones Beach out in Long Island. Although only a short ride away, our dad refused to go to Orchard Beach. He insisted it was much too crowded to allow us any real privacy, and as far as he was concerned, the one we frequented was not so far away.

Dad drove like a snail, and it always felt like some light-years had passed before we would finally arrive. Naturally, we left early in the morning to avoid traffic, and we also returned home early in the afternoon for the same reason. Ricky and our mom were never with us, so we three had the day to ourselves. Once in the water, our driver would swim out and practically vanish from view. At some point, all you saw was a very shiny bald spot which from time to time would briefly disappear.

Out of the blue, one day, our father announced we would have a real summer vacation. If I recall correctly, it was the beginning of August when we arrived at Long Branch in New Jersey. He had rented a small bungalow for the entire month, and we four settled in. Our dad resumed work a few days after our arrival but would join us every weekend, and he appeared a bit more relaxed and quite happy to be back among us.

One Saturday night, he did the unthinkable. We ate out! It was something that hardly ever occurred, unless we were with relatives celebrating some important occasion. We dined at a place called Chicken in the Basket. The meal was good and affordable, but our father insisted that while American food was delicious, it was unhealthy and quite poisonous. Oh well, the very next afternoon, he returned to the Bronx.

We four vacationers lived in a Cape Cod type house. It was shared with another family, and as our schedules differed from theirs, we hardly ever saw them. The rooms were comfortable, and the kitchen was in the basement where we ate at our own large table.

The beach was within walking distance. We took ourselves there at nine every morning loaded down like mules. I carried the beach umbrella, one beach chair, and some beach towels, whereas Peter had the other chair and the cooler with a bag with filled with sandwiches and water. Of course, I had also stocked up on books and a magazine, and lots of other crap, like our dad's transistor radio, which was highly prized by us kids. For some strange reason, we always squatted in the same spot.

As Peter and I had experienced the rough Atlantic waves at Jones Beach, we felt at home in our new environment. It seemed only right to perfect our swimming, and we both learned to ride the waves to shore, which was fun but could also be troublesome as we got tossed and battered once a wave broke. Sometimes you would hit the floor bottom and the pain was unmistakable. Nevertheless, ours was a dream vacation, and as our mother had let up pestering us over every little thing, we all felt very much at ease.

Ricky was restricted from staying in the sun. Once we two swimmers had had our fair share of aquatic activity, we would join him under the umbrella and dedicate ourselves to perfecting sandcastles, which we worked on with diligence and cooperation. Of course, once finished, our masterpiece would be abandoned as it was usually time to head home for lunch.

In the afternoons, it was Peter and I who returned to the beach. I usually read extensively, but one day some guys perhaps a few years older than us introduced themselves. They had been tossing a football around and had now invited us to join them in a game. Football was a new sport to us, and it was certainly becoming rather popular. We caught on quickly and showed our new friends a bit of potential. Soon enough, we two awaited their arrival daily, quite eager to play this game which had certainly taken us in.

Mom and our little brother always joined us around four thirty. We never got off the beach until the sun began to dip. Dinner was never a big affair. We were very happy with whatever our mom had previously prepared in the afternoon, and it simply got heated and devoured. Then we all headed off to the boardwalk for an evening stroll, and it seemed impossible not to run into someone she knew.

One would have assumed Long Branch a favorite family resort going way back. For no matter whom she spoke to, they were somehow related to someone mom knew, and those folks were acquainted with other people, who knew who we were and so on. A brief exchange of details regarding the mutual friends and some analysis was to be had before we could finally resume our walk.

On that boardwalk, Peter and I discovered the arcade. We had only caught a glimpse of it on our first night out, but the next evening we were allowed to explore it. From then on, whenever we managed to get a few coins out of our mom, we happily engaged those exciting pinball machines. Now mind you, there were other interesting attractions, but those flippers had a magnetic feel which pulled us right in.

Sometimes we got lucky and won a free game. One rainy afternoon, we hit the big times. It was as if that machine had gone totally berserk for it just continued to pile on extra games by making a popping sound, and it just kept on popping away for dear life. My brother and I were almost dancing on air as a load of onlookers settled in to witness our outstanding good luck.

Unfortunately, a few hours later, we had to abandon our gold mine. It was dinnertime, and we could not afford to be late, at least not too late, as our mother had been truly good to us, so why ruin a good thing? Consequently, we, most unhappily, turned over our enterprise to one of the kids standing by. He was quite shocked, but thankful, and very happy to see us leave. Of course, we ran right back a bit later hoping to regain control of things, but our operations had been abandoned as that machine was no longer being super generous.

Our August holiday eventually came to an end. Our last week was truly rewarding. We two kids, totally inexperienced in anything which smacked of romantic entanglements, got a first taste of what never fails to please the human heart. It was a rewarding and joyous affair, and the kind you most often never turn back from.

We had convinced our folks to let us meet up with the guys we played football with. It was the first time we went out at night on our own. It may have been a bit after eight on Saturday when we left our bungalow, made our rendezvous, and then headed off with five other boys to an area by a new motel.

Our hosts had mentioned some phrases which were not part of our dialogue. They described the girls we would meet as "fine" and then mentioned something called "making out." Oh well, after a brief introduction and a few casual words, it was decided that we should play something called "this or that" which was another foreign concept to us as the two boys from the Bronx had no clue what was in the making, pardon the pun, but we very quickly caught on.

A girl stood behind a corner wall and decided if she wanted "this or that". The words equated to one of two guys on the other side of the wall who were both hidden from her. The one chosen then brought himself to her for a make out session. For the young lady, it was either a pleasant surprise, if she found you cute, or somewhat burdensome, being forced to kiss some ugly duckling. Either way, both parties gave the best of themselves or faked it very well.

Now please allow me to state the facts and with much pride. I love this country! Every aspect of life seems so well-thought-out, and everyone is just so eager to please. Well, the shy fool in me and my innocent younger brother may not have been acquainted with any kind of luscious games, but once a pair of delicious lips were to be had, and with so much passion, there was only one thing to do—rise to the occasion. And I certainly did. As a matter of fact, there was much rising.

Folks, my shyness simply evaporated as my teenage spirit popped into fifth gear. Perhaps there are humans who insist that expertise can only come though experience, but I am here to disqualify that concept. Furthermore, kissing is the healthiest, most natural and enjoyable pastime ever, for it not only exercises the lips but also simply warms the heart.

What a perfect summer we had! Our time away from the Bronx had been exciting, truly enjoyable, somewhat constructive, and perhaps even educational. For our last adventure had certainly brightened our spirits and given me some hope that more of these encounters would perhaps soon follow.

Peter returned to P.S. 47, whereas I now began sixth grade at St. Anthony's. The school had made a small change regarding the class. They decided to mix up the students. Some of the ones previously in 5B were now in 6A, and a few from our old 5A were now in 6B. Maybe the intent was to separate the problem students, hoping to see an improvement once in their new environment.

My first day of class went well. There were some new faces, previously seen here and there, yet I hardly knew anything about the individuals attached to them. Among the new folks was Shamus, a popular guy known for being tough, and he was also someone my brother had gotten very close to in third grade. It seemed like Shamus was someone you did not want to have as an enemy. Yet from day one, once in class formation before entering the school, my new friend revealed a part of him most folks hardly knew. The guy had a big heart. Before the school year came to an end, we were practically inseparable.

Scholastically speaking, little had changed for me. Except that my very radical views on religion, strongly formed in Sicily, had regressed a bit. That is, although my outlook was basically the same, my mind hardly dwelled on the subject or gave much thought to it. Just like my classmates, everything hammered into us in class seemed reasonable and not worth challenging. After all, why rock the boat?

Now if I am not mistaken, that year our class was scheduled for the sacrament of Confirmation. Perhaps you are not familiar with the Catholic Church's religious traditions, and believe me, things called sacraments are a big deal, and they follow a certain order somewhat relevant to age. Please allow me to clue you in.

After birth, Baptism is the first milestone. Here, a horrible sin is removed from your spirit through a quick non-invasive action performed by a priest pontificating a bit of religious jargon and using just a few drops of water, which is blessed. The infant participating, believe it or not, is living in an evil state, but the ceremony sets things right, and therefore that child will then have a more conducive and righteous life until the next intervention.

At a much later date comes Holy Communion. This is a rather straightforward affair as the participants simply allow Jesus to enter their spirit through what is basically a thin wafer-like bread. It tastes pretty good, but sometimes can be a bit annoying if it gets stuck to the top of your mouth. However, before allowing Jesus in, you are responsible for cleansing any evil deeds stored up within you.

So, you must simply declare all sinful thoughts and transactions committed to the local priest. This act, known as confession, is accomplished inside a private booth, and is usually a weekly practice, and for some folks it can be a rather long process. One must remove all sins, no matter how big or small, before being able to receive Communion regularly at Sunday mass.

Then comes the sacrament of Confirmation. If I am not mistaken, this reaffirms that you still merit keeping Jesus within you. Please forgive me should this not be quite the case for it certainly is not my intention to mislead anyone. Anyhow, this sacrament is also important, but unfortunately, and due to no fault of my own, Confirmation was put on hold for me.

My folks could not produce a certificate of baptism. Technically speaking, there was a strong possibility that my soul was still engulfed in the "original sin" and everything which came after it. The school principal insisted on seeing the document, although I had made Holy Communion back in Palermo and even had some nice photographs to prove it.

Well, my father believed I had been baptized. Perhaps a document existed somewhere but was simply not available. And so, as Dad could not produce it, Father George, who would perform the upcoming ritual of Confirmation, was not a gambling man and decided to baptize me and get it over with. Maybe in my case, two baptisms were better than one.

It was late afternoon when a nun informed me that the good father awaited me in the rectory. As a witness was required, Mike Smart, who was sitting closest to me, gladly volunteered, and so we quickly departed. Soon enough there were three of us attending to my salvation, and it was over in just a few seconds. My spirit had now been cleansed of the so-called "original sin", or, as some of my classmates referred to it, "the dirty deed."

I certainly did not feel any different. Oh well, we two students returned to class in a somewhat cheerful mood, but not at all for what had just transpired. Both of us were too busy discussing how the New York Giants needed to establish a better running game if they were ever to make the playoffs. And we also agreed that Homer Jones, the offensive receiver, was simply the greatest!

Chapter 25

One morning while heading to school, Frances, my agonizing love interest, stood at a small distance ahead of me. My feet casually accelerated. We greeted each other politely and exchanged a few words. After a bit of laughter had ensued, my foolish assumption, believing everything was proceeding rather nicely, favored doing the unthinkable.

I told Frances how much I liked her. She looked a tad startled, and then via two cold indifferent eyes, she calmly informed me that she thought I was a creep. A sudden knot in my throat impeded me from spitting out any more stupidity as we now proceeded to school under a blanket of silence.

While my composure had been completely shattered, she seemed just fine. Almost immediately, my intuition laid down one solid decree—that my relationship with members of the opposite sex would probably tend to lean toward shaky grounds. It cautioned me to tread carefully, and after this bumpy encounter, I certainly kept my distance from Frances. If we did cross each other's path, without any hesitation, I either slowed down or speeded up in order to completely avoid her. Nevertheless, it was impossible to get her off my mind. For my foolish heart would not act reasonably and simply call it quits.

Fortunately, my romantic plight began to suffer less. She moved on to high school, and I still occasionally caught a glimpse of her, but not often, for that gorgeous creature was no longer in our neighborhood after school hours. She and her best friend Mary began a daily trek over the Cross-Bronx Expressway with destination, Archer Street. A different neighborhood had become their new stomping grounds. I was informed they returned in the latter part of the afternoons, retracing their steps while heading straight home.

Back at home, I continued to revel in the medicine of music. It had been the Beatles' music which kept us singing in our room. And having now fully inherited my dad's transistor radio, I slowly got exposed to a wide range of rock melodies. Every evening, after all homework had been properly attended to, it was Cousin Brucie on an AM radio station, who excited my spirit.

Enjoying a variety of rock sounds was my new cup of tea. One evening, a Rolling Stones' tune stopped me in my tracks. It began with a slow introductory pounding drumbeat followed by a powerful and unique guitar rhythm. While I turned up the volume and sat back to enjoy it, a harsh voice sang somewhat rebelliously about life on modern city grounds. That glorious tune cemented my new love affair with a band I hardly knew.

A few months later, an article on the Stones enlightened me. It defended the band's image as the author insisted the musicians did not deserve such criticism and outrage over their looks. After all, they were musicians, not apostles. Plus, their music spoke for itself as the group was rather successful. Besides, the musician's lifestyle was not on sale. This converted me even more, and soon enough, I devoured all the Stones' music.

While this began my maturing beyond the Beatles, Peter was off and running on a completely different path. His school environment was apparently influencing him, although he was one of the few White kinds there. At times, he sounded like Mr. Soul, as he would sing and even do some kinky moves which made me take notice. I must admit that this genre of music was usually heard on a program called the Ed Sullivan Show, and it did absolutely nothing for me. It seemed to lack harmony and was a bit raw, yet my brother was quite at home with everyone from Aretha Franklin to Sam and Dave and many others.

Not only had our music profoundly changed but so had our neighborhood. Many of its permanent residents or familiar faces had mysteriously vanished without a trace, and the evening gatherings in front of the building, from young to old, had ceased a while back. Even the loud teenagers had moved on.

There was simply a more diverse crowd residing in the community with, perhaps, a somewhat similar agenda but with a totally different approach to things. That street and its surroundings had slowly given way to people from a completely different part of the world, and it consisted mostly of Puerto Ricans and Cubans but also other Hispanics.

Perhaps my inner vision tends to be blind. I had failed to notice where the difference was. Oh well, such was life on Rosedale Avenue. One person who also remained completely oblivious to his surroundings and their composition besides me was our dad. The man was comfortable, maybe slightly concerned, but certainly not ready to budge from our current premises. However, curious but true, a few years later he also threw in the towel and headed to a completely different domain.

Before moving on, one peculiar incident merits mentioning. There was a knock at our apartment door late one afternoon. Mom was busy with Ricky and had told me to get the door. When I opened it, two huge men who looked like professional football players stood in front me. These fellas were gigantic and wearing cheap suits. One of the two asked to speak to my mother. That is why she quickly came to the door, and as both men immediately identified themselves as detectives, they were shown in. I was instructed to take Ricky to our room as she accommodated the visitors at our kitchen table.

Not long after their departure, Dad arrived home. He was filled in about the unexpected visit. Apparently, there was a drug dealer living in our building. The officers claimed someone had found a burned spoon on the roof, and they identified the individual in question as an ex-dealer and believed that, although just released from prison, he was back to his old ways. Mom was asked if she had witnessed any suspicious activities going on in the building. Of course, she was quite clueless about anything, or at least that's what she told the detectives.

It was about a week later when Rosedale Avenue made the headlines. I had just arrived at school that morning, and while in line with my classmates, someone mentioned the morning news. He asked if I had anything to say about the big-time junkie arrested in my building? And so, making a complete fool of myself, the million-dollar question was asked, "What's a junkie?" Believe me, for days to come everyone pretty much laughed at my good name.

That incident must have had something to do with what had just occurred. For those detectives may have been surveilling their man with more precise methods. On the day after their visit, I had picked up the phone to call a friend regarding a question about our homework. The lines must have crossed, and my ears were now listening to two women with strong Hispanic accents. They lived in our building, for sure, and I had seen them quite often.

What startled me was hearing, in detail, what they would do to each other on their next encounter. Believe me, their exotic romance got all my attention! My teenage manhood raised its steel flame as their carrying on solidified my groins to the extent that a bulging mast was now exerting itself through my pants. It was impossible to put down the phone. Why, you cannot imagine how I longed for something to say hoping to get invited to their next encounter.

Unfortunately, my luscious fantasy dream was cut short. Our mother had walked by, and her presence disrupted my composure. I immediately put the phone down and made a dash for the bathroom. It had already become my romantic safe-haven, and that afternoon, my needs kept me within its confines for some extra time.

Chapter 26

At school, my friendship with Shamus solidified. He often shared a tale or two about life in his neighborhood. They included some of the people he looked up to, and a few were in some of the higher grades at St. Anthony's. My chats, even though spruced up some, seemed rather insipid compared to his funny sagas.

One day, Shamus invited me to his neighborhood. He lived on Beach Avenue but hung out with a crowd on Archer Street, a name he mentioned a lot. Associated with that name were a few peculiar incidents which indicated a bit of rough ways in how things usually were conducted. Well, the following afternoon, once home from school, I ventured to his neighborhood.

It was while crossing the bridge over the Cross-Bronx Expressway that it hit me. I was now following in Frances' footsteps. It also highlighted a most peculiar situation. For quite some time, she never left her house after returning home from school. It was still a heartwarming feeling seeing her occasionally, but why she was now locked up at home was a bit peculiar.

Oh well, my first day in Shamus's territory had me in awe. I was walking on Taylor Avenue, near the P.S.102 school yard, and very close to our designated rendezvous area. A small group of guys were gathered there, and they suddenly circled two people who now began fighting. My good friend Shamus stood out from a distance as I approached him. Almost immediately, I noticed the two contestants were from our school, but only one of them was in our class.

It seemed incredible. Both guys were circling each other like professional boxers and then they were landing some heavy blows, which was a bit tough to watch. Growing up in Palermo, we kids wrestled and quickly determined who was stronger or perhaps the strongest among us, but the idea of punching someone in the face was completely unheard of. Whereas here, some serious blows were being dished out, and it looked a tad vicious to me.

While maintaining a bit of a distance, the two would move closer to land a blow or two. Their faces bore strong looks of hatred for each other as the fight dragged on, and both fighters were certainly getting many encouraging words from the audience. It continued for some time until an adult going into the nearby building came over and brought it to an end. Upon separating, both guys, tired but certainly not defeated, at least by their looks, went off in different directions with a few fans complimenting them.

Minutes later, Shamus introduced me to some of the spectators. We strode into the schoolyard and began a game of touch football, which had seen my initiation back in Long Branch. The best of me came out, for being very fast I could easily outrun anyone trying to cover me. Every pass thrown my way, even if overthrown a bit or slightly underthrown, was somehow caught and often taken in for a touchdown.

Points accumulated for our team. Our defense was also solid, and we won big time. So, having covered myself in a bit of personal glory, I beamed with joy, but unfortunately, or fortunately, someone mentioned the time. I needed to run home or risk being late. My speedy gait got me to our place very quickly, and the following day I resumed my new love in that schoolyard.

Life remained decent with its guaranteed ups and downs. Soon enough came a down. Our darling little brother fell ill again. Ricky was recovering at Jacobi Hospital and remained there for a long while. It was then when Peter and I became aware of his specific ailment, he was battling a form of lung cancer.

Our mom became a desperate soul. She spent her entire days at the hospital, and that cheerful and fun side of her which we had once known and enjoyed simply disappeared. The woman became so withdrawn and morose, she appeared a bit lifeless. When home, she did her best to be a mother to us two, but her spirit was just not in it, and sometimes it was best to keep our distance.

Peter and I struggled with this scenario. It was impossible to avoid our friends, for they were the ones giving us a bit of relief and joy from our personal tragedy. Our sport games with them or just simply being together made us momentarily forget everything else. Nevertheless, our brother's absence left a vacuum to contend with once back in our room. His absence was profound.

On one occasion, we visited him in hospital. He was in bed with a tube attached to his chest to help him breathe and a needle in his arm feeding him. Seeing him so very thin and lifeless truly devastated us both. I immediately left the room and broke down uncontrollably.

It was almost unbearable to witness my brother in this state, so I turned to my refuge—my friends. We no longer hung out at the P.S. 102 schoolyard. We were now part of the Archer Street crowd, but truth be told, we were hardly ever on Archer Street back then, but that was a name everyone wanted to be associated with. Football still dominated our lives, but other interests were beginning to surface.

This may sound odd, but everyone smoked except me. Once finishing a few football matches, Marlboro cigarettes were on everyone's lips. It seemed like smoking was a national pastime back then. People smoked at home, at parties, outdoors, any public or private work environment, parks, restaurants and diners, sporting arenas, and just about anywhere someone wanted to light up.

TV ads bombarded society with advertisements which sort of glorified the deed. My favorite commercial had an individual wearing a pair of sunglasses indoors and eventually removing them to reveal a very black eye. He "preferred to fight rather than switch" brands. Well, somehow, I managed to get by without indulging for a few years, but eventually, the fad finally sucked me in.

One day, while still abstaining, a more sinful craze pulled me in. It was a rainy afternoon when a few of us went off to Macy's in Parkchester. We made our way to the music department, and a rather bizarre LP caught my attention. It was Frank Zappa's "Freak Out." The whacky cover and the fictional character named Suzy Cream Cheese captivated me, as it was both attractive and funny. But unaffordable as I had no money.

Something unexpected then caught my attention. A guy not too far off opened a large Macy's shopping bag and slipped a bunch of LPs in it. He moved quickly and nonchalantly, then casually walked away looking very sure of himself. It seemed incredible, but I had just witnessed someone stealing and making it look quite easy.

About a week later, that scene came back to me. Surely my conscience knew better, for it was certainly wrong, and yet something compelled me to consider it. A stupid initiative, which begs the question—where did I find the courage? It was wintertime, and I was in Macy's music section. I removed my coat. Not only because it was warm, but this move would also assist me in my caper. I draped my coat over my left shoulder, allowing it to hang down for it would hide the LPs chosen to steal. Then while browsing various records, I began collecting the LPs which interested me. I placed them together, and once certain no one was watching me, they got shoved under the coat.

My legs carried me forward, but my nerves were on fire. Nevertheless, this was just the beginning, as the gig would continue, soon becoming a weekly habit. Sometimes, once the store clerk distanced himself from the sales counter, it was easy to get my hands on a Macy's shopping bag, reenacting the very scene which got me started. It felt less risky with the LPs in a bag although my nerves were always on edge until exiting the department store.

In the neighborhood, some of my friends were soon placing orders with me. Of course, my financial situation began to prosper and so did my personal collection of music at home. However, one day I got caught. An employee, some distance from where I stood, had been eying me and followed me as I exited the music area. He suddenly pounced from behind, grabbed my left arm and twisted it behind my back. It hurt a lot. He took possession of the bag with the LPs and forced me to walk forward while never loosening his grip one bit.

The guy was practically attached to me. My mind began anticipating the horror at home once this deed came to light and realizing something needed to be done to somehow free myself, I moaned a bit to signal his grip was hurting my arm. Although it was, the very moment he slacked off a tiny bit, a powerful yank freed me, allowing my legs to run like mad.

If my speed was that of a rocket, so was that of the person behind me. We flew right through that department store, bumping into a lot of people. I accidentally knocked one down, yet neither one of us slowed down, and while continuing through what felt like a maze, something in me believed I would not leave that store a free man.

We were outside Macy's, both still running. And folks about us witnessing this scene, must have taken in what looked like two track athletes striving toward the finish line. Now for all my incredible speed, this older man remained right behind me, just like a true bounty-hunter refusing to give up his fugitive. Eventually, while the cheetah in me continued its race, my head turned slightly to look back and finally saw him standing some ways back.

My assailant had stopped. He was bending down, hands placed on his knees, apparently exhausted. This allowed me to also stop being as much out of commission as he. I then began walking at a somewhat fast pace while heading back to the neighborhood digesting a simple fact, my initiative as a petty thief had just fully terminated.

While my stupid endeavor came to an end, it was Peter's turn to perform an unusual stunt of his own. A while back, our dad had purchased a movie camera and a projector. Before Ricky became ill, he had started filming the usual birthday celebrations, outings at Aunt Mia's house, and other events deemed momentous.

I had never learned how to work a movie projector, but my brother had apparently taken good notes. Somehow, he also came across a pornographic film in our dad's closet. Peter was highly resourceful and well-informed, and that led to an incredible undertaking on his part. Fortunately, like me, he somehow miraculously came through without a scratch.

The young critter had a bunch of school friends over for a personal viewing. Of course, bless his entrepreneurial spirit, a small fee was charged, and the event came about when no one was expected home. Ricky was hospitalized again, so our mother was there. Our dad was scheduled to return home from work in the late afternoon. The young lad had just begun setting up the projector when quite unexpectedly someone attempted to come in.

What saved the day was the extra lock. It was a police lock which had been installed just a few months back. For once the front door was closed, it was held in place by a rod bolted to the floor. Without a key, you would have had to remove the door to enter. And it remains a mystery why Dad did not have the key on him that day. Now the man immediately understood one of us two must have been home. He eventually retreated downstairs to the courtyard hoping to see the culprit leaving.

Meanwhile, everyone took refuge in our bedroom and Peter cowered behind the window hoping to see Dad leave. The man's car was parked across the street and remained put for quite some time, forcing an overwhelming silence throughout the apartment. Eventually, Dad got into his car and drove off, which prompted a mad rush to the front door. However, according to the facts revealed to me many months later, some of the fleeing spectators, now unhappy customers, began to demand a refund once back on the schoolgrounds.

That very evening, the usual silence prevailed at the dinner table, but something felt different to me for the man of the house stared at each one of us for the longest time. Nevertheless, not a single word came out while he continued eyeing us so suspiciously. I had no clue what was amiss, but the conspicuous situation made something within me grasp the fact that something was wrong.

A few weeks later, Peter confessed his sin. Well, we both enjoyed a good laugh, and he thanked his lucky stars that nothing had come of it. It was not long after his revelation that yours truly was home, alone, and when the coast was clear, I tore that closet apart but found nothing. The only films available were family events which were the last thing on my mind.

Chapter 27

Shamus always shared some news with me. One day I was informed that Sal, the neighborhood butcher, was looking for a delivery boy. Dad no longer gave us any money, and living without new records or an occasional snack was rough. It seemed only right to pay a visit and inquire.

The store sat on Archer Street next to a laundromat. Sal was busy with a customer which allowed me to hear him practice his trade, as he mesmerized the couple in front of him. I waited patiently, and the man soon appeared delighted to have someone inquire about the job. He interviewed me right there on the spot asking about my academics, family make-up, and a few general details. Maybe he was impressed or maybe a bit desperate because he hired me immediately.

I began work the following day. My hours were four until six thirty on weekdays, but nine to seven on Saturdays. My last chore, right before the store closed was to sweep the floors. It was brought to my attention that occasionally the laundromat next store needed help with a few deliveries. My readiness to please all was in full gear.

The only means of transportation rested right outside the store. It was a bicycle with a huge metal box up front, and the entire contraption weighed a ton. Nevertheless, things began very well. The weather was picture-perfect as it was fall, a great time to be on a bike, and I had learned to ride in Palermo from a bike Uncle Luca had purchased for Peter and me. My rides were not usually so distant for only a few customers required some serious peddling to get to their neighborhood.

Most of my clients were elderly folks or a few housewives who were stay-at-home moms. Everyone seemed happy to see me arrive. Some were more than thankful for my services, especially when it rained, and they all expressed a bit of gratitude via a few kind words, and usually a nice tip. A couple of the elderly ladies appeared more than desperate for a quick chat, sometimes not such short ones.

As a matter of fact, once some of these ladies opened up, there was no holding back. Often, the topic included their grown children who were successful in their careers and making their way most diligently in a grandiose manner. It may have been my easy disposition or cheerful attitude which encouraged them to yap away, for they treated me as if we had known each other for years.

Now Sal was never absent, but he once missed work for an entire week due to a severe flu. His son, who toiled alongside him on Saturdays, was attending college classes full-time and not able to fill in for his dad. Consequently, a young and rather talkative individual, who seemed very well-informed on most things, ran the shop like he owned it.

And it was he who provided me with some peculiar news one evening. While sweeping the floors, I asked if he would have his own store one day?

"Absolutely not" he answered. This quick reply, delivered so very matter-of-factly, forced me to inquire why. He replied, "These stores are finished. The supermarkets have taken over." It would be many years later, when Peter and I drove through the old neighborhood, that his prophesy was fully confirmed. Sal and everyone else were long gone.

When I wasn't working, I was hanging out with friends from the neighborhood. Growing up in Palermo, we two boys had never had a serious fight with anyone. Yet from our arrival and going forward, we had learned that in the U.S., one needs to be ready to defend himself at any given moment. In my new neighborhood, a good fight seemed like a normal pastime. If someone dared to turn the other cheek, something was very wrong.

Outside of a one-way bout in school, no one had ever truly challenged me. Then, so unexpectedly, it occurred on a Sunday afternoon. A bunch of us Archer Street guys were at Cardinal Hayes High School to watch a football game. Some of my close friends and other folks from the neighborhood were huddled together enjoying the moment.

Now you would have thought Notre Dame was playing considering the names of all alongside me. The list is long but let me give you a tiny taste: Murphy, O'Brian, O'Reilly, Maguire, McCarthy, Flanagan, Sullivan, O'Donnel, Kelly, and many others. While we all wanted to see a good match, we certainly wanted our team to win.

Well, there we were, maybe a dozen or more, sitting in the first two front-row benches. What separated us from the field was a small wooden fence. It stood maybe two feet tall and was approximately three feet in front of us. One could have easily stepped over it to get on to the field.

Shamus, myself and a few other guys were in the very first row. The match had not yet started, and the sunny cold day was welcoming more folks to fill up the bleachers. Out of nowhere, a huge stocky guy and his friend, much smaller, came over and stood a few feet in front of us. They then began cheering for the opposing team. Soon enough, the bigger one started insulting our team while his friend appeared to be on standby.

Perhaps both were enjoying the performance given while our silence held steady. It seemed incredible to me, but nobody uttered a word, as I began to suspect that the Fighting Irish, from the notorious Archer Street neighborhood, were in a rather peaceful mood that day. Nobody, not even any of my oversized brethren sitting right alongside me, dared to respond or challenge the giant who was now hurling a storm of insults.

I was somewhat concerned. This fellow was not only super big but also appeared rough, and he voiced his opinions with too much confidence. We remained poised, calm, or at least appeared to, and then, much to everyone's relief, the two intruders suddenly left. No doubt, we all thanked the heavens above that the overcast storm had simply moved on, but to my chagrin, the giant returned. This time, he was alone. He was now holding a set of pennants on slim wooden sticks, and almost immediately began his tirade again.

Out of the blue, he came up to me, stuck his face in front of mine, and began cursing me out, loudly and clearly. I was petrified and began pleading with higher forces above to please let peace prevail, but to no avail. And who can say why? Maybe it was my skinny frame and tiny face which encouraged the immense-sized bully to continue. He just kept yelling, probably convinced the dud in front of him would not reply. I was on my own to sink or swim!

Now I have no recollection of my words to him. But they were not pleasant. The big prick hit me rather hard across the face with the pennants. My unexpected reaction struck like lightning. I threw a powerful left hook which, truth be told, shocked the both of us. My guts quivered as the massive guy backed up a bit from the small wooden fence and challenged me to step out onto the field.

Again, without thought I swung into action, quite literally. Instead of stepping over the fence to get on to the field, I jumped on it. Simultaneously, I kicked him in the face as hard as possible with my leg coming upwards and hitting him under the chin. The impact was swift, strong, and it even lifted him a bit, for he went flying backward landing on his side. Like a mad cougar, my rage was totally uncontrollable. I jumped on him and started punching his face mercilessly, having pinned him down on his side as he struggled to move out of that position. I pounded most savagely for my fury was greater than my being.

A few coaches and others standing nearby came running over immediately. They assumed that I was the guilty culprit, and so they yanked me off him rather hard shouting and threatening me. Finally, my fellow kin came to life. A few were now on the field loudly explaining the circumstances, but the folks who had intervened were not so convinced, nevertheless, everyone began to slowly move on.

It had been a modern David and Goliath affair. The dazed and bruised Goliath was now retreating, while the proud David returned to his seat, still somewhat stunned but very much alive, especially inside. Now please forgive me for admitting this, for I am not boasting, but I felt rather good. And as incredible as it was, the bruised giant returned with three other guys. Well, he no longer looked so tough, and his face, visibly scarred, showed less signs of one anxious to fuck with anyone. Just the same, we were warned by the three that they and their friends would be waiting for us after the match.

Well, we finally got to watch the contest on the field. It had just started and turned out great. The home team sustained itself nicely, in fact they played incredibly and won. After our victory, we left the stadium, and no one confronted us. Our crowd headed home, feeling ecstatic about our victory on and off the field, if you may.

That evening in the park, by P.S.102, Julian Di Stefano was in demand. Anyone who had witnessed my performance was encouraging me to speak up. Of course, my tale was retold several times. There were many requests, yet it felt only right to stick to the facts, while others who had been in attendance began contributing and lightly embellishing the tale. Oh well, I even admitted having been a bit scared before the brawl began. Why not? It changed nothing in the narrative.

I was a neighborhood celebrity and was getting kudos all around. Naturally, this did inflate my ego, yet yours truly managed to stay somewhat low-keyed. Then someone handed me a can of Budweiser which I gladly accepted. For the first time in my life, the overgrown kid in me basked in a bit of personal glory and drank a beer. I felt so very American. Oh well, it was a long night! Oh, by the way, this may be pushing the envelope a bit, but man, can those Irish drink!

Chapter 28

Our parents would have never gone to bat for Peter and me. Why, if someone came to our door and informed them that either one of us had stepped out of line, they would thank the source, close the door, and the matter would have been settled very quickly.

Such a situation never occurred. Thank heavens! And yet, although coming from such a background, it did not keep me from venturing into the unknown and, once again, into dangerous territory. For some reason, when in my mid-teen years, I, today completely bald, began to let my hair down. Not literally speaking, of course. Not at first. And truth be told, no one is to blame for what ensued but my stupid old self.

Why do we start getting high? Someone once asked me if I could have gotten by all those years without something stimulating me. Probably not. But let me bring back a famous punch line from a 1960s TV series that claimed, "The devil made me do it." So, perhaps, my personal demon is a rather indifferent Lucifer, at times exploring the forbidden and ultimately painting his world with a light shade of black.

One Saturday evening, a bunch of us gathered at an empty lot where Beach and East Tremont Avenue meet. Someone had bought us two cases of beer. It was time to party, which included drinking plenty with the intent to get high.

This sort pf excessive celebration was not part of life at home. My mom and dad did not drink. Sure, our father had a glass of wine with his evening meal and when dining with guests, but that was basically it. At any feast or celebration, something now long behind us, neither of my folks ever participated in any type of excessive behavior. They were both straight as nails.

Anyhow, there were six of us yapping most cheerfully, and I had decided to participate in the activities my friends were now engaged in. Getting through my first beer was no problem, however, I felt rather full. My keen senses detected it would be no easy task finishing the rest of the six-pack at my feet. Miraculously, however, a second beer went down, but while struggling with the next one, something forced me to take matters into my own hands. When no one was looking my way, some beer was spilled out. Then, I began making trips to a corner of the lot to relieve myself, and more beer went overboard.

Everyone kept talking loudly, excessively, and terminating each tale with a clever ending. Sometimes we laughed over any foolishness being shared, and then suddenly Brian, who had just arrived, challenged me to drink some wine he had brought. After all, as he put it, I was the only "eye-talian" among them. So down went entirely too much Bali High wine. It was a huge mistake. My stomach protested and my balance no longer cooperated.

Someone labeled me drunk. Although not yet there, jumbled words flowed out of my mouth as things about me moved at their own pace. I giggled, while having a difficult time explaining myself, and right about then, Brian advised me to stick my fingers down my throat and let it all out. I may have done it but cannot remember. Getting home that night remains a vague and obscure mystery.

You would think that awful experience should have terminated my wild endeavors. No sir! I soon pursued a long-time obsession, something which had been brewing within for a while. Once again, taking a rather giant step forward, or backward, depending on your outlook, I decided to smoke pot.

And why? First, because we teenagers suspected that all our idols got high. That is, rock bands, Hollywood celebrities, stars on TV shows, and even a lot of athletes appeared to indulge in this gig. There was a guy named Timothy Leary who advocated for the use of LSD. In school one day, while in recess, we debated the lyrics of a song which sounded like it proposed using that drug. Eventually we discovered it was not so. A good outcome for we all had sworn to never experiment with that foreign substance. The word grass had a more inviting and gentle sound.

It was with a bit of trepidation which saw me finally partake. There were three of us on an abandoned bridge. As a pipe was being passed around, someone instructed me to take a deep puff and hold it. That is what I did. Good Lord, it nearly killed me. Coughing uncontrollably, as my lungs were screaming for help, two guys eyed me curiously and asked if I was okay. The inhaled smoke felt so harsh and dry as we continued our powwow. Things improved, and we finished smoking, but nothing at all happened to me while my buddies were chuckling and smiling quite happily. I began to wonder what all the hoopla was about, and believe me, unlike a certain president, I had inhaled it for sure!

My next smoking session worked. It was just Shamus and I on that same bridge. We smoked a joint he had just rolled. He mentioned that this was some potent weed. My friend was definitely right, for we were suddenly laughing uncontrollably with absolutely no clue as to why. Life was just a bowl of cherries, and why not?

Eventually, we left that bridge. Our destination was a nearby candy store. Like peppy little children, satisfying our cravings for something sweet was our only ambition. A bit later we parted ways, Shamus headed home, and I on to Rosedale Avenue to my usual evenings of dinner alone as everyone had already eaten. I would later tackle my homework, and ultimately enjoy my brothers and a bit of music.

Chapter 29

My last few days at St. Anthony's School came and went. Cardinal Hayes High School was my new destination, a nice accomplishment, but unfortunately my dad informed me he could not afford to pay the tuition fees. This was a small problem as my income at Sal's did not amount to much, but a week later someone came to my rescue.

Uncle Timothy was my grandmother's only brother. A real gentleman, and someone who always wore a warm smile. He came to visit us and proposed a job which would pay me a lot more cash. There was absolutely nothing to think about. I jumped on it and a week later began work at Massa's Delicatessen located on Buhre Avenue.

It was a part-time job, but it killed my weekends. The erratic work hours included Tuesday, Wednesday and Thursday afternoons from four until closing at ten, Saturdays from eight in the morning to five in the afternoon, and Sundays from noon to ten in the evening. So, those fine glorious Sunday afternoons with a few good friends immediately became a thing of the past.

My responsibilities were twofold. It was to run the deli section and, when necessary, restock the store shelves, preferably in the latter part of the evening. Most of my time was spent slicing cold meats and the large portion of that work was for takeout orders. I caught on quickly and was fast, however, some folks who bought tons of cold meats caused a few people to queue a bit. In that case, Gloria, the cashier, would come over to assist me.

Sandwiches were in big demand, especially on weekends at lunchtime. What people preferred between two pieces of bread sometimes baffled me, like liverwurst, salami, ham, Munster cheese, a layer of lettuce, pickles, and some mayonnaise. Now, it seemed only right to prepare these extravagant concoctions without adding a word, but while observing the strange faces awaiting their treat, it made me wonder what these people were smoking.

The job continued just fine. One day, Uncle Timothy dropped by to buy a bit of cold cuts. He also took a few minutes to inform me that my boss was very happy with my work. By the way, in the back of the store was a bakery, and my boss, Ernie, and his brother kept the baking business booming. The two began their day at 3:00 a.m. and once all the bread rolling out of the oven had been properly stacked and wrapped up, it was ready for delivery. It was Earnie who spent his mornings and a part of the afternoon cruising throughout the Bronx and beyond.

While work progressed splendidly, and life at home was good, once again, things were not faring so well for my brother. Just like the cartoon character, Mr. Magoo, Peter had done it again. Go figure. He and a few classmates had played hooky one day and went to a friend's house. They all drank excessively. My brother drank himself close to death.

He was rushed to a nearby hospital. There, his stomach was pumped, and our father arrived home later that evening, appearing as a truly broken man.

The silence at the dinner table was palpable. Dad looked confused, and throughout our meal, his eyes expressed total agony. Perhaps his entire world was slowly collapsing, and nothing could alter the outcome.

Sometime after this incident, Peter began seeing a school psychiatrist on a regular basis. Occasionally, he would share some of the more interesting parts of their sessions. It surprised me when one evening, long after the maniacal drinking bout, he informed me that the good doctor had initially suggested he smoke pot instead of going on a drinking binge.

It seemed impossible to me! Marijuana was categorized as an illegal drug, at that time, and a dangerous one. My brother swore he had only stated the facts. Oh well, it was sometime after this bizarre episode, when Peter, out of the blue, began to come to the park near P.S.102. I shall never know why he chose to abandon Noble Avenue. His arrival was somewhat concerning, as most of the guys in my crowd were a bit rough. And sure enough, my brother got kicked around a bit, maybe even a bit too much.

One thing which had plagued him for years was his stuttering. It came about in Palermo when a stray dog attacked him and pinned him against a wall. Fortunately, someone intervened, and he was not hurt but quite shaken up. Since then, he had a small speech impediment which would flare up if he was nervous. It was one of my friends who nicknamed him Put-Put, and for a while the name stuck. My brother still managed to fit in and very soon found a different crowd to run with, who immediately welcomed him with open arms.

Peter's troubles may have abated, but mine did not. And my setback had nothing to do with whom or where I hung out. It occurred in the bathroom every morning. When I combed my hair, large amounts of it would stick to the comb or cascade in the sink. It certainly frightened me! A teenager coming of age and confronting baldness equates to a catastrophic future, almost like knowing you may never get laid.

My concern led me to seek advice, and I consulted my father, a knowledgeable and very bald man. He advised me to shave it all off. This was not the solution I had hoped for. However, after considering it for a few days and seeing nothing would change, I became rather desperate, and decided to do it. For best results, according to the expert, it was crucial to continue the process for years. This would strengthen my scalp, and maybe my head would not start to shine so early in life.

I sat on a kitchen chair on top of volumes of encyclopedia books. Dad diligently went to work and quickly terminated the session, and the man's face beamed with such joy as he happily dismissed me.

Chapter 30

A new year arrived, and January had a few of us at Madison Square Garden to see the Doors. It was my first rock concert and my circumstances had me donning a wool cap to sort of hide my crew cut. This at a time when hair was all that mattered.

There were about six or seven of us, and before leaving the Bronx a few of us took some LSD. It came on as we rode the subway heading downtown. Suddenly, everything felt very strange indeed. It is rather difficult to explain, but things were not as they should be, for an eerie sensation within was somehow slightly distorting my reality. It felt like my mind was trying to convince itself of what was going on all around me and that my participation existed and mattered, yet everything seemed odd and somewhat unreal.

Then the incredible occurred. Me, a rather conservative one, was now the comedian among us. And no one could shut me up! All-of-a-sudden, the most outrageous things gushed from my mouth, and all my friends, although shocked at first, were soon enjoying the hilarious performance. They laughed uncontrollably while my tongue dished out bizarre and absurd thoughts that my brain was continuously fermenting. Quite unexpectedly, even some of the passengers in that noisy railcar were now listening, smiling, and nodding their approval.

It was one hell of a show! This unusual but hilarious state of affairs traveled with us all the way to the Garden. Before exiting our car, someone handed a small doll to our friend Sara, and it came with us. Now, once we got to our seats, an impulse to silence the comical engine running wild in me slowly took hold. It was still no easy task, and soon enough, a few of the people around us were enjoying my craziness as Sara then happily gave up her doll to someone sitting next to her. It was Sara's brother, Roger, who was a big Jim Morrison fan. He had taken the initiative to buy our tickets some weeks back, and he now ran off to the bathroom. It seemed like just a few minutes later the stage lights came on, and the band walked out. What a tragedy! Would they begin to play while one of their biggest fans was taking a leak? My case was pleaded loudly, to the amusement of the audience about me, and there were some stares from the band on stage. But almost immediately, and much to my relief, my good friend was back and right next to me.

Jim Morrison walked up to the microphone and said, "How's everybody feeling? Fucked up as usual?" A thunderous applause followed, for we, having assumed he was alluding to our state of mind, certainly agreed and wanted him to know it. Then in a degrading voice he said, "Yeah, right, sure." I now felt somewhat insulted, as if we had been taken down a notch or two by being labeled a bunch of miserable bastards. Oh well, it was hard to know who was doing the thinking, me or the acid.

What a spectacular show we witnessed! I had never been a big Doors' fan but knew and liked some of their songs. That night, I was fully converted.

Every tune sounded great, and those I recognized had been performed to perfection. Some tunes from their new LP were delivered with such force and good rhythm that it was hard to sit still.

The song which spoke directly to me was, "The End." While its melody and lyrics orbited my mind, my body seemed to float off somewhere, with me watching it from the side of an enormous lake, yet never touching its waters. Someone was now asking if time really existed, and while favoring a positive reply, some uncertainty led me astray. Then I saw myself sitting cross-legged on top of a hill and appeared frail, old, very tired, as if sitting there forever.

What an experience! Jim Morrison was my new idol that evening. He mastered his trade both as singer and performer, and he made the stage his personal world to recite in, while we the audience were fair game. He sang divinely, at times moved in a dance pattern, and once even fell to the stage floor and played dead for a while, but he never left you completely to yourself. You sensed he had a distant personality.

The performer was the act itself, within and without you. And once "Light My Fire" came on, there was what felt like a human explosion of relief and joyous endorsement, and suddenly folks were lighting up matchbooks as if to participate in the ordeal. It was a completely wild moment, but even crazier was later discovering that Sara's doll was now in the singer's hand.

To say we were all hypnotized when exiting the concert hall is a misnomer. Much was said about specific moments and certain songs. However, on the long ride home things changed abruptly. The jester in me had died sometime during the show, and now a lengthy period of silence engulfed us all. My body was completely exhausted, and when Roger asked how I felt, I quickly replied, "Like I have been beaten with hammers."

On the subway ride back to the Bronx, across me sat a stocky short Black woman. It was difficult determining her sex, but she seemed to be a woman. I then sensed a dismal bit of pain around a rather subdued face and could not help but wonder if her sexuality or its mixed gender or just what was it that seemed to be tormenting her? Oh well, I did not want to dwell on negative thoughts, and it seemed better to look elsewhere.

Yet a bit later, tears were flowing from her eyes. It led to my own personal minute agony for her, and it began strangling my cool composure. For some strange reason, now my very own existence was being questioned, and the more my life got analyzed, the sadder my spirit felt. Something within, not sure where it came from, whispered to me that I, Julian Di Stefano, was just living a fucking illusion.

Chapter 31

The school yard behind P.S.102 was a thing of the past. When not working, I would join my friends on Archer Street by Taylor Avenue where we congregated for hours. In front of us stood the corner delicatessen, and we sat on the hood of parked cars debating every imaginable topic.

Everyone in my group was an expert in some field. If you were not sure about something or had limited knowledge, you could simply make it up as you went along and hope no one called you out on it. Our main curriculum on weekends was deciding what to get high on. In winter, we abandoned that corner and huddled in the buildings on Taylor Avenue. Back then, the entrance doors were never locked, and it was a good thing as we often had absolutely no other place to go.

Our trespassing inside those buildings never lasted too long. Some pesky residents, either arriving or departing, would usually chase us out, and we would quickly head to an adjacent building. There, we squatted, continued whatever topic had been breached, and remained until either we were again asked to leave, in which case we sometimes went right back to the premises we previously vacated, or it was time to head home.

The Archer Street neighborhood was still predominantly Irish. A few Hispanics now resided there but on the outskirts. Overall, it was a White neighborhood, and to some extent, tolerant, as long as it remained White. There were exceptions, albeit very few, but one stood out a mile away. It was our new friend, Aaron.

Aaron was the only Black guy who hung out with us. Nobody was quite sure where he lived or could remember exactly when he joined us. He was such a pleasant individual and very easy-going. He stood tall and thin, and a great smile was always on display. Our friend would speak slowly and appeared to think carefully before confiding his ideas. On no account was there an unkind word toward anyone. Oh, by the way, he always possessed a joint or two.

Of course, there were different crowds scattered about our neighborhood. What brought or held any group together was basically their age and their interests. A few of the guys in my crowd longed to be hippies. A couple already were. There was one peculiar thing we all indulged in. We smoked plenty of pot, quite regularly.

We often lit up in the nearby empty lots. We smoked and drank in those lots for hours. One summer, when grass was hardly available, we resorted to just drinking or the occasional upper or downer. Most of us avoided LSD, which never sat well with me after that first and only experience. Our culinary drug use, however, was not a fixed menu, for it was prone to change depending on availability and what we could afford.

A completely different bunch of folks inhabited the bars on Beach Avenue. They were an older crowd, strictly against using any kind of drugs. They seemed mostly interested in drinking, sports, and an occasional brawl. Yet, they were slightly tolerant toward most of us. A few were very friendly with us, and a couple of them did occasionally smoke some weed.

The outcasts always remained by the handball court in the park behind P.S. 102. They were the junkies. Like a class unto themselves, when these people got high, they were quite stoned. A few of them, when not high, were either begging for money or trying to sell something. What certainly stood out, at least to me, was that most of them had some fine-looking girlfriends. Also, sometimes one came out of prison looking like Mr. Universe, but of course it was part of a lifestyle which did not last very long.

Not all the guys in our crowd had girlfriends. However, Roger, the big Jim Morrison fan, was with Susan permanently, as they were inseparable. No matter what the occasion, place, or time, there they were, all smiles, occasionally kissing, and always hand in hand. Everyone insisted they had been together forever. One had to wonder if they had met on their tricycles.

I am not sure why, but one day Shamus shared the name of a prospective and rather passionate young lady. She had been in our class back at St. Anthony's. It would have been rude to question his intentions, and so my randy spirit simply jumped on the opportunity. For a while, lucky me began to visit Nancy. Her residence was on a side street which I passed on my way home from work. That is why I began dropping in on Saturdays after work, just for a few hours when she had no plans.

It soon became routine. For Nancy kindly made life easy for me as she would invite me indoors with a great big smile. We hung out in the foyer and talked a bit but always ended up glued to each other and kissing so passionately as my hands quickly found her perfect breasts, which were always warm and readily available. She would inform me her parents were at home, but no one ever came out to check on our subtle but passionate affair.

Sometimes our sessions would terminate much too quickly as dinnertime was approaching. Occasionally, we would reunite later, go out for a few hours, but happily return to her place to resume business as usual. My, what I would have given to possess a small apartment, even a tiny room for that matter, or any place where we two could have accommodated our insatiable cravings. And mine, once energized, always insisted on releasing my pent-up volcanic seed a bit later.

Chapter 32

My freshman year at high school was coming to an end. It had started off well, yet it nosedived toward the end of the semester year. My biggest problems were not just scholastic ones. Life at home was miserable. Once again Ricky's health was not faring well, and Peter was drowning in academic issues. At times, my initiative toward anything felt slightly off course.

In school, surviving chemistry class seemed impossible. Not only was this subject totally boring but also quite incomprehensible. Our teacher, who looked like a goofy Jerry Lewis, assumed I was just plain lazy. It became apparent he did not fancy me one bit, and every chance the man got, he joyfully went out of his way to make me look like a complete idiot.

It sometimes seemed like that Sicilian kid in class had resurfaced completely intact. At least my history class was a different matter, and so was Italian. The latter one had me in the hands of a most beautiful teacher, a Greek goddess in my eyes. She certainly brought me back to life. However, it was a bit of a challenge participating, for yes, Giuliano Di Stefano, now known to the world as Julian, could not form a complete sentence in his once native language. What a shame, for all I yearned to impress that gorgeous Aphrodite.

While my academic progress was slowly sinking, Peter's was on life support. Nothing had changed since his arrival at P.S. 47 a few years back. The school principal and counselor had now advised our parents to place him in a trade school. Our folks, who were quite clueless as to what route to take, and desperate to try anything, agreed that he should pursue a vocational skill, hoping it was the right remedy.

In late December of that year, my father and I accompanied Peter to Lincoln Hall. The school is located in upstate New York, and I believe it is somewhere near Lincolndale. Upon arriving, we were certainly impressed with the campus grounds, as they were extensive and well-maintained. Plus, everyone we encountered appeared very polite and were talkative.

My brother's expression now betrayed a sense of loss. This saddened me even more than when we had left home that morning. It was to be our first separation since his birth. A counselor now stood next to my brother. Our hug was long, and my goodbye came out slowly, yet my emotions were in check. As our car later exited those academic grounds, I kept looking back hoping to see him, but Peter was no longer anywhere in sight.

The ride home felt like a long funeral procession. Neither of us spoke at all. My emptiness raged. I was feeling distraught and lightheaded and wondered how this could be happening. Just the same, Dad got us back to the Bronx, his eyes constantly taking in the road via his own agonizing thoughts while mine had finally produced a tear or two.

Chapter 33

If not on Archer Street, I was often in the nearby park by the handball courts. It was a new crowd which had me among them. One person I was now close to, who lived on Noble Avenue, and whose sister had been in my class at St. Anthony's, was Jimmy O'Conner.

Jimmy had an absurd way of looking at the world. He was a tad cynical, somewhat slightly critical of life in general, but super funny. At times, he seemed like a child who cannot sit still too long, yet it was easy to overlook this for his repertoire included a punch line to sort of legitimatize any rough issue we had taken on. One evening, he introduced me to his brother, Kevin.

Kevin was much older than both of us. He had recently divorced, was presently living at home with his parents, and had expressed an uncomfortable sense of not being able to move on in life. He was back to passing time in the very park he had left behind years ago. Plus, seeing some of his old friends now using heroin, made him feel a bit lost and perhaps somewhat confused.

It was a month after Kevin and I met that she came into my life. He and I had been to see one of Woody Allen's first movies at a cinema in Parkchester. Once back in our neighborhood, Kevin had stepped inside a store for a pack of cigarettes, and while exiting, two incredibly attractive girls were passing by. Both young ladies were lost in a happy chat, but my friend simply stepped right up to one of them. She immediately exploded into a fit of joy, as they then hugged and prattled on using hand gestures and pronounced facial expressions.

Apparently, they had been in high school together. After an introduction all around, I gave my undivided attention to this gorgeous girl standing next to me. She was a bit older than me, but her angelic look and gorgeous smile reeled me in. After all, does age ever really matter? Her name was Emilia, and her friend—much taller and well rounded off, still happily chatting away with Kevin—was Betty.

We walked to Betty's place which was close. Betty was a bit curious about my age, and I, the youngest by several years, informed everyone they could help me celebrate my turning nineteen in a few months. The venue was yet to be determined. Kevin flung an approving smile my way for my quick thinking, which to be honest was not one of my strong features. Both girls seemed somewhat satisfied.

The girls met us late Saturday afternoon on East Tremont Avenue. We rode the subway downtown to Central Park. Emilia looked stunning. A blonde with a creamy complexion, she appeared to radiate above and beyond the light blue dress she wore. Her sparkling blue eyes made me feel somewhat happy or, at least, happier than usual.

It was incredible! Our every word and thought created a most pleasant and warm feeling, sometimes followed by quite a bit of laughter. Our ride, although long, had us again in a tad of ecstasy, and we soon took in the park where some people were enjoying a casual stroll. Although the day had begun well for us all, it would not continue. We had sat on a bench in a slightly secluded area when things between Kevin and Betty began to sour.

Betty appeared somewhat uninhibited and was now challenging my friend. He looked puzzled and slightly irritated. She insisted they climb the tree behind us, but it was not to be. It sounded far-fetched, but it was my friend's solemn face which spoke volumes. Soon, neither one spoke at all, and it was apparent this date, their first, would be their last. As a matter of fact, they abandoned us and traveled back to the Bronx. It was the last time they saw each other.

Emilia was incredibly soft-spoken and volunteered few words, yet she was brilliant and ready to tackle any subject, especially my request to know the ideal place to settle down, which according to her was a small town in Massachusetts. We walked a bit, then left the park and got something to eat. No matter where my eyes took themselves, everything appeared to be so perfectly divine.

I had even mentioned my past from abroad. It was after we had left the park when Emilia inquired if I thought about my real mother. Her request slightly embarrassed me, and it seemed better to change subjects for I was clueless as to a reply. She then kissed me, pulled away while staring at me with a grin.

We returned to the Bronx early the following morning. Once off the subway we walked to her place. Outside her house, it seemed only right to share one last enduring kiss. On my way home, a few lines from "And I Love Her" began flowing out of me so perfectly. It was now 3:00 a.m., and my overactive mind would struggle to invoke a peaceful rest once in bed. Maybe a small slumber would ensue and give Emilia a leading role, like some unscripted aspiration flirting in my dreams. Oh well, life was good, and I certainly knew it.

I spent all my weekends with Emilia. We would go to the movies, eat out, catch a play at a nearby high school, or just talk and get to know each other. My folks met her, quite by chance. They were not supposed to be home. They appeared totally surprised, and the following day, they could not stop saying enough about her.

Everything was proceeding just fine. Then one evening my beautiful girlfriend unexpectedly questioned my age. As we had just celebrated my birthday a few days prior, it felt ridiculous to continue this lie. After all, what difference could it possibly make? Such was my line of thinking when something entirely unexpected came forth. Emilia wanted to get married and have children. Lots of children.

Now, in my scheme of things, marriage was still light-years away. It seemed wise to try to avoid the subject, one which had slightly alarmed me. Nevertheless, Emilia wanted to hear some kind of commitment, and she appeared rather anxious, almost as if she were making up for lost time, at least, that's how it seemed. Was there some cutoff date to contend with? Obviously, my silence did not much help her gloomy mood.

As we walked to her home, I quickly grasped that we had taken a road to nowhere. What can I say! My entire future lay in front of me, but it felt like a blank page. Someday it would certainly flourish, like some Renaissance era, but in my mind, that time was far off. Truth be told, yours truly was a bit clueless about many things. In my last year in grammar school, everyone had already mapped out their lives. Most students had chosen a profession they felt suitable to pursue. Why, some even knew exactly where they would live, and marriage was also an essential prospect to align with. I, on the other hand, was not just clueless, but simply nurtured the thought that tomorrow will bring everything, just wait and see.

The very next evening Emilia and I parted ways. We had spoken on the phone, and she sounded so far away. It felt awful concluding a relationship which had given me so much joy. A few months later I ran into Betty quite by chance. Now how absurd; she informed me that Emelia had joined the Air Force, which sounded so unlike her. Betty was convinced that she just wanted to somehow erase her past and start life anew. And yet, it was so bizarre, her exact whereabouts were completely unknown.

Chapter 34

School had become my worst nightmare. My body occupied a seat, but not the rest of me. It had felt a bit inappropriate at first, but my decision to drop out was now solid. Of course, presenting such a rash decision to my folks would be no easy task. Somehow, my need to speak up and be heard came forth.

My father heard me out and claimed he was not angry, yet his tone was a bit loud and bitter. Mom just nodded as if agreeing with his every word. She looked confused and shocked with my decision. Sure enough, an ultimatum was handed down. If I no longer wanted to go to school, I needed to move out.

Insisting I could find a decent job was useless. Dad had closed the issue. Well, was this not always the case? Peter and I were simply expected to obey house rules, family traditions, and improvised requests, for such were our commandments, most sacred, and never to be questioned. Our lot in life seemed to border on that of medieval times. Serving and pleasing the lord of the manor was our only function.

Regardless, my silence closed the issue. I would move on as soon as possible. On the following morning in school Shamus got a full report. After a small laugh over the details, he came to my rescue. Had my ears heard correctly? My friend calmly invited me to live with his family. Perhaps this was a prank? And once I accepted the offer, he would burst out laughing.

No, sir. My super close Irish friend was dead serious. Upon grasping this fact, it became almost impossible to stop thanking him. It was decided my move would occur that coming weekend. If there is something to state about Shamus O'Riley, which was a stone-cold fact, he was tough to the core, but he had a huge heart.

The O'Rileys lived on Beach Avenue. The maintenance of their building was their responsibility. I quickly observed it entailed quite a bit of work, but there were many of them. They occupied a large apartment in the basement of that edifice, and near the boiler room area was a small fully furnished flat which was my new quarters.

Shamus was the youngest male member of the family. He had an older brother and three lovely sisters. The man of the house was hardly ever home, having two jobs to contend with, but we occasionally caught a glimpse of each other, and he seemed a most serious person. Shamus' mom would sometimes invite me to dine with them, but it did not feel right to accept. They had already thrown me a lifeline; hopefully, I would be able to pay them back one day.

Well, right after moving in, a job, a real job, came my way. My new employment was with the Hudson Bay Waterways Corporation in the administrative department of the maintenance and repair shop in Co-op City. The job title was messenger, but having been told there were few messages to deliver, other tasks would come my way. So was the information given, which was happily accepted.

If you are not acquainted with the Bronx, allow me to expand. Co-op City is a large dwelling which consists of townhouses and high-rise buildings. It is practically a tiny city unto itself. There are parks scattered about, parking garages in each section, sports facilities, a firehouse, and, back then, its own security detail. If I understood correctly, the residents had to leave a down payment for their units after meeting some strict qualification requirements. Eventually, they would own them.

My co-workers called it "the city." In those days, it was considered an innovative and well-designed housing project to accommodate lower middle-income families. Each morning, after leaving the subway stop to head to section one (there are five), my eyes took in what looked like a quaint modern oasis. It was somewhat peaceful and clean, basking in its own light of freedom. At least such was the view from a distance.

Now what truly baffled me from day one was not my job but my ride to work. It began at the subway station, West Farms Sq./East Tremont Ave. For it was there, while awaiting my train, that the painful exodus going in the opposite direction befuddled my eyes. It simply shocked me. Were these commuters on the ride to hell?

A line of cars would briefly stop at my station to collect riders. No one within appeared to exchange a few words with anyone else, and some faces hid behind oversized newspapers, as if trying to stamp out their presence there. Other passengers seemed lost in thought, some perhaps meditating, while standing, or perhaps they were suffering quietly, and a few looked angry and confused. It was as if they had suddenly discovered there would be no Resurrection, at least not in their lifetime.

I had once read a bit about Dante's Inferno but was not acquainted with the poem. It appeared that here, I was witnessing a glimpse of its tale. It startled me. My school had provided us with a ton of positive facts, and we were made to understand that our country was the greatest in the world. I foolishly believed it. But weren't our Founding Fathers keen on claiming the right to be happy? This fundamental truth was often presented as if it had been handed down by God to George Washington up on Mount Vernon. Oh well, maybe it had become totally insignificant, for everyone just looked so fucking miserable.

It was better not to think. Hiding behind a book kept me intact. Reflecting on the meaning of life, modern employment, and its peculiar features while heading uptown, was immediately drowned out. Yet one thing was certain. Julian would never join that cattle ride heading in the opposite direction.

Chapter 35

Quite by chance, I ran into Betty one afternoon. She seemed most happy, and we chatted for a while. Once again, there was no news of Emilia. It seemed a bit peculiar that her friend had sort of vanished, but I let the matter drop. My information regarding work, or the lack of it, had me slightly complaining over the long days as my manager had not yet decided how to fully utilize me when not running messages.

Betty carried on about life at home and her closeness to her younger sister. It soon became apparent she did not want to part just yet, which is why I very diplomatically threw out my, "not seeing anyone," after which she was invited to catch a movie with me that weekend. She offered me a warm smile and stated she would certainly join me.

I saw much less of my friend Kevin nowadays but still felt an obligation to receive his blessing, so I mentioned our date to him. My friend sighed, wished me the best of luck and nicely insinuated that it would be the date from hell.

It certainly wasn't! That Saturday evening, we ate at Jack's Diner on Westchester Square. The date proceeded smoothly, and not being asked to climb any trees was somewhat invigorating. Betty was a good listener, and quite good at contributing most freely. Plus, she appeared happy to be with me. Now please forgive my arrogance and simplistic ways. She was not Emilia; and so there would be no magic air happily bringing me home. Nevertheless, like two good friends, we shared a wonderful time together and agreed to do it again.

Summertime had arrived quickly, and one weekend Betty and I had gone downtown to catch a movie. The timing of our companionship was auspicious. Although I still hung out in the neighborhood, I now hardly ever saw my friends from Archer Street. Some of them hung out in the park by the handball court area. Getting high was still very much everyone's gig, yet they all kept their distance from the smaller crowd nearby, the heroin users. Their weekend sins consisted mostly of a lot of pot smoking and some light drinking, plus there was always a bit loud rock music blasting on someone's radio.

Anyhow, the film we saw was by Jean Luc Godard in which the Rolling Stones were captured while recording "Sympathy for the Devil." We anticipated something interesting because we both loved the Stones' music, but we exited the cinema hall slightly disappointed. The Stones appeared like innocent bystanders to a message of revolution which we two did not fully grasp.

Back in the Bronx, by the handball court area, the totally unexpected occurred. This incident is being mentioned mostly for one reason. It goes to the moral core of who we were and how we lived—a bunch of young people with no hostility or violent intentions toward anyone—but always hoping to have some fun time together and get by. Unfortunately, I missed the action that night.

One of my friends in the park that night was Jim Messina. Jim was an extremely jovial and lovable character, someone who radiated sheer innocence. He was stocky, if not a tad overweight, had long curly hair, and wore such thick glasses. The guy, being mellow and rather laidback, made us all see him as a bit passive in his persona.

Suddenly, a small group of people had approached the handball court area. These were the guys from one of the bars on Beach Avenue. They took themselves over to the park benches where everyone was gathered, and Fred Dunnegan, the leader that evening, very loudly said, "The nigger needs to leave the park."

He was referring to Aaron. And just like my fight at the football match, a veil of silence seized the entire crowd. It was Jim who spoke up and stated that Aaron was our friend. He had been coming to the park for years and was certainly not bothering anyone. Now, Jim's words were delivered in a very upright and soft-spoken manner, but it was not what Fred wanted to hear. Obviously, he had not come to parley and so went into action. He quickly removed his shirt, exposing a well-formed muscled physique, and he challenged Jim to fight him. No one, and I mean no one, thought Jim stood a chance.

Fred now became arrogant and insulted Jim for refusing to fight. After a minute of excessive verbal abuse and realizing he had little or no choice in the matter, Jim, cool to the core, removed his watch and eyeglasses. After carefully placing them on the park bench, he began boxing. In no time at all Fred Dunnegan was annihilated. Everyone was completely shocked!

As per facts revealed to me the following day, Jim looked like a professional boxer. He delivered fast pounding blows which Fred simply could not block, and he very quickly moved in close and hurled more devastating powerful punches. He managed to quickly grab his opponent and violently flung him to the concrete ground while continuously pounding him.

It was over very fast! The beaten fighter had been completely overwhelmed and was forced to throw in the towel rather quickly. Although badly bruised and barely able to stand up, he insisted there would be a rematch.

They fought a week later. Once again, yours truly missed all the excitement. As in the first encounter, our friend tried again to avoid the confrontation. Everyone there agreed he was just so fucking cool, but it was no use, for the beaten champ needed to restore his good name and obviously thought he could. However, everyone witnessed a rerun of the previous encounter. Jim Messina simply pulverized his opponent. Someone said it was too bad Aaron was not present that evening, as he would have again witnessed how loyalty to friendship and dedication to what is right are symbolic of humility and kindness, for that is the American way.

Regrettably, the only Black friend among us never returned to the neighborhood. We all missed his warm smile and friendly ways and even wondered about his whereabouts. Whereas Fred's arrogance, although no longer on display for a while, may have never totally abated, and who can say if still today he feels a need to determine who should be where in the scheme of things?

Chapter 36

Work began to improve, albeit slowly. A few easy assignments would occasionally come my way. While doing some filing one morning, my mother called. She wanted to know if I had seen Peter. This slightly puzzled me. He was in Lincoln Hall, wasn't he?

Apparently, the restless critter had taken a small vacation. My brother and two other kids had run away. Our mom was now up in arms and could not contain her hysterics. It is a curious thing, it was John Cariaccio who first brought the incident to light. He now drove a truck delivering gas and the previous day had just parked it somewhere on Leland Avenue.

The delivery man spotted Peter nearby, so he called out to him suspecting something was wrong. My brother and a few friends were all loaded down with fishing gear as they were heading out to City Island for the day. Of course, the fisherman in our family assured John that life at home was just great, and he was happy to be back.

Mom was now pleading for my assistance. Someone from the school would need help in getting to the neighborhood but also identifying which crowd to look out for. It was very important that he bring Peter back to the school! I was tempted to ask, dead or alive, but my humor would not have been appreciated by our despairing mother. Well, although imbued with a small sense of betrayal, she got me to try and help out.

Late afternoon on the following day, a stocky Black gentleman met me. We began to cruise the neighborhood in his large station wagon, specifically the park area around Leland Avenue. There was no sign of my brother. When approaching a few of his friends, feeling a bit foolish and very out of place, I inquired of my brother's whereabouts, and some sly devil craftily insinuated that he was upstate in a reformatory school, wasn't he? The search continued as we toured that neighborhood. Eventually, the very silent driver next to me decided it was fine for a day's work, so he took me home, and I believe he returned upstate the following day.

While on the phone the previous day, my mom's apprehension had finally abated. So, I mentioned the need to come home to retrieve some clothes left behind which would come in handy now. She was fine with me coming over at my convenience as she and Ricky were practically home all day. A few days later that peculiar building on Rosedale Avenue stood in front of me.

Inside the courtyard some loud Latino music had a few guys jumping. There were also a few professionals in uniform moving some furniture, and Spanish was the only language spoken. Obviously, in no time at all, a complete transformation had occurred, and for a moment it felt like no one had bothered to inform me.

Once inside our apartment, I felt so out of place. It was as if my feet were now desecrating some sacred grounds. While walking cautiously, a nagging feeling inside me would not subside. My heart almost skipped a beat. I had entered our room, and my brother's appearance completely devastated me. A lump formed in my throat.

Not only was Ricky completely bald, but he was thin as a rail. He acknowledged my presence but was too weak to show any feelings. I somehow controlled myself, and we sat on his bed, me caressing him some. He placed his head on my chest, and we remained like that for a while. A bit later, after some hugs and kisses, I spoke to him while getting my things and packing them. I kissed him again and soon left.

I have never forgiven myself for not staying. He began to belt out one of our favorite Beatles' songs, and we gave it a lovely rendition. Maybe it would have given him a bit of pleasure even if he had not participated. I can be such an idiot. My selfish and ignorant lifestyle had completely blind-sided me. It was my era of living only for me, and, too often, in a blind fog.

Chapter 37

Occasionally my office appeared truly bizarre! It felt like a war zone. Too often, some of the employees would argue, occasionally shout a bit, and tended to exaggerate with our customers, the very folks who were seeking our help.

Co-op City residents would arrive to complain about problems in their apartments. They were either scheduling an appointment for service or rescheduling an appointment as the maintenance crew, who constantly worked behind schedule, had never made it to their unit. A few folks, especially those who lost a day of work, could not contain their frustration.

And they were right! Why were the Co-op City units so inundated with problems? It had been called a residential mecca and promoted as a cooperative housing dream, yet we endured the numerous complaints. The usual ranting covered everything from intercoms that did not work properly, leaky faucets in the bathrooms or the kitchen, water leaking from the toilets, water leaks under the sinks, windows that did not close properly, and so on.

My fellow co-workers were hardly moved by any of this. They appeared more than ready for the good fight. I simply observed, listened attentively, and often got to witness loud shouting matches. What certainly startled me was the lack of sympathy toward the residents' complaints and also having to watch the complainants get an ear full.

Our office was responsible for responding to fix the problems in the units. They recorded the request as a work order and passed it to the maintenance branch after first scheduling an appointment. However, my co-workers were not about to be pushed around. The branch was manned by some stocky middle-aged women, who were full of fire. Consequently, they did not put up with any crap.

Those iron ladies had spent years as stay-at-home moms. And now that their darlings had gone off to college, they had merrily rushed back into the work force in excellent fighting spirit. Ferocious and fast, those burly seasoned fighters seemed to fully enjoy and embrace the customary shouting matches which occurred.

One day, the usual fray erupted, and it was apparently just the opening act. Here was a pesky and irate elderly couple going on and on while refusing any interruption by the staff member, who was beginning to lose it. Unexpectedly, while standing at the counter where I was previously chatting with our clerk, I foolishly intervened in a rather delicate tone and cleverly inserted a few amiable words. Miraculously, it worked, as no verbal melee ensued.

My fast-thinking might have avoided another fatal fiasco, or so I thought. However, the manager, who had been standing nearby, called me to the side and quickly reminded me, in case I had forgotten, that the counter was not my area of business. And, by the way, didn't I have any messages to deliver?

It seemed only right to bow, smile, and leave. While walking, I wondered if all work organizations were so demeaning and brutal in function or process. Fortunately, I ran into one of the guys from the maintenance branch whom I often spoke with. All were high school graduates and quite proud of their accomplishment, and we had a brief, friendly chat. I never indulged fully into it for it seemed wise to be cordial but keep my distance.

If work seemed a bit stormy, life at home was sheer bliss. In the evenings, Shamus would drop in, and we would scrutinize everything—sports, my job, the guys in the neighborhood, getting high, music we liked, the war in Vietnam, and when the rare occasion occurred, our latest romantic encounter.

Shamus seemed a bit reserved with his tales of the heart. I, on the other hand, trusting him entirely, opened up once his ears were all mine. Truth be told, I had never gone all the way. However, for all my bogus romantic flings, once again, my heart knew true love. It was a sealed matter and known only to me. I was crazy about Shamus' oldest sister, Fiona. And it was not some precipitous fall, like with Frances. This had developed quietly and over time.

She was graceful, composed, and had a soft voice. She was also quite beautiful. Whenever we shared a few words, she made profound statements, and there was no subject she shied away from. Once, we briefly delved into the arena of injustice—social and political. Big mistake, for the fire in her lit so strongly as she spoke about the plight of her people in Northern Ireland.

Yet one day, Fiona startled me. She admitted feeling unhappy living in the U.S. What bothered her most was the lack of social communal warmth and cheerfulness, like what she had grown up with. In her town, she had special bonds with childhood friends, who had always been there and would always be there, whereas her few friends here were nothing more than mere acquaintances.

Although I dished out a few encouraging words, I hated myself for not being able to do more. Like a cog in a wheel, unless propelled to move, I sat still and proposed the obvious. Oh well, perhaps my presence and sincerity may have soothed her some. Now the following day, it was Shamus who shocked me. He calmly informed me he had joined the Merchant Marines, and having assumed he meant the military, I sat there quite speechless.

He soon explained he would be working on ships transporting commercial cargo. It was his big chance to travel, see the world, and get out of the Bronx for a while. And according to him, there was good money to be made. My friend appeared so sure about his new adventure, yet something in me suspected he may have been pressuring himself to move on. But why? Had his life perhaps been put on hold and this was the only way forward.

While listening, Shamus suddenly jumped up and ran to raise the volume on the radio. The room reverberated with a very delightful tune, and we may have both closed our eyes for a few seconds. The beat had me swaying some, and the lyrics claimed that at times traveling airs out all symptoms. Wow, a life gone by being revaluated through musical poetic justice.

We both remained glued in place, enjoying the melodious narrative. Once it finished, a thought registered. When a voice within calls for movement, then the body must simply comply. Shamus' choice now made a bit more sense for at times traveling airs out all uncertainties.

Chapter 38

It is impossible to explain why I tried heroin. From my perspective, it was considered a dangerous drug to be avoided. Shamus had been gone for a while, and that day Betty, her sister, and her dad had gone to Long Island to visit family. Was it simply the right moment to experiment? But why with something so dangerous?

Approaching the heroin users in the seedy section of the park seemed unreal, and I risked being ripped off. But Louis, one of the few Hispanic guys among us, was an ex-addict who sometimes swore he was clean for life, yet he did not always convince us. My request left him speechless for a few seconds. He outright refused to assist me and began preaching a familiar sermon finishing with, "You know, once a junkie, always a junkie."

And yet, upon mentioning a small sum would be his if he complied, the guy slowly changed his tune. That took him to where a few folks already stoned were sitting, but he returned to inform me no one had anything. However, he now knew where to get some, and it would take about an hour. So once money transferred hands, he was gone and returned after a very long time. Truth be told, my uncanny mind had envisioned him telling me he had gotten ripped off.

All my friends were truly shocked. Jim Messina appeared somewhat upset as he simply could not fathom what had gotten into me. But Louis eventually returned smiling, and we immediately departed for a nearby empty lot. He shot himself up, whereas I sniffed a white powder that came in a tiny aluminum foil packet. It was bitter and had a medicinal taste. The effects struck so quickly.

On our walk back to the park, I was very high. There was a feeling of being slightly off physically with not a care in the world within. It was a bit later, once rejoining our friends, when I began to feel sick. While sitting on a bench, I spoke slowly, did not always finish my thoughts, and even slightly nodded out a bit. Then, I jumped up and ran toward the nearby trash bin but did not make it. Everything in my stomach was now on the pavement.

A bit later, it hit home how wrong this was. Although still a bit groggy and slightly incomprehensible in speech, it seemed foolish to experiment with heroin, something so addictive and destructive. The proof was all around me in that park from guys who lived a lifestyle quite beyond their control. Then, a more peculiar notion hit hard. How was it possible that people continued to use it and become addicted?

I may have found one of the answers to that more quickly than I would like—tragedy. It seems that tragedy begets more tragedy.

Fiona woke me up one morning. It was a bit strange seeing her standing by my bed. Having turned in a bit late the previous night, I was lingering under the covers semiconscious. She looked terribly sad. Apparently, something was wrong. She stared at me as hesitating to speak.

Finally, Fiona found her voice and told me I needed to go home. She took a deep breath and informed me that Ricky had died. I do not remember much else. My walk to our building on Rosedale Avenue is also a blank page. Once in the apartment, a few of mom's relatives were gathered in the dining area where my mother was desperately crying. Dad was in his chair in the living room just staring at the wall. A couple of my mom's relatives sat nearby.

After shaking hands and humbly greeting everyone, I sat next to my father. The silence was slightly unbearable, and very soon, perhaps feeling uncomfortable, the men excused themselves and went downstairs. While sitting, my mind struggled with trying to comprehend why a merciful God takes the life of a child, especially after his long suffering. Was it to finally relieve him of his pain and now extend ours?

For some reason, not one single tear flowed from my eyes. Just like the man next to me, my mind was numb, and my spirit was buried elsewhere. It was like an impenetrable wall surrounded me, and its structure would stand solid forever. I did not stay long but cannot remember where I went off to.

The following day, Fiona offered to accompany me to the wake. I needed to be alone. My walk proceeded fine, but once inside the morgue and entering the room where my brother lay, something began to suffocate me. I felt so out of line, especially with so many eyes observing me as I faltered toward the coffin. I began to wonder if I was guilty of something.

Aunt Mia approached. She gently embraced me and guided me toward Ricky. We knelt together. She slightly sobbed while holding me tight. Then my aunt said, "He loved you so very much, Julian." Nevertheless, my isolation remained solid, my lips sealed, for nothing seemed to touch me. Eventually, we left the casket and sat not too far from her sister. My father's figure came into view, as he appeared so vulnerable, and just plain worn out. His face racked in deep pain. The man had just lost his son. Then a fleeing thought surfaced so quickly—he had lost three.

That night, I drank a beer at a bar on Beach Avenue not far from Shamus' place. No one asked for any ID. Maybe the neighborhood grapevine had my back. Some guys who played for the local football team, the Archer Rams, came over to express their condolences and offer me a few kind words. It was tough to speak freely, but after thanking them most sincerely, I finished the beer and went home.

Fiona was soon in my room. What a gentle and kind soul she was. She must have fully embraced my situation from day one, a grown teenager, coming of age and yet still young, somewhat naïve, over-sensitive, and full of faith in life, but maybe born to suffer. Her presence nurtured my silence. She was a truly beautiful spirit in a perfect body. A woman who would never flaunt her strength, but her radiance glowed and soothed. I loved Fiona, desired her immensely, and needed her comfort so badly, but for now, I desperately sought to be alone.

Ricky's funeral was held at St. Anthony's Church. My mother's relatives, and there were many, and a few of our dad's friends were in attendance. Peter was present, and so we sat next to each other. Once the mass began, my mind kept reshuffling my dilemma with a good and all forgiving God.

Our parents were engulfed in a sea of pain. Ours was not a sinking ship, it already lay on the ocean floor. As we left the church, our mother once again completely lost it. A nun approached us, and rather than comfort her, she very sternly said, "Mrs. Di Stefano, you must get a hold of yourself. Richard would not want to see you like this." Such is human folly at its best. Too often, we fail to truly acknowledge someone else's pain.

We arrived at St. Raymond's Cemetery. It was a sunny and warm June day, and it seemed like the weather welcomed us to those sacred grounds as if to embrace our brother's departure on a light note. The burial was over quickly, and once the casket was lowered, our mother began to bawl, and she refused to leave her son's tombstone. Some of her relatives and our dad assisted her as best as possible.

A few minutes later, we got into our limousines and proceeded to leave the cemetery grounds. Throughout this entire ordeal, my petrified heart had outright refused to acknowledge our reality. Never once had a single tear been shed, and just why it was so I cannot say. Only when the limousine exited the main entrance did Julian Di Stefano crumble. A striking force of spiritual lightning pierced my heart. I began to weep uncontrollably and could not contain myself.

My beautiful brother had just touched me. Of this, I am sure. Yes, that angelic little soul whom we all loved so much was gone, now leaving me to continue to walk alone. This was our last moment in the final act of our personal journey. I now finally grasped an unbearable truth. I would never see him again.

Chapter 39

My personality, at times, borders on aloofness and contemplation. It can also perform delightfully and leave those around me feeling cheerful, but with Ricky's passing, my penchant for fun regressed dramatically. It made me more of an observer than a participant, for anything I did was simply because I had to.

A couple of classmates from St. Anthony's played guitar. And it was a few months before the funeral that I had joined their band as the lead singer. We practiced in the drummer's apartment, which drove the tenants insane. Yet every Saturday afternoon, the four of us religiously went through our gig of rock songs. "Five to One" was my favorite. It allowed a bit of my anger to get properly rendered in the final phase.

My voice was good, somewhat melodic but also strong. After Ricky's death, it became difficult to go practice, and even though I would show up, I wasn't truly there. My weekends became empty as participating in anything seemed unexciting, and I began to devour books in the evening. Someone had mentioned Jack London's *The Iron Heel*. It was now in my possession and absorbing my mind completely.

Fiona would come by often. She always provided me with a healthy time-out from too much reading. One evening, she confided in me that she was seeing someone from the neighborhood, but she suspected it would not last. She mentioned how he did not have a serious bone in his body. Of course, he was fun and funny, but much too plain and limited in thinking, real thinking.

Once Fiona moved on, Shamus came to mind. I was a tad curious. Just what sort of work did sailors do on those merchant vessels? We knew so little about what he was doing for he was not one prone to write, and I was informed his phone calls home were few and brief. Before his departure, Shamus had been specific about his new travails, he had joined the SIU (Seafarer's International Union), and then jokingly remarked that like Uncle Sam, they too were looking for a few good men.

My curiosity in his venture had remained dismal. Yet somewhere in my notebook, existed a phone number and name he had given me of a gentleman located in Brooklyn. He would be my point of contact should I ever feel the need to call. And for some time now, that thought from the Doors' concert bothered me some. Was I just living an illusion? If yes, how to break free was still a bit of a mystery to me. Should I escape? Even though there were people around me, I felt so very alone.

Peter and I would run into each other from time to time. For quite a while we had become a tad estranged, but our stern childhood bond had never vanished. I knew of his whereabouts, and we occasionally sought each other out and gave it our best to stay in touch.

The young critter had returned to Lincoln Hall but ran away again. The institution must have simply written him off as no one contacted me to try to locate him. He now lived with a Chinese friend, and just like me had been comfortably accommodated in the basement area, but in a small older house. He and his host worked out of his friend's van delivering bean sprouts and other vegetables to various Asian restaurants throughout Manhattan and Queens.

Peter was a happy camper! At times, he slightly filled that image of a modern-day Huck Finn. He cherished his freedom, could never be cooped up by any scholastic institution, and the unusual antics he stumbled into pushed him onward to more wild and whacky adventures. And as the two delivery workers usually finished their runs by early afternoon, they were then masters of their day and nights. Weekends were sacrificed some but not entirely, and who really cared?

We met one late afternoon and headed off to Manhattan to see the movie *Gimme Shelter*, which had just been released and was getting excellent reviews. Upon arriving at the cinema, a long line snaking around the corner from the theater assured us we were in for a worthy treat. And soon, we enjoyed the movie's opening scene which introduces the band on stage while catching a photo shoot elsewhere for it seemed very cleverly done. Well, we caught the band's 1969 tour in the U.S. hearing an incredibly loud and perfect soundtrack for each performance that made it feel like we were at those concerts. We also witnessed the group's daily movements, along with those sponsoring them, which gave us a realistic insight into the life of rock musicians.

Unfortunately, the film ends on a painful note. It terminated our joyful viewing with some violence, which felt too close for comfort, and that may have created a sense of vulnerability. The so-called love generation, having proudly fed itself mostly on music and getting high, was witnessing what felt like the collapse of an idealistic world. What we could not have fathomed was that, in reality, this was the beginning of a new industry, outdoor concerts for a massive crowd.

What a great night out. We parted ways back in the Bronx somewhere on East Tremont Avenue. And while heading home, my mind reflected on our past and how we had been raised with a heavy hand of discipline in Sicily and at home here in the Bronx. Peter had been hit more severely than me by both our grandmother and dad. Yet his cheerfulness and immense love for all seemed to cancel out that horrific upbringing. Later at home, in bed, my mind strongly hoped I had inherited some of those same glorious genes.

Chapter 40

Betty and I had been together for some time. The people who knew us in our neighborhood assumed we were a real couple. After all, we seemed inseparable. One Saturday night, we headed off to see Mountain, my favorite hard rock band, which was playing at the Fillmore East.

Now if any rock group should get top honors for creating what would soon be called heavy metal, it is certainly Mountain. They had gotten recognized at Woodstock, and their fan base grew very quickly, but although they emerged as a powerful rock group, the band did not remain in the music scene very long.

We were close to the stage, and it felt impossible to sit still as we were overcome by the raw energy and overpowering melodic songs. My favorite tune, "Theme for an Imaginary Western" put me in sheer heaven as the group continued to fiercely blast us away and that rhythm held us in a sway. Sometime between tunes Betty and I would look at each other as if hoping the evening would never end.

It was well after midnight when we exited the concert hall. Our eardrums were still vibrating, but all sorts of positive facts came to light about the show. We now faced a small dilemma, a long noisy subway ride uptown. Then someone called out my name. Why, it was Harry, one of the guys from the maintenance branch in Co-op City. He and a friend were soon at our side, and my co-worker appeared a bit surprised to see me there.

Almost immediately, Betty, who looked quite sharp that night, was scrutinized. Perhaps Harry even grasped our relationship, as we were not a real couple. Yet he held off intruding for we immediately began carrying on about the outstanding performance. It was upon mentioning our dreaded ride back to the Bronx that my friend insisted he would gladly drive us.

We happily accepted and soon got into a new black Camaro. Almost immediately, the Woodstock festival became a topic of discussion. Everyone agreed it was unforgivable not to include Mountain's performance in the movie which followed. None of us had been to Woodstock, but the film had mesmerized everyone plenty and perhaps convinced promoters that outdoor musical venues were here to stay.

Eventually, we were in front of Betty's digs. Sure enough, Harry let on that he was single and available, and yes, Betty got the drift but remained the charming noncommitted soul she was. Once on our own, we sat in front of her building as neither of us was ready to part ways. Something in me threw caution to the wind and kissed her.

A cool breeze accompanied me home a bit later. Then quite suddenly a peculiar thought surfaced. Perhaps, it had been brewing for some time, and it was now encouraging me to act boldly. I would join the Merchant Marines. Yes, this was certainly a direction into uncharted waters, and yet sustained by the belief that sometimes the unknown is not to be feared.

My father was not buying it. It made no difference what I said, the man was not at all moved. Neither was his wife. Not even making good money seemed to faze them in the least. We had spoken briefly on the phone the previous evening. Dad, of course, sounded like his usual serious self, and I was now in their apartment hoping to win my argument.

Obviously, my presence would not change anything. He refused to bless my initiative, for according to him, it was all very simple. His brief experience out at sea had given him a negative view of sailors. Part of a world of poor and sinister souls who would never fit in anywhere nor find their true calling in life, is how he labeled them. Simply put, this was a world of losers, and no son of his was a loser.

My disappointment followed me home. Nevertheless, a few days later, I resigned myself to the fact that this venture did not require my father's approval or consent. I called Mr. Chase at the union hall in Brooklyn and instructed him to mail me the application. Finally, it truly seemed like my stalled existence was now turning a corner.

Chapter 41

It was a weeknight which had Betty and I in a pizza shop. She was shocked hearing of my upcoming adventure, going to sea. Like me a few months back, she also suspected the Merchant Marines was somewhat affiliated with the military, and she then stated most eloquently that this was not my cup of tea, however after some explanation, she blessed my initiative.

My friend seemed sure I would be okay and was curious to know if my new venture was a career move or just temporary. A tough question to answer. Oh well, later we parted ways and agreed to keep in touch, yet something in me suspected it would not happen. Just the same, we embraced, said goodbye, as I offered a few silly words thanking her for having been there.

Leaving Betty was not easy, but Fiona was in a completely different category. I found her a bit too quiet. It felt as if she had known this was coming and had understood nothing could impede it. After hearing me out, she admitted not being happy with Shamus, for he had sort of temporarily vanished. She requested I not do the same. For a moment, we simply stared at each other. I hugged her having noticed her sad eyes as she said, "Please remember, always be true to yourself."

A few days later, I was in Mr. Chase's office. My eighteenth birthday had just passed. At first it seemed everything was off to a good start. However, upon finishing all the administrative work, nothing which followed was even close to what I had imagined. One big surprise followed another, and most of the other recruits were just as shocked as yours truly.

We were all accommodated in a building near the union hall. This was the processing center, and the following morning, I and six other guys were issued military clothing, Navy work blues and boots, khaki pants and shirts, along with black shoes to match, plus a duffle bag. It felt more like being prepared for boot camp than having joined a union. That afternoon, someone marched us down a block to a barber shop where we were razed like sheep.

More newcomers continued to arrive every day from every imaginable city in the continental U.S. A few days later, a large group of the recruits left Brooklyn. We were on a private bus heading to the Harry Lundberg School of Seamanship located in Piney Point, Maryland. While eying the road out of New York and making myself as comfortable as possible, a small sense of grief unexpectedly grabbed me.

I missed Ricky so much. Not having been at his side in his last few days was so unforgivable. And upon considering my dad's pain, mine was almost immediately deemed insignificant. Our brother had spent his last few hours in our father's arms. The man continued telling his son stories he wanted to hear until the boy's final last breath. He died in his arms at three in the morning.

The guy sitting next to me began talking. Perhaps he sensed my discomfort. The chap was much older than me and for some reason appeared like a soldier. He began talking very politely about having just attended his sister's wedding in Minnesota. His expansive joy was knowing she had married a man he truly admired. According to him, knowing how much his new brother-in-law loved and respected his sister was all that mattered.

I was even informed about him. He now lived in Connecticut with his lovely British wife. They had met in a small town in England, and he wished they were still back there. People were so full of life, friendly and helpful, and quite merry, especially in the pubs. Perhaps my eyes begged for a moment to myself, for he now asked if I was okay. I assured him an unpleasant moment had just passed, and so he allowed me some rest.

I quickly dozed off. Soon, the Doors' concert opened up again. This time, I stood behind the stage looking at Jim Morrison. The transgender person who had sat opposite me on the subway was at my side. It felt as if we knew each other, and we understood this was the band's final performance. Then the singer on stage, whose back was to us, went to the microphone and said, "Life is just a fucking dream which will one day awaken you."

Almost immediately, Long Branch came to me. I was riding a wave, and Peter was watching me from the shore, happily shouting out to our new friends, "Look at Julian. He is so fucking good! He will ride that wave until it breaks, but he will never break." Now, was it the acid speaking or him or me? And was I truly just fucked up as usual?

My eyes opened. We had just exited the New Jersey Turnpike and were now entering Delaware. My life was such an unpredictable trip. Like a never-ending rollercoaster ride. It had begun in Nuneaton, taken off in Leicester City and hurled down to Palermo, turned around and headed uphill to Barazzetto, only to slide back down and up again, then once more down for a layover in Palermo—yet the engine was kept running. And soon onward to the Bronx, only to now begin to glide down to Southern Maryland.

Part 3

Chapter 42

The Harry Lundberg School of Seamanship is in St. Mary's County. It faces St. Mary's River and has its back to Piney Point Road. Upon arriving we felt a bit uneasy about our whereabouts. There was a tall fence running along the road surrounding the school. A portion of St. George Creek jutted out by the pier, and the entire school grounds seemed like a cage.

The school had all the makings of a small military base. We now understood our lot for the next three months. This crabby-looking camp was home, and we discovered that any idea of getting somewhat acquainted with the nearby town and its surroundings was highly improbable.

Sure enough, the following day, our worst fears were confirmed. That morning we were taken to a large parking lot where a wiry fellow in a khaki uniform with one hell of a Southern accent began shouting out orders. Assisting him were several guys dressed the same. They were ready to instill discipline in anyone not ready to fully cooperate. Yes, sir, we had joined a union, but it felt like we were in the army, and would now be put through some basic military drills.

The entire morning consisted of practicing different maneuvers. They instructed us how to march, do an about-face, open and close ranks, and other exciting soldierly drills. If anyone failed to respond quickly and properly, they were yelled at viciously. Our morning was full of verbal jargon applied soundly, as our instructors appeared to be truly enjoying themselves. It was later that evening that we discovered they, too, were trainees, only with little time left to serve the school. Go figure!

At noon, we were led to a long rectangular bungalow called the chow hall. And we had to remain perfect soldiers, for the smallest infraction or a tiny fluke in our movement triggered the ire of our superiors. As we waited to enter the dining facilities, a bunch of students, who were without a doubt not new trainees, marched by in perfect coordination. They certainly had the look of professional cadets. All that was missing were weapons, a drill sergeant, and a guidon.

Well, when you are hungry, you will eat just about anything. I took up a tray along with other starved students and formed a line that turned around a long counter. We chose various food items in front of us, and while nothing looked too appetizing it was all definitely edible. One of the guys sitting next to me introduced himself. He was Sean Blatter, from San Francisco. I soon came to realize how nothing seemed to slip by Sean without him attaching a proper label to it. Once through eating, we stepped outside the dining facility to enjoy a cigarette, the only befitting pleasure to crown a quick meal with. And curiously, it was a somewhat decent habit which was not restricted.

Shamus came over to my bungalow that evening. What a pleasant surprise. It had only been three months since we separated, but it seemed like a lifetime. He briefly acquainted me with some of the school dos and don'ts. He did not stay long because students were not allowed to be in bungalows they were not assigned to.

A few days later, Shamus returned to Brooklyn to begin life at sea. Before his departure, we spoke briefly. He instructed me not to go over the fence at night, should the occasion arise, as there was absolutely nothing of interest anywhere in the vicinity. He appeared certain of this and had probably found out the hard way.

Our bungalow bordered the fence by the Piney Point Road. There were several of these small type cabins, which although comfortable, deprived us of any privacy. We trainees also shared a large bathroom attached to our living quarters, and not far off was the so-called chow hall, which we punctually visited three times a day.

There were about seven or eight guys in my bungalow, and we were referred to as a squad. The squad leader was called a bosun, and he bore the responsibility for leading the group around. Ours appeared capable enough and seemed like an okay guy, even though he bragged of being from New Jersey, as if to exalt his status in life. To me, it seemed like we all shared one common trait. Although we were all from different cities and circumstances, our objective was the same—to make it out of this school and ultimately improve our status quo.

The blue uniforms we wore may have assisted us in starting a clean slate. And maybe they also served to keep order within the institution's ranks. We wore blue jeans and blue work shirts and boots, but our bosun wore khaki pants, a black polo shirt, and black shoes. He looked sharp and certainly stood out, but he always kept his cool and treated us all with warm kind words.

It was the month of January, and it was cold. Our heavy coats, gloves, and caps with fur lining protected us from the rather crisp incoming winds, and sure enough, on our first week of training, we were on the pier facing the creek and a bit of harsh weather. Several instructors stood by, none in any uniform, and our only purpose that morning was to learn how to use a lifeboat. In total, we numbered about twenty lost souls, and, man, did we look awful.

As we stood near two huge lifeboats, everything was explained clearly before boarding those boats and being lowered into the water. Navigating those boats should have been easy. Yet it seemed a rather curious thing, they must have had a mind of their own. My, if we were not the closest thing to a motley crew. Two guys dropped their oars into the water and retrieving them seemed an impossible task. In attempting to do so, one nervous rookie almost fell into the river. No one knew what anyone else was doing, and getting everyone synchronized was like pulling teeth.

Our instructors remained on board the ship. They watched from the deck, assisted verbally, and gave us very sound advice. Perhaps they were slightly exasperated, yet they remained calm throughout the ordeal. Unlike our drill instructors on land, these guys refused to shout like madmen, something which was noted and appreciated. Now how they managed to keep a straight face I will never know.

A few days later, we were scheduled to return to that pier to get some kind of hands-on training on the freighter, but it never happened. A student came to our bungalow that morning right after breakfast to inform our bosun that five of us, including him, were to report to the administrative building, which some of the junior trainees referred to as "the hotel." It was certainly a most appropriate name for that is exactly what it looked like.

Our bosun was concerned and could not fathom what was up. We were soon standing inside and were greeted very nicely by a pretty young lady who also had a strong Southern accent. Sean whispered we had won a free trip to South America, but most of us did not laugh. And once escorted into an office and nicely accommodated, a very huge man, all smiles, entered and slowly closed the door.

Now please allow me to provide some significant facts about our school. For this will give you a sense of where we were and its predicament. Once upon a time, and not so long ago, sailors were considered the scum of the earth. In many places throughout the country, in hotels and restaurants, there were signs posted which specifically spelled out they were not welcomed.

As you can imagine, St. Mary's County was not overly thrilled with our school of sailors. The county had originally been established by English Catholics and named after the mother of Jesus. Folks in this part of the world were apprehensive about who its inhabitants ought to be. Perhaps Jesus Christ would not have agreed with them, but those practicing Christians had some serious limitations on board.

The local community consisted mostly of farmers and fisherman. However, all its citizens were still upset with the SIU's acquisition of a parcel of their land a few years back and then establishing the school. There was some resistance and pent-up hostility toward our union. What the county had failed to take into consideration was that Paul Hall ran the SIU.

Paul Hall had succeeded Harry Lundberg as president of the SIU. Back in the early 1930s, he was a prize fighter, and at the age of fifteen he became a sailor. By 1962 he was elected to the AFL-CIO Executive Council, and this man certainly mastered the skill of winning and walking away from the bargaining table with a bargain.

The union leader had a vision and soon began realizing it. He established the school in Piney Point in 1967 for the sole purpose of preparing and providing young people with a career at sea. Once the school had been founded and was operating at full speed, he recognized the need for it to grow, and it would do so by improving its curriculum. Paul Hall made sure this happened.

Now the colossal man in front of us was Mr. White. He spoke to us in a friendly and warm voice informing us that we all had one thing in common. And what was that? We were all high school dropouts, and the school we were now attending had just begun implementing a GED program. He proudly announced that we would be among its first students.

Mr. White seemed rather sure we would all participate. Looking around the room and taking us all in, he continued his very mellow speech. This endeavor would provide us with a bit of scholastic education and establish the possibility of going to college one day. It could also entail an exciting future, if we chose to, within the union's ranks. And, last, but not least, upon finishing the course, we would receive $100, even if we did not graduate. And, in 1971, that was a nice chunk of change.

I immediately took a silent vote and decided against it. Studying was the last thing on my mind and something I did not look forward to. Besides, what good would this do me on a ship? The idea of being a well-educated chap, and maybe even a union delegate to boot, did not interest me in the least.

Perhaps the soft-spoken burly gentleman read my mind. He terminated with a final statement, "For those who think this is a waste of time and wish not to volunteer, you can pack your duffle bag when you return to your room. Tomorrow morning, you'll be going home."

We left that room very quietly and in deep thought. Everyone seemed just as pensive as I was in considering the benefits of a high school diploma and what to do with some extra cash.

Chapter 43

Life at the Harry Lundberg School of Seamanship was not an overly rewarding vocation. All the trainees were assigned different tasks in the upkeep of the school. Some had kitchen duties; that is, they were either assistant cooks, assistant bakers, or bus boys. The rest, for the most part, maintained the school grounds and its facilities.

Any training regarding working on a ship had pretty much been summarized and practiced in the first few weeks upon arriving, which was mostly that brief lifeboat odyssey and what basic instructions we got regarding some of the vessels at the pier. Once at the end of the three-month course, the graduates were treated to a day trip at sea on one of the schooners. These lucky chaps experienced a bit of real navigating, in the small league of course—within the Chesapeake Bay.

The scholastic group I was in consisted of six students including our bosun. Being in the academic program spared us the rigorous trainees' functions, and now we attended school most of the day. It seems only right to admit that my initial inclination to decline the GED program, diplomatically dispelled by Mr. White, was soon reaffirmed as a good idea by Sean. He casually pointed out that sitting in a classroom and being separated from the other trainees was a wise move, especially as we did not have to scrub pots and pans.

Our school sat on the creek. We had the good luck to board the Charles S. Zimmerman every morning and head to class. It had once been an excursion ship called the Mt. Vernont, and it used to cruise the Potomac River right outside Washington, D C.

The SIU had purchased the craft some years back after it sank. It was given an impressive facelift and you could say it came back to life. To us students it felt like a luxury hotel on water as everything about it was so stylish. Remember, most of us were either city slickers or harmless ruffians, but once on board that vessel, we sort of felt a slight air of importance and even somewhat useful in the scheme of things.

On our first day on the Zimmerman, we met Hazel Brown, the school director. She spoke so candidly and caringly that we all immediately sat up and listened. I, for one, was now convinced that both the school and its hierarchy truly cared about us as individuals and as future sailors. It was a great way to start, especially after having now chosen to give this new challenge my very best.

Our teachers were wonderful. These ladies were enthusiastic about their undertaking and seemed to appreciate and like us all. We began our classes regularly at nine and continued until noon. We usually finished at three after having lunch and doing homework. If something did not click, they remained with us until it did.

It was not just the Zimmerman which had put a spell on us. That pier was simply a bit magical and had a mesmerizing effect. It made the rest of the school grounds seem insignificant. We would look around the pier, and docked in front of us was every imaginable small type of vessel to have hit the high seas or common waters.

I have already mentioned the freighter for our lifeboat training. Alongside it, there were schooners, yachts, sailboats of all sizes, canoes, a steamboat, and even the very famous Matinou which was so special to President Kennedy and had been nicknamed "the floating White House." And let's not forget our very own Zimmerman, as it was equipped with state-of-the art classrooms, a library, and a huge auditorium. When at that pier, we felt certain of who we were and our objective.

We had a lot of time to ourselves when not in school. Near our quarters there was a bowling alley and a gymnasium with a boxing ring, which most trainees often used, but we, the academic bunch, did not exert a lot of physical movement besides marching to class and chow.

By the way, one afternoon in our bungalow, a couple of guys lit a pipe, and we all joined in. I and the others were simply keeping faith with our lifestyle, which was just a small dose of recreational herbal fun. Was it our downfall, or our salvation? Who can say? But at times it seemed impossible to go without getting high. So not too often, but occasionally, our books and reality itself were simply put aside as we would enjoy a small time-out.

The bosun had a guitar. Often, we all made the best of our voices by singing, and it always began when one of us initiated a line from the song, "Don't Bogart that Joint." The singer would begin and immediately hold that first word for the longest time, allowing everyone to join in. After this lengthy introduction we would go from one tune to the next, one of my favorite songs being "The Weight."

I soon got to know a chubby jovial Black guy named Willie. He was not part of our academic group but had taken a liking to me, and so we always shared a few words. His laughter was simply contagious, and he had a warm and friendly smile. The guy could fire off one crazy line after another, leaving you in stiches and wondering what came next. Not sure when or why, but one day, he nicknamed me Jaded Jewel Julian, or simply Jewel. I may have been somewhat jaded and jeweled to my more intimate friends and a few others, yet my outlook always remained simply jovial to all.

Chapter 44

Three months flew by, and it became time to tackle the Maryland State High School Equivalency Exams—a rather nerve-racking affair. If I am not mistaken, it lasted four days, and I think we took our exams at the Leonardtown High School.

No one thought they had passed all the tests. They were just too long and rigorous, and it was frustrating sitting through them. Our results were available a week later, and the good news was that only one student had failed. It hurt a bit knowing someone did not make it, but he swore to remain and retake the ones he failed, and at least, he too, had a hundred bucks for his troubles.

Well, it was our last week at Piney Point. The school had recently added a music program to its curriculum. The intent was for the students to express or begin an appreciation of music, and so various instruments had been purchased and were available after school hours. One of the guys I knew was preparing for what he described as a rock concert. None of us students had given it much thought, but what a show we got!

The band opened with a couple of well-known popular tunes. It slowly built up a tempo, and when they did "I'm Eighteen" by Alice Cooper, the entire auditorium exploded. A few old blues tunes, which they had slightly modified, followed. Not to sound too negative, but while White folks can certainly play the blues, they should not sing them.

Anyway, what happened next pleasantly shocked me. Sean got up from his seat and went on stage. It seemed unreal. He took out a harmonica and made his way to the mike. Man, Sean played from his heart and was in perfect tune with the band. We were all impressed, speechless, and slightly taken aback as my close friend had never expressed the least inclination toward a musical instrument, but there he was deftly belting out harmonious tunes. The band eventually wrapped up with "It Hurts Me Too", and Sean could not be contained. The truly happy crowd and a few teachers present closed the show to a thunderous applause and lots of happy eyes all about.

Please allow me to express my most candid opinion. Okay, so the local folks in Piney Point had not been keen on welcoming Paul Hall and his kind. Had they succeeded in keeping us out, they certainly would have. It is sometimes curious how history plays out. Much too often, the heartless, ambitious, and blind carry the day and fail to see the cultural change of seasons all around them. Yet at times, the inevitable triumphs.

Ours is a nation of tough and sometimes rugged individuals. And I take my hat off to those who have vision and guts. A great American boxer once remarked that a true champ is simply that individual who has a heart. Someday, maybe our schoolbooks will recognize and appreciate the great name of a sailor whose legend began with boxing and finished with enriching the lives of others; for such a man was Paul Hall.

Chapter 45

We graduates departed our school on a sunny April morning. Our destination was New York City, specifically back to Brooklyn where we had departed three months earlier. A limousine picked us up in front of "the hotel" that morning, and all on board were proud of their small accomplishment and quite happy to leave.

Having participated in the school's academic program, we were also entitled to catch a ship out of any U.S. port of our choice. The union would pay for our transportation there once we were finished at the processing center. I had chosen New York, whereas Sean could not wait to get back to San Francisco.

Our driver was in his mid-twenties. The limousine had exited the school gate, and what happened next was totally unexpected. The man at the wheel asked if anyone wanted to get anything to drink. Naturally, the limo stopped at the nearest liquor store, and he filled all orders. I, much to everyone's surprise, chose to abstain.

As we headed north, the guys around me were merrily chirping away. It was not long before everyone was a bit too lively, and some loud singing and occasional chaotic argument ensued. Nevertheless, the ride proceeded smoothly in terms of driving, and my eyes took in such natural green beauty all about me, but it slowly disappeared once the Baltimore skyline came into view.

Someone suggested we make a brief stop in the city just to stretch our legs. It seemed incredible, but our mild-mannered and friendly chauffer was happy to oblige. So rather than pass by what appeared like a rather grayish metropolis, we descended into its vortex as the late noon sun guided us in.

The plan was simple, and so were some of the folks on board. We parked, synchronized our watches, and agreed to return in an hour. A couple of guys took off immediately. Sean said he was only interested in drinking a Harvey Wallbanger, and I tagged along, foolishly assuming most bars would be closed, and we would just enjoy a bit of a walk.

Sure enough, a bar not far off had just opened. It was a bit dark and somewhat empty, except for a pleasant bartender and a devoted alcoholic at the counter. I ordered a ginger ale, and Sean ordered his drink. We discussed what came next in our adventurous careers. The local drunk insisted we explain ourselves, but we thought it best to ignore him.

My line of thinking was that a trip off the east coast might get me to Europe. Sean thought it a wise choice, but then whispered in my ear he would only make one trip—to South America. Once there, the ambitious lad would buy a ton of cocaine, come home, and retire. Well, his work ethics certainly made me raise an eyebrow, yet any judgement over his ambitious adventure was immediately dismissed.

A couple of hookers came in. One immediately approached Sean, and a bargaining session began. Although I was a bit uncomfortable, not the least interested, and fending for myself as best as I could, the other female now strutting her credentials, would not take no for an answer. As a matter of fact, the voluptuous lady claimed she could make me touch the sky.

I first claimed that I didn't have money and then added that I was not ready for so much attention which must have annoyed her. For the well-proportioned madam, who eventually gave up on me, began insisting I was foolishly missing out on "Baltimore's finest pussy." Oh well, I had always expected sex to come with love from the heart, but then I was still a teenager.

Sean did his thing, and then we two proceeded to the limousine. A couple of guys had returned, but two folks were still unaccounted for. We sat and waited patiently while Sean gingerly carried on about his adventure and how his lady friend had strongly complimented his superior romantic power. Our driver raised an eyebrow while looking in the rear-view mirror. Little old me had to somehow defend having turned down the lay of a lifetime.

A cop on foot came by and informed us parking there was limited, so we needed to move. Hoping to spot the sailors not yet on board, we circled the block a few times. Our driver then drove up and down some streets and took a wrong turn somewhere. He did his best to return to our rendezvous, and we cruised for the longest time but failed miserably. Eventually, our chauffeur admitted being very lost. At some point, he decided to head north, and so we headed for the highway and on to Brooklyn, consequently abandoning two students.

I am certain the entire country knows who made the expression popular. But I know who coined it first. We arrived at the SIU office at about eight-thirty that evening, and upon entering the front door to the school center, a union delegate approached our driver and screamed, "You're fired!" Perhaps he had expected as much, for he did not seem the least bit concerned.

Our accommodations at the SIU center remained exactly as we had left them. Perhaps the school at Piney Point had provided us with a small upgrade, but we were now back to basics. I was too tired to hop on the subway to the Bronx after getting out with Sean to eat a pizza. We made it back to our digs and soon took to our bunks. After a nice chat, we turned in early.

The next morning around nine, Sean and a few others were handed plane tickets, and the group proceeded to JFK. We shook hands, hoping to run into each other again. Sometime after he had left, the abandoned missing trainees, who had caught a bus from Baltimore, shuffled in and got an earful, but nothing too drastic.

At that moment, one of the union delegates working for Mr. Chase handed me my union book. He instructed me to walk across the street to the union hall and register for work. It is crucial you have some information about the union's file and rank basis regarding its sailors. I was a B member.

The SIU had a three-tier membership system. At the lowest level were the C book members. Back then, these were mostly senior sailors who did not fare well in the scheme of things, whereas all the graduates from the Harry Lundberg School of Seamanship were B book members. At the top were the A book members—the cream of the crop. These were mostly folks who had been with the union for years and had upgraded themselves to higher-paying jobs.

Registering at the union hall to find work was a simple procedure. You showed your membership book to a union delegate. They were behind a long counter, and they gave you a card which was stamped with the date and time, your membership seniority, (A, B, or C), and the position for which you had registered. Once a ship arrived in port and its crew members terminated their jobs, the union was notified to recruit new employees for those positions.

Job announcements were posted on a gigantic board, and hourly calls were made. The ship in question would recruit the needed personnel, all non-officers, which included everyone from chefs to electricians. Sailors interested in a position would throw in their cards on that long counter, and the card registered first in chronological sequence, both by date and time, won claim to the job. Naturally, the A book members came first. If they were not interested, then those positions were available to the B book members, and last came the C members.

That morning, after registering, an hourly call was made. The few jobs announced were in high demand, and the few positions available were all scooped up immediately by A book sailors. Some guys, who looked very unhappy, and others even more desperate, claimed they had been anxiously waiting for work for several months.

It seemed like noon rolled around rather quickly, and it was time for lunch. While getting ready to leave, the delegate who had given me my union book was near, and he informed me I was to attend a meeting at two o'clock. He also proudly let me know that Paul Hall would be speaking.

After a pleasant walk, I indulged in a meatball hero and a cold Coke at a nearby pizzeria. I returned to the SIU building and made my way to the conference room, which was enormous and packed with an enthusiastic crowd. Consequently, some of us had to stand in the back of the room. As promised, the main and only speaker was our president.

Paul Hall began his agenda by first outlining the provisions of the Merchant Marine Act of 1970. It was incredible how he slowly worked the group, casually presenting the current situation regarding shipping and the applicable laws he had fought for. He wasted no time in fingering their opponents. His description of them was not pretty by any means, but what seemed precious was his flawless jargon, well-prepared and delivered with passion.

Suddenly, the room exploded in wild applause. Most union members could not contain themselves, and I was enjoying some political theatrics but was also slightly concerned about finding work in the port of New York. Well, once the speech terminated and our president left, everyone around me made the rounds to share a few words.

There was so much buzz and wild chatting in that room. Mr. Benitez, who had informed me of the meeting, came over. The two of us agreed the president was an incredible man. I expressed some concern over finding work, and the Spanish gentleman asked if I was willing to travel. I said that I was, and he informed me there was a job available in Houston, Texas. Was I at all interested? It seemed foolish to dwell on this but much smarter to simply jump on it.

Chapter 46

My plane landed in Houston that very afternoon. A short bus ride brought me downtown, and another bus took me to the area where the union hall was located. The union representative who had been informed of my arrival was waiting for me. And soon after I made his acquaintance, he escorted me to a boarding house a block away.

All that was with me was my duffle bag with most of the school clothing issued and a bit of my own clothes. I suspected my stay would be short, and it didn't seem necessary to unpack. Once the proprietor got me to my room, I washed up and took her up on having dinner. She informed me there were other guests, as we shared a bathroom, but they were out in the town.

Dinner was on the table a bit later. Believe me, my stomach was in such a frenzy that I dug in without the slightest hesitation. Goodness gracious, I almost killed myself! My delicate constitution was not accustomed to spicy food, and this was beyond "muy caliente," to the ninth power. Suddenly, my entire body was paralyzed, my face was on fire, smoke poured out of my ears, and tears were quietly flowing down my cheeks. That I did not pass out was a sheer miracle.

The very polite yet startled host, a true Southern gal and now an overly concerned matron, asked me, "Are you ollllll riiighhhhhhtt?" I could not answer but attempted to nod and simply lie, yet she must have grasped the truth as she noticed I was "reyd as a beeeeet."

Well, after that close call, the cool evening breeze invited me out for a walk. The dinner from hell was now behind me as all my wounded organs were slowly recovering, and my soul was pleading with my brain to pay attention when using my careless mouth. Oh well, it was onward, leaving my temporary premises behind but with no particular place in mind, just a need to get out.

Soon, an uneasy feeling began to set in. For some unexplainable reason, my surroundings began to worry me. It was not only the wear and tear of the homes around me which stoked my concern, but everything looked a bit too rugged. Then, a few sinister looking chaps, obviously wasted, came tumbling out of a bar, laughing very loudly, and looking like they were ready for trouble. Some cautionary note within, while remaining somewhat composed, urged me to reverse my direction, bringing me back to my safe-haven, hoping to arrive with my sails fully intact.

The next morning, my breakfast was simply a cup of coffee. There were several mysterious looking things on my plate, but I claimed an upset stomach and so probably kept one at bay. The madam may have understood yet remained her "Southernly kind ole sielf" and even more polite than the previous evening.

At the union hall, I registered and received a card. The nine o'clock call was a brief affair. There were only a few work announcements, and I was the only person to present a card for a position on the ship, the Seatrain Maryland.

It seemed strange that nobody else was interested as there were quite a few sailors all around me. Then once the process terminated, the union delegate gave me directions to the Beaumont shipyard where the ship was docked.

My employment as a wiper would begin once aboard the ship after signing a contract with the ship's company. The word is certainly not appealing or may even sound slightly demeaning, so perhaps it is best to inform you of the positions on a merchant ship.

There are three categories which divide the ship's functions. They are the steward department, the engine department, and the deck department. On every ship, there are two types of workers filling in these categories, officers and crew members. In my case, I was part of the latter along with all the sailors provided by our union.

The steward department ensures the sailors are fed well. It only consists of crew members. There is a chief steward who bears responsibility for the food operations, prepares a daily menu, and requests food and laundry provisions when a ship is in port. There is also a chief cook, his assistant, and the baker, who keeps everyone happy with bread, desserts, donuts, and various types of pastries.

Mess-men is the name of the waiters. One serves the crew members, and one serves the officers, and both make coffee for breakfast and break time (10:00 a.m. and 3:00 p.m.). Alongside them is a dishwasher and a pantry room person who ensures everyone has clean linen and towels.

The engine department personnel keep all systems below the main deck both operational and in top shape. The officers consist of the chief engineer, who is the highest-ranking person and is responsible for the overall maintenance of the engine room (anything which needs to be done, he makes it happen). And there are three regular engineers (referred to as third engineers) responsible for a four-hour watch in the engine room to ensure all systems continue functioning accordingly. By the way, when a ship is in port, the four-hour watch changes to eight.

Working on the same watch with a third engineer are two crew members. There is an oiler who makes steady rounds controlling everything throughout—the electrical systems, the lubrication of machines, and the generators—and once finished, he spends a lot of time chatting with the third engineer. Whereas the fireman-water-tender is in the boiler room and his work consists of monitoring the gauges indicating the amount of water, air and fuel that keep the boilers going. Again, when a ship is in port, the four-hour watch changes to eight.

The eight to five workers in the engine room along with the chief engineer are the wipers. The two wipers are the slaves who do everything spelled out to them by the chief engineer, but most routine work entails keeping everything clean. Last but not least, there is also an individual who, believe it or not, occasionally changes a light bulb, and that is the electrician.

It seems best to take a moment and outline some of the ship's structure. Above the engine room is the area called the deck, and the room where there is a navigational wheel to steer the ship is called the bridge. The front of the ship is the bow and the back, the stern. If you are on the right side of the ship facing the bow, this is called starboard, and the left side is port.

Back to the workers. The deck department also has officers and crew members. The chief mate, just like the chief engineer, is the capo of the deck department. He oversees all operations on deck, and he also stands a four-hour watch on the bridge navigating the ship, and so do the second and third mates. Again, once in port, that watch becomes eight hours.

The deck crew has a boatswain (bosun) as its boss. Whatever jobs are deemed necessary by the chief mate, the bosun will coordinate who gets it done. This includes various maintenance and cleaning duties, but most importantly, the crew is responsible for tying up the ship when arriving in port, assisting it going out to sea, and navigating when at sea. Carrying out these functions are the able seamen, known as ABs, and the ordinary seamen, OS, who also stand a four-hour watch when the ship is at sea, alongside one of the mates.

At the top of the chain is the most important person, the captain. He is the grand master who is responsible for the ship's journey. And just like God Almighty, he simply ensures that everything continues to run accordingly.

Chapter 47

The Seatrain Maryland was tied up at the Beaumont shipyard and obviously being repaired. An infinite number of workers were everywhere, coming on and off the ship, and a few were discussing some serious work concerns. Once I made it up the gangplank, the OS, Tim, who was on watch politely greeted me and then showed me to my room. It was tiny and in a pitiful condition. There were double bunks and two small metal lockers, but what immediately caught my attention were several ashtrays overflowing with cigarette butts and a small trashcan topped with empty beer cans. Some were scattered on the floor.

The room stank terribly. I immediately opened the porthole to air it out and then put my clothes away in the empty locker. One of the two beds, the bottom one, had not been made, and the top one was obviously mine as there was a mattress with no linen on it. Tim had already informed me where to get linen and towels, and so I quickly got that out of the way.

Once ready to go to work, but not certain whom to report to, I foolishly returned to the gangplank to ask Tim. He laughed his head off and suggested I change into my work clothes. He then indicated which door to use to make my way below into "the bowels of the engine room." Well, I felt rather silly, but at least I could now head off in the right direction. I slowly descended to the bottom level of the engine room. The third engineer was on watch alongside the oiler, and it was the latter who then accompanied me to the machine shop.

We crossed the lowest part of the engine room area. All about were large cables and electrical lines crisscrossing the deck, as well as groups of workers gathered around discussing something. A few were obviously assisting others with some repairs, and someone was shouting, trying to get someone else's attention. My goodness, this chaos was not exactly what the school had prepared us for.

The chef engineer, my boss, looked me over quickly. He was rather tall, in his late seventies, had a strong accent, and gave the impression of someone who never smiled. His instructions, or orders, were to get a wrench, bucket, and a long screwdriver, and report back to him. I had foolishly forgotten to bring my gloves, so he suggested that I return to my room to fetch them. While exiting the engine room, my body felt somewhat sticky. By the time we finished work that evening, it was completely wet.

We needed to remove a valve. It was huge, and now that the water running through it had been turned off, we proceeded. My boss called the shots, and I obeyed. Apparently, I was not fast enough, and this irritated him. He made some unkind remarks. Removing those bolts was no easy task. They seemed permanently stuck to that valve, and so my boss jumped in to help.

We somehow managed to get the bolts off. Eventually, using a pulley set up over the valve, we got it up and out of the way. It must have weighed a ton! The two of us returned to the machine shop where he quickly finished making new gaskets for the valve. Eventually, we removed the old gaskets, placed the new ones in, and put back the valve. At about 5:45 p.m., we finished, and he thanked me for not leaving at five o'clock for dinner. If the man was pleased with my work, it certainly did not show.

Once I exited the engine room, my first stop was the bathroom to clean up. The entire portion of my upper body was soaked, and my shirt was glued to me. I removed my gloves, and as I had not always worn them, my hands were filthy. Oh well, such was the life of a wiper, and one who had only put in a few hours of work.

Dinner was both good and abundant. The waiter was friendly, talkative, and made it his job to point out that he and the chief cook were both from Alabama. As he and the rest of the kitchen staff were preparing to go into town, he asked if I desired anything else. Feeling rather full and quite satisfied, I declined and soon returned to my room.

Once my bed was in order, it seemed only right to do some reading. So having laid myself down with my pillow propped up, I retrieved my book—a popular novel making the rounds, and just when my level of comfort in reading was at an all-time high, the door to my room opened, and my roommate walked in.

The individual in front of me was a skinny older Asian man. He had a six-pack in a shopping bag. The guy was not yet completely drunk but would soon be. He immediately offered me a beer. My declining it made him a bit uncomfortable, yet he insisted on making some small talk. He noticed my intention to be left alone, but—nothing doing! Once he settled in, yours truly became his private audience. It must have been close to eleven when my light was finally turned off, but he continued to drink.

The following morning, after breakfast, I reported to work at eight. My roommate, however, did not. During coffee break, I returned to my room and found his locker open and empty and his linen gone from the lower bunk, which of course became mine. At lunch, the waiter informed me he had been fired. The waiter believed once the chief engineer saw the likes of me, he was probably happy to go with one wiper for the time being. For a moment, my dad's words came back to haunt me, leaving my mind to consider that perhaps he knew the score quite well.

Our ship left Beaumont a few days later and headed down the Neches River. We had not yet sailed into the Gulf of Mexico, but something was terribly wrong with me. My stomach was throwing a tantrum, and a strong need to fling my well-digested lunch overboard tormented me.

My boss was all smiles and advised me to take some time off and come back later. I went up on deck thinking this would somehow help, but for the next few hours, life was hell.

A few days later we stopped at another port in the Gulf, and once again, in the earlier part of the evening, the crew members were all heading "ashore", but my room and my book were my only interest.

Suddenly, the door opened, and in walked my new roommate. His name was Ted Allen, also from Alabama. That seemed a bit peculiar to me. Yes, it is a small world, but hopefully not overpopulated with the usual species from the same well. Anyhow, my impression was that my new roommate was certainly less obtrusive and ridiculous than the drunk whom he was replacing.

Ted was just a few years older than me and looked like someone who kept himself in great shape. He had barely finished putting his things away when he began filling me in on his love life and the few broken hearts left behind in Mobile. I listened and feigned some interest for a while, but my mind was stuck on that book, specifically the chapter where several murders had occurred.

Our ship left that night heading toward the Panama Canal. Our destination was the West Coast, and we would stop at the army pier in Oakland, California to pick up some military cargo bound for Vietnam, our ship's ultimate destination. I was a bit excited with the idea of going to Vietnam, a place which had commanded the TV headlines for some time, but Ted seemed indifferent. His mind was stuck at home, and visions of his few ladies traveled with him.

Chapter 48

We two wipers must have been ideal workers. Every assignment given to us was carried out quickly and efficiently. Our boss had us clean up every part of every compartment within the engine room and beyond. Now, once we had left Beaumont, the machine shop, which looked like a war room as every tool and various type of equipment were scattered about, was returned to order by yours truly.

Out at sea, a dreadful job awaited us two every afternoon. It was done at exactly four o'clock. It was referred to as blowing tubes. Call it what you may, it entailed a filthy task which, once accomplished, forced us to leave the engine room just to get fresh air into our lifeless bodies.

It was necessary to wear gloves and a mask as we worked in the back area of the two boilers. Basically, we had to pull on chains attached to those boilers, which forced steam to blow out on top. This action removed whatever soot had accumulated there that day. Naturally, some of it headed downward, and between the unbearable heat and the crap dropping on us, we were super filthy once finished.

Ted would work the four chains on one boiler, and I would do the ones on the opposite side. Until the engineer gave one of us the go-ahead, we waited by a side door which allowed us to breathe normally. Once we were given the okay, one of us moved to the first chain near that side door and began pulling. Those chains were scorching hot. Often, even gloves were insufficient, and you needed to wrap several rags around them to protect your hands.

Breathing with a mask on was difficult as you felt like no air was getting into you. At times, I would desperately yank it off and continue to pull the chain until ordered to stop. Then I would return to the ventilated door with only one thought in mind—survival. Sweat poured out of my entire body, and there was always a nasty taste of soot in my mouth. Only that fresh air by the side door kept us on our feet. The engineer, on the other side of the boiler room, observed through a scope, and once he determined sufficient cleaning had been done, you could take a break, while the other wiper attended to a chain on his side.

The task lasted half an hour, and we made our way above on deck. We usually headed to the stern, half conscious and quite happy to breathe fresh air. Our horrific gig was finished, but the pungent taste of soot remained in our nostrils and mouth, forcing us to spit out globs of black saliva. We were both totally exhausted but always found the strength to head to our room after cleaning up in the bathroom, and it was then on to the dining area.

One early afternoon, The Seatrain Maryland docked in front of the Panama Canal. The bay where we dropped anchor was inundated with ships from all over the world. We were just another vessel among competing naval traffic and eventually ours was allowed to enter the canal the next morning.

That evening, Ted and I chose not to go ashore and explore the city of Colon. From the many stories highlighted during our meals, we may have been shortchanging ourselves. Almost everyone on our ship seemed to have had been there, and we heard so much about the natural beauty of the land, the excitement of the city, but even more was discussed regarding the gorgeous senoritas to be had. Well, we two newbies just wanted to get to the West Coast and explore our native beauty and babes.

The ship finally entered the Gatun Lock. This is the first of three locks, and once inside, the ship is temporarily pulled along by an electric train car. Then once it leaves the last lock, it again navigates freely on a river-like waterway and makes it to the other side of the canal, eventually entering the Pacific Ocean. The entire journey pretty much took most of the day.

While being towed through the locks, something peculiar caught my attention. Almost all the dock workers were Blacks. I had expected to see Panamanians; that is, people of Spanish heritage. No, sir. And while these workers did not look exactly like folks back home, there was a definite strong similarity. That is why my curiosity got the best of me. I queried the AB standing nearby. According to him, the deck workers were descendants of Black Americans who had slaved away and practically killed themselves in building the canal. As no White person in their right mind would work under these oppressive physical conditions, our Black citizens were sort of forced to volunteer. Consequently, their offspring were now running the show, something which did not sit well with the Panamanian people.

Our ship left and soon arrived in Oakland. Ted and I finished work at five, and then we caught a bus into San Francisco. Crossing the Oakland Bay Bridge was quick, and in no time at all we were at the central bus station. I was finally in the city immortalized by a popular song. My blood pulsed with excitement, however, once we took to its streets, it was not a very welcoming scene that greeted us. Some rough-looking characters squatting on the sidewalk were drinking cheap wine. Three girls, very similar to the ones in that bar in Baltimore, were standing nearby, talking loudly and wildly. It appeared they were waiting for customers or preparing for a busy night.

We two sailors were turned off. It was tough accepting this ghastly scene. In my vision or fantasy, San Francisco was wrapped up in love and happiness, filled with people with flowers in their hair. My eyes were now correcting things, and my mind felt slightly put out. Nevertheless, we soon stood on Powell and Market Street and then caught the cable car to Fisherman's Wharf. Now, a somewhat majestic feeling rode with me to the bay while my eyes took in buildings with a slight touch of antiquity about them. They were rich but not plush, serene but never sleepy.

Once at the bay by the pier, we ate some fish and chips. I discovered a place called Tower Records. It was a huge store where music in LPs and cassette forms abounded. A bit later, we walked around, gazing at the serene bay, and so I expressed my excitement to Ted about our trip to Asia, a place practically unknown to me. He seemed completely indifferent. His only concern was our salary, and he was hoping we would work lots of overtime while crossing the ocean. He was also somewhat upset that he had received no mail upon our arrival in Oakland.

Eventually, we two sailors sat facing the ocean water with the Bay Bridge at our side. Everything looked so wonderful, and my inner rumblings were asking if I could live comfortably and happily in a city like this. Oh well, for the moment, there was a long trip ahead, and who could say where it would leave me? One thing I knew for sure—my union grade allowed me six months on a ship, and if, upon return from overseas, that amount had been exceeded, the union would force me off.

Chapter 49

The steward ensured our vessel was fully stocked for our trip to Vietnam. On the day before departing, all sorts of provisions were loaded aboard and stored away. For the next few days, our chefs provided us with some truly delicious meals prepared with fresh meats and vegetables. Ted and I made all three meals and the two coffee breaks, where donuts or pastries were abundant, and man we ate like two starving souls.

When the Seatrain Maryland pulled away from the dock, the able seamen and ordinary seamen, under the direction of the bosun, were busy with all operations on deck. The ropes tying the ship to the pier were pulled back on board and others were thrown out to the tugboats which now pulled our ship out to the end of the bay. On the bridge, the captain oversaw all operations. The chief mate and an able seaman stood by ready to take over once the tugboats allowed us to proceed on our journey.

In the engine room, the third engineer and the fireman-water-tender were busy getting the boilers to perform to perfection. Their mission was to create the right amount of steam to run the generators properly and get the engines rolling at a faster pace, while the oiler made his rounds and checked all gauges throughout.

We were finally on our way to Asia. Within a few days, the immense Pacific Ocean began graciously displaying its vast blue empire, consequently reminding us what tiny trivial creatures we truly are.

There was never a dull moment for us two wipers. Our daily routine quickly became a bit monotonous as we began our days with a bucket in hand, full of soapy water, and made the machinery in the engine room spotless. And we also swept all the floors throughout each compartment every morning. After, we attended to any task assigned by the chief engineer, who always found something.

Our boss was a Swede from the old school. He sternly dictated orders, and we, of course, simply obeyed. The man was not so young, yet he sizzled with energy and had an overdemanding personality. He sometimes reminded me of my dad, who often felt that Peter and I either moved too slowly, by his standards, or not fast enough. And my new boss, like my old boss, could easily be angered over any frivolous thing.

One morning, Ted and I were complimented by the waiter serving us breakfast. He reassured us that the chief engineer was lucky to have two workers like us. Apparently, there had been some problems with the wipers on the previous trip. And yet, the engineer did not show us much appreciation. Nevertheless, he was keen to get down to serious business once we left Oakland. He made us an offer we couldn't refuse, which certainly made Ted one happy camper. All the bilges throughout the ship would be cleaned up and painted, and this was expected to be accomplished after regular work hours.

Once back in our room, Ted immediately began calculating. According to him we would both be very well-off once the trip terminated. That is, upon arriving back at the original port of embarkation. The trip had begun with its departure from Oakland, California, for we had been paid upon arriving there for our work. Now a new trip was under way, and what mattered most to my roommate was for us to remain frugal sailors and not go wild once in port.

The new assignment began the following evening. Every day, we still concluded our daily work when facing the four o'clock massacre behind the boilers. Then at four thirty, we headed up on deck just to breathe and revive ourselves. At five o'clock, having already washed up, we sat down for a full meal. At exactly six we were back in the engine room at the very bottom of the ship. And can you guess just who was already there waiting for us?

Our boss had pumped out any water that had previously accumulated in the bilges. We two now crawled in to set up portable lights and face years of accumulated sludge. Of course, there were boots on our feet, and we were armed with gloves, scrapers, and metal dustpans to scoop the crap up. We also had plenty of buckets. You can say we came well-prepared.

It was uncomfortable work as our space was so restricted. We had to remain on our feet but were basically bent over so low that our butts almost touched the filthy floor. It was difficult to remain in such a position for a lengthy period. Everything began to ache and our legs would stiffen. This forced us to crawl out, sometimes even before having filled as many buckets as we wanted to.

Once the buckets were all lined up, we headed above to the deck to dump the contents overboard. And those buckets weighed plenty. We could only carry two at a time, which meant making several trips in order to dump all of them. After arriving on deck, the cool breeze and dark skies restored us mentally and maybe even physically. Plus, the overwhelming silence coupled with the slight whining from the tiny waves created by the ship's propeller may have diluted the sense of our precarious circumstances. One thing fully grasped now was what the engineer on duty had replied to Ted's boasting that we were in the money when he replied, "Yeah, but that's blood money."

Sometimes we took a cigarette break by the bilges or up on deck. We smoked quickly because we feared that our boss would sneak up on us, which was not beyond him. This may have been what Ted and I found a bit extravagant. The man hovered above us like a hawk. Every evening at 6:00 p.m., he stood by the bilges, awaiting our arrival. Once we disappeared below the floor rails, he would leave but return punctually at 8:00 p.m. to allow us our coffee break. He stayed below to wait for our return and came back at 10:00 p.m. to dismiss us and ensure we did not leave a minute too soon. Ted soon nicknamed him master.

Oh well, no matter what new task or emergency arose, we got it accomplished. Once, our ship was going to navigate through a severe storm. We were ordered to bring below all the fifty-five-gallon barrel drums (full) which were on deck. Our boss wanted them secured in the machine shop. We immediately saw that just moving those barrels to the stairs, which were close by, was no easy task. Getting them down the stairs was even worse.

We tied a thick rope around the individual barrel and took turns guiding it down. One of us held the rope at the top of the stairs and bore the brunt of the barrel's full weight, while the other guy controlled it firmly while guiding it down the stairs. Lowering each barrel down those steps with iron railing around us was very risky. The person lowering them had to pass the rope around the railing to contain the full weight and keep tight control of the barrel. One slip and the other person could easily have been crushed or hurt very badly. It took forever to finish, and, incredible but true, once the storm passed, we were ordered to bring them all back up.

The two of us worked our butts off, and it was certainly recognized. Ted and I kept going full steam ahead, and our relationship was healthy, perhaps mostly because I talked little and am a good listener. My co-worker revised and slightly spiced up some of his past amorous tales. Sometimes, he even included explicit details which always seemed more fascinating once certain peculiarities were explained.

I, on the other hand, had limited and somewhat insignificant tales from the Bronx. Yet my spirit was being fully entertained and it often truly enjoyed Ted's hilarious narratives, while at the same time we both continued working our fingers to the bone.

Chapter 50

Tim was a hippie who fit the image of a sailor. He was tall, robust, had long blondish hair that cascaded down below his shoulders. He wore an earring and had a tattoo of the devil on his left arm. One day after lunch, he surprised me on the bow as I was just killing a few minutes but also enjoying the beauty of the immense blue surrounding me.

We shared a few words, and very soon, with my happy approval, he lit a joint. After my first inhale, my eyes must have expressed some surprise and curiosity, and Tim simply said, "It's from Thailand." Now I understood, from hearsay, and presently participating in the ritual, that we two were smoking some incredibly top-of-the-line weed.

As many times before, my attempt to be a law-abiding citizen fell to the wayside. Although having behaved for a few weeks, I was now recharging some inner craving, and it did not feel so bad. There were now three of us laughing uncontrollably on that bow as my roommate had joined us. It soon became our very sacred personal smoking grounds.

You should know that for recreational activities on the Seatrain Maryland, well, let's just say, they were few. If you were not applying your trade, reading, or playing cards, there was not much else to turn to. However, although I was getting high, my love for reading never abated, and one day, while browsing through the ship's library, which was minute, I spotted an unusual title. It was written by Jim Garrison, whom I knew was the district attorney of New Orleans when JFK was assassinated. The title of the book was, *A Heritage of Stone*.

I had been in third grade when one day, a nun interrupted our class to inform us the president had been shot. She had asked us all to stand and say a prayer along with her, which I recited and took seriously. Although I was still young, the killing of a president seemed like such an impossible and strange occurrence. Once at home later that day, Pino La Casa had come over, and he and my dad were silently discussing the circumstances. My father said we would never know the truth and stated it so matter-of-factly.

A few years later, we witnessed Jim Garrison on TV arguing his theory that the president was assassinated under odd circumstances. The panel there considered him a quack and his conspiracy theory totally absurd. They branded him a lunatic. It was soon apparent how much hostility everyone bore toward the man that you would have thought he had committed the crime.

Well, the so-called experts attempted to discredit Mr. Garrison and shut him up. However, it became apparent that the man had done his homework and often left the panel members speechless. It was when the show concluded that my father looked at us all and said, "I always knew there was more to this than the nonsense we have been told."

I could not put that book down. It was apparent that Lee Harvey Oswald was just a scapegoat, and some powerful forces had carried out the assassination. Unfortunately, I made the foolish mistake of sharing my new knowledge with the bosun, who was from Dallas. He was a tad crude but always appeared well-informed and was often a good source of information.

The man agreed to the conspiracy theory. He even quickly rattled off a few names of those he believed were involved, but his next statement horrified me. He basically said he was happy that our commie president got what he deserved. I could not make sense of this and felt terribly hurt, as if it were personal, and so I chose to drop the subject. That peculiar incident for sure led to my new mantra: if it is not work-related, leave it alone.

Chapter 51

If my memory serves me well, our ship crossed the Pacific Ocean in a bit more than two weeks; however, I may be incorrect on the exact time. Working all day, seven days a week dulls the senses. We stopped in the Philippines at a U.S. naval port in Olongapo City. The ship needed to refuel, stock up on fresh food provisions, and other miscellaneous items, and of course, at least in my case, take a break from a long haul.

Tim was on watch that afternoon, so he was not available to tag along. Ted refused to budge. It seemed hard to believe, but facts are facts. His harem back home was not corresponding with the now frustrated young sailor. Not one letter since his departure, and my friendly pleading to come ashore with me served no purpose. The frustrated wiper would continue to sulk in our room, so the small town to explore was all mine.

My exit from the base was through a well-guarded gate. Once outside and heading to the center of town, I noticed that there were plenty of bars and some very pretty girls. Everyone appeared in a rather festive mood. This attractive yet sinister scenery made me a tad nervous. I saw so many people just hanging around. A few looked a bit suspicious, plus there was some loud Filipino music pouring out of the bars.

Now please remain neutral. My virgin existence since reaching puberty was now being considered for an overhaul. Those luscious smiles coming my way were edging me on. It felt only right to sort of close my eyes and pick a bar at random, which is exactly what I did. And sure as shit, once I was inside and heading to the bar counter, a flock of young ladies started chirping around me. They appeared rather excited to have me among them.

One immediately inquired about my status. According to her, I did not look like a GI. The others smiled, stared, and finally allowed me some elbow room once it became apparent that yours truly just wanted a drink, for now. Then, quite unexpectedly, another attractive young lady walked over and sat right next to me. She began strutting her stuff, insisting she could make me a happy man, and she even described her credentials as simply the best.

She pushed her image, but something did not seem right. Plus, the girls who had welcomed me a few minutes earlier were now eyeing us curiously and smiling a tad deviously. Suddenly, my companion placed my hand on her chest. Perhaps she wanted to reassure me that all was in good condition and genuine, but to me, it felt like things were moving too fast. So once I finished my beer, I got up and began to exit the bar.

Not so fast! My new friend was right by my side and appeared intent on following me to the end of the earth. I moved on and felt a bit uneasy wondering how long the madam would stick to me. It seemed a bit wise to pick up the pace and head back toward the naval base. Out of the blue, a couple of guys who had been eying us began to laugh loudly. They asked if I liked Billy Boy.

My already apprehensive gist was now on high alert! Perhaps the Olongapo vernacular was not part of my repertoire, but having somewhat understood where things stood, I now opted for full speed ahead and dared not look back. And believe me, there would be no kind of boy, or girl, or boy-girl, or whatever was under that fine appearance for the likes of me.

I found Tim in the dining room drinking a coffee. My slightly agitated mind did not allow me to share my brief and sorry state of affairs. However, once in my room, as Ted began demanding the facts about life abroad, and although still slightly shaken up, my version of things got out. First by describing this incredibly exotic mystic beauty I had just met. Naturally, he was told, my loins were ready to burst at the seams, but possessing her both body and soul was just beyond my possibilities for her fees were extravagant, plus her very wild side seemed a bit untamable.

Ted's eyes lit up. He wanted to hear more. Instead of complying, I mocked him for living like a hermit and consequently missing the opportunity of a lifetime. He could have passed the night with this very exceptionally beautiful mature queen. My roommate began to brag how she could have been treated to some genuine Alabama charm. Oh well, it seemed like a match made in heaven, Alabama charm and Olongapo camouflage. It was time to crawl into my bunk, get back to reading, and thank my lucky stars to be in bed alone.

Chapter 52

For an eighteen-year-old kid, life was good. Financially, that is. Some years back, my dad had taken me to the Dollar Savings Bank in Parkchester, and he opened a bank account in both our names. Since then, my frugal ways persisted in saving a portion of my earnings. To me, it was the simplest of equations—stash away as much as possible and live frugally, and you'll have something.

On our merchant ship, the captain was both our banker and our accountant. When we arrived in port, you requested an advance from your salary. He would look at your earnings, subtract any allotments or previous advances made, and allow you to withdraw what was left. If you demanded less than what was available, he was only too happy to keep you in the black. And when the ship arrived at its final port after completing the voyage, the captain would settle your account.

Upon joining my ship, I had initiated an allotment to my bank in the Bronx. This ensured my funds grew and continued to gain a bit more interest. Now, almost on a weekly basis, having been influenced by my roommate, a calculation of overtime work gave me a better picture of my current financial situation. And guess what, folks? Things were looking pretty darn good!

One day someone gave me some incredible news. They informed me that as Vietnam was a war zone, our basic pay doubled for each day spent there. This forced me to estimate days in that country and recompute an approximate total. The sad part of all this was never even considering that a war was going on. Oh well, after getting a more precise picture of my financial status, I patted myself on the back.

Now if you think it is impossible to spend money on a ship, well, you are slightly wrong. You may be asking what is there to buy out at sea? Absolutely nothing. But once the ship arrives in port that scenario changes drastically. In order to get about, you need a taxi. Then once you are in any city center, you begin to shop around for things like souvenirs, music, food, drinks, books, and most often, certain women. If the woman you are with is charming and making you happy, she will come shopping with you. That, for sure, will include perfumes and some personal accessories. Pretty soon, your cash begins to diminish, and unless you have a financial life jacket to keep it afloat, it sinks rather quickly. I had sworn to remain the frugal fool I was, but it was a gig which was not meant to last.

Anyhow, we arrived in Vietnam and navigated up the Saigon River to Newport. This was a small port very close to Saigon. As the amount of military cargo that had been arriving daily had put the capital city under much pressure, Uncle Sam had built its own docking facilities. Here, too, were many ships coming and going.

The Seatrain Maryland, like all Seatrain ships, was equipped with two huge cranes. Once the ship docked, the longshoremen would take control of working the cargo onto the docks. The cranes facilitated the loading and unloading of cargo faster than old freighters that had no cranes and had to rely strictly on the port facilities. And in Vietnam, these were ancient and quite run-down.

The entire area seemed to be overwhelmingly run by Vietnamese workers. My first impression upon seeing the local longshoremen was strictly appalling. Most of them were dressed in raggedly worn-out clothes and aging flip flops on their feet. Some even walked barefooted. It was also surprising seeing the color of their skin which the sun had turned to a dark crisp. Just the same, they appeared friendly, and a few who smiled lacked a full set of teeth. It was impossible to not feel sympathy and a sense of pity for those folks and their super rugged physical conditions.

Well, believe it or not, Ted agreed to come see the city with me. Oh, even more important, once again, there had been a slight change in my physical appearance. Heeding my father's former wise counsel, suggested so happily, I decided to reinforce my scalp via a total shave.

Ted used his razor and applied a few quick swoops leaving me with a new shiny look up top. Of course, it was not necessarily something I looked forward to, yet it seemed like a healthy ritual for me to conform to. And my roommate, pleased with his performance, informed me he would be quite happy to dish out another scalping and appeared ready to continue practicing his new skill.

It was after work hours when we left the port area. Both South Vietnamese and U.S. soldiers well-guarded the exit gate. Immediately, scores of taxis and other vehicles were at the ready, but Ted insisted on riding a rickshaw. It may have been a wise choice as it allowed us a better view of our surroundings, but you cannot imagine the chaos we found.

Traffic was horrific everywhere. The streets seemed infested with a huge number of scooters, bicycles, a few motorcycles, lots of rickshaws, and occasionally even an overloaded cart pulled by a donkey. Cars were practically nonexistent, but a few, belonging to a wealthier class of people, could occasionally be spotted, and sometimes a jeep or military truck would rush by, and it seemed like they had the right of way over everyone.

Upon arriving at our destination, a small problem arose. Ted insisted we were being taken advantage of and refused to pay what he called an astronomical fare. Who could say, but it felt foolish to be arguing with this poor looking individual, especially as some useless back-and-forth "baby English" had not accomplished anything. Ted finally paid the scruffy looking chap, and so we moved on.

Just so you know. Anything deemed good or very good was expressed as "number one." The very opposite was "number ten." It was my roommate who had sort of baffled the rickshaw guy, having insisted the fare was "number twenty." The man's face appeared puzzled, and he began to look my way for help. Once paid, the chap seemed relieved and even somewhat grateful.

My glowing head received plenty of attention as we strolled around. Some folks walking in proximity to us seemed to stare forever. A young kid snickered, and a couple of schoolgirls slightly bowed to me.

Ted was all for browsing at a souvenir shop. We managed to bargain with the store owner and left with a few trinkets. Apparently, we must have been in the center of things as there were small shops and street vendors everywhere. Most of them were supplying food to folks at their stalls or on the go. And as in Olongapo City, every time we passed by a bar, a choir of sweet voices tempted us to go in, and so we finally did.

The house rulers were as follows. The bars were owned by a mamasan. That is, the woman in charge of the premises and the girls who worked for her. The young ladies lived upstairs in their own tiny rooms and were paid a commission for their services. A customer chose a girl and decided whether to remain "short time" or "all night." Your choice determined the price paid to the mamasan before going upstairs.

Sometimes these girls would ask you to buy them a drink. If you did, your bill would set you back plenty. They drank a glass of Coca-Cola, but you were told that it was rum and Coke, and it came at a very stiff price. Perhaps war can make people do all sorts of desperate things, sometimes even when they are not so hungry.

My buddy and I were not enjoying the ladies' chatter. At least in Subic Bay, English was spoken, and rather well, whereas here all we heard was "You, number one" and "me like you so much." It was slightly annoying, even though the girls appeared well versed in their trade. Obviously, their only interest in us was the few dollars we could give as we were basically a human commodity. Necessary but also dispensable.

Well, believe it or not, after ordering our beers the senator from Alabama was getting all the attention. He was tall, solidly built, and a rather handsome devil. Obviously, everyone wanted a piece of him (pardon the pun). And you cannot imagine how cleverly the prince played his part, using few words but smiling and leading the girls on. For a moment, he seemed like a celebrity madly in love with his own image. Whereas I, not so bold but very bald, sat quietly, allowing the merriment to proceed, and accepting a bit of self-imposed isolation. Then the girls, seeing no real action occurring, took a small break and left us to ourselves.

We enjoyed our beer and chatted about life under the tyrannical rule of our very "Sveeedish boss." Ted's incredible imitation of our aged, fearless, and cranky ruler earned a few happy winks from the bar's plump matron. In the meantime, three GIs walked in, and the girls immediately welcomed them with more smiles and a few words. Our soldiers were considered steady clients and maybe even a one-way ticket out of their rotten trade.

Eventually, it was time to move on and hardly anyone noticed. Our brief visit to Saigon allowed us to experience the city's pulse, yet it was difficult to provide a prognostic. To me, that city, back then the center of attention in the U.S. media, in some ways was a bit like Palermo. The Vietnamese people's agenda was nothing more than attending to their personal needs. They were quite busy working, hustling, or doing whatever it took to make ends meet. That a war was going on seemed so far from our reality. As a matter of fact, the only evidence of fighting I had ever witnessed was on the nightly TV news back home.

However, something rather peculiar had caught my attention. It was the blasting music that seemed to shake the foundation of wherever we went. Apparently, American rock music was driving the local folks wild, and it was not the Doors or Hendrix or the Stones, for they were practically unheard of. It was Creedence Clearwater Revival. This band had certainly captured the heart and soul of these people, and they simply could not get enough of their music.

Chapter 53

Just so you know, our ship was owned by a private firm but chartered to the Military Sealift Command (MSC), an entity within the U.S. military. Once all the cargo picked up in Oakland, the originating port of embarkation, had been consigned, the captain would then receive new orders from MSC and either proceed to a new port or various ones or return to the port of embarkation.

Our new destination was Naha, in Okinawa. Tim assured me it was quite different from what we had experienced and seen so far. He was right. Naha had all the makings of a small jewel to be worn and admired, and my brief visit after work hours filled me with admiration for everything I saw.

On the day after our arrival, Tim surprised me. He invited me to tag along to an outdoor rock concert the next day, Saturday. It was my day off, so I accepted and extended the invitation to Ted. However, that critter was moping and carrying on about being home sick, which to me was the perfect reason to make the trip with us. Oh well, once again I simply could not grasp why my roommate was refusing to budge from our ship.

Tim and I had no one back home to report to, so off we went. Late that morning, a taxi outside the Navy base we docked in carried us southwest and rather slowly, as if in no hurry to escape the city heat. Once outside the confines of that city, a bit of thick dense vegetation became our entire surroundings, but then our taxi started hugging the coastline. We could now see light blue water invading the bay area, and we began to plead with our driver to stop so we could soak up this colorful display. It was a pristine aquatic oasis, so refreshingly clean. Why, you could clearly spot the floor of the sea, and if I had not known better, I would have been tempted to scoop up a bit and drink it.

An hour later, we arrived in a huge park. Some people were roaming about, and it was not long before the first band opened the show with Led Zeppelin's "Immigrant Song." It was delivered with an abundance of energy and raw passion, and what followed was one American rock song after another, but quite mysteriously, for whatever odd reason, every band to take the stage also began with that Led Zeppelin tune. Now, did they simply love it so much or was there more to this? It got old quickly, but no one seemed put out by it, and so we two laidback, lit up, and let our minds rest.

At some point during a brief time-out, we attempted to chat with a few hippie looking guys. Nothing doing. Apparently, English existed only on the stage and was limited to the songs we heard. We two then discussed a bit of our past, me rehashing life in the Bronx and Tim about Tallahassee, Florida. My mate then assured me he intended to make another trip on the Seatrain Maryland, whereas I wanted to explore San Francisco. He showered me with lots of useful tips and pertinent information regarding the city which he knew very well.

Suddenly, the sky darkened, and an avalanche of rain poured down. A bunch of us scrambled toward a huge tent not far off. It looked like an immense tepee, and it was held up by a thick solid wooden center pole. More and more people joined us, and it quickly became overcrowded, but it was the only place to be. Then, as the rain persisted, the ground around us became muddy, and in no time at all, it was very slippery inside that tent.

The center pole appeared to give way. Tim immediately took himself to the center of the tent, grasping the pole and holding it steady in its place. Unfortunately, no one else moved, and after a short while, he requested my assistance as he began having difficulty holding it. Like everyone around me, I simply remained paralyzed, both mentally and physically. My buddy began begging me to step in. He appeared a bit exhausted, but for some strange reason, I never moved. Now my friend's eyes were lashing out at me as he appeared furious with my inability to act, and his frustration began to show. Truth be told, all of us huddled there were like Morlocks, simply awaiting our fate and never disputing its arrival. How pathetic!

Fortunately, the rain soon stopped. Miraculously, that pole held, and Tim was much relieved we had come out okay. He joined me as we left the tent and walked around the wet grounds. My friend was certainly irritated with me, but he never uttered a word, while I quietly confronted my gutless, reckless, and unexplainable indifference.

Sometime late that evening, we turned in and slept where we were—in mud. The next morning, we two and many others looked like spectators out of Woodstock—muddied, hungry, but somewhat happy. After, we encountered what felt like a long ride back to the Navy base in much silence, and we got quite a few stares from the soldiers at the gate.

Tim never once mentioned that incident to anyone. It was almost as if it had never occurred. And as incredible as it may seem, a few days later he approached me and carried on like the true friend he was.

Chapter 54

Our ship visited two more ports before returning to Olongapo City. Again, provisions and fuel were procured, but this time yours truly did not budge from his quarters. It was time to return to the West Coast, and once on the high seas, we two wipers resumed rubbing everything clean, blowing tubes, and even returned to our evening residence in the bilges, which were now becoming more habitable.

It felt like in no time at all, we docked at the Oakland Army terminal. My roommate and I would not make another trip. He had decided to return to Alabama, and I would reside in San Francisco. Now if our impudent boss had just once shown a sliver of appreciation for our hard work and not have been so unbearable, I may have made another trip. Anyway, as soon as word of our moving on reached him, he was in our room.

The man's expression spoke volumes. It bore an incredible sense of loss and betrayal, almost as if we had moved to a sister ship docked next to ours. He obviously knew replacing two healthy young slaves like us would be challenging. He promised us more overtime with less supervision. Nevertheless, we, very diplomatically, stood our ground, being convinced of our plans elsewhere. Consequently, having lost all hope, the beaten man retreated, bearing a look of sheer disgust.

That afternoon, Ted and I shook hands and parted ways. I also said goodbye to Tim, and we both hoped to run into each other again. The captain had terminated the trip late in the morning and had paid everyone a few hours after the ship had been tied up. My, what a change of scenery would do for me, having gotten plenty of cash from him and knowing my bank account looked healthy. It was now on to face the SIU representatives onboard to settle my union dues. A trivial obligation, you would think!

The union delegates were huge guys but very friendly. Mine was also full of surprises. In addition to several months' dues, there was also a mighty steep initiation fee, not to mention the flight from JFK to Houston. Remember, I had initially chosen to ship out of NYC. And finally, there was also a charge for the clothing provided when enrolling into the union and going to Piney Point.

The bill was catastrophic! What an idiot I can be. That is, for never asking the right questions at the right moment and then listening. Just the same, I left the Seatrain Maryland still feeling somewhat rich but now wondering if all that calculating some months back had been worth the time and effort.

I tried not to focus too much on my lapse of foresight, and instead, I thought about my new hometown. Unfortunately, the San Francisco of my dreams did not exist! Nor did it conform to that once popular song. Like all cities, this one had its own rhythm and pace, and it offered a unique central urban environment. Yet, in some ways, although more minute, its outlook appeared and felt a tad like the one which had me in its paws for almost eight years.

Nevertheless, its actual charm soon emerged. It caressed the coastline by the bay and was also visible in the lovely Victorian homes resting nearby, scattered about nicely. My favorite ones adorned the Haight-Ashbury neighborhood, where a good cup of coffee and a chat could easily be had.

I lived close to Powell and Market Street. Tim had recommended an inexpensive hotel which was old but in good condition, plus, it was close to the main cable car stop. This allowed me a nice walk to the union hall, and there were a few affordable and tasty restaurants nearby, which is something extremely important to someone nursing a healthy appetite for daily walks with no specific deadlines.

Tim's suggestion was a bit strange. The hotel entrance was nothing more than a long corridor. That hallway was super clean and quite empty, simply displaying a sign with instructions to ride the elevator to the first floor. There I found a large and well adorned lobby, and standing guard behind a counter were both the manager and two huge Doberman dogs. This made me feel safe and slightly uncomfortable at the same time.

The gentleman in front of me was very polite and extremely feminine. He provided me with an inexpensive room and some useful information about my new digs and the surrounding area. The dogs did not appear too friendly but remained attentive and quite ready to pounce if necessary. The room was large and cozy, and although it did not have a bathroom, one was right outside. The view from the only window available zoomed in on a somewhat busy street, and across that street stood a shop with a peculiar sign—Franks A Lot.

I consulted a map the following morning and headed off to Chinatown. It was sunny, so walking felt pleasant and rewarding while a blue sky above and elegant buildings caught my attention. Folks appeared ready to exchange a greeting, and so it felt only right, if nothing else, to dispense a slight nod in saying hello.

Well, Chinatown is just Chinatown, no matter what city you are in. It entails various shops selling inexpensive colorful trinkets, a lot of herbal stores supplying remedies in existence for thousands of years, cookware galore, fruit and vegetable stands sitting side by side, and let's not forget the many restaurants emitting a captivating scent of fried food.

Everything smacked of a unified collaboration. Almost like a collage, casually displaying the colorful and unique lifestyle of China's immigrants abroad. Here, as in the Asia I had just left behind, was a lively movement of folks brandishing their existence through well-anchored traditions. It seemed to me that everything was laid out as it should be, neatly and strikingly.

Soon it felt like a late lunch was in order. Besides, food prepared in the latter part of the midday seems more appetizing. My waitress was an older attractive Chinese woman who displayed an uncanny seriousness and was a bit limited in her knowledge of English, or perhaps afraid to use it. A simple décor with an overabundance of red infused the restaurant's dining room.

I ordered and was served rather quickly. The food was delicious with all the ingredients fresh and crispy. My meal, which I scarfed down, enhanced my love for food and delighted everything within. Once finished, I was not so full and would have gladly surprised my unhappy server by requesting the same dish again. Well, maybe another time.

A bit later, Union Square stood in front of me. Here, the change of scenery seemed self-evident as fashion and wealth appeared to reign supreme. While observing the rich vitality, the park across the way from the St. Francis Drake Hotel was calling my name, and so I strolled over there, sat and opened a San Francisco Chronicle. One of my new objectives was to stay well-informed about the world around me.

Apparently, my initiative would have to wait. In the upper section of the park, a young man had created his own stage. He was a juggler and a canny entertainer, or so it seemed. His dialogue scratched the surface of most current events, and he easily captured everyone's attention with his acrobatic skills and sharp tongue.

He was funny, somewhat charming, and his repertoire proceeded flawlessly. After entertaining us for a while, he asked if we were at all curious to know how a juggler found time to eat while working at his trade all day. He then promptly inserted an apple into the flow of juggling pins and continued his act with much ease.

Our young artist proclaimed that life is nothing more than the art of improvising. Having said so, he began to bite the apple while it still circled with the pins. It was incredible! He was fast, and this captivating stunt seemed to create no problems as he proceeded to work and eat.

What an enticing performance we got! Everyone there had witnessed a superb acrobatic comedy, and it came free or via a donation. It felt only right making a decent contribution to this young man's tax-free salary. And why not! He had certainly given us a bit of time-out from ourselves and both lightened and enriched our moods. Anyhow, a bit of reading was eventually completed there in the park, and I left feeling content with a peppier bounce in my stride. Who could say, maybe this show would be available again.

Back at the hotel, I first treated myself to some music while watching the crowd below. Then after several hours of reading, I felt the urge to include a small nap to the rest of my day, which is not something I normally indulge in. A few hours later, again, the view from my window brought me back to life, though it was somewhat limited as it was turning dark outside. I slipped out to explore the neighborhood.

Now life was good! However, while continuing to promenade, a slight inconvenience cornered me. It confused me at first, for a rather big Black man—who looked very feminine, but was a man, dressed in women's clothes, including a lady's wig—stood on display on a street corner. While passing by, he gave me a huge smile and licked his tongue in a most provocative manner. My pace slightly picked up as this made me feel a tad, a big tad, uncomfortable.

It seemed like a good idea to mark my surroundings, hoping to bypass it the following night. Well, the very next evening, while on a less exotic scenic route, I faced a similar experience. I passed a slim but handsome guy with flowing blond hair who wore red hot pants, white boots, and a tight turtleneck blouse that displayed a small bust. My curiosity deliberated the vision. This was a man, but he could easily have been a woman.

It was all too much for me. Why, my sexual fantasy world only came to life when my loins demanded immediate attention, which was rather often. But while my repertoire only knew the "five to one" method, it was always over an image of a member of the opposite sex. And a few years back, the finest memento used in a workout session was a Playboy magazine found in my aunt and uncle's bathroom in Long Island. Life at night in this city was somewhat bizarre.

Oh well, the union hall was my destination the following morning. It seemed only right to acquaint myself with its exact whereabouts and see what work prospects were up for grabs. After getting a registration card, I stayed a while to witness a rather busy hourly call as several ships in port needed quite a few people in all three departments. It was sort of a bullish sign, which made me happy while hoping it would continue into the coming weeks and beyond.

While leaving the premises, a guy standing nearby walked over and introduced himself. He seemed a few years older than me and had long brownish hair and a thick droopy mustache. He could certainly have used a shave. His pungent Southern accent accentuated his every sentence, which rolled out in a rather slow nonchalant drawl.

We shook hands, and my few words came out with a refined ease. Almost immediately, he stated he had just found work on a ship going to Vietnam and would board it this afternoon. His was a very pleasant smile as he briefly described his love for a part of a world which I had just visited but hardly knew. He appeared ecstatic with his return to what he called home. It seemed only right to feign interest while wondering if this poor chap was not swimming in a sea of dreams.

Anyway, it was on to the Haight-Ashbury District that afternoon. Upon arriving, the bus ride provided me with a glimpse of vibrant colors, and the homes all displayed a simple but somewhat architectural elegance. Then it hit me. They reminded me of playing with a colorful wooden construction toy set as a kid in Palermo.

My wandering about that area did not last long. An old bookstore tucked away on a not so busy street grabbed my attention. My eyes were soon besieged by the immense collection of old books stacked everywhere. This simply delighted me so very much, ecce homo. A few books appeared a bit dusty, one had slight yellowish pages which gave it a dab of antiquity, but all this was just fine with me.

Quite by chance, my eyes spotted a paperback whose title was somewhat peculiar. It was called Tropic of Capricorn. The author's name seemed familiar, although I was not certain where exactly from. The first few pages grabbed me immediately, for they were practically toxic! I knew right away I would buy it, and I did for such a cheap price. It was soon on to a nearby coffee shop, and once accommodated I ordered something to drink and gave the book my complete attention.

Why, Henry Miller was a sheer genius! He was someone who delved into the essence of everything about him while brilliantly laying out his struggles with such verbal supremacy. This book almost felt poetic. At some point, it was put aside. A very lovely Asian woman had sat close by and was browsing the latest issue of Rolling Stone magazine. Although I tend to be quite shy in front of beautiful women, and she was super gorgeous, it seemed worth the gamble to ask if the Stones were coming to town any time soon. She smiled and politely said, "You are from New York, aren't you?"

My Bronx accent was obviously greater than its mentor, and perhaps too much for its spectator. She gave me a brief update on the present music scene on the West Coast, particularly at the Fillmore West that weekend. We briefly compared notes on life between the two coasts. As she was a local and well grounded, we happily concluded that California was a world onto itself and a real trend setter. Recalling the exotic street display of the two previous evenings, it forced me to wonder if such fads were here to stay.

She appeared to want to return to her magazine and so I concluded our small talk. After I left and enjoyed a pleasant walk, a bus brought me back to the Tenderloin area. This neighborhood was my new home, and the very stage where a nightly exotic combo of human flesh would be on display and continue to slightly puzzle me. It ultimately became less imposing as I may have finally grasped how the streets at night belong to those who know no boundaries.

Chapter 55

A month after arriving in San Francisco, I revisited the union hall and immediately landed a job. My new employer was Sea Land Corporation, and the ship was called the Sea Land Adventurer. I was now feeling good about going back to work, and my lively steps carried me home rather quickly.

Once at my hotel, something within finally corralled me to patronize Franks A Lot. It was just a hot dog shop, interestingly though for they served every type of frankfurter imaginable. Now my hunger never took long breaks, so I ordered three Viennese hot dogs and a Coke and gave no thought to junk food being at the bottom of my list of nourishment.

Well, my eyes immediately confronted a rather peculiar scene. The employee behind the counter, a rather portly and balding man, was transforming himself into a woman. This was obvious, and my mind began to question how one takes on such a challenge. It must certainly take courage to leave behind the gender assigned at birth knowing it would lead to a point of no return. Anyhow, the chap appeared slightly morose or maybe even a little unhappy.

My delicious food arrived rather quickly, but my curiosity would not leave me alone. Why was he so sad? Was it uncertainty over his decision, or were folks like me, hiding behind a façade of indifference, a small hindrance to his serenity? Or maybe both. It began to feel unnecessary for me to contemplate his decision, but something in me asked if he would truly ever be any happier than the rest of us. Wasn't his fix nothing more than what often eludes us all, an attempt at happiness at all costs?

Oh what the hell! All this thinking served absolutely no purpose. I was devouring my franks, slurping down my Coke, and it now dawned on me I would soon abandon this great city. But my brief stay had enriched me with its metropolitan uniqueness and easy access to the bay. Those exotic male/female illusions were like an education outside the classroom—a street world yet to be understood but very apparent.

I eventually headed into my hotel. The sailor in me now fully realized how my present existence relied on the livelihoods of the vast oceans beside us. I would soon discover that my new ship carried containers that were loaded and unloaded onto a vessel in a matter of hours. Consequently, after a long spell out at sea, you barely get your lips wet while in port, and it is already time to return home.

My vessel was certainly in outstanding condition, but very quickly, my eight-to-five-schedule became a dreadful, long, and unbearable routine, and overtime after regular work hours was unheard of. Please forgive me for mentioning this, but I now missed that ancient Viking buccaneer boss from my previous trip. He not only had kept Ted and I truly busy but had also made a nice contribution to our personal wealth. If only his approach toward us had not been so rough.

Once again, I shared a small room. The other wiper was either from North or South Carolina. Those accents sound the same to me. We were two complete strangers in outlook and personality, and we hardly saw each other most of the day. I had no clue where he hibernated, but it was far from my area. After work hours, he drank a bit, and the guy could talk forever and say absolutely nothing, an art I have yet to master.

Perhaps the idea of reading was not totally foreign to him. Nevertheless, my strict diet of literature and solitude did raise an eyebrow, but thank heavens, he liked some of my music, especially Janis Joplin. He would request to hear her while my nose was in a book. This was a bit of a problem, as I was not capable of doing two things at once. Often, I would abandon our room and head off to the bow for a bit of solitude.

Out of the blue, I became friends with one of the oilers. We had previously chatted, with me complaining about lack of work and he consoling me, understanding the issue having come up through the ranks. What impressed me most about him was the fact that he, too, like Tim, fit my image of a real sailor. He sported a gold earring, was built like a middle-weight fighter, and had a light goatee under cascading dark hair, which he sometimes wore in a pony-tail. All he lacked was a tattoo or two, but that seemed okay.

Just like my roommate, the oiler, Matt, could go on for hours. However, he constructed interesting and meaningful sentences to engage in. On one occasion, he was artfully engrossed in painting the entire premises of his room, and while applying a variety of paints he was listening to Dylan's "Mr. Tambourine Man." I entered and heard well known lyrics which got us talking a bit, most animatedly, and sealed our friendship.

Chapter 56

It felt like a long haul to our first and only port, Busan, South Korea. My restlessness stemmed from two things—the lengthy trip with little work and having made a major decision in life. Love and sex are two great complementary elements, but is there a universal law forcing their union? Absolutely not!

My spirit, having consulted my mind, had decided that the time to satisfy my hard-up sexual needs was at hand. These two human components reassured my striving heart that no grave universal sin was being committed. All three had concurred and given me a right to some carnal pleasure, or, if not, Julian Di Stefano risked exploding.

Once in port, my indoctrination into becoming a man soon unfolded. One of our waiters introduced me to a local Korean guy who he knew from previous trips. This well-dressed individual, probably just a hustler, was described as reliable and inexpensive for his services, and one who could get you anything you wanted. Such was the reputation he enjoyed.

What his real function on that ship was, I will never know. Sometimes in life you have no choice but to just trust and go with the flow. We met and spoke briefly, his English practically nonexistent, but the peculiar looking man got the message, and soon enough we got going. We rode off on his scooter to the outer center of town. Of course, my nerves were working overtime, as they usually do when facing new circumstances or a testy situation. He parked on a long side street with plenty of bar signs everywhere. I assumed he would earn a commission from the bar for his services, and of course, the bar girls would make something off me.

We entered, and the lady of the house accommodated us in what looked like a well-laid-out parlor. She immediately retrieved a beer and handed it to me. A few minutes later, several pretty girls, who may have been napping, came in and lined up. My goodness, they all looked good to me, and not wanting to offend anyone, I simply chose the one closest to me. She seemed just as shy as I was.

Her English was equivalent to my Korean. But was there really anything to say? We went up to her cramped quarters and began working in perfect harmony. Soon, we were like two crazed animals who could not be pulled apart, and once that first and only round concluded, I rested a bit. She then made a gesture to inquire if I was hungry. With my yes, she left and returned with an egg sandwich and tea. It was so unexpected and appreciated, but it also terminated our session.

As the ship was scheduled to depart prior to midnight, it was time for me to leave. My tour guide had left, and I now exited the premises through the front door to board the taxi waiting for me. Suddenly, a voice called out. It was a stunning female goddess in front of a bar not too far off, gesturing for me to walk over and keep her company.

Why didn't my foolish pimp work for that bar? Oh well, time was not on my side. I also suspected we would not be quick. While boarding the taxi, feeling regretful in having to depart, General McArthur's words came to me: "I shall return." That is why my inquisitive eyes began scrutinizing every minute detail of the area, for once back, I would know exactly where to go.

Our ship was soon back on the West Coast. I decided to resume my stay in San Francisco to catch another ship but certainly not one carrying containers. My pay off would be meager, however, considering that most eventful experience which had temporarily satisfied my loins and slightly soothed my spirit, the richness in me was quite exuberant.

Matt approached me a few days before arriving in port. He convinced me to join him on his trip across the country. It was a simple but adventurous plan that seemed worth the ride. We would visit his friends in the Bay area then fly to L.A. to get his motorcycle and ride it to Dallas, where his car had broken down the year before. The final part of our journey—in his vehicle, as the bike would be towed—was to Ft. Lauderdale, Florida, his hometown. After a few weeks there, I would make my way to the Bronx to visit family and see my friends. It seemed like one hell of an intriguing trip!

Matt's friends lived in Santa Rosa. What a great bunch of folks. All well-mannered, cool, and, without a doubt, young hippies. Well, perhaps their hipsterism was only in appearance, for they all had day jobs, except our hosts. The husband was also a sailor and presently not working. Now everyone seemed to share a very laidback attitude, which would have equated to a motto claiming, "Why do today what you can leave off for tomorrow."

These folks smoked a lot of pot. Naturally, once again, I saw wisdom in relaxing through smoking and participated religiously. However, those smoking binges would ultimately bring a slight change within, forcing me to silently confront a peculiar side of myself. It arose after much laughter and casual chatting, for suddenly my outlook and personality tended to turn inward, consequently abandoning any attempts to communicate with anyone. Matt, the persistent conversationalist, would manage to wisely embrace my mute spirit and somehow always got it back on track.

We two unemployed sailors did get into San Francisco on one occasion. My only plan before going to L.A. entailed a visit to Jack London State Park. I had once read about its beauty and the London family's presence on it and what they had left behind, but it did not happen. However, prior to leaving Santa Rosa our guests gave a party for the two sailors preparing to travel strictly on land.

Most guests arrived in the early part of the evening. A few with demanding jobs trickled in much later. It was a quaint event with endless wine, delicious sandwiches, and non-stop rock music in the background. While I was busily conversing with someone, a very attractive girl smiled at me so warmly. It certainly seemed like an invitation, but I failed to move quickly enough.

Matt was now at her side. He was apparently doing the talking, but I casually made my way over, remained composed and managed to get a few words in. Soon the conversation bordered on idealism, or the lack of it, and my contribution simply stated that societies thrive best when new ideas generate creativity. If not, then complacency, or lack of change, stifles innovation. I even added, "This is like, I sit, therefore I am." For a while we played with words.

Of course, the gorgeous smile in front of me was irresistible. Perhaps my friend caught on, and soon appeared as if being crowded in, therefore forcing me to excuse myself and join the others about the room. Soon enough, someone lit a pipe of some good grass, and then a bit later, quite unexpectedly, as the stereo was not moaning very loudly, I began singing "Hey Jude" and immediately everyone joined in.

We ended partying around midnight as folks were leaving en-masse. I had just said goodbye to Sheila, the beauty who now appeared a bit stifled by Matt, and once again her fierce inviting look spoke volumes. Plus, her brown eyes were so addictive. But then she was gone, and so we turned in for early the following morning Matt's friend was bringing us to the airport in San Francisco.

When our plane landed in Los Angeles, we hopped in a taxi and made our way to a hotel. Sometime later, we went and picked up Matt's motorcycle. It was a BMW R75, which looked brand-new and took us to some of the more interesting sights to be seen.

The huge city did not impress me much. Nothing stood out or attracted me entirely, not even Hollywood. Maybe because as Jim Morrison once so poetically stated, that city, very female, appeared much too lonely. The following afternoon we headed out to the San Bernardino Valley to visit Matt's friends, Terrence and Julia.

Our sojourn was in what appeared like a home by the desert. The couple were friendly enough and gentle, but somewhat peculiar. They did not always seem to connect very well, not just verbally but as if they were in different time zones. At times, Terrence looked a bit lost, almost like wondering what he was doing in this relationship. Perhaps their significant age difference was to blame. I also suspected their newborn child may have been what had forced them together.

Fortunately, we did not stay long. By the way, a desert environment leaves one feeling too silent and void of any nurturing feelings, unlike the ocean, which happily gives of itself but also hints possessing a tiny role in your personal journey while remaining in the background.

Now one enjoyable pastime was our music. Terrence put on something so different from anything I had ever heard before, and we two newcomers could simply not get enough of it. Every song on this LP had a somewhat mystical tone, and all were brilliantly composed. Each one stressed the individual personal life while prophesizing future dreams and everything in between. The LP was Cat Stevens' Tea for the Tillerman. A mental note formed stressing to pick it up once back on real land.

Chapter 57

We left California early one morning and flew through Arizona and New Mexico. Riding a motorcycle can be an exhilarating experience, even if you are sitting behind someone. Not only are you on the road, but you become part of that road.

After traveling for some long hours, we would stop to take a short break. My legs felt a bit tired and my mind a tad dull, and, thinking it unnecessary to rehash the road just traveled, few words trickled out of me, whereas Matt's vibrant tongue made up for my inconsistency. With the exception of a couple of overnight stays in some cheap motels, we simply kept going.

It had not yet become a problem, but soon enough Matt began to take a stand against my silence. It came on sometime after our smoking sessions ended, and it would slowly censor all lines of communication. My super talkative buddy was now somewhat concerned. He once even asked if some mishap in my past could be the cause and then politely stressed the importance of getting to the bottom of things.

It wasn't long before we arrived in Dallas. It should have been a brief stop, but it became a small bump in our journey. Matt's car, a 1957 Ford Thunderbird, was supposed to have been repaired, at least considering the check which had been mailed to the mechanic, but nothing had been accomplished. The vehicle needed a new piston which was impossible to find. Although it looked great, it just wasn't going anywhere anytime soon. At least the mechanic was still trying to find the missing part.

We settled in at a nearby motel and rode around most of the time. We sneakily engaged in some casual drinking and smoking sessions, but they did little to get us by. And, if you must know, adversity often comes uninvitedly. Our relationship began to dwindle, however, my friend, always cordial and plenty talkative, remained so until our last day together. He took me to the airport, had little to say, and we parted on friendly terms. Something within suspected we would not see each other again, unless by chance. In retrospect, things had started going downhill from the moment we had entered Texas.

On that flight, my mind attempted to explore my inadequacies. It was no easy task. The incident back at the concert in Okinawa resurfaced, and it was hard to grasp my lack of motivation in helping a good friend at a crucial moment. Failing to share myself sufficiently with Matt, a fun and spontaneous person, now had me somewhat concerned. For the moment, it was evident that there was a fixture in my personality with its own agenda, and maybe not a healthy one. This quandary traveled with me all the way to JFK.

I was soon in the heart of Manhattan which was not overly familiar to me. There was a bustling movement of noisy traffic which kept me wide awake while moving around, and it even reminded me of the chaos in the Asian cities my ships had brought me to—people on the go, plenty of vehicles moving them, and everyone too caught up in their own agenda to slow down.

I had just entered the subway station. My plan was to head uptown to the Bronx. I asked for some tokens from a gloomy looking employee behind the glass cage. She continued staring at me, while I waited patiently and smiled courteously. Seeing no action on her part, I dared ask again. Big mistake! The woman screamed super loudly, "Where's your money!"

What an idiot I can be! I had not put any cash under the tiny slot in front of me, and so the craggy employee, who had been eyeing me suspiciously, snapped at me. My guilt was obvious but not its cause; for having been gone for a while, one can forget some of the city's institutionalized safeguards which keep it going. Oh well, my inability to catch on woke me up rather quickly.

It was a long and noisy ride uptown. Yet soon enough, there was Beach Avenue, and Shamus' building stood in front of me. It was Fiona who had been dominating my thoughts for some time, but it was Evelyn, the youngest family member, who greeted me at the door. After we exchanged a few words, she gave me the unexpected news. Her oldest sister had moved back to Ireland. It seemed unreal and more than a little painful, but at least Shamus was nearby. He now shared a flat with some friends nearby on Taylor Avenue.

Shamus and I hugged like athletes who had just accomplished the impossible. What stood out immediately were my friend's physical changes. He had put on a bit of weight, donned a fine-looking mustache, and appeared more serene. Why, he even looked a bit older. Once we settled down in the living room, we began comparing notes. It wasn't long before Shamus grasped that I was homeless, and he insisted I stay as long as necessary, offering me the living room couch for a bed, which looked almost new.

The ex-sailor in front of me had only made one trip. It took him to the Persian Gulf. He had worked as an OS, a job he found very boring, but even more troublesome was sharing a room with an arrogant and rough roommate whom he eventually came to blows with. He stated so matter-of-factly that he had seen enough of a solitary life at sea, and he had no regrets about abandoning a profession which was not for him. He had just started working as a firefighter and seemed quite pleased with himself.

The following afternoon, I caught up with some of the guys in the neighborhood, but I struggled a bit to fit in. Their jargon was just a rehash, delivered verbatim of all the nonsensical things which kept them going—getting laid, getting out, getting on, getting high, and getting by. If Dallas had somehow shut down my ability to chat at length, my old friends did little to bring back a more talkative part of myself. That was a tad disappointing.

Oh well, it was on to Co-op City the following evening to call on my folks. They had moved there during my first journey out at sea. Both Mom and Dad were totally shocked by my unexpected and unannounced visit, yet quite delighted to see me. My mother was very complimentary, insisting she found me more mature, and, perhaps, I even looked somewhat happier. She liked my well-trimmed beard and crew cut hair, and insisted that I keep my appearance, slim and trim to the core.

My folks got a bottle of wine from me. Dad thanked me plenty and decided to put it aside for a special occasion. There was a box of chocolates for mom, which she later happily shared, and we soon sat for coffee in the kitchen area. Much was said about how more than an entire year had slipped away. They happily informed me Peter was back in Lincoln Hall. All they wanted was for him to learn a trade to be able to have a decent job.

It was during a lull in our conversation that my old man made himself heard. He was happy to see me and hoped my work and personal experience was off to a good start. Nevertheless, he felt a need to caution me again: life at sea could ultimately have me in rough waters. According to him, the full experience of wandering about the planet, even though my cavalier spirit was in full bloom, was a risky endeavor, for life at sea begot loneliness. He strongly hoped I would return home and settle down.

What could I possibly say? Sure, life was not perfect for me. However, neither was my ship sinking. It seemed wise to smile while reassuring both that overall, things were fine, and they would remain so. If not, I certainly knew my way home.

Chapter 58

I left the Bronx a few days later. Who can say why, but I rode a Greyhound bus across the country. I guess, at times, the simpleton in me takes over. This impulsive trait to run with things might be my worst enemy. Either way, the trip lasted a whole five torturous days.

Much too soon, sitting on that bus became a tedious task. There is only so much reading one can do. I was trying to watch the scenery rushing by, but to no avail. My mind began to despair over my lack of direction in life—something which had remained buried while nicely charming my overly concerned parents.

In theory everything seemed okay. Sure, I was a union member, could choose when to work, earned a good salary, and traveled to places far from home, but something was not quite right. Was mine just a temporary gig which would ultimately lead to nothing? Then suddenly, a quote from Tropic of Capricorn came back to me: "Once you have given up the ghost, everything follows with dead certainty, even in the mist of chaos."

It was late afternoon when a passenger boarded the bus somewhere in Ohio. She sat next to me and easily opened up. It seemed a bit odd, but she delved into her personal narrative. Could she feel that comfortable with me? Her father drank too much and had often turned violent, and while her mom feared him some, she too had a penchant for a few too many cocktails, and it seemed like pleasing her aggressive husband was all that mattered.

The young female had run away from home years back and lived with an aunt. Things had now improved tremendously, for God had seen to it. Someone special had recently come into her life, her fiancé. She was heading to Ft. Carson, Colorado, where he was stationed, and they would soon marry. It was his gentle ways which had attracted her, but he was also funny and fully dedicated to her. She then said something which sounded odd, "He is my best friend."

We carried on for hours. She got an earful of life at sea according to Julian. My transition from being a messenger to walking about in Saigon impressed her. Being present in what seemed like a totally foreign world was gallant and something to be proud of, no? Discovering that the South Vietnamese loved Creedence Clearwater Revival had her laughing a bit, and she thought it strange that our music attracted them. Well, her appreciation of my travels got my not so upbeat attitude flying high again.

It was much too soon when my pleasant traveling companion left me. Once she was gone, my attempt at sightseeing resumed. A small town would pop up here and there, and then just as quickly disappear, but its skeleton frame sort of highlighted a sense of isolation. My goodness, was this a vestige of our pioneers' frontier?

How was it possible that hundreds of years ago, settlers had arrived with practically nothing? Perhaps some scant provisions, their sheer determination to survive, and obviously a stubborn ambition to forge a living anywhere possible. These folks were deprived of everything that renders a brutish life more bearable. It suddenly hit me. Why, they were just like me—happy loners who just wanted to be left alone.

Oh well, I faked some indifference to all my thoughts and tried to read again. Soon enough, I dozed off, and sometime later awoke as the bus window rekindled my vision of the world outside. What a vast and empty land. In its most pristine state, it offered a natural beauty, but it appeared too void of human life, and it lacked spirit. Then a tune from my stay at the San Bernardino Valley hit me up, and it reminded me that in some ways being alone means being free.

Chapter 59

San Francisco revived my weary spirit. The manager at the hotel was delighted to see me back, but the dogs did not share his enthusiasm. My presence was merely a familiar smell. And the room which became my new abode was better than the previous one. It was on a lower level, had a bathroom, and the view of the world below appeared a tad within reach.

The following morning, I arrived at the union hall. After registering for work, it seemed only right to witness the next hourly call. Incredible! Several ships were recruiting practically entire crews. It seemed a very positive sign. Again, my hope was for this to endure a while. Once I exited the building, an older sailor standing nearby questioned why so many crew members were jumping ship. It seemed better to avoid speculating, so my smile and a nod allowed me to get going.

Sometime that afternoon, a bus had me on my way to Santa Rosa to see Matt's friends. It was not only to pay a brief visit but also to retrieve some clothes which had been left behind. The couple were surprised to see me, especially without Matt. Nevertheless, they were so accommodating, and later that afternoon, I was informed about Sheila. She had run into them and had expressed an interest in me.

Sheila was from Sacramento but had been residing in Santa Rosa for years. We met that evening when she got off work. Perhaps the gorgeous young lady was a bit tired, but her charming mood was upbeat. I became acquainted with such a pleasing attitude and her slight philosophical thoughts which came and went at random. Plus, she stated life was to be enjoyed, full stop. It certainly made my take on things a bit easier to pitch. We soon headed off to a club, both to dine and see her friend who worked as a bartender.

Dinner was simple and plentiful. Our chats were cordial but fun and very interesting. We had also spent a few minutes at the bar talking with her buddy, who, although busy, found time for us and was hilarious, so we agreed to all go out one evening. We eventually left, and Sheila took me home, and there is no doubt, we were very comfortable with one another.

Quite soon a romantic mood began to set in. The entire premises, as lights were dimmed and some classical jazz played in the background, were simply perfect. I was next to Sheila on the couch, having finished a glass of white wine, and now her bewitching and seductive eyes invited me to be a bit rash and affectionate. So, I blew her a kiss, but she insisted it be delivered a little closer. My, how all things come to those who wait.

Well, I had certainly experienced a wonderful encounter upon my return, but one should always be fully prepared to expect the unexpected. This concept ought to be stamped, in bold letters, on all currencies, especially the all-mighty dollar. For one thing, it could stimulate a sound financial and social rectitude and might also make citizens more cautious in their outlook toward all matters, not just money!

I say this as one late afternoon, something snapped me out of my peppy daydreaming mood and shell-shocked me. My walk on Geary Street had me heading to Union Square, and my step was in perfect harmony with my surroundings, particularly the stillness that accompanied me. As always, past incidents were getting rehashed mentally, depriving me of my full consciousness of the surrounding world.

Suddenly, a human body landed and pounded the top of a car just a few feet away from where I was. That very powerful impact nearly put my startled heart out of commission. The huge body, whose crash stopped me in my tracks, rolled off the vehicle and fell onto the sidewalk. It was a man who had obviously fallen from way above.

People began to run toward my direction. I simply froze. Blood was now flowing out of the man's battered head, and although he may have still been alive, it certainly did not look good. What an awful sight to contend with. My immediate instinct was to turn away and keep walking. There was absolutely nothing to do but stare. A bit later, at some distance, my curiosity began to vent.

Was it an accident? Or perhaps a suicide? And one quite damning to us viewers. Or maybe that individual had been pushed? He was practically naked. He only wore a T-shirt, and there were some strange scars on one of his legs. Maybe he had been ill. My goodness, how quickly life can wound the body it dwells in without the slightest bit of warning.

My legs somehow bypassed my destination eventually landing me in Chinatown. And although life there was in full progress as usual, for a slight moment, things seemed grayish and dull as I sat on a street bench. Then so unexpectedly, Ricky's laughter penetrated my ears. Was my dead brother reminding me to live each day, wisely, fully, and happily? Isn't each moment merely a test to render our time here worthwhile?

It seemed only right to walk and catch the cable car to Fisherman's Wharf. There, all my inner worries disappeared as the beauty of the Golden Gate Bridge compelled me to appreciate its immense and attractive work of art. And what a perfect color red is. How is it that I had never quite noticed its elegance? This perfectly modern architectural structure simply wears its façade so well. But why is it called Golden? Is it because its true value lies in the majestic embrace of the land it touches?

Chapter 60

I sailed on the Seatrain Carolina in 1972. The new itinerary was very similar to that of my first ship. One peculiar difference, however, was with my new outlook regarding sex, especially once back in Asia. My prudish and shy teen ways had fully expired. It was now my duty to practice love-making more often and improve wherever necessary.

On this voyage, we revisited some of the ports I was already acquainted with. However, one issue plagued me quite a bit—my profession. That is, being a wiper. Once again, the chief engineer was hardly around, and so my days were very long and quite boring. A mental note began insisting I return to Piney Point to upgrade myself to a higher position once this trip terminated.

My roommate was from Yemen. He was a laidback individual, soft-spoken, and a man of few words. Could I have possibly been luckier? Almost every evening, while my nose was in a book, he would quietly revisit parts of the Koran, reading, and sometimes informing me on the essence of living a good clean life. It seemed only right to listen and show some interest.

There was another Yemeni on board, and he was our waiter. Once he had served dinner, this tiny man, would often invade our narrow quarters. There was not much room for just two people, so it forced me, but most happily, to allow them to chat in their native language while making my way to the bow, weather permitting, to simply meditate for a while.

Soon enough, I made friends with Jimmy, an oiler, and Frank, an AB. We became close. And just what do you think brought us together? Yes, we shared a voracious interest and love for marijuana, which is nothing more than an herbal cure for boredom. And believe me, we smoked excessively and would ultimately find out that we were not the only ones.

One unique individual on our ship was Frank's boss, the bosun. He was an old-school tough gentleman from Dallas, full of manners, and some interesting stories, but always ready to brawl at a moment's notice if deemed necessary. The man was up there in age, but his heart seemed to verge on puberty. He loved putting on a performance, no matter what the environment. Frank had nicknamed him "the duke" and it seemed a title rightly earned and one to respect.

I encroached on the duke in the cargo hold one day. My mission there was to kill some time and familiarize myself with some of the cargo going to the troops in Vietnam. Of all people to run into, I bumped into the bosun. From the expression on his face, he appeared to be in a galaxy of his own. He was placing rat traps throughout the area we were in and identifying them with huge letters on the nearby wall so no one would accidentally step on them.

The word "mouz twap" was everywhere. Of course, it begged the question as to what was with the crazy spelling, and he very happily informed me, "That's so the mice don't read it." Need I say more? It may have been his expression, my state of mind, or both which made me burst out in uncontrollable laughter. For a moment, we were like little children, finding joy in the silliest of things, for laughter brings out the best in us. And yes, the duke had just made my day.

Our ship soon docked in Olongapo City late one afternoon. I definitely knew which bar to avoid. That evening, Jimmy and I went ashore together, but Frank remained behind. In some ways, he reminded me of Ted, whose dedication to someone at home was uncompromising. While in Ted's case, there were several anonymous ladies, Frank only loved one woman, and, as he referred to her, she was "the one."

There is little to reveal on my revisiting what was then called, "Sin City". The following day we proceeded to Vietnam, and this time the ship went directly to Saigon itself. Several GIs were scattered about the pier, and once we anchored, a few soldiers came on board to guard the ship. My eyes again caught a vision of the raggedy-dressed Vietnamese longshoremen on the dock and on the ship, going about their work with pride and tenacity.

The incident now being revealed is to provide a brief explanation on how things stood. You should know that on our ships, the kitchen staff always prepared entirely too much food. Perhaps it was to ensure an abundance of nourishment to all and not deprive each hungry sailor of something on the menu. It also led to excess food getting thrown overboard when we were out at sea and thrashed when in port. A classic example of good intentions but wasteful results.

This never sat well with me. As a kid in Italy, and at home in the Bronx, and in my personal outlook, food is a sacred commodity. Why, we were taught that if you dropped something you were eating, you picked it up and washed it as best as possible and continued eating. To me, watching food hitting the ocean waves in early evening, which fed the seabirds following the ship, disturbed the very core of my moral fiber.

It was after an afternoon coffee break when the incident occurred. My roommate and I were ready to return to the engine room, and I had asked the waiter if it was okay to give the leftover donuts to the Vietnamese longshoremen sitting on the stern. They too, were taking a load off. He approved my initiative and even provided me a tray quite full of those buns.

A few female workers, wearing their non-la hats, were sitting by their male co-workers. All were chatting most happily. By the way, just so you know, the heat and humidity were unbearable, and nowhere else but inside our ship was air-conditioning available. After I stepped out into the stern, and once seeing me approach, tray in hand full of treats, some smiles already on display became huge.

Then all hell broke loose. An AB, quite old, came rushing out of nowhere, yelling like a madman. He was cursing me out, and he then grabbed the tray out of my hands and continued with his verbal barrage. Naturally, the frightened dock workers quickly disappeared, and the old prick headed into the dining room to return the donuts. Sure enough, that very evening, they were thrown out.

The event forced me to my room, finding it impossible to return to work. I was so fucking angry but had heeded Jesus' call to "turn the other cheek." I hated myself for doing it. Arguing or yelling with the old prick would have been useless, and who knows, maybe the fool would have taken me on. I felt a bit bruised, both morally and philosophically, but my ego soon managed to heal. I consoled myself by ushering in the notion that a generous heart is better than no heart at all.

Chapter 61

Our ship left Saigon and hugged the Vietnamese coastline while heading to Cam Ranh Bay. The cargo consisted of a few military trucks and jeeps and plenty of supplies for the post exchange, including a lot of beer, which I had discovered a while back. Consequently, so had some of the elderly sailors who were happily enjoying free brew in the privacy of their rooms.

It was a bit strange arriving in a puny and practically empty port. Yet that is exactly what we found. There were just a few Vietnamese longshoremen on the dock to tie up our ship. Even more baffling was that although we were inside a Navy port, it was being manned by army soldiers. We soon came to terms with the lack of dock workers and practically no vehicles of any kind moving about, for most of the Vietnamese personnel were on strike.

While the pier may have appeared skimpy, it was nothing compared to the oblivion right outside the main and only gate. Barren land extended for miles. No matter which way one looked, there was absolutely nothing—no paved roads, no traffic or destination signs or lampposts, just a dirt road heading in two different directions to the nearest villages and the army base. How anyone got about was a sheer mystery to me.

The problem with the emptiness and a lack of transportation was soon touched on. A soldier on guard duty on our ship had begun a brief chat with me. Mack soon revealed that only by getting a lift from the GIs driving a few trucks and jeeps in and out of the port, could you get to the nearby villages, or anywhere for that matter. And he, from North Dakota, and only in the country for the past three months, looked me up and down carefully while inquiring why in the world I would want to go anywhere. His description regarding our surroundings was stated with, "what you see, is what you get."

Perhaps my curiosity can be somewhat ruthless. Was it possible to get to one of the villages? At first, Mack was not big on cooperating, but he finally came around. Late in the afternoon, after work hours, we rode to the Cam Ranh village. We were in a military truck with two of his unit buddies, who had finished their shift and were ready to head off to their base. The driver had eyed me suspiciously, and he even checked out my merchant marine card, presented with a sliver of pride, after which he branded me as "legit".

We bypassed their base and headed to the village. Listening to these three soldiers bitch and moan was disconcerting. They apparently hated military life. The U.S. Army had forced them to adhere to strange rules of engagement, and even more disheartening was the oppressive environment they had to contend with. Each one agreed Uncle Sam had dragged them thousands of miles from home, and then sort of abandoned them. They also disliked the Vietnamese, whom they did not trust, and often referred to them as lazy stupid gooks.

Soon enough, we arrived in the village. Goodness gracious, what was I thinking? Mack had certainly tried to warn me. First of all, it was more of a hamlet than a village and an awful eye sore. A series of bamboo huts on dirt ground were scattered throughout with folks slowly going about their daily routine. Poverty is too modest a word to describe our surroundings, yet the locals looked happy, especially seeing the likes of us among them.

In one area stood several women. One had a wooden pole on her back to transport her wares, and all wore those cyclical hats. In a nearby pen were some chickens, and some small kids there were playing a game, oblivious to the world around them. An older man on a bicycle rode slowly by us, and my companions said something in Vietnamese which brought a smile to his lips and a slight nod. I could not help but notice how here was another wretchedly dressed individual with hardly any teeth in his mouth, but he appeared to be one of the better off members of the tribe.

What immediately hit home was the lack of anything modern. Something we Americans simply take for granted. Here, bathrooms did not exist, refrigerators were something to dream about, and electricity was a limited commodity reserved for the far away city of Saigon. The dirt path we were now walking on was the town's heartland.

You cannot imagine how we stood out. Of course, not so much the soldiers but me, the slightly bearded civilian in colorful civilian clothes with just a bit of long hair. It certainly felt like all eyes were on me. Some folks were pointing to us, chatting happily and looking inquisitively but with smiles on their faces. Almost immediately it hit me to return to the ship. Mack had that "I told you so" look piercing me.

On our way back to the port, we lit up and smoked some very good local weed. Perhaps it was to erase the misery we had just witnessed. My hosts let me off by the pier gate as they went off to their base. Once the MPs checked my ID, go figure, the road leading to my ship ran straight ahead and was all mine. I walked a bit, and at a distance further up, it appeared that someone was on the ground, and two soldiers were severely stomping him. The poor soul was obviously taking a very severe beating.

It was impossible to avoid the fracas on the tiny road leading to where the ship was docked. I approached the duo and foolishly asked, "Hey, what's going on?" One soldier immediately came toward me. His rifle slipped from his shoulder, and he pointed it in my direction. He was fucking angry, and like a madman, he began ranting furiously as he moved in my direction. His eyes looked evil, the veins in his neck seemed ready to burst, and it was apparent that I represented everything he hated.

I froze! We both stared at each other as he rambled on. Then his buddy spoke up urging him to calm down. His exact words were, "Let go, Tommy. Come on. Just let it go." He repeated this again, and what stood out was how young they both looked. In fact, they were too young to be in uniform and ready to kill at a moment's notice.

I'm not sure how much time passed. Fortunately, the weapon pointed at me returned to the guy's shoulder. I walked away cautiously while eyeing the soldiers, and so a slow retreat was on. The victim then got up. He was elderly, shoeless, scruffy to the utmost but was now allowed to walk away. My gait continued at a snail's pace but then slowly picked up. I noticed both GIs continued taking me in until I turned my back on them. After taking a deep breath, I resumed my walk to the ship in full gait.

Once up the gangplank, I headed to the bow. It was impossible to even breathe normally. I lit a joint but then almost immediately chucked it. Nothing made any fucking sense! Why was there so much hatred all around me? I must have sat there for the longest time feeling so empty and even sorry for myself. Just who was I? Where did I belong? Why was I in the middle of a country at war? For a moment, my outlook on my own citizens was questioned.

Eventually my angered confusion slightly abated. It seemed strange to not find my roommate in our room, so I sat and stared at the locker for a while but then decided to turn in. A bit later there he was, and happy as a pig in shit! For the first time in his life, he had played poker, against his buddy's warning, and had won a few bucks. What could I say? I just smiled, gave him a nod, and attempted to bury my misery.

It was Mack who had a bit of a laugh the following day. He had heard some talk regarding something similar back in the barracks but had not heard all the details. Learning that a rifle had been drawn seemed incredible to him, and he would never have imagined me the victim. The guy immediately apologized for the "hot heads" who according to him had gone too long without R&R.

Even his apology could not justify what had occurred. It dawned on me what war does to the human spirit. It criminalizes it. Oh well, those soldiers represented a madness we civilians could not possibly fathom, and so it seemed better to let the matter drop. Now according to Mack, I was one lucky person. Things could have gotten out of hand and finished badly. Yet, what immediately floored me was discovering the nature of the incident. The ragged Vietnamese man had been caught stealing a pallet. That is basically it. A wooden platform which holds cargo, so it can easily be moved around using a forklift. That starving old man had stolen a fucking piece of wood, and that is what merited the brutal punishment he endured. The only thing that consoled me was that had I not stumbled by the beating could have been worse.

The following evening our ship quickly pulled out. The strike continued, but it was something entirely different which had us beat a retreat. A few of us were on the bow in the evening having a powwow. Jimmy had requested to hear Sticky Fingers, which was slipped into my portable stereo set, but before it played, some firecrackers went off at a distance. That is what it sounded like. Then some popping sounds ensued, and now a siren was going off, and guns began blazing away. Apparently, a gun fight was on in one of the nearby villages.

Soon, total chaos resonated from nearby. The vestige of a battle was at hand. And as quickly as it began, it was over. We three left the bow and dashed to the dining room. Most of the crew was there, and a few guys were talking rather anxiously. Then the bosun entered. He seemed indifferent to our concerns as he began taking a head count to determine if everyone was on board. About half an hour later, the ship left the pier and dropped anchor in the middle of the bay, quite some distance from shore. We believed we were safe.

Early the next morning the captain received orders to sail to Da Nang. Our ship left immediately, and later that day, the radio operator got news of what had occurred and so informed the captain, and soon even the bosun knew the details and shared them. The Viet Cong had attacked the Cam Ranh village. It was a nightly hit-and-run tactic, and a few American soldiers who were in the village had been slightly wounded. One was dead.

Chapter 62

Da Nang was unbearably hot! A few of us did not want to leave the ship. Having just arrived for morning coffee in the dining room, Frank approached me and asked if I could step outside on to the stern. One of the soldiers on board had told him that a Vietnamese guy on the nearby tugboats was selling some incredible weed from Cambodia. Top-of-the-line shit. Was I at all interested?

Frank had been generous with us when we had left the West Coast and headed out to sea. Almost everyone had purchased some weed back in Saigon, and so I saw no need to go on an unnecessary shopping spree. I told him so, but my friend began insisting this was some truly great stuff and even referred to it as El Supremo. He had not requested an advance of funds and was without cash. He was hoping I would score, so he asked if I would willingly pass up this golden prize, sounding a bit like a desperate housewife.

Later that afternoon, I skipped the coffee break and walked over to the tugboats. My hands were shaking, and my heart kept questioning why I was doing someone else's dirty work. There was only one person on one of the two tugboats, and he looked like a young kid. After boarding, we managed to miraculously communicate, me indicating smoking a pipe, and he showing a price using his hands.

He got paid and handed me a brown package neatly tied up. My instincts demanded a quick inspection be performed, but this was shut down by the paranoid salesperson. He began gesturing for me to leave, and he seemed slightly agitated, which had me feeling very jittery, super suspicious, and returning to my ship with a package with no idea what was in it.

Fortunately, there was no one on the gangplank. I quickly made it to my room, and my hands desperately tore into that package. Sure enough, my heart almost skipped a beat. It did not look like weed, at least nothing my eyes had ever seen before looked similar. It had a golden color, lacked the right texture, and almost made me think of something like hay. I immediately went below to the engine room and got a bucket. Once back in my room, the package was placed in the bucket and slightly camouflaged with some old rags. Then, it was on to an area in the forward part of the ship, and once there, I took myself to one of my favorite places to hide anything. The package got stashed there after stuffing some of that hay in my pocket. I would soon find out just what we would or would not be smoking.

Frank was in the dining area. We casually made our way to the bow, but my mood was rather dismal. So was my dialogue, for it bordered on serious paranoia, not being sure just what to make of all that had occurred on that tugboat. Frank was not convinced I had been ripped off.

Now what can I say! Never judge a book by its cover. Once the first intake hit my lungs, I knew we had hit the big times. El Supremo or not, this grass was perhaps triple A grade, and to the ninth power. We were very relieved, and even before finishing the little bit of grass in the pipe, we started laughing uncontrollably. Perhaps finishing the pipe was overdoing it, for in no time at all, we were both super happy and quite paralyzed.

A few days later, we proceeded to Naha in Okinawa. Our ship docked in the early afternoon. My roommate and I were on deck watching our crew secure the vessel to the pier. Everything on that dock was such a major upgrade from what we had just left behind. Here, efficiency and coordination were very visible, and nobody appeared poor or struggling to survive.

My roommate suggested, and soon insisted, seeing me hesitate, that we dine together that evening. That is, him, me, and his Yemeni buddy. This is what brought us to the USO club right outside the port gate entrance. My two hosts had guaranteed it would be an English-only session. Consequently, once the waiter finished serving dinner, we three went off to the club and found it fully packed. Lots of soldiers, some civilians, plenty of Navy sailors, and a few Japanese officers were all about, and that raucous environment took a bit to get used to.

Miraculously, we got a table. Just a few minutes after sitting down, someone tapped my shoulder. Why, of all people, it was the guy from the union hall who had claimed a profound devotion to Vietnam. The lad was all smiles and seemed genuinely happy to see me there. We briefly exchanged notes, his ship was docked next to ours, and he insisted we join him at the bar once through eating. I promised to do so, but my mates did not appear so keen on this.

Soon enough, plenty of food came our way. My explanation regarding this acquaintance had been provided but perhaps had not convinced my two hosts. Oh well, my Yemeni friends had chosen well, for our dinner was exceptionally good, and our chatting continued in English, mostly about what entails good food, while all the folks around us were apparently igniting their fun via the consumption of booze, and plenty of it.

My roommate and I had ordered beer, but his friend refused to drink, and he did not approve. A few native words came out but were soon replaced with English and an apology. Eventually, the two gave me a brief lesson on customs and traditions back home, and even touched on some aspects of the Muslim religion, which prohibits drinking. At that point, my roommate jokingly informed us he had taken the evening off from his religion.

Both guys emphasized their devotion to the family nucleus. In their upbringing, it was more than just a tradition. It was like a religion. They proudly claimed it a privilege to support their family members back home and announced it so cheerfully, and then the waiter, from our ship, wearing a huge smile, mentioned that one day soon, they would both return home to live like kings.

Their revelations flowed out like a catechism. Quite surprisingly, they mentioned their unhappiness living in the U.S. They felt terribly lonely, out of place, struggled to fit in, and had no American friends. So, for the moment, all that mattered was ultimately returning to the intimacy of living in a small village where everyone is truly your neighbor. It sounded like a blessing. Out of the blue, my roommate made a positive remark about the U.S. He smiled and said, "But the money is good."

Eventually my mates moved on. This allowed me to go over and properly meet my mysterious Southern guest. Sam Bloodrock was from South Carolina, and he had the accent to prove it. Next to him were a couple of American guys who looked like hippies, but with no accents, or at least nothing easily distinguishable.

I assumed they, too, were sailors, and perhaps on the same ship. No, sir. The two flower children look-alikes were ex-soldiers (Air Force folks, to be precise). Only now they were living on the island and somehow fending for themselves. This truly baffled me. From what Tim had once told me, Japanese culture was a tad hostile toward foreigners among them, especially guys who looked like the sixties had entrapped them. Now just how had these two gotten past the authorities?

We all found much to talk about and continued drinking. While the chaos around us between bar and restaurant kept us four talking quite loudly, one of the two Okinawan residents suggested we leave. A taxi was flagged down and in no time at all we were at their dwelling. The flat they shared, though small, was quaint and super clean and inundated with rare tropical plants. Plus, there was a large Buddha statue dominating the center of the living room. All around, one's eyes were greeted with a soothing ambiance with a touch of Asian fusion and some modern but small Western furniture. True to tradition, we had all removed our shoes before entering, for it seemed only right.

Now my vision of the mood in the flat was on target, but it was quickly shattered once some music came on. It was Jethro Tull's "Stand Up". Sure enough, one of our hosts lit up a pipe, and while it did not compare to my Cambodian gold, we were soon laughing loudly and chatting radically about anything while also sipping some very sweet Japanese wine. At some point, Sam looked at me, smiled, and then said, "Is there any other way to live?"

As always, time runs off too quickly. It was way past three in the morning when Sam and I headed back to the port in a taxi driven by a super silent native. Sam later revealed he thought the driver disliked Americans as he appeared old enough to have been in WWII. Well, we shook hands and parted ways on the pier inside the U.S. military base in Naha. His ship would leave early that morning to return to California, whereas mine was scheduled to sail to Saigon in the latter part of the day.

While boarding my ship, it seemed odd having run into the guy. We were practically strangers, and yet I instinctively knew how much I now liked him. It was his easy-going, super friendly, and sincere attitude which stood out and made me feel like we had known each other for ages. Then the word destiny sort of redefined itself. For do we really control ours? Or are our personal dice in life tossed long before we even get our hands on them. If we ever truly do.

It soon hit me! Sam's love for this part of the world, especially Vietnam, was not a devotion toward any specific nation. His was an appreciation for all people, especially those who have little and fight against tough odds. At this point, Asia was simply our unique landscape to explore. And strangely, it was because of an ongoing war that we had somehow been brought together. Yes, I, too, now shared a strong sentiment for people living in circumstances beyond their control. It sealed itself in me for good.

Our ship did not return exactly to Saigon but went to Newport. My needy loins were desperate to be attended to, but having exceeded my financial possibilities, the captain had refused my request for funds. For some time now, my once prudish ways had completely vanished, which is why I, and a few others, would be staying on board.

Frank, as always, was not going anywhere. He was a stay-at-home sailor. James, on the other hand, like me, made each port visit count, but he was also laying low. The three of us met on deck and decided to head to the bow and were even joined by the baker, who occasionally partied with us, and sometimes a bit excessively. Our guest soon surprised us by insisting we mix some of his opium with my El Supremo weed.

No one objected. Off we went, and once our smoking session terminated, we were mentally, physically, morally, and maybe even philosophically pulverized. I just wanted to go lay down, but the kitchen worker had other plans. He suggested we make it to the soldier's club as it was located on the pier right next to our ship. Surprisingly, he even offered us a round of beers, which even Frank, so unlike him, agreed to participate in. The four of us made it down the gangplank, most cautiously, and we may have looked a tad like Dumas' heroes, except in a fog, for we certainly adhered to the motto "one for all and all for one."

The club was nothing more than a large wooden canopy. It was held together by thin bamboo walls and was next to several tugboats at the end of the pier. Once inside that wooden shack, a large room full of tables and chairs faced a huge movie screen, and there was a bar right by the entrance as if to greet newcomers filing in. Lots of soldiers were everywhere and sounded quite rowdy. My how we merchant marine sailors always stood out for all eyes were now on us.

A movie was scheduled to begin in just a few minutes. We got our beers and made our way to a table. The overhead lights had been dimmed when my vision suddenly began to fail. Then, my sight was completely gone. I sensed doom and disaster as panic forced me to head back toward the entrance area. But I could not see! Voices were now barely audible, and there were some murmurs as I accidentally bumped into people who were strongly pushing me out of their way. My feet kept moving my body, but then a silence engulfed me.

A powerful force grabbed me and pulled me into an infinite black space of emptiness. I was traveling at a meteoric speed, body quite motionless and in a state of unconsciousness. An inner voice was desperately screaming, pleading to be spared. It was like a call to a higher power while being sucked into the endless vacuum of the unknown, as my ego refused to be pulled in.

I suddenly came to! My body was between the entrance to the club and the edge of the pier. I was on the floor and my knees touched the ground. I began to raise myself back up, as my heart slammed in my chest and my mind slowly dispelled the horrific trance which had transpired. Once standing, I began to head toward the ship as an immediate thought kept regurgitating; I would never get high again.

Unfortunately, the new me lasted only three days. And, if not mistaken, tragedy struck a week later once the ship was on the Pacific Ocean making its way back to the U.S. That is when my super fantastic grass disappeared. It almost gave me a heart attack. My Cambodian weed was no longer where it had been hidden. A desperate and frantic search of the area led to nothing, and I could only blame myself for having somehow slipped up.

Chapter 63

It was terribly hot at the Harry Lundberg School of Seamanship. However, the very fact that I was not wearing a uniform or had to march anywhere or salute anyone was tremendously rewarding, like bypassing an unnecessary silly routine.

Those of us that were there to upgrade ourselves were staying at the hotel. Monday morning saw me eventually on the Zimmerman to greet my old teachers. The program was proceeding beyond anyone's expectations. All appeared so proud and rightfully so. It was tempting to thank them all again, even that huge gentleman, who I discovered was no longer there. After all, I had attained a small investment which could one day bring a bigger one, and it was achieved so quickly, which made me now feel a bit proud and very grateful.

We had perfect weather the entire next two weeks, the duration of our class. And on the very first day of school a student behind me inquired about taking out one of the large-sized sailboats. It got approved! So, on our very first weekend, early that Saturday morning, six of us, accompanied by the chief, an old hand at sailing, cruised the bay and ultimately made it out to sea, but always within eyesight of the coastline.

It is such a pleasure to be on a small vessel. One enjoys a peaceful serenity which only gets slightly disturbed by the sound of the waters' constant tugging motion as it hits the sailboat. Unlike our work experience on cargo ships, we six put in some real work hours handling the sails and navigating under the chief's orders, but it never felt like we were working.

Back in the classroom, my course was more in-depth than expected. Nevertheless, two weeks flew by quickly, and little old me now qualified for two positions, oiler, and fireman-water-tender. Who can say just exactly what sparked my preference for the boiler room? It may have been because someone in class had mentioned such work could equate to jobs on land if one chose to abandon a life at sea or after fully completing one as a sailor.

It was already time to leave the school. A limousine, which would take myself and two more students to Leonardtown to catch a bus, had just arrived. It stopped in front of the hotel and suddenly, a very familiar face stood before me. It was the maestro himself, Sean Blatter.

We warmly shook hands and started complimenting each other. Sean was obviously following in my footsteps, except that having worked in the deck department, he was now upgrading himself to an AB position. One assumes he had abandoned his wild scheme to strike it rich. After all, here he was, attempting to improve his life at sea.

Unfortunately, the hasty driver who looked nothing like that person that somehow miraculously got us to Brooklyn two years ago was in a bit of a hurry. So, we two old buddies had to cut it short and parted ways but promised to try to catch up in San Francisco.

Running back to the West Coast without a quick trip to the Bronx did not feel right. Something always pulled me back to the Big Apple. And this time around, Shamus' place was fully inhabited, which is why my present destination had me going to a place called the Apostleship of the Sea, located somewhere in lower Manhattan.

My new digs afforded me a comfortable stay. The institution was nothing more than a sailor's home away from his ship. It was basically an inexpensive hostel. However, lodging there required some minor clean-up chores. And certainly a tad more annoying, they had a curfew, which the administrative personnel took too seriously. This soon became a real problem for me.

Nevertheless, my stay in the southern tip of the island allowed me to get somewhat better acquainted with the city. Soon enough Manhattan's immensity and its inhabitants' chaotic movement frightened me much less. This quelling of my fear led me to discover the New York Public Library and a Japanese author, Yukio Mishima. His book Spring Snow was the most beautiful thing I had ever read. Perhaps one day, his tetralogy, the Sea of Fertility, would also be taken on.

Well, it was bound to happen. I had returned late one evening, and the following day, the manager had much to say. Entirely too much. So, it was goodbye to Battery Park and hello to the Bronx, a place whose open arms greeted me nicely, although too often I hardly noticed it. It was my grandmother who had come to my rescue as we had spoken on the phone a few days earlier. She was now a widow and had suggested her apartment, if the city, as she often referred to Manhattan, became inconvenient in any way.

The woman lived on Rosedale Avenue not far from our old bunker. I knew there would be a few errands to run occasionally, and no elevator to the fifth floor, but my grandmother was a happy camper. She lived by a simple rule—look for the best in everyone. And she could certainly bring out the best in anyone. Her phone was constantly ringing, for her chats were warm, full of concern for all, and rarely was there an unkind word toward any family member, friend or foe.

There was just one instance in which she expressed some negative thoughts. It was over the movie, Midnight Cowboy. This film had truly disgusted her, for she felt completely outraged over its language and vulgar insinuations, and her exact words were "having witnessed such filthy scenes and hearing so much vulgarity was simply repulsive." She asked me if people really lived like that.

Hopefully, my silence did not give me away. I had seen it in San Francisco at a cheap theater, as a rerun and had enjoyed it very much. It was nothing more than a modern saga of two vagabonds, one rugged beyond recognition and one simply new to the core in his updated take on life. Both were trying to survive without surrendering their freedom. And yes, some people did live like that. Sad but true.

Oh well, the lady of the house played bingo every Wednesday night. It was in the local church auditorium and she often, hopefully not too often, came home with the evening's winnings. I tagged along once, and we eventually left and brought home a large pepperoni pizza with her winnings. Oh, by the way, after finishing breakfast every morning, she savored a small shot of Southern Comfort. Her physician had said it stimulates the heart if taken in the morning, which she always did.

Chapter 64

You may remember that my father, Adriano Di Stefano, had become Adrian. Well, his brother Roberto had become Bob. He had left Sicily several times returning to the Bronx and would then go back to Palermo looking a tad disrupted. Yet once again, he was back among us.

As a kid growing up in my dad's home, we rarely saw him. This was a familiar Di Stefano trait back in Sicily and abroad. Just what brought us together I do not recall. We met for coffee at Jack's on Westchester Square, and I immediately noticed how shy and quiet he always appeared. He was an observer, and if I am not mistaken, he lived alone and worked in a pizzeria.

My uncle was soft-spoken, super calm, and well-composed. Once he opened up a bit, there was much to admire, like his love for literature, which at first puzzled me. Never had any of us at home seen our father reading anything. Whereas this man was apparently well-read and shared a keen interest in world politics, and he certainly knew his facts.

Upon exiting the diner, I had mentioned my new initiative, getting a driver's license. Being clueless behind the wheel, it seemed prudent to attend a driving school. My uncle volunteered to help out and insisted spending money on a school was out of the question. I thanked him, declined his offer, but nothing doing—we started the following morning.

The empty parking lot where we began was close to the delicatessen where I once worked. I must say, the man was an excellent teacher as his approach was well-thought-out, and he would give a basic but thorough explanation. He first highlighted the various parts of the car, how to use them, like breaking carefully and not exaggerating in using gas, and soon pointed out what to observe as he slowly drove about the lot. The process was repeated the following day, but this day, he pointed out various safety tips and made sure I understood.

I began driving in that lot. Two days later, we moved on. His prudent guidelines stayed with me as I cautiously anticipated what lay ahead in order to prepare. My confidence increased daily, although slowly at first, but it quickly picked up pace, and soon enough We were cruising small side roads and regular streets throughout the Pelham Bay area and eventually beyond.

My uncle's ability to teach properly impressed me, and I liked that he spoke enthusiastically about a variety of topics. One day he mentioned that he was reading, Il Gattopardo, written by Tomasi Di Lampedusa. It sounded foreign to me. He certainly had my attention but soon lost it. He revealed having fully grasped the essence of that book's theme: "the more things change, the more they stay the same." Folks, my eyes covered the road, my ears processed his words, but nothing registered within, so I left it at that.

In one of our last driving outings, his passion for technical skills came out. Weeks back, he had repaired my folk's TV set and was now working on someone's stereo. It felt great being with him, including getting acquainted with his various interests and talents. Thus, began a small relationship for that man had made a driver out of me. He had also enriched my knowledge of the world, and maybe one day that book's bizarre concept would hit home.

In the meantime, I was spending less time in the old neighborhood; however, I would occasionally frequent it. One evening Shamus informed me that Betty was in a serious relationship. She and her boyfriend had moved to Oregon and were doing quite well. On the other hand, I had run into Kevin O'Conner and his brother and learned they were using heroin quite frequently. My, we had once been so close, and I had always found them so much fun to be with.

Shamus was still my best friend. We met one evening at one of the bars on Beach Avenue to catch up. Upon entering, a most bizarre sight puzzled my eyes. It was like a scene from the *Twilight Zone*, its meaning quite vague and rather daunting. A long shuffleboard table was situated in the center of the bar with a motorcycle on top.

James Easton was on that motorcycle. He was clad in a black leather jacket and wearing a WWII German helmet. About a dozen guys were marching around him singing something that sounded like, "Once again the Panzer tanks will roll." Shamus must have read my face. He began explaining that the Northern Irish, who had no love for the English, had favored the Germans during the Second World War.

Now that ghastly scene made a bit more sense. Nevertheless, it still felt somewhat overdone. A few minutes later, the biker scaled down from the contraption, and we became acquainted. It soon felt like the person I met and the one on that bike were complete strangers.

James was rather popular in the neighborhood. He was the only biker and considered a free spirit. The lad was also good-looking, and in demand by the ladies. According to legend, he often rode off and vanished for months at a time and left someone heartbroken. So here was this very jovial, extremely charming, fun guy, and yes, he bore no resemblance to the previous image on that motorcycle.

My new friend prattled on about a recent trip to Toms River in New Jersey. His new escapade included a trip to upstate New York to visit some old friends. I was briefly considering asking if I could tag along as I wanted to visit Peter in Lincoln Hall. It felt like ages since we had separated. Oh well, I could ride some with him and ultimately catch a bus, but it then felt like too much of an imposition. Plus, my only motorcycle voyage had left me a bit high and dry. It was a wise move, for a few days later someone informed me my brother was back in the neighborhood.

Chapter 65

My only straight friend was Jack Le Braunt. He was hardly ever in our neighborhood having moved quite a-ways from the Bronx a while back. One day I was exiting the delicatessen on Taylor Avenue when he spotted me and ran over. The lad could not contain his surprise and happiness in seeing me.

Jack was a bit of a riddle to most of our friends. He never got high on anything, which was simply inconceivable to just about everyone. Nevertheless, here was the picture of pure happiness. It was as if he was overdosing on the joy of living. The very same person who had branded Peter that awful nickname had also labeled him as Happy Jack, and it seemed to suit him perfectly.

My latest news was about my trip to Maryland, and in a week, I would head back to the West Coast. Jack was very curious about life out at sea, especially as Shamus had so quickly abandoned the occupation. I suggested we meet over the weekend and grab something to eat but instead he told me that he had an extra ticket to the Stones' concert at Madison Square Garden for that coming weekend, and it was all mine. I was floored!

Sometimes one's calamity is someone else's blessing. His girlfriend had to run off to Vermont as her father had been hospitalized. My happiness was immense, not over the incident, and so we soon synchronized our plans for that upcoming evening while anticipating the concert of a lifetime.

If I am correct, the Rolling Stones 1969 tour had proceeded flawlessly. Until all hell broke loose at their final gig at Altamont. Whereas this time around all the band's performances had been plagued by violent outbursts. Fights, brawls, overdoses, and all sorts of wild flareups had become a common trend. Jack had expressed some concern because it was one of the band's closing shows, yet it seemed right to insist lightning never strikes the same place twice.

Well, there we were! My how the Garden's infectious excitement grabbed us both by the collar. It was like a dream come true. Plus, our seats were very close to the stage. Soon the band came out to thunderous applause which lasted a long time. It was surreal just to be there.

Unfortunately, my wild enthusiasm plunged rather quickly. Sure, this was undoubtedly now the "Greatest Rock and Roll Band in the World", a title proclaimed a few years back. But this evening, the same band did not show up. Just what had happened to all those great songs I loved? No "Get Off of My Cloud" and "Jumpin Jack Flash" or "Gimme Shelter" or anything in between.

It felt like someone had put on the LP Exile on Main Street and maybe fallen asleep. I had to ask myself if the great Rolling Stones were lip singing. And my idol, Mick Jagger, practically never moved the entire night. Something was just not right. This was not a live concert, at least not until the end when Stevie Wonder came on stage, and they all did an awful version of "Satisfaction."

The media came to Mick's rescue the next day. He had been terribly ill and should not have even performed. It still did not exonerate a very uninspiring performance from a band I loved. Even more bizarre was Jack's take on things on our ride home after the show. He was completely baffled hearing my negative and rather disappointing comments. For a moment, as absurd as it would have seemed, I was tempted to ask if we had attended the same performance.

Oh well, a few days after the fiasco at the Garden, I had my last driving lesson. My uncle assured me I would pass the test. A few days later there was a mandatory driver's education class which was scheduled for a couple of hours in the early part of the evening. A few others and I arrived a bit early and waited for the instructor in what looked like an old conference room.

Soon the classroom filled up. The instructor arrived ten minutes late, and there was someone right behind him but got turned away. It seemed absurd, especially as the late-comer even pleaded for some consideration, which to me seemed only right. The instructor had not yet even introduced himself, which is why I foolishly expressed a sense of leniency for the tardy student. Big mistake!

The instructor looked at me in a threatening way. And so, the ousted student left, our class began, and our lecturer soon enough made some incredibly arrogant statements. It was regarding what he called an intrusion into the American automobile industry.

When my brother and I had arrived in the U.S., there were practically no foreign cars. Unless, of course, you were going to college and your parents had bought you a Beetle. Those vehicles had been around forever. However, a small car was just not part of the American psyche, for the word small plays no role at all in anyone's line of thinking. Well, except our dad. But the Japanese had broken this golden rule by introducing a few compact model cars at the end of the sixties. It was certainly a risky initiative.

Our teacher claimed these "bugs" had no right to be on our roads. He insisted they would not last more than a year or two. It was a stupid initiative according to him, and he added that the Japanese people were simple and small, both mentally and culturally. I could not help but recall growing up where small cars ruled the roads. He drove home his point by finishing with "And by the way, folks, when a tiny Japanese bug meets a Cadillac head-on, going fifty miles an hour, who do ya think's gonna win?"

I am an American, but for some reason this bothered me. And it looked like his eyes were dancing most happily upon predicting our competitors would ultimately fail. Of course, yours truly was clueless about the future, especially the auto industry. Wouldn't you know it, once the class terminated, he gave us our insignificant diplomas, and mine was full of coffee stains. Naturally, while handing it to me, he delivered a childish and idiotic smile so triumphantly, as if he had had the last laugh. Go figure!

A few days later, I was scheduled to go to DMV and get tested on my driving skills. Unfortunately, my uncle, who was more than happy to assist me, fell ill, and no one else was available. So, no uncle, no car. Oh well, my driving career was on hold, but at least a stained diploma to testify to my hard work and effort was now in my possession.

Chapter 66

I left the Bronx by plane this time. Once back in San Francisco, my new line of work as a fireman-water-tender was launched. It was an old freighter, the Potomac, that I sailed on in the latter part of 1972. We were heading to Bangladesh.

Perhaps it is not totally wrong to say our destination may have been imposed on us and the world at large. One individual responsible for this was George Harrison. His concert at Madison Square Garden for a people we Americans hardly knew existed, won us over. For the U.S., like many other nations, was now assisting a newly formed country which had been devastated by a horrible war the prior year.

Our ship was ancient, or as we sailors referred to such antiquity, an "old rust bucket." However, unlike on my other voyages, this crew consisted of mostly young sailors. Why, one quick glance in our dining room and you would have thought you were looking at a hippie commune. All that was missing was a guru figure handing out flowers on deck. Of course, I did a bit of partying once we left San Diego, the city I had traveled to where the ship was docked. And one evening, something totally unexpected occurred.

I pierced my left ear. My image had sort of changed drastically, it now being expressed mostly through lifestyle, looks, and fashion. It felt right to now seal it with a ribbon. My hair was long, although thin on top, my beard was fully grown, sometimes neatly trimmed, and so complementing the overall look with an earring made me feel in. And why not? Keith Richards wore one.

Oh well, that awful ship broke down several times. Suddenly the main generators were dead as our vessel sat in the middle of the ocean for a while. Through an emergency generator, a bit of life returned and, soon enough, the chief engineer and others got things back on track. By the way, our ship had no air-conditioning. Cool air, if you can call it that, came via open portholes and being up on deck. Now we all certainly knew life would be even more uncomfortable once arriving at our destination. Hopefully, we would not stay long.

My room was quite large. James Henderson, the oiler, was my roommate and a Black American, but one who spoke little. However, he played lots of jazz on his stereo, especially Coltrane, which did absolutely nothing for me. I would have loved to hear him speak more often, for anything he played, strictly jazz, sounded so gloomy to me. It lacked the type of harmony and style familiar to my ears, and Coltrane's music wandered aimlessly, musically speaking of course.

James may have been an introvert, but while on watch, he would always stop by the boiler room and briefly chat with me (very briefly) about anything which came to mind. His thoughts were positive and shared with a slight shade of fun. My work as a fireman-water-tender entailed a four-hour routine, including keeping an eye on all the gauges to ensure proper levels of water and air going into the boilers and occasionally checking the fires blazing away in the fire chambers. This most certainly felt like a long shift which led to too much thinking, plenty of walking back and forth in the limited space there, and sometimes talking to myself.

Of course, real work was accomplished when the ship entered or left a port. Then, I was super busy with required maneuvers. The engineer on watch was alongside me giving instructions based on orders coming from the captain, who was on the bridge overseeing the steering of the ship. If the captain wanted the ship to slow down, the burners, which allowed fuel into fire chambers, needed to be changed with smaller tips and vice versa to speed up.

You had to be fast in replacing the burners. So, the engineer would tell me what size tips to prepare on burners going in, and once given the okay, I would shut off the fire under the chamber, remove the old burner, and insert the new one. Then, I would relight the fire. After this, it was on to the next ones. I worked like Speedy Gonzalez. Once we left port and were heading into ocean waters or had finally arrived somewhere and docked, the process terminated, the engineer left, and it was time to think about the next meal.

After three long weeks out at sea, we finally arrived in the Bay of Bengal. There were ships everywhere, each one proudly flying their nation's flag on their stern. Of course, this huge congestion prevented us from docking at the port, but we could visit our new environment via the many small boats around our vessel.

It seemed like an everlasting waiting period before operations began. Unloading the cargo onto barges which were lined up on both the port and starboard side of our ship also took forever. Now why the likes of me wanted so badly to go ashore is impossible to explain. Perhaps it was a need to confirm my legs could still navigate on land.

My roommate was not the least interested, but I talked him into it. After all, if the city was not worth the visit, we would not go back. Our means of transportation ashore was via one of the many old decrepit boats scattered around our ship. They looked beat up, and so did the sailors in them, who were apparently happy to make a few bucks out of us, and they sure did.

It felt good to leave the ship. However, the most direct route went against some powerful currents, which is why the two boatmen, practically naked and mute to the core, rowed around the entire bay before finally docking at a tiny pier. Well, they may have been slightly exhausted, but we two passengers were drenched in sweat as the blistering sun had nearly melted us.

The very moment they tied up their boat, we encountered a problem. We had agreed to a round-trip amount before leaving the ship. Our sad-looking mariners were now insisting on the full amount up front, while reassuring us they would be at the dock once we returned, but I sensed a devious pitch in their eyes. Many unhappy ragged-looking natives surrounded us, so we had no choice but to comply.

Chittagong was an awful sight sore crammed with squalid living conditions. Most dwellings were nothing more than light metal frames held together with string. The unpaved streets were full of beggars and hustlers, and even folks going about their business eyed us suspiciously, indicating we had no right to be there. On one long and crowded street, a corpse lay on the side of the road as if it simply belonged there.

Wanting to purchase some souvenirs, we walked around for quite some time. There was little to be had, and soon enough, we were back at the pier as per the time coordinated. However, our sailors were nowhere to be found, which forced us to make offers to others for our return trip. The folks about us made it perfectly clear there would be no bargaining session. It was take it or leave it, for they certainly had us by the balls. Our return trip cost me quite a bit. After all, this foolish trip was all my doing.

Eventually, we headed off to South Africa to take on provisions, fuel up, and then head home. James shared some information about our destination, Cape Town. He had been there before, and what he told me sounded preposterous. We could not be together! This seemed impossible to me, but a few days later we arrived and faced this sad reality.

Knowing the ship would shortly be docking, I had taken myself up on deck. A coastline came into view. There was a vestige of a modern metropolis, still off a bit, but once within close proximity, it appeared nicely complemented by palm trees along its shores and a majestic mountain protecting its sprawl. Such was the spectacle, and quite far from what my mind had conjured up as a city in Africa. My, I was still so naïve.

As per my roommate's info, we headed in different directions once leaving the port. It seemed unreal, but very true. I caught a taxi, and my driver had an incomprehensible accent, but the chap was talkative, and he appeared a tad confused upon learning I was uncertain of my destination but simply requested a club or bar. Nothing too fancy but no dive either.

My tension eased up when we crossed the city. The surroundings truly impressed me. The city boasted immaculate cleanliness, orderly traffic, modern building structures, and regular looking people, Black and White, all on the go. It defied my simplistic expectations. Soon enough, we stopped in front of a modern and somewhat plush bar/nightclub. The driver wished me, what sounded like a "bagkat of u thime." My thanks came out spontaneously, me being relieved of dishing out one yes after another, even though the gist of his chat was hardly ever clear.

The club was full of young folks, reminding me of a similar one in San Francisco. It looked plush and well decorated, with lots of tables about and plenty of folks carrying on at the bar counter. I strolled over to that counter, and almost immediately, three very friendly chaps drew me into the midst of their conversation. Of course, my ears had to perk up, but fortunately, ours was mostly a casual chat which came in friendly tones, yet my nationality was immediately questioned but got highly approved, me being a "Yank."

All was proceeding extremely well. Until my inquisitive mind took a wrong turn. It ventured out boldly into a risky factor once I dared ask, "Just why was it necessary to separate my mate and I?" Well, all sorts of comments were rolled out, and the word apartheid, very new to me, got tossed about quiet freely. It sounded like some traditional social code applied to all ailments and uncertainties. Apparently, according to my instructors, keeping the races separate was due to the inequality between them, and looking at my plush surroundings it was easy to acknowledge.

Everyone defended the Afrikaners' right to maintain control over their nation. After all, their forefathers had found only wilderness but forged a country. They had fought against tribes which were not easily subdued and had strongly refused to accept the intruders. Then came a lengthy sermon delivered with pride and a sense of patriotism, and soon enough, the chap right next to me stated that South Africa would not become the next Rhodesia.

The conversation had turned too political and terribly solemn. It dawned on me that I had initiated the frenzy, and so, hoping to bring about a more positive note, I quoted from Bob Dylan's "The Times They Are a Changin" and foolishly asked if all people could not share the fruits of their labor. My idea was that of a "naïve critter." So went the chastising, and then the same person leading the charge asked, "And just what did the American pioneers share with the tribes they encountered?"

Chapter 67

Our ship would not return to San Diego, the port of embarkation. The company had finally recognized it was time to retire the old rust bucket. After departing Cape Town and before beginning the long trip across the Atlantic, we received orders from the ship's company to now head to Chickasaw, Alabama. It would be the final resting spot for our vessel before going to the scrapyard.

We arrived early one morning. I had just finished my routine with the engineer who had me working like a madman in order to provide less spunk from the boilers. I was happy to have finished. Now that the ship was tied up to the pier, our nostrils were suddenly infested by a most acrid smell. Good heavens, was there a chemical plant nearby poisoning the entire county?

Fortunately, the captain paid everyone off rather quickly. There was a mad rush downtown, then on to Mobile to catch any means of transportation available out of Alabama. I called Ted Allen from a phone booth at a diner in Chickasaw. It was a gentle female voice that greeted me. She sounded somewhat hesitant to continue speaking. This was Ted's sister. She eventually informed me her brother was on a ship, but the two had not communicated for some time. I was reassured he would know of my inquiry once they touched bases.

It would have been great to have seen Ted and shared a nice chat. But it was now time to get out of town. I hailed a taxi. Just like a few weeks back, the driver was a person with much to say, and in a not so comprehensible language. He immediately inquired which part of our country was home, and so, speaking somewhat proudly, New York City took the honors. Apparently, this further rallied his mental reflexes as he now looked at me through his mirror and then said, "Now y'all up there are the problem. See, down here, we keep our niggers in line."

South Africa was far behind. Yet I now felt disgusted here on my own soil. Just why is my country, a nation born from the elegant concept of equality for all, so infested with vicious hatred? A cloud of emptiness plagued me as my mood darkened. The only consolation rescuing my now sagging spirit was knowing that this foul-smelling little town, and its contagious hatred would soon be far behind.

It wasn't long before I was back in San Francisco. Incredible! There was Sam Bloodrock at the union hall carrying on with a union delegate in a rather nonchalant way. They both appeared to be savoring their chat as yours truly walked over. His voice was music to my ears. Sam's harmonious Southern rhythm and his meter certainly exterminated that vile jargon back in Chickasaw.

We soon left the union hall and went to a nearby bar. It catered mostly to us sailors. Oh, the sacrifices one makes for good friends! The place was packed, but the beers came quickly, and we found a corner to hustle into as Sam began filling me in. He had recently been home where everyone had smothered him with cheers and family warmth. However, everyday life was lacking something.

He claimed the friendly jargon he found sounded old though delivered with plenty of enthusiasm. Apparently, if your body is parked in one place but its spirit is elsewhere, your settings are somewhat out of whack. He was among family and friends, and yet Sam again felt a need to return to Asia, especially Vietnam. For a moment, he appeared like a modern-day Robinson Crusoe, desperately hoping for any ship to come rescue him.

Unfortunately, shipping was very tight. The longshoremen on the West Coast had been on strike forever and were practically crippling the maritime industry. We two unemployed mariners soon became close, and we would often leave the union hall in the late afternoons and, like two castaways, cruise the city with no particular place to go. We often spent our evenings in the Tenderloin area, very close to my abode. Eventually, once the night came to an end, I headed off to my hotel and Sam walked home to a rental room in an old house near the union hall.

Sam was my only friend, but a damn good one. His slight meditative flair and positive outlook was what attracted me most. We could chat for hours or sometimes get about in complete silence for quite a while. He apparently possessed a vital philosophical belief, love what you have, and look no further. This sentiment made me feel better about myself.

Soon enough, however, a peculiar side of him began to irk me. Sam consumed too much of anything and everything. How he remained on his feet was a mystery. It was no easy task helping him get about. Nevertheless, it was impossible to overlook his kind ways, simplistic approach to things, and his good heart.

One afternoon, we headed to my place after purchasing a bottle of bourbon. At first, he simply savored it, but it came with us when we left, this after smoking quite a bit of grass. We eventually ran into someone he knew, and he bought some LSD, which he immediately ingested. Mixing weed, whiskey, and acid defied all logic to me, and to say he became very wasted and acted truly strange is to be gentle.

He was my guest that night. We turned in rather late, and yet the following morning, he was gone. I did not see him for several days. Then one morning at the union hall, an older sailor filled me in on his whereabouts. Sam had been arrested. The guy had passed out in a bathroom at the airport. No details were available as to how he got there or when or why. It seemed best to not ask. And just so you know, when taken in, all they found on him was an empty wallet, three joints, and a picket sign.

In any event, we two soon resumed our routine lifestyle. One day, somewhere on Market Street, a group of Hare Krishna folks accosted us. One nicely attempted to inform us on the righteous path to salvation, but we both settled for brochures. Before leaving, the one who seemed to be in charge invited us to dine with them at their home. I wanted to decline but Sam would not hear of it. A date to participate was provided.

It was an early Wednesday evening that saw us in front of an old Victorian row house somewhere in the Richmond District. While the exterior appeared somewhat plain, its interior far exceeded those outer lackluster features by a long shot. The room which accommodated us was large but completely empty as if furniture seemed an unheard-of commodity to the few super silent hosts of the place.

We sat on spotlessly clean wooden floors in the lotus position. I had some trouble remaining in that position but not my mate. What began to disturb me almost immediately was not the drab accommodation, but the unbearable silence. It felt like having been accidentally locked up overnight in a church. There is only so much praying one can do, and then one needs to come up for air.

Sam and I had had a skimpy lunch that day. We foolishly believed we had been summoned to an abundant feast of vegetables and exotic teas. So, there we sat, waiting anxiously and somewhat hungry, and soon other guests arrived. Then a few group members descended the living room stairs to join us. Finally, someone came forth with a gigantic pot. She placed it in the center of the room, and we were handed bowls but no silverware. Nevertheless, my stomach was thrilled as my intestines welcomed the rescue effort on the way.

The meal consisted simply of soup. It was the main and only entrée, and as far as soups go, it was tasteless! It lacked salt or any kind of broth stock. And please forgive my over demanding ways. All I could see in that bowl were overcooked and sogging vegetables floating in a brownish dense liquid. Of course, not knowing we were indulging in the only meal to be had, my tiny sense of optimism had not yet fully abandoned me.

We ate, or rather drank our dinner slowly and, of course, very silently. Upon realizing we had finished, we two had the good sense to graciously thank everyone and casually made our exit. Now believe me, once out of sight and far from all that melancholy hush, we stopped at the nearest McDonalds to make amends. We were low on funds, so we skipped soda but doubled up on fries, and we each happily scarfed down a delicious cheeseburger, which brought us back to life.

Chapter 68

Sam was practically broke and a tad demoralized. He had been put on notice where he lived for back rent. It was mainly his silence which concerned me and the fact that he looked so lost in thought. It seemed only right to invite him to move in. He was in my hotel room the very next day.

Everything proceeded well for a week. As a matter of fact, the lad appeared a bit more laidback. However, one Sunday morning, there was a bit of laughter and random words coming from the right side of my bed. My sleepy eyes opened to an unexpected sight, and something certainly smelled awful. The lingering chatter now seemed a trifle uninhibited.

On the floor was my roommate sitting comfortably and cross-legged. Next to him was a homeless person. Our guest had apparently not seen a barber in ages, but it was his lack of hygiene which made his body stand out quite repulsively. Anyhow, both gentlemen were concentrating on the chess set in front of them and were even assisting each other in the moves to make or not make.

A large bottle of Gallo wine and a slab of cheddar cheese sat on the floor. The two contestants very nicely insisted I eat something once my eyes fully focused on them. After declining the offer, I buried my head under the pillow, hoping to delay the rising dawn, and continued to ignore the two ambitious amigos who appeared to have found their safe-haven. Fortunately, they moved on once I left the room to shower.

A week later, an unexpected ruse created some real havoc. Sam and I had separated at the union hall around four in the afternoon. Feeling horribly ill with the flu, I dragged myself home, sent down some aspirin and went right to bed. Sam was left in good company and insisted he would be in early. As to when he really stumbled in, not early for sure, is impossible to say. It must have been very late.

Once the room light switched on, I was now somewhat awake. My buddy was barely able to stand up, but not from illness. Although I felt a tad paralyzed and unable to move, I felt something strange cascading on my legs. Slightly turned to better look in his direction, there was Sam, totally oblivious to his surroundings, as he was diligently urinating on the bed.

The following morning, I stated the facts most viciously. He had to go. Of course, he could not remember anything and sincerely apologized for what was revealed to him. But something in me insisted I stick to my new course of action. Taking a deep breath, I remained silent, refused to hear anything else, and soon watched him leave. I then put it all behind me.

Four days later, I saw him at the union hall. We both acknowledged each other's presence from a distance, yet neither one of us made a move toward the other. He appeared very sober and even a bit more reserved in his demeanor. He sat at a table with two older sailors, both of whom spoke freely and continuously. His eyes may have acknowledged their presence, but no words were forthcoming.

Perhaps we both wanted to speak to each other. I would like to believe so. Sometimes pride writes its own solemn script without an inkling of a proper finale. I never saw Sam again and have occasionally asked myself where he may be today and just what road took him there.

Chapter 69

In the latter part of 1973, violence was crippling the serenity of San Francisco. A series of killings carried out by a group known as the Death Angels seemed so incomprehensible and quite senseless. Every morning, I religiously read the newspaper only to discover more gruesome details.

The crimes were carried out by a radical group of Muslim Black Americans. Apparently racial tensions had been fermenting for some years, and that various factors were to blame was becoming quite evident. To some extent, some of the atrocities in my beautiful city may have been partially stoked by the propaganda of the Black Panthers, whose home base was right across the bay in Oakland.

Once again, I took to the high seas, relieved to abandon this awful chaos. My new ship would scuttle back and forth in Asian waters for a long while before returning to the West Coast. The idea of an extended journey suited me perfectly. However, it may seem a bit odd, for here I was distancing myself from a city plagued by brutal murders and yet anxiously and happily heading to a part of the world where one nation was still being battered by a devastating war.

Well, work had me taking on a new enterprise. Having failed to land a job within the three-month period allowed and having to register again and compete with folks registered longer than me, I took advice from an older seaman and signed up to work as a waiter. Quite frankly, the change seemed just fine. For some time, my dad's contentious counseling a while back was making its point—a lifetime at sea was just not for me.

My first few days in my new line of work did not proceed well. Taking several orders at a time was no easy task, and once inside the kitchen area, it was easy to forget something or mix up the orders. The crew members were a bit restless in having to wait for something they had ordered but carrying several dishes together, therefore satisfying more than one diner, was no easy task. Fortunately, my daily performance improved and, soon enough, things ran much more smoothly.

Now most sailors at my tables were a happy bunch. While devouring plenty of food, a few tales, old or new, were rehashed and always fancily decorated with intricate bits of details to perhaps harness the adventure being shared. It became apparent to me that some of my most unusual escapades paled compared to theirs. One incredible tale came from Armando.

The Hispanic sailor was an AB. He was short and rotund with an overabundance of thick black hair. According to the facts revealed, that gentleman, originally from Peru, was at the airport in Chicago on his way to Houston, which was his residence since arriving in the country years back. In his own words, which he most happily stated, "I had drunk a lot, you know, a lot."

His flight was ready to depart, but he was still at the bar, intoxicated and charming a few other travelers. His name was announced over the speakers with instructions to proceed to a gate. Our hero, carrying with him a toy doll which was inside what looked like a violin case, ran like crazy. In the 1930s, similar cases carried machine guns, at least in gangster movies. He was soon driven to the plane awaiting his arrival. Once up the stairs and on the plane, as the door closed behind him, he loudly said, "Let's go to Cuba."

These not so well-chosen words raised an eyebrow with the crew members and the captain. Back then, airplanes were hijacked much too frequently, and Cuba was considered a-safe-haven for most hijackers, especially if they were anti-American. The man was drunk, but I assume it was the violin case which probably triggered the concern.

Very soon, two huge FBI agents escorted Mr. Armando Cruz off the plane. After methodically checking him over and grilling him for hours, it became apparent that the sloppy sailor was just a mild-mannered victim of his intoxicated state. In the meantime, the federal agents had been collecting data on him, and as he put it, "My whole life was there on a desk, on paper. They knew everything, even when I took a shit."

Across from Armando sat a quiet gentleman from Panama. He stood out due to a strange habit of his. Each meal began with him first drinking a glass of milk. But before indulging in the beverage, he would scoop in two teaspoons of black pepper and then diligently stirred it for the longest time to ensure the concoction was properly mixed. Once the chap sent the exotic beverage down, his entire body seemed to come to life with a small jerk, then back to total stillness.

I was tempted to inquire about the benefits of his tonic, but the man was too reserved and often appeared more like a statue, solemn and frozen in place, almost as if all that pepper had absolutely no effect on him.

The steward, my boss, was truly minute. He was also delicate in his ways, but he ran a tight ship. Not once did he hesitate to put his foot down if deemed necessary. Yet it was always done in a gentle manner and dignified tone, as if you were not being scolded or reprimanded but coerced with a degree of gentlemanly reproach.

He maintained a grand policy for us kitchen workers. While our ship was in foreign ports, we could take a day or two off as long as we hired a reliable and qualified foreign seaman. As he had been on that ship for ages, he had a list of responsible native sailors in most ports we visited, who were willing to work for practically nothing. Of course, yours truly, on more than one occasion spent several days far from my chores on that ship and in some pleasant company.

I embarked on a most destructive course that trip. It did not affect my daily performance, for to a large extent, I have always been a perfectionist regardless of the circumstances. Just like my dad. Yet everyone around me soon noticed, for it was impossible to hide or deny just how sad and pathetic I looked.

My stunt had begun the previous year in Thailand. I had tried heroin again. This time, unlike my first fling back in the Bronx, no sick feeling plagued me. It occurred in a bar, upstairs with a young lady who got high. We shared what I had purchased, and we smoked it. She had removed some tobacco from the tip of a cigarette, dropped in some of the white powder, rolled it so it would mix well, and then lit it. For the next few days, that is pretty much all we did.

I returned to sniffing it. It tasted so nasty at first, but within a few weeks it was just fine. Of course, my co-workers caught on. For when not working, my speech, my eyes, and me constantly scratching myself gave me away. Nevertheless, I attended to my chores, and managed to fit in, which perhaps was what mattered most. Now there was something uncanny about its impact. Like my need for cigarettes! I now constantly craved one and smoked like a chimney. As soon as one was finished, a new one was lit, and going through a pack by early afternoon was the new norm. However, I confronted a more treacherous dilemma every single morning. Constipation! Fortunately, the pantry room was overstocked with boxes of canned prunes. Before serving breakfast each morning, a large bowl of this necessary treat got scarfed down, and it certainly kept things moving.

The biggest physical change was discovered while in port. It was with my sex life. Initially, it seemed like my manhood was on strike. Yet once this drug had fully invaded my body, mind and spirit, things changed so drastically. It was as if my romantic power had a mind of its own. Each encounter had me going non-stop way into the night. Mine was a vicious erection which refused to quit. Sometimes I was forced to take a pause, light a cigarette, and sit back, and no one ever complained, although my mates were somewhat exhausted.

You may be thinking how grand to keep chugging all night. Well, not really. For while the wild stallion in me was galloping most happily, hurling forth my avalanche of love was practically impossible. I simply could not come. It was such a joyful miracle when occasionally, finally, my volcano would erupt. It not only brought an overdue moment of ecstasy to two exhausted bodies, but it also terminated much overtime work and therefore allowed my lover and I to finally turn in.

Chapter 70

One of the guys in the engine room took me to a bar in Saigon. That is where I met Thuy. Her beauty captured me immediately, but something about her spelled out her finesse. We spent three entire nights devouring each other and part of two days getting about the city. There was a steep fee to pay at the bar for her daily freedom, but it was a minor nuisance.

The young woman was above money. Being with her was worth any price. She had a warm smile and a kind heart, and she was gracious, well-mannered, and carried herself flawlessly, never overdoing anything or coming on indifferently. Nothing about her seemed out of place. It felt so wonderful to ignite a spark of love with someone who had truly touched me within.

We took to certain parts of downtown Saigon hand in hand. It was frowned upon. Apparently, a foreigner with a local girl usually meant she was a prostitute; this being a word which no longer meant anything in my vocabulary. The next blunder, all my doing, was dragging her to an Italian restaurant. Seeing one had surprised me, and I wanted so badly to introduce her to my culinary culture. So, in we went, and after ordering, it was soon apparent how foreign such food was to her.

Thuy struggled with everything in front of her and practically ate nothing. Oh well, upon leaving, we stopped at an outdoor food stand where I sent down a few beers, and she took on some familiar grub with much enthusiasm. The next morning, we stayed in and later cruised around.

Later in the afternoon, I got the silly idea to see the movie Patton. We had passed by a cinema, and a poster of George C. Scott standing so proudly there in Saigon struck me as ridiculously funny. Thuy was concerned over my not understanding Vietnamese and so remaining clueless and perhaps quickly bored. Truth be told, my biggest problem was me constantly nodding out, yet once back, there was George C. Scott speaking Vietnamese flawlessly.

It was our last morning together. My intent was to leave early. Thuy had so pleasantly talked about the tiny village she came from the previous evening. She had even suggested taking me there once I returned. Before departing her room, she handed me a note with the bar's address and also a lovely photograph of herself. Once downstairs, someone gave me something to write with, and I reciprocated with my folk's address in the Bronx, but of course no photo. We then parted ways.

I was preparing to board the scooter waiting for me when a pleasant aroma of fresh baked bread hit my nostrils. This had me walking to the bakery just a few yards away. I purchased a half-dozen baguettes, which appeared to startle the Vietnamese baker, and just like in Palermo, he neatly wrapped it in a light brown paper bag and tied it up with a string. Now a scooter was taking me back to my temporary home, a freighter ready to return to the U.S.

Breakfast that morning was one joyful event. Watching everyone spread butter and jam on that crispy mouthwatering bread made for a more pleasant start to the day. The steward asked if he owed me anything, but it seemed petty accepting money for a small thought, especially seeing such happy customers. Why, even the milk and pepper guru managed to silently thank me with his almost cheerful but downcast eyes.

Chapter 71

Julian Di Stefano was now a different young man. He still lived by an important principle of his—help if you can or get out of the way but never hurt anyone. The introvert within was trading places with a chap who enjoyed constant small talk and some idle chatter. At times, while partying, and in the middle of a conversation, he would simply nod out a bit and even briefly fade away.

Books were no longer his cup of tea. Money was still a valuable commodity but not to save or use wisely. It was there to be spent. Most often, unsparingly, like simply being too generous with any bar girl with him. And to think not long ago, he saw them as vultures, simply waiting to feast on a live carcass for what money it could bring them. Now, they, like he, were victims dealt the same bad hand. The only difference was that they played from circumstances way beyond their control.

Most mornings, once awake, our hero was plagued by anxiety. It disturbed him just knowing how strung out on heroin he was. He felt slightly useless and only once high would that negative sentiment be erased. Sometimes, he would try to overcome his destructive ways. Only to eventually fall victim to the only game in town, getting high for the sake of being with others and enjoying the moment. One morning, while looking in the mirror, he noticed how much Dr. Jekyll had transformed himself into Mr. Hyde.

Well, once again, a year had come to an end. Safe as always, I was lodged in my hotel room but now facing a horrible bout of cold turkey. My abode became my sanctuary for several days, helping me cope and recuperate after seven months of recklessly abusing myself with drugs, alcohol, and tobacco. I suffered with an aching sick body and unhappy mind which demanded rest plus an internal cleansing.

Why was I attempting to read Henry Miller's trilogy, *The Rosy Crucifixion*? Something different would have been more appropriate. Oh well, one afternoon the hotel manager paid me a visit since he had not seen me leave my room. It seemed best to blame a nasty flu, which rendered a look of relief. He returned later with some soup and a sandwich. It rekindled my faith in the world.

A few days later, I finally ventured out. It entailed an aimless wandering, more to improve my strength and enjoy my surroundings. Yet, soon, while on other excursions, my simple existence appeared so drab. I was simply going through the motions—get up, eat, walk about, go home, read, and start the process again. My life was a routine lacking its most important element, the pleasure of living it. Anyway, I soon got back on my feet and went several months clean as a whistle.

Chapter 72

Franco lived somewhere in the Haight-Ashbury area. Being in proximity to his neighborhood, my feet carried me right up to his townhouse. It was Jimmy who had introduced us, perhaps more than a year ago when our ship had returned to Oakland. We simply paid him a visit one evening. My mate had even informed me of his sexual orientation, but not to worry, for he said, "The man is harmless."

On that visit, it was the art-work of Pablo Picasso that grabbed my attention. Not the originals, mind you, but fine copies, and our host gave us a complete run-down on Guernica, which to me felt a bit crude and hard to grasp. Franco's words sort of reiterated war's ugliness and savage totality, plus, he informed us that the original was huge in dimensions and could have never adorned the walls around us.

Our host was a sailor, an older gentleman, and worked as a chef. That evening, Jimmy and I were treated to his culinary proficiencies. He had insisted, so we happily accepted and soon dined on salmon with a crunched layer of cooked almonds and a buttery squash, complemented with some white California wine. Well, our meal was par excellence, and our host was opiniated with unusual and interesting observations. He was super polite, a bit charismatic, and very gay.

I found Franco at home. He was with a guest who was being interviewed. The young lady was there to inspect the premises, mostly the spare bedroom which was for rent. Not wanting to disturb, and sensing the ongoing session could last, I chose to cut my visit short promising to return some other time. My friend stopped me in my tracks and invited me to return Saturday evening. A few of his friends were hosting a party and had guaranteed him an exceptional time, plenty of food and wine, along with a heathy mix of "lovely San Franciscans."

When I rang the doorbell that Saturday evening, I was surprised to discover that the previous female guest now lived there. She and her boyfriend, sitting nearby, would also be attending the evening's engagement, and both appeared very glad to do so. Franco soon appeared, all dolled up and sporting a look strongly that insinuated a—wait till you see—smile.

We two, along with Paul and Kathy walked to a nearby rowhouse. The brief stroll allowed me to become acquainted with the couple, me being classified as the only out-of-towner. Paul volunteered at a soup kitchen when he was not writing fiction and still lived at home with his folks on the bay. Whereas Kathy, who was from Sacramento, had been teaching political science in Frisco for years. She claimed she loved a good argument.

I soon came to terms with the nature of the party. For upon entering, we could see men everywhere, and two were dancing. This did not strongly affect me. After all, wasn't this a room full of adults? My intuition sided with the idea that unwanted advances would not be forthcoming, and if wrong, my verbal skills would come to my rescue.

There were plenty of wine bottles on a nearby bar counter. As Franco was immediately sought out, we three headed toward the wine and indulged nicely. There were some folks in the kitchen area placing food on a long table. Paul thought it was safe to inspect, and we were soon admiring some grand culinary works of art. Everything from lasagna to cheesecakes, homemade of course, got a passing grade, and we three soon returned to the living room.

It was the lasagna which got me going. Italian food was simply the best, no? Soon enough, it came out that Sicily had once been my home, and some of my grandmother's culinary treats were mentioned. Paul questioned why that southern island didn't really produce much wine, unlike the areas in the north. My ignorance on the topic did me in. Oh well, the California wine we were drinking was excellent according to Paul, and I certainly agreed.

I had to excuse myself. Not to go refill my glass but to use the bathroom. My hand soon opened a door, and I began to enter but stopped dead in my tracks. A large semi-lit bedroom came into view. Goodness gracious, on a king-sized bed were quite a few women. Fully clothed, beautiful, gorgeous, exotic, sexy, savage fucking women, all lost in a passionate frenzy for each other. No one even noticed me staring so vividly.

My mind was quite stunned, my groins aflame, my heart in heaven, but my spirit was a bit confused. Perhaps all my other organs had "tilt" as their status for at that moment it felt like every single part of my internal mechanism had skipped a beat. Now my full-time ego began digesting the luscious scene, as my manhood, already on call, contemplated what to do. However, my brain knew better and forced my exit.

The plain bathroom was right next to that vigorously engaged room. Realizing how carnal pleasure comes in all sizes and shapes, once finished there I got myself another glass of wine. There was now a mix of folks all about, and an older woman seized my attention. She politely inquired into my line of work. I decided to entertain a bit. My words flew out slowly as no narrative was awaiting to be launched, yet my words now claimed, "He who stands before ye has sailed the vast oceans."

She and a few others heard an improvised tale about having been thrown off course, only to be rescued by a rather wicked wind, very female and over ambitious. It saved me by washing up my lifeless body into the waters by the Golden Gate Bridge, where, fortunately, air was breathed into it, and a happy gale soon landed it on the shores of an island known as Alcatraz, once a seabird habitat which was taken over to accommodate villains and criminals. Being of neither flock, I refused to remain on board and so joined the party now in progress.

A few smiles encouraged me on. Someone asked if I were a sailor, insisting I looked like one, and then demanded facts about lonely men at sea. It seemed best to assure everyone that loneliness, at times, is a familiar concept, not just at sea.

I then chose to bring them to Saigon. With it came the plight of a poor people struggling to survive, yet they seemed happy. My tale even included the sleepy Cam Rahn Village, carefully pointing out the sheer misery of the place, but it being wiped out by the happy faces of its residents. My audience appeared to sympathize with folks striving to survive and having little or nothing to live on.

Someone then mentioned the Pentagon Papers. She included her sense of outrage over the deception which brought us to war. There was a consensus condemning our military venture into south-east Asia. A rather tall individual stated, "This tragic war is finally over." He also felt a need to add, "Hopefully we will never again go destroy countries that have nothing to do with anything."

Politics was shoved aside. I inquired if the BART system would ever be completed. Some laughter and plenty of comments ensued, and a bit later I excused myself, hoping to find Franco. I found the man happily carrying on with a male couple. We spoke briefly and agreed to see each other soon as I was moving on. After locating Paul and Kathy, one of the two gave me a phone number and insisted I keep in touch.

It was a breeze of fresh air which rejuvenated my slightly toxic spirit. What an experience, and perhaps a good one, having been made a bit wiser regarding human relations. Something in me insinuated that life was both an experience and an experiment. Perhaps I was just not putting in a lot of overtime, but I was certainly getting out plenty.

Chapter 73

On Monday morning I made my way to the union hall. Suddenly the McDonald's on Market Street came into view. I chose to stop, not simply because I was hungry but more because my eyes noticed a small congregation of loud disgruntled employees who were on strike. It seemed reasonable to observe an old English tradition.

Those workers were demanding higher wages. And while approaching the entrance, it was impossible to not fully dwell on the ruckus about me. I have always found it somewhat peculiar how a large part of our nation manages to run on cheap labor. Couldn't such a system possibly shed a sliver of frugality, especially when doing so would cause little or no financial pain to profits? And why is the word profits so sacred in the scheme of things?

Anyhow, my delicious breakfast was served rather quickly. Eating healthy was put on hold that morning. Once I exited, the rather angry crowd was making itself heard very loudly. Their expressions were not of hunger, but of those starved for nothing more than a tad of dignity. This was plain to see. They had my sympathy, as their plight seemed to stem from our system's failure to acknowledge their predicament. Career ladders are not available to all.

Jobs at the union hall had their own shortcomings. Ships were again scarce, and the hourly call seemed a useless announcement. Most sailors appeared to be hanging around but hardly paying any attention. I was reading the newspaper to acknowledge how the rest of humanity was fairing when someone tapped my shoulder.

It was Steve. We had met at a nearby bar months back and saw each other from time to time. He embodied cool maximum. Here was someone well-off financially and very indifferent to the world around him. He owned a small flat somewhere on Telegraph Hill, drove a new sporty car, and knew the city from top to bottom. If I suggested a place to eat, he knew a better one nearby and would even offer to pick up the tab. My friend had this incredible smile. He displayed it rather casually with women but would quickly follow up with a perfect opening line, sort of a rainbow script, which usually led to a date.

Steve had one hang up. He strongly distrusted the news, both on TV and in print. "They tell us what they want" was how he put it. To him, TV was just trash entertainment, and the news media nothing more than a circus act with too many rings to contend with. Tough words to fully accept but often hard to dispute.

We stepped outside the union hall and went to our local bar, where Steve ordered a beer for himself and a Kahlua with milk for me. My concern over the lack of ships on the West Coast got tossed out, and Steve confided in me that he was considering giving up sailing. The vast oceans no longer interested him. I wanted to hear more but the raucous voices made it impossible to continue. For the bar's other patrons were fiercely arguing about the Patty Hearst saga.

If you are not familiar with that name, here is the scoop. Her father was William Hearst, a millionaire and news media publisher, but it was his daughter who was now the headline news. A radical urban guerilla group, the Symbionese Liberation Army, had just kidnapper her. After the abduction, the kidnappers forced her father to initiate a food program. It would feed the needy both in San Francisco and Oakland. This obviously did not sit well with most people around the bar. They were not only venting their frustration but seemed quite ready to take matters into their own hands.

And just what was causing the present uproar? It was a scene from the previous evening news. The media had broadcast coverage of people arriving to collect food at the distribution centers. Some of the recipients looked very well fed. Others had driven their fancy El Dorado cars. A guy was now shouting that this was nothing more than, "forced welfare" and the closest thing to Communism, in Black bodies of course, and how could this be happening?

Steve invited me to play a game of pool. I was forced to decline. After excusing myself and promising to return shortly, I walked over to the opposite corner of the bar. Sometimes my impulse appears to spring to life on its own. Someone had caught my attention. She was a very pretty lady who appeared to have been eyeing me and had now given me a most inviting smile.

Patricia Johnson was a soft-spoken young Black woman. Surprisingly, she quickly identified me as a sailor, although it was her first visit to the bar. She admitted it was the peculiar daily congregation standing outside the bar which had sparked her curiosity and brought her in. However, her present concern was over the uproar on the other end of the bar. I quickly assured her it was just an airing out of nonsense.

I discovered that Patricia was attending a class right across the street from the bar. It was training her for office administrative duties, and it would finish the following week. Then almost immediately, her love of Shakespeare came to fore. She was apparently a big fan. Of course, that name was slightly familiar, but not overly so, which forced me to pay attention. Patricia apparently loved theater, and she even revealed her dream as a kid to be on stage and recite "Old English".

Well, there I was. My hair was long, but my top was covered by a fancy cap hiding its fight for survival, and my trimmed beard looked perfect, plus a golden earring in my left ear waved a flag of total freedom. I dressed well and knew I looked good, and I hoped the beautiful woman in front of me had accepted the whole package.

She asked if I was acquainted with theater. Sure, in my first and only year in high school, Arsenic and Old Lace had made me laugh plenty, but that was basically it. She thought the movie with Cary Grant was excellent and gave us one of his best performances. Patricia then opened her handbag and took out a thin book, The Tempest. She handed it to me and was sure I would enjoy it, and we could eventually compare notes, yes?

Steve came over to say goodbye. After properly introducing him, I offered an apology for having run off so unexpectedly. We agreed to see each other at the union hall the next day. Patricia soon asked me a bizarre question. She wanted to know if sailors were merely the oceans' gypsies, constantly traveling to appease their restless bloodline, and perhaps never finding a perfect port to call home.

Wow! After a brief thought, I claimed a simple heritage running from merry old England to a hollow borough called the Bronx. If anything, my wandering on land had been appeased, forcing me to now test the ocean's temperament. Yes, my ship had quietly left its harbor but was steering close to shore. And did she care to come on board to share the view of land all around me? My new friend, who smiled so sweetly and very convincingly, said, "I'll gladly join you no matter what you look like under that hat."

Patricia and I saw each other daily in the afternoon. She soon terminated her course and immediately began a job in Oakland, her hometown. Our encounters were now limited to weekends, but not always, for sometimes, a bus brought me across the Oakland Bay Bridge for an overnight stay. Whereas on other occasions, she happily came to Frisco with an old car in desperate need of a paint job but still a worthy commodity.

We enjoyed being together and our chats moved steadily. We always found comfort in our warm bodies, so it was a huge surprise when, one evening, my friend revealed some disturbing facts. It was totally unexpected and a bit difficult to grasp. Apparently, she, too, had had her ups and downs. The young lady first brought me back to her mid-teen years.

She had fallen madly in love with the guy next door. They became sweethearts and were quite inseparable. However, once in their late teen years, the relationship began to change, and not for the better. He began to demand something Patricia would never do. He wanted her to prostitute herself, and he would be her pimp.

So, the happy child who had dreamed of being on stage refused to change her role. She may have been in love, but she was nobody's slave. It was this outright refusal which led to loud quarreling and a physical fight, in which she was roughed up a bit. Even though she loved the guy, she could not continue to tolerate his violent ways.

Patricia eventually sought assistance through a community service program. Her counselor convinced her to immediately terminate the relationship and assisted her with steady therapy. Then, quite by chance, the shabby persistent boyfriend was busted on some serious drug charges and imprisoned for a while.

After all this, she foolishly rushed into marriage. The new relationship fared fine at first, but it wasn't long before she felt completely unhappy living with a rather sedative and much too mellow husband. It was she who became a bit aggressive in her behavior toward her man. This often led to long verbal battles, and so they soon separated and ultimately divorced.

What came next was even more erratic. Although she had some experience with getting high, a bit of weed and some casual drinking, she began exaggerating and slowly losing control. In no time at all, she got high on just about anything, except for heroin, and finally hit rock bottom and then attempted suicide.

I sat there very speechless! Then my arms embraced her. We kissed quite passionately. She was to be admired for her strength, but even more so for bouncing back from so much adversity. It seemed wise to not admit to my own nightmarish lifestyle once overseas. After all, if she had pulled through, so would I.

Later that evening, we went out to catch a movie. We both loved Woody Allen, so we headed to the cinema to see Sleeper. Now in those days, there were not many White guys dating Black women. Certainly not in Oakland. Quite a few eyes took us in, a few even stared as we sat up front and were soon laughing hysterically, very much in tune with Mr. Allen's eccentric ways while loving what the comedian does best—say the unthinkable.

A month after we met, I found work. My phone conversation with my girlfriend was not received quite well. She asked how long the voyage would last and even admitted having some concerns over our relationship. Sailors were known for being rather wild once in port. She also wanted to know if our lives would ever be a bit more well-adjusted, like me settling down to a regular job in San Francisco.

We joined up in the early evening the next day. After a small meal, I assured her that we would always be a couple and even promised to write. If I am not mistaken, it was mid-April when we kissed goodbye after I had informed her the ship would probably return in late summer.

Perhaps you recall my career at sea began on the Seatrain Maryland. Well, it ended on this ship as my sailing days were numbered. But right now, heading to the Far East had me looking forward to an enjoyable trip. And do forgive me if my ruthless male character does not conform to your standards. Yes, Patricia was my lover whom I strongly cared for, but Thuy was my true love. Now just how the human heart reasons will always be a vast mystery beyond my simplicity.

Chapter 74

The trip on the Seatrain Florida had me laying low after work hours. It did not last. There was entirely too much drinking in the evenings. On most ships, it usually occurred once we left port and would then quickly die down. That was not the case here.

A few days after leaving Oakland, one of the oilers invited me to join a party in his room. Later in the evening, I faced a small crowd of people, abundant beer everywhere, and two whiskey bottles on standby. Plus, the tune "Superfly" was blasting away while everyone was talking at the same time or trying to while the two portholes were open to let out clouds of smoke, mostly from cigarettes but some weed too.

A guy named Ray handed me a beer. Then someone else opened one of the whiskey bottles, Chivas Regal, and slowly walked over to the porthole and gingerly flung the cap out. My curiosity inquired as to why he chucked the cap to which he replied most convincingly, "Cause we don't need it no more." Enough said. The wild crew huddled in that room was taking their drinking very seriously.

More celebrations were to follow. Fortunately, they did not include me. Once again, the kitchen was my area of work. However, I was now washing dishes. Such were the consequences of grabbing a job, any job, just to get back to Asia. In my spare time, a few books again had me practicing an old interest, which had been brought back to life in a small bookshop in the Haight-Ashbury area. An interesting book on the Russian Revolution rekindled my love for history, especially on the genius of its main protagonist, Trotsky.

Our ship soon docked in Sattahip. My evening outings consisted mostly of visiting a bar I was already well acquainted with. The young ladies who knew me commented on my healthy look, and one hoped it would last. However, the taxi driver, also my connection from the last trip, had already provided me with a small vial of heroin. Rather quickly, it was back to basics—sniffing heroin, drinking beer, and pleasing the companion passing the night with me.

He had taken me to Bangkok on that trip. My main but not only interest was to see some of the temples. It was Steve who had described them as incredible works of art. And he was so right! The first one we saw displayed such majestic vibrant colors. Once inside, an almost mystical feeling engulfed me, something which no church had ever accomplished. After lighting some incense and kneeling, a flow of spiritual energy rolled through me. A few others were also colorful, well-laid-out, even bearing stunning gold and red colors, and I agreed with Steve that they sort of forced a sense of divinity in you even if you were the planet's biggest atheist.

We eventually returned to Sattahip. After two more delightful nights, our ship left and headed to Vietnam. Once in Saigon, I almost had a heart attack. Thuy's card with the bar's address was nowhere to be found. How was this possible? And the more extensive my search, the more my heart despaired, until I finally accepted having lost it somehow. This had my spirit sulking a bit just like Achilles in his tent.

My roommate appeared confused to see me moping over a bar girl. He happily suggested I tag along with him and meet some gorgeous ladies. Then the baker, a super talkative man, came by. Upon learning of my circumstances, he proposed a plan. Perhaps ridiculous, so he claimed, but his words were, "It's worth a try." I would show the photograph to the taxi drivers outside the main gate. It was a million-to-one chance that they knew her, and it seemed absurd to me, yet my weary soul gambled on this apparent long shot.

The taxi drivers appeared confused at first. Then one of them spoke animatedly with the others in Vietnamese, and soon they all laughed hysterically. That same individual looked at me as if I were the world's biggest loser. He said he would bring me to the "number one" bar in Saigon. I simply returned to the ship.

We left Vietnam a few days later and went to Yokohama, Japan. My misery over Thuy held steady, and there was no relief in sight, so I remained high all the time. I was again addicted to sniffing heroin, and my persona felt exhausted both mentally and philosophically, just like on my last trip. I once even tried going without getting high but couldn't even last an entire day.

The only thing that I looked forward to was seeing Patricia again. She and I reunited in late July. We met at the port terminal in the late afternoon after we had spoken earlier that day. She arrived with open arms, a huge smile, and a long narrative of her advancement at work. The proud young woman had also changed cars! Our embrace on the dock was genuine, yet something did not feel quite right, but who was I to talk?

She must have certainly suspected some infidelity on my part. Neither of us had ever pledged to remain faithful. Nevertheless, we were certainly glued to each other over the next few nights. My ship would leave Oakland some days later, but it was on our first evening together that my friend got a rude awakening.

We had planned to get something to eat after she picked me up. However, Patricia wanted to first stop at her flat as she needed to make a phone call and drop off some documents. I was so happy to see her, perhaps a bit too excited, and somehow forgot that it would not be a short fling. So once home, we took to her bedroom and finally separated a few hours later. She stared in disbelief and simply said, "My goodness, what happened to you?"

It was then that Mr. Hyde fully revealed his true nature. The subdued woman was slightly shocked and, at first, refused to believe anything about my addiction. To prove it to her, I took out a small piece of tin foil, opened it, and began sniffing some heroin right in front of her. She immediately shut down, became sad and insisted I needed to stop sailing and clean up. Patricia was adamant she would help me get through my addiction. I now fully realized there was more to our relationship than I had cared to acknowledge.

The ship pulled out of Oakland two days later, and it would revisit many of the same ports. I was up on the bow, on my own, when the previous evening's scene forced me to reflect. Patricia had pleaded with me to acknowledge the damage being done, both to body and mind, and then insisted I join a rehabilitation center. She was certainly right. I assured her that this would be my last trip, and once back, I would clean up.

Back in Sattahip, a big surprise awaited me. My taxi driver was in prison. At least such was the news from the one driving me who claimed to be the brother of my driver's girlfriend. Of course, he was not well versed in our language, yet he was happily bringing me home, a place I had previously been to for a few minutes on my last trip. Upon arriving, both his mom and sister appeared surprised but also quite happy to see me there.

My new driver motioned that he would buy some food. The lady of the house had me follow her as she brought me to a large washroom. The woman gestured what was expected of me. It was easy to grasp, having been given a towel and a silk bathrobe and being surrounded by huge round vats. The heat in Thailand is oppressive, and apparently, it was time to wash it away. I stripped and began using a large pan to pour cool water all over my body, and upon finishing donned my silk robe.

It was now on to the porch area in the front of the house. The lovely girl sitting there was beautiful, but communicating was an impossible task, yet I did not stop trying. While giving it my best, I wondered about her age. Perhaps she was eighteen. Then much too soon, there was silence and a bit of embarrassment but fortunately her brother soon returned.

The mom was the chef on the premises and was soon complimented. Fortunately, body language is universal, as everyone acknowledged my gestures and had a nice laugh. We dined on fish and rice, plenty of odd vegetables, some unfamiliar condiments, and there was lots of beer for me. The food was truly spicy, but I survived.

After our meal, the taxi driver brought out an instant Polaroid camera. Everyone seemed keen on a few photographs of yours truly and the beautiful young maiden. So, we posed quite innocently as he snapped away, and then gave me a couple of photos to remember the event by. Perhaps it was just a flash, but my thinking centered on this event. Was it their intention for me to become serious with the girl? And perhaps there was something to this, for the reserved mother, who hardly ever spoke, at times, smiled at me as if suggesting she approved of my presence there. Such was the scenario, and the ongoing event concluded early.

My chaperon was paid very well for transportation, food, company and miscellaneous. It did not seem right to go to my favorite bar, at least not that evening. And while he drove me back to my ship, it was rather apparent that my new driver would not do for the plan I had in mind. Oh well, I certainly knew exactly who to turn to.

Chapter 75

Joe was what we called a deck-hand. We had become acquainted one evening when Patricia dropped me off at the terminal gate. He was joining the ship, having just landed his job, and we had shared a few words while walking toward our vessel. Almost immediately, he complimented me on the attractive woman he had just caught a glimpse of and claimed she looked like someone with a head on her shoulders.

Once out to sea, it became apparent that Joe was a bit of a loner. No drinking, card games, or long chats, yet he remained friendly and gracious with me, and we occasionally talked. It shocked me to the core when he revealed that he also used heroin. He informed me about his attempt to cure himself via methadone, which he claimed accomplished nothing. I now discovered he knew Sattahip very well having been there on various trips and confided that his connection was solid and super reliable.

It was Joe who would fill in for my missing taxi driver. My plan was to finally adhere to a constant request back in the Bronx. Too many folks had often suggested I bring back some of that killer weed, the Thai grass, following up with, "Man, we could really make a killing." It had never once crossed my mind to do so as smuggling was both dangerous and just plain wrong. Plus, getting caught scared me plenty. And yet Joe would be the one to consult in carrying out my new plan.

It was on the stern of our ship that I approached him. He heard me out and said he would introduce me to someone he trusted. That afternoon, a Thai soldier and I spoke briefly, and he returned the next day with plenty of Thai sticks and enough heroin to keep me going for a while. And so began an even further descension into a point of no return which would ultimately bring me to my knees.

Our ship sailed to Saigon. For some time now, we all understood the war in Vietnam was coming to an end. Most U.S. troops had been pulled out, and the South Vietnamese army had fully taken over all combat operations. Once in the confines of that city, my childish mind kept hoping for the impossible, an encounter with Thuy.

Joe and I took in the city. The congested and noisy streets were still loudly vibrating, but most folks were not going anywhere very quickly. Some faces could not hide their sense of gloom or perhaps despair. Did they know something we didn't? Was it the lack of trust in their military forces, the ARVN, Army of the Republic of Vietnam? Along with an impending fear of a dark future?

We two sailors stepped into a bar. Every girl there, and there were plenty, practically stormed us. They tugged our sleeves, each one desperately pleading to be chosen as a companion, and the chaos only died down when the mamasan intervened. Joe looked so uncomfortable, and I had a strange sense of guilt over their predicament. The human spirit will grab on to anything when it believes it is sinking.

Joe soon abandoned me and returned to the ship. Too many desperate eyes had been bearing down on us. I chose someone, we made our way upstairs, and the following morning I moved on. Before departing, I emptied out my wallet and handed almost all my cash to a very surprised and unbelievably grateful person. It was a small gesture, although huge in Vietnamese currency. It was all I could do.

At breakfast, some guys were fuming. They had visited a bar the night before. After consuming plenty, they had paid and left but were marched back in at gun point by two South Vietnamese soldiers. The mamasan insisted they had not paid for their drinks. They were forced to empty their pockets and were practically robbed of everything. One guy was now thoroughly venting his frustration, and stated most angrily, "We should have abandoned these bastards long ago."

It may sound hypocritical, but Thuy did dominate my thoughts. Was she back home safe or another victim whose future was a blank narrative? Years back, one of my roommates claimed that bar girls were either from farm villages or the mountains and usually working off a loan their family had received from the bar. Of course, once they were accustomed to money, although little, and some material things, few, if any, ever returned home.

I had once mentioned Thuy to Joe. He inquired why I had not married her. Perhaps I missed my calling. But then my mind quizzed his logic. Just where would I have brought her? And how? Certainly not to a hotel room in San Francisco or the Bronx. Why, my folks, if somehow acquainted with her past, would have disowned me for sure, especially seeing a small semi-American-looking child who looked nothing like me. It was better to forget her, yet it felt impossible.

Chapter 76

The Seatrain Florida was returning to Oakland. A guy from the deck department startled me one evening with an incredible revelation that came out quite by chance. We had been laughing about something when his change of expression over my previous statement startled me. The moment he heard me mention having sailed on the Seatrain Carolina, he asked me if I knew a certain Frank Salvetti.

Frank Salvetti? A guy in his mid-forties with long brown hair, trimmed beard, and could do a great imitation of Cheech and Chong? Why, we had been good friends! He also knew Frank, having sailed on a ship with him, and they occasionally would get high together. Apparently, Frank had once bragged of having stolen someone's Cambodian weed on a previous trip.

This immediately dimmed my spirit. He was the last person I would have suspected. Well, the eager beaver tried a similar stunt on that ship, but this time he chose the wrong person. Perhaps his bragging gave him away. The new victim played his cards perfectly. A few nights after the ship had docked and the trip terminated, Frank left the pier believing he would soon be home, but several custom agents grabbed him. Apparently, the man's suitcase had much more weed than what he had stolen.

What incredible news! Perhaps I lack faith. But upon hearing the ending, something forced me to clutch the Buddha medallion hanging around my neck. It had been with me since my first trip, and it felt right to thank those spiritual forces guiding me onward. For a second, something within insinuated karma had given me a tiny but well-merited reward.

Although this was a welcome development, life, in general, was not giving me its best. In fact, my drug addiction had taken a turn for the worse.

My fear of needles was a permanent thing. As a kid in Palermo, a cold always had me in bed for several days. If absent more than three, the school required a trip to the nearby hospital. My grandfather took me and always comforted me while I received an injection that would allow me to return to school. Both the sight of a needle and the hospital smell always put me in tatters.

Yet, my time had arrived.

Joe, at first, outright refused to even hear me out. In retrospect, my somewhat cautionary and fearful inclinations to use a needle had been tossed aside long ago. I did not shoot up but was quite ready to start. Nevertheless, my friend would not cooperate and began lecturing on how much graver my circumstances would be.

Now, nothing was going to put me off. Even being informed I risked getting an infection which Joe had encountered a while back. And we had nothing to clean the syringe with. So, eventually, I rolled up my sleeve and began trying to do it myself. It was a disaster, and that is why, after calling me an idiot, Joe quickly found a vein, and now this incredible feeling of warmth and lightness penetrated my entire body. All tension and every thought bottled up inside me simply melted away. I just felt so relaxed, so good!

A few days later, his warning came to fruition. There were two huge boils on my back, very painful and nasty looking things. I failed to connect them to Joe's cautionary words and did not realize I developed an infection. The second mate, the ship's supposed nurse, had absolutely no medicine to administer, and so for several days, even putting on my shirt was a painful experience, as the slightest touch on those things made me jump.

About a week later we arrived at the army terminal in Oakland. While the boils had retreated some, a new one formed on my leg. Once off the ship and in my old quarters in the Tenderloin area, I went to a clinic. An older Asian-American doctor prescribed an antibiotic and assured me things would be back to normal in a few days. And yes, while on that medication those intruders withdrew, but this new malady would soon return, on more than one occasion.

I invited Patricia over one evening, and we went out to a Chinese restaurant. Immediately after, we made a dash to the hotel. Our reunion was like a lusty physical ritual where two hungry bodies refuse to be satisfied. We eventually fell asleep in each other's arms and were up early the next morning in order to ensure she got to work on time.

The following evening, however, began with an argument and almost turned into a verbal fight. Patricia wanted to talk seriously about our future, and she was a bit irate. A commitment that led to something meaningful to us both was all she wanted to seal the evening with. I pleaded with her to be patient. I planned a quick trip to the Bronx, but once back, everything would fall into place.

She was slightly put out. My calmness may have infuriated her more. Then, rather unexpectedly, she informed me about an admirer who wanted her and would do anything to have her. He was a co-worker, an older gentleman, well-off, kind and understanding. And although she continued to refuse his advances, he had no intentions of giving up on her. It was a message which my silence slowly discarded.

Our last night together played out okay. The next morning Patricia drove me to the airport. We embraced gently but warmly, and I assured her I would return in a few weeks. She may have suspected differently from her looks. Perhaps we were both a bit on edge, so I thought. However, as we separated, she looked at me most seriously and said, "I will wait, no matter when you return."

Chapter 77

I was back in the Bronx. My grandmother was delighted to see me; however, she immediately professed some concern over my pale face and much too slim physique. I had looked so much healthier when she last saw me. She briefly spoke about the importance of eating properly, and soon enough there was a delicious asparagus soufflé in front of me which I scarfed down.

Almost immediately, my plan to no longer go out to sea came forth. Perhaps she was a bit indifferent but happy, and she told me I could stay as long as needed. After all, a bit of company would be good for her. So once all my things were put away, and she gave me a set of keys, I happily took myself out for a walk.

I was soon looking at that gloomy building which had once slightly confused the two kids from Italy. It had not changed at all, whereas the lot across the street now had a series of townhouses which were certainly more impressive than our old dwelling. Once over the Cross-Bronx Expressway, the old neighborhood came into view. The closer I got to my old stomping grounds, the more my mind became inundated with different thoughts.

The most important task was to get things moving quickly. Mine was a simple plan which involved only dealing with someone I knew very well. We would meet once a day, preferably in the morning, and he would hand me cash and then receive the number of bags being purchased. Of course, I would keep some grass for personal use, but mostly for my friends as I no longer smoked that much.

A small problem would certainly ensue. Once word got out that I was back and high on heroin, a few junkies would seek me out to insist on buying some. I swore I would not sell any and try to keep my distance from everyone. Hopefully this would hold true. But one thing I knew for sure, once the heroin ran out, this cold turkey would be a real killer. And it was now time to truly turn the page.

I often recall when one of our teachers at the Harry Lundberg School of Seamanship made an unusual announcement. One morning, she said, "Today I would like to initiate a discussion on the drug problem." Almost immediately someone behind me answered, "But drugs are not a problem."

Well, drugs had impacted our neighborhood dramatically. Almost everyone, either in their mid or late teens and a few years above got high on something. Long gone were the days when drinking on weekends was most people's favorite and only pastime. And we had certainly been cautioned in school, once you begin experimenting, you may never stop.

This epidemic was not just an Archer Street gig. It had no boundaries, and it seemed to have caught on like wildfire or a silent deadly outbreak, for it was overwhelming most young people in the inner part of cities, some of the suburbs and even small towns. Just about everywhere one looked, the appetite for drugs was beyond anyone's control.

Most of my marijuana vanished immediately. Once word got out that some weed from Thailand was making the rounds, the demand quickly overwhelmed the supply. My dealer was somewhat disappointed having to close-up shop so quickly. I realized almost immediately that my slim personal reserve, which I hardly used, would not last very long as my smoking friends were few but demanding to see me more often.

Chapter 78

James Easton and I had become rather close over the years. My time in the Bronx was always brief, but we often went out and enjoyed each other's company. He now lived with Sheryl. She had a small flat on Taylor Avenue, and he had moved in. My friend was a lovable character, super charming, sincere to the max, and his gracious smile was contagious.

One Friday afternoon we met at their place. I learned that he now worked as a salesperson for the Fuller Brush company. My friend happily provided a full display of products, explaining their make-up in detail and stating that the job allowed him a flexible schedule and the possibility to make more acquaintances, something he thrived on.

We had just opened a bottle of wine when Sheryl returned home. She appeared a bit worn out and complained about a long day at work. Although she had been introduced to me some years back at a party, we hardly knew each other. A small but tasty dinner was served, and I divulged that my sailor life was over. They inquired about my present plans. There were none.

James then truly shocked me! Our conversation had somehow steered off course. He claimed he wanted to get high on heroin and shoot up. I was baffled. This request was incompatible with the person I knew. I strongly objected, but he claimed he just wanted to try it. Then, remembering my own issue with Joe, I threw in the towel. If not with me, he would do it with someone else.

The amount in the spoon was tiny. Good heavens! He overdosed immediately! He lay quite motionless on the living room floor. Sheryl began to cry wildly, while I, although startled, started to slap James' face and jerk his body around. Sheryl soon joined in.

James was in limbo. He turned slightly blue, and I feared we would lose him. Suddenly, something Joe had once mentioned entered my mind. I had Sheryl get some ice cubes, put them in a plastic bag, and once she was back, it was she who pulled down his pants and underwear. I then stopped hitting his face and placed the bag on his testicles. A slight movement of one eye was a tiny but positive sign.

My assistant now held the bag as I returned to my previous tactics. Suddenly, our victim's mouth twitched and began to open and so did one of his eyelids. We were finally seeing slight facial movements and soon our victim groaned a bit. This certainly made me feel a lot better. Mind you, the chap was still far from normal, but it appeared like the worst was over.

I foolishly attempted to stand him up. The intent was for us to make him walk as movement would be helpful in reviving him. However, when a chunky body is unresponsive and not helping in its own recovery, it is not an easy task to accomplish the impossible. Yet, he had begun to respond, if only in tiny doses, and so with his girlfriend's help, on our third try, we somehow got him up.

It felt like James weighed a ton. We managed to walk him around the living room but were both soon exhausted and yet not ready to quit. At least we had succeeded in keeping him alive. And now while continuing to move about the room, a slightly revived man began to slowly murmur, "If you wanna play, you gotta pay."

A few nights later, I revisited the couple. Sheryl appeared slightly unsure what to make of my presence. She attempted to be cheerful while trying to put the past behind us. Her boyfriend had sworn it was a lesson learned for a lifetime.

Our plan that evening was to go out to a club with a few other folks. Anyhow, I found the two relaxing in front of the TV as it was still too early to leave. Apparently, they were watching a boxing match but neither appeared interested. I inquired about our escapade as the chaotic noise from the match now caught my attention. Soon the round ended, and the camera zoomed in on one of the boxers returning to his corner.

The announcer insisted this fighter was obviously upsetting everyone's expectations. Suddenly, someone on the television screen captivated my eyes! No, it couldn't be! But yes, it was him! There was Sean Blatter providing gestures of tactical moves and obviously urging his boxer to continue his excellent performance. My friend appeared to be fully enjoying his new gig.

My exciting roar shocked the two viewers. I informed them that this was an old buddy from the SIU school in Maryland. He was coaching a Jewish boxer I had never heard of, and sure enough, we three were now happily cheering for a complete unknown while the commentator was proudly proclaiming this boxer, "the underdog." Well, this proclaimed underdog was definitely giving his adversary one hell of a fight.

Apparently, Sean was still working for a living. Now, isn't it incredible where life may take you or where you may take it? Is it a small world, or perhaps is it our individual roles which are minute until we choose to blow them up? Though in each personal race, all aim high, we ultimately find ourselves wherever the finish line takes us.

The match had terminated, and we joined some of Sheryl's friends at a nearby bar. Our group headed to the area close to the Throggs Neck Bridge, and I do not recall for certain if we went to a club called the Hollow Lake. If so, that is where I met Rita.

She was at the bar with a friend. What a gorgeous smile! I walked over to inform them there was a cemetery nearby. The two women looked a bit startled. I asked if the quiet souls lying in perennial bliss might be wondering what we mortals, near their residence, were doing to make our evenings matter? Rita smiled and allowed me to continue. A bit later we took to the dance floor.

It is so strange! Whenever I got high, I would dance with feeling and purpose. And if the rhythm pleased my spirit, my body moved with great ease, abandoning me to its pounding beat and moving my carcass in perfect harmony. We continued dancing until Rita felt a need to come up for air, and we settled in an area all to ourselves.

The beautiful young lady was Puerto Rican. She revealed a few details about her job and love for tennis. She also mentioned her divorce from the guy who had been her lifelong boyfriend. It had seemed like the best years of her life had been passing her by, whereas now she felt free to live it up. So, we danced again, and then a bit later she accepted my invitation to leave.

A taxi took us to a cheap motel on Westchester Square. Perhaps she was making up for lost time. Immediately, our bodies became entangled, and our daily pain vanished into thin air. It was a divine celebration. An animalistic passion engaged by two well-matched specimens. It was a deep dive into a fertile sea, where beautified waters force you to engage the divinity of living.

We worked in perfect harmony for hours, but at some point, my mind wandered off. It was not Rita's fault, for my ego refuses to lie still too long. We two were now lost in a forest. Did we need stars to enjoy the perfect night we had created. Our crazed fever poured out a passion which refused to surrender. It was immaculate! We finally fell asleep early the next morning. Later on we visited Jack's Diner and I eventually put Rita in a cab and took the subway home.

A few days after this tryst, my folks invited me to lunch. I never saw myself as a junkie, and they would have never suspected me of being one. My appearance conveyed a financially stable man, and I carried myself with a sense of pride.

It was a cold but sunny winter day that accompanied me to their flat. Once at the dinner table, as per family tradition, out came the latest news. It was regarding Peter. One of our father's close Sicilian friends, who knew my brother from his pizzeria, had run into Peter unexpectedly. He looked very thin, a bit raggedy, and in the gentleman's words, "In the company of some shady characters."

Our father had located his son and convinced him to come home. A few weeks later, Peter boarded an Alitalia flight with a one-way ticket to Palermo. The initiative was to separate him from his "bad environment." Well, here was the full circle tour of the Di Stefano family saga. Of course, there was a major undeniable change. The once healthy and happy boy was returning as a struggling and somewhat dispirited young man.

Oh well, lunch was superb. Afterwards, while my mom brewed coffee, my father invited me into the living room, where his love for opera was on full display. He insisted on playing an aria from something called Rigoletto, and although I was an ignorant bystander to this musical genre, he got my blessings to proceed.

My untrained ears, once tested by jazz, were again confronted with an unpleasant harmony, and the lyrics were in a foreign tongue quite hard to grasp. It seemed better to fake it, as Dad's expression shined, almost as if in a happy trance. Fortunately, once the song finished, as if on cue, Mom announced coffee was ready and so we joined her in the kitchen.

Chapter 79

Whenever I was in the neighborhood, I was usually on Archer Street. I always carried a few joints and a piece of aluminum foil filled with heroin in my front left pocket. It was late afternoon and my carelessness made me disregard the most important lesson in life, never undermine your surroundings.

Sara approached me and wanted to buy some heroin. It was completely out of the question. She was once part of the crowd by the handball courts, but she had moved to Long Island and only came around once in a blue moon. She casually came on to me and admitted being strung out and hurting. She began pleading incessantly.

Although she appeared a bit untrustworthy, my instincts failed to protect me. Why, I will never know. We began walking together, and not wanting to hear anymore of her agony, I had decided to turn her on. She suggested we step into the hallway of the building right in front of us. It was a colossal mistake! The moment we walked in, as she stayed behind me, was when my intuition said, "You fucked up!"

A guy pretending to be drunk and laying on the first set of steps was now on me. He had a knife to my throat. Sara started going through my coat pockets, found nothing, then hit my pants, front ones first, and smiled once she had what she wanted. She then reached behind me for my wallet. Fortunately, my somewhat long coat was impeding her attempts to get to it.

Suddenly the lobby door opened. They were never locked back then. A middle-aged man, obviously a resident, entered, and before he could even blink, the knife disappeared, and the two ran out like the very wind. The puzzled looking guy in front of me, slightly frozen in his steps, wasn't sure what to make of it all and asked if I was okay. I briefly stated all was fine and moved on very quickly myself.

My anger knew no limits. I headed to Sheryl's place. James was in the kitchen cooking spaghetti while enjoying a beer and some David Bowie. He was happy to see me, but my red face instantly gave me away. Once informed of the facts, my friend attempted to calm me down. It was useless. Something within demanded revenge.

James owned a gun. He had shown it to me a while back. He insisted I take a minute to wind down and think about the consequences of overreacting. It was to no avail. Incredible! How quickly the human spirit can easily fail. Anger is that uncontrollable fuel which triggers our impulse to right what is deemed wrong, sometimes by doing the wrong thing when you are already in the wrong.

We left the flat and headed to Archer Street. How stupid! The chances of running into either of them were practically zero, but my rage perpetuated my foolishness. The very moment we stepped outside the building, it began to snow. Just a few drops at first, but it quickly accumulated fast and heavy. At the corner of Archer Street and Taylor Avenue, we came to terms with reality.

Very few folks were anywhere, and people were hurrying home as the weather was forcing everyone indoors.

I now fully grasped what a true friend James was. His attempts to keep me from doing something fatal were matched by his now being at my side. Perhaps it was to prevent the unthinkable from occurring, and yet in just being there, he, too, could have been involved in some aspect of my craziness. It hit me. He was right, and so we headed home. Once indoors, James put the music back on, and Bowie's charming tune resurrected a livelier version of myself. James resumed cooking while I now admitted being a complete fool for trusting someone my intuition had warned me not to. My friend advised me to never trust anyone, unless it was someone you were sleeping with. Such was the philosophy of a man who was never without a woman at his side.

That night the city was hit by a heavy blizzard. The following afternoon I got the news. Sometime late in the morning, Sara's body had been found in an alley not far from the park area. The person who informed me believed she had overdosed elsewhere, and then someone, previously with her, brought the body there and dumped it.

My sense of guilt was evident even though I was not directly to blame. Few words flowed from me as my friend thought it best for me to disappear for a while. It was December and very cold, and yet Long Branch in New Jersey did not seem so far away. It felt strange heading off to a summer resort in wintertime, but perhaps wise. And did it really matter?

Chapter 80

I bumped into Kevin a few days before Christmas. He was one of the guys at the Doors' concert who had not taken acid. Nevertheless, we were now carrying on about old times, and he soon proclaimed he still enjoyed smoking pot, good pot, and then looked at me a bit curiously. Message delivered.

Oh well, his folks passed winter in Florida and so he was king of their domain. Having already invited several people to a Christmas party, no religious connotation involved, he was more than happy to extend an invitation to me. It was a feast to simply bring some folks together. Most were friends going way back, and, in his words, "Let the night reveal its true face."

Now the façade of that house reminded me of the opening scene from the TV series, the Addams Family. And upon entering through the basement door, a familiar face stared at me. It was a poster of Frank Zappa. The one where, of all places, he is sitting on a toilet bowl, doing what all humans do, think and stink. Now, off to one side was a long table stacked with snacks, cold-cut meats, and breads. Close by were several coolers full of beer. The couch had been moved by the wall to leave some room for dancing.

A few people were standing around and chatting. From their looks, it seemed as if some were uncomfortable to see me there. Kevin came over immediately with two folks I did not know. The trio began to swear allegiance to the Bronx, mostly because some folks we grew up with had recently moved to L.A. Yes, our neighborhood had somehow maintained its original identity, lots of Irish folks still dominated its everyday affairs, and apparently this was still important.

Kevin left us for a bit, and the couple inquired about my occupation. Not wanting to say too much, it felt right to claim being happily unemployed and presently hustling a bit. Then while groping for a better topic to hang on to, someone changed the music in the background and raised the volume, going from soft rock to an LP by Mott the Hoople. I lit several joints, one for us three, and the others got passed around.

It was not long before other people arrived. Rather than celebrating Christmas, the ambiance began to feel more like a New Year's Eve party. A couple was dancing, some girls were singing loudly to the tune of "Sweet Jane", and it became impossible to talk above the now chaotic sound around us. The food appeared to have been forgotten, but beer was in high demand. It was an enthusiastic crowd which had turned that basement into a disco lounge.

Soon, some of my old friends from St. Anthony's were chatting with me. They had heard about the Thai grass making the rounds, had now tasted it, and so wanted to barter. I was offered some Seconal pills for grass. It did not interest me in the least, until it registered how those pills would come in handy going through cold turkey. We struck a deal, a bit of grass for a bunch of pills.

James and Sheryl were now among us. We tried to chat, but the loud music would not allow it. Oh well, the party finally began to wind down. It may have been around three a.m. when we left, and both my friends insisted on having me over, telling me, "Mi casa es tu casa." Once there, the living room couch was all mine, and it was simply grand, for in my condition, walking to my grandmother's was not an option.

Chapter 81

Christmas Day arrived. It brought a completely different sort of pleasure. My grandmother and I joined my folks in Co-op City, thanks to my dad's taxi service. We spent a fun day listening to my father share some of his adventures growing up in Palermo. After a delicious meal, we enjoyed an amiable chat in the living room, with a bit of opera in the background. My mom even took a few photos to record the wonderful occasion.

A few days later, Shamus and I got together. We had dinner somewhere in the Parkchester area, and eventually made it to his favorite bar on Beach Avenue. He talked of his sister in Northern Ireland, who was doing grand, and my good friend was planning to visit her, which almost tempted me to invite myself to tag along. We soon carried on about what constitutes a healthy and happy lifestyle, and when one truly recognizes it has arrived.

We separated rather early. My destination had me heading to my grandmother's place. Suddenly someone called out my name. It was an ex-classmate from St. Anthony's. His brother was the great Doors' fan, the guy who had gotten us all our tickets. We spoke briefly, but he said something which simply shocked me. He wanted to buy some heroin.

It made no sense! The guy in front of me did not fit the bill. Perhaps my stare may have embarrassed him some, for he explained that he would never get hooked, and this would be just a one-time thing. I informed him that I had nothing left, and although he may have suspected I was lying, he began sharing some interesting news about his first year in college. We soon parted.

I was still stunned. How could this be happening? Something forced me to now recognize the unthinkable. Outwardly, to most folks, I appeared a man of the world. Someone who had been on his own for years, well-off financially, and there was a cool image about me. I was certainly the furthest thing from those folks who were strung out that you dreaded running into. It now hit me. I was probably influencing a few people who perhaps looked up to me. This truly shattered my serenity.

Now one thing was certain. This unreal performance would now be terminated. The actor in me was slowly dying, and, truth be told, he had been carrying a heavy burden for too long. My walk held steady, but somewhere on Leland Avenue, I just stopped in front of a corner drain-hole. I took the bag of heroin on me, my very last one, and threw it into the sewage hole. It was time to face my self-imposed crucifixion.

The morning began just fine. Once out of bed, I ran out to buy some donuts and returned to a simple but delicious breakfast. My grandmother soon joined me. She shared some negative news about having a verbal altercation with one of her sisters. It was so unlike her. I guess from time to time, some petty circumstances led to an unnecessary argument.

Later, I got out and rode the subway to Pelham Bay Park. It was super cold, but I enjoyed a brief walk and eventually found a diner and feasted on a second breakfast. I returned home feeling slightly weak, knowing what was in the making, and now faced my grandmother who was surprised to see me back so soon. After a nice chat, we separated as she was joining an ex-co-worker whom she had not seen in years. I headed off to my room.

My music did absolutely nothing for me. Concentrating on anything was tough, and so reading was out of the question. My body felt exhausted, and I soon fell asleep. When I awoke several hours later, my back ached terribly, my nose was running, and again nothing seemed to interest me. A bit of diarrhea had set in, so I was constantly scrambling for the bathroom. Eventually, I popped some Seconal pills thinking this would assist me in bearing my agony.

It is impossible to say when my eyes opened. The curtains had remained closed making it difficult to distinguish morning from evening. The room was dark. My wristwatch showed thee o'clock, making me assume it was morning. I again needed to get to the bathroom, but my attempt to leave the bed failed miserably. How strange! This was not my first stint at cold turkey, but nothing like this had ever happened before.

My eyes continued to stare at the darkened ceiling. An eerie feeling began to trouble me. Time dragged on, and my lifeless self was sort of drifting in a vacuum, blocked in place. I then lost control of my body, and it just happened so quickly! My bowels opened and out came everything. Even urine poured out from my body.

Later that morning, my grandmother knocked on the door. She was assured all was fine. She resumed her business, only to return much later. My grandmother was apparently a tad concerned and perhaps somewhat curious. The door opened a bit, and that awful stench must have horrified her. The woman disappeared but evidently got a hold of my father.

The human spirit is both flexible and resilient. When those whom we love need help, it will bolt into action. My father stood by my bed and never uttered a single word. He pulled up the shades, opened the window a bit and left the room. He returned well equipped with a roll of paper towels, a large brown shopping bag, a bucket, gloves to wash dishes with, and a huge sponge.

I was given a thorough cleaning, and he somehow managed to carefully get me up and escort me to the bathroom. While slowly and carefully being lowered into the tub, I understood my body was being catered to, and now buckets of warm water began to pour over me. Once again, he used the sponge more thoroughly, and then somehow got me up and turned on the shower. This may have revived me.

Throughout it all, I remained in a fog. Yet, for a quick moment, I saw a side of him that rarely came out, but it existed. It was his caring attitude. Eventually, my dad threw a huge towel over me and patted me down. Once finished, he took me back to the bedroom, and he dressed me. How we got down five flights of stairs is not in my memory banks. Once in his car, my father's apprehensive look remained on display. It certainly stood out, as he occasionally turned to face me while driving to Jacobi Hospital.

The emergency room was not so crowded. I could barely walk and still felt sort of lifeless. The staff accommodated me on a chair but soon moved me to another area where a nurse came over to attend to me. She was attractive, I remember that distinctly in the midst of my fog. The nurse drew blood from my left arm while politely listening to a bit of my incoherent babbling.

Suddenly, my right hand slowly extended forward, touching her breasts. My dad's exasperated look spoke volumes while the nurse, somewhat angry, protested loudly and moved back some while pleading for Dad to intervene. He simply managed to say, "I've never see him like this." My goodness, in some ways Dad was still such a foreigner.

When she was finished, two nurses arrived and put me in a wheelchair. I was moved to a different area and parked outside of an office in a small hallway. My father and I shared a long silence. At times, he seemed so disappointed, and his concerned expression almost begged to know how this could be happening.

It felt like a long wait but eventually a male nurse took me into the nearby office. A bespectacled doctor, middle-aged, was sitting at a desk. And after I was placed in front of him, he introduced himself and calmly began a series of questions. At times, he waited patiently for my answers, which were forthcoming but slowly and inconsistently.

One question baffled me. He asked me what day it was. I had no clue. The only bit of information to offer was that Christmas had passed. Of that I was certain. Yet my mind could not recollect if the new year had begun. After some hesitation, I very clearly stated, "I am not sure what day it is, but it is either December 1974 or January 1975."

The doctor continued to scribble on his notepad but suddenly stopped and removed his glasses. He informed me I had come close to being in a coma. This meant nothing to me, and my expression remained blank. However, he inquired if I was ready to stop taking drugs and consider rehabilitation. I informed him that I genuinely wanted to change my lifestyle and finally leave behind the mess I had found myself in.

My sagging body remained in the wheelchair but outside that office, and my father left to go home. Two nurses, who appeared somewhat grumpy, tied me to the wheelchair and took me to an isolated area. It was only when I needed to use the bathroom that I was allowed some freedom. Eventually, they brought me to bed and again restrained me. Laying there semiconscious, exhausted, and with a terribly aching back made for a long and miserable night.

The following morning, I was tied to that wheelchair and moved to another remote area. My wardrobe consisted of a white robe, and my clothes were neatly stacked on the chair next to me. A bit later, it became apparent that with work it would not be difficult to set myself free. And that is exactly what I did. I took myself into the nearby bathroom, dressed slowly, and once finished I made my way to the main entrance and walked out.

A taxi took me to my grandmother's house. My host was totally shocked! Of course, she allowed me in, offered me some coffee, and then immediately called my father. He arrived pronto. We then went to Co-op City as my presence at my old lodging was no longer desired.

While on the Cross-Bronx Expressway, the man revisited bits and pieces of our past. He even suggested that Peter and I should have remained in Italy and never have come to the U.S. It was a country which had certainly welcomed us but had also transformed us into two roaming and restless personalities. While listening, nothing truly registered, for my mind could not acknowledge what the truth really was.

My father parked the car. We walked toward a rose-colored building as my mind registered the irony of it all. Here was the very gloomy residential mini city I had so eagerly abandoned a few years back. It appeared just as lifeless and insignificant as it did then. Perhaps it had even slightly contributed to my moving on. How absurd; I was back, quite empty-handed, in the very place where my quest to embrace life had begun.

My folks lived on the eighteenth floor in section 5 of Co-op City. The room I took up residence in was simply a place to park myself. My daily morning walk to Perham Bay Park became routine. Then after purchasing a newspaper, I would return home. A few articles always managed to grab my attention, yet nothing truly interested me.

After my experience at Jacobi, my father had taken me to Manhattan to a rehabilitation program. It lasted two whole days. The folks running the facilities, mostly ex-drug users, frightened me. Both they and some of the volunteer workers appeared untrustworthy and rugged. Sure enough, my locker was broken into the very morning after my arrival.

It was then on to Daytop Rehabilitation Center in New Rochelle. The counselors and the folks in recovery appeared friendly and were very talkative. My contribution was somewhat limited but decent, and it felt like my first day ended much too quickly. Unfortunately, and quite mysteriously, I soon shut down and everyone's warm approach did absolutely nothing to alter my now miserable personality.

One evening, my father insisted that a job, any job, would save me. In his analysis, my boredom and pathetic outlook were self-induced, and once involved in some type of work, my spirit would rise to the occasion. I would then be able to find my way. So, the following day, I began checking the wanted columns and quickly recognized that nothing truly interested me. Mine was a lost cause.

Well, my old man had one more trick up his sleeve. It was an Italian woman, an ex-customer whose couches he had serviced. She taught at Fordham University, and my visit there was to hopefully arouse my interest in the higher world of learning. Now believe me, she was certainly a most attractive lady, and spoke like a well-cultured individual, which was why she had me listening.

She taught a class on the Renaissance period and quickly zoomed in on her love for her profession. After a while, I was inclined to believe she was sizing me up to get a better sense of my interests. Then, after speaking at length, with practically no participation on my part, she appeared to have finished, but she went on to share one last thought.

Did I have any interest in computers? This was a completely foreign topic. Computers were some strange mechanical objects, like noisy robotic machines the size of a small room, well-hidden somewhere in an office that very few people were allowed to use. She expressed her belief that one day they would play a key role in life. Was I at all interested in looking into the field of computing? A few minutes later we again shook hands, me leaving and feeling more useless than when I had first arrived.

Chapter 82

I called Patricia late one afternoon. In our only conversation since my departure, we had both struggled to convince each other of anything concrete in terms of a future together. Yet she had intimated that she was happily awaiting my return. It seemed only right to connect again, especially as something in me was now suggesting a return to the West Coast to begin a real life.

A man answered the phone. The voice seemed elderly and very polite, and I suspected he was the one who was mad about her. Patricia was out running an errand but would soon be home. Did I want to leave a message? Well, the phone was put down. My first thought acknowledged what an idiot I can be. Someone had wanted me in their life, appeared sincere in dedicating themselves to our happiness and future, but I had chosen not to participate.

Perhaps that phone call summarized my foolishness. Yet the next evening, someone else's brand was accidentally put on full display. We had finished eating, and the TV was now on. Mom was heading off to the bathroom as I began to ask my father something. Then seeing South Vietnamese troops on the news and hearing of them retreating from devastating assaults by the Viet Cong, my attention slightly focused on what was being shown.

My mother returned and sat next to Dad. They both began talking about the present drama from Asia. My thoughts regarding Thuy came forward. Mom's sudden frown and sinister look made me a tad suspicious. She asked me about Thuy. Of course, the information was limited to what was necessary, but I certainly expressed my love for her. That is when the woman looked at my dad again and said, "Maybe we should tell him."

Apparently, a while back, a letter had arrived from a Vietnamese girl. I was still out at sea, and my folks had not heard from me in a while. Believe it or not, my overly concerned and vigilant family, always ready to safeguard my predicament in life, had decided to terminate the sinister relationship before it began. After all, the girl was obviously just a gold digger trying to find a way out of her circumstances. She was just another foreigner, like many, hoping to somehow sneak in.

I was stunned by what followed! Apparently, mom had been given instructions and so had gone right to work. She diligently penned a letter back to the ambitious maiden informing her that, unfortunately, Julian had been in a terrible car accident and had not survived. And now both the author and narrator looked at me apprehensively, perhaps understanding my disappointment and strained look. Both insisted they had acted out of concern for me. My folks were simply trying to help. I retreated to my room but did not sleep very well that night.

Chapter 83

In was early March 1975. Jimmy and Kevin O'Conner crossed my path. We met by chance, and both admitted to being strung out but insisted it was time to clean up. The new year had seen me drug-free. Mentally and psychologically, however, I was on a crutch, but certainly adhering to solid abstinence. Now I suspected I was doomed to fall.

An hour later, someone drove Kevin and me downtown. Jimmy did not want to tag along. Once the car was parked, the two left me to wait for their return, and you cannot imagine what paranoia engulfed my personality for the next ten minutes. Just what was I doing, and why? They soon returned, smiling a bit, and so we ran back to the Bronx.

We reunited with Jimmy near a park close to my old dwellings on Rosedale Avenue. A couple of syringes did the trick, but while my friends were feeling great, I hardly felt anything. Then there was much talk about the need to stop this madness. And so, while my once close friends were again pledging the impossible, I knew I had lost an important battle.

Was it possible I could never get out of this mess? That evening I sat down with my father and asked his advice. My dad was a man of few words, but he saw clearly and far. His decisions were usually the right ones, especially when it came to counseling others. Like Peter, the year before, I would now go to Sicily and remain there. Once completely cured and able to live a normal life, I would return home.

A few weeks later, we drove to JFK. My eyes were glued to an Italian language book. It made me grasp how desperate my situation truly was. The Italian language was somewhere inside my skull but retrieving it was a rather solemn affair. I practiced some phrases while my father chuckled, insisting I sounded like a real American. Yet, he encouraged me to continue. After all, in a few weeks my natural native flow would return. Was he sure? I asked. "Sicurissimo!" was his reply.

We hugged and said our goodbyes. The man was gone. All around me were many passengers enjoying an effervescent Italian. Although my ears perked up, hoping to comprehend something, nothing happened. It all sounded Greek to me.

Once on the runway, the irony of it all hit me. Here was August 1963 in reverse. Once again, Alitalia would carry me across the ocean. This time, first to Rome then to Palermo. However, this journey had no flowers for anyone. What came with me was just a suitcase, a slightly frightened outlook, and one totally exhausted body and mind.

The airplane reached the skies. I looked out my window at a rather grayish day. Beneath me was the very city which my spirit had once struggled with. It was an urban sprawl tightly knit together and independently laid out. The very city I had never felt truly at home in. But now, from above, New York seemed more attractive, less busy, and totally indifferent to my departure.

I reached for my book, Hemingway's *The Old Man and the Sea*. It held my attention for a good while. Then, needing a small break, I placed the bookmark in and allowed my thoughts to roam freely. A Rolling Stone's tune came to me. It still sounded as good as the first time I heard it. It was almost as if the band was singing directly to me, when Mick Jagger intoned.

Part 4

Chapter 84

"Americanu. Che mi raccunti?" My young cousins, who were many in number, were all over me and demanding to hear anything, as long as I spoke. It was my intention to be heard, or at least to share a few words, something, anything, but nothing flowed out of me. My tongue was mute to the core!

I had arrived in the afternoon, and it was Uncle Luca and my grandfather who were at the airport in Palermo to greet me. "Buongiorno" and "Come stai?" was all my voice could offer. So, it was a very long drive back as my endemic reserve allowed my two hosts to carry on in Sicilian quite excitedly, and we soon arrived in front of a tall building very close to where we once lived. My grandparents occupied a flat on the second floor.

Unfortunately, my Sicilian and Italian were like a barren desert. Soon, my muteness chased off my aunts and uncles in attendance, who, up until a few minutes before had happily overcrowded my grandparents' living room. Uncle Nicola's kids remained and were certainly amusing me. Some were happily jumping up and down on the couch next to mine, all just horsing around, madly lost in the joy of the moment.

Then my grandmother appeared. She stood at the entrance to the living room. A curtain of silence fell as the many kids about me had now frozen in place. Her expression penetrated every face there, including mine, as she looked us over, and her eyes conveyed the message that things had gotten slightly out of hand. Order needed to prevail.

Nonna Vincenza did not have to say anything. She simply made a well-known gesture. She hit her right hand in a horizontal position against the palm of her left two times. It was a Sicilian message, and it signaled for the young kids to move on. What an incredible scene! They scrambled off the couch, lined up in a single file and began exiting after first kissing me on the cheek to say goodbye.

Their ages ranged from ten to six. A couple of them risked sharing a parting word, in a whisper, of course. Their eyes flashed a sign of resistance and happiness while then moving forward like tiny soldiers, each one following the one in front, keeping silent and heading down the long hallway to the entrance door of the apartment. Once outside its confines, they resumed being kids, innocent, wild, a bit loud, and happy in their world. One thing which struck me as funny—the oldest and tallest led the procession.

My grandmother seemed happy to have me back. She said something and gestured sleeping, and I gladly followed her to a room down the hallway by the front door. It was rather tiny, its walls bare and grayish with a single bed next to the window. A tiny desk in the corner accommodated her old sewing machine, which was accumulating a bit of dust. Such were my new quarters, and as in past settings, they would do just fine.

Once she closed the window shutters, ensuring the afternoon sun would not keep me awake, she was gone. I slid under the covers, and exhaustion engulfed my body. Before closing my eyes, I caught a glimpse of a small statue of the Madonna sitting on the tiny chest of drawers adjacent to the bed. Was this the work of my old hero, Il Professore? It seemed to be greeting me back to Sicily, to my new home, in an old and once familiar environment.

It was much later when my eyes opened. The room was pitch-black, very quiet, and although making out my surroundings seemed tough, it registered that the island of Sicily was dead to the world. I got out of bed and headed down the long corridor to the bathroom. Once there, my grandparents' well-synchronized snoring chorus from their bedroom was very audible.

Upon finishing in the bathroom, my throat pleaded for anything to soothe it. My body cautiously navigated the hallway toward the kitchen, and the refrigerator came into view. I opened it and found a somewhat comical scene which was well-known to me. Not a morsel of food anywhere, but a dozen or more liter bottles full of tap water crowded the fridge. The lack of food was due to Grandma's frugal ways, accomplished daily, but the abundance of water was a completely different ball game.

As a kid, I had often witnessed my grandmother performing a morning ritual. It was imperative to store as much tap water as possible as the city authorities punctually turned it off at noon. She usually filled a half dozen or more. Water in Palermo was a precious commodity which always stopped flowing at exactly the same time each day. Obviously, nothing had changed, and so our abode, like all the others, kept up with the trying times.

Much later, my grandmother was up and about. We Di Stefanos are early risers but also early to bed. Apparently, her day was set in motion, for I smelled the pleasant aroma of espresso, which had made its way to my minute cubbyhole. That is why I put down my book, forgot my linguistic predicament, and returned to the kitchen. We two managed a very warm "Buongiorno." She added a few extra words, and I simply shook my head in agreement, but don't ask me why. We drank a cup of espresso, mine super-sweet, and I had forgotten that this would be my breakfast in its entirety. However, there was plenty of water to be had.

Later that morning, my destination was the train station. Before running off to work, my grandfather had provided directions very slowly, repeating them twice, and then left looking so very proud. Of course, the station's location was somewhat familiar to me. I had wanted to check on an itinerary to Termini Immerese for Uncle Andrea and his family who resided there.

Walking down Via del Vespro felt like old times. Almost immediately, a small sense of belonging overcame me, making me feel a casual attachment to the once familiar sights. Those same street vendors, camped out in the same old area by the hospital's main entrance, were still happily plying their food wares in loud Sicilian dialect. And there was now a gas station not too far off from where a car had taken me down, but not out.

Corso Tukory came into view. It was awfully noisy and totally inundated with tiny automobiles. Some of the passengers appeared packed in like sardines in a tin can. All the vehicles were presently at a standstill, with some impatient drivers blowing the car's horn and cursing most devotedly. It dawned on me that not even downtown Saigon at its finest moment had the luxury of such a chaotic state of affairs.

I spotted a fancy coffee/pastry shop nearby. It displayed a variety of delicious sweets, which my eyes diligently approved of, and so the word colazione joined what little bit of Italian was now in me. The breakfast consisted of a glass of fresh orange juice, a cappuccino and a tasty croissant for a just few Italian lira, a currency of huge, old, worn-out, and nasty-smelling bills.

It was a delicious treat. And the barista was very shocked with my gesturing for another round of the same, minus the juice. His startled look indicated that some golden rule had been broken, and he said something to the customers near me, and they too looked me over making me feel like the foreigner among them. It must have been my quick and well-toned response, "Non parlo molto Italiano" which may have confused him. It was delivered too perfectly, whereas my initial request for food had stumbled out a bit inconsistently. The phrase attracted the attention of the two men next to me at the coffee counter. It seemed like almost everyone was now smiling politely, a bit affectionately perhaps, and so feeling the mood had changed, I smiled right back.

Chapter 85

My first days in Palermo proceeded well. All my relatives were certainly delighted to have me back among them. My aunt and uncles were all married with children. And when I visited, all their kids treated me like a celebrity. However, my inability to properly correspond a bit bothered me, even though that language book accompanied me and did help some.

Uncle Nicola lived in my grandparents' building, on the eighth floor. He was the first one to invite me over for lunch. Upon entering the flat, he, Aunt Lisa, and their six children—that's right, six—were queuing inside their hallway giving me a most cordial royal greeting. Now believe me, my concern over the lack of literary skills was quickly put aside for the culinary feast which followed blew me away. A few compliments delivered in a slow mixture of words was dished out quite appreciatively.

One immediate observation needs an explanation. My aunt and uncle possessed an immense love for their children, but there was a disciplinary code which kept them in line, something very well-known to me and quite normal back then. The kids did express themselves but never went overboard. I was also informed that it was my aunt and uncle's desire for a girl that kept them going until finally blessed with one, the last child. I had to assume my aunt, a devout Christian, was also happy to take some time out from the faithful religious concept of procreation.

Sometimes, the children's queries were delivered too hastily. My frown revealed slight confusion, which prompted my uncle to repeat the question, dragging out each word as to properly accentuate it, thinking this would explain everything. The children listened attentively, bearing wide grins and joyous eyes, obviously appreciating their dad's serious but silly spectacle. At times, one of them would chip in, imitating Dad.

Uncle Luca had me over next. His apartment was close to my old elementary school. By the way, that strict gender division my brother and I had been indoctrinated with in school no longer existed. It was astonishing having witnessed it first-hand as school had just let out. The infectious and joyous chaos that the mixed schoolkids shared on their way home was very endearing, although it had startled me at first. They may have been a bit too loud and raucous, but those boys and girls were plenty happy.

My aunt was delighted to finally meet me. She claimed to have heard so much about Peter and me. Her kids, two boys and two girls, appeared slightly more reserved than my other cousins, yet they also showed much enthusiasm for their American guest. I was treated to another food fest to die for. It was clear that meals were an important part of Italian family life, a tradition I had forgotten.

The following day, I took myself to the other side of the city to Aunt Felicia's home. If my grasp of what my grandfather had revealed was accurate, my aunt's husband, Gino, had wanted to pick me up. But my need to experience traveling beyond the periphery of my digs forced me to decline his kind gesture and catch a bus. Once among her and her family, tons of hugs and kisses were shared all around.

My aunt's young daughter appeared a bit shy but was quite lovely. After a brief apology for not being able to express myself fully and properly, we sat and attempted to converse some. My small audience accepted my words with, at times, a few giggles from my aunt and uncle. That is why a grammar lesson came my way because apparently my conjugation of the verbs was not always accurate.

I must explain. You see, to conjugate verbs accordingly, you must first determine the status of the person or persons being addressed. For common folks you are acquainted with, there is one form of the verb, but with strangers or people somewhat highly elevated in social status or their profession, it changes. Therefore, it is either "Ma, tu vieni?" for the former or "Ma, lei viene?" for the latter, in asking if someone is coming.

Apparently, yours truly was treating his three relatives like the rich and famous. Nevertheless, they gave me a passing grade insisting my problems would soon be far behind me. Oh well, it was another wonderful day in good company, great food, and as the evening came to an end, I accepted a ride home, which allowed me to practice conjugating some verbs with my uncle.

It was Uncle Andrea who phoned me the following day. My plan to take the train to his town was disregarded. He was in front of our building by noon, as per his word. We soon took to the tiny highway heading east. My goodness, it seemed like everyone drove like madmen! And when I expressed some concern over the driving etiquette in Italy, or lack of it, my uncle laughed and replied, "We are not in Italy." It would be many years later before this bit of satire registered completely.

Upon arriving, we snaked around the city center, then parked in front of a somewhat run-down building. Actually, all looked a bit worn out, and yet, while not impressed with the façade, once in the main hallway, a different scene welcomed me up. The lobby boasted a very clean and splendid marble floor with a staircase that made me think of medieval times, as it was rich in artistic layout. Plus, the walls, which had recently been painted, appeared so solid.

The large apartment we entered was very well decorated. While I casually took in my surroundings, Aunt Anna appeared. We hugged each other rather strongly and kissed in the Southern Italian ritual on the cheeks, which was a daily gig now. My intuition sensed something a tad peculiar about the woman, but that thought almost immediately vanished.

She introduced her three children, who seemed well-mannered. We congregated in the living room and a middle-aged woman coming out of the kitchen joined us. I walked over to meet her, and I was completely shocked when she treated me to a familiar language. In perfect English she said, "It is a pleasure to meet you. I have heard so much about you and your brother."

Well, it was certainly going to be a great Sunday. My caged-up spirit began speaking slowly, freely, and non-stop. Her name was Silvia, a close friend of my relatives, and she soon informed me she had lived in Chicago for many years with relatives. Having fallen in love with the city, and in no hurry to return to her small town, she stayed there for ten years. We now communicated fervently, with much translation going to our audience.

My aunt moved on to the kitchen but promised to return quickly. Soon, we gathered at the dinner table where a blue vase with flowers sat in the middle. Gold-plated silverware along with rich-looking china were at our disposal, creating a touch of sophistication. My uncle must have read my face. He insisted they were just an average middle-class family, but with good earnings. And yes, he was the breadwinner, but he then proudly stated that his wife's love and dedication to the family was the most important element. It provided a warm human anchor making the family rich beyond money.

We began our meal with a Sicilian dish, pasta with sardines. We continued with more local dishes and my stomach demanded I never return to the U.S. Later on, once the children retired to their rooms, my aunt revealed a past incident regarding the oldest boy. Well, not really him, but his name. She and her husband chose not to follow tradition in naming their first male after our grandfather. He would not be another Giuliano. There were now three of us cousins bearing that name. Well, me on and off. This gesture did not sit well with some members of our clan, especially my grandfather.

I expressed my opinion. Changing long-standing traditions is never easy. They often bear a similarity to religious virtues and so become untouchable and unquestionable. It takes lots of time to secretly bury things once deemed sacred or divine and allow humans to forget the past and live in the era of their making.

A bit later, some problems women faced in modern Italy came to fore. As I was a bystander in a new country, it seemed only right to listen; however, things got off to a shaky start. The issue was women in the work force, or the lack of them, and my uncle took a stand regarding some roles as inappropriate for women. The two ladies were adamant that jobs, no matter how demanding or demeaning, should go to any woman who qualified.

It was not my intention to object. However, considering my experience with the filth, sweat, stink, and grueling pain in the bilges of my first ship and the massacring fumes and unbearable heat behind the boilers, it seemed inconceivable to me that any woman in her right mind would want to take on such ghastly work. I asked if any rational woman would choose such a horrible occupation like crawling down into the bowels of the earth to dig for coal.

My aunt appeared more agitated than her friend. She insisted women belonged in any occupation they qualified for. But my next question may have silenced her a bit. Should women participate in the barbaric madness of war? Where killing other human beings is your only means of survival and you kill, not even truly grasping the act committed. Did women long to become as barbaric as men, living a spartan lifestyle dedicated to excelling in body and spirit to better annihilate life when ordered to do so? Well, perhaps I had gone a bit too far.

Fortunately, out of the blue, perhaps to change the topic, my aunt asked if I wanted to speak to Peter. I certainly did! What kind of a question was that? I knew my brother was living in Milano with our mother, but I had no clue how involved our aunt had become in getting to know the very woman we practically knew nothing about. Anyhow, it seems only right to bring you up-to-date on my brother's whereabouts.

Back in 1974, my father had located Peter and convinced him to come home with him. Then very soon, Adrian Di Stefano persuaded his son to leave the Bronx behind. He would return to Palermo to live in a good environment, and, more importantly, also have family support to assist him. And unlike in the Bronx, our family in Sicily was now quite big.

My brother's arrival excited everyone, but our relatives were quite stunned to learn he could not communicate. After all, he had only been away a bit over ten years. However, the young lad soon caused an even greater sensation for a few months later he found his tongue and spoke like a true native. Not only was his Sicilian perfect, but when he lost his cool, his tone was complemented by some tasty words which he deftly pronounced.

Uncle Luca took him in at work. This got my brother out of the house and provided him with the possibility to learn a trade. It even put a few coins in his pocket. However, the lad's new venture came to a complete halt after a few weeks. Peter had no trouble fitting in anywhere, but the unruly rough bunch he worked with went out of their way to make life miserable for him.

One would think a newcomer would be assisted and slowly brought into the scheme of things. No sir. His co-workers enjoyed watching him struggle with his functions and laughed behind his back. Of course, this led to an occasional verbal outburst. But one day, one of the workers made a provocative remark about our mother, who according to legend had abandoned us. Well, just like Samson, the young man almost took down the walls of the entire shop, but then walked out to never return.

Now, you would think life without work would make for a long day. Perhaps, but not in Peter's case. He had become acquainted with Gianni, a florist, whose shop was near the cemetery entrance. Gianni was the only son to one of our father's childhood friends, and he admired my brother's jovial ways. The two were practically inseparable. And Gianni's friends were no different. Soon, the guy referred to as l'Americanu was quite at home, for they all bonded like true friends who had previously lost sight of each other.

Peter was also quite the survivor and master of his gig. Lunch at our grandparents was still just a dish of pasta. Well, once finished with that meal, he would head to Uncle Luca's home. There, as in all Italian residences, food was vital and in abundance. Once they sat down to their lunch, the still hungry lad would be treated to a culinary feast fit for a king. Now his only real interest was eating more pasta, and not just one serving. Of course, like elsewhere, he compensated everyone thoroughly, making it impossible to not laugh uncontrollably and wholeheartedly.

After a year in Palermo, Peter was preparing to return to the U.S. He missed the place where he felt he truly belonged. No doubt, much had changed inwardly, and he was certainly more content with life in general. And with inner changes sometimes come some physical ones. The young man stood over six feet tall and had filled in nicely. His long wavy hair cascaded down to his shoulders, and he was simply one good-looking devil.

Our grandmother approached him one afternoon and handed him a postcard. It was addressed to both of us, Giuliano and Piero. It was from our grandmother in Barazzetto. He discovered, much to his surprise, that she had been sending cards religiously for years to inquire about us. In them, she expressed her desire for some news from us. But apparently, it had always been a one-way correspondence.

Peter was truly touched. The card rekindled an erased memory of a distant past. He may have even sensed the love and devotion given to us by our folks and the simple townspeople who one day witnessed our departure and eventually knew nothing more about us. Peter decided to make a trip up north as our grandmother happily encouraged him to do so.

Well, Piero Di Stefano, or Peter, boarded a train a few days later. He traveled twenty-four hours to reach Milano, it being the main train hub. After a few hours there, he caught another train for about six hours with the last destination being Udine. There he took a taxi heading to the tiny town of his birth.

The taxi driver, a local, was slightly confused. His passenger spoke with a strong Southern accent, but the bizarre thing was just how anxious he appeared to be to arrive at an insignificant hamlet. A tiny town in the very heart of the vast Friuli farmlands. A place where practically nothing of any interest ever occurred, and most young folks happily exited at an early age, often never to return.

He was dropped off right in the center of Barazzetto. Now you may not believe it, but this incredible critter, who had left at the age of four, walked right to our grandparents' house and recognized it immediately. Just like a tourist returning home from a very extended holiday. And curiously, the entrance to the house does not face the main road he was on but is located inside a courtyard area adjacent to the neighbors' dwellings.

Peter knocked loudly on the front door several times. Apparently, no one was home. The somewhat curious neighbors, now seeing a strange looking individual near their premises, became a bit concerned. He continued rapping on that door, and then a voice from a few yards away inquired just who he was seeking. The young man answered very matter-of-factly, "My grandmother."

It was a troublesome moment for the old couple. They both froze, and the woman began crying. There was an exchange of kind words and handshakes, and my brother was invited into their home, where the couple brought out a bottle of homemade wine, which may have helped settle Peter's speech impediment. The happy farmers began to share news of our family's whereabouts.

In no time at all, the town came to life. Human history was being made, and at the heart of it all was one of its citizens who had vanished many years back. People were arriving at the house, and all seemed to recognize Piero. Much was said about this incredibly good day. Curiously, Peter was mostly well versed in Sicilian, but his Italian came to fore. It may have been the local wine that kept all communication lines fully open.

He discovered our grandmother was now a widow and lived outside of Milano. She lived with our mom, who resided with an elderly gentleman, and the three had recently left Barazzetto to return to their home there. A small crowd escorted him to the only bar in town, where the only phone available could be used. They then provided Peter with our mother's phone number. He dialed it and a woman's voice pierced the receiver. He asked to speak to Ms. Zoratti. The somewhat annoyed voice inquired just who was seeking her, to which he answered, "I am her son, Piero."

There was a brief silence. Then the woman spoke but immediately stopped and began to search for words. The struggling voice, although hardly audible and somewhat strained, found its footing. That was our mother, and the two spoke briefly. Once Peter had identified his whereabouts and circumstances, he was instructed to make his way to Milano Centrale, the very place he had been at that morning.

One of the townspeople took him to Udine. He left on the first train available and upon arriving called our mom who informed him that she would be there soon. He placed himself close to a large model ship on display outside the arrival area for those had been his instructions. Yet once close to the expected moment, he slightly distanced himself from the rendezvous spot, wanting to first size up his guests before they spotted him.

Eventually, three people approached the encased model ship. Our grandmother, whom Peter recognized immediately was embracing our mother, and an older man was engaging both women in small talk. The young man simply popped out of nowhere, and they all warmly and strongly embraced. The magic of the moment did the rest.

Peter remained with his new family for a week. Much was discussed regarding our cruel past which had separated us all, and they agreed it was now time to embrace the future. At the airport in Milano, which is close to where our mother lived, Peter promised to keep in touch, and our mom invited him to return whenever he chose to. After a series of strong embraces, and a few tears, the lad was on his way back to the Bronx.

My brother settled in at Co-op City. However, our father was not at all thrilled with this new version of things. Years ago, he had brought us to the U.S. to relieve his mom of a demanding responsibility in raising us. He had also embarked on a course to completely obliterate our past, and our mother's very name. To him, his wife was our mother. After all, it was she who had been there for us.

Peter soon landed a job as a boiler attendant somewhere in Hunt's Point. He also worked on weekends at a pizzeria owned by one of our dad's friends from Sicily. This job afforded him ample time to be a Sicilian again and entertain his co-workers. He certainly kept himself busy and avoided old friends and the neighborhood. But to a large extent, the young man was a bit lonely.

Now life within the confines of the Di Stefano household was no piece of cake. My brother spent too many evenings at home. Unfortunately, some problem or contentious issue always ensued, and although insignificant, it would get elevated to a litigious category, one which would then be analyzed, scrutinized, over dramatized, and diligently fermented into some type of unbearable discord by two argumentative parents.

Soon enough, the hereditary hostility and threats accompanying the accusations became a bit too much. And please understand, my brother if pushed enough, could easily lose it. He tried his best to hold back on more than one occasion, but one day he said the unthinkable. He dared insinuate why our mother had been unable to live with our father. This, of course, was like a declaration of war.

My brother was immediately asked to leave. He had absolutely no place to go and feared returning to his old ways, so he profusely apologized and kept the peace for quite some time. Unfortunately, more incidents occurred, and he again misspoke, only this time he held his ground. A few days later, he bought a one-way ticket to Milano. He decided to move to Italy on the spur of the moment and allow destiny to fill in the rest.

Chapter 86

Aunt Anna looked so delighted as she handed me the telephone. My brother's voice brought a slight feeling of relief, for as bizarre as it seemed, it felt like we had separated centuries ago. The two kids from Italy were now both carrying on in English and had entirely too much to say. After a while, it appeared as if I were ignoring my hosts. We decided to cut it short and leave the rest for our next reunion.

Peter sounded so happy! In a few days he would be in Palermo. Before we hung up, he spoke to our aunt and thanked her. I found out that she was the one who had sought out and contacted our mom the year before once my brother had gone off to Barazzetto and settled in for a few days with our mother. The two women had spoken again on other occasions, and my aunt had recently informed her friend of my presence in Palermo. Oh well, such were the circumstances, and it was now time to give my undivided attention to my hosts.

The rest of the evening slipped away. Uncle Andrea brought out a cassata which should have been served after finishing our meal but was forgotten, and he now began cutting huge pieces. The kids joined us, and although it was late, no one refused a thick slice of this super-sweet treat. I felt so very welcome among all my relatives and my new friend. It had become apparent that my Sicilian family members were warm, generous, and loving people, who were nicely enriching my stay in any way possible.

In the mornings it was on to my grandfather's place. He was no longer a barber. His shop, where so many faces and heads had been catered to, now held a large variety of various items to adorn the graves and mausoleums in the nearby cemetery. I always found him doing a crossword puzzle.

Grandfather Giuliano was a curious character. The barber who had so much enjoyed his clients, and all they had to say, allowing their contribution to make his day, was now passing his time pen in hand, eyes on a booklet with his mind searching for words. He appeared a bit desperate for a customer to drop in. So, just why had he stopped doing what he loved? If age was an issue, couldn't he have hired someone to work for him?

The next stop was a just few yards away. Years back, Uncle Luca had relocated his business right by the cemetery's entrance. An indiscreet family issue, something better left unsaid, forced him to move. The shop was huge, and he still employed the same faithful workers who had been with him from the start, minus my favorite person who had passed away years back. Several customers were always in his office.

An elderly couple was chatting away while my uncle scribbled in a notebook. It seemed better to wait outside by the glass window so he could see me. Upon finishing, he stepped out and we went next store for an espresso. I informed him of Peter's arrival, which generated a delighted smile. My uncle even expressed a bit of guilt for not having intervened over what had transpired in his shop, but he insisted that if Peter had simply disregarded the crap from his co-workers, he could have stayed and learned a useful trade. We returned to his shop, and as a few customers were waiting, we embraced, and I then moved on.

I proceeded to the train station to confirm Peter's itinerary, just to be on the safe side. My grandfather had suggested a visit when we spoke that morning. If I understood correctly, he insinuated that Italy's trains only ran efficiently in the days of Mussolini. Then he added that in Sicily anything was possible, and the impossible usually reigned supreme.

Outside the entrance to the station was a kiosk selling lots of magazines and newspapers. In my best Italian, I asked for an English newspaper, and the scruffy looking chap handed me a folded Herald Tribune. He appeared a bit leery, but maybe it was just me seeing the unusual in people. Although it was a bit thin, having some news of the world, even if limited, made me feel like something good was being accomplished that morning.

Now how curious! I paid with a large bill, in size only, and along with my change there was a stamp and several pieces of candy. This seemed odd, and caused me to briefly stare at my palm, uncertain of how to demand an explanation. A bit of Sicilian, which sounded a tad crude, was loudly belted out to me. I did not truly understand what had just transpired, but it seemed better to move on and even thank the shabby looking chap.

Once home, my grandmother greeted me most cordially while continuing her house chores. It was a perfect day to sit on the terrace and listen to the small creatures chirping away while catching up on daily world events. I made myself comfortable on an old chair and looked at the front page of the paper. My enthusiasm collapsed immediately. The newspaper was more than a week old. My grandfather's words and their insinuation rang so loud. It is imperative to not fall asleep at the wheel, certainly not on this island.

Chapter 87

Peter arrived early afternoon the following day. His train was only fifteen minutes late. I had gotten to the station a bit early, and believe it or not, I returned to that kiosk but with a completely different objective—to purchase an Italian newspaper. It was time to get serious with the language, mostly due to my fear that we two Yanks would now only communicate in the one we absolutely mastered and truly loved.

Incredible but true! Again, I noticed my change consisted of more than just coins. There was a caramel, no stamps, but a fancy paper clip. And this time, that gloomy face suddenly displayed a huge smile, leaving me to wonder if he considered me a complete idiot. Or perhaps the guy was simply happy that I patronized his shop. It was no time for trivialities. The mystery of my exotic change would need to get resolved some other time.

Peter was soon on the platform and walking toward me. We grabbed hold of each other's shoulders and embraced in a warm hug. Without thinking, our English flowed out quite naturally. It may have raised a few eyebrows with the folks around us, it being a recognizable language but hardly heard of back then. There was much to say, when I suddenly proposed an unexpected task. We took a horse and buggy home. And why not? It seemed only right to participate in a trade we were once partially acquainted with.

Our grandmother's happy eyes more than welcomed the newcomer. Not so much our grandfather's once he got home later that day. It was eventually revealed to me that the two had had a few run-ins during Peter's long stay the year before. In one incident, a few unpleasant words came out of my brother's ire, which is why our grandfather reminded him that he had not been invited to reside there.

Nevertheless, the young lad had us all in stiches! My brother could imitate anyone and everyone, and his funny fictional dialogues were delivered in perfect Sicilian. I could grasp some of it, although I was not familiar with everything, and while our grandmother was begging him to stop, no one truly wanted the lively entertainment to terminate any time soon.

Peter talked non-stop for the next few days. He even mentioned how ironic it was to be there—the very home we had departed for good. He insinuated that it was our very destructive lifestyle which had brought us back. We wondered if things would have gone differently had we remained in Palermo. Just what would have become of us? It was then almost unanimous that moving to America, regardless of the ultimate outcome, was probably the best thing which could have occurred.

We decided to spend time exploring the city together. Peter's one-year residency came in handy for he certainly knew his way around. He also mastered the art of the deal. If there was a store where a bargain could be had, we stopped there. And if not treated properly, he would argue, raise his voice, and walk away. We occasionally got called back as the item was now available at a new price.

One evening, we had just left a pizzeria. On a nearby wall was a poster of that individual, Adriano Celentano, who was now making movies. Peter claimed to have seen one but was not terribly impressed. Then he suddenly changed the topic. Wasn't I at all curious to know anything about our mother? My response was a tad hostile. After all, she had abandoned us. Case closed. In my book, it seemed that on her last trip to Palermo, having failed in bargaining for money, she left to never return.

My brother viewed things differently. He had now been with her for three months, and she expressed how strongly she regretted not having taken us away. Apparently, she feared bringing us back to her town, knowing she could not live there for lack of work, and she had not established a home anywhere. So where could we three possibly have gone to? My brother even stressed that some things which had been said about her had certainly impacted our outlook. Nevertheless, she was our real mother. Wasn't a bit of consideration in order? I answered but failed to defend my beliefs and insisted we close the argument.

It got rehashed the following day. At Uncle Andrea's place. Our aunt suddenly took advantage of us three being alone. She asked me if I intended to go to Milano to see our mother. It was a tough question to answer. Our aunt soon exclaimed her strong conviction and backed it up. The woman casually stated that all mothers, even the most awful ones, love their children. Some do so differently but most profoundly. And did I know for sure if our mother had not been devastated in not seeing us again and knowing nothing of our whereabouts?

My aunt did not insist but very calmly pursued her point of view. Our mother had gotten a rotten deal in the Di Stefano household. Especially the issue over her attire when last in Palermo, which, according to our aunt, showed how pathetically ancient some people's outlooks remained. She advised me to make the trip to Milano and added, "It will bring you the peace of mind you have long been seeking."

Chapter 88

The two Di Stefanos were on the road again. Only this trip had us in first-class rail. Peter outright refused to pass an entire day in an overcrowded and worn-out second-class car. After all, wasn't I at all curious to see how the other half lived? It seemed superfluous to disagree with a good idea, and once on the train, the various accommodations confirmed his precise prognostic.

There would be no reading on this journey. My brother saw to it, and with the exception of a small nap, much about our arrival in the Bronx in 1963 was discussed. He recalled the Coca-Cola bottles enterprise and how quickly it came to an end. He spoke of other events delicately glossing over them with some rather funny intimate details.

Eventually we arrived in Milano. I was soon acquainted with the very spot where the family reunion had occurred. Peter called home to confirm our arrival, and we soon exited the station to wait for Mr. Rossi. All I knew about the man was that he was rich. But absolutely nothing else. My brother never mentioned him. He had simply referred to him as "un signore". In English this equates to gentleman, but in Italian it connotates much more.

A brand-new Buick arrived a bit later. Upon seeing it, my brother and I sauntered toward the car. The driver greeted us nicely but not too excitedly, and this was Mr. Alessandro Rossi. He was well-dressed, both in style and the richness of his clothes, and he appeared somewhat reserved, almost as if he had been forced to perform a rather delicate mission and was cooperating but not very enthusiastically. After a handshake and kiss on the cheeks, we departed.

My brother sat up front, so the back seat was all mine. We crossed the city center and entered highway A4 heading in the direction of Torino. Once on that highway, something peculiar stood out immediately. The signore's driving style was like that expression—put the metal to the pedal. He made his way into the left lane, and it seemed as if it was his personal space, for the man had no intentions of slowing down. Any vehicle in front of his was warned of his arrival through a touch of high beams, while the left turn signal remained active, and every driver cooperated and quickly moved into the center lane.

It felt like we were traveling at the speed of light. I was convinced we would tap or hit those autos which did not immediately allow him to proceed. Somehow, miraculously, there was a means to the madness as everyone did their part. I asked my brother just how fast we were traveling, and he told me it was over two hundred kilometers an hour. And while our vehicle rode smoothly, and the driver knew the road, my hands were grasping anything to hang on to while my heart hoped for a quick and safe arrival.

Once off the highway, Mr. Rossi resumed a normal speed and soon entered a small town. We parked near a huge wooden door that looked like something out of medieval times. Our driver opened it and then drove us in. We were now in Villa Rossi; my eyes had never seen anything so enchanting.

What a splendid palace! It embodied nobility. There was a crunching sound as the car drove over the gravel that surrounded the entranceway. Once I had exited the car, my eyes continued to admire the entire premises, which had once been a monastery. Everything about it held me in check. I quickly spotted the stone shield representing the family emblem. It made me think of the importance of history as a whole.

The monastery's walls evidenced its sturdiness yet smooth elegance. A trimmed lawn bordered the buildings' sides, and a mini enclosed garden with a fancy well stood in the center of our surroundings. A slim cement wall protected this little garden area, and a few statues of Cupid sat on them, with two long rows of rectangular pots of peony flowers at their side. It was all so endearing.

Peter and I grabbed our luggage. Mr. Rossi informed us that he had to run an errand. An overwhelming sense of curiosity about the venerable structure that stood in front of us had my mind on fire, yet Peter had few details to share. Two women now appeared by the atrium. Our mom stood out like a sore thumb. She was tall and slim with straight long black hair pulled back in a bun. Plus, she was smiling and had asked if we had traveled well. But just who was that other woman by her side? Could that be our grandmother?

In my mind, Nonna Melania should have looked much younger. She once had dark hair always worn in a chignon, whereas this curly gray-haired woman with glasses did not fill the bill. Oh well, we four approached each other and finally my mother and I embraced. My words had a tad of warmth to them, yet my heart was not fully there. She was suddenly quite moved, and her face fully confirmed it. She said something and Peter translated "Eventually, there will be much I shall explain."

My grandmother and I hugged and held on tightly for a while. It seemed like in no time at all, Mr. Rossi had reentered. He approached us and insisted we all move indoors. We accommodated ourselves in a very quaint area near the kitchen. A brief chat regarding my stay in Palermo was given with Peter at work translating. A bit later, I asked for a tour of the house.

It began on that floor where most rooms were rather large and a bit dark. The furniture was mostly antique pieces yet preserved like new, and there were many precious decorative objects everywhere, including some incredible paintings. One peculiar thing struck me as odd. The dining room was far from the kitchen area, which according to Alessandro was designed so that the lower ranking monks served their higher echelons who ate there.

We returned to the kitchen area. Our mother resumed a bit of work on dinner and proudly claimed she would serve us rice with saffron. Mr. Rossi excused himself and headed to the cantina to procure a few bottles of a local homemade Barbera wine. According to my brother, the wine would certainly get us all better acquainted. Our grandmother expressed feeling truly ecstatic to see us all together. Too much time had separated us, and we were so happy that it was finally behind us. Alessandro returned and quickly opened a bottle of wine. He had three, and that exotic grape juice was to die for.

My stay in Palermo came up for discussion. My responses had Peter putting in some overtime. Now if it wasn't a dandy, that incident over the change at the kiosk got properly explained. According to my host, Italy was facing a shortage of coins because the metal used was scarce and very expensive. Consequently, store owners and others were improvising. And according to him, in Italy, anything was possible, even candy and stamps for change. He then laughed and defined it as Italian ingenuity, if you may.

We touched on various subjects, even life in the U.S. Mr. Rossi mentioned being a prisoner during WWII, in custody of American soldiers, who according to him, were pretty much drunk every night. At first, it was tough detailing life in the U.S. The Vietnam War had caused much grief, hatred, and separation, but at least it was finally over, and it seemed better to change topics.

Dinner was served. As promised, the wine did its job. I certainly could not speak much Italian, or very well, yet it almost seemed like a forgotten problem. Sometime later, my brother and our mom accompanied me upstairs to my room. We faced a long corridor once at the top of the stairs. My room had antique but sharp looking furniture, and the carved angels on the door panels of the wooden closet stood out. There was also an old mahogany desk bearing a few books bound in leather covers. Our mother used her best English in welcoming me to my new home. I slept well that night.

Villa Rossi was sort of a dream come true. Living in style was not necessarily the only delightful part. Although my rich surroundings made me feel a bit lavish, being reunited with my family was having a very positive impact. Nevertheless, much too soon life became a bit too routine.

At about eight-thirty, my brother and I would come down to a breakfast of coffee and milk and a few biscuits. In the background, the radio's speakers belted out the morning news. It became part of a brief morning session with Alessandro. Although my contribution was still in need of my brother's assistance, my views were still fully expressed at length, as no one else showed any interest in world affairs. And my host and I had much to say.

Perhaps our breakfast was a simple staple, but not Mr. Rossi's. He, too, had biscuits, but his beverage defied all expectations. He waited for our mother to make a small pot of espresso coffee just for him. Once that coffee was put into a large cup, he poured in a half glass of Barbera wine. A purple foam adorned the top of the cup as the man most happily stirred the concoction insisting this was a real morning banquet.

We two guests always left the villa around nine thirty. However, when it rained, we confined ourselves to our rooms, and it was a long day. Our mother began her daily house chorus in taking apart and spotlessly cleaning a section of the huge mansion. Grandma either took to the garden behind the house or found something to do indoors. She never worked alongside our mom for the matron of this small empire was too feisty in her expectations, and the elderly woman would simply not do.

Mr. Rossi was a lawyer who had never practiced his profession. Every morning he secluded himself to a section of the villa where his personal office awaited him. The man obviously attended to his affairs as he was a wealthy landowner. He was constantly pounding away at an old typewriter, yet no one knew exactly what he did. Once through, his morning tasks consisted of consulting with our mother as to lunch and dinner, and he would then exit the villa to procure fresh provisions from the various small stores in town. He also purchased a newspaper which he fully digested in the afternoon.

Peter and I would trek most mornings. Our long walks got us to some nearby towns while immersed in our usual chats. My brother's world of improvised entertainment kept things going smoothly. He would comment on everything and everyone, including executing excellent imitations of real people. When appropriate, he occasionally even tossed in Richard Nixon's "I am not a thief".

We ordered an espresso in every town we visited. Sometimes we splurged and dined on a cappuccino and croissant. The latter were on display and hard to pass up. And, if there was a pinball machine in the location, we would spend hours improving our old skills. Our trips would eventually terminate back at the villa punctually at twelve thirty. Well, actually give or take a few minutes.

Every day at precisely one o'clock lunch was served. Our mom's culinary skills were excellent and much appreciated. We ate by the kitchen area and would remain there long after the meal terminated as some topics always needed to be further ironed out. Later on, I usually took to my room and read, an incomprehensible pastime to my brother. He, on the other hand, did some incredible sketching, and he was quite good! He could draw anyone, especially folks we knew, and he placed them in the most unusual settings. It was apparent that with a bit of training my brother might have found his passion in the most unlikely of all places—the world of art.

Our evenings were most annoying to me. Villa Rossi was locked up at eight. Our host would secure those ancient mighty doors by sliding a long solid iron bolt into a hole in the side wall making our premises impenetrable. So, usually around nine we two and our grandmother headed upstairs to the long hallway where a large TV sat. Soon after, our mother joined us, but not Alessandro. The man claimed TV was stupid, and simply not for him.

Now we two Yankees abroad inquired into work options. It was no easy task. First of all, it seemed like we had no valid skills to fall back on. And although Italy's economic sector was rather weak, our biggest problem was our status. We had been informed that hiring foreigners of countries that were not part of the European Union Community, was almost impossible.

So, it was a most welcomed request when Alessandro recruited us for work. During the latter part of a long afternoon, we were asked to do some bottling. That is, a recent delivery of local homemade wine needed attending to. In the cantina were two large kegs of that superb Barbera wine. Our task, which we most happily accepted, was to get the wine into the hundreds of clean empty wine bottles neatly lined up. Our tool to accomplish this mission was a thin plastic tube about four feet long.

We tossed a coin, and sure enough, faith granted my brother the privilege to start. Peter stopped yapping and happily placed one end of the tube inside one of the kegs Alessandro had unsealed. I handed him the first bottle, and he began to suck the tube. Immediately, he got a mouthful of wine yet managed to place the tube in the bottle without spilling much of it. My turn came next, and it was impossible to not taste and send down a bit of that wonderful beverage.

Seeing his enterprise off to a good start, Mr. Rossi allowed us to continue. Soon enough, Peter began to complain that I was spilling too much wine and insisted on taking over the entire operation. Believe it or not, he yapped away for dear life while also continuing the sucking function becoming both hilarious but also a bit sloppy as the wine going inside him was having an effect.

It was not long before we were both singing. Peter brought us back to those delightful days in our room with Ricky. He began to belt out and we gave it a lovely rendition. We had no audience, but there was no stopping us as we simply went from one Beatles tune to the next. At some point, I realized my brother was drunk.

A bit later our boss returned. Peter was imitating an Italian TV personality, but our host's presence calmed him down. He asked me to take over because he needed to get upstairs to use the bathroom. He departed in a bit of a hurry but unfortunately took the stairs too quickly. Peter fell and hurt his ankle. So, the injured worker, in much pain, found it difficult to walk and needed our assistance.

Alessandro and I helped him up the steps and out of the cantina. We three ultimately stepped into the kitchen area. Our mom and grandmother joined us in assisting the wounded wine-bottler. And although insisting he was in a lot of pain, the brilliant comic managed a wonderful imitation of John Wayne, in Italian, of course, pretending to be wounded and asking if the battle had been won.

Chapter 89

A month after my arrival things changed drastically. Life at the villa was proceeding just fine, at least such was my take on things. Never had anyone said anything to the contrary. However, apparently, some hidden underlying issues were creating a bit of discomfort for our host.

On one occasion, Peter had said something a bit loud to Mr. Rossi. It had quickly been sidelined. And yes, the young guests from the Bronx lived most comfortably, but we certainly created no problems to contend with. Truth be told, outside of a daily outing to Milano, we had hardly ever ventured very far from our home base.

One morning our mother told us two to pack our things. Her tone and mood were a bit hostile, but no explanation came forth. Sometime later, the entire family nucleus entered Alessandro's Buick with suitcases and small bags, as we were heading to the highway with destination Barazzetto. It would be a long and silent ride, and although still clueless, it was apparent that something was wrong.

Now my conclusion is sheer speculation. Mr. Rossi, a single gentleman, very well-off and quite independent, had happily accepted our mom into his life. Some years later, with my grandfather's passing, he also gladly took in our grandmother. Then quite unexpectedly, two young adults, unemployed and a bit clueless about their future, had now become a part of his domain. Perhaps his concerns over us two were minor, but we lived in a small town, one with a very effective grapevine highlighting all the news not fit to print.

It was after gassing up somewhere near Verona that a small eruption surfaced. Mr. Rossi and our mom, sitting up front, were barely speaking, but were now disagreeing over something. It led to quite a bit of arguing back and forth. We passengers remained quiet in the back seat, hoping our journey to our destination would continue without any unexpected changes. Apparently, at times, our mom would not let go of some insignificant issue. This was the case now, but fortunately we resumed our voyage.

Barazzetto is incredibly tiny. You can drive right through it and not even realize it. The local bar was in the center of the town's main and only road. A corner grocery store and a cheese factory at the other end of that street were basically it. As usual, few people were about carrying on with their daily routine.

We arrived and settled in that afternoon. Almost immediately, the few natives who had spotted the fancy car parked by the side of the house began their brief invasion. Once word got out of my unexpected presence, it may have rattled a few folks knowing the entire family was reunited. Suddenly I was in high demand, but my star faded quickly due to my limited speaking ability. Even though my Italian had improved, I had no knowledge of their dialect.

Mom carried on as if all was well. Mr. Rossi, very much admired by all, chatted most amicably with our guests by the front of our premises. The following morning, the gentleman left us after a late breakfast. I, unfortunately, woke up to an old problem. It came and went at random. A huge painful boil was on my back. This mysterious ailment that occasionally revisited me was becoming unbearable. Neither the cure in San Francisco nor a medic in the Bronx had been able to properly exterminate it. Those carbuncles came and went as they pleased.

My mother insisted we visit the local physician. A bit later, someone drove us to a nearby town, and my mom would later reveal he had never worked a day in his life. Surprisingly, the doctor's office was a huge apartment. We entered a large room where three patients sat on chairs lined up against one of the walls. Mom asked who was last, and a woman raised her hand, indicating we would be seen after her. Once sitting, my mother began to chat about the awful weather we were having.

Eventually we entered the doctor's room and met the physician. He was wearing a military uniform and was a substitute as the regular doctor was on holiday. We were greeted cordially, and the man had an uncanny resemblance to my Uncle Robert. Not only in appearance, but his tone of voice and slow speech were practically the same. He may have been a junior officer in the Italian military, but I saw my uncle's twin, just a tad slimmer.

The physician examined me and inquired about the ailment's history. Once becoming acquainted with my past, he ordered a series of blood tests, which were done the following day, via the goodness of the Italian people for I had no health insurance nor an Italian medical card. My mother's card was used. Back in those days, providing a helping hand whenever possible was more important than simply obeying the rules.

I returned on my own a week later. There were a few more people waiting this time, but the gig was the same. The doctor gave me some not so pleasant news but nothing too worrisome. My liver was infected, yet the culpable source was not identified. Plus, I also had a strong case of anemia. My instructions were to follow a very strict diet, but more importantly to avoid alcohol and limit wine intake to only a small glass with meals and, if possible, to give up smoking.

It certainly seemed doable. Yet the two lists he handed me had me very concerned. One showed food to eat and the other what to avoid. All fat was to be eliminated. Therefore, things like sausage, salami, gorgonzola cheese, and many other such delicious delicacies that I loved, were out for good. Replacing these were lean meats and fish, preferably grilled or baked, nothing fried and plenty of green vegetables. The greener the better. My what a punch to the stomach this was.

There was one last issue. Having complained of always feeling tired, the good doctor prescribed vitamin B12 injections for two weeks. He also informed me that once cured and finally free of the boils, an occasional deviation from the diet was allowed. My mind accepted the cure, my stomach not so much, for the idea of limiting that wonderful Barbera, or the excellent white Friuli wine, felt like an unjust punishment.

Peter referred to my diet as a persecution. It certainly felt like one. But my disciplinary skills, now somewhat better engrained, got me through it all okay. I even began to enjoy something I was at first reluctant to try. It was beef tartare. Raw chopped meat, from a nearby local butcher, who swore to its excellent quality, which my grandmother prepared with minced garlic and chopped parsley. The name and ingredients had not thrilled me, but after my first taste, I was hooked and remained so for quite a while.

Folks, the diet worked! The nasty boils no longer plagued me. I even felt much better. However, while dieting and remaining alcohol and drug-free, the unthinkable occurred. And why? It is such a paradox. The incident took me down a few pegs and to this day remains an unsolved mystery. Perhaps there was much invisible pent-up anger which unexpectedly took me down.

Chapter 90

My grandfather's bicycle, old and worn-out, still functioned. It only needed a good solid cleaning, new tires, and the care and dedication that keeps anything going. After giving it some attention, it still looked a tad rickety, and could certainly have used new brakes, but that was not crucial because I certainly wasn't speeding off anywhere.

The bike became a part of my morning workout. It hauled me around the Friuli area, usually going off to some distant towns while on main roads which hugged vast farmlands. After several hours of riding and a small break for a cappuccino, I usually headed back home. My afternoons consisted of reading, whereas Peter entertained all who came by to chat. Often, some of the local girls riding their scooters home from work to have lunch would stop and share a few words with my brother.

What happened one morning defies any explanation. I had left early for the lovely town of San Daniele. It sits on a hill, and after taking in the view below me, it was time to pause. Perhaps it was sheer boredom which had me on edge, or maybe it was a feeling of uselessness, but whatever it was, it caused me to make a bad decision. After my coffee, a glass of grappa was ordered and my it went down so smoothly.

I then drank another grappa before heading home. At the very next town on the main road, I visited a coffee shop but just for grappa. One was not enough, and I chased the second one down with a glass of white wine. This ritual continued in the very next town. The bartender, a lively elderly woman, got me talking some. She never said a word about my excessive drinking so early in the morning, yet her expression signaled slight concern, but not too much, me being a stranger.

Sometime later, our town's church and its steeple came into view. My bicycle, however, was not cooperating as it had me in the middle of the road and tottering. Peter spotted me once I arrived closer to our residence, as he stood by the front of our house chatting with a girl on a bicycle. My precarious circumstances were obvious. He helped me off the bike. The girl who had eyed me curiously said a few words and left.

My brother escorted me to the entrance door. Suddenly, our mom was next to us. She began to yell at me, but her voice seemed to be arriving from so far away. She appeared a tad ridiculous. We could both hear her, such was my thinking, so why all the shouting? The irate woman demanded to know if I understood why we were now living here. Did I realize just how much she was forsaking for my brother and me?

My response flew out. "Where the hell were you when we needed you? Do you know what they did to us in Palermo? I bet I know where you were." A hand suddenly struck my face. I grabbed my mom's arm and squeezed it while pulling her toward me. Peter grabbed me, forcing my hands to release her as she walked away holding her arm, obviously in pain. My brother then let go and escorted me toward the bathroom, located outside the house near the entrance.

Something gushed out of me like a geyser. All that liquid poison hit the bathroom door as I struggled to remain standing. Our neighbors were now taking it all in and they kept staring. Peter held me up and walked me inside the house. He struggled to get me up the stairs to our bedroom. Once my body was laying on the bed out came, "If you wanna play, you gotta pay."

It seemed impossible to get out of bed the next morning. A bit later, I somehow made my way down the stairs. There was complete silence in the kitchen. Our grandmother sat by the table as if waiting for some awful news to be delivered. She remained motionless upon seeing me. My voice was practically inaudible, but it managed a greeting.

Then, someone's voice could be heard outside. The person was chatting with my mother, and this broke the stillness of the moment as I sat at the kitchen table. Once my mom entered, her expression changed dramatically, and she refused to acknowledge my presence. Her bruised arm, now practically black, evidenced the horror of what had occurred. While the awful saga of my drunkenness registered, I only managed to say that I would soon leave for Palermo. No one responded.

Peter arrived a bit later. He found me by the house on the main road. As he approached, my expression said it all. My shame knew no limits. I shared my decision to move on, but he insisted I not do anything. He had lived in Palermo a whole year, and he was not convinced it would accommodate me. We walked over to the garden area behind the house. My brother convinced me to sit tight as he would try to patch things up.

Later in the afternoon, my brother proposed a trip to Switzerland. After arriving at the villa, my aunt Sofia, our mom's oldest sister, had spoken to me on the phone and had insisted that I visit her. I had also spoken with her daughter Angela, whose English was perfect, and she too seemed happy to have me join them in Geneva. So, Peter suggested it was best to head north instead of south. He also believed what had occurred could soon be forgiven.

My brother's wise counsel had been delivered so candidly. And as he knew Angela well, they had traveled a bit in Italy some months back, he described her as friendly, kind, and very bright. It was his concern for me which made me appreciate him so very much. He was truly a loving person. Peter then looked at me and simply said, "You need to let go of the past."

It felt strange waving goodbye to my brother so soon. Once the train pulled out of Udine, out came a book which had been purchased in Milano. It was Twilight of the Idols. And before I dove into it, Peter's remark, when he had spotted it on my desk, came to mind. He looked confused, maybe even concerned, and then said, "Just what the hell are you reading?" My, we two certainly belonged to different universes.

Well, Nietzsche's ideas struck a chord with me. The culmination of great culture comes about when nations have arrived at the highest level of their personal glory, be it Rome or Great Britain, or any country for that matter. It seemed a profound truth and had me asking if it was also applicable to the individual. If yes, well, it appeared as if I was still light-years away from any moment of greatness.

My train was eventually some ways outside Geneva. My view from the window basked in soft sunshine and all around was an immaculate countryside, which had properly soothed a patch of the restlessness brewing in me. Some moments before, my inner spiritual domain had posed the million-dollar question: Where are you going in life, dear Julian?

Soon enough, a partial view of the city center prepared me for my arrival. My cousin and I were complete strangers. Yet once off that train, it was she who noticed me. Although a bit cautious, she walked over, smiling so intently, and in perfect English asked if the gentleman in front of her was her American cousin. We quickly embraced, exchanged a few compliments, and rode a taxi home.

The moment my aunt laid eyes on me she said, "You are the spitting image of your dad." We hugged most affectionately, and she insisted that although she had only seen my father once, we were identical twins. She then suggested how Peter, on the other hand, was her father Zamparo incarnate.

We enjoyed a simple dinner and spoke mostly in Italian. At times, my cousin briefly improvised with English to ensure I had fully grasped a few things getting a bit drawn out. My cousin's brother, Vittorio, joined us rather late. Almost immediately, he complained about being a slave to his job at the bank. Once at the dinner table, in a somewhat jealous tone, he mentioned the great benefits Italian employees enjoyed, and how the Swiss would never have them, at least not in his lifetime.

Afterwards, our chat in the living room was quite lively. However, my aunt was the first to abandon us. She claimed she had to head off to work very early. We three eventually got on to life in the U.S. My cousins appeared eager to discuss all things American. This, of course, included movies, music, politics, and President Nixon's resignation the year before. My answers created more in-depth discussions, and some general aspects were compared to life in Europe, or, at least, how things got done in Switzerland. Vittorio was next to leave, having some papers to review, and so Angela and I continued our chat a bit longer.

The following morning, Angela took me to the Art and History Museum. It is impossible to recall how we got on to the subject of Vietnam. It may have been because I mentioned falling in love with Thuy. My cousin stated the Vietnamese had been through a horrible war, and she did not hesitate to blame the U.S. According to her, in too many instances American soldiers had fared no better than savages.

Those words hurt some! Yet they were delivered by a cheerful and serene person, at least that was my impression. According to her, too many horrific atrocities had been carried out in both North and South Vietnam, mostly through our bombing campaign. Were Americans at all aware of what they had done? I felt a need to mention that Jane Fonda had certainly attempted to speak out. However, both the media and TV quickly silenced her.

A bit later, we strolled around the lake. The sunny weather brought out the best features of the city, providing an impressive view. I also enjoyed my cousin's immense knowledge of what we were viewing. One of the sights that quickly grabbed my attention was the splendor of the lake and the far-off Alps which appeared to be crouching in the background enhancing a natural soft charm.

It was late afternoon when we returned home. Angela asked me if I liked jazz. Now this was music that was still quite foreign, even though a bit had passed through my ears years back. While she put something on, my eyes took in her immense collection of LPs. There was a huge variety of American music along with some classical. Here was everything from Beethoven to the Beatles, and many familiar names, Ella Fitzgerald, Ray Charles, Chet Baker, and even Liberace.

How strange! Did we not have choices galore in just about everything back home? So why was my interest in music limited to one genre? It seemed only right to inquire about her appreciation for all music. Angela informed me that Switzerland only had one radio station. Consequently, it had to please everyone. You could very well hear Bach, followed by Edith Piaff, or the Who, maybe Johnny Cash, and just about everything under the auspices of music.

My cousin asked if I liked Nat King Cole. It was somewhat embarrassing to admit that I was only familiar with the name. She put on an LP and said the tune now playing reminded her of me. Well, it began rather slowly and with a somewhat touchy feeling. I felt the need to look at the album cover. The song was "Nature Boy."

My how those lyrics grabbed my attention. A request to hear them again made Angela smile. Soon enough, a bit of reflection occurred as the opening line spoke of a child who was shy but wise. I felt like those lyrics were speaking directly to me. But gee, would I ever really be wise?

Oh well, my stay in Geneva came to an end rather quickly. One day, Peter called, and as we had just chatted a week before, I assumed he was just checking on me again. There was some real news to be shared. Everyone but our grandmother had returned to the villa. She remained in her town claiming a bit of solitary confinement would do her good. Although this would never be the case, as constant daily visits from some elderly and overfriendly townsfolks kept her company.

Peter then informed me he was returning to the U.S. He would be leaving in a few weeks. I was debriefed that Alessandro had returned to Barazzetto. Apparently, he and our mom had spoken on the phone, and they were obviously back on good terms. Peter had also taken the initiative to share with them my long years of drug use and my struggle to find some peace of mind. They both agreed to help me by providing some crucial support to ensure a successful return to a normal lifestyle.

Even our mom got on the phone. She sounded happy and in good spirits. So, that very evening, my news was shared with everyone. That is why a few days later my wonderful vacation in Geneva terminated, and I again boarded a train, this time heading back to Milano.

Chapter 91

Villa Rossi is not far from the town of Magenta. This town is associated with a famous battle fought there when Italy began to seriously strike out for its independence from Austria. It, too, is rather small but much bigger than the one I was returning to. It was a rainy grayish day when Peter and Alessandro picked me up at the train station.

We chatted as we headed home. It felt good returning to the villa. And having done some research, Mr. Rossi confirmed what I then related. That his home, once a real monastery, spurned out silk to be sold on the clothing market. According to our driver, the monks were surely a busy lot, but so was the Vatican. He very happily informed us he was rather proud to live in the house which had long ago been purchased by his parents.

My mom and I hugged for a while. Of course, she demanded information regarding her sister and family. After a lengthy chat, I eventually took myself upstairs to my room. Peter soon joined me and spoke of his decision to return to the U.S. He claimed there was no future for him in Italy. Why, he even admitted to never feeling really at home. He had made no friends, had never gone on a date here, and often longed to return to the Bronx.

The following day, we resumed our usual daily activity. It would continue for two more weeks. That morning, I confided to Peter my concern over my hair. My brother, who still had quite a full scalp, and had recently cut it short, admitted that mine was certainly in dire straits. Why, he even referred to it as Custer's Last Stand. Later that day, as per my request, he performed the same tune-up our dad had so happily introduced me to long ago.

It was on a Wednesday when the four residents at the villa headed to Malpensa Airport. My brother had lived in Northern Italy for six months. Although he had cemented a good rapport with our mom, and even Alessandro had accepted him (though at times they butted heads), it seemed like his take on it was that of mission accomplished. It was time to move on.

And he looked fantastic! He was dressed impeccably smart, although casual, and was an attractive young man. A few of the girls about were certainly admiring him. Much too soon we two embraced and said goodbye as he boarded an Alitalia flight to JFK. We promised to keep in touch and had even worked out a schedule to communicate when the coast was clear. Once my brother was gone, we three returned home.

Chapter 92

My former walks were replaced by jogging. For someone who had always believed in both physical and mental health, I had taken too much time off, especially as a sailor. Every morning saw me on the main roads running slowly between the small towns. This ritual was only forsaken when the weather failed to cooperate and if it rained excessively.

One morning, once back from my run, Alessandro guided me to a room behind his office. Against a wall under a closed window was a long rectangular wooden box. It was quite dusty. He pulled a latch, and presto, there was a rowing machine, which he pulled out. It was an old paraphernalia, but it worked perfectly and so became part of my routine when I returned back from my runs.

A few days later, we two headed off to Milano. Mr. Rossi had an engagement with his veteran's group. WWII may have been somewhat far behind, but the ex-soldiers celebrated coming together often throughout the year. My destination, however, would be the U.S. Consulate Office, hoping for some positive information regarding the possibility of being able to work in Italy.

We swiftly arrived in the city. Mr. Rossi parked somewhere near the Piazza del Duomo, very close to his mechanic's shop. He had grown up there, and so he knew the area rather well. At his mechanic's shop, we were greeted by a short stout individual who looked a bit rugged, spoke to us most cordially, and had even extended his forearm to shake hands, not wanting to dirty ours with his. Later that day, it was revealed to me that it had been his wife who introduced my mother to Alessandro some years back.

At some point, Alessandro and I synchronized our watches and agreed on a time to meet back at the shop. Not far off was Il Duomo. It is no doubt the most splendid example of a Gothic church in Italy. I froze in my tracks. That light but uplifting structure was so captivating and impressive. Its slim architectural elegance prepares one for what it houses within.

Upon entering, I felt a need to kneel-down. Here was a vast shiny attractive marble floor which ignited the words of a lovely poem from my school days. Once I walked down the center aisle, a strong feeling of serenity enveloped me. I am not a religious man, yet my soul was enthused by everything, especially the elegant columns on both sides which rendered my presence small, in the immense scheme of things, but not at all insignificant, just a part of some grand design.

Eventually it was time to move on, and I carried a sense of optimism with me. The staff members at the American Consulate were polite. An elderly woman spoke to me and confirmed my biggest fear. As a U.S. citizen, it was quite difficult to work in any member nation of the European Community. My quest for work seemed futile unless one was highly skilled in some unique profession. In this case, a firm would willingly incur the imposed extra cost of hiring an outsider.

While listening, a staff personnel who had joined us noticed my passport. She began looking at it and saw my place of birth as the United Kingdom. She stated that as a British citizen, by virtue of birth, things changed a bit. I could apply for a British passport, and being already a Brit created no problem with the U.S. It would allow me to reside and work in Italy. Wow, for a moment, finding out I was first, of all things, a British citizen, sounded incredible.

It was great news! Yet, something in me did not feel right. After all, I was a naturalized American, with some Italian still in me, but absolutely nothing British. Then, the employee holding my passport added, "Well, being born to Italian citizens, if you reside here, you may be required to do military service." That certainly created a problem. A U.S citizen swearing allegiance to a foreign country back then was not possible.

What a circus of circumstances! Here was someone with a Bronx accent, wanting only to reside on the very soil he had once inhabited, but maybe as an Englishman or, if possible, as a Yank. Oh well, I soon left and headed to the nearest coffee shop. I forgot my liver issue and had a grappa with my coffee, and then remembered I had occasionally confronted some rough seas and somehow always got to shore safely.

Back at the mechanic's shop, my ears were treated to a bit of the local dialect, Milanese that came from one of the other mechanics and two customers. In our little town, it was all one ever heard, quite contagious, and always spoken with a slight delayed sense of passion. Unlike Sicilian, which to me came off as a bit crude, this language had a mild tone, one with a slight Asian incantation but a French intonation.

My news, good or bad, was soon shared with Alessandro as we headed off to a restaurant. He strongly suggested not being exposed to going into the Italian military. He believed it was just a waste of time, and an entire year at that. His advice was to be patient a bit longer for he believed things would fall into place. Oh well, it was now time to eat.

We went to a restaurant he sometimes frequented. Once inside, we were immediately accommodated among what appeared to be mostly businesspeople. Of course, most were sharing loud jargon regarding work but not in the local dialect. Alessandro revealed some news from the veteran's meeting for they had agreed to less meetings, something all were for.

A waiter came over, and Alessandro ordered a wine. The wine was brought to our table, uncorked. Then once opened, a small bit of wine was poured into his glass for approval. It was not given. My very composed companion was a man of all seasons, and he certainly knew wine, and this had been exposed to air. He assumed the cork may have had a defect, making the wine rather flat.

Immediately, the proprietor came to our table to make amends. He soon returned with another bottle, which received a favorable vote. We now drank a Barolo, and while my knowledge of wine was practically zero, my eyes opened some and my gut was cheering. It was a bit dry and a tad bitter, but so pleasing to the palate, which made it difficult to limit my consumption to just one glass.

Mr. Rossi appeared in his proper element and was a real gentleman. The man carried himself with pride and dignity, but his manners, joyful mood, and his sense of humor always stood out and were truly appreciated. We enjoyed a great meal and a pleasant time. The gentleman informed me that I was very welcomed at the villa, and he hoped I would remain. But he then, using a serious but favorable tone, mentioned my aggressive behavior with my mom in Barazzetto. He looked at me and stated he was certain it would never reoccur.

My most sincere guarantee came forth. I excused myself for that mad escapade, expressed how awful I felt when remembering it, and the issue was buried immediately. We raised our glasses and drank to my future, while I thanked him most kindly. I felt so fortunate. For the first time in a long time, something convinced me things would turn out well. And wasn't I in really good hands? Here was a man who was not even my stepfather, yet he treated me like his favorite son.

Chapter 93

In July I had made plans to visit my aunt, mom's youngest sister, in Salerno. We had spoken via phone on one occasion when she insisted that I vacation there for a while. We agreed on a date, and so I decided that Salerno would come before returning to Palermo.

Before my departure, we three at the villa attended a party long in the making. It took place at a restaurant on the outskirts of Milano, and the cooperative weather gave us a warm and rather pleasant evening. We were a good number of people, all friends of my mom and Alessandro, who wanted to meet me. Someone in our crowd chose the tables outdoors under a lovely wooden roof off to the side by the restaurant's entrance.

All was proceeding well with introductions and a few words. However, we soon confronted an unexpected dilemma. Out of the blue, a colony of pesky mosquitoes attacked us most viciously. They appeared intent on making life miserable for us, and everyone began to fend for themselves as best as possible. Yet, we refused to heed the waiter's suggestion and move indoors. It was a fight we had self-imposed, and there would be no shying away from it.

A slapping contest soon blossomed. Occasionally, folks were even slapping whoever sat next to them to try to be helpful. It was a tough clash. Those bugs were getting the best of us, and perhaps it was the wine which motivated us to not surrender. Then, quite unexpectedly, our aggressive enemy simply vanished, leaving us feeling relieved and hoping this truce would hold.

Our meal began with an abundance of appetizers. It was followed up with a taste of small portions of various dishes of pasta, and they were all so good. Right about then, the gentleman sitting across from me, an accountant by profession, asked about my growing up in the U.S. This allowed me to briefly summarize life in the Bronx, but I kept it clean, and I even mentioned my love for American football. The sport was practically unknown back then in Italy.

Eventually, the years out at sea were included. Here too, with much censoring, I highlighted various jobs worked and some of the places in Asia my ships had taken me to. I received compliments regarding having experienced so much at such an early age. Then, the mechanic, who was at some distance from me, asked how Italy was treating me. Well, life was just grand, was my reply, but it would be so much better if I found some work.

Right about then, something peculiar struck me. What an odd mix we were! A mechanic, an accountant, a shop-owner, two office employees, and of course, everyone accompanied by their spouse. Our union seemed to defy something Mr. Rossi had recently shared with me. Italy was deeply steeped in strong traditional customs, and very hierarchical in terms of people interacting with each other. Full integration across different classes or professions was practically unheard of.

Apparently, this table defied tradition. It was my mom's contagious laugh that made me grasp our reality. Here was the matron at the villa, a cook, a fanatic for cleanliness, a simple woman, but most importantly, the key person in Alessandro's life. And yes, it was she who had given him access to most of these folks, professions excluded, for it was who they were which really mattered. I now fully grasped something peculiar, how you carry yourself may always be your biggest asset.

Chapter 94

My train was still quite some distance from Salerno. A few thoughts of my childhood in Barazzetto had just resurfaced. That is why my book was put aside. Consequently, out came a magazine I had purchased that morning at the train station. Perhaps browsing through it and enjoying photographs of military action would maybe get me back on track.

Since my only year in high school, the Second World War had become my sole interest in military history. It sort of put a spell on me. On the front cover was a picture of the German general, Heinz Guderian. He looked so brilliant. He possessed a set of falcon eyes, alert and sharp, and he wore an expression reflecting his own importance, which certainly proved him right in military matters. His uniform adorned him perfectly and elevated the man to the highest standard of great generals.

The article spoke of his early commitment to the use of the tank in modern warfare. He had truly understood its role and, even more importantly, the need for speed of troops and machines in attacking, something soon categorized as blitzkrieg. Quickly thereafter, while totally emerged in my reading, there was a small distraction. An elderly woman had entered the compartment. After settling herself in, she began to casually look my way.

The lady was elegantly dressed. Upon entering the car, we had simply said hello, perhaps more so with our eyes than voice, whereas now we caught each other's glance. She asked me if my interest in the magazine was simply about the general or history per se, or the war and its horrible consequences. I claimed it was history in general that fascinated me, but there was no denying my addiction to that specific period.

She heard my slight accent, inquired about it, and so we soon spoke English. It seemed a bit unreal, but the woman began narrating her days in Berlin before the war concluded. Her vivid recollection, particularly the fear instilled by the daily bombing raids which had decimated the entire city, soon had me rapt with interest. According to her, life was a nightmare as living conditions had drastically deteriorated. Food and water were scarce, almost nonexistent, and the shelters were completely overrun. Lots of dead bodies were constantly carted off and buried.

People sensed the entire world sought Germany's annihilation. However, no one truly wanted to surrender. She had even begun to pray daily for some miracle to make things right. But in those last days before the capitulation, everyone knew the war was lost. Once again, Germany had been defeated. Nevertheless, Goebbel's propaganda did revive them, but also, the Fuhrer's spell held them captive as a message of resistance had been delivered by him. In that man's isolated mind, the impossible did not exist, and all needed to simply believe and obey.

It was fascinating to listen to history by an actual participant. Getting such descriptive details of everyday life seemed incredible, but my traveling companion then shocked me. She admitted having been a member of Hitler's administrative staff. She had seen him from a distance on several occasions but had never actually met him. And when I referred to him as a madman, she appeared a bit surprised and responded, "History shall be the judge of that."

This truly puzzled me! I had a bitter taste in my mouth. Here was a very charming and intelligent person, obviously well-educated, poised and serene. But she had just made a most sinister remark. It was better to change subjects. I dreaded having to discuss a man who was so evil. It was the general who was mentioned again, and my admiration for him, especially as he certainly did not share any guilt of the mass human carnage. He had even been highly respected by most modern historians.

My companion soon excused herself and returned to her newspaper. A long period of silence followed, but she spoke again before arriving in Naples. She was heading to Capri, and she affirmed her love for Italy and the Italian people. It was a country cleverly clinging to its past while chugging along craftily and doing well in keeping up. Whereas her country had its foot stuck on the gas pedal of modern capitalism, Italy participated but refused to surrender its grand origins, regardless of the progress being made.

Her statement was a bit beyond me. I asked the woman for an example. We had practically arrived, and so she flung her parting thoughts quickly. Germany, like Japan, had been pulverized by the war. Consequently, its culture, traditions, and outlook were buried and would never resurface, at least not to the same level as before. In Italy, however, one could still see and breathe a harmonious lifestyle which slightly changes from city to city. This was true freedom according to her. In Germany, everything was now the same everywhere.

She soon left and so did the train. In no time at all it pulled into Salerno. And perhaps it is necessary to inform you how my aunt went from the very northern tiny town of Barazzetto to the somewhat overcrowded small southern city of Salerno.

It was 1960 when Aunt Maria and our mom came to visit us. Peter and I had been in Palermo for several years and had completely forgotten our family up north. We were very surprised to see them and a bit unsure how to act. Upon entering the living room to join them, my brother hid behind our grandmother. She stood a few feet away from her seated guests and refused to sit. I attached myself to our aunt as if holding on for dear life. This person had been my constant companion, a mother to me, and so my head was now placed snugly on her chest. Something in me hoped she would never leave. Unfortunately, my personal sanctuary did not last. A few hours later, the two were gone.

Our mother had spoken to Uncle Luca and our grandmother. It was a process of negotiating our residency status, but no deal was reached. We two kids would stay put and were available to anyone who wanted to visit us. It hurt profoundly to witness both women leave, yet the very next day things returned to normal at home, in school, and with friends.

Sometime that year, Aunt Maria moved to Geneva. Many Italians were immigrating then, and some still to the nearby promised land, Switzerland. It was apparently just a continuous exodus as the Friuli farmlands could not accommodate all its inhabitants. No factories or any form of industry existed there yet; therefore, a lot of the locals were heading in different directions.

In her home, it was practically a ritual. Her father, an ardent Fascist and tough man, sent everyone out to work at anything at an early age. Our mom began her servitude for a wealthy family at the age of thirteen. Aunt Maria, now an elderly teen, was just joining her older siblings—Sofia, Giorgio, and Bruno, the youngest one, and of course our mom. She moved in with Sofia, whose husband had passed away, and was immediately received with open arms.

My aunt soon discovered that no "promised land" is a golden rainbow. The life of an immigrant is never easy. One may feel bedazzled by the improved surroundings, yet much too soon there is a bizarre culture to contend with, few incomprehensible traits, and a sense of isolation, especially when among the host citizens. All that luster once shining so brightly from afar darkens rather quickly.

Fortunately, there was a strong family tie bonding the sisters and brothers. Aunt Maria soon found work in a beauty salon, along with other newcomers. There she improved her French, began appreciating some of her customers, and developed a healthy attachment to her co-workers. This led to weekend outings mostly to explore the city and engage in a passion my mom also had—dancing. It was on a dance floor where she met the love of her life.

The man was a southern Italian from the city of Naples. Now racism is not always associated with skin color, for the northern and southern Italians were worlds apart, and their color had nothing to do with it. Anyhow, although the times practically forbade the union of a southerner and a northerner, my aunt and future uncle immediately knew they would never separate.

Sure enough, that bond resembled a modern version of Romeo and Juliet. For it encountered a familiar problem of strong opposition but from only one family, ours. That is right. Their biggest challenge was not their unmatched ethnicity, today so much less visible, as habits, speech, manners, customs, and different local food is ubiquitous throughout Italy. No, it was the rumblings of contentious family jargon which created their biggest obstacle.

Antonio, the young man from Naples, presented a rather severe problem. This was not the concept of southerners as, quick to anger, quick to fight, quick to deceive, and somewhat lazy. No, sir. While this northern ideology may not have been discarded in establishing the gentleman's standing, it was his name which created a family scandal. He was a Di Stefano. Here was the very name my mother had married into and found adversity, and she was not going to allow her sister to follow in her footsteps.

Nevertheless, the couple married and moved to Naples. Sometime later, they transferred to Salerno where Antonio went into business for himself. And while the two love birds had arrived with nothing but the clothes on their backs and a bit of savings, both adhered to the will to endure and love each other permanently. Their refusal to accept misery from our northern clan was as solid as their love.

That was their story—now back to mine. Once off the train, there they were, the Di Stefanos! My aunt approached with a huge smile, and we held each other firmly. This was followed up with a handshake and kisses for Uncle Antonio and two lovely children, Alessio and Stefania.

We rode home in a tiny car. There were many and all navigating through some very narrow streets. Once we arrived at their apartment and settled in a bit, my aunt dove into some fond memories of our wonderful past. She recalled me falling and burning my arm, and how horrified she felt while out searching for the mailman. Then we both touched on other stories, and my take on things was that Barazzetto had given us two kids some great years in starting out, after which I included a bit of what came next, in summarized fashion.

We rehashed a few more tales over coffee the following morning. Later when we separated, my aunt and her children headed out for air and movement while I took myself to the city center. It was on to see a bit of central Salerno but also to pay a visit to my uncle's shop. Upon entering, my eyes were testimony to some incredible works of art. He made picture frames. He had just finished one, and it looked so perfect. There were tons of incredible paintings on canvasses with frames that seemed to revive the art. Everything from modern to abstract art, and some incredible scenes of the Amalfi coastline and its lovely towns quickly penetrated my curious spirit.

I revisited there most mornings. And while that man certainly kept busy, we always found a bit of time for Italian politics. He chirped away while working and I chipped in. At times, we disagreed about the nature of things in Italy. To me, the Italians lived well, complained continuously, and deprived themselves of nothing. However, there was one issue we both saw eye to eye— the inability of the present government to tackle terrorism.

A group called the Brigate Rosse was almost a household word. These young criminals would strike at random and appeared invincible. Perhaps they held a political initiative, but their killings labeled them as terrorists. There were also Fascist elements to contend with, yet they appeared more like street gangs than politically motivated groups. While nothing was resolved in our discussions, regardless of our great intentions, we certainly did not lack solutions, and some were vividly debated as we headed next store for a cup of that enhancing Italian ritual, espresso, which we both drowned with lots of sugar.

Chapter 95

Well, Julian Di Stefano, or Giuliano, as everyone called me, was again a happy camper. Living in Italy had quietly taken the wind out of my restless sails. And yes, a direction or some clear sense of where my future lay was still missing, but for the moment I harbored a love for all things and a belief that everything would ultimately work out.

Time flew by. After two months in Salerno, I was heading south to visit my other relatives. They had been expecting me to arrive more than a month ago. Undoubtedly, when humans find their comfort zone, the notion of abandoning a happy nest which feels like home or a home away from home seems impractical. Oh well, in no time at all, the train arrived at the tip of Calabria.

It was while watching our rail cars make it onto the ferry to cross over to Sicily that it hit me. Mr. Rossi had once said, "Italy is like a third world nation, and nothing will ever change." It was a rather harsh statement. Of course, I was clueless and quite ready to discard it. However, now, while watching the present operation, which took forever, it did feel slightly antiquated for a European nation considered modern and competitive.

My train eventually got to Palermo. Once at my grandparents' place, we casually resumed our roles. I was again welcomed while informing them I would remain for the rest of the summer. Neither of my grandparents demanded to know anything about my stay up north and so it was never shared. As in my first days upon arriving, my visits to the area by the cemetery resumed, after which it was on to the beach.

It seemed like such gorgeous weather had followed me to Salerno and to Palermo. Practically every day had me enjoying the calm Mediterranean waters, and once again enjoying the pleasure of reading in Italian. My mornings began with a visit to Claudio. This was Peter's friend, and he usually placed flowers in various vases and attending to his customers. The guy appeared all business with each of his clients, but once a purchase was made, he displayed a rather playful side which enhanced everyone's presence.

Our chats included some information regarding my brother. Claudio was certain Peter was better off in New York City. Italy was simply not for him as life here moved much too slowly. Plus, unless one had connections who could guarantee results, you were destined to remain at your current job for a lifetime.

Claudio's father arrived unexpectedly one morning. He looked me over and knew immediately I was Adrian's son. My resemblance to the man he had grown up with intrigued him. He informed me that as teenagers they were inseparable, and both had done unthinkable things during the war. They separated once my father was called into the Navy and was stationed in Venice, after which he returned home but soon headed off to England.

According to the man in front of me, my dad had a huge heart. However, on the downside, too often, he was at war with the world at large, even with the Almighty himself. In a grueling instance, my father was getting beaten badly in a fight. His opponent had him down on the ground and completely blocked, yet my dad grabbed his leg and sank his teeth into it and almost came away with a piece of flesh. He stood up looking down at his adversary, now in agonizing pain.

After this narrative, the man insisted on having me for dinner that weekend. The family was far from well-off, but the meal put together was worthy of the many compliments I offered throughout our long culinary session. From appetizer to dessert, it again hit home that Sicilian food was truly outstanding, and the Sicilians were a very generous and kind people.

On the following day, I had just returned home from Cefalu when my grandmother approached me. She gave me some unexpected news. My mother had called. It was surprising to hear my grandmother's casual attitude in describing their brief but warm chat. Well, at least in a couple of Di Stefano households, the woman was no longer the evil Knievel of old times.

I called the villa, and it was Alessandro who picked up the phone. He was happy to hear my voice and let me know it was he who was seeking me out. Apparently, some American military personnel were coming to the villa, and he feared a communications problem. Although not terribly concerned about the visitors, Mr. Rossi thought my presence would help a lot. He had spoken to a colonel a few days back, in Italian, and it left him feeling somewhat uneasy.

Apparently, a group of U.S. soldiers were coming to take possession of a large library. Well, rather than questioning him to death, I promised to return that coming weekend, cutting short my holiday. My mother then came on to inquire about my vacation. She got a bit of daily life in Palermo and was reassured I would soon be among them.

Consequently, my new agenda forced me to visit everyone rather quickly to say goodbye. My summer vacation which had just entered the first week of September was closed. The traveler in me was on the road again via first-class rail.

Chapter 96

Mr. Rossi and mom picked me up at the train station in Milano. They had made reservations for a late lunch at a nearby restaurant. Afterwards we spent some time roaming around the area and even enjoyed another espresso. On the highway while heading home, my hosts were again demanding more facts about my stay, as they put it, "abroad", which helped diminish my present level of concern over the excessive speeding.

At the villa, I was shown the library in question almost immediately. It was located in an area behind Mr. Rossi's studio, the right wing of the monastery. He opened a door and turned on the lights. The entire room, quite huge, was inundated with books on various shelves, accumulating dust and starting to show their age. They were also contained in boxes scattered about against the expansive walls.

The owner was Alessandro's cousin, Tomasso Taisamario. The man was a historian, and apparently an avid reader. He was also the author of several books. Each book thereabout was associated with some period of history. Some were about WW II, and a few dealt with the Italian resistance that strongly came alive toward the end of the conflict. The library had been entrusted to Alessandro by his cousin when the man had moved to Switzerland. This was part of a tiny exodus by a few wealthy Italians who feared the rise of the Communist Party, which had become a powerful political force.

Mr. Taisamario had now reached the latter years of life and decided to donate his entire library to the U.S. Army, mostly because he had remained thankful to our military for having saved Europe from Nazism. He was also grateful for something he had never forgotten—the initiative to feed the starving masses in certain parts of Italy—especially in very needy and remote areas, for food was truly scarce. Apparently, he now deemed it only right to give his treasure to the United States.

The historian arrived on a Thursday morning. He was accompanied by his lovely administrative assistant. It was the day of the move, and they had driven from Lugano, the Swiss canton, which had been formalized in the late nineteenth century and where Italian is spoken. Once on the premises in the villa, it was the charming Swiss woman who immediately fell in love with her surroundings and was given a small tour.

Our guests were then accommodated in the living room. Mom served espresso and grappa and was the only one not to partake in the ritual. Perhaps Mr. Taisamario was a man of few words, but he spoke highly of my mother, right there in her presence. I asked his opinion about NATO's future role in Europe, seeing how much he revered the U.S. military. He smiled and said there was one thing he now knew for sure, American soldiers would never leave Italy.

It was an hour later when the villa's very loud doorbell rang. I excused myself, exited the house, walked to the front area of the mansion, and opened the large wooden entrance gate. Two officers neatly decked out in their green military uniforms smiled as they stood by their car. We introduced ourselves and shook hands. I opened the larger gate-door, anticipating the entrance of the military truck behind them. But soon it was apparent it would not pass the low curved ceiling over the door.

One of the officers then spoke to a sergeant standing behind them. He and a couple of soldiers by the truck would take a break, and so they very happily took themselves to the nearby corner coffee shop. We three entered the villa and Alessandro joined us. After introductions and some translating, we agreed the cargo would have to be carried out to the truck. It was now time to join the others.

Our guests were both colonels. The taller gentleman came from the American Embassy in Rome. The other officer had flown in from the U.S. and was stationed where the books would go to, Carlisle Barracks in Pennsylvania. They complimented the splendid surroundings and the house as we slowly moved indoors.

Naturally, I addressed the officers in English, then translated in Italian to everyone. The colonel from Rome began using his Italian, rather slowly and with some difficulty, yet we all communicated just fine. My mother was again serving espresso and grappa but not everyone was on board. We discovered that U.S. military personnel cannot drink while on duty. The two elderly Italian men among us were shocked! Both insisted this would cause a revolution if proposed to the Italian military, especially the Alpini, who basically live to drink.

Eventually, we men headed to the library. The officers briefly revisited their plan, and once we exited that area, we were now standing in front of the huge villa. As the main large door remained open, the multitude of people outside passing by and stopping to admire our surroundings stood out. Undoubtedly, much was being discussed about the soldiers, and perhaps different theories were being proposed. For sure, today Mr. Rossi's home was making the local verbal headlines.

The colonel from Pennsylvania now consulted the sergeant standing by the villa's entrance. Then the three soldiers on standby began their mission. We returned to the living room. It was the officer from Carlisle Barracks who asked me if I lived in Italy. I first claimed being a permanent tourist, but then my real circumstances came to the forefront, emphasizing the difficulty of working as a foreigner.

The colonel from Rome suggested joining the army. He appeared serious and thought I could perhaps be stationed in Italy. I was a bit surprised. Until recently, I had always believed the U.S. military was mostly in Germany with few, if any, in our backyard. The colonel spoke up, proudly informing me the army could provide me a great career, and if I were not happy with military life, once my tour terminated, I could go back to being a tourist.

My mother's ears perked up. Perhaps she had grasped very little, but something regarding my future had been mentioned. Apparently, her English had not fully perished. When the officer mentioned the benefits of the G I Bill, the idea of a college education certainly struck a chord with me. The colonel even revealed he had left home at an early age, a bit clueless about anything, but wanting to serve in the military. He happily stated he never regretted his decision.

That is when my mother attempted to speak some English. She was not faring so badly. Had she heard correctly? Giuliano could be a soldier here in Italy? Even Mr. Rossi, with no knowledge of my language, perhaps hearing the word NATO, had certainly begun paying attention. It was as if a solution to my circumstances had just been proposed. But joining the army was the furthest thing from my mind.

Several hours later, all those books were ready to travel. The military crew took their leave. So did the two colonels who were both heading to Rome, one back to work and the other to enjoy one more day abroad before returning to Pennsylvania. The officer from Rome had given me his calling card and invited me to stop in at the embassy if ever in the city.

Since the mission was accomplished, our Swiss guests also moved on. We three resumed our daily activity, and that evening went out for pizza. It was over a glass of wine when Alessandro questioned my interest to work for NATO as mom looked on. In their scheme of things, the word had a sort of mystical tone. Both appeared to be watching me closely to see my reaction. Well, without making any definite statements, I promised to consider it and stated that I thought it impossible that Italy would be my military residence. Who could tell where they would send me.

My two consiglieri were not buying it. Hadn't the good colonel given me his calling card? Surely, he meant to help in some way. Mr. Rossi touched on the issue of the one-year obligatory duty in the Italian military, which he again categorized as wasteful. Whereas he felt rather certain that working for NATO was a different ball game. He now asked me if something had been mentioned regarding school or an education.

I felt trapped. Oh well, our delicious pizzas arrived and so we moved on to the pleasure of food. Later that evening in my room a sense of isolation plagued me. Reading was always a pleasure for me, but tonight one thought strongly implanted in my mind stood out, I was certainly not soldier material or in any way military oriented.

Chapter 97

I was out jogging early one morning. Our small town was soon far behind me. Not having slept much or peacefully, I questioned working out at this hour. Soon a fragment of my dream early that morning flashed back. It was a scene from the movie, *The Bridge on the River Kwai*. In it, a British colonel swiftly cuts the throat of the frightened young Japanese soldier in front of him, for the British soldier at his side had been frozen in place and unable to do it.

Further on, while trotting at a steady pace, various thoughts began to plague me. My trip to the consulate office came to mind and how they had proposed getting a British passport through the English Embassy in Venice. It could open a door to employment. Now a different situation had presented itself—the army. Just what the hell would I do in the army? Hadn't Alessandro thought something would surely come my way sooner or later? This certainly could not be my future. Julian Di Stefano, a soldier?

My jog accelerated while I was running through my dilemmas. Perhaps my stubbornness was now blocking my wisdom. Who could say? It suddenly dawned on me, too much thinking is unhealthy, and as my impasse left me, a scooter approaching from behind sounded their horn to warn me of its proximity. I turned to get a glimpse of the rider, and my head managed a graceful nod to a very gorgeous smile from a pretty young girl probably heading to work in one of the nearby factories.

I was now running fast but eventually slowed down some. Perhaps this morning I was putting in some overtime, mentally and physically, and then it fully registered. My goodness, Julian had been standing still too long. Shit, I had not even gotten laid in almost a year.

Chapter 98

1975 was coming to an end. My grandmother was still in Barazzetto. Perhaps she was enjoying her sleepy town and the company of folks her age. Some who would stop by daily for a brief chat or to play a game of cards.

My visit was made to keep my grandma company, knowing Mom and Alessandro would soon join us. I found the lady of the house napping in her favorite sofa by the wood burning stove. She appeared so serene, perhaps somewhat regal, like nobility subdued on their throne. She was certainly the queen of her surroundings, and this town had been her domain since birth.

My gentle tug of her shoulder slightly broke the spell. She was surprised and so happy to see me as we shared a few words. We stepped out to fetch some wood from the nearby shed to feed the fire in the ancient stove. She inquired about my trip to Salerno and was anxious for news about her daughter and family, and soon questioned why they never came up north for a visit.

Once back in the kitchen we made plans for dinner. I would help with the simple meal she proposed. It sounded good enough. Then, my grandmother complained a bit about all her sons and daughters being so far away, one in Milano, one in Salerno, and the rest in Switzerland. Plus, her dilemma here at home was having to go use the phone at the bar in the center of town, the only one available. At times, she remained in the phone booth a bit too long, and someone would be standing by waiting and looking her way as if to insinuate, haven't you said it all yet?

Oh well, such was life in the mid-nineteen seventies in our small Friulian town. And to some extent, it was pretty much the same throughout all minute townships in Italy. Yet, just like my grandma, one simply went through the motions and soon felt somewhat satisfied having accomplished the task at hand.

Mr. Rossi and my mom eventually joined us. Apparently, the duo had quarreled in the car and were now avoiding each other. Nothing new there. Mom could be prolific in arguing, and it always led to a silent period which never lasted too long. Nevertheless, the couple had a solid relationship as they had been together a very long time.

Early the following morning, Alessandro invited me to tag along with him to Yugoslavia. My invitation was to take the ride and enjoy the scenery and the company. Once there, Mr. Rossi would gas up, for petrol was super cheap there, and he claimed he never passed up a good bargain. If I recall correctly, he was off to Gorizia and would then cross over into what is now Slovenia.

I declined, and that surprised him. My passport had brought about my decision. Somewhere in one of the back pages, instructions specifically prohibited visiting countries the U.S. had no diplomatic ties with. There was Cuba, Vietnam, and, of course, Yugoslavia. It felt wrong to turn down Alessandro, for his company was delightful, yet the idea of a fancy hammer and sickle stamped anywhere on my passport concerned me.

That morning, I chose to walk rather than bike. The Friuli countryside is lovely and has a variety of small towns scattered about. Often all one sees is a tractor coming from or going to the fields but hardly any people getting about in the towns. As a kid, my eyes had always witnessed an engaging group of local farmers heading out to the fields together, super talkative, and quite ready to pass judgement on the town's news. My, how things had changed.

Once back home, I found my mother ironing. My grandmother was not present. A goulash was cooking. The fragrance was so good, and Mom stated that once her mother arrived, she would be the one to make the polenta, a food I was beginning to like. Soon enough, my grandma was among us and shared news about one of the old farmers in a nearby town being terribly ill. She began to cook that bread substitute, and we soon sat to eat.

I expressed my curiosity over Alessandro's trip. My excellent rapport with the man simply flowed out. He treated me like a son and was a world of knowledge and a fun person to be with. My grandmother mentioned she had remained especially grateful for assisting her and mom, when my grandfather, who was afflicted with gangrene, had to have both legs amputated.

Mom then mentioned that Alessandro could be a bit stubborn. Almost immediately, she added that compared to what she had experienced with my father, he was a saint. Now perhaps my words were delivered too quickly. I stated that my father was a difficult person, however, he had intended to start a family when you married him, no? My words had specifically stated, "His intentions were good." They were barely delivered when my listener disagreed.

My father had only married her because he was forced to. She was single and pregnant by him. The man risked being forced to leave the country had he chosen to not marry her for she would have informed the authorities. It sounded preposterous, but more news followed. Dad had given her some liquid concoction to drink to terminate my existence. And she drank it. Obviously, the task failed, but the woman had been poisoned, suffering agonizing stomach pains for several days. Mom then finalized her narrative with "I thought for sure I would die."

I sat there quite mute. My grandmother's expression confirmed she had heard this story before. One detail which was not mentioned was that I, too, bore the brunt of their foolish decision. Oh well, at times life is a sheer chance, a toss of the dice. Perhaps, it is merely a detachment from a spiritual energy cruising the universe. Arriving in a body by any means is the objective. My mom eventually placed her hand on my shoulder and said, "You are here. That is all that matters."

Chapter 99

In December, we all returned to the villa. I felt extremely restless. Even reading was a slight problem for it was difficult to concentrate very long. Some strange dreams were again hounding my nights. The latest one was incomprehensible.

One morning, after my jog, I found my grandmother in the back of the villa. She usually tended to her small garden there, but now the ground was frozen. We chatted, and she wondered where our turtles were. There were four or five in the back of the house, but they had been underground for some time. Almost immediately, one of their past performances came to mind.

Peter and I had witnessed a huge male turtle demanding an accommodation. It continuously bumped into the back of a female turtle and persisted until the chosen mate came around. It took a while, but that horny turtle never stopped trying. Eventually, the male mounted the female and began making these soft lengthy screeching sounds. It seemed like the turtle was struggling to keep going while its neck protruded from its shell. Once the mission was accomplished, each critter went its separate way. Today I felt somewhat like that desperate male turtle, only minus someone to pound into.

Alessandro came over. He suggested we take in a movie that evening. He handed me the Corriere Della Sera and the task of choosing a film. I took that newspaper, which frustrated me, for it felt I was reading some ancient language that I would never master. A few minutes later, once back indoors, I looked over the movie section and chose The Eiger Sanction. It starred Clint Eastwood, who also directed it. He was my past hero from an old TV series called Rawhide, which was big at home in the Bronx.

I also noticed an article in the paper that caught my attention. It was about the leader of the MSI, the Italian Fascist party. This was Giorgio Almirante, one of the few icons from the Fascist era, and someone Mr. Rossi truly admired. According to what was written, the politician was keen on blaming most of Italy's problems on the system, a useless parliament, and the incompetent governing political party. He also insisted Italians had lost their patriotic spirit, and discipline had been replaced by love of money and TV.

Once through reading, I headed off to the living room. The newspaper was cast aside for an unexpected urge took over me. My cousin Angela had given me an LP that I had yet to listen to. Classical music was still somewhat foreign to me, and this was Dvorak's "Symphony for the New World." After making myself comfortable on the couch, the music took over.

What an incredible symphony! From the very opening to the powerful ending, it never let go of me. The first movement would explode into some overpowering orchestral bits, and then it would cascade into soft, almost timid pieces, which made me think of something Angela had told me. One could visualize and almost feel the power of nature, like waterfalls cascading or the stillness and beauty of vast forests.

It was so true. Once the music concluded, there was a warm feeling in me, as if a huge stone had been lifted off my back, allowing my body and spirit to feel much lighter. After putting the record away, an instinct within quickly arose. I would join the military. Later that evening my announcement was made. My grandmother had chosen to stay home. We three sat in a restaurant enjoying our wine when Mr. Rossi and my mother seemed a bit mystified, almost as if they had witnessed a miracle. Alessandro insisted mine was a wise decision, and he happily offered a toast. We drank to my new mission as both my hosts seemed to be in sheer heaven. Yes, it was time for me to move on, but right now, we had a movie to go see.

Chapter 100

My conversation with the soldier on the phone, who was knowledgeable and polite, went rather well. He was the local recruiter at the army base in Vicenza. Apparently, there were a series of placement tests to take which would determine the kind of work I qualified for. If I accepted the work offered, based on the results, I would serve a few years in the army.

Then came some more details. My first mission would be to attend basic training to learn fundamental soldiering. It would be followed up with the AIT, the Advanced Individual Training, which would prepare me for my line of work, and then an assignment to a military base followed. Based on his knowledge of army regulations, he was rather certain it was impossible for me to be stationed in Italy, my country of origin and where I presently lived.

That is why I called our embassy in Rome the next day. My voice may have surprised the colonel. It took a while before stating the reason for the call. Yet, the officer remained neutral, and never committed himself to any promise, but he continued to express his joy with my decision. He even assured me that military life would reward me tremendously, especially if I returned to school. The officer sounded so positive, but not ready to come to my rescue over my base assignment.

Our conversation came to an end. It seemed imperative to me to continue with my plan. If Italy was not to be my duty station, so be it. And who could say, perhaps Germany would welcome me on board. Being a soldier seemed so far from who I really was, but what the hell!

Chapter 101

My mother's oldest brother had invited us to Marseilles. Uncle Giorgio had been living there for ages. It was the latter part of December when four of us were on the road to southern France. Alessandro had made hotel reservations for he believed we were too many to invade my uncle's flat.

My uncle was a chef and very fortunate to have a few days off near Christmas. He insisted that he was being compensated for having forsaken any vacation for years. And believe me, both he and his wife were delighted to spend a few days showing us the city, which, if you must know, did not impress me much.

At home, my uncle was the cook of course. His wife smiled and mentioned, "It's what he does best." He certainly cooked up a storm every day, especially for the holiday, which was soon behind us. The man returned to work but had apparently made some plans for New Year's Eve. Perhaps my apparent restlessness was being attended to. Mom informed me I would spend New Year's Eve with some people my age at the home of my uncle's boss.

Not much other information came my way. I was delighted to be with younger folks to bring in the new year. And so, late afternoon on December 31st, my uncle and Alessandro drove me to the city's suburbs. We parked in front of a large fancy-looking house. I was introduced to the family members, mom and dad and their daughter, Marlene, who was assisting the maid with a final touch at the dinner table.

My host did not speak a word of English, or perhaps it is kinder to say her English was equivalent to my French. Yet, it felt best not to panic, at least, not just yet. A bit later, Marlene's parents departed, her dad to his restaurant and her mother to a family gathering.

Soon after the parents exited, Marlene's friends began to pour in. They consisted mostly of couples, including Marlene's boyfriend. No one spoke a word of English. Yet these folks were talkative, laughing wholeheartedly, and appeared a great bunch. I felt quite left out, but my will to give it my best remained intact. It seemed only right to take a-not-so-great-situation, fiddle with it some, and make finalizing the year a passable scene.

Our food was served by the elderly maid who appeared friendly. Large trays full of clams, oysters, and mussels were served. Not a bad way to start and accompanying such delicious sea life (very dead), someone put on music which immediately took hold of my attention. It sounded like folk music, yet somewhat poetic and very French. I made a gesture indicating my appreciation, and one of the girls showed me the cover of the LP. The singer's name was Georges Moustaki, and the record was *Le Meteque*. I made a mental note of the album title to eventually purchase it.

The feast continued as we ate and drank plenty. My wine consumption knew no limits, and many hours later, we finally terminated the long-lasting delicious meal with an assortment of mouthwatering pastries. Soon came coffee and some after-dinner liquor. Then, rather unexpectedly, we were grabbing our coats, leaving the house, and piling into cars. It seemed a bit odd, and in my most perfect Italian, I demanded an explanation.

Marlene pointed to her watch. Perhaps she was insinuating we were late and may have said so. It was the couple sitting next to me, in the back seat, who both announced "Party." Our drivers were obviously anxious to arrive at a destination, wherever that was. They sped through the French countryside and on some rather narrow roads. At times, it felt like our car would slide right off them into the dark farmlands coasting us.

In no time at all, Aix-en-Provence was just a few kilometers away. Our cars slowed down once we entered the city itself. Midnight was fast approaching as my guests appeared to be searching for an address. Marlene attempted to enlighten me, but her words were put aside. I suspected we may have been lost as our cars were moving very slowly, and all eyes were glued on the houses nearby. We continued and soon turned into a street where a large crowd of folks were assembled.

This avenue was practically empty of vehicles, but not people. Apparently, everyone around us was preparing to celebrate the coming new year, now just a few minutes away. We stopped, got out of our cars, and joined the excitement. It was contagious. People were blowing into party horns, chatting away wildly, and some, with champagne bottles in hand, were passing glasses to those around them. A bunch of children were running wildly while parents appeared on standby, and all seemed happy with the night's magic.

A loud boom suddenly went off! It was like a signal giving consent to begin the hugging and kissing that followed. I happily joined in, and although it sounded silly, my "Viva la France" was happily accepted, along with handshakes, kisses, and the very passion of the moment. It all felt so natural, and what stood out were people's eyes, overloaded with happiness, believing a new and better tomorrow had just arrived.

Soon after, and feeling somewhat energized, we resumed our journey on a different road. It was not long before we pulled up in front of a huge mansion and parked on the front lawn. There were so many cars everywhere. We strode behind the mansion and entered a small house which was actually a party room. It was huge and certainly overcrowded, and the lights had been dimmed. An avalanche of young people quite lost in the wildness of the moment were dancing to the sound of loud pop music. My evening friends soon melted into the fray. I stood for a minute or two before someone came over and offered me a glass of champagne. My "Merci bucu" earned me a big smile. Then suddenly, I saw her.

Not far off was this beautiful angel. She was not very tall but had cascading hair, a gorgeous face and a complementary body. Her smile radiated. What a way to start the new year, so I thought, but at times, my shyness does me in. While my heart may have slightly panicked, my mind insisted on moving in, hoping for a pleasant encounter. So, I introduced myself in English, and believe me, it worked its magic.

A very bright and infectious smile followed. Her eyes sparkled while she made a sign with her hands. This did not immediately register with me. But after she followed up with another one, I now understood she was mute. The dazzling young lady took me by my hand and brought me across the room. We both faced another incredibly attractive person who was laughing and talking with someone.

This was Adele, the sister of the young lady still holding my hand. She spoke perfect English. She officially introduced herself and her sister, Brigette, who could neither speak nor hear but was well versed in English and so we could communicate by writing. Then Adele excused herself and soon returned with a notebook and a pen and said, "This is a good start."

Now I am no Shakespeare, but there is no holding back an inflamed heart. Monsieur Julian felt like a sturdy vessel heading out to sea, its course set, and its sails properly adjusted to the winds around them with no adverse weather anywhere in sight. My mind was an arsenal of fun ideas which became my ammunition to gently bring on board this beautiful spirit now a captive in the vast and playful ocean around us.

Once again, I was in love! Brigette's inner beauty glowed vividly, and so did everything about her—her smile, reflective eyes, slow and delicate moves, and beautiful literature. She bewitched me completely, and it felt exhilarating. We were off in a corner all to ourselves scribbling volumes of warm and happy messages personally dedicated to our hearts. No sooner had she expressed herself than my response brought a unique smile to this beautiful individual.

Our notebook was soon filled out to the max. I went searching for anything to write on, but I failed and eventually returned with a roll of toilet paper, having discovered the bathroom was well-stocked. Her smile and dancing eyes encouraged us to resume our unchartered script, bringing us even closer in heart and spirit as the morning rolled away on its own. We were simply glued to each other's hearts.

It was soon 4:00 a.m. Someone from my group came over to inform me we would now return to Marseille. Well, I could not possibly just leave. We three located Adele in order to work out a plan that would allow me to see Brigette again. Although I was scheduled to return to Italy the following afternoon, some unforeseen arrangements could certainly be made, like taking a train back on my own.

It was Adele who gave me some rather sour news. Brigette was in a relationship and had been with someone for years. Her boyfriend was away serving in the military. My happiness deteriorated immediately. Perhaps my disappointment showed as I began slowly shaking hands all around. I also parted with a friendly kiss to both girls.

Somehow my body managed to exit the party room. My face, parting unhappily, must have advertised the wound within. Oh well, I had survived a previous knockout in the Bronx, so being romantically pierced was no foreign scar to me. Anyhow, our group drove back to our city in silence. I thanked everyone upon arriving at my uncle's place.

It was at that moment that Julian or Giuliano suspected the new year could bring some disappointments, although no clear problem stood out. I had struggled with drug addiction the previous year. Now a less destructive malady challenged me. A strong feeling of loneliness coupled with a lack of female companionship, was taking me down a peg or two. Maybe a change of scenery would somehow help. Who could say if serving Uncle Sam would bring some stability in a profession and a place to call home? It all seemed so simple but just so far away.

Chapter 102

In the new year I set out for Vicenza. It seemed best to arrive prior to the testing date at Caserma Carlo Ederle as Alessandro had spoken so highly of the city and its charm. He had even mentioned the name of Andrea Palladio, totally unknown to me. Apparently, the man's splendid architectural works had strongly influenced Thomas Jefferson. It seemed worthwhile to take in a few sights.

Once there, the person at the train station's newspaper kiosk told me how to get around. He disclosed which bus to take to the base, and frowned when asked if one could walk, yet informed me it was doable and would maybe take an hour. I headed toward the center of town where my hotel was located. My plan was to check in and then explore the city.

I first encountered the old city wall which once protected its inhabitants from invaders. It was then on to Corso Andrea Palladio which runs through the heart of this small but very attractive city. On both sides stood captivating medieval buildings, reminding me of this nation's Renaissance glory. The solid structures and their pleasant designs imparted a sense of stability and enduring tradition, sort of like being well-anchored to something.

Just as noticeable were the many stores in the area. There were fancy clothing and coffee shops, electronic and music stores, and all seemed to fit in so appropriately. Even the main delicatessen neatly displayed a variety of tempting cold meats and cheeses. Everything was laid out in an eye-catching fashion.

A feeling of déjà vu hit me. It made me feel connected to a far-away past, long gone, yet strangely still present. Once off the main road, I found myself in the piazza, that civic spot where human activity still flourishes and will always remain on the go. Andrea Palladio's Basilicata stared at me. Yes, this was the city hall of its times, which now confirmed Alessandro's view—there was an incredibly gifted energy behind this man's works.

I began to wonder if spells of artistic greatness arrive by chance, or are they simply echoes of many past baby steps? Italy was a treasure-house of excellent antiquity, capped in a blanket of artistic sensuality and architectural stability.

My hotel soon came into view. It was tucked away in a remote corner close to the city plaza. After checking in, and even confirming it was possible to walk to the base, I took a stroll to see more of the city and find a place to eat.

As a true Sagittarian, my restless legs always impose their right to fully explore. While moving on, and contending with quite a crowd, I spotted something a tad sinister. On a side street, there was an infinite number of tiny cars parked, some even on the sidewalk, as if it were the private property of the car owners.

Nevertheless, all the buildings and some of the fancy new shops there were still worth taking in. I eventually stopped a well-dressed passerby to inquire about a good restaurant. The elderly woman with sparkling eyes suggested avoiding restaurants for the few available were very costly. Her suggestion was to try Righetti, a trattoria by the main post office behind that gorgeous piazza.

Just so you know, a trattoria is less formal than a restaurant, but more formal than an osteria. The latter is simply a place to drink and have a sandwich or two. I dashed to Righetti, which had once been a pub but had been remodeled to a rustic, fashionable place to eat. It contained several individual cozy rooms attached to a large area where the kitchen was located. It ran on a self-service basis, which had me feeling quite at home.

I found a seat at a large table with several professional looking workers. They were fine with me taking the empty chair, and so then it was on to get silverware, paper napkins, and bread from a nearby area. The moment I placed all my items on the table, one of the occupants indicated that if football was of no interest to me, they would all sound a tad boring. They were assured I could be a good listener.

In the kitchen area there was plenty to choose from. Behind a large glass counter various dishes were already prepared, or ready to be handed out by the head chef and his assistant. Several plates of spaghetti with Bolognese were placed on the side, and as if on cue, three customers were there to retrieve them. The assistant cook informed me there was a bean soup ready to serve, or more pasta would be ready in ten minutes.

The bean soup was fine with me and served immediately. Before leaving, I requested a pork chop, which was tossed on the grill, and the assistant cook smiled and informed me it would need ten minutes. I took a glass, filled it with red wine and headed back to the table.

The guys there were all business, that is, sports business. It was Vicenza Lanerossi, the city's football club, that was being scrutinized, analyzed, and slightly chastised. One of the guys sounded like he knew the players personally. Knowing little besides how to play and having difficulty deciphering the dialect, my mind concentrated on the tastiness of the soup.

Eventually, my meat was ready and with it I was also given some Brussel sprouts. As I carried my food back to the table, something puzzled me. Just how was the bill settled? It was revealed by the football experts that you simply went up to the cashier and told him what you had consumed. Upon finishing my meal, the cashier heard me out and rang up the bill. It was not at all expensive. How very civilized this seemed to me.

I returned to my hotel, and it hit me how the place where I had eaten did not resemble anything in the U.S., the country I had left behind almost a year ago. I felt a sense of longing for it. Oh well, the military service would bring me back.

The following morning my eyes opened at 5:00 a.m. I read for a while and sometime later went out for a walk. The empty streets and stillness all around filled me with a sense of personal morning glory. At around eight o'clock, I checked out of the hotel, grabbed a cappuccino and croissant, continued my walk to my destination, and arrived about half an hour later.

At the gate stood a carabiniere alongside an MP. The MP escorted me to the entrance booth and checked my passport. He then called the recruiter who arrived quickly. Perhaps it was half hour later when my mind began to struggle with various aptitude tests, which seemed even more challenging than the GED back in St. Mary's County. There were also three soldiers, in uniform, retesting, hoping to improve their scores.

If upon arriving my confidence level had slightly soared, it had deflated once departing. Fortunately, right outside the entrance to the base was a bus stop. You see, walking invites my thinking, and at that moment it seemed better to abstain. Soon enough the train station was in front of me. It would be temporarily bypassed for I planned to walk to Monte Berico and feast on what Mr. Rossi had defined as "the interesting view of the city."

I tackled a long series of infinite steps to ultimately reach my objective. The scenery was a bit peculiar but not so grand. From a distance, Vicenza appeared to be napping. Perhaps because the presence of its inhabitants and traffic gets hidden by the splendor of the city's narrow shell, very silent, still, and surreal. However, a most positive feeling lit up within me as I glanced at the nearby church. It sponsored a slightly mystical touch reassuring me that I would certainly return. In the meantime, it was back to the villa to await my results.

Chapter 103

The call came one morning while I was out jogging. Upon reentering the villa, my very excited mother notified me to call a number left by "the good sergeant in Vicenza." She didn't offer any more information as she had difficulty understanding his English.

Well, the news was not so surprising. My scores were rather low; however, it was incredible to hear that my math results were outstanding. It was a subject that had never appealed to me. The army was offering me the possibility to attend a finance course at Fort Benjamin Harrison in Indianapolis. It would qualify me as a 73C20; that is, a Finance Specialist. It came with a commitment requirement of four years. I would complete basic military training, also referred to as boot camp, at Fort Dix in New Jersey. After that, the city of Indianapolis awaited me, and, finally, I would be off to my permanent duty station.

There was nothing to think about. Why, if I declined, my mother and Alessandro would have shot me. I was in great physical shape and of sound mind. Plus, a spirit willing to test the unknown boundaries of my new adventure was driving me onward.

Some weeks later, in March 1976, my wonderful hosts escorted me to Malpensa Airport. For a slight moment, something in their serene attitude made me think that, perhaps, they were responsible for my new migration. We hugged and said our goodbyes, and I must admit feeling a tad nervous, I flew out of Milano to JFK. Apparently, crossing the vast oceans was becoming a small part of my unique odyssey.

Once in the air, almost immediately a Bob Dylan tune came to mind. It reminded me that I am probably bound to just keep moving on.

Part 5

Chapter 104

My first week at Fort Dix was similar to those few days in Brooklyn, when I was waiting to leave for Piney Point. Only this time, the uniform color was army green, both in dress and fatigue uniforms, along with the familiar khaki shirts and pants. We newcomers passed our time filling out all sorts of forms and soon got our heads razed. And just when everyone was getting a little too comfortable, it was time to move out.

We were ordered to secure and pack all our clothing and personal belongings. Then, about thirty of us reported to the sergeants in the parking lot behind our building. They informed us we were about to see the "real world of soldiering" as a few old school buses, referred to as cattle buses, pulled up. Some of us may have been apprehensive about our new destination and what life there would be like, but we had gotten this far, so there was no turning back now.

Our buses traveled about a mile and then headed into a parking lot. There, several drill sergeants anxiously awaited us. The very moment the vehicles stopped, two drill sergeants ran onto our cattle bus and started screaming like madmen. The thunderous and crazed command "Get the fuck off my bus," was continuously belted out.

This screaming forced us all to instantly grab our stuff and make a mad rush to the bus door. We moved to the tune of insults and furious verbal assaults. They lined us up into several files, and it was apparent that our drill instructors desperately hoped someone would say something out of turn or forget to include "drill sergeant" at the end of any reply while being grilled.

Believe me, there was hell to pay when someone screwed up. However, this theatrical farce did not intimidate me in the least. One well-known fact was that they could not touch us. And even if they did, so what? I had been schooled in the art of getting hit at an early age, and by the best. I now felt slightly intimidated but certainly not at all concerned about whatever they could dish out.

We were ordered to place our duffle bags over our heads. Absolutely nothing was to remain on the pavement. This forced me to put my small personal bag between my legs and then grab the duffle bag and raise it up in the air. Although the one being held above me was not so heavy, holding the other one, small as it was, became a bit cumbersome and created a problem in balancing myself. Plus, there was a sergeant screaming in my face.

Did they know just how long we could hold out? A few guys were having problems with their bags, including yours truly, and once two guys dropped theirs, the highly animated instructors hit their tilt button. They insisted we were the lowest scum, perennial shit, men without dicks, and so on. Then they told us to drop our bags, open them, and empty their contents onto the concrete pavement.

One of the drill sergeants off to my right began kicking about the clothes in front of him. Another one joined in, and soon enough, this was their new distraction. I felt someone's presence behind me, and he soon faced me and yelled "I smell weed!" The nutty bastard continued with this absurd insinuation. He bent down and began to diligently search my belongings while mumbling some verbal rubbish.

He then threw my clothes all around. Now just what was this madman looking for? Once he unzipped my shaving kit, the guy flew into a rage and insisted I turn over the grass. Though I was slightly annoyed, not a sound left my sealed lips. After all, as I had no reason to believe such foolishness, my composure remained intact and my mouth continually shut, which the angry sergeant did not appreciate one bit.

My accuser, Sergeant Johnson, was a Black man, and I mean black. He looked me straight in the eyes and said, "I know weed when I smell it." And although he decided to abandon his fruitless search, he warned me that he would be watching my every move, which forced me to make a mental cautionary note to keep out of his way.

The ritual may have lasted more than an hour. Eventually, the harassment, now a bit less intense but still overplayed and quite redundant, came in lower tones. We were being assigned to our barracks, the many bungalows behind us. But first, a fit and athletic-looking drill sergeant with a serious killer smile on his face asked if anyone wanted out of his army.

This seemed like such a stupid question. Yet three soldiers immediately raised their hands. Back in our previous quarters, one of them had been constantly bragging about life on the streets of Philly, and I had foolishly thought the guy could eat nails.

Chapter 105

By the end of March, Ft. Dix was not super cold, but spring still seemed far off. Our alarm clock was a drill sergeant coming in around four, turning on the lights, and screaming a morning tune at the top of his lungs. It always included mentioning our mothers, who had shamelessly put us on the planet. And believe me this got everyone up.

Being an early riser, I was almost ready for this morning ritual, and it got me out of bed rather quickly. What we then faced was not so easy to grapple with, but eventually, we all did. Our drill sergeants marched us over to the nearby sports field while the morning was still pitch-black, and the stillness around us reminded me it was too early to be doing anything. They ordered us to remove our clothes—hat, gloves, field jacket, and our shirts—and we placed everything on the frozen grass. It was not so terribly cold, but the wind reminded you it was still winter.

A sergeant standing by began our morning exercise drills. We did quite a few repetitions while several other drill sergeants kept tabs on us. If they were not happy with anyone's performance, that poor soul was forced out of the formation, made to "get it right" under some close scrutiny, which usually led to even more exercises until you "got your shit together."

Once we finished with our workout, we began jogging as a single unit with one of the drill sergeants leading us. This run, referred to as "the airborne shuffle" was nothing too demanding at first, for the formation moved at a slow pace, singing cadence along with the sergeant in the lead, and we would soon venture off quite a way from the sports field. Eventually, the sergeant leading us picked up the pace, and soon enough we began to run pretty fast. When satisfied with our progress, our leader slowed down, resuming that shuffle pace and song, finally finishing where we had started. It was a five-mile run, but it never felt too long.

Every one of us was thoroughly drenched in sweat. We began to dress, putting on our practically frozen clothes, and it did not seem like a smart thing to do. Nevertheless, they marched us to the mess hall, and no one gave it any more thought, for food replaced a large portion of our misery. But a week later, most soldiers in all the units were seriously sick with severe lung and throat infections.

I woke up one morning thinking I had died. My body was inflamed and ached terribly. My throat was so dry and painful, and my chest was full of phlegm which shot out at random every time I sneezed or coughed. Oh well, it seemed all of us were coping with the same malady and on the verge of extinction, but once they had us in formation, we were warned not to go on sick call. Our unit drill sergeant, who looked like a spartan soldier and a natural born killer, laid it out in plain street language that only "pussies" went to the hospital. Were any of his soldiers, pussies?

That early morning routine continued uninterrupted. Only a few of the guys took themselves to see a medic, and we all somehow survived and refused to be branded as weaklings. I believe we may have all learned an important lesson about life as a whole. It is mind over matter. You see, those crazy drill sergeants, most of them Vietnam veterans, were absolutely right. The body should never control the brain.

For the next two months, we marched everywhere. Our drill sergeants' everlasting shouting, occasional stomping up and down, and the somewhat brutish jargon, usually over some insignificant issue, reminded us we were being prepared to endure and never quit. Yes, just like my Sicilian grandmother, they, too, were instilling toughness to prepare us for life's most daring challenges.

Soon it was time to go out on bivouac. That is, live off the land for a few days where the primary mission is survival. The actual exercise was not quite as discomforting as I had expected, and it felt like our only real objective was not to survive but to keep our rifle spotlessly clean.

Nevertheless, I woke up the first morning to a slight aching back. Plus, my entire body felt rather dirty. Things could certainly have been better with a decent breakfast. But no, sir. They trucked in stale tasteless eggs, lukewarm coffee, and other unappetizing precooked nasty crap which we all ate very diligently, but not through choice.

My tent was shared with someone I had made friends with. Diego was a cheerful Mexican guy, a few years older than me. He had informed me of his true objective back at the processing center. It was to become an American citizen. That same ritual my brother and I had accomplished so easily back in 1966 by answering a few questions and very seriously swearing allegiance in front of an elderly and smiling judge.

My companion certainly knew how easily citizenship could be obtained because his son had been born in San Diego. However, his accreditation was certainly more demanding. And we both agreed that becoming a real American took a bit of work. You see, my amigo, myself, and a few other Hispanic soldiers all shared one common trait. We did not much care for some of the things the "gringos" all around us did.

What a bunch of losers! Such overgrown babies. Constantly bitching and moaning about any task assigned, and even more so when getting their hands dirty. The only time they seemed to exude a bit of enthusiasm was when they headed to the commissary to buy candy and soda. In theory, I was one of them, having become a U.S. citizen. But in practice, it was tough convincing myself of this.

Oh well, as the weeks slipped away, most of our instructors harassed us less, however, there was still hell to pay if you screwed up. But the change in attitude was evident, and we even seemed to have a bit more time to ourselves. It allowed us soldiers to bond more easily and get to know each other better.

One evening, I called home and my stepmother answered. She was surprised to hear from me, and even more so to learn about my new status.

Then my father came on the phone. He immediately expressed a sense of horror in discovering my whereabouts, and according to him, though stated gently, I was simply going nowhere in life. Peter, on the other hand, sounded super happy to hear my voice. He promised to visit the base the following weekend. And he sure did.

Peter arrived with his girlfriend, Mary. They drove her new Mustang, and both seemed madly in love and quite right for one another. Yet, they were a bit physically mismatched, for my brother stood over six feet tall, but his mate appeared almost half his size. It was again pure pleasure to catch up with him. Only when life at home was mentioned were a few sour notes shared. Peter was again working seven days a week, but he now swore he was almost ready to move out having finally saved some cash.

A few days after my brother's visit, our unit marched to the firing range. All of us trainees were very certain we would perform well, and most of us simply could not contain our enthusiasm. After all, we were to become experts on using the M16 rifle, which was never referred to as a gun. In the military, a weapon will save you, whereas a gun is for fun.

I was unaware of it, but I was blind as a bat. The sergeant watching me fire away at the target was flabbergasted and remarked, "Di Stefano, you can't shoot worth a fuck!" This is what caused me to visit the oculist the following day. I discovered that my right eye had been damaged and was now causing the problem on the range.

This had occurred at work on my first ship. The third engineer and I had been up on deck. He was on overtime, whereas I was just carrying out one of my many duties. Our task was to straighten out some of the old bent rails, and he started using a torch, which he was qualified to handle. Now please do not ask why no goggles protected my eyes.

After the engineer heated the center part of the rail to loosen it some, he asked me to use the hammer to force it upright. On the third strike, metal fragments hit my face, especially my right eye. Some chips immediately lodged in my eye, creating plenty of discomfort which lasted for several agonizing weeks. There was no relief until we arrived in San Francisco and I got to the hospital. Using a magnetic tool, a young female doctor cleared my eye of all that metal crap.

Chapter 106

Our stay at Fort Dix was coming to an end. Diego and I were in good standing with a couple of the drill sergeants, especially our unit sergeant. Quite by chance, one afternoon, he asked us if we played soccer. What was that? It sounded like music to our ears, and not just to us two, but to all the other Hispanic guys in other units.

Folks, you cannot imagine how volunteering for an assignment was a dream come true! That very afternoon, on that familiar field where we began our morning exercise, it was us newbie soldiers against some of the drill sergeants, and as they could not field a full team, a few of our guys were on their side. My, how we all ran like crazy and gave the best of our physical selves.

It always feels divine to participate in something you love. Why, even our opponents looked ecstatic. Some showed a few good moves, especially the guys who had been stationed in Germany. Apparently, they had watched some of the local teams play and had become hooked on the game. They were now keen on proving themselves as worthy opponents.

My teammates sounded a lot like the Sharks from West Side Story. I quickly adopted to the new lingo, although some words were a bit familiar. I made some very useful contributions, having somewhat grasped the verbal messages being flung my way. Perhaps the sergeants had stamina, no doubt, but we had talent, and both teams played their hearts out, but we "non-gringos" scored big-time.

Well, our opponents certainly got a game and a half out of us. They had probably not expected to be beaten so badly. Yet they were somewhat grateful, maybe even more appreciative of who we were—young, eager, energetic, and always ready to bounce back. Although we were now short-timers, from that day on, we were treated a bit differently, and even those sergeants that were not from our units seemed to remember a few of us by our first name whenever we crossed paths.

Just as I was beginning to not completely despise my time there, my days left at Ft. Dix were now very few. And while I did not expect anything, I received a big surprise as my drill sergeant promoted me. I was now a private first class. He personally expressed how highly he thought of me. And quite honestly, Julian Di Stefano would never have expected such a compliment. I was almost tempted to ask him to speak to my dad.

That bit of good news boosted my confidence. However, there was someone complaining. And just who was making a bit of a stink? It was one of the guys who, on day one, had wanted out of the army. He was insinuating that he deserved that promotion more than me, yet it was hard to see why. He was physically big, but that was basically it. And he was even part of that Mickey Mouse club hooked on candy and soda. He expressed his frustration in front of me one day, so I told him to take it up with our drill sergeant.

It was the very day before my departure when a mystery was resolved. Diego and I were in the mess hall finishing our lunch. He would be leaving for Ft. Benning in Georgia to master jumping out of planes. From the corner of my eye, I spotted Sgt. Johnson, who had just entered the premises, and he was happily yapping away with another sergeant. Then it hit me! How could I possibly have been so blind? Why, that old dog had certainly been on to something!

His wild tantrum over weed he could not find when I first arrived now made sense. It was more than a year ago when there actually was weed in my shaving kit. Whenever I rolled a joint, some grass was always spilled, but rolling a joint over the empty open zippered case proved super useful. What had been spilled was there to be included in another joint. So yes, one day, I had removed my various items in it and replaced them with quite a large amount of grass.

Although the kit had served me well, it had also been cleaned properly. Once I was home from Jacobi Hospital, while living with my folks, I gave it a thorough washing. It even got blow dried and returned to its proper use. Yet the good sergeant's nose had been right on target. His perfect scent was only off by a year.

Chapter 107

Life at Ft. Benjamin Harrison would be very different from the premises I had just vacated. No one was going to yell orders or try to make a warrior out of me. This was very much appreciated. The soldier within was quite delighted to simply concentrate on learning a profession.

The barracks atmosphere would not change much. Yet, a less rigid lifestyle would ensue making me forget my present station in life, for I still bore a slight sense of reservation about being in uniform. And by the way, my stomach, once accustomed to food, real food, was now surviving and hoping some relief would follow after my scheduled eight weeks in Indianapolis.

The base was well-maintained. One interesting attraction that immediately caught my eye was the large number of officers from different countries, allied with ours, of course. They appeared super sharp in their uniforms, reminding me of those elegant folks in Italy—mostly office workers always looking so stylish, or just about anyone on Sunday, for that was a dress up day. Whereas, here, in my mind, my army dress uniform fell way short. Man, we looked so drab, unattractive, and just plain ordinary.

My first Sunday had me heading downtown. After two months of military confinement, seeing a bit of the real world becomes a priority, for a change of scenery, especially one that thrives on city life, is simply a must. It was the latter part of the morning when a bus took me to the city center. The plan was to walk as much as my legs would carry me, and as I now possessed a camera, I could capture some of the more interesting sites.

Now just what was I thinking? Few stores were anywhere and hardly ever in proximity to each other. The charm of souls interacting and carrying on was nowhere to be seen. Most buildings looked plain and lacked an inherited sense of construction, one which would have said "This was made by dedicated professional hands." This metropolis looked a bit too grayish and lacked its own unique city glamour. Fortunately, after a long walk, a diner provided me with a wonderful grilled cheese sandwich, a coffee, and a truly delicious cheesecake, which certainly lifted my spirits.

The next day, I began my financial training. My class kept me busy from eight to five. Then came an hour of an intense workout at the gym, which was not always followed by food at the mess hall. They closed at six, so I would occasionally grab something to eat at the club. Back in my room, I would read, but far too often, loud music shook the walls, which would force me out for short walks.

Those strolls were very brief, for there was a unique problem to contend with—a safety issue. It was something no one dared discuss as it bordered on racial tension. Quite a few White soldiers, off duty, had been mugged by Black soldiers, also off duty, right there on the base. It may not have led to any entanglements or voiced hostility, but you sensed the tension. Fortunately, things remained under control. But one simply felt a bit of hostility. After all, weren't we all here to improve our lot in life?

Soon enough, some personal frustration came my way. Not only was my locker broken into, but a few days later my camera was in the hands of three Black soldiers standing near the entrance to my room. They were unable to figure out how it worked. It did have a tricky start button that was practically hidden, and they were casually arguing that there was nothing wrong with it. Good thing my anger immediately took a back step. Perhaps sometimes a cowardly act hurts on the inside, but it may make a hell of a difference on the outside.

My school days, on the other hand, were progressing very well. Our teacher was simply the best. He knew his facts and shared them quite professionally with incredible motivation. The man was always well-prepared, highly enthusiastic, and he made the class fun. He used our time so wisely. We covered all the intricate aspects of work in a finance office, posting financial data, such as soldier's pay and allotments, disbursement of funds, and we also tackled the more complex travel reimbursement tasks.

One day, our teacher advised us to absolutely avoid working in a travel section. This work involved reimbursing soldiers and civilians for (TDY) temporary duty travel and (PCS) permanent change of station moves for both soldiers and their families. He informed us that the TDY computations were based on extensive complex regulations and prone to interpretation. According to him, most folks working in the "travel twilight zone" found it a living hell.

Once class terminated, there was nothing too exciting to do on the base. Occasionally, I caught a movie with one of my classmates. He had befriended me as soon as he discovered I lived in Italy. He was a bicycle enthusiast, who worked out religiously on Sunday mornings, and could spit out all the great names associated with the sport, many of whom were Italians. It sometimes sounded like he was pontificating about the various national cycling tours throughout Europe, a sport quite foreign to me, and, truth be told, a bit boring.

One day the guy shocked me. He admitted to being an ardent Fascist. I had assumed we soldiers were sworn to believe in and love democracy. Well, at least to some extent. Even more bizarre was when he mentioned Ezra Pound, another foreign name to me, which appeared so out of place for we had been discussing the Second World War. Pound sounded like the name of a political figure, yet I discovered the man was a poet, and a Fascist. My, it all seemed so absurd.

We may have had little in common, but occasionally we got off the base some. My mate, who was from Indianapolis, insisted I discover the beauty of the nearby outdoors. So, it was on to a lake one morning, and absolutely nothing bit my bait as my love for Italy was all he heard.

Chapter 108

One evening, as I was watching the news, a report was delivered that there had been a series of earthquakes in my mother's hometown. A phone call to Villa Rossi relieved me of my concerns. It was my second call within a few days, as on the first one, no one was home. The news on TV had shown a bit of damage from the persistent earthquakes in the Friuli region. Not too much information was given, and although my grandmother was again living with my mother, it seemed best to check on everyone.

When we spoke, mom informed me no serious damage had occurred in Barazzetto. She quickly switched topics and wanted an update on my arrival. Getting her to grasp that my return to Italy was not guaranteed was no easy task. Just the same, we did speak at length, and Alessandro was standing by listening, and eventually we were allowed to chat for a few minutes. Upon finishing, my mom came back on and signed off with "a presto", which means "see you soon."

It may have been two weeks later when PCS orders for my unit began to arrive. Now, wouldn't you know it, no one was truly happy with their assignments. Folks hoping to be stationed in the U.S. were being transferred to West Germany or somewhere in Asia. The two Asian guys, both from South Korea, were heading to Ft. Huachuca and Ft. Campbell, respectively.

Incredible! It seemed unreal, but a week later, Julian Di Stefano got his assignment to Caserma Carlo Ederle in Vicenza. What a miracle! It may have been a bit unusual, and it surely got our unit sergeant's attention. The man suspected some hanky-panky or what he labeled as "sheer nepotism", and so he began to outright harass me for information.

You cannot imagine how much this upset the sergeant. Why? Who can say! Fortunately, my stay was limited to three more days, and although a few unpleasant work details came my way, it was insignificant. Knowing my destination, my happiness came in bucketsful. After all, I had a new job, a supportive family not so far away, and a gorgeous city to live in. It suddenly felt so easy to do what the English are most famous for—keep my chin up.

The near 8-hour flight back to Italy seemed quick. I promptly arrived at my assigned base. The main entrance to our army base was on Viale Della Pace. It is very close to the neighborhood called La Stanga. Across the street stood an old grocery store and a few feet away, a movie house which showed triple X pornos. Now one would think plenty of lonely soldiers would have flocked there, but it appeared to have no customers at all.

Caserma Carlo Ederle had been there for ages. It was now my new home and would be so for a while. It seems only right to shed some light on its origins, its make-up and its purpose.

Major Carlo Ederle, who was from the nearby city of Verona, was an Italian WWI patriot and war hero. The man was beyond courageous. He was incredibly fearless and daring. On two occasions, he refused to leave the front where fighting raged wildly, or to even acknowledge being severely wounded. But his luck did not hold out. He was killed on the front line of battle at the young age of 25 in the year 1917.

The base was built in his honor. It was constructed between 1942 and 1943. It initially housed an Italian infantry regiment, then years later an artillery regiment was added, and the base remained under Italian authority until 1955. This was the year when all Allied occupational forces in Austria were pulled out. A contingency of U.S. soldiers stationed there were sent both to Vicenza and Camp Darby. The latter is a U.S. military base in Livorno named after an American general killed in action there in April 1945.

For the most part, U.S. troops had never completely left the European theater once the Second World War ended. Most soldiers were stationed in Germany, and some in Austria, France and England. But a limited number were also in Italy. It was in 1955 that the 350th Infantry Regiment, also known as the Red Knights, arrived in Vicenza. They were well-known in that area, the Veneto region, having bravely fought retreating German soldiers ten years earlier.

During my stay on the base, beginning in August 1976, there were two major military forces there, the 559th U.S. Army Artillery Group, and the 509th Infantry Regiment Airborne Battalion. My mission was to take care of their financial situation and theirs was to engage in combat if hostilities ever broke out. They continuously participated in military maneuvers with other member countries of NATO. The enemy then was the Soviet Union, which eventually disintegrated in the early 1990s.

Caserma Ederle—now don't let the name fool you—is a mini-American city. The base houses single soldiers but also maintains a housing area nearby called Villaggio Della Pace, the Village of Peace, for soldiers with families. Whereas U.S. government employees working on the base, single officers, and other soldiers not in the housing billets are all provided a rent allowance and can find places to live through the so-called housing office on the base.

The base is huge. It has a chapel located near the entrance, a supermarket called a commissary, and what is equivalent to a small department store known as the post exchange. There is also a cinema house, a cafeteria, a gym, a large sports field, a couple of banks, a library, a hospital, clubs, and the University of Maryland. And to ensure all the comforts of home, you can even find plenty of junk food in a couple of eateries. Now what else could one possibly need?

Chapter 109

I signed in at my barracks, met the unit captain, and was eventually given a room. The accommodations here were not much different in substance from those on my ships, but the room was large and had four bunks located in each corner. I took up residence next to an empty locker after getting linen and towels, then I changed into military clothes and went to the finance and accounting office.

Once inside the two-story building, someone at the counter escorted me to the sergeant-major's office. He, in turn, immediately brought me upstairs to meet the major, the officer in charge. Both soldiers' eyes expressed their happiness to see me, and the major claimed they desperately needed people in the travel section. That is, the very branch my ex-instructor had warned us to avoid at all costs.

Apparently, that entity was losing a key figure—a soldier now preparing to return to the states. They had a heavy workload and needed more people. What could I possibly say? My smile may have perhaps misled them, but my silence spoke volumes. Nevertheless, that very line of work became my new position. Of course, the major stated he was certain things would work out just fine. And so, a few minutes later, after a brief introduction to others in nearby areas, I sat at a desk in that branch. Oh, let me mention, two Italian civilians from the accounting branch were there. After seeing my last name on my uniform, they greeted me in Italian, and so you could say it was like a true homecoming.

Two people in that section were Flavio and Sergeant Rump. The Italian gentleman was a local national. Such is the title of all Italian employees working on the base, and it seemed that by virtue of seniority and experience he sort of carried the workload. A few minutes later, an Italian woman arrived from her coffee break. She, too. worked there, and so began explaining her administrative tasks. Believe it or not, after a quick run-down, she began to complain of a headache and left on sick leave.

Sergeant Rump was officially in charge of the branch as of the previous day. He seemed completely lost in his work and spent most of his time reading various regulations to better understand the computations prepared by Flavio, who had worked there for years. It was impossible to not notice how the sergeant's desk was inundated with vouchers and other forms and stacks of papers, along with several thick volumes of regulations. It looked so very disorderly.

The soldier who would train me, the very one to soon depart, was off that day. He had spent the previous night on guard duty at the barracks. Well, neither of my two co-workers were sure what to do with me, but the ailing employee, before abandoning us had mentioned that the travel cards needed to be filed, and that was pretty much how I spent my first day at work.

It was sometime after six when I finished and returned to the barracks. The soldier on guard duty by the entrance door introduced himself and asked if I played soccer. My positive reply prompted him to bring me over to the bulletin board to point out a sign-up roster, which he had previously signed. It was for the SETAF company soccer team. And that was exactly who now owned me, both body and soul—the Southern European Task Force.

I distinctively recall being told that soldiers who came from foreign countries could not be stationed in their country of origin. The names in front of me read like an Italian sports team; Liberatore, Mazzei, Formica, Mazzotti, and others. I was not sure if they were American Italians or Italian Americans, yet it certainly felt good as those names convinced me that Julian Di Stefano would fit right in.

Chapter 110

A month after my arrival, a few startling incidents occurred. The many tasks in the branch kept me super busy, but one early afternoon the ground under me trembled. My desk, chair, and I shook, as apparently some exterior natural force was flexing its muscles.

It concluded rather quickly. I immediately realized it was an earthquake. The soldiers around me stared at one another while noticing the accounting personnel running out of the office. By the way, Flavio had also moved just as quickly as they. Now every soldier throughout the office began to move away from their desks, yet we awaited orders, for at times such is military foolishness.

Suddenly, the sergeant-major arrived and screamed, "Everybody out!" There was an immediate dash for the doors, this being a few minutes after the previous exodus, which of course gave the Italian workers standing outside a good hearty laugh. Someone even said, "Hopefully they move more quickly in combat." It seemed only right to agree but not join in the raucous laughter.

Approximately a week later, Bianca arrived. Our female co-worker had changed jobs a few weeks after my entrance. Now please do not make assumptions. Anyhow, Flavio was super delighted to see her go as he claimed she was either at home ill, or when at work, unhappy with her tasks and always complaining. That is why he was now interviewing candidates for the vacant position, and the last person was this very attractive young lady.

The girl was slim but well-built and had dark seductive eyes and long cascading brown hair. Throughout that interview, it was difficult to not occasionally gaze in her direction. My best attempt may have lasted a couple of minutes. She eventually left and gave me a grandiose smile on her way toward the door. Oh, I was tempted to run after her just to escort her back to the entrance to the base.

Flavio eventually hired someone else, but a few months later I spotted her in the parking lot near our office. This time it was impossible to not zoom into action. She happily informed me she now worked at one of the offices close by. My happy soul sputtered a few words inviting her to share a coffee later that morning. It would entail a brief walk to the Italian mess hall where, at ten a.m., all the Italians on base were having an espresso or a cappuccino.

Bianca gladly accepted. However, she insisted we go to a nearby coffee shop off the base. So later that morning, we met. She drove us off the base, and our time together was both rewarding and endearing, as we laughed plenty while getting acquainted. We had to return to the base rather quickly, and it felt like we had run right back. Now what can I say! Yours truly was once again in love. Soon enough, our encounters became a wonderful daily ritual.

I boarded a train going to Udine that very weekend. Mom and Alessandro met me at the train station. They had been in Barazzetto at Grandma's for over a week. We three began to cruise the city to look for a place where my mother could purchase a new pair of glasses. Alessandro found parking in an area abounding with shops, including a store that sells glasses, and after a casual walk, we decided to stop at a bar they both liked for an afternoon drink.

Mr. Rossi ordered three glasses of Picolit, a very distinguished Friulian white wine. The gentleman behind the counter, a rather talkative chap, was now blessing the great weather we were enjoying as he attended to our glasses. While listening to the chap, a rather peculiar light sound, hardly audible, came to my ears. It made me think someone had just turned on an engine in the area below us. The chandelier began to rattle, and the ground began to shake. Our bartender, like the tardy sergeant-major, screamed loudly, "Tutti fuori!"

My instincts ordered me to run, but my body struggled to move. When the pavement under your feet begins to tremble, you can't go anywhere. Thinking the end was here, my mind's only concern was survival at all cost.

Fortunately, the earth calmed down. Nobody was hurt, and no apparent damage was visible in the premises around us. We three and the few other customers quickly made our way out of the bar. My mom was quite ready to chat with some of the now fleeing survivors, but Mr. Rossi insisted we get back to the car and go home.

A few days later, back at the office, work was truly demanding too much of me. My main responsibility was processing the PCS travel. This entailed attending a weekly in-processing session inside a large room adjacent to the chapel. There I filled out travel vouchers for the newly arrived personnel and their dependents, if they had also moved, and then all those vouchers came with me to the office.

Unfortunately, the system was stacked against me. A bus with a large number of soldiers assigned to SETAF, plus their family members, would arrive from the air base in Aviano every Wednesday afternoon. The following day, the in-processing session began at 2:00 p.m. It was inside the chapel area where a series of desks were set up. Each soldier stopped at one desk after the other, and for some strange reason, ours was the last one they visited.

Everyone appeared rather tired and a bit bored. But as the expression "money talks" bears out, myself and Todd, a guy from one of the other sections in our office who assisted me, were treated very friendly and with a degree of importance as we accommodated the soldiers in front of us. We first collected all their pertinent financial documents and then filled out their travel vouchers. The process seemed to take forever.

We never left the chapel before seven. My assistant would return home to his family at the Villaggio Della Pace, whereas the office awaited me. I would compute the vouchers for payment on the following day; such was the office policy. Consequently, my Thursdays terminated around ten thirty in the evenings. I had forsaken dinner as once I was back in my room, I went straight to bed.

Another important task required reviewing TDY vouchers which had been computed and needed to be processed. Sgt. Rump had either checked Flavio's computations, or vice versa. I needed to acquaint myself with the work done, ask questions, and then type the computation from the work sheet onto the voucher to be paid. Once through, all the documents were brought to the disbursement branch for payment.

Now my questions were endemic. And whereas Flavio supplied brief answers, Sgt. Rump would show me the applicable regulations, and if a new question came up, he would usually get back to me whenever possible. Once those vouchers were out of our branch, we had completed our task. But there was a cog in the process. Our customers never went directly to the disbursement branch first, although a payment date had been provided. Some first came to check on the status of their payment. At times, not all payments were ready on the day promised.

These constant interruptions soon began to frustrate me. Going to the counter to assist someone deprived me of precious time to fully learn other functions that were part of our work. Plus, some itineraries brought a misery of complexity with them, and the applicable regulations applied to make a legitimate payment were based on some very challenging reading material.

There were also visits from soldiers located outside of Vicenza as they had no administrative staff. They needed to be provided with a voucher and required help in filling it out. They often inundated me with too many questions regarding their TDY travel. And once their voucher had been filled out, most soldiers wanted to be paid immediately as they were not all stationed near our base. These interruptions put my regular work on hold as I attended to the matter at hand.

Sometimes, while I was assisting a customer, my phone would continuously ring. Different office personnel throughout the base had a question or needed assistance in preparing travel orders for itineraries with unusual circumstances. There were also situations where the unhappy faces at the counter were customers dissatisfied with their payment. A few would even demand to see the applicable regulations before finally accepting that they had been paid properly.

You can imagine my happiness when a new employee arrived to replace the woman that had left us a while back. She spoke very little English, so Flavio and I communicated with her in Italian, but she caught on quickly and worked accurately. More importantly, she had a pleasant attitude which allowed me some peace of mind while still being pulled one way or another.

So, stepping out to meet Bianca no longer made me feel guilty. However, returning to my office was not always a pleasant experience. Bianca and I now met briefly, both for morning and afternoon breaks, but she was not available after work hours. This frustrated me. After laughing wildly and enjoying each other quite nicely, even if only for fifteen minutes, how could she move on? As the workday terminated, my soul felt burdened over this bizarre arrangement.

Fortunately, unlike my nonexistent love life, the soldier within was faring well. Outside the excessive office work, my military life was in tip-top shape. I worked out at the gym with light weights and jogged around the sports field on a two-mile track at least three times a week. And my love for football, or what we Yankees call soccer, had me on that same field quite regularly to improve my skills.

Our team consisted of a few sharp players. They not only played well but were also fun to chat with once off the field, and just like me, some guys had Italian last names and had grown up in the U.S.

On the first day of practice, it was agreed that we would have a strong defense. Our two forwards were fine, the mid-center field held up okay, and I, along with the other full back had sworn no one would get by us. Believe me, hardly anyone ever did.

During a match, I would sometimes get carried away. Intercepting the ball came rather easy, and it seemed only right to fly off to the other side of the pitch, try to score, or pass and then assist the forwards in scoring. It was difficult to pass up such opportunities. However, Sgt Rump, our goalie, would immediately bitch and moan. He insisted I was hogging the ball and not showing good team effort by just staying put on defense.

After one of our first matches, a carabiniere befriended me. He worked on the base and was impressed with my playing. When he heard me talk his native language and discovered my last name—he was also a southerner—we soon became rather close. As a matter of fact, he invited me to join him daily for lunch at the carabinieri cafeteria, which happened to be right next to our barracks.

His mess hall became a place to enjoy some great meals. And it seemed best to arrive as lunch was finishing, for this was not my place to eat, and I followed the same rule for enjoying dinner there. The meals came at such an affordable price and were prepared by expert hands using all fresh produce. In the evenings, the cook dished out plenty of food not wanting leftovers to contend with. Such were a few additions to my daily routine now, and I had no complaints whatsoever.

Chapter 111

The year seemed to terminate rather quickly. A few Italian employees from the payroll office and the accounting branch staged a Christmas party at a nearby restaurant. Incredible as it may sound, Bianca happily accepted my invitation.

Our rendezvous occurred in front of the base on a Saturday in the late afternoon. We met, and Bianca drove me home to meet her mother. It was quite unexpected but fine as there was ample time before the engagement began. Although this gesture initially baffled me, it generated a hope that maybe some progress was finally being made. I discovered that Bianca's dad had passed away many years ago, and she and her mom lived in an area close to the restaurant we would be attending.

I was surprised to see Bianca's mother dressed in all black. At first, she was a bit quiet, yet soon enough, the lady of the house began to open-up a bit. Perhaps she felt more comfortable with me, and so she spoke but strictly in the Venetian dialect. It was the language she mastered, which Bianca certainly knew but never used, and although I understood it, it was not my forte.

Sometime later we left. All proceeded well. The food was excellent, the social entertainment was engaging, and the young lady at my side was nicely accepted. Later in the evening, someone suggested we head off to a disco, and so we did. This allowed me to dance with Bianca and a few other girls, and it was sometime after one a. m. when we all separated.

My night out on the town had gone well. However, it soon still felt like a real date with the person whom I loved so dearly was still light-years away. Anyhow, I returned to the villa to celebrate Christmas and New Year's Eve. During the first holiday, many of Alessandro's family members came over. Of the various guests among us, it was Adriana, Alessandro's oldest sister, who impressed me most. She was a woman of few words, yet she mesmerized me with her glorious eyes and casual brilliant chats.

Year-end was an entirely different affair. This time we joined Alessandro's brother on his large estate, not too far from the villa. This feast consisted of some family members and plenty of their friends. Even my grandmother participated in the festivities for part of the evening. There was much merriment, quite a bit of drinking, and a few hilarious guests who simply could not contain their need to entertain. My, how we laughed hysterically most of the night and into the following morning.

Overall, my mind gave the old year a positive vote. My personal life was not faring so badly after all, having made some friends, being somewhat well settled in at work, and maintaining a great relationship with my folks in Italy. And, unfortunately, I had even fallen in love. Perhaps with the wrong person? Who could say? Yet quite unexpectedly, this one-sided romantic puzzle took an unexpected turn a few months into the new year.

Chapter 112

It was early spring. One evening I was with my new roommate, Frank. We were downtown in a record store looking at an endless number of LPs. Some were quite familiar to us both and we purchased a few. He picked up Led Zeppelin III and IV, while my eyes insisted on Jimi Hendrix's Greatest Hits.

Soon enough, we were happily heading off to Righetti for dinner. It was once we turned a street corner that Bianca stood in front of us. She was just a few feet away and with someone, a male someone. The much taller gentleman had his left arm extended across her shoulders, and both were happily conversing without a care in the world. If the music purchased had raised my sense of joy, the scene I was now witnessing had just buried it. I wanted to crawl into a hole.

What can I say? Should I have been dismayed because someone on the base who had acted friendly and kind and was fun to be with had a boyfriend? Absolutely not! But the child in me felt totally devastated, so Monday morning I did not meet Bianca for coffee. She soon called to inquire about my whereabouts. I gave in and continued my hangout sessions with Bianca. Need I say more?

It was the month of May, and the army gave me my second promotion. I was now a specialist four, this being equivalent to a corporal. It seemed only right considering the excessive work and stress that went with it. I mention this for an entirely different reason, for on that day my world got turned upside down. During our coffee break, Bianca informed me she was taking a small vacation. She was going to Spain for a week. There was no need to ask with whom. Since it was her last workday before departing, she invited me to lunch at her house. This nice gesture came along with a bit of joking about her mom often inquiring about me. Apparently, the lady of the house wanted to provide me a most splendid meal, and although I wanted to refuse, it seemed silly brooding over her vacation plans. Why put the two ladies out?

We met at twelve o'clock. In just a few minutes we arrived at her residence. Upon entering the flat, a pleasant fragrance of home cooking hit my nostrils as her mom was finishing up what was an appetizing culinary feast. We laughed wholeheartedly over her stories of some peculiar family members. It was soon time to leave as I reminded Bianca of my need to respect my hourly lunch break.

As the elevator was heading down, I had simply wanted to state that my coffee breaks would be less exciting. Perhaps I used the wrong words. Thank the Lord! My brief sentence exclaimed, "I am sure going to miss you." The woman next to me moved very close and said, "I will miss you even more." We then embraced and kissed most passionately. Well, it certainly felt like it had been worth the long wait. It was a delightful and satisfying moment that ended much too quickly but end it did.

With Bianca now gone, I decided to execute one of my New Year resolutions, which was to obtain a car. It was delayed for some time because it was first necessary to have a license. My driving with my uncle back in the Bronx had certainly prepared me, but I was out of practice, and it was impossible to find a car that was not stick-shift, which was not in my league. Nevertheless, it seemed only right to remain a true optimist.

Frank insisted he was available to help me out. His vehicle had manual transmission, and the lad appeared quite willing to assist me in my endeavor to learn. Unfortunately, it fizzled out very quickly. My first attempt at practice was a total fiasco. Having difficulty shifting gears properly, that awful grinding sound turned my roommate completely off. After too many of these awful noises, he simply called it quits.

It was my carabinieri friend who came to my rescue. One day he introduced me to one of the MPs he knew quite well. The very soldier responsible for issuing licenses. Please forgive me, it would just not be right to go into details, but let's just say a license was soon in my possession. Nevertheless, my driving skills needed a touch up, so I decided to buy a used inexpensive car and get acquainted with shifting gears and driving comfortably. Then one day, when I had mastered stick-shift, I would splurge on a fancy vehicle.

As luck would have it, the perfect car was parked near my office. Actually, the entire body looked like shit. It was an old beat-up Fiat 600, and it was rusty and needed new tires. Truth be told, the entire body was begging for help. Yet, it was the sales pitch which had won me over. It read, "I am riding. You are walking. Make best offer." It is things like this that makes me appreciate the best of Americans, their sense of humor, and willingness to deal with any issue while not losing touch with reality.

The owner met me that afternoon. I took possession of that dilapidated auto the following day. With some assistance of course. It was a bit curious to hear this elderly soldier speak perfect Italian as he drove my new beat-up car to my barracks, where it sat for several days. That Saturday morning at around 6:00 a.m. yours truly got into his voiture, turned on the engine, and miraculously got it to the sports field area. There, on the road around the huge field, I practiced and incurred a few noises while switching gears but soon familiarized myself with it.

A few weekends later I was ready to venture off base. On a lovely early Sunday morning, I casually exited Caserma Ederle and drove onto Viale Della Pace. And perhaps because the roads were empty, I felt so very at ease, and it went rather well. Soon enough, I was on the lovely outskirts of Vicenza, and for one who was somewhat of a beginner, and a tad nervous by nature, my driving proceeded rather well.

Chapter 113

Our office had a new leader, Major Deitrick. The man walked with sense of urgency and was quite friendly. One of his first initiatives was to announce he was fine with changes, especially when improvements followed. Well, one morning I took myself to his office and proposed one—changing the in-processing of new arrivals. The officer heard me out, asked no questions, and told me to get on it.

My plan was simple. Rather than soldiers continuously arriving at our station once through with the other personnel with most of them waiting for us to accommodate them, they would all come to our section at exactly four o'clock, having by then finished with everyone else. They would be accommodated at a large table where I would provide instructions to them on filling out their travel forms, what documents to provide us, and answer all their questions.

My proposal met no opposition. The major replied, "Julian, you have my blessings and my complete faith in you." However, he insisted this process was not for officers. They would be told to proceed to our office and be taken care of promptly and individually by Sgt. Rump. It was a piece of cake, for there was never more than one or two officers on Thursday.

The new plan worked like a charm! My instructions were delivered clearly, slowly, and concisely. I provided very simple instructions. No one could write until given permission, and at times, it seemed only right to be a bit silly as to what possible information to write down or not. My approach, humor, and attention to each person won them over. Once finished, everyone seemed pleased with their own accomplishment.

What had been an almost three-hour process was now down to half an hour. This allowed me ample time to compute their entitlements without burning the midnight oil. Not simply because of the change, but also for cutting corners. If there were several soldiers, sometimes as many as ten, from the same base (example-Ft. Benning Georgia), one calculation was made for the monetary mileage due, and the applicable per/diem was put on a computation form. Then nine photostatic copies were made, each one labeled with the pertinent soldier's name. All that remained was to compute the leave taken by each soldier. I was now able to have dinner at the carabiniere mess hall which closed at six.

The following morning, my work was checked and then given to Cristina, our co-worker. She typed all that information onto the vouchers, and then had those documents ready within a couple of hours and brought them over to the disbursement branch for payment. Everyone was paid in the afternoon, and unlike some issues with TDY payments, the newly arrived personnel never contested their reimbursements but a few even came by to thank me.

Well, some things had improved at the office. But outside the office too. My beautiful friend and I were now also meeting after work hours. We found some isolated area where we shared a passionate and fun-loving time together. It was so divine. Our coffee breaks were more fun than ever before. And yet, one morning after separating from her, quite happy and carefree, things back at work went south.

An officer at the counter had come to inquire about his TDY travel pay. My co-worker, always on top of things, could not locate it. It had been registered but finding the travel voucher seemed impossible. I returned from the disbursement branch empty-handed, but the voucher had now been located. It was under a bunch of other vouchers that needed to be computed. As Sgt. Rump and Flavio were both absent, I took the initiative to process it, but I noticed it had been marked on top to be paid the following day. The document had been logged in the day before, so I expressed my opinion that it was not yet due.

The high-ranking officer's vein on his forehead bulged upon hearing my explanation. Through gritted teeth he stated, "Specialist Di Stefano, suppose you call my wife and explain to her why she can't go shopping today." I chose not to speak. My response would not have pleased him or his wife. Apparently, the simpleton who outranked me was in a foul mood. Soon enough, my co-worker checked my computation for mathematical accuracy. She typed it and brought it to the disbursement branch to get the officer paid. That pathetic individual never even thanked us. Actually, when I began to work on it, he was kindly asked to return in a few minutes, but he sourly stated, "I am not going anywhere Specialist Di Stefano."

It was not the pathetic insulting attitude that angered me most, but rather it was the fact that two of our office personnel, our captain and a sergeant, who heard everything never attempted to deflate the tension or put in a good word for us. Incredible! It was once through that I put on my cap, abandoned my duty station, as military terminology would state, and eventually received the punishment meted out in such cases. Oh well, at times such is individual military foolishness at its best.

Chapter 114

Not sure why, but Sgt. Rump was moved to another section. The branch was now down to three, Flavio, Cristina and me. TDY vouchers, however, continued to stream in every single day, and so much time was spent on the phone or at the counter where everyone had a unique itinerary. Also, my Thursday afternoons were still in full bloom at the chapel.

We certainly managed to keep our heads above water. Major Deitrick stopped by to see us one afternoon. He expressed his appreciation for our hard work and informed us a new soldier would soon be on board. The chap was experienced in travel work, and, incredible as it may sound, he had expressed a desire to join the branch. His rank would entitle him to be the branch chief, and we would again be fully staffed.

A month later, our new branch chief was among us. He too had grown up in Italy, a small town close to Pompei, and moved to Brooklyn at a much older age. His name was Gregorio Severo, and his awful Italian accent backed it up wholeheartedly. The guy was definitely a few years older than me, but quite often it was hard to believe. For at times, he would do the unthinkable, talk forever about anything, and occasionally would even become a tad obnoxious.

As a matter of fact, one day both Flavio and I witnessed some slight mischief. A major at the counter was inquiring about an upcoming travel itinerary. Gregorio was at his desk, reading a regulation, but he soon joined us and began to question our discussion. The officer would soon be escorting his wife to Germany as she would be receiving medical treatment which was not available at our base.

Our new boss simply took over. He provided various possible scenarios and ranted endlessly, quoting regulations left and right, and almost put both of us to sleep. And as it had now become a one-way conversation, I thought it proper to simply move on. That is when the officer politely thanked him and very diplomatically terminated the one-way discussion.

So, the new guy in town walked back to his desk slightly exalted. Upon leaving the counter, he began scratching his rear end most casually and very innocently, as if it were a very appropriate and common thing to do. The major looked at me and smiled. Not appearing too surprised, he quietly inquired, "Where did they find that guy?" Did I previously mention there was never a dull moment?

It was the following morning when Gregorio accosted me. I had just returned from my joyous coffee break and was informed the major wished to see me. The officer was at his desk, and he happily invited me to sit down, which brought on a slight feeling of concern. Had some complaint been made about me? The major then asked if I would object going to a small base in Turkey. Temporarily, of course!

It was almost advertised as two casual weeks away from the office. Gee, how nice! However, my destination was our military base in Cakmakli, an isolated small town located somewhere in the mountains in the northern part of the country. Apparently, the travel branch needed help. The clerk in that section was overworked, under pressure, and struggling to comprehend some of the regulations, so, consequently, he was not always making payments on time or correctly. Well, it was easy to grasp the rather harsh situation.

My boss claimed there was a benefit to be had. The trip would expose me to what most of my customers experienced when traveling, the ups and downs of being on official government business. This meant experiencing and gaining an outlook on one peculiar travel circumstance, but somewhat applicable to others. But most of all, I would be helping out. It seemed only right to jump on it, which made the major super happy.

Exactly a week later, a tiny plane, an Army C12, flew out of Dal Molin Airport in Vicenza and headed to Athens Greece. The following day it would depart for Istanbul, Turkey. After which I would be on my own to get to my final destination by bus. On that flight with me were three people—an officer on his way to Athens and the two pilots, both familiar to me as they often came to the branch to get reimbursed.

While we were flying, some agonizing moments had me in distress. It was my relationship with Bianca that now irked me. Like two loving souls, we laughed plenty every day, and our time spent in her car after work hours was sheer heaven. She refused, however, to discuss her other relationship but would neither end ours. Whenever I questioned if our affair was simply that, she would quickly shut down and become a tad morose.

Anyhow, the tiny plane arrived in Athens rather quickly. As we four exited the aircraft, oil began to pour out of the engine under the left propeller. One of the pilots summarized it wisely, "Oh shit." There was certainly some serious concern over our means of transportation. We proceeded as scheduled and registered at the Basic Officer's Quarters to lodge for the evening, as we were supposed to leave in the morning. Now, I was not an officer, but I was accommodated just like one.

Sometime the following morning over breakfast, I was informed we were stuck in Athens. The aircraft needed a new part which would be flown in, but as to when was anybody's guess. Both pilots seemed quite happy when revealing the news. I soon contacted the sergeant-major in Vicenza, and he heard me out and put me on hold. Once back, he ordered me to proceed to Cakmakli by any means possible.

It was no easy task. A few years back, Turkey had conquered the island of Cyprus, and so diplomatic ties between the two nations had been severed. There were absolutely no commercial flights between the two nations, and the only other solution was brought to my attention by an Air Force employee at the transportation office. It would require traveling on two military planes over nearly three days to finally arrive in the middle of nowhere outside Istanbul.

My second call to the sergeant-major stated the facts but in limited mode. I was stranded in Athens. It was not received well. He heard me out, questioned me and eventually accepted my unhappy circumstances. I then ran into the pilots, and both seemed rather thrilled with our misfortune. One, while smiling, pointed out how we simply needed to make the best of a bad situation.

Our lodgings were situated near the sea, and traveling around the city was a breeze. Now Athens is not Rome by any means, but it, too, has its charm and ancient history. It would have been an unforgivable sin to not soak in as much as possible. The Acropolis was my first destination that day. I felt extremely enthusiastic, assuming I was sure to be impressed. However, my imagination failed to properly ignite and invoke the glory of its ancient past. The ruins about me were exactly that—terribly ruined.

Nevertheless, my unexpected vacation excited me in other ways. Every morning, its majestic sea invited me in. Having now purchased a bathing suit at a nearby shop, it earned my full participation. Also, a few days after our arrival, this very beautiful young Greek lady, Bruna, who worked where we lodged, introduced herself. She was super useful in acquainting me with the better places to eat, both nearby and in the city center.

By the way, the Greeks eat late, very late. Dinner in Southern Italy starts at eight, but here, that was entirely too early. Well, Bruna and I went out to dinner on my last night in Athens. She was not just attractive but also cheerful. We enjoyed our night, but my intuition suspected I was perhaps a distraction from something or someone else. At times, she seemed a bit too far away in thought and personality.

We dined at a family-run restaurant. It seemed everyone there knew her, and throughout our meal, several people came over and cut into our conversation. Only Greek was spoken, and they obviously had much to say. Finally, a bit around one in the morning, we headed to a nearby club and danced quite a bit. Time ran off too quickly, and we eventually grabbed a taxi, which first brought her home and then brought me to my quarters.

The following day a C12 from Vicenza landed at the air base in Athens. It had the needed part for our aircraft. However, we three happily stranded soldiers on standby, then boarded that aircraft, and my now close pilot friends took over the controls and began to ascend into the skies. Thus began our journey back to the Dal Molin Airbase.

If a bit of stress had taken me to Greece, it was sheer terror which brought me back home. For some time, our aircraft had flown in bright skies with a few white clouds below us. But somewhere out over the Adriatic, we ran into the bowels of a nasty storm. There was a blackness all around us which felt very ominous as our aircraft was getting tossed around and was quite helpless against the brutal force of Mother Nature. The pilots seemed unfazed and continued joking loudly and talking non-stop, but their brave act brought me little comfort.

My heart was in my mouth every time my butt landed back on the seat and then went back up again. The spirit in me believed the end was here. As a matter of fact, as baffling as it will sound, something within was now suggesting the possibility that God may actually exist. Yes, as a matter of fact,

I was now sure. And who knows? Hopefully, that supreme being was watching and listening and perhaps voting in favor of our safe return to Vicenza.

Miraculously, we eventually returned to our base in one piece. And once settled in at my desk, I had sort of created a scandal. As my time at the Air Force base in Athens was that of a military personnel in transit, the housing office which put us up gave me a form (Statement of Non-Availability) for meals, which entitled me to get reimbursed, both for food and lodging. A nice chunk of change came my way for the entire trip, and, I had done the unthinkable, lodged where only officers were accommodated.

Oh well, such was the reimbursement coming my way. Apparently, it looked like the U.S. Army was now paying me for a week's vacation, but such were the circumstances that had befallen this now very at ease and happy soldier.

Chapter 115

An Italian friend of mine had once filled me in on the country's past. One peculiar custom back in the Middle Ages was the city-states' competitive drive with its neighbors. From Rome to Florence to Venice to Genova, each city government attempted to outdo the others in terms of distinguishing itself as an independent state. Its aim was to appear superior in building, managing, and showing off its small empire. This is why no two Italian cities look anything alike.

A major component reflecting the inner city's unique façade was what the Italians call "la piazza" or the city square. Here, buildings did not simply house commerce but also proudly reflected the unique architectural elegance of their era. Competition, along with a dislike toward their neighbors, was the objective in designing and erecting a diverse environment from folks only a few miles away. The human pulse of each city could be felt in congregations galore, chats and juicy gossip, and other aspects of their citizens' personal agenda.

In the heart of Vicenza is Piazza Dei Signori. Most evenings, it was either the Bar Garibaldi or one of the other coffee shops across the way where my friends and I hung out. Oh, by the way, let me explain. In Italy, a "bar" is generally a coffee shop, although alcohol and all sorts of drinks and small portions of food are also served. Whether you desire a cappuccino, or a glass of wine and a snack, or simply a bit of down time with others, you say, "Andiamo al bar."

It was in that piazza that I met Renato. Here was a truly brilliant individual, and prone to talk with anyone and everyone, for such was his cheerful disposition. No doubt, he was the intellectual among our small crowd, yet he never made anyone feel inadequate. Our group certainly enjoyed some fun chats, and no topic was ever off-limits. We would also occasionally engage in walks about the city center just to enjoy moving a bit while soaking in our fascinating surroundings.

Julian Di Stefano was a bit of an enigma to some in the group. One of my older friends, Carlo, had labeled me as an American without a country. Such was his take on things. He believed that my American accent when speaking Italian was the only feature qualifying me as a Yankee. Of course, there was also a U.S. passport and the army uniform I wore, never after work hours of course. Yet my older buddy insisted my composure and outlook were not that of an average American. So, he claimed, and he seemed convinced and very convincing.

My friends saw me most evenings but not always on weekends. For most Saturdays, after a healthy morning workout on the base, my car had me exploring some of the nearby cities in the Veneto region. The city of Verona, which was nearby, was voted my favorite. Here is a jewel of a gracious town, and not just because of a popular balcony scene related to Shakespeare's imagination. In my book, the city center and its immediate surroundings is best described by a word Italians rarely use, "incantevole".

The Verona Arena simply mesmerized me. Unlike Rome's Colosseum, it is a work of art which remains quietly nestled in perfect antiquity, and it simply preserves its unique parlor like setting. On some occasions, a few of us attended an outdoor jazz concert there, and on quite a few pleasant summer evenings, Verona's splendid beauty and its people's charming ways kept bringing me back. I was one happy tourist who loved the city's charm and would occasionally arrive in my old creepy voiture.

I also made trips to Belluno, Lake Garda, Padova, and the nearby mountains. In that same car, of course. The only attraction which had me arriving by rail was La Serenissima. And once leaving the train station, the usual trek to Piazza San Marco never became old. My walks would reveal partially hidden alleyways, old looking but unique, and perhaps housing a quaint shop displaying a variety of colorful souvenirs. In instances where I engaged a store owner in a chat, at some point, they claimed that although tourists were more than welcome, they felt that the masses were also ruining the tranquility of their small quaint city.

It was Carlo who had once suggested seeing the island, Giudecca. Once in the Venice train station area, I took the ferry there, and it was a brief ride. One senses being far from the madding crowd and happy to promenade quietly while taking in a few interesting sites, especially the once famous institute, Le Zittelle. It sits next to the immaculate church Santa Maria della Presentazione. Le Zittelle was a hospice for very young beautiful girls from poor families, and they were sent there so they would not become prostitutes. One of my friends at the Bar Garibaldi was not convinced they fared much better there.

My weekends were great as I was getting out plenty. For one always senses a unique feeling of happiness when touring historical sites, being impressed by beautiful monuments, and learning some peculiarity of that area's historical past. It was usually on my return ride to Vicenza that a bit of moody blues grappled my free spirit. They would vaporize the happy sentiments coming home with me, once I recalled that the person I wanted to be with or would have loved having at my side while on my escapades, was with someone else.

Chapter 116

My mother and Alessandro usually saw me once a month. Not in my car, mind you. It seemed like too long of a drive to put that old voiture through. Also, I wanted to avoid a bit of embarrassment entering the villa with such a sad-looking vehicle. It would have certainly raised a few eyebrows from the town's inhabitants. And why give those folks a bit of fodder to entertain themselves with?

Mr. Rossi always received a treat. The man did drink, although he was always a perfectly composed gentleman in complete control of his faculties. His favorite beverages, via the Class VI store on base, were Bailey's Irish Cream and Johnny Walker Red. Not together, of course, nor in that order. My treat was in complete disregard of the base's policy prohibiting any of our benefits being shared with or sold to the country's citizens. Oh well, he had done so much for me, and his smile upon receiving a bottle justified it.

It seems awful to admit there was never anything for my mom. All she wanted was to do my laundry, and so I cooperated. Whenever I purchased something for her, it was highly appreciated but usually put aside and hardly ever seen again. By the way, my grandmother had remained a permanent member at the villa. She enjoyed the company and still maintained the garden in the back. Although she now smoked a few cigarettes, she did not appear to be fully inhaling them.

In September of that year, no dirty laundry came with me. My suitcase was fully packed for my trip abroad. Peter and his girlfriend were marrying. That is why the day after arriving my folks brought me to Malpensa Airport. We arrived with plenty of time to spare before my scheduled departure. However, an unexpected announcement soon informed us that my flight was delayed.

Thinking it a brief setback, we accommodated ourselves and indulged in small talk about the upcoming matrimony. About half an hour later, a second notice via a loudspeaker informed us of a mechanical problem with the plane, consequently forcing us to sit tight for further news. Suddenly, I spotted someone who looked familiar, like a soldier from the base in Vicenza. I then remembered her from my in-processing session.

The Black lady was a nurse at the hospital. I took myself over to her, and we shared the awful news, for she too was on that flight, it then having been recast along with a free lunch and a complimentary bus tour trip of Milano, all offered by the airline. Apparently, the flight would not leave for some time. Mr. Rossi came over and suggested we return home. And so, Sally, the portly woman at my side, most happily agreed to tag along. Of course, with Alessandro at the helm, we made it back home quickly. And you cannot imagine how much those enchanting surroundings impressed our guest.

After the car was parked, we two soldiers took in the breathtaking sunny palace basking before us as the sun amplified the beauty of the mansion and its surroundings, Sally looked at me and rather curiously asked, "You live here?" Well, what could I possibly say? It felt only right to not exaggerate, be a tad humble, and right to the point, so I replied, "Sometimes."

I suspect most humans have no idea what an abundance of Barbera wine will do. Over a late lunch, that beverage was not spared in the least as Mr. Rossi was feeling generous. Our nurse opened up rather quickly, and boy was she funny! She rattled on with much confidence, awaited my translation, laughed with a happy heart, and immediately moved on to another tale. The abundant wine did help. Both my mom and grandmother, who had never been in the presence of an African descendant, were most impressed with her enthusiasm. Consequently, they encouraged her on with more wine and huge smiles, and Sally cheerfully accepted their generosity.

We eventually returned to the airport. The flight was again delayed. It was late in the evening when we finally boarded the aircraft, and once everyone was seated and seat belts were latched, all the lights went out, so we sat very quietly for several minutes. Finally, sometime afterwards, having regained power, the aircraft was soon heading down the runway with me very much holding my breath!

When I arrived at JFK, I found a very annoyed brother. My fault for sure. I had made no attempt to phone him, fearing someone else would answer and know I was at my mom's place. My mother had suggested calling him when we had returned home. But I had assumed that the airline would have informed all concerned parties on the tardiness of their flight. Not these folks!

In the meantime, a highly overworked and tired Peter waited at JFK. He eventually made some inquiries and was told the plane was behind schedule. They even misinformed him on the arrival time. Which is why he returned home, but unable to sleep and then remembering the inconsistency of things, and wanting to be there for me, he returned to the airport where he may have managed to sleep a bit, but not much.

We finally greeted each other and immediately ran home. Later that morning, Peter ran off to work, and our father, usually the first one out the door, went to his new job downtown as a doorman in a rather fancy building. Our stepmother was home as she had taken a few days off from work. Soon enough, over a late breakfast, she unleashed. The complaints about Peter were aired out and there was no letting up! Choosing to remain polite, only once did I dare interrupt her sermon by asking the frustrated speaker to just stop and breathe for a minute. My words were certainly not appreciated. She made an unpleasant statement which forced me to head to the bathroom, shower, shave, and move on.

I took the subway to lower Manhattan, Battery Park specifically. The ferry carried me to the Statue of Liberty. The impressive monument was photographed, and that scene from one of the Godfather movies, briefly highlighting the immigrants it accommodated, came to mind. So many of us were or have been welcomed, directly or indirectly, by this very inspiring statue at one time or another.

Reentering the lovely island of Manhattan was a breathtaking fling. The modern buildings hugging the southern westerly coastline complement each other rather nicely. Well, my morning was off to a great start as I then decided to head off to Central Park. Once inside that enchanting garden, and having walked a bit, some classical music could be heard and invited me in its direction almost immediately.

My vision of things soon noticed a couple dancing, both well-coordinated and moving so freely. They kept in tune with the music and looked fantastic. Yet, a most absurd scene came into view once getting closer to it. A young man, dressed in a tuxedo, was on roller skates and dancing with a life-size doll. Yes, it was a dummy in drag carrying on so devotedly that was now being fully taken in.

Isn't the Big Apple so full of surprises? Even when offering an improvised version of life. In this case, it stemmed from a tad of creative ambition, something New Yorkers abound in, and at times, so easily put on display. It was fun to watch a dummy keep in step with a human. I was almost tempted to walk over and congratulate the artist. Oh well, I moved on while enjoying a somewhat lively feeling from a city welcoming me back. Something which I had not always felt in my past.

Chapter 117

Peter and Mary were married in the Bronx. It was a picture-perfect day. Everyone looked incredibly happy. Yet there had been a small mishap back home that morning. It was quickly buried via a few unpleasant Sicilian words. In some ways, Peter had preserved his Sicilian street-upbringing and used it quite sparingly.

While putting on his tuxedo, the groom-to-be noticed several stains on his vest. And they were not coming out. He vociferously cleared his soul of his frustration. I, too, was somewhat put out. But for an entirely different reason. In Vicenza, a stunning gray suit had been purchased, plus, as my buying spree continued, a light blue shirt, a dark red silk tie, and top quality Italian black shoes. Gee, I would have looked fantastic! Unfortunately, I was informed that there was a rental outfit in the closet for me. It seemed best to just bury the issue.

In the meantime, life on the eighteenth floor of a high-rise in section five of Co-op City was progressing nicely. Last-minute preparations were being tackled as Aunt Mia and family, and grandmother, had just arrived. Everyone looked their very best. We soon got on our way. Peter rode a limousine to Mary's home in the Fordham area. The rest of us were driven directly to the church where family members from both parties waited. Now, as far as the religious ceremony at hand, it went rather well. Nevertheless, I must admit, whenever I participate in a church ritual, my mind tends to wander off, and is only again fully present once exiting those sacred grounds.

Outside the church, I began shaking hands and exchanging a few words with most of the crowd, many of whom were relatives. It felt like ages since we had last seen each other. Then we were off to the Eldorado Country Club, which was in New Rochelle. Eventually, after the newlyweds were photographed in a garden area, we in the bridal party descended to a large private room. It was located below the room where we would dine. I was with one of Mary's cousins, who was not so talkative, and we sat next to Aunt Mia's kids, who were quite grown up.

It was a bit peculiar being with my cousins. Peter and I had first seen them as small children back in 1963. In my mind, they had remained our small cousins, whereas these two young adults, both a bit reserved and apparently on their best behavior, were also quite funny to chat with. Of course, not wanting to startle anyone, I, a man who had traveled the world, sometimes in company of thugs and loose ladies, measured my words carefully.

All proceeded well, but our isolation was much too long. Eventually, we retraced our steps and ultimately entered the dining area announced as a couple and received a warm round of applause. I felt slightly relieved to be moving on from a somewhat tight situation below, and the entrance was a wonderfully staged performance! It was both theatrical and so very typical of American hype. We love entertainment and are at our best when a bit of accumulated wealth is being easily displayed, perhaps rather nonchalantly and with little concern for what gets dished out. At the very moment of our entrance, one positive fact registered within. Such an over-celebrated monumental stunt accompanying my marriage would not occur.

The newlyweds entered last to a super thunderous applause. It continued for a long while. Our party now sat facing many round tables consisting of families and friends. There were many young faces among our relatives, which were unfamiliar to me. Eventually, I would check out a few. Such was my strategy.

We enjoyed an excellent meal served at just the right pace. My conversations were aimed more at my cousins, John and Sophia, but also, when possible, with the young lady next to me. I was not the best man, yet I was informed that I would give a speech. And someone even pointed to the stage where the band would play, insisting I use the microphone. It seemed so unnecessary for my tenor voice has never failed me. Soon enough, a few well-chosen words were delivered from where we sat.

Mine was a simple and rather short message. I pointed out that throughout the planet, it was just an ordinary day for most folks. However, not so for the newlywed couple who were now sharing a sacred element, one which if nurtured properly and brought to the fore in every aspect of their relationship, would thrive forever and keep them happy. That was basically it.

It garnered a nice round of applause. Someone even yelled they would vote for me. It took a while, but our delicious long dinner terminated, and it seemed right to now visit a few tables. There, something quite unexpected began to reveal its true nature. A few of my stepmother's relatives, knowing my blood line differed from theirs, may have been eyeing me as the perfect candidate for their attractive and angelic looking daughters. Apparently, a few were ready to settle down, something which, at that moment, for me, was still an event far off into the future.

Most conversations with parents and female cherubim were fun and concluded nicely. It was after having showered everyone with smiles and pleasant ideas, that the moment to make my move had arrived. I had previously danced with Aunt Mia, and we had the floor practically to ourselves and swung very nicely to "Proud Mary." I noticed a young lady had been eying me. So, when we finished dancing, I headed off to a table where a few of Peter's colleagues sat.

The girl and I spoke and then shared a slow dance on a rather crowded dance floor. We were both a bit reserved, but she stared at me as if ready to follow me to the ends of the earth. The harmonious dance kept us glued to each other for a while. Once through, it was on to her table for a fun chat. We eventually agreed to meet the following evening. It was a most divine and savage-like night.

Peter's co-worker was slim, blonde, had a creamy white complexion, and was very chest-less. But she had those Bette Davis's eyes. Her features were totally insignificant and had not mattered one bit. For my intuition had brought me to her, and it was a very wise move. The girl was all fire and fury throughout the entire long entanglement. Our intertwined physiques simply refused to dim their magic glow. And by the way, years back it had been the heroin which kept me going. I obviously no longer needed help from any drug.

Chapter 118

The memory of my brother's wedding was now behind me as work demanded my full attention. The soldiers in administration at Caserma Ederle had to qualify in using their weapons. That is, we needed to prove we could still shoot properly. Therefore, all the office folks clad in uniform, rode a rented commercial bus for several hours just to get to an Italian military base, somewhere near the city of Trento. It was always an all-day affair, and the only time we ever got to handle a rifle.

I was asked to participate as an interpreter in the team making the arrangements. There were three soldiers and one officer with me as we drove in a military vehicle the day before the exercise began. We met the Italian officers in charge of the base, and once the perimeter was checked out and deemed satisfactory, finding a place to lodge for two evenings was our only other exercise. The shooting drill lasted two days as two different groups were to be accommodated.

On both days, two Italian soldiers escorted me about the base. Once they saw my last name and heard me speak their language, you would have thought me one of them. Perhaps it was also my carefree attitude which may have endeared me to them, for they were suddenly showing me all around and carrying on quite freely. They even insisted I eat at their mess hall for free. It felt rather nice to be in the limelight, but a bit less so upon hearing their many complaints.

In those days, military service in Italy was obligatory. It lasted a year. A soldier's daily salary equated to about a dollar. This forced most of them to beg for funds from home just to buy cigarettes and occasionally go out to eat a pizza. If this seemed unjust, it was nothing compared to their gripes about being assigned useless and insignificant tasks, almost as a form of punishment. Sometimes it was just to keep them busy, but no matter what they did, they claimed most officers looked down on them and spoke to them very harshly.

Hearing this reminded me of Alessandro's past counsel. He had cautioned me not to chance being drafted into the Italian military, which could have happened once residing in Italy. My, things had turned out rather well for me. First of all, I was among guys who grew up under similar circumstances, but also, my daily work function was important and quite useful. It suddenly dawned on me that a bit of military madness on the Italian front had been witnessed just recently.

This soap opera occurred right there on our base. One afternoon, our team came together to practice, usually an hour or more. We had just arrived on the pitch. However, it was impossible to pass up the chaotic game in progress in front of us. A company of Italian troops from the base downtown were fiercely playing a match of football. There was a lot of shouting and threats in perfect Italian coming from the troops' commander. The lieutenant was a distinguished looking chap bearing a walrus type mustache.

He was playing but also directing the game as if on a battlefield. He screamed out orders to his men, especially to whoever had possession of the ball and would immediately threaten anyone who had failed to comply or moved too slowly. This included everything from excessive kitchen duty to not granting leave for months on end. And the officer was serious. He resembled a pissed off kid ready to retrieve his soccer ball and go home.

We bystanders were certainly having a good laugh. His soldiers, however, looked so disgusted, and one team member pleaded with us for assistance. It was a striker, who upon coming to the sideline to retrieve the ball that had just been kicked out, asked if someone could trip up their annoying leader when he ran by us. My teammate Tony looked at me as if he was considering it, and I urged him on. After all, he would just be doing his good deed for the day.

That match soon terminated. The Italian soldiers certainly kept their distance from their overbearing leader. Well, the show had made me appreciate my present circumstances most vigorously, even though occasionally there was some griping to air things out.

Chapter 119

The year was coming to an end, and my birthday was just a few days away. Would Bianca have me for lunch at her place as she did the previous year? Over time, she had invited me over on various occasions, and her mother, always clad in black, was very happy to see me. It was highly appreciated. However, what transpired that Monday morning was so bizarre and incomprehensible. It truly destroyed me.

Bianca and I always met briefly before stepping into work. That morning she exited her car and walked right past me, ignoring my presence. Just what was going on? I was shocked and quite confused. Nevertheless, I followed her to her desk, but the woman refused to even look my way.

At five o'clock, our eyes finally met. She immediately said, "Whatever happened between us is over. It should have never occurred." I dragged myself to my room and did not even acknowledge Frank, who was his usual cheery self. The confused soldier was puzzled over the devastated look on my face. My lips were sealed as nothing flowed out of me, and having dinner at the carabinieri cafeteria was not an option. I had been drug-free for over two years. Now I just wanted to get high.

The junkies had always hung out in a particular part of the piazza. Everyone knew who they were. They were tolerated but looked down upon. I took myself to the side steps near Palladio's monument, and though the folks there had seen me around, they were not cooperating. Asking to buy some heroin generated some strange looks my way. Apparently, those folks felt uncomfortable and avoided my requests. One guy insisted I was addressing the wrong folks. So, I parked myself next to those people not wanting to give up.

A guy named Marco soon arrived. We had once been introduced by, of all people, Renato. He had complimented him on looking healthy after returning from a rehabilitation program. It was a very new practice in Italy but one taking off quickly. The individual now came over as if we were old friends. We shook hands and after he heard me out, he suggested we take a walk. There was a park nearby, and once there, I began to shoot up. Nothing else mattered anymore.

Such was my new life. It came on sometime after work hours for the next two months. Occasionally, it required traveling outside Vicenza, especially to the town of Arzignano. There was always plenty of heroin to be had in that minute place, and once high I would usually spend a few hours there. However, back at the barracks, most folks around me were totally shocked when they realized my new circumstances.

Everyone was accustomed to an athletic Julian. I was either on the soccer field, or jogging, or at the gym. I looked like an athlete. So, watching me scratch myself, and at times, unable to finish my sentence made everyone a bit uncomfortable. At work, it was a totally different story. Once again, it was Dr. Jekyll dutifully getting through the day while Mr. Hyde came out at night. And the love of my life, Bianca, kept her iron wall distance, never once acknowledging my presence when we accidentally bumped into each other.

One evening, at the piazza, Renato came over to where I sat. He insisted we go for a walk. My friend's concern was on full display. In a gracious and caring way, he asked me to stop this "destructive foolishness." Which is what had me in front of my captain's desk the following morning. The officer had recently taken command of our unit. He too considered me a jock, which is why he appeared stunned once hearing my request to rehabilitate myself.

Mine was a simple call for help. Once I admitted to using heroin, the captain appeared quite dumbfounded and even asked a few questions. He calmly assured me he would help, but he quite emphatically stated that once rehabilitated, there would be no second chance. If I screwed up and got back on drugs, he would oust me from military service, which meant a dishonorable discharge.

Our hospital did not have a rehabilitation program. Consequently, a few days after my chat with the captain, I was provided TDY orders which got me to our military base in Nuremberg. While traveling, I pondered some about my new misery. Not long ago, in the Bronx, my heart was on fire for someone who hardly knew I existed. Then, more recently, a night in France got quickly turned upside down and took me with it. And now someone I loved quite madly had simply brushed me off. Oh well, for the moment, I needed to change my ways and return to Vicenza a stronger and better person.

Chapter 120

The rehabilitation program in Nuremberg did wonders for me. The staff were friendly but also super strict. After all, we were patients but still soldiers in uniform, and we were expected to act accordingly. Most of the guys in my room appeared a bit withdrawn, but not John, who immediately came over to shake hands and introduce himself upon my arrival.

He was changing the linen on his bunk while whistling a Rolling Stones tune. I filled in the lyrics, and this brought a huge smile to his face as he complemented my singing, and at that very moment we two cemented a friendly and strong month long relationship.

A bit later, having settled in, I was off to the barber shop. After all, John Lennon had razed his head when he went through detox. Why not me? The gentleman there, a middle-aged German, was reading the newspaper but seemed more than happy to accommodate a customer. He heard me out and then began his chat, one which may have been well rehearsed.

I sat comfortably to his informing me that once home from work, his wife would instantly get him a beer. He would then sit down to enjoy it, but first he put sugar in it. Hearing this had me a tad concerned over the man holding a machine over my scalp. The barber continued, and so I allowed him to recite his narrative. My ears perked up, as he claimed to always add sugar to everything in his meals. That's right. He put sugar on meat, vegetables, and whatever else was on his plate. And are you ready for this? Why, he even put sugar on his dessert.

Now believe me, it was not the electric razor which had me a tad concerned. My curiosity over this mystery demanded a proper ending. So, finally, out came the million-dollar question for the "Barber of Nuremberg," who for some mysterious reason needed to sweeten everything going in him. So why was he using sugar so recklessly? He answered briefly and most harmoniously. He said, "Because life can be so bitter." In some odd way this made sense to me.

My stay in Nuremberg proceeded rather well. It is incredible what healthy personalities can accomplish! At the rehabilitation center in Manhattan, the staff around me, which seemed thuggish and incapable of inspiring any confidence or trust, had chased me off. Whereas at the cozy vibrant center in New Rochelle, it was me who simply could not properly participate in the process. Why? I do not know.

Here in Germany, from day one, I communicated most happily and felt rather comfortable in all my encounters with my counselors. Even more rewarding was hearing John express similar thoughts and feelings. We both gave it our best and did it most sincerely while engaging in coming clean.

Why was this program such a success with me? Our counselors were simply two incredible women. They emanated an abundance of serenity and a tad of severity, if necessary, but never in an angry tone or rashly throwing anyone off balance. It was as if they were richly versed in life's agenda, not necessarily from books, though they may have read tons of them, but from something within. Also, perhaps, just like a man named Jesus, their love of others truly stemmed from the heart.

Each session began with a thought or idea generated by one of the two. Our task was to fill in the details but never in general terms. We were challenged to back up our opinions, which often were not forthcoming from some of the guys, yet no one was accommodated. Everyone had to practice the art of communicating, often through disputes or slight arguments. But we always emptied out the basket of our feelings, good or bad, and faced our individual challenges from a rational point of view.

One morning, we were asked to explain why we got high. John and I, always ready to fully pounce on things, may have outtalked everyone else. It is not just problems or adversity which lead most people to forgo sobriety, but sometimes, it was just plain boredom. A Jimi Hendrix song strongly stated "Well, I think I'll go turn myself on, cause I'm down." Wasn't this usually the case? Hadn't most of us lost our way in life but also all interest in what makes it most rewarding?

My relationship to Bianca came to the forefront one day. It was difficult, and I felt somewhat uncomfortable eventually revealing she probably did not love me or ever would. Yes, I was just the guy who had provided her some excitement, and perhaps, someone good at fulfilling her sexual desires. I was told that that was not love. It was simply satisfying a craving. Then out came another issue that had me in crisis mode. She was now pregnant, and I was certain her child was ours, but both counselors cautioned me to not rush to judgement.

Soon, an unannounced guest was among us one late afternoon. He was the husband of one of the counselors. Can't recall for sure if he was a psychologist. However, he performed a miracle, at least for me. The guy eagerly shared a bit of information about himself, his profession, his interests, and even his love of literature. We were then asked to reciprocate. Once we all finished, what followed was an incredible feat, which almost hypnotized me, and it certainly enhanced my ability to properly listen to others.

His brief introduction had provided some explicit information about the man. We were now challenged to do the same, and he specified we should include our hometown and some peculiar information which we deemed right to impart. It could include anything from our favorite hobby to our favorite snack or whatever we felt was worth sharing. The more information given, the better his understanding would be of a small part of us.

The talk progressed in a clockwise movement, and one by one we all spoke. We were a large group. Most guys were too brief, others a bit too long. I simply stated my name, being born in England but having grown up first in Italy and then in the Bronx. My accent certainly bore testimony to the latter. Having spent four years at sea in the Merchant Marines, which is not a military institution, and seeing many Asian countries, I had gotten a better sense of how the other half lives. To conclude, it seemed only right to include my love for music, especially the Beatles, and my favorite song being "In My Life." And by the way, I was stationed in Vicenza, Italy.

Seventeen of us made our voices heard. When finished, our guest returned to the first speaker, and he repeated the exact information we had all heard without missing a beat. He even played with it a little bit. The fact that he could recall every minute detail and then spruce it up when appropriate was an astonishing feat. He proceeded to do this with every single one of us.

Maybe in ancient times such deeds were called miracles. Our fantastic counselor had certainly caught my attention. For you see, I am one who quickly loses his way and not always present in the moment. Could I possibly learn to pay attention, even register the audible, not so much as a mechanical feature but as proof of having been present and having heard? It was no doubt one of my new challenges.

Chapter 121

Upon arriving at the hospital, we were not allowed to leave the base. As the month came to an end, a bit more freedom came our way. During our last weekend, the staff was rather generous in giving us some time to ourselves. We could wander off to explore our surroundings far from our medical confinement. It was very much appreciated.

One gorgeous Saturday morning, I met John and his wife. The couple lived outside of Nuremberg. Our escapade was a planned hike with no equipment or maps. We simply joined a crowd on an outing in a countryside favored with plush green hills and fresh air. We three valued the courteous and friendly local folks whom we had joined, even their German sounded okay. Some big warm smiles and a willingness to chat a bit with us made for a superb trek.

We were relishing our day of freedom, but at one point, John and I inherited a small problem. It came about while on a break in one of the small towns we had arrived at. After enjoying a beer at one of the large outdoor tables, we resumed our walk and spotted a couple of guys from our group in the hospital. They appeared to be hiding and were smoking a joint. Hmm, what to do? John was for turning them in. It seemed a bit harsh to me. Mine was a personal dilemma based on the idea of never creating a problem for anyone. Anyway, turning them in did not feel right, and so my buddy agreed to look the other way.

However, the following day, I came to terms with a new fact. Not all patients were recovered on a volunteer basis. Some among us had been busted, and were forced to attend the program, and were here unwillingly. Apparently, their participation could simply be a bit of a farce. Just an act to get them through the program. John's harsh inclination toward these guys was somewhat now more in tune with my changed outlook.

It was the day before leaving the hospital when this issue resurfaced. I was in a private out-processing session. My two counselors had asked about my plans once back at work, and when my scanty details terminated, they both suggested I request a transfer to another base, like the one in Livorno. Then, very unexpectedly, they asked me who in the program was getting high. Wow, it seemed only right to follow up on my previous decision, and so I simply opened up.

Now please forgive me for hardly mentioning the beautiful city of Nuremberg. My one day in its lovely city center mesmerized me. The pure cleanliness all about simply stood out, and there were rows of quaint and colorful homes, structurally solid, which slightly reminded me a bit of some of the ones on the hills of Vicenza. The coffee shops appeared to be in a class of their own. In most, either jazz or classical music was playing, and though still not that acquainted with either, both sounded wonderful, especially the jazz from the early sixties. But it was the immense selection of cakes and pastries which put a smile on my face.

That smile soon disappeared. I confronted the area where the Nazi rallies occurred. My mind tried imagining the columns of soldiers, and the sense of belonging which they must have felt. Yet nothing truly touched me in any way, until I was departing. Then a sudden thought flashed through my mind. It made me grasp how the masses of any nation, at any time, long for law and order, the meticulous alignment of soldiers, and a strong belief in a better tomorrow, which sometimes can lead to an unrecognizable future.

Chapter 122

I was back in Vicenza and excited to return to work. Flavio was happy to see me, and even my supervisor commented that I was looking great. Everyone in the finance office and beyond knew of my whereabouts, but no questions were asked. It was time to return to office basics, but I had also promised myself to fully enjoy the summer.

And it certainly began very well. I was again working out daily, felt fantastic and looked great. The nearby cities were calling to me to return, and on some occasions, a few folks from the base tagged along to the beach in Jesolo. Those enjoyable evenings in the piazza were back on, keeping me busy and quite happy.

It seems only right to mention Piero and Giglia. They were part of a completely different crowd. Of course, it was Renato who introduced me to them. The guy simply knew everybody. The couple, so cordial and laidback, were big on meditation and very keen to recruit me. They were apparently part of a large group, maybe fifty or so, who shared a strong interest in the inner glow of spiritualism, and my new friends insisted I give it a try.

Now, my curiosity is such that anything deemed beneficial is worth trying. Therefore, on a Saturday morning, I was in a flat which served as a center for meetings, the initiation ritual, and some group meditation. However, once inside, it was the many peculiar surroundings everywhere which served as a sort of cautionary note. It seemed best to put things off for the time being. Why? Well, the main room was inundated with strange looking objects. Along with various statues and symbols, there was a huge poster of a human form sitting crossed-legged in a trance, but it had an elephant head. Nearby was a large poster of the group's spiritual leader, a man named Sai Baba. And in my eyes, he simply did not look spiritual. Perhaps it was best to get better informed and then decide if meditation was worth doing.

A few days after this brief excursion, Renato introduced me to someone else, Brian Sheen. Here was someone with a gracious and contagious smile. Like me, he was a Brit, but a real one. I discovered his profession, he sang opera, which is what had brought him to town. Well, it seemed like such a small world that we live in, doesn't it? And could it ever survive without music?

Brian now lived in Vicenza. He was part of the cast for a movie on the opera, Don Giovanni, by Mozart. The film would include many parts filmed in the piazza, while most of the other scenes would be shot in the city's surrounding areas. And, strangely enough, at least to me, the complexity of all this was a bit astounding. Here was an opera written by an Austrian; sung in Italian by an international cast that would become a movie being directed by an American, Joseph Losey, and filmed in the very city which was practically my new home.

I was eventually briefed on the story of the Don. It made me go out and purchase the opera, an older version, but that was a big mistake. Getting beyond the first act was impossible. To simple little old me, the music lacked harmony, and the singing, though the lyrics were comprehensible, made no sense at all. However, Brian had insisted I first read the libretto before listening to it. And the story, as related to me by him, is actually very interesting.

Don Giovanni is a curious character. Perhaps by modern standards, some would consider him a scoundrel. Obviously, his sexual appetite refuses to commit him to just one woman. And his only interest in women is sex. The libertine's conquests, if this can still be said without burning down the planet, are in the thousands. Spain is where he apparently worked the hardest. Brian had mentioned an aria where the Don's servant, Leporello, catalogues his master's busy schedule. It gives the number as 1,003 women in Spain alone. According to my friend's interpretation, that song is sort of an affront to whom it is being sung to, one of three ladies angrily pursuing Don, but secretly wanting him all to herself.

Oh well, my initiation into the world of opera was a total flop. Nevertheless, Brian and I got to see each other on various occasions and enjoyed some nice chats, in English, right there in the bars by the piazza. And just as life was treating me grand, a few peculiar issues arrived out of nowhere. They were not inundated with moral dark forces, or lyrical in any way, just laced with a heavy sprinkle of drama. In one case, Di Stefano drama.

Peter and Mary were now parents. It was joyful news to my ears. Yet it came with a huge problem. The baby's name. Truth be told, I like the name Margherita, and so did my brother and his wife. But it is our mother's name, and this created a real war in the Adrian Di Stefano household in Co-op City. Apparently, our father was beyond furious, and nothing would abate his ire.

Although thousands of miles from the scandal, my dad and stepmother would soon be in Sicily. And believe me, his full overblown anger was fully exposed. I witnessed something so harsh and ruthless, but now began to see that his overblown tantrums would always be a way of life with us. And truth be told, I also slightly questioned my brother and his wife's wisdom.

Another significant event, not one bit tragic, was over another birth. One of the Italian girls in the accounting branch, who knew Bianca, had informed me that she had given birth to a baby boy, Francesco. It seemed like a fine name, and my curiosity over the child had me truly hoping to somehow be able to see him. However, almost immediately my rehab instructor's words came back to me. It was better to not be so presumptuous, but just go with the flow.

Chapter 123

Palermo greeted me warmly. Once again, my grandparents accommodated me and were happy to have me on board. My folks would arrive the next day as they were in Rome for a week visiting one of Dad's friends and roaming around the Eternal City.

They arrived and were staying at a hotel. We soon met at some relative's home, and I witnessed an extremely sulking couple plagued with anguish while sharing the overblown tale on a daily basis. Fortunately, my mornings began at the flower shop with Peter's old friend. It was a lovely way to start the day, for we indulged in much joking and friendly chats, and touched on a bit of Italy's politics and some of its exciting cinema.

It was later in the day when my eyes confronted my father's tormented look. He was totally consumed with anger. His eyes flashed dark bitter feelings of hatred. Our stepmom, apparently very much in ca-hoots, simply sat back and allowed her husband to continuously relive the narrative. At times, the telling would include more details but always summarizing the totality of the sin. Just how could those two have done this? To have named their baby after the very woman who had abandoned us.

They had also managed to keep it a secret. It was on the day of the baby's birth when the truth was exposed. A slap in the face to our dad and certainly a declaration of war! That is why he outright refused to go to the hospital to see the newborn. And there was plenty of blame to go around. Mary's parents were Sicilians, born and bred in Corleone. How could they have forgotten the importance of family honor, traditions, and, most of all, a sense of allegiance.

It was too much for me to take. The same melancholy melody was played daily to a new startled and shocked audience. So, I chose to return up north sooner than planned. I was accompanied to the train station by my dad and two of Uncle Nicola's boys. My father was silent and distant in thought, and he would sometimes appear on the verge of saying something but then choose to keep it to himself.

My cousins, though young, sensed his dilemma. To me, it looked like a personal agony gone wild. What could I possibly say? However, what happened next while preparing to board the train shocked me to my core. For it was then that the man made a solemn oath: he would never forgive us two for having established a relationship with our mother. Tiny tears formed in his eyes while revealing he had wanted to deprive her of ever seeing us again.

Chapter 124

It is my opinion that changes are not only inevitable but sometimes necessary. They can sweep away burdening routines, stagnant processes, and, occasionally, even thrones that people latch on to forever. The major was promoted to colonel, and he walked with a bit more swagger in his stride, happily continuing his friendly and resourceful style, which served us all very well.

Our office again gained some new personnel and lost a few. Some soldiers returned to the U.S. while others arrived from there. There was another Italian-American soldier among us, much older than my section chief but purely Italian-bred and of higher rank than most office personnel. Plus, a rather unusual and somewhat entertaining playful individual, Sgt. Jack Julian Hope, kept us all laughing plenty.

Sgt. Hope was talkative, and no subject was off-limits. His wild chats made him a favorite with us in the travel branch, and his contorted facial expressions came along with a hearty chuckle or two. Now, the good sergeant almost immediately took up an issue which irked the office authority and so was promptly castigated. Everyone smoked cigarettes back then. The office air was horrible, and it was suffocating most folks, smokers and non-smokers alike, but it was a way of life. Our co-worker, Cristina, had often complained, but as both Flavio and myself diligently indulged in the ritual, she never pushed the issue, and neither did our boss nor any of the other non-smokers.

Flavio had attempted to quit. He had done an acupuncture session, a very expensive therapy according to him, and so we had assumed he had been cured. However, he practically cursed himself out for having spent a bundle on what he described as a foolish venture. The following day, he began begging me for a cigarette, and he eventually got one, and so life returned to normal in our branch.

Now Sgt. Hope swore he would clean up the office air once and for all. Which is why he had taken the initiative to request an air quality test. About a week later, the hospital sent one of their personnel to check the air in our office. A strange looking device was used, and we failed miserably. The air surrounding us was unhealthy and catastrophically so. So, the good sergeant took himself to see the colonel, who was quite angry over not having been consulted about the scheduled test yet was now being informed of the results.

No one will ever know exactly what occurred in that meeting. However, the next workday, a Monday, Sgt. Hope was given an order to move his desk outdoors. That is right. The soldier was now working at his desk but in the area behind the office, his back to the finance office building wall with him facing the ten-foot wall that separated the base from the outside world.

It was certainly a scandalous affair. Actually, at first, it seemed a bit funny. Not too much, of course, but it was mostly because the good sergeant appeared so indifferent, as if it was just a casual thing to do. There he was happily shuffling paperwork at his desk. However, the crazy ordeal did not last the entire day as our castigated silent hero eventually returned indoors, desk and all.

The Italian employees were having a good laugh. It was mostly the ones in the accounting branch, for they never held us in very high esteem. Some were now proclaiming we were truly an army of misfits, and someone even wondered how we had won the last war. Oh well, considering our on-and-off shenanigans, how could anyone argue with them?

Outside of that scandalous but trivial affair, things ran well at the finance office. But not according to the new Italian-American soldier, a sergeant-major in rank, and one who found much to criticize no matter how perfectly any process worked. In no time at all he began to get on everyone's nerves for almost daily he attempted to reinvent the wheel. That stubborn individual insisted rules and regulations were not being adhered to. Plus, he constantly barked that our processes needed a complete overhaul, and he had a perfect remedy for everything. Most of his ideas seemed a bit far-fetched, and quite a few had already been tried but provided hardly any positive results.

One day he came over to my desk. He ordered me to exit the area by the counter and address the officer standing nearby. But let me first clue you in as to why. The army has a regulation for every issue under the sun. For example, in this particular case, soldiers in uniform are not allowed to put their hand in their pockets. I was being dispatched to bring about regulatory finesse, and it required me confronting an officer who was doing the unthinkable—putting his hands in his pockets.

The individual was standing by a window and looking outside at the gloomy rainy day. Perhaps he was lost in his thoughts. My approach was cautious, my tone very polite as I spoke like a gentleman. The officer seemed quite surprised as he turned to face me, and my eyes bulged. The soldier was not only a colonel, but a highly decorated one. Believe me, there were medals everywhere. He heard me out, kept his hands where they were, and then said, "Specialist Di Stefano, I've never heard of such bullshit."

Oh, it was like music to my ears. Real religion! Like an unexpected Christmas present in the fall season! I was so tempted to both salute the officer and shake the gentleman's hand and maybe offer him a coffee or something, anything just to acknowledge his personal greatness. I was like a happy kid. My warm smile came forth most graciously as I returned to my desk. After all, mission accomplished.

My butt had just been placed on my chair when someone stood over me looking mystified. Well? So, I informed the sergeant-major of the encounter. My happy eyes claimed a small victory, but he refused to believe the outcome, which allowed me to state that maybe he needed to approach the officer himself. His face turned red as he retreated to his work station to hide behind a document.

Oh well, life was good! And one day I saw Bianca. It must have been two months after Francesco was born. She had obviously just resumed her work, and she smiled at me as if seeing the most wonderful person on the face of the planet. What could I do? What did I do? That afternoon had us going off the base as in past times to get a coffee. Pretty soon, after work hours, we again distanced ourselves from Caserma Ederle to fully embrace and resume our frantic passionate ways.

Chapter 125

My new roommate was from Kalamazoo, Michigan. What a strange name. I found it hard to believe such a place existed, but he insisted, and the map we eventually consulted, which he brought out to prove my ignorance, confirmed his statement. Just why was it that those settlers could not accept the very folks whom they had vanquished but then used their names?

Anyhow, Harold was assigned to the accounting office, which meant this guy was pretty smart. I soon became testimony to the fact that he was not just all numbers and statistics. He also had plenty of common sense and used it accordingly. Plus, a few of us had noticed how proudly he wore his airborne qualifications on his uniform, and one who jumps out of planes and can also add properly must certainly be treated with a high dose of respect.

The guy was neat, super clean, serious in his work, and, as I said, wore his uniform well. He was also somewhat talkative and fun but not always. A few months after constantly giving the best of himself, he would sometimes turn inward and refuse to show any side of him. This would last for several days, and it made no sense to me. My falling into a similar trance was only when I was going through cold turkey, which was something far behind me.

Fortunately, his time-outs were rather brief. It was easy to overlook them for just as quickly as he had vanished, he would reappear. Present Harold always liked whatever music was on, which back then was pretty much rock. Things proceeded well between us, and it was easy to overlook the fact that he was straight as a nail.

One Sunday, he got a complete tour of the city. Then after a grand lunch in a rather expensive restaurant. We decided to visit the piazza and sit on the cement steps outside the Bar Garibaldi. Perhaps we were confronting just what had driven us to join the army. Suddenly, a swift movement brought us a filthy mess to contend with.

Out of the blue, one or several of the pigeons overhead unloaded what must have been lunch. It was an awful sight to behold. My friend was hit dead center by plenty of ammo. He appeared startled, mortified, and perhaps wanted to blame me for having chosen our concrete seats. We rushed into the bar to use the bathroom, and even the owner, after approving our request, chuckled over my friend's misfortune, but then immediately stated that city hall needed to stamp out those awful creatures.

Our trip back to the base was a rather silent one but the following day all was well. Now just so you know, my other close friend on base was Richard. This somewhat noble fellow was also a true comedian. A very warm, funny chap, and he would always cleverly kill you with his closing lines. Nothing was off-limits in his repertoire, which was simply brilliant. Unfortunately, a few guys in the barracks thought Richard sometimes crossed the line. But in his world, boundaries did not exist as laughter was a sacred commodity, and it was hard to dispute such philosophy.

Perhaps he did exaggerate on one occasion. It occurred early Monday morning during the weekly linen exchange. Most of us dragged ass in turning in our old linen for clean ones. Typically, everyone who had just pulled off their linen from their bunks carried it hanging loosely from their hands while other people would fling it over their shoulders, as if it were a clothing garment.

Richard had just exited his room. He was moving quickly down the long hallway and bypassing others going to turn in their linen. Mind you, it was early, and everyone was pretty much dead to the world. Suddenly, my friend tossed his sheets entirely over himself and asked, "Am I late for the meeting?" A bit risky, and perhaps a dry sense of humor, for it certainly did not thrill everyone, but it seemed innocent and fun and was delivered by someone who did not have a racist bone in his body. To me, it was simply funny, just once, which was the way it went.

It was sometime after that gag when he performed at our small theater in Man of La Mancha. My, he was so natural on stage, moved gracefully and sang beautifully. And while I watched him perform, something which had once baffled me came to the surface, and it now made sense. It was a quote from a bizarre book of poetry by Jim Morrison, where he stated something peculiar regarding cinema.

In theater, one never forgets that before you are human beings. That is, other members of our species. It remains glued to you throughout the entire performance, and male or female performers are the same in their raw, real role, dressed cleverly and delivering lines they have mastered. Theater, like the male animal, no matter how expertly transformed in clothes or jewelry, never loses its crude form, for that is our true nature.

Whereas cinema cons the audience. The cast of actors and actresses deliver a part, yet the screen fenagles the viewers as they eagerly swallow and believe the fancy tale being given. It is similar to our female counterparts. They are so attractive, at times, gorgeous, often impossible to resist our longing for them. In reality, theirs too is a white washing of our senses, as they easily fake their true form, which requires that they shave, bury their odors, clean their mouths, hide sagging facial lines, and cling on to their desperate need to be loved.

Chapter 126

My faithful but rugged, beat-up Fiat died. That is correct, it failed to do anything. The ignition key turned but absolutely nothing happened. Which is what got me over to my mechanic, an Italian guy who worked on the base but also out of his large garage at home.

He came by my office that afternoon. We went to look the vehicle over, and the man smiled and suggested towing it to the junkyard, so that is what I did the following day. Fortunately, there was a nice car available.

It was a sporty small Alfa Romeo, a Giulietta 1600. It looked great! Although it was a bit overpriced, I did not feel like haggling over it, so once again I was driving but this time truly in style. My new means of transportation allowed Bianca and I to go much further out to the city's suburbs and countryside.

It was usually after having been on guard duty all night that the following day was all mine. Bianca and I would meet. She had taken the day off, and we would then have a pleasant trip to Asiago, which was always a good time. The serenity and fresh air of a mountain environment always created a laidback attitude with us, and it became almost impossible to return to the city. It dawned on me one day, how giving up drugs had not been easy, yet accomplished, but terminating our peculiar relationship was impossible.

Occasionally, I tried. Sometimes, when we met after work hours, she would bring Francesco. He was a gorgeous blond boy, and our time together at the park, even if brief, was worth every minute. Nevertheless, it was never easy to separate. He would look at me from inside her car and appear to be wondering why I was not there next to him. Then, as the vehicle drove off, his expression was one which could not comprehend my remaining behind.

Chapter 127

It was spring of 1979 when my roommate and I took an improvised trip to Rome. We boarded a train heading south to go explore one of Italy's oldest and most interesting cities during the Easter weekend. Once at the train station in Rome, we were queuing to enter the exchange office and get some Italian lira for our dollars.

Harold was merrily cataloguing which sites to see first when a monk approached us. He asked if we intended to convert dollars. Of course, we did, but my buddy looked a tad perplexed. Dealing in the black market, and with a stranger? His expression said it all, but the man in front of us looked like a monk. At least, such was my take on things. The elderly fellow was rather short and stout, had an angelic expression, wore a frock and sandals, and just seemed on the level. The monk suggested we follow him to his nearby quarters.

My roommate began to protest strongly, fortunately in English. Wanting to trust in God and his humble servant, I somehow managed to get my good friend to relax a bit. We three then walked out of the station. My buddy asked if I had completely lost it. Now, once on a side street behind the station, well, even my casual outlook took a slight turn, and as we continued walking on some small avenues, Harold was pleading with me to come to my senses.

That is exactly when the monk stopped and took out a huge ancient-looking key. It was very similar to the one Mr. Rossi used on that large door at his villa. And here too, a door opened to reveal a huge monastery behind a well-maintained garden. No doubt, we two gringos silently breathed a sigh of relief, perhaps most divinely, and then happily followed our host. We marched up a flight of stairs leading to his room.

I'm not certain why, but it was practically impossible for Italians to have access to foreign money back then, especially dollars. Unless you were heavily involved in commerce and the funds were strictly related to your business. However, there was also a messy bureaucratic process to navigate through, especially for dollars, a most prestigious and sought-after currency, and so this system kept most folks in need of foreign cash at bay.

Now believe me, our saint from heaven was in a buying spree. He wanted all we had, and he floored us with the rate he offered. I began to curse myself for not having taken more cash with me. Oh well, the two soldiers on holiday were certainly happy campers having gotten the deal of a lifetime. But wait, there was more to come! Once money changed hands, our beneficiary inquired about our lodging. Good question. We two homeless duds had simply embarked on our journey on the spur of the moment. So, the monk made a phone call and got us some very inexpensive rooms close by. Well, we now certainly felt lucky having been approached and enriched by this saintly person. Perhaps the soldier next to me would begin to show a finer appreciation for all our fellow neighbors on the planet, especially those who wear sandals.

We thanked the generous soul and our lucky stars. Now that kind abbot made another small contribution. He opened an old wooden cabinet and insisted on giving us lots of food items, like canned tuna, mackerel, and whatever else he could get his hands on. Apparently, when it rains it pours! So, while we walked along the street heading to the hotel, I wondered if more good luck would follow.

It certainly did as our accommodations were old but super clean. Plus, one of the staff members spoke excellent English, something a bit uncommon back then. Once we checked in, we put our things away and headed right out to explore the city's local sights. It was on to the Coliseum, the very first place in Rome to have served Christians, for this was at the top of Harold's list.

We set out on a stroll, knowing our destination but with no sense of how far off it was. Soon enough, there was that ancient entertainment gallery, and we both agreed this amphitheater was a great reminder of a long past glorious era. However, it certainly needed a facelift. Oh well, next came the Spanish Steps and a few other interesting places, and it stood out that the city was overwhelmed with visiting Christians and others, all here to attend Easter mass the following day.

Having moved around plenty, both our stomachs were rumbling. A nearby restaurant, which appeared inexpensive, grabbed our attention. Once inside and seated, it was impossible to not notice the customers at the tables close to ours. There were two distinctive cultures. To our right was a Japanese family, mom and dad and a little boy and girl, close in age. On the other side sat an Italian family, a middle-aged couple and two young boys.

One scenario left us a bit inquisitive. The Asian family members appeared like perfectly carved statues. It was an admirable but somewhat unusual scene. Not only were they mute to the core, but their bodies hardly moved. Perhaps the parents were lost in thought, apparently far from each other mentally, as if traveling in a twilight zone dimension of their own, and the children were certainly following in their footsteps.

Harold commented on their superb table manners. He said he wanted his children—future ones, of course—to resemble those kids. This was a bit difficult for me to grasp. But on the other hand, the folks on the other side, a Southern Italian family, carrying on loudly, made me also favor the silent Asian clan as soon enough, the boisterous four were starting to get on my nerves.

The smaller child was under the table. He was playing with his little plastic car and making loud engine noises. The brother, lacking a toy of his own, was using his silverware like an airplane and casually landing it and taking off from the table as his airport had expanded to the outer limits of that table. The parents had made a small attempt to still their kids, but they had failed miserably and appeared totally unconcerned and occasionally even managed to send a smile our way.

You can imagine which group I preferred. Yet not completely, for while any future children of mine would resemble them to some extent, never would they come under the auspices of the Nonna Vincenza harsh etiquette. If they needed to act like saints in a public environment, they would learn by virtue of seeing and accepting their parents' ways. And if a stricter method was necessary, then a bit of coercing would do, but never with ample severity.

Anyhow, Easter Sunday arrived. We came down to a late but hearty colazione. Back then, breakfast was simply a cappuccino and a croissant. That was it! But we, to the amazement of the hotel staff, had seconds, which we were charged for. We probably would have had another stab at it but sort of feared our reputation would suffer. It was for the sake of our nation, considering we have never been truly loved anywhere, that we chose not to exaggerate.

As we two soldiers were in good physical condition, our excursion that morning began with a walk to the Vatican. Boy, did we screw up royally! According to our map, it appeared to be a doable trek. And if the walk became impossible to finish, there would certainly be a taxi to hop into. Such was that morning's plan. There were no taxis.

Somehow, many exhausting hours later, we arrived at our destination. Mass had apparently just finished, and very soon we stared at an almost empty Saint Peter's Square. That is why that attractive site, quite astounding in architectural elegance, but now quite empty and practically all ours, felt slightly trivial. It was almost as if its spiritual significance could not absorb us properly, for something was certainly lacking.

Even our next plan failed us miserably. It was to dine at a restaurant called La Parolaccia. That morning at the hotel, we had assured ourselves that mass at the Vatican would cleanse us of our few insignificant sins. This would then have allowed us to commit some new trivial ones. For the restaurant allows its waiters to abuse the clients, both via insults and nasty jokes, and the customers can certainly push back and insult fair and square to their heart's delight. We were quite ready to do our part using what few Italian curse words we had prepared.

But it was Easter Sunday. Life had come to a complete standstill. We discovered that everything was closed as we desperately searched high and low for a place to eat. Our legs were quite exhausted when we finally spotted a bar run by Egyptians. We happily feasted on several sandwiches and downed a few bottles of Cokes. All this without one "parolaccia" coming out of either of us two weary travelers.

Such was our brief Roman holiday. The following morning, we were heading back up north. It was once past Florence that Harold stopped reading, lowered his magazine, looked at me and said, "Freud is the guy who believed everyone desires his mother." Perhaps something was slightly off in the wording of that sentence, for I simply replied, "Well, he certainly had a problem."

Chapter 128

We had a new branch chief. The Italian-American fellow was moved to another section. Our new sergeant was from South Carolina. As a matter of fact, I am not certain, but one thing I do know, we two certainly did not look anything alike. This is a fact of which I have absolutely no doubt. If a thin sliver of similarity existed, it was hard to see, yet one day our images almost created pandemonium.

Flavio and the Italian woman were on their afternoon coffee break. This is practically a religious custom on the base with all Italians and many others. Having attended a training class in administering first aid, I had just returned to my desk. Mason, the sergeant, ran over, greeted me most cordially but then ran out of the office. The bathrooms were located outside the building we were in, and he was obviously in quite a hurry to get there.

A few minutes later a soldier stood at the counter. The chap did not look too happy. I took several strides toward him and very politely asked if I could help him. The young Black man looked annoyed, put a form in front of me and asked if that was what I had requested. This certainly confused me, which is why I immediately followed up with "I don't think I have ever seen you before." Apparently, those words were not what he wanted to hear.

The soldier stared at me most incredulously. He stepped back an inch or two, making me a bit uncomfortable, and he very loudly said, "Yeah, I know. Cause we all look alike. Ain't that right?" Sensing we had gotten off to a bad start, and being somewhat concerned, I excused myself. The lieutenant's office was very close, and that sharp officer heard me out, and we soon walked over to where the soldier stood. As we arrived, Mason was back and making his way to the counter. Once there, he looked at the guy and most politely asked "Did you get that form?"

The lieutenant's eyes and smile signaled having grasped the facts. We both returned to our work, me less confused and perhaps even feeling comfortably numb. Thank heavens my calm had prevailed. A bit later, I reflected on what had occurred, and a tiny voice suggested our customer had some issues clouding his way of thinking. It was also apparent that racism is obviously not a one-way street. For some time now, my foolish mind believed we White folks were to blame for all the apparent anger aimed at us.

Oh well, once Mason got all the facts, we both had a good hearty laugh. He then returned to his desk and continued reading some regulations, but a few minutes later he came over and looked at me quite startled. Mason then lit a cigarette and curiously asked, "Damn, do you think we look alike?"

Chapter 129

Caserma Ederle was suddenly on the map. Headquarters SETAF was now a safe-haven to our military personnel evacuating Iran. At our office, no one had anticipated such a huge number of arrivals from a part of the world we hardly knew. Nevertheless, we rolled out the red carpet, and provided funds, a comprehensive attitude, fun chats, and anything else we could furnish to the soldiers now in transit while awaiting a new assignment.

The problems in Iran had begun manifesting themselves some years before. Whereas now, a small revolution had fully escalated. And yet, unlike most radical movements which sometimes generate necessary changes, those at the helm in Persia were promoting a way forward, but via a return to ancient ways. For some time now, I had witnessed on Italian TV what looked more like acts of sheer fanaticism. Oh well, we at the finance office were useful, and at times we felt like we heard it all.

It was during these trying times when Lorenzo sought me out. He was at our counter and looked like a man on a mission. My friend worked at the Italian bank on the base. We had gotten acquainted by chance a few days after my arrival in '76. It was mostly his love for all things American, especially James Brown and soul music, which had pulled me in, but also had me wondering how this was possible, for modern Italian music was so different. Anyhow, after a cordial greeting, I was informed he was here to recruit me.

A friend of his managed some cultural and linguistic classes. It may have been for the Partito Liberale, as that political party ventured into more than politics. The manager was desperately seeking an English teacher, and what struck me was hearing that no experience was required. Just how was this possible? An institution would gamble hiring any member of the human stock, as long as they could ramble on in English? I simply refused to get involved.

It was Bianca who convinced me otherwise. Once we met that afternoon, she was overjoyed with my friend's proposal and insisted I was perfect for the job. She advised me to contact Lorenzo once back at my desk, which I later did after wondering about her true objective. Was it simply to ensure herself that my evenings entailed work, versus me pursuing whatever came my way? Oh well, the next day I phoned the lad seeking a teacher. I did this with hesitation for the idea of facing students who depended on me to learn a subject I mastered but knew nothing about, had me slightly concerned.

I even recalled what had once puzzled me back in school at St. Anthony. When the teachers tackled analyzing grammar, they would draw a horizontal line, placed the subject, the predicate, and an object, if one was to be had, on that line, separating each one with a small vertical line. They then included other lines under one of the words on top with words associated with it. Now just what did it all mean? And here it was many years later, and my lack of grammatical sense was still solid.

Nevertheless, I met with the manager. He asked very few questions and offered me two evening classes and one on Saturday afternoon. It seemed only right to mention my lack of experience, however, once the salary, tax-free, was mentioned, we shook hands rather firmly.

I would simply give it my best. So, feeling somewhat blessed and ready to start teaching English, Bronx accent and all, it was now onward into the unknown. After all, who could say what this new adventure might lead to?

Chapter 130

My trips to Villa Rossi always felt like a homecoming. Alessandro not only treated me like a son but always made me laugh. Now he and my mom, although of a completely different breed, got along nicely, unless she had some issue to gripe about. And my grandmother was enjoying a rather casual lifestyle well-groomed to someone her age.

Unfortunately, there was now some concern over my future. Four years of military service would soon end, and my old quandary regarding work was again challenging me. Returning to the U.S. was out of the question. But what next? Alessandro accepted that a career in the military was not for me, and he even asked if I had considered getting a British passport. It would allow me to work, and perhaps the military requirement in Italy would get overlooked, considering my age. I had no answer to offer.

The matter, however, was set aside for the time being. Some members of the Rossi family would soon be with us. My favorite person, Adriana, the only female Rossi, but the one whom I treasured most, was among our guests. She was elderly, yet not at all old in any way, most serene, and wise beyond her years. What had truly captured my heart and soul were her excellent manners and impeccable speech, especially those soft pauses between thoughts, as if slightly contemplating. It was all just so captivating.

Adriana sat opposite me at the dinner table. She occasionally gave me all her attention. Which is why my upcoming venture into teaching had me mention being concerned. My fears were quickly cast aside as my listener suggested finding a good grammar book to work with. She somehow got on to Esperanto, the invented international language which had never truly taken off. According to her, it fared badly for it lacked the fluency and natural progress of a real language.

She even stated that one day English would play a large part in the world of communication. For its linguistic gift was expressing much but with few choice words. She was certain of this and claimed it was the U.S. which would internationalize it. Just as American music, like jazz, rock and roll, and various forms of entertainment had so easily been accepted and appreciated, now even the language arriving from a nation dominating the world stage would strongly impact everyone to use it.

I then asked her about something which baffled me. Did she think Italy's dialects—all countries have plenty—would continue to endure. Adriana believed all Italian dialects were strongly engrained as a major social communications channel, and yet it was possible they could one day lose their appeal. For as nations modernize and various sectors of their industry globalize, the national language would certainly become much more relevant and would soon prevail over the dialects. She concluded by saying that only time would tell.

It was while listening to this gracious lady that something caught my attention. Everyone at the dinner table, with the exception of myself and my mother, were all highly educated people. Therefore, they held a strong desire for diverse cultural knowledge, and they also mastered a keen sense of traditional etiquette, so they understood the world we lived in very well. Whereas I, somehow simply got by. But what about my mom? She hardly ever participated in our discussions. Perhaps they even caused her a bit of discomfort, which she certainly hid well. Yet, she often smiled at me, appearing happy to see me there. It felt like a hidden message being displayed. I was not a true member of the class around me, but via her presence, a small role had been forged.

Chapter 131

There was not an empty seat in the classroom. It would have been impossible to accommodate a new student. Every face looking my way appeared to be evaluating the carcass standing before them. I had no book to work with, so that first evening was almost complete improvisation. And somehow, miraculously, it went rather well.

We began with the basics. This led to plenty of repeating small sentences, and sometimes I wrote on the board to instill the idea expressed. Occasionally, my horrible Bronx accent, although used most diplomatically, cleaned up some students' pronunciation, and some lingering smiles led me to think that maybe some progress was being made.

It was not so Tuesday night. I was improvising again, bookless, and clueless. Only this time my students, some a tad well versed in English, were very demanding, and there was a constant challenging request for explanations of grammar and its proper usage. A few questions even confused me, and a couple of students appeared bewildered and perplexed by my inability to provide answers. But somehow, again, as perplexing as it was, I survived, but barely.

Thank heavens the conversational class on Saturday restored a bit of faith in me. We talked about any subject that the students found interesting. Plus, sharing my knowledge of rock music, visiting Asia in the early seventies, and the Vietnam War brought a sense of wonder to their faces. They told me what they knew, and everyone contributed in some form or fashion. A bit of laughter would ensue at various times. It appeared my overall performance throughout the session had gone very well.

Two new students joined the group the following Saturday. Both females, both gorgeous, one's English a bit more fluent than the other. Our first subject, suggested by one of the students, was the million-dollar question, what constitutes a healthy marriage. Now, occasionally one of the two new women appeared a tad annoyed, not sure with whom, myself or the other students, yet, she had much to say. And unless mistaken, she appeared to be carefully observing me.

Our session felt a bit long. At the end of the class, a few students were at my desk just to chat some more. Perhaps they also had some questions over something which had been said. No one appeared in a hurry to leave but eventually did, and then one of the two new women approached me, smiled, and asked me to join her for a glass of wine. Well, now, what could I say? And that is how I met Francesca Zanini.

We became slightly acquainted over a glass of Pinot Grigio. Unfortunately, I had a previous commitment with a foxy female soldier on base. Therefore, I claimed to be returning to guard duty, and that someone was now filling in for me. I even dared to complain about the injustice of military life. We agreed to meet during a weeknight and so we did.

Francesca was not over talkative. She appeared rather serene, not immune to challenging my take on things, which was fine, and she certainly began acquainting me with other possible outlooks. Her sunny smile, beautiful face and perfect outfit had me very interested in seeing more of her.

We soon met regularly. Then quite by chance, she discovered my bond to the Friuli region. It obviously shocked her. She had assumed that I was a true Yankee, but not from Connecticut, and certainly not in any king's court. It was upon revealing my plan that she frowned. My mother had just purchased a flat in Udine for her and Alessandro's final years of retirement. Francesca then insisted on joining me, as her folks lived in a small town not too far from that city.

It was early Friday evening when we took to the highway. Almost immediately, Italian substituted English, and it then became our permanent language which suited us two just fine. I discovered that Francesca had grown up in a small town, only this one was near the city of Padova. Years later, her folks had moved to the town of Martignacco—our present destination. And quite amazing, or amusing, was discovering that her family had arrived there the very same year Peter and I had been whisked away to Palermo.

Upon finishing school, she had moved to Vicenza to join her eldest sister. She found work with a high-fashion clothing firm, and believe me, her impeccable attire was testimony to that firm's rich clothing apparel. Now, the young lady next to me not only dressed divinely, but she also spoke most enthusiastically about her line of work and her co-workers. She was quite happy with her decision to have abandoned a small town for the lovely city she now resided in.

During the somewhat long drive, she turned inwards for a while. It was a brief pause, a time-out. And sharing a bit of silence just seemed quite natural, fully acceptable, and felt okay. Eventually we arrived at an old farmhouse. After a few minutes together with her folks, it was time to go join mine in Udine. During the last part of my trip, a thought within surfaced to the forefront of my mind. I was certain she was the woman I would spend the rest of my life with.

Chapter 132

The new year had us two love birds in a strong relationship. Actually, it was three. Now, please do not judge me too harshly, for it was so unlike me to multitask in matters of the heart. Nevertheless, my companion at the base continued to play a role in our weekday affair but much less.

On one occasion, while we were heading to the coffee shop, Bianca startled me. She mentioned having seen me downtown with a very beautiful woman. What could I say? It was my turn to clamp down, look away, and wait for the coast to clear, as she had done with me in the past when I would plead with her to leave her husband. Our relationship would now certainly terminate, for my military time would end soon, and although we two did not want to let go just yet, it was inevitable.

Our last encounter was not so grand. She dropped me off in front of the entrance to the base. I felt a little dirty, almost as if I had betrayed my wife. It was not said but certainly understood that we were parting ways. And while reentering the base, Harold's wise counsel, once offered to console me, now truly hit the mark. I was the person who brought her fun and a healthy dose of passion. Things which were obviously missing at home. After all, what is life without laughter and excitement?

A few weeks later, I was on my way back to the U.S. The deputy post commander had refused to grant me a European Out. Under this program, soldiers in Europe were allowed to remain in the country where they were stationed upon finishing their military service. This forced me to return to Fort Dix to separate from the army even though I had joined it in Vicenza. Once finishing there, the Bronx once again accommodated me.

Co-op City was my temporary home. I continued to avoid the old neighborhood and my former friends. At times, my spirit felt empty and deprived of serenity and hope. My daily outlook was rather void of anything that mattered. It was almost like looking at a painting by Edward Hopper. Even the folks in the area where we lived appeared like total strangers, among themselves also, and if a slight greeting could be shared, it was usually disregarded rather than given.

Then something rather unusual occurred. My father, a man of good intentions, did the unthinkable, he set me up on a blind date. This unexpected initiative simply shocked me. However, it seemed only right to fully accept the gesture and thank him. The nonchalant explanation provided ended with a million-dollar question, what did I have to lose?

Barbara was a few years older than me. Yet, it seemed insignificant. We chatted in a friendly tone as she drove us to New Rochelle, and after a pleasant walk, we dined at an Italian restaurant. She was curious about my long stay in Italy, and most of my information dealt with a bit of customs and traditions and a tad of family history in a country full of talkative folks. I'm not sure when it exactly occurred, but she delved into her personal life and offered it with much humor and enthusiasm. Nevertheless, she did mention having recently divorced an abusive husband who was too controlling. Then out came her immense love for their small daughter whom she occasionally shared a bit with her ex.

Perhaps one who already gave himself to two women could easily embrace a third, but that was not to be. Having promised Francesca that upon my return we would continue our relationship forced me to conclude my date on a friendly note. We two New Yorkers parted amicably, but Barbara's eyes flashed a disappointing glance for she had happily given me her phone number, but there was no commitment forthcoming.

My startled folks diligently grilled me the following evening. It was never said explicitly, but my manhood was being questioned by a somewhat angry father and a rather confused stepmother. I had nothing to prove to anyone and managed to talk my way out of committing to anything. And the next day, a phone call made me realize it was time to leave. For upon arriving, my folks had suggested contacting a placement agency which had just informed me of several exciting positions available. One was with a travel agency offering annual trips to visit and rate some of their more exotic resorts.

So, why not jump at one of these jobs? My folks were truly baffled with my plans to return to Italy. Explaining my dilemma left the two interrogators quite confused. They could not fathom my sense of isolation here, and although never uttered aloud, I could not be in a relationship where there was already a child. After a bit of silence, my father looked at me and angrily asked, "And just what the hell are you going to do in Italy?" That, my friends, brought my day to an end.

It was Peter and Maria who offered a sense of warmth during my visit with them. They invited me over several times and, and they both grasped my need to move on. Not only did I enjoy their company, but their baby was such a beautiful child. Peter brought me to JFK, and he assured me that once the baby was a bit older, they would come visit, and we would catch up at Mr. Rossi's villa.

Chapter 133

Although Vicenza is an enchanting city, the section I had to visit, called the Questura was not so charming. The institution which decides the faith of immigrants in country had already seen me several months prior, once reentering from my brief visit in the Bronx, and it would now accommodate my stay in country.

The officer in charge, Maresciallo Di Salvo, had given me a three-month visa. I simply needed to find a job, and he would then extend my visa for five years. My heartfelt thanks had been delivered most sincerely. Now mind you, a friend of mine, Giorgio, had prepared me for that visit. Years back, he, too, had left the army, but with a European Out, and had been through the process. He was now happily married and worked near the base, so it seemed quite possible that I could attain a similar outcome.

Giorgio had warned me about the maresciallo's theatrical pranks. It included a steady dose of very loud verbal jargon to instill the fear of God in the poor folks outside his office waiting to see him. My friend's advice had been to remain calm while nicely insisting Italy would be my new home. After all, I was born to Italian citizens and had left the country as one myself.

Unfortunately, there was no job under my belt. Oh, just so you know, my stint as an English teacher the previous year had lasted only four weeks. Much to the disappointment of the students, I threw in the towel. But truth be told, I felt unqualified to teach that subject. Now, over a period of several weeks, hundreds of resumes had been mailed throughout the city and beyond. The miracle I had been hoping for was not forthcoming.

My only interview was with a firm outside Vicenza. A total failure! The administrative assistant, a middle-aged woman, had greeted me most cordially. Yet her boss, owner and kingpin, had acted very indifferently and was even a bit rude. It was apparent that he was a no-nonsense type for her whole demeanor changed once we entered his office. She appeared ready to bow and expected the same from me, which yours truly had not fully grasped but later regretted.

The firm had some lucrative contracts with two companies in Libya, and they desperately needed someone who spoke English.

The owner sat at his desk with a clenched jaw and furrowed eyebrows. He curtly provided some information about the office, and then asked me what skills I would bring to his firm to improve their lot. This caught me off guard, and my inconsistency and amateurish follow-up did not win the man over.

Therefore, I was jobless and preparing to face Maresciallo Di Salvo, but life is full of surprises, and one had recently occurred. I had run into Brian Sheen. While we were enjoying a cappuccino and I was whining about my upcoming visit, he proposed the inevitable. Brian told me to quit stalling and get a British passport. Having been born on British soil, I was a Brit, so why delay a reality? Besides, they were great-looking documents, and the English embassy was in nearby Venice.

The following morning, my past concern about dual citizenship was laid to rest. At the British embassy, an elderly and well-dressed lady, slightly regal looking and not so easy to understand, inquired about my need for that document. Once my story was revealed, gently, briefly, and in my best English, she simply stared at me and said, "How sorry!" Her words were the least of my concern, for Brian Sheen had me off and running, and there was simply no stopping me now.

Well, there I was, facing Maresciallo Di Salvo. I was actually sitting. My hands and underarms were drenched in sweat even though it was not a damp day. The light chewing out of three months ago was still fresh in my mind. The man had insisted he could not comprehend why any intelligent human being would give up the U.S. for Italy. Now, he certainly remembered me and asked if I had found work. That was when, after taking a deep breath, my practiced pitch was delivered with much hope.

It began with an explanation of my new circumstances. Then, rather casually, my British passport came out, and although I was ready to explain its origins, I got no further in stating the facts. The man exploded like Vesuvius. The entire ceiling above us shook. Perhaps some paint chips landed on my head as he bellowed out like a sailor of old having spotted a whale! With his shocked expression, he now refused to face me as he turned and looked away, almost as if he could hardly bear to acknowledge my presence.

For a moment, he reminded me of a historical documentary I had seen on TV. Mussolini was addressing a huge crowd and appeared to be inspecting them to see if they appreciated his words. Maresciallo Di Salvo screamed for his assistant to come over. He invited the officer to now witness "un miracolo." The man's face was now cherry red, and his penetrating eyes were instructing his assistant to concur. It was as if some unthinkable sort of crime had been pulled off right under their noses. Then he belted out, "Yesterday he was American. Today he is British. Next week he'll be Russian."

Oh well, Giuliano Di Stefano, as my British passport identified me, was given a five-year visa. Soon a work permit came my way, then a health insurance card, which granted me not the best but free medical care. Now believe me, things were starting to look up, and the wonderful woman I was living with seemed to have expected as much. She was always so cool.

Some days later, I shared the news with Renato. My, he was truly happy for me. He even suggested that I make a trip to a firm on the outskirts of the city. The company had a lucrative contract with the U.S. military base in the movement of household goods for all the personnel, both military and civilians, sent to or leaving Caserma Ederle.

Francesca lent me her Fiat 500. The following morning it took me to the firm Roiatti, located some distance outside the city. The company not only catered to all American personnel in Vicenza, but even to soldiers in some of the other small bases scattered about in the northern part of Italy. And though unknown to me, there were military personnel in some of the most remote places one could imagine.

The manager appeared thrilled with me. He had begun to speak in an awful broken English, but we soon converted to Italian, and things proceeded rather well. My new line of work included everything associated with packing and unpacking household goods. I was also to greet and communicate with the customers, act as a translator for my crew, pack and label items, and then bring boxes to the containers they would be stored in. But, most importantly, I was responsible for all inventory, and it was crucial to ensure the customers were satisfied with our work.

It amounted to plenty of grind for what were measly hourly wages. No problem! Work had never hampered my outlook based on earnings. It had simply challenged me to always do my best. I thanked the manager for his time, my being hired on the spot, and we both shook hands.

Meanwhile, Francesca and I were enjoying the comfort of living together. She loved music and had introduced me to some Italian artists, but she simply could not get enough of ours. Especially Simon and Garfunkel, whom she hardly knew but now adored.

She was an artist. Her paintings looked fantastic, something she did not always agree with. When she explained the technique and form, they became even more interesting. Just as rewarding were instances when she would point out specific details of a church's ceiling, explaining the figures and their historical importance. At times I felt a bit plain but at least quite ready to participate with my limited knowledge.

It was her love for fashion and elegant clothes that also made her a star in my eyes. Every suit, outfit, dress, or anything she matched and put on appeared to have been designed just for her. Often on Sundays, as was the fashion back then, we both dressed to the nines. You would have thought we were Hollywood celebrities off to receive an award or two. And very soon came an introduction to books.

I certainly read and enjoyed what literature I tackled. But she acquainted me with books I would never have picked up, like the chronicles of the Courtney family. The author, Wilbur Smith, had written a series of novels, my favorite was *Rage*, where he flings you into some rather intriguing and brilliantly told narratives of life in South Africa a while back. The books provided a great depiction of the first Europeans settling in that foreign land, and it made me reflect on what I had seen in just two days there.

At times, we seemed to be a perfect couple. Our bond, subtle yet strong, though not overly steeped in physical passion, complemented our days together in a rather soothing and cordial manner. One Sunday afternoon while driving back from her folks' place, it dawned on me that I was one lucky person to have friends like Luciano, who indirectly got me to the very place where Francesca and I met. But a greater sense of luck was based on this now growing relationship on which to build a solid foundation.

Chapter 134

I commuted to work by bus. That beautiful Alfa Romeo Giulietta was long gone. Keeping it would have been a bit too costly. But also, if you ask me, a tad ridiculous. It was easy to buy an Italian car and bring it on the base. It then got converted to an AFI (American Forces in Italy) licensed plates. However, doing the opposite was no easy matter.

Several steps were involved, and one was a bit extreme. It entailed putting the vehicle on a ferry, sending it out to sea, and then returning it to the port. As if you had cleansed it of some impurity, sort of like a sacrament. Plus, the amount of paperwork processed and money required was infinite. How Bizarre!

Oh well. In instances when I needed to get to work super early, for we occasionally traveled far, Francesca would lend me her car. She could easily catch a ride to work with a colleague.

And my being employed as a mover proceeded very well. My only complaint was not having learned the Venetian dialect. Most of my co-workers spoke it quite naturally, of course, and a couple outright refused to speak Italian.

Every morning, we were separated into groups and given a different assignment. There were two other interpreters, both American military retirees, and so three squads had a daily mission to accomplish. The firm contracted out truck drivers. They provided their own vehicles and were paid a fixed amount for a day's work, which occasionally created a problem. We, the movers, were paid by the hour, and so we were in no hurry to finish a job. The truckers wanted to get home as soon as possible, allowing them to work on the family farm. If we returned to the warehouse by 3:00 p.m., the drivers headed home most happily, whereas the rest of us were not so thrilled to have the remainder of the day off.

A few employees appeared a tad rough. Some months after coming on board, an unusual situation brought us all a bit of entertainment. It was over someone named Giacomino. He looked rugged and a bit thuggish, but he was a small-framed and smelly individual. Although a bit elderly, he had recently bragged of having seduced his second wife's youngest daughter, who was still in her mid-teens. His constant boasting and rude remarks, plus his double-crossing ways, kept us all at a distance.

We had just terminated a job somewhere in Rimini. The packing of things had begun at exactly eight, and we finished a bit after two. Our driver got us to a nearby trattoria, which was beginning to empty, and we were seated among a few other customers. By the way, my co-workers certainly knew where to eat and which places to avoid.

I was sitting next to Dino, someone I truly liked and often talked with, me in Italian and he in Venetian. He had expressed a surprise with the immaculate cleanliness of the house just serviced, for this was not always the case with some military folks. Then, quite unexpectedly, Dino stood up and walked over to where Giacomino, sat. He picked up the large ceramic wine vase on the table and dumped the contents on the head of the scoundrel. We all watched wide-eyed with our mouths hanging open and so were some of the nearby customers who had witnessed this. There was now an unbearable silence permeating throughout the trattoria.

Giacomino jumped up. Although drenched in wine, he began to swear, and we all assumed he would start swinging. The customers at the nearby tables were now focusing on us and commenting on the unfolding scene, all probably wondering how it would end. Dino, the much taller and well-built one, and a no-nonsense guy, simply asked the very irate wet co-worker, "What is it you had to say about me?"

Fortunately, it ended there. There was a bit of mumbling by the smaller man while he headed to the bathroom to clean up. Everyone was much relieved, and the no-nonsense guy among us appeared happy, for in our eyes he had been decorated a hero for services rendered. My curiosity regarding what had transpired to bring about this scene was gnawing at me. But Dino and I were not yet that close, so if a proper moment arose, I would inquire at that time.

And so, we hungry souls raised our glasses in a small toast for a job well done in record time—the packing of household goods that is. We ate like famished workers, chatted very happily, and eventually rode back to Vicenza. Suddenly, everyone began shouting, and the person by the right-side window rolled it down to let in some air. We were confronting a well-known problem that I was not yet aware of. The truck driver, having drank too much, was now falling asleep at the wheel.

Our chorus lines were conveyed in fair unison. We continuously belted out any topic without letting up until the problem appeared somewhat resolved. Yet we all remained vigilant. We each kept one eye on the road and one on our fucking driver. Occasionally, our voices resumed a full volume pitch, and I felt like an opera star, delivering volumes of foolishness while performing most intently.

Chapter 135

August was the month when all Italians flocked to their vacation holes. It was typical back then to arrive in any city and find it nearly deserted. Almost everything would be closed for their owners would abandon their enterprise to retreat quite far from their city.

It was the first week of that month when Francesca and I boarded a train to Palermo. While we were both happy with our vacation plans, we were still devastated by a recent tragic event. A bomb had gone off at the train station in Bologna. Eighty people had lost their lives and more than twice as many had been severely hurt. What a sick and senseless act, for the idea of killing innocent people just made no sense to us.

Watching the ghastly scenes on TV the day after the explosion brought a lump to my throat. Listening to some agonizing comments made by the journalists on location was just as painful. What became most disheartening and truly hard to comprehend occurred as our train pulled into the station at Bologna. We got a sense of the gruesome massacre from the destruction still visible.

I had never fully understood the young people fighting the Italian government. And since my arrival in 1975, it was mostly a group called the Red Brigades who made the headlines and appeared almost untouchable. Their crimes were dreadful, mostly against civilians at random. And for some time, it seemed like no one was ever truly brought to justice.

Fortunately, our train quickly left the station. We shared a chat with the folks in our compartment about what we had just witnessed. The overall opinions referred to those responsible as animals, having nothing human within, and being totally deprived of compassion. Eventually, I put it all behind me and returned my attention to Ken Follett's *Eye of the Needle*, a small gift from my beautiful girlfriend which now completely possessed me.

It felt like a long haul down the Italian peninsula. Finally, after passing Calabria and then crossing over to Messina, we arrived in Palermo. At the train station, a bus took us to Passo di Rigano, the neighborhood where Aunt Felicia lived. We had spoken by phone when I had announced our plan to visit and asked for help in locating a good hotel. My aunt was adamant that we stay at her place. She and family would be away vacationing elsewhere, so the flat was ours for several days until their return.

After settling in and making ourselves comfortable, we went out. It was mostly to pay a visit to my grandparents and Uncle Roberto who was now living in that small room I once occupied. Again, it was rumored he might not return to the U.S. Remembering the pleasant days spent with my uncle in the Bronx, I looked forward to a friendly encounter at my grandmother's, but that was not to be.

Something was terribly wrong! Upon entering the flat, we confronted two sullen faces that refused to speak to us. We newcomers felt totally put out.

What could be the problem? Oh well, their icy silence forced us to cut our visit short, and we simply moved on. Yet, we did manage to shake hands and kiss cheeks in entrance and departure. After all, traditions always surpass expectations, no?

It was then on to see some of the city. Plus, it seemed wise to find a hotel before my aunt got back. We soon stumbled on an old but clean place not far from the train station. Our room came at a reasonable price, and so we registered to move in later that week. The owner, an older gentleman, who was quite helpful in some ways, even suggested we visit the nearby restaurant Da Ciccio, and so we did. That evening, we allowed ourselves to feast like celebrities pulling out all stops and its culinary glory had us coming back a few nights later.

Palermo was a unique visual treat. Its mix of Western and Arabic architecture creates a mesmerizing effect on the senses. We took in everything from Norman palaces to Christian churches. And what would a visit to Palermo be without experiencing the Vuceria. My grandmother had once dragged me there as a kid. Absolutely nothing had changed. One could still hear the constant frantic yelling from the food peddlers, who were lively and entertaining. We even got a small treat from one of the happy vendors, for it was obvious we were not locals, but to some extent among our own people, at least that seemed to be the case.

Francesca was a big hit with all my relatives. Well, with the exception of you know who, but you can't win them all. We two enjoyed such appetizing meals with all my uncles' families, but more palpable were the long conversations regarding the local traditions and what distinguished Sicily from the Italian peninsula. My Uncle Nicola remarked that Sicilians consider themselves "scaltri"—shrewd, sort of—and therefore, so is their approach to all things.

Soon enough, two of my uncles' boys attached themselves to us. They tagged along to a nearby beach which they knew well. Later, we explored the nearby rocky shores for mollusks, which they called "patiedde". They were delicious but not sufficient to make a meal, which is why on the way home we ate a few arancine. Back then this was strictly a Sicilian treat unheard of anywhere else in Italy.

Francesca and I were down to our final days before returning home. Along with other members of the Di Stefano clan, we were invited to pass the day at Uncle Luca's country estate. My uncle had obviously done well for himself as his business had flourished throughout the years. With his move by the entrance near the cemetery, his business had acquired a lot more space, but he had also purchased a new flat in the city and, a few years later, the summer home we visited that day.

Boy, did we eat! To say food is important to Italians is an understatement. It is what we live for. Our meal began at two in the afternoon and simply kept going. From a large assortment of appetizers to pasta and various light meat dishes in tomato sauce, to fried fish, eggplant parmesan, and other in-season vegetables from their garden, there was just so much food—not to mention plenty of homemade wine.

An oppressive heat wave was devastating the island, but the abundant shady trees and a pleasant breeze kept us cool. My goodness, I must confess that I have never seen my relatives so cheerful. The wine certainly helped. We two northerners discovered that the occasion for our union was to send us off most happily so we would return, soon and often. This simply confirmed how wonderful my relatives really were, especially Uncle Luca, who had always had a fancy for both Peter and me.

It was Uncle Nicola who drove us two tourists back to the hotel. We got back late that night or early the next morning, depending on your perspective. Now can you believe this? The front door was locked, like bolted shut to keep criminals out. I rang the doorbell for quite some time, but there was no answer. Then my uncle, being a tad mellow from the drinking, but still quite his old self, took over and suddenly began pounding strongly on the old wooden door.

Perhaps the man felt the need to make a statement to his local countrymen. For he certainly got someone's attention as a window above us opened, and an elderly woman stuck her head out to see who was causing all the ruckus. Before she got a word in, my uncle who was facing her with an unbelievable look in his eyes, bellowed out, "Is this a hotel or an army base?"

You cannot imagine how much we hated to leave. Yet, my holiday was limited, being expected back at work Monday morning. Oh, by the way, that evening at Uncle Luca's place we came to terms with the harsh encounter at my grandparents' place. Although no one commented, it confirmed my personal suspicion that traditions have an agenda all their own.

How could we have been so naïve? In the eyes of some of my relatives, we two visitors were living in sin. Venial or moral, who can say, but my grandmother and her son, not necessarily a practicing Christian but certainly one with morals, considered our union scandalous and totally unacceptable. So be it, I thought. And yet many years later, this issue would resurface, leaving me quite speechless but slightly overjoyed.

Once back in Vicenza, Francesca's mother came to visit. Naturally, having learned a valuable lesson in Palermo regarding the nature of relationships, we prepared accordingly. It was crucial not to repeat our foolishness. We coordinated a plan in order to not raise any suspicion over our bonding ways.

It was Francesca's sister Anna who picked up her mom at the train station and drove to our place. Our plan consisted of me casually arriving much later as if just visiting to say hello. Mine would be a brief stay, somewhat well-thought-out and delivered with a most sincere effort to present myself as I was, a simple lad who just wanted to get along and not put anyone out. It would have worked perfectly had it not been for Alessio.

I arrived approximately an hour after our guests had settled in. All were in the kitchen area sharing coffee and a few recent events from the Friuli region. My contribution to their chat keyed in mostly about work and fitting in with my co-workers. Surprisingly, Anna's five-year old son, Alessio, was among them, but as always, not sitting still for very long. Soon, no one was paying much attention to him, and the boy had sort of disappeared but reappeared again, holding a pair of my shoes.

My swift improvisation did not fool anyone. I mentioned we had gone shopping for shoes a few days back. My new shoes were so comfortable I simply kept them on and had forgotten the old ones here. I removed them from the young critter's hands, feeling slightly embarrassed, and asked Francesca for a bag to put them in. It was evident, however, that the elderly woman, wise beyond her years, was way ahead of me. Being the gentle soul she was, plus, one who always measured her words, my future mother-in-law chose to change topics.

We two love birds enjoyed a laugh later that evening. Nevertheless, a week later, the real issue surfaced unexpectedly. Francesca and I were in a coffee shop when out of the blue, our future was being questioned. Like, what would it entail? I responded that we would marry. Her sparkling eyes certainly approved. She then asked me when. This would be her decision, according to me, and so the beautiful young lady next to me began making plans.

It must sound so unromantic and perhaps shoddy. There was no engagement ring, and I did not drop to one knee to inquire if she would have me. And it seemed only right. We both understood one thing—our long search for a compatible one was finally over. We were meant to meet, remain together, and wed. And we both wanted to start a family. November 22nd was the chosen date. It sounded fine to me until a bit later when I recalled that JFK was killed on that day. Oh well, we were far from Dallas and the reach of American politics.

Chapter 136

Work was demanding. Believe me, Giuliano Di Stefano was busting his butt. My colleagues certainly noticed and respected me for it. Perhaps, a few even admired me for having chosen to reside in their city and accept my lot alongside them. They could all see I was always giving it my very best.

Whenever we arrived at a residence, my friendly tone quickly won over the clients. It may have been my most important asset, verbally that is. Regardless of a move in or out, I would roll up my sleeves and begin working alongside my crew. It did not take long to master the art of packing or unpacking. But most important, it was crucial to follow the others in taking inventory as they finished with their boxes.

Eventually, those boxes were moved outside by the truck. Next came storing them inside the wooden containers which would carry them across the ocean. This appeared to be the most skillful part of the overall operations—storing everything properly inside those containers. It required good judgement of space and assessing items to determine where to place them. This was the truck drivers' function, as he stood inside the container calling for individual items to be handed to him.

Dino had a keen eye for this. Sometimes he would insist with the driver inside the container to place a different item than the one asked for, and he was always right. For whenever the driver chose not to listen, he would later be moving items around previously placed inside and then had to reconfigure the space while cursing like a madman but never admitting being at fault. Dino would then look at me with a tiny smile which needed no explanation.

One time, we finished a job early. The military family moving out was in the very area where Bianca lived. My co-workers, true drinkers but never drunk, insisted on stopping for a small one upon finishing. Quite miraculously, that day our driver was in no hurry to run back to the warehouse. Once in the bar and at the counter, we began talking away when I suddenly informed Dino that I would not return with them. He was asked to process my timecard once back, and I assured him I would call the manager to notify him.

It was a brief walk to my destination, Bianca's place. I was gambling on finding everyone home, minus the husband, and I lucked out. Initially, it had been a mystery to me why that man had moved in with her and her mother, but one day my lover informed me that he was having a fancy small villa built. Once finished, they would all move to the outskirts of the city.

Well, there I was! Bianca was surprised to see me and greeted me nicely but a bit indifferently. Her mother appeared slightly stunned, whereas that beautiful boy immediately threw himself on me. For quite some time, with him in my arms, my hosts got to hear a few fun anecdotes of the crazy antics my co-workers pulled off. Francesco would not budge from my side. I had attempted to put him down for it was now time to leave, but he simply clung to me, quite comfortably and most devotedly.

Right about then, Francesco's grandmother, in a most diplomatic but direct tone, claimed it was time I found a nice girl and settled down. A bit of sound advice but presented more like an indirect farewell gesture with a hidden clue to not return. Now, everything would have been fine, even the unnecessary hint, as we headed to the entrance door, but it unexpectedly opened, and Bianca's husband walked in.

We had previously met some years back. A few words were now exchanged as I stood facing him. Francesco was still in my arms, his arm wrapped around my neck, and the boy never once acknowledged the person in front of us. That is when his grandmother intervened and attempted to take him from me. Then all hell broke loose! The boy threw a tantrum, crying hysterically. And once his feet were planted on the pavement, he attached himself to one of my legs and refused to let go.

Bianca began speaking to her husband. I felt most uncomfortable. The grandmother took physical hold of Francesco and began scolding him, all to no avail. His tune only exalted. Having given my farewell to all, I managed to finally exit, leaving behind a screaming child and three solemn faces staring at him. While in the lift heading down, my curiosity found it incomprehensible that the man of the house could not see the obvious. For that handsome little devil was not simply attached to me, but he was also the spitting image of me.

Now, you cannot imagine my fully blown mental anguish! It followed me all the way home. Once inside the building, something completely different laid on more adversity to contend with. We lived on the fourth floor, the top landing, and there was no elevator, but it was not the lack of a lift that now angered me. There was a pungent odor wafting from the apartment directly across ours.

While walking up the spiral staircase, my handkerchief covered my nose. This revolting smell was the work of two elderly ladies as they had taken it upon themselves to feed the neighborhood cats. Each meal consisted of boiling large pots full of scrap pieces of meat the local butchers would throw out. The vile stench coming from their premises was a weekly ritual they had no intention of ending.

Francesca had recently spoken to the elder of the two women. So had our neighbors, all to no avail. I rang the doorbell, and it was the younger of the two, the one who looked a bit like a bulldog, that now stood in front of me. She not only appeared terribly annoyed but soon became sarcastic over my request to bring this ordeal to an end. Well, my response, which began when hers terminated, did not hold anything back.

Things quickly got out of hand. She slapped me rather hard across the face. I immediately grabbed her by the collar as she fought back, and we were suddenly by the staircase rail, me contemplating throwing her off it. Someone screamed loudly! Francesca had heard the commotion and had opened our door to check on things. That scream snapped me back to reality. I backed off and allowed the terrified woman to run indoors, as she threatened to go to the police.

She must have contacted the authorities sometime after. Fortunately, in those days, there was a different approach to such entanglements. Perhaps it was the very appearance and attitude of the little boxer which kept the police away. No one actually came that day, but a week later, our neighbor, whom we were very close to, informed us that two carabinieri had called on her and other families in the building to inquire about me. What sort of chap was I, and just what had happened to create such a fiasco?

They had one version of things but were now trying to put together the facts. We two never heard from anyone. Of course, that incident prompted me to open-up about my real problem. My beautiful mate was only acquainted with bits of my past, specifically my drug use, and had discovered it quite by chance. Nevertheless, she had put her foot down, and it was not necessary, but appreciated, for I had long ago terminated that lifestyle.

She now discovered my past relationship with Bianca. It was fully closed for sure, but the issue over the boy hurt me profoundly. Francesca disputed the question over his fatherhood, and she stated most convincingly that he could not possibly be mine. Later that evening, she urged me to consider what had been proposed a while back, meditation. Which is why a few days later, she tagged along with me to the meditation center.

It was a new person who greeted us two. She described the process and the results, and ultimately quoted a price. We were then given a different date to return for the initiation and instructed to bring a brand-new handkerchief that had never been used and a non-citrus fruit. This seemed a bit odd. Nevertheless, eventually, there I was fruit and handkerchief in hand as per scheduled date and time.

In a semi-darkened room, surrounded by objects which had previously startled me, I learned to meditate. A word was given to me with instructions to never share it with anyone. After lighting quite a bit of incense, my instructor sat in front of me and had me close my eyes and repeat the word loudly and fast. She told me to slow down my repetition, and a bit later, I was to only chant it inwardly, and then even more slowly.

Once twenty minutes terminated, she brought me out of my trance. My mind had never known such a relaxed feeling, a sort of purity inside, and there was also a sense of happiness in me, as if tons of worries and lingering concerns had somehow been properly flushed out. The woman handed me the handkerchief and the fruit and sent me on my way.

I descended the stairs slowly. It was as if I were not really participating in my own movements. The building's front door suddenly opened, and there stood Piero, my very personal connection to this incredible gig. For some unexplainable reason, after shaking his hand, or as we began to do so, I started laughing uncontrollably. Not at him but simply because I was super happy. He, too, joined in, and without ever knowing why, we laughed for quite some time.

Piero then proceeded upstairs allowing me to move on. Although uncertain as to where to head to, my wandering about the premises was on and soon my memory banks recalled my holding a handkerchief, which got put away, and a pear which I bit into. It tasted so divine. Why, it seemed as if the flavor of that fruit was being revealed to me for the very first time.

Meditation then became my daily ritual. However, that incredible heartfelt joy and uncontrollable laughter, even if only brief, never again manifested itself. The twenty minutes was just a quiet time-out, far from all the daily chaos, and a movement inward to simply flow away for a short while. It was my way to unwind and, in pure poetic terms, keep the bright candle of light inside well lit.

Chapter 137

We two love birds took ourselves to see the parish priest, Don Lorenzo, to arrange our marriage. He was a bit younger than us, appeared a tad cocky, but he was certainly unhappy with the church we had chosen to be wed in. The cleric attempted to persuade us to have the ceremony in his church, the one servicing the area where we lived. But Francesca and I had fallen in love with a small temple to seal our union.

It was the church of Santa Chiara. Why, the moment I had laid eyes on it, we both agreed it was perfect. It had a circular structure that did not exude finesse, but its light red brick façade felt warm, perhaps humble, but uniquely attractive. And once we entered, missing were the excessive frescoes and paintings which bombard too many ancient Gothic walls. It would nicely accommodate the minor congregation that would be in attendance.

Our priest may not have been thrilled with our choice, but he soon gave us a lecture on the concept of a sound matrimony. He appeared to be more pontificating than speaking while disclosing what consisted as good relations between a bride and groom. The man even provided details on maintaining a solid and fun bond as husband and wife, and never neglecting it. It was a bit strange, but he seemed so damn sure of himself as his speaking continued flawlessly. At some point, I began thinking we were very well bred in most of his prescribed marital theology, and his words felt slightly excessive in both narrative and scope. Although, had he known more about our present union, he would have certainly wanted to save our souls right then and there, or perhaps even refuse to wed us.

The meeting, otherwise, went rather well. Don Lorenzo appeared satisfied, and once he finished, we were instructed to return the following week at the same time. Which is exactly what we did. We arrived there punctually Saturday afternoon. Why, we had even debated what topics to discuss and had prepared a bit. However, no one was able to locate our overly talkative minister, and to me, that did not seem so bad.

Don Lorenzo was not in the room where we had previously met with him. Nobody in the sacristy knew of his whereabouts, although a few people had just seen him. We checked all around and eventually returned to his office, hoping he would show up. After about fifteen minutes, we headed back home. Once we were on a side street near the local church, Francesca spotted him in his car leaving and even speeding a bit.

Now get this. The following week, the very man who would marry us asked why we had not come the previous Saturday. It was truly shocking. His words left me speechless for a few seconds, yet it seemed best not to tangle with this mysterious priest. We then briefly, and most diplomatically, stated our case, yet neither of us insisted, but he reassured us he had waited for us in his office, and his face expressed a sense of wonder as to why we had not shown up.

Chapter 138

It was an early Saturday morning when we newlyweds-to-be left for Milano. My girlfriend's Fiat 500 would not do, that is why we borrowed her brother-in-law's Mini Cooper, which was not much of an improvement, but it had a trunk big enough to store a suitcase or two. And it would travel much faster than the Fiat. Our destination was Malpensa Airport to pick up my father and stepmom.

We were still a bit sleepy as we left Vicenza behind and faced a pitch-black highway. Francesca was discussing the flower arrangements which had recently been taken care of when the car began to decelerate on its own, and pressing my foot down on the gas pedal was not accomplishing anything. Sure enough, our vehicle was soon coasting the emergency lane, having lost all power.

In my mind, it is a big waste of time to open the hood of a car and stare at an engine which is not cooperating. And although it was quite dark, that is exactly what we did. After feeling a bit useless and closing the hood, I got back in the car and turned the ignition key. The vehicle, to my surprise, started up and allowed us to move on. I held my breath while the Mini drove nicely for a while.

Not sure how far we got, but we started to slow down again. I eased up on the gas pedal then gave some gas, not excessively, but soon we again came to a complete stop. The engine was shut off, and after a few minutes I turned it on, and we again took off. Fortunately, after another bizarre interruption, the vehicle got us to the first gas station we came across.

The mechanic's shop was not open, but one of the two attendants was a mechanic and agreed to look at the engine. He, too, was puzzled yet concluded there may have been a bit of water in the gas tank that could have gone into the engine. Soon enough, he sent us on our way, and after one more malfunction, the car finally transported us to the airport intact.

Our guests were so happy to see us. Francesca received quite a few compliments as I took their luggage and eventually put it in the trunk. The two ladies were now in the back, and my father sat up front. Once we were all on board, a new glitch occurred. I could not close the door on my side. The latch was either broken or malfunctioning, and so it was time to improvise.

The trunk had plenty of miscellaneous crap, so I found a couple of elastic ropes and attached them to the inside handle on my door and ran inside the car to the other door, where my dad sat. This kept my door closed but not shut entirely. Of course, entering and exiting the vehicle now required instructions, so we decided not to stop unless necessary. Even though my door was now somewhat secured, and it would certainly not open, I can state most emphatically that my dad was not impressed.

My folks were staying in a small hotel in the heart of Vicenza. Upon my visit the following morning, they expressed how content they were with the accommodations which Francesca had made. Miraculously, I was off from work that day, but my companion could not get away. My plan was to show my guests around, but they had little interest in seeing any of the local sites, or some of the nearby attractions, like Venice or Verona. Oh well!

We went off to the Bar Garibaldi. Once we were seated at a table, out came the usual family satires. It was apparent that a middle-of-the-road approach in family matters would never exist. I insisted that it was my duty to provide them a small tour of our beautiful city. They were shown the piazza and given a tad of history. Yet neither seemed impressed with anything. After a few more interesting sites, at some point, we went off to Righetti's where we had an excellent lunch. The idea that one could eat and then pay the cashier based on telling him what you had, seemed quite preposterous to both my guests.

The day of the big event was soon upon us. Early that morning, Francesca's tiny apartment was turned upside down. Her sisters were present. The one from the Friuli region had arrived the previous evening and had stayed with Anna. Our neighbor, Sara, who was the bridesmaid and her mother also joined us. It seemed best to allow the ladies proper access to our tiny premises. So, I, the groom, all decked out in a light gray suit, headed to the nearby hotel.

My Uncle Andrea had arrived the prior evening. His lovely wife was battling a health issue, so would not be present. We hugged and exchanged a few words, then we four walked to a nearby coffee shop. My father informed me that a friend of his, also Sicilian, would join us as he had left instructions of our whereabouts with the hotel clerk. The gentleman from Palermo was an old friend who had been living on the outskirts of Vicenza for years.

Eventually, the Randazzos were among us. The Sicilian gentleman was married to a much younger woman, yet they acted like newlyweds. They shared a few stories of their past life in Sicily and carried on about how much they missed it. The wife had even suggested that living in the north was like being in a foreign country, but their young daughter, pretty and angelic-like, furrowed her eyebrows and squinted her eyes in disagreement.

At some point, we took ourselves to the church. It was a fifteen-minute walk, and we arrived at eleven thirty, the time assigned by our priest. It was crucial to be punctual before commencing my, well, sort of, new life. After all, Giuliano Di Stefano, a British citizen who had left Leicester, grown up in Barazzetto and Palermo, came of age in the Bronx, and traveled the vast oceans to then become a soldier and again a civilian, now residing in the city of Vicenza, was quite ready to consecrate a permanent union with the beautiful Francesca Zanin.

As we approached the church, we found several people standing by. They were dressed impeccably well and chatting amicably. None of them were familiar to me, but considering their attire and circumstances, all were obviously there for us. These folks were Francesca's relatives from the outskirts of Padova, most of whom I did not know, and they, like my small group, were making the best of things while awaiting the bride's arrival.

I felt a bit awkward introducing myself. Nevertheless, we shook hands and exchanged a few words. And if my intuition served me well, they appeared to approve. Don Lorenzo arrived punctually, and the priest in him seemed a tad withdrawn, as if his mission was more crucial than divine. Finding me alone, he quickly inquired about Francesca's whereabouts and was reassured she would soon join us. He did not answer, but he began to look around and beyond me.

Francesca finally arrived in Mr. Rossi's car along with my mom. She was a bit late. However, the woman looked gorgeous and her contagious happy eyes ignited mine. She joined me at the church entrance door where we now faced a slightly irked cleric. With his back to the church door while looking at us two, he glanced at his watch and, very business-like, said, "I can now only give you fifteen minutes of my time." It sounded incredible. For my mind immediately vibrated a religious message: "Blessed is the Lord, for he works in mysterious ways."

Brian Sheen sang Schubert's Ave Maria as we entered and approached the altar. It was in the original version, the only one he knew, and it simply opened my heart. For music, all music, especially when sung by a beautiful voice, provides a quaint mood to soothe the spirit. We continued walking slowly and once at the altar, our priest requested that we turn to face those in attendance to acknowledge their happiness for us.

There were many bright faces in the church. Just not in the first pews. There, like two opposing forces, sat my family members. My mother and Alessandro on the right, and my father and stepmother, his friends, along with my uncle were on the left side. And if you had not known this was a wedding, you would have assumed it was a funeral.

Nevertheless, the beauty and affinity of that quaint church enriched our union. There were abundant colorful flowers all around us shedding their lavish glow, and it must have been the audience, not necessarily us two, which fired up our priest. For the very person who had sworn to be brief could not contain himself, and his verbal spin on things knew no boundaries.

Don Lorenzo delivered a most appropriate speech. He pointed out that we both had traveled and moved about in our youth. But now, the mature adults at the altar had arrived where God wanted us. Why? Because in his universal design of things, we two were meant for each other, and no one could deny this. He even included the role of the flowers sacrificed for us but happily in attendance here with everyone else. For this was part of a mysterious plan beyond the individual's power of comprehension.

The threat to be brief was lost to the pleasure of hearing himself. And finally, once our priest concluded the ceremony, he helped himself to quite a few of those flowers, previously there for us but which were now going home with him. It was fine. After all, the man's perfect staging was being idolized in everyone's eyes, and my wife and I were simply too happy to care. Oh well, consuming our now legitimate union was moving forward rather nicely.

It was the restaurant, Lovise, located in the town of Costabissara, where the reception was held. That eatery was popular for its good cuisine, rustic environment, and reasonable prices. Our reservation was for two o'clock, and having finished in church before one, our guests had extra time to contend with.

Most folks in Francesca's clan had not seen each other in ages. Quite a few were somewhat acquainted with Vicenza, so they briefly took in the city center. My small group of friends headed to the Bar Garibaldi, while my folks from abroad and those with them, were now on their way to the only Sicilian bakery in the area, which also served as a coffee shop.

Mr. Rossi drove us newlyweds to Parco Querini for photographs. My friend Giorgio and his wife, and the photographer, a close friend of theirs, led the way in their auto. Traffic was light and we soon entered the park. Although it had slightly rained earlier that morning, there was now just a slight trace of grayish clouds casting a subdued but calm sky.

It was late autumn, but we found a perfect fall setting. Along the lovely path coasting the inside of those quasi-empty grounds, fallen orange leaves sat at the feet of bare trees. It was a splendid contrast to my gray suit and Francesca all in white and a light brown cape. Our photographer worked from different angles at various spots, and he continued inviting us to try new poses here, there and everywhere.

At the restaurant, everyone sat where they pleased. Our bridal group faced them, and from the corner of my eye, I noticed my father and company were quite a distance from my mom and Alessandro. Thank goodness! All proceeded well, and I did my best to keep my wine consumption in check. Eventually, with tummies fully satisfied, we newlyweds began to visit different tables.

Francesca introduced me to relatives I was not yet acquainted with. Everyone was keen on hearing any tidbit, especially regarding the U.S. Goodness gracious, we are certainly a popular nation with some people. Oh well, my chats, although brief, were appreciated as we continued making the rounds.

Apparently, my father was not pleased. His forlorn expression stood out. No matter what topic we tried to share with him, it was a complete failure. My uncle helped by throwing in a few playful comments, and we reciprocated and even delved into the outstanding speech by our priest. Regardless, my dad was unfazed, remained silent, and simply appeared unwavering.

At my mom's table, life was pulsating. Francesca and I were drawn into a hilarious chat about our priest and some specifics which attempted to justify him leaving with our flowers. That divine soul had certainly earned his keep according to my mother. We had a hearty laugh, and it was then that my mother, sitting next to Alessandro, moved a bit closer to me and placed my right arm across her shoulder.

A gesture that certainly devastated the sulking Mr. Di Stefano. The irate man was ready to leave. It was my uncle who interrupted us to inform us of their departure. He was so apologetic and understanding, and certainly down-to-earth. I felt a need to express my regret, for no seating arrangements had been made, and so apologized thinking his table may have vaguely felt isolated from others in attendance. Oh well, we would catch up the following day.

Later that evening, a dozen or more of us were in our tiny apartment. How we managed to fit remains a mystery, but there was an overabundance of happiness being shared. It was a festive mood running on its own as we participants were moved by much wine consumption and happy hearts. Lots of wine taken along with lots of food will brighten your outlook.

And just who was getting all the attention? Yes indeed, "me mom." And it certainly made sense. She was a showoff, someone who needed to be heard and liked, and told so, but she was also funny and rather adventurous in all her present bits and pieces. I am not sure when things finally came to an end and everyone left, but eventually my bride and I enjoyed the rest of the night on our own.

Chapter 139

There would be no honeymoon. That was my decision. My job did not allow me many days off, but truth be told, my old frugal ways were demanding austerity. It seemed wise to bank all the funds which came my way. We had decided to buy a flat, furnish it nicely, and soon there would be children, perhaps several of them.

Both my parents had been quite generous, and so my financial situation was advantageous. On my mom's behalf, Mr. Rossi provided a huge sum of money, for which he was thanked infinitely. My father had given me an envelope, an American-Italian tradition, which had several donations from he and his wife, and Aunt Mia and her mom. Believe me, any concern about putting down roots was quickly eliminated.

And when it rains, it pours. A few months later my boss called me into his office. The firm had another warehouse near the town of Aviano servicing our Air Force base. The manager's position would soon be available. Was I at all interested? He specified that the present employee, an older American, was retiring and with the job came a house, rent free, next to the warehouse. So, my only expenses would be to pay utilities.

You would think it a very worthy offer to consider, no? Perhaps everyone expected me to jump on it. I did not do so. You see, a week before, an old friend from the base, an Italian employee who worked at the personnel office, ran into Francesca and me in the city center. We had hardly shared a greeting when I was given some incredible news which could lead to a rewarding opportunity on the base.

The army had changed its hiring policy regarding veterans living overseas. Previously, the doors to the base were shut once you terminated your service. Whereas now, a veteran could be considered for any position they qualified for within a year from the date of discharge. There was little time left to apply, so a visit to Caserma Ederle had recently been carried out.

Now, perhaps the question is, hadn't a lot been done to make Italy my home? Why return to the little America inside that base? Well, it may have been the Yankee in me insisting on a comeback. Perhaps I had discovered how precious and significant my work environment there had been, regardless of its ups and downs. But more important, that domain was still part of who I really was. So, in a way, it was like a home coming.

A position became available in the accounting branch. It was for a file clerk, the lowest grade in the federal government, GS-2. (The GS is for General Schedule—Please accept it at face value.) Yet it meant a foot in the door, the possibility to advance, and there were benefits to be had, for both military and civilian personnel, which were most definitely worth having.

My interview occurred with the branch chief. He seemed very friendly and most agreeable, and according to him, I was overqualified and had the job sealed. The man virtually appeared apologetic to not be able to do more for me. We shook hands, and before leaving, a brief tour of the premises seemed only right. I just wanted to say hello to my old co-workers, and last but not least, see the good colonel.

Colonel Deitrick must have put in a good word for me. He was on his way to a meeting, so we spoke briefly, and he appeared super happy for me. However, the officer warned me that he would not tolerate any mischief. If he so much as suspected me of reliving some of my past sins, the position would be terminated. My facial expression, along with a few words sealed a binding contract assuring him that would never happen.

A few days later, the personnel office called to give me the good news. Not long after, I was back on the base but now as a civilian. The personnel office had me first, and my good Italian friend was all smiles over my latest accomplishment. We briefly touched on my luck, and he then turned me over to an Italian woman who would process my paperwork. She spoke to me in Italian, which was fine, and soon enough had me on my way to work.

It was prior to my departure that a last-minute detail startled me. Within the next few weeks, it was imperative that I travel to the Questura to register myself as being employed on the base. Good Lord! This truly frightened me! The maresciallo had not been very thrilled that I obtained my British passport. He had predicted that I would return as a Russian, but being reborn as a Yankee would certainly cripple the poor soul.

I decided to disregard those instructions. Sometime that evening, my five-year visa, ID card, work permit, and healthcare card were placed in a large envelope and filed in a folder on the old bookcase in our tiny living room. My sporadic outlook on national identity favored that I now stop jumping around from one to the other.

Chapter 140

Life at the accounting office was great! My new environment consisted of many Italian employees, and all knew me. There were also a few Americans, and everyone there was quite friendly and fun to chat with. This branch was busy, yet all my co-workers enjoyed an easy and laidback attitude as if life there never put them under a lot of pressure.

I was in the same room as my boss, the head accountant, and Piero, the second in command. One would think that sharing the premises with them would bring me knowledge of that office's main functions and workload. After all, they were the two kingpins. However, it was not so, for both men were super busy but for completely different reasons.

Piero was continuously reading manuals and operational guides. He was basically acquainting himself with his new responsibilities as a vice manager. The chief accountant was always on the phone, but work seemed to be the last thing on his mind. My assumption that he was knowledgeable, and to be consulted when necessary, was hardly the case.

Anyhow, I found a ton of documents on my desk. Several months-worth of filing were scattered about, but everything was soon in the pertinent cabinet drawers. Consequently, as this allowed me plenty of free time, I requested to become acquainted with the work of the accounting technicians. It was approved, but my boss insisted I would only familiarize myself with the process and not do any actual work.

It was very beneficial to learn what had never been fully digested. I was informed about the accounting classification, something once a bit insignificant. Previously, it was only the fiscal year and object class which meant anything to a travel clerk, whereas now, everything from the type of funds being used, which office paid for the services or items purchased, and other important details were drilled into me. It certainly kept me busy and enthused. Eventually, contracts and purchase orders were being scrutinized, and suddenly, the world of accounting seemed less far-fetched.

On one occasion, the colonel stopped by. He found me alone, doing some filing, and he inquired about the work and my take on things. Then before leaving, the man suggested that I consider going back to school to obtain a degree in accounting. He matter-of-factly stated, "I am sure one day you will be running this office and doing a great job." Well, that is exactly what brought me to the University of Maryland registration office the very next day.

Another great bit of news—sometime before my return to the base, Francesca had given me a truly wonderful notice. She was pregnant! Oh, what sheer joy she passed my way. A child to love and nurture was my manna from heaven. Not to please anyone or to have it be imposed on me, but if it were a boy, he would be named Richard.

Eventually, the great day had arrived but at night. I was now attending evening classes when someone interrupted our teacher. A soldier had knocked on the door and opened it. She stuck her head in and asked for Julian Di Stefano. The smiling woman then informed me I needed to run home quickly for I would soon be a dad. Well, a round of applause accompanied me to the door as a sense of urgency carried me home in a flash.

Francesca had chosen the hospital in the town of Arzignano to conceive the baby. It was approximately eighteen kilometers away. My concern was mostly due to her size and timing, for my huge but beautiful wife was a bit behind schedule. And she now appeared ready to give birth at any moment. With my nerves on edge, we departed immediately. I drove fast but cautiously.

Once at the hospital, a nun, who was in charge, insisted Francesca was not ready and informed me I could return home. It was not my intention to comply, but that feisty religious creature persisted while assuring me she would call immediately if things changed. I gave her our neighbor's home number, as we did not have a phone. Sara had become super close to both of us after we married. So, I departed and sped back home convinced that once back in the flat the Mother Superior would be calling our neighbors to have me return.

Richard was born early the following morning. I was not present. No one had called. That evening and the early morning, I paced the floors of that tiny place, wondering why no call yet. Eventually, I took myself to the hospital, and the staff on duty were reluctant to let me in as visiting hours started much later. Fortunately, Italians are good-natured folks, and in those days had a healthy knack for grasping what is truly important.

Once in the delivery ward, a nurse accompanied me to my wife's room. She still looked somewhat big, and no one had yet told me anything. It was her happy eyes which gave her away as she asked if I had seen our beautiful Richard. The nurse then accompanied me to the baby's crib, and that is when my full-blown enthusiasm quickly vanished.

Goodness gracious, what a complete shock! Here was a child with such a terribly red-colored face and an overwhelming scalp of jet-black hair, like tons of it were just sprouting all over his head. It made me think of an ancient Inca king or the picture of a Peruvian child seeking adoption. While slightly staring and, yes, feeling somewhat happy but also a tad confused, I said a few words to our little boy and then returned to my wife.

"Isn't he beautiful?" my exultant wife boasted. I agreed, and let's just leave it at that. Three days later we brought our son home, and the critter's hair was no longer so blackish, and his cheeks had begun to mellow into a nice creamy color. Now, talk about two amateur parents worrying themselves to death every inch of the way home, that was us. Well, truth be told, I was the worse of the two.

Chapter 141

1981 closed on a sad and rather terrifying note for Caserma Ederle. On December 17, at 6:00 p.m., an American general was kidnapped from his apartment in Verona. It was the work of the Red Brigades. These terrorists continued to appear unstoppable and untouchable. They caused havoc at random and were responsible for some ruthless murders.

They had kidnapped the ex-prime-minister Aldo Moro two years earlier. He was serving as president of the Christian Democratic Party when apprehended. His entire police escort was killed immediately, and he, too, was murdered sometime after. The media was informed that a sort of people's court had tried him behind closed doors and that he had been executed. His body was found in the trunk of a Renault 4. It was a horrible crime, so senseless, and it left everyone quite stunned but also clamoring for an end to this madness.

General James Lee Dozier was stationed in Verona at the NATO headquarters, in charge of the Southern European Land Forces. He was seized in his apartment by four terrorists posing as plumbers. His wife was held at gunpoint, which forced the general to comply with the outlaws and be taken prisoner.

News of the incident immediately put us all on alert. The base initiated cautionary maneuvers which became routine on our base and throughout all U.S. military installations worldwide. Everyone on our base, both American and Italian, were truly concerned over the possibility of another senseless killing. And as time lagged on and the general remained in captivity, it began to weigh heavily on everyone.

The FBI sent some of its people, and they were soon in our office. There is not much I am free to say regarding how the finance and accounting office played an important role in what happened next. However, there is an old saying which claims that "money talks." Suffice to say, sometimes it can speak volumes.

Early one morning in the month of January, the NOCS, an Italian Special Force team, liberated our general. He had been held in captivity for forty-two days, chained to a steel cot under a tent in a small apartment, and forced to wear earphones and listen to extremely loud music. The news of his liberation brought a small but hearty elation throughout the entire base, which would actually repeat itself on a much larger scale in the upcoming summer.

That kidnapping was the straw that broke the camel's back. As one of my old friends from my getting high days would occasionally remark, "You mess with the bull, you get the horns." The Red Brigades had picked a fight with the wrong people.

With the capture of these terrorists, the Italian law enforcement agencies accomplished what was long overdue. In no time at all, more and more terrorists were apprehended. Soon enough, they were tried and imprisoned for long periods of time. The Italian police agencies were now unstoppable in their pursuit of these criminals. Finally, they would be at least somewhat accountable for the horrific crimes they had committed.

Chapter 142

It seemed incredible! More than a year had flown by since my return to the base. It was June of 1982, and I certainly had a busy schedule. After work, I went to the gym from five to six, then it was on to an evening class at the university. My family only got a bit of me, but hopefully the best. Weekends, when fully together, ended much too quickly.

The office felt more like the news media was running the show. All comments and opinions were about the World Cup matches. The event was being held in Spain, and Italy had not fared well in their opening matches, so their fan base was convinced they would not advance.

Of course, the two office experts on the world of football had their own theories as to why. Antonio, a supervisor, a bit older and perhaps wiser, was sure that the main problem was the absence of Roberto Bettega. He was a forward who played for the team Juventus and the national team, but as he had been injured during the regular season, he was not in Spain. According to our expert, it was a lost cause, case closed.

Roberto, one of the technicians, insisted the main problem was Paolo Rossi. Rossi had previously been involved in a betting scandal and was, therefore, disqualified from playing for two years but had been assured a place on the team by the coach. According to the Gazzetta Dello Sport, the sports paper that Roberto studied religiously every morning, Rossi should not have been playing. Yet he was on the pitch, though hardly visible, sort of there but not there.

Well, the team somehow made it into the second round of the tournament. Now it faced a real challenge—Argentina. The daily comments prior to the match were awful, and our office looked like a morgue on the day of the event. Absolutely no one believed Italy could win. Roberto, along with a few others, were not only predicting a sure loss but were voicing strong hope for the team to lose with pride, like a score of three to one or two nil. Anything similar was being invoked to save face.

I played the game but knew little about professional football or the Italian national team. However, while watching some of the highlights of the Sunday matches on TV, someone caught my attention. There was a player who seemed quite good, and that was Giancarlo Antognoni, who played for Fiorentina, and he was in Spain fully participating.

It must have been my overall ignorance forcing me to slightly object to the office's sense of prevalent doom. Stating on one occasion that Italy could perhaps win the game, I got thanked all around for my wishful thinking, but mine was branded as naïve optimism. Oh well, it was on to the gym after work, then to my accounting class with the University of Maryland. Consequently, I got home too late to have seen the match on TV.

Now believe me, the euphoria the following morning was just incredible. The name on everyone's lips was that of Claudio Gentile, a defensive player who had kept the Argentinian phenomenon Maradona at bay, quite often laying him on the pitch. Italy had accomplished the impossible. It defeated the superior playing Argentinians by a healthy score of two to one. Everyone agreed that in the second half, the team had simply played a superb game.

Apparently, Paolo Rossi, once a local star who had played for Vicenza, had still not come through. His appearance at the World Cup would again be slightly questioned. Oh well, I truly enjoyed the cheerful mood and verbal melee that morning. But it was not long after, when silence and fear again prevailed as an even greater challenge confronted Italy. We would now play the unbeatable team of Brazil.

The office news was again just plain awful. Overall opinions predicted a disaster, for sure. Even the so-called experts, the old giants in the world of football, from Beckenbaur to Pele, now speaking as resourceful commentators, considered the Brazilian team an unstoppable powerhouse. So, everyone insisted this was the team which would win the cup. And as they had defeated every team they played—it looked like a done deal.

I was again tied down at the gym and my evening class. That is why I missed what was described as a nerve-racking match. It may have been one of the best in the 1982 competition, as, just like Super Bowl III, it perhaps provided the world with the greatest upset of all times.

And what occurred the day after that win is certainly a peculiar thing. For unlike the victory over Argentina, I was now fucking ecstatic. Just like everyone else around me, it felt like something personal had been accomplished. Perhaps, like most Italian folks on that base in those truly stressful but exciting days, the sheer joy over that team's victory may have somewhat grounded my allegiance to the country. Like my co-workers, I was experiencing a sense of belonging to something great!

Not only that, but that morning everyone was so excited over Paolo Rossi. He was back, and in perfect form. The Pablito had scored all three goals for Italy, an incredible feat against the mighty feared Brazilians. Actually, even my hero Antognoni had put one in, which unfortunately was not allowed as he was mistakenly called offside.

We now knew the cup was coming home. It was written in the stars, according to Antonio and company. By the way, those doomsayers, from journalists to guys you met at the coffee shops, had all become the most loyal Italian footballers and were now predicting more victories and the cup, and they were quite ready to celebrate beforehand.

It was Sunday, the day of the final game. My family and I were with Francesca's folks on their farm. As always, a culinary feast had been prepared for lunch with almost everything coming from their garden and chicken coop. During these meals, my father-in-law always quizzed me on life and traditions in the U.S. He seemed so fascinated with our big country. Especially our capacity to produce an abundance of everything. To him, we represented a sort of modern mecca for both food and industry, and let's not forget entertainment.

After putting Ricky to bed and once glued to the TV, nothing could come between us and that game. Well, Italy went on to defeat West Germany. It was with the team's third goal in the second half when the demoralized Germans appeared to have accepted the inevitable.

However, we had suffered throughout the entire first half of the match. Germany attacked furiously but I witnessed an incredibly talented Italian player, someone I had never heard of, Bruno Conti. He was all over the field, consistently making things happen. If in a defense role, he easily recovered the ball, began the attack, and supported the offense with persistent ball control. This incredible athlete was not just moving the ball and forcing the plays but had cleverly raised the skill level of all his teammates.

Oh, what a feast the following day! Italy celebrated like never before, and I was witnessing something extraordinary. Everyone, everywhere, was kinder, sincere, and helpful. Why, even the idea of turning the other cheek rather than the usual unnecessary loud arguing seemed to have become a common value. Italian flags, hardly anywhere back then, were seen in various places.

Italy had just won its third World Cup. But I sensed a joyous relief which was almost personal and long coming, as if dispelling years of national frustration. I had to ask myself if this victory was not a bit similar to winning a long and bloody war, for it seemed to have briefly instilled that patriotic sense driving all to forge a greater form of unity and national pride.

Chapter 143

Ricky shared our tiny and only bedroom. Almost every morning, especially on weekends, I had the joy of taking him out of his crib and bringing him in our bed with us. He slept most of the night but, like me, was up early. And just so you know that carpet of thick black hair had turned completely yellow some time ago.

My wife had terminated her employment. While on maternity leave, she collected her entire salary up until Ricky's birth and then a nice portion of it for a few months after. She was certainly a dedicated mom, and she lavished her baby with an overabundance of pure love. He was stylishly dressed, plus she took tons of photographs, and most importantly, fed him like a prince, making all his meals entirely from scratch.

Anyhow, it was August and time to splurge to take a much-needed vacation. My father was happy to host us and visiting New York City was big on my wife's agenda. Soon enough, there we were, and once settled in, we made the best of things. Our small bedroom had a crib for Ricky, and although a bit tight for space, we certainly lacked for nothing.

Francesca and I rode the subway to Manhattan almost daily. My folks, who were both employed full-time, took turns staying home to attend to the "cute little Italian boy," as my stepmom referred to him. This allowed us tourists, often but not always, the chance to spend the entire day in the city, and that is when the Big Apple finally won me over.

I now took in a more majestic side of it. Even the chaotic, loud, hustle and bustle of getting about bothered me less. Its immense proportion when seen from the top of the Empire State Building was rather glorious and captivating. For Manhattan appeared to show off its incredible layout and its buzzing vitality, which when seen from above, seemed to flow rather smoothly.

My wife loved everything. Especially those wonderful shops on Fifth Avenue. One day, we visited the Metropolitan Museum, and it consumed our entire morning. After, it was on to Central Park, which feels like a natural museum itself. Then, we shopped around the Rockefeller Center area. And as there is such a variety of international food everywhere, we certainly ate well, and plenty, returning home later in the evening, not at all hungry, just simply exhausted.

Aunt Mia had us all over that first weekend. She was now divorced. My lovely aunt was just as gentle and charming as ever and simply the perfect host. She never allowed you to wander off mentally, but neither was she overly intrusive. The woman spoke plenty, but all her chats were somewhat sprinkled with a nice dose of fun and laughter. And so, between the pool, which kept us cool and busy, the delicious barbeques, and lots of catching up, we two guests certainly felt quite at home and would have happily stayed longer.

There were other plans. As Long Branch had become a thing of the past, my folks took us to Wildwood in New Jersey. Both our hosts insisted they preferred their new beach resort, and it was a tad peculiar but throughout the entire stay, the couple appeared a bit more relaxed. My father still noticed everything occurring around him and judged it accordingly but less aggressively.

We two were even given a night off. Which is what brought Francesca and I to a fancy steak house. Almost immediately, after being seated and ordering, we tackled the immense salad bar. Our chatting was non-stop, and so I had simply not paid attention to my wife's selection of greens. Soon enough, our creative salad bowls were being dug into as Francesca mentioned that all those salad dressings were a bit of an over kill. Now just what was wrong with plain oil and vinegar?

She suddenly froze! Her face turned red as she began gasping for air. I sensed trouble but did not comprehend. Then she pointed to her dish, in tears and unable to speak. What she had mistaken for pieces of red bell peppers were in fact bits of serrano peppers, and they were taking her down. It took several glasses of water and a few minutes before she revived herself some. Then came a tiny reprimand, for apparently, I never paid attention to things that really mattered.

Our last weekend arrived much too soon. My wife and I took a trip to Washington, D.C. The fancy bus left from Port Authority and eventually stopped in Delaware, where a late lunch was in order. We got to the capital in the afternoon, and our driver parked in front of the Air and Space Museum, informing us that he would return in two hours. The bus door opened allowing us to step out into a murderous summer heat which is why we practically ran in and thanked our lucky stars for air-conditioning.

What an incredible museum! Its sharp layout and various items on display gave us much to chat about, especially the landing on the moon, at times a bit of a curiosity. Not long after, we prepared to reboard the bus, and absolutely no one in our group dared step outside the museum's doors until our means of transportation arrived and opened its doors. Later that evening, we lodged in the Rock Creek Park area, near the zoo, and eventually feasted on plenty of Chinese food, a cuisine which my wife was now slightly acquainted with, it being somewhat available in Italy, but mostly in the bigger cities.

The following day was dedicated to sightseeing. First came Iwo Jima, which received plenty of attention, but the changing of the guard at the Arlington National Cemetery kept everyone spellbound. Watching our soldiers move in a robot-like fashion made me wonder if perhaps everyone's DNA had a lingering bit of spartan gleam inside. We two also followed their every move, and those soldiers appeared just a bit too mechanical and so far from a mortal-like existence.

It was the Vietnam Memorial which was most sought out. That incredible monument appeared so soothing, unique, certainly the perfect temple to quietly remember those who perished in a horrible war. Recalling how veterans and politicians had severely contested it always puzzled me. So strange. For here lies a massive tomb placing us so close to those we lost, yet without losing it.

Maybe an Iwo Jima type rehash, flag adorning fighting and falling soldiers, would have made those folks happy.

On our final morning in D.C., our bus cruised toward Mount Vernon. While proceeding down Highway One, my eyes cherished the silent Potomac, so serene and refreshing to look at, and it seemed to travel with us nicely caressing the slightly contagious residences resting alongside Mother Nature. Plus, in the background were a few pleasant white clouds garnishing the sky above us.

I asked myself if perhaps one day we would live here. My thoughts were shared with my wife. Her eyes exalted a sense of approval, yet almost immediately she quickly added, "Wouldn't we be far from home, no?" I returned to a bit more daydreaming, still savoring my surroundings but remembering we would soon return to Vicenza.

Our holiday was practically over. In a few days, some very wonderful memories of two fantastic weeks would accompany us home. We also had tons of photos to remind us of the Big Apple's magical effect, and our other visits, plus all the folks who had contributed so wonderfully to a magnificent vacation.

Chapter 144

The Di Stefanos had upgraded their standard of living. I purchased a flat which came at a fair price, and having prepared for it, I did not need to apply for a loan. Once again, it was that clever fox Lorenzo who had mentioned a new condominium where the apartments were not too expensive.

We now lived outside the city in an area surrounded by farmland in the town of Sarmego. The apartment was spacious and well-designed. It had three bedrooms, two bathrooms, a large living room/dining room area, and a kitchen which allowed us to comfortably dine there daily. There were also two terraces, a fairly-sized garage, and of course there was a cantina. And as my wife's folks generously complemented all our visits with homemade wine, it stayed well-stocked.

Top-of-the-line modern furniture was purchased, and once residing in our beautiful new enclave, all seemed just grand but not for long. One morning, Francesca got a slight shock in the living room. In one area, the wooden floors had risen creating what looked like a small camel hump, leaving her quite flabbergasted. Fortunately, after much finger pointing between the construction company and the firm which installed the floors, the problem got fixed.

It was after this incident when my gorgeous wife informed me that she was pregnant! Once again, mine was happiness galore! Who can say why, but something in me believed this child would be a girl. So, my preference for names like Melissa and Viviana were revealed to my companion. She, however, insisted it would be a boy. It was stated with such certainty, it forced me to inquire why. How could she be so sure? Francesca looked at me and said, "I know you only make boys, and Eric will be our last one." I was almost tempted to give a military salute.

Sure enough, Eric was also born outside Vicenza in the same hospital. Only this time I did not leave. Upon arriving, my wife was immediately brought into the delivery room. Now please accept my take on this. I was not wanted there. That is correct. Francesca had insisted there were some matters she could attend to without the likes of me standing by uselessly. It seemed only right to respect that woman's wise counsel.

So, I was pacing a long hallway. Waiting anxiously, but certainly very present in mind and body. For a few minutes, some words had been going back and forth between the doctor and Francesca. He would instruct her to push, she would respond accordingly, although she was obviously now in much pain. After all the commotion there was a stretch of silence. It seemed to have lasted too long.

My feet carried me closer to the delivery room door. Our son then confirmed his arrival. It is such a joyous moment when a newborn has established its presence, regardless of whether Dad is fully participating in the room or not. And by the way, can we men ever truly come to terms with what that new critter has just put our companion through, even if standing by holding her hand.

A nurse soon arrived with this beautiful baby resting in her arms. He was truly handsome and appeared so at ease that my thought simply popped out most innocently. I stated, "What a small treasure we have here." Now the very surprised looking nurse corrected me immediately. She very seriously responded "A treasure yes, small no, for he is huge."

Eric came home a few days later. He was blonde, serene, and still bore the category of heavyweight. A month later, we three went off to Friuli for the weekend. Ricky had remained with his aunt Sara, my wife's older sister, for about a month. I found him playing in the backyard, and apparently, he may have had slightly forgotten us. Seeing me suddenly approaching him, brought on a most hurt look to his face. It was as if he had been abandoned for good. I immediately picked him up, kissed him, and we resumed right where we had left off.

Now the new member in our family was a big hit with my wife's folks. However, those elderly farmers had absolutely no knowledge of English. They had no trouble whatsoever pronouncing Ricky, but simply could not get his little brother's name right. It came out sounding like RERIK, and they seemed to insist on it! Oh well, both boys were showered with love and admiration, and pretty soon, we four became regulars at the farmhouse visiting often and staying for long periods, especially in summer.

Chapter 145

Sometimes I view my lot in life as vexing. Occasionally, it appears to bask in a bit of unexpected glory. The year of my return to the base, Ronal Reagan became our fortieth president. He may not have much impressed me as an actor, and my expectations of the man as president were not exactly sublime, but his arrival at the White House did wonders for my pocket.

It was the administration's commitment to capitalism that helped me plenty. If a motto could be pinned to their policies, it should have been "Full speed ahead, and man the currency." For the economists advising the new president decided to tame inflation; lower taxes, both corporate and individual, and ultimately bring unemployment to very low levels. And President Reagan himself soon insisted the U.S. dollar would become a most valuable commodity, as good as gold.

That the national debt would skyrocket was understood, but it was not something to be immediately concerned about. Plus, the Pentagon was given a green light to modernize and be ready for action, for there were still powerful nations which posed a threat to capitalism, although the word democracy is often used. It was mostly the Soviet Union we needed to fear, and their unhappy allies, the Warsaw Pact Nations, or so the U.S. believed.

Consequently, and as predicted, the value of the U.S. dollar against other currencies began to rise. As more money poured into our country in the form of investments, including everything from military hardware to rubber duckies, its rise seemed unstoppable. Actually, only the event of the Falkland War, which we were not involved in and lasted a total of seventy-four days, kept the dollar in check until all hostilities finally ceased. Then once again, our currency resumed its upward trajectory and would eventually anchor itself at an unprecedent high.

Back in 1975 and throughout my military years, the exchange rate of Italian lira to the U.S. dollar had always held steady. A dollar earned you six hundred lira. But this was now a thing of the past. Our currency rose almost daily, consequently expanding my purchasing power and that of all Americans living or stationed in Europe and throughout other countries. It was a great thing, yet it soon became a sour note. For having to listen to my Italian co-workers, at times was simply more than an earful.

Someone would categorically state that the dollar would destroy them. Every single day! Why, even a supervisor sitting near me mentioned how unfair it was that I now out earned her, especially as her grade equivalency was much higher than mine. A few people also dragged our benefits into the talk and categorized us as a privileged class of exploiters. Just how the hell I was exploiting anyone was not clear to me. Yes, it was true, we Yankees on that base were now much better off than ever before, but how this was hurting anyone was a mystery to me.

My one attempt to point out that a strong dollar led to a rise in imports by the U.S. did absolutely nothing for them. Why, the proof was right there by the entrance to the base. My friend Giorgio, working at a car dealership, was certainly keeping his Italian boss very happy. Lots of folks on our base who wanted an Audi, Golf, or BMW, autos with a very high sale value back home, simply went over and purchased one as the Credit Union on base was more than happy to provide them with a loan.

According to my friend, soldiers would visit the showroom and get details. They then went right to the Credit Union. The following day they would return to make a purchase. Giorgio, who occasionally sold a car or two a month, was now doing that every day. He was in pure heaven as the buying spree from Yanks in Caserma Ederle seemed a permanent fix.

That spending binge was not just within the vicinity of our base. Many stores in towns on the nearby outskirts of Vicenza were also cashing in. Most Americans had for years avoided what was called the economy. This referred to the bundle of Italian fiscal activity which most Americans had totally disregarded as they only shopped on the base. However, now practically everyone was flocking to the butcher stores, supermarkets, clothing shops, and were also eating out a lot more often. Most officers and high-ranking professional civilians were even accumulating an abundance of expensive furniture.

However, it was not just my Italian co-workers who were up in arms. Some of my American colleagues had taken a stand against our "Ungrateful allies." According to them, the army treated the Italian employees much too well. After all, they had good salaries—and they did not receive twelve monthly checks, but fourteen. And just who paid for all this? Uncle Sam. Plus, wasn't the Italian mess hall, which had become my dining facility for lunch, subsidized by us? We Americans paid for our meals, but they ate for free.

It seemed like there was no containing the madness. It flared up mostly among folks who loved to gossip for a living, and there were plenty. Nevertheless, I, Julian Di Stefano, working as a federal employee for the U.S. Army on Caserma Ederle, but still registered in the Vicenza City Hall as Giuliano Di Stefano, a British citizen, did my best to keep a low profile, maintain the peace, and stay far from the unnecessary verbal melee.

Truth be told, it was the best of both worlds for me. I was one happy camper and not because of money. My only complaint was not speaking English at home, therefore depriving my kids of a very important language. Yet, it was they, my beautiful children, and my lovely wife, who had grounded me to a world of love and happiness. Now, there was no denying it, we lived so very well, and the benefits helped plenty. But it was settling down in Vicenza and working on that base, that was the best thing that had ever happened to me. This was my abode, and I loved it.

Of course, life in the small town of Sarmego was not bad. Yet our U-shaped building was far from perfect and looked a bit pathetic. In the original plans, there was a splendid garden in the middle of the building area, which was still nowhere to be seen. And whenever it rained, the muddy ground around the condo, not yet paved, made everything look plain dirty.

If I felt a sense of frustration with Italian punctuality, it was due to the lack of it. Especially when provided a date for the delivery of a service or finishing a project, which was the case with our building. You could rest assured a new date would follow, and perhaps even others. Consequently, when something finally terminated, you hardly noticed as you had sort of forgotten all about it.

Most of the apartments in our condo were not sold. The local folks were not interested, and the city dwellers found the town too far away. Perhaps, life there was deemed too provincial. So, the owner of the construction firm had now begun to rent. Sure enough, folks whose rent was paid by the army became our new tenants. That is, they who were not accommodated in the Villaggio Della Pace and entitled to a housing allowance were soon arriving in droves.

One of the first families to move in lived on the west side of the complex. It was a young Black couple with a small child. Both adults were prone to what was once referred to as party-hardy. This led to some miserable weekends and the occasional wild weeknight, as music blasted away non-stop. Also, the participants continued screaming at each other, perhaps hoping to be heard above the pounding chaos which made life for the rest of us a tad frustrating.

The military police on base came over on several occasions. Life would quiet down for a while, but once they left, things would return to normal, if that's what one could refer to it as. We were again at the mercy of those savages, that was the very label a few Italians in the building had branded them with. Fortunately, the newer arrivals were a bit like us, quiet and somewhat reserved, and most lived on our wing of the building.

Above us was Terry. He was an officer who worked as a dentist, and he religiously jogged every weekend in the area surrounding our town. His apartment was super huge and had been empty for an entire year, which is why the owner was thrilled to have him and even happier with the exuberant rent he got. Terry was quiet as a mouse, and you hardly ever knew he was home. Occasionally we ran into each other and always shared a few words. Courteous, cordial, and always smiling, he appeared a happy camper.

In the apartment next to his was an elderly couple. She was German, and he was a retired army officer now working on base as a civilian. We met them by chance and got to know both quite well. Directly below them, a small family took up residence there for about a year. The husband was a soldier, and his wife, who did not work, dedicated herself to their two lovely children. Perhaps we once shared a chat but never truly became acquainted with them.

The Italians among us were few and of a totally different breed. Next to our apartment was a young couple, just married, and always fussing about something. He was a carabiniere and his wife may have been employed at a clothing store in one of the nearby towns. Sometimes we could hear them from inside our kitchen, as the walls in the condo were not anything like those in Mr. Rossi's villa.

Apparently, the lady of the house was continuously fighting off her sex-crazed husband. For once home, he could not keep his hands off her. She pushed back rather loudly, clearly standing her ground, and sometimes told her love-sick Romeo to calm down. In one spat, the randy companion was called an out-of-control loose cannon, and the fair maiden even insisted he was a pig. We two listened, chuckled plenty, shared a word or two, but I sometimes wondered how much different my sexual predicament really was.

On the first floor was a peculiar couple. The old woman there, Bonina, lived with her overgrown and not-so-young unemployed son. Describing her as the Wicked Witch of the West is being a stifle modest. Mother and son always appeared to be loitering outside by the entrance to the building. This forced us to be sociable when encountering them, yet the two had little to say, making us feel uncomfortable and quite happy to be moving on.

Once in my car, however, I sort of revisited my take on things. This was strictly to provide entertainment to the boys. It was with a song penned for Bonina, by me, in Italian, and fervently sung to the tune of Goldfinger. The lyrics were strictly mine, but they even included a line or two from a silly Italian tune claiming someone was using the eyes of the police while spying for the CIA.

My voice created an instrumental sound introducing the song. The lyrics made Bonina a spy, and of course her eyes were helping out those folks at Langley. It was delivered delicately and with a sound conviction. The boys would then burst into hysterics. It became impossible to render only one take of it. No, sir. Those two super happy kids demanded an encore and persisted until arriving wherever we were going.

Chapter 146

The teacher at Fordham University certainly had it right. Truth be told, I shall never know her true relationship to my dad, for he did not have female friends, and she was certainly an attractive woman. Anyway, the future had arrived, and as per her prediction, computers were about to change our entire work process.

Our office had recently purchased a lot of PCs, still in boxes, but they would soon be on our desks. The lengthy and tedious procedure of recording accounting data on long sheets of paper and then sending those to an office where it was key-punched into small cards with a move of those documents to ultimately be input into a computer the size of a large room, had reached its final stage.

By the way, I was now an accounting technician at the GS-5 level. It took a while to land this job, but it was a significant upgrade that felt long overdue. My supervisor Angela, who ran the Accounts Maintenance Branch, was very thorough in acquainting me with my new work, although I was somewhat familiar with various aspects of it. Occasionally, it seemed like too much information had come my way too quickly, but she was quite ready to make sure I understood it.

It was on a Saturday morning that three of us accounting folks were on our way to Zweibrucken in Germany. It was to attend a computer class to familiarize ourselves with those machines which would soon take over our desks. Piero drove his Alfa Romeo, and Luciana sat in the back seat. We chatted about various topics. It seemed incredible, but just like Mr. Rossi, our driver must have thought he was at the Indianapolis 500. Any hope to catch a glimpse of the scenery outside that automobile was a lost cause as it instantaneously became a flash behind us.

Eventually, Piero put on a cassette. It was *The Wall*, and it certainly seized my attention. Pink Floyd and their music was somewhat familiar to me. Yet, for quite a long while, the very rocking sounds which had once sustained my merry existence were no longer doing so. It seemed a bit peculiar that the man introducing me to this music looked like someone who had bypassed the late 1960s and 70s, but apparently not.

We enjoyed the melodic tunes, but it was lowered to allow for some more conversation. Piero surprised me with some of his ideas. He made a rather convincing argument why Communism, or any government strongly administering its economic system, was doomed to fail. Capitalism flourishes very well on its own and usually prevails in economic fluency, although some government moves do make a difference. However, he then switched topics entirely when he stated how our role on Caserma Ederle, although highly appreciated, was a tad superfluous.

According to him, a horrendous conflict, the likes of WW II, could simply never happen again. He was certain that the top brass on both sides of the aisles certainly knew it. However, no general would ever admit this. For a basic strategy of all professional top-ranking soldiers is to never abandon a position once taken. Piero insisted that our military presence in Italy, as in other parts of Europe, would continue for a very long time. And of course, this made him one happy camper.

Eventually we arrived. I am not certain which base our class was in, it may have been Keuzberg Kaserme. We stayed in a rather fancy hotel for the two-week course. Truth be told, none of us understood exactly how this training would be used once back at the office. Anyhow, the class was partially military and civilian personnel, and our teacher, super knowledgeable, was an attractive woman. Plus, she certainly stood out for her ability to present the material in a well-thought-out manner.

On that first day of class, Piero was making a strange facial expression as he pointed to a soldier sitting nearby. Apparently, the guy would close his eyes, head nodding slightly forward or sideways. He certainly appeared to be sleeping. And yet, when the instructor moved on to a different subject and consequently turned to the next page in her manual, he too, would automatically turn the page in his booklet with his eyes closed. The student, like the rest of us, was fully participating but, at the same time, was napping so very naturally.

This scenario triggered an infectious laughter. Piero, Luciana and I promenaded around the town after dinner, and that soldier's discipline and steady permanent absence would infuse our conversations. His solitary vocation was invoking the importance of being there, both in body and mind. After all, who says you need to be awake?

Now, for all you folks not acquainted with geography, the city of Zweibrucken is in southeast Germany, and not far from Belgium and France. Consequently, both Angela and I had foolishly assumed we would sample a mix of culinary dishes for dinner at the local restaurants, but it was not to be. Signor Piero, a true Southern Italian and food connoisseur, dragged us to the same Italian restaurant every night.

We chose to cooperate because our co-worker was truly a fun chap. So, outside of Saturday, a lovely day passed in Belgium, pasta of every type, along with well-known Italian entrees, became our evening fare, and every meal concluded with a desert and an espresso. Upon exiting the restaurant, a different route would bring us back to the hotel as this allowed us to briefly explore the city center. It had always appeared so empty and left us wondering just where everybody was.

Then one evening, it seemed like the entire metropolis came alive. Apparently, everyone was participating in an annual event. Wherever we looked, in front of private homes or apartment buildings, we saw old and not so old items placed outdoors for folks to cart off, and, believe me, the place was jumping! Cars, vans, small old trucks, bicycles, and just about anything which could transport a body was in motion.

People would stop to examine the oddest things. Some even jumped out of their vehicles very soldierly like, as if immediate action was imminent. Even whole families were going at it. And, whether a couch or a hand mirror needed a more thorough inspection, it certainly received it. Of course, we also kept our eyes open for a souvenir worth claiming. And wouldn't you know it, Angela spotted an old leather suitcase in excellent condition, and as no one had yet claimed it, that item came to the hotel with us and then on to Italy.

We eventually graduated and zoomed back home on the highway like our initial journey. Some months later, once everyone was trained, those PCs came to life. As our office fully implemented using them, their value was undisputable. It took so much less time to record our financial data or change erroneous entries, and we were all deliberating how we had gotten by without them. By the way, that machine called a typewriter very quickly vanished along with the job of typist.

Chapter 147

My friends at work were few. One person I truly cared for was Dawn. She was just passing through, that is, working temporarily because she would soon return to the U.S. I believe her mom was a local who had married a soldier many years back, and both were now living in Vicenza where they had met. Dawn worked in Antonio's branch and, at times, looked slightly baffled.

The young lady certainly kept to herself. Although her co-workers, all Italian, had much to say, she hardly ever joined in their conversations. She suspected her contributions were not truly understood. To me, she seemed most graceful, articulate, and open-minded. Our brief exchanges were quite endearing. One day she even confided in me her dating dilemma there on the base. Considering the few qualified suitors available, her outlook was sort of "to date or not to date, that is the question."

Then there was Gifford. He was stationed in Athens and worked extensively with me. The budget shops in Greece and Turkey were a two-man operation, budget chief and clerk, and they had no access to our accounting system. Consequently, I input their data from documents they sent to our office which arrived by mail and provided them with monthly reports to ensure all was fine.

Gifford reconciled his accounts on a quarterly basis with me. That brought him to Vicenza. He was from Ohio and of Italian descendancy. It seemed like after a few days in our gorgeous city, he loved everything about the country, including Italy's ancient monuments, culture, cuisine, fashion, and its laidback lifestyle. It all had truly won him over. Was he perhaps searching for his roots and had glimpsed a small remnant of this yearning? Oh well, we two became very close and talked often in and out of the accounting environment.

Now I must include an office peculiarity. Once a month on Fridays, a bunch of us had lunch at a nearby pizzeria. It was mostly the accounting personnel and a few employees from the budget office. We were seated at a long table, and for some unknown reason, Italians were always on one side while Americans on the other. It looked a tad like a diplomatic encounter. Fortunately, our only business was food and conversations totally deprived of work-related issues.

I'm not certain why, but I always sat with the Italians. And once our delicious pizza was devoured, along with the beer and soda, it was time for an espresso. This was simply a ritual. For that tiny cup of coffee is a long-standing tradition which all Italians abide by, for breakfast, lunch, both morning and afternoon breaktime, and some folks even have it after dinner. However, my compatriots were not espresso drinkers whatsoever. All the Americans, except moi, ordered cappuccinos.

So be it! But Italians have a powerful sense of etiquette much like law and order is to Americans. Back then, drinking a cappuccino any time after eleven in the morning was considered a barbaric act; however, this was never uttered aloud. Yet, the expression and smiling eyes on faces to my right and left made for a silent but implicit laugh. On one occasion, while stirring sugar in my espresso, I considered changing sides on our next outing, just to simply spice things up.

Chapter 148

It was Olga, the German woman who lived above us, to request my wife's assistance. She needed help to travel downtown to the only phone company that existed in Italy back then, TIM. Once her husband would depart for work, she felt stranded and isolated in our rural region, but also frustrated to not have the ability to communicate with family abroad or anyone nearby without a phone.

In those days, you visited the phone company in the city center to order one. Then you waited forever. Well, on that trip the two ladies became better acquainted while spending a few hours in Vicenza. It was sometime after that outing that she and her husband came by one evening to thank us. With them came an assortment of delicious Italian pastry which the kids, and we four, quickly scarfed down.

It had completely shocked the couple to learn a phone would be installed almost a year later. How was this possible? Neither I nor my wife could explain that. For such was life in Italy. Fortunately, there was someone on the base, a true Italian gentleman, who had once worked as a communications expert. If you were in good with him, and I certainly was, you got a phone at home within a few months, which is exactly what happened.

We had a wonderful conversation once the kids disappeared into their room. The ladies revisited Francesca's dislike of our town. My wife felt a little too secluded and far from civilization. Apparently, both women had sworn to get to the city more often versus just to run an errand. Then, quite unexpectedly, life on the base got aired out. Our guests had assumed I was a professional, in a career-oriented position, and therefore at a high-grade paying job. They were surprised to learn my actual circumstances.

Olga's husband mentioned he would speak to someone. Apparently, he did. Now, just exactly what was discussed behind closed doors is a mystery to me. A few weeks later, the personnel office notified my boss that I would be detailed to the SETAF Budget Office. It was then rumored that two positions with promotion potential to the grade GS-11 were being requested by the comptroller. Of course, with me working there, plus my present experience, I would certainly qualify for one. Why, it felt like a miracle come true, provided by some divine force here on earth.

You can imagine that not everyone was thrilled. A couple of my Yankee co-workers, though they never voiced it, were perhaps not eagerly enthused with my presence. I was one of them, but I spoke the native language perfectly, was in good standing with the locals and took my coffee breaks with them. I appeared too much at home in Vicenza. Consequently, while my Italian colleagues all congratulated me, a few of the other folks did not approve.

I soon reported to the budget execution shop. My basic function there included interacting with other budget personnel from various offices. They provided us documents to obligate funds for present or future ongoing activities. Rather quickly, and most enthusiastically, I had a good grasp of all the various aspects of my job, and I liked the analysts I interacted with. I also won my boss and co-worker's approval. For a moment, it felt like a miracle come true.

But adversity is never far away. My initial departure from the accounting office had some folks up in arms. Not only there, but also in other sectors where a bit of monetary tasks were performed. After all, there were quite a few of us desperate souls seeking a promotion and perhaps a career. Some were called lifers, that referred to personnel married to ex-soldiers who intended to remain overseas permanently. One of them had claimed the budget shop was a male-dominated private club promoting its own personal agenda. And so, she filed a discriminatory complaint against the so-called budget club.

Time passed, and it became apparent the new positions would not come about. They were first put on hold, which is exactly when a co-worker informed me that the previous year that office had barely survived a discriminatory investigation. Sure enough, those jobs were eventually terminated. Nevertheless, my new boss insisted I remain on board, and I certainly agreed for returning to my previous job felt like taking a giant step backward.

Then the shit hit the fan. One of my customers was the budget analyst from the 509th Infantry Battalion. We had just established funds for the battalion's upcoming NATO maneuvers in Germany. He was adamant that the main document for various fuel expenses was not to be closed out when the first pertinent bill was processed. A few more would soon follow.

Eventually, once all charges were processed, a minor amount would remain and could then be reversed. This was due to bills being encountered at different intervals and some uncertainty as to the quantity of fuel acquired.

I had hand carried all the pertinent documents to the accounting branch. My specific instructions provided to the technician regarding that issue appeared to have been understood. Perhaps my English was not so good? A few months later, I noticed a very large amount, previously set up to pay for the NATO exercise, had been returned as funds available for other expenses. Something was definitely wrong. After a concise review, it was obvious that the technician had closed the account which needed to remain open, after paying the first invoice.

The following morning, I approached her desk. It seemed only wise to ask questions, speak cautiously, and then carefully point out the error. Well, the morose lady was no doubt an ex-bar employee from those Asian places my sailor years had me in. She also appeared a tad annoyed and very clueless. Eventually, she understood the problem which I would now have to fix. Unfortunately, prior to my departure, my joking did me in. I had foolishly said that if this incident occurred again, I would return to handcuff her. That my laughter was not shared should have put me on alert.

Well, the offended accounting technician went home and cried to her husband, a very high-ranking officer. For such was revealed to me during the chew-out session the following day. The meeting between myself, her husband, and our colonel, was held behind closed doors and was a one-way session. It felt like basic training at Ft. Dix, where being marginalized was the gig, as my superior now shouted, while I sat still, mouth shut, eyes simply glued to both soldiers who appeared quite put out.

Well, if office encounters were a tad rough, life at home was not always a bowl of cherries either. For any bowl may have a few undesirable bits of fruit which can ruin the whole. In most, if not all relationships, people eventually come to terms with their differences. Sometimes, more often than not, they begin to detest them, or the circumstances leading to them, or perhaps, even each other.

Francesca and I had first butted heads some years back. It occurred after a weekend visit to her parents. Ricky, still a baby, had been properly fed before our departure and had slept soundly during our trip back home. Once in our tiny flat, he awoke and began to cry uncontrollably and would simply not stop. As someone who had lost a small brother, I tended to become overly concerned quickly, and things immediately got out of hand.

My suggestion that he was perhaps hungry was deemed ridiculous. So, I was told. The baby was now in my arms, screaming wildly, and terrifying my limited peace of mind. Nevertheless, my wife, who was putting some things away, refused to accept he needed to be fed. Soon enough, as the commotion continued, I began to insist and persist, which led to an outburst from the irate lady. She began to bang small pots while reaching for the right one, and also throwing things around for she had finally decided to cooperate, but not so happily. She even carried on about my many interfering ways.

Francesca sat down with Ricky in her arms. He was still making himself heard. The moment the bottle-nipple entered that baby's lips, he drank the entire contents non-stop. Without as much as a small nod to thank me, he was then out like a light. Not a word from the mom, and I am not one to play up on what is past. Mission accomplished, that is simply all that registered. I then returned to a book which had me on its last few pages, and I must admit feeling somewhat vindicated.

It was now a totally different issue that occurred after our move to Sarmego. The flat and all that adorned it had cost me plenty. We had two automobiles, not new but not cheap, and I was the only one working. So, having dished out nearly all my savings, it seemed wise to become a bit prudent. That is why the lady of the house had been asked to curb her spending habits, unless for something truly necessary.

The message was buried. My wife one day informed me she wanted to buy a fur coat. It made absolutely no sense to me. When exactly would she wear it? Of course, no answer was provided, and it was apparent that practicing a bit of frugality was rather inconceivable to her. This was simply not the woman's style. She and her sister Anna went off to the city of Ferrara to purchase similar fur coats—to the tune of two thousand dollars each. Maybe I was furious, maybe not, but I was certainly not very fucking happy.

Her fancy pelt was only worn once. For on the first occasion, Francesca spotted someone else wearing an identical one. The two furry ladies exchanged notes, and the stranger informed my wife that her husband purchased them in Romania, very cheaply, then sold them in Italy for a lot more. Apparently, its real value was nothing compared to what she spent. And so, the new but now highly undesired clothing was hung up in our bedroom closet to stay there permanently.

Oh well, materialistic things should not be so important. They have value, yes, but add little to the welfare of a household. However, at times, one tends to notice certain things. One evening I realized that the bed frame, a lovely mahogany wood, super expensive, was warped in several areas. Apparently, something had struck it continuously and damaged it. Our Ricky was allowed to ride his tricycle in the house. He had accidentally rammed his bike against the bedframe more than once. Such was the information provided. And well, what could she have done about it?

I chose to look the other way. During times like this, my inability to blow up accordingly was questioned. One day I finally lost it. Ricky's tonsils, like mine, much too often had the boy in bed for several days. He would appear a tad lifeless, and the only solution was to administer what the doctor prescribed. And the doctor's office was right across the street from our building. It seemed incredible—he was hardly ever consulted, and back then, doctors made house calls. You cannot imagine my anger after returning home from work and finding our son exactly as I had left him that morning. After a bit of slight hysterics, I insisted she contact the doctor the following day. It was accomplished, and Ricky was back on his feet immediately.

My assumption was a tad devious. Perhaps the woman feared a visiting doctor would lead to a few rumors. After all, life everywhere mostly consists of any news that thrills its spectators. Anyhow, I no longer recall the circumstances over what occurred next. One evening we began to argue loudly and incessantly. I belted out like a madman that I was leaving. That is when Ricky, sitting in his highchair, looking both shocked and very concerned, asked, "For good?"

I took myself for a long walk. And believe me, I would have massacred anyone or anything getting in my way, but it soon registered that such is the way of most marriages, if not all. Upon returning home, my son was in my arms, and he gave me a warm kiss, which is why I promised myself to avoid verbal rampages, as they serve no purpose. Our lady companions have us wrapped up neatly and soundly, such is the way of all things and may remain so forever.

Chapter 149

It was Henry Miller who once claimed that to be happy one needs to be a selfish bastard. Otherwise, you must accept your fate at the mercy of others. My only complaint with our sleepy town was over the church bells. They rang so loudly, especially on Sunday mornings when life at home was moving slowly. My wife, however, most desperately wanted out of Sarmego.

Francesca was a city slicker and was now quite miserable. At times, upon arriving home, I found her looking terribly withdrawn and almost in tears. Soon enough, out came her ailment. We needed to move back to the city or within the city limits, so we would be close to family and friends. I decided to sell the flat and purchase one within the urban paradise of Vicenza.

Our first exploration took us to Torri Di Quartesolo. A small town, not exactly in the city but not far from it either. Our expedition was just to feel things out. After picking up my family, we drove to a neighborhood very close to Piero's home. We found a vast green area right by the small building in question. I parked by the building and seeing a sand box and a sliding pond in the park right by it, we two parents thought it safe to let Ricky and Eric play there. After all, why bore the children with looking at walls and living space. Italy was a very safe country back then, with the exception of Italian terrorists killing Italian politicians.

In we went but very soon came back out. The flat needed a lot of repair work. The floor plan was limited in lay out, plus the owner was renting it, and the person at home did not appear like the type to move out as per notice, which in Italy was a common problem. Upon exiting, we immediately confronted a different scenario which seemed a bit peculiar. Our boys were facing a dilemma.

Ricky was at the top of the sliding pond while Eric stood by below. Both kids looked rather frightened. Two boys were blocking Ricky, as he could neither slide down nor come off using the steps. The unnecessary encounter was the work of a group of Black American kids. The two on the sliding pond refused to move as a bunch of friends were standing by enjoying the ongoing contest. The rowdy lot on the side were yelling and insisting the Italian kid do something or else. Of course, my children only spoke Italian, but that was not the issue here.

I marched over there and asked the boy blocking Ricky to come down. This would allow my son to slide down and be finished with it. Now, my manners are always impeccable no matter who stands before me, and my tone was rather pleasant and calm. The boy in the middle of the sliding pond, perhaps eight or nine years old, was obviously not about to move. He looked at me and then said "Ain't no bald-headed nigga gonna tell me what to do."

Well, my upbringing in the Bronx did not instill such shenanigans in me. I grabbed his arm, carefully brought him down, and then forced him to bring me to his dwellings. He immediately began yelling, and his friends were protesting, loudly and not so politely, while following us, but we continued to walk. Once at his condo, the kid started crying and insisted I let him go. I didn't comply with his request. When we arrived at the floor where he lived, I rapped on the door he indicated was his.

A short stout White woman opened it. She looked unhappy and quite ready to provide manners immediately. My speech, pleading for leniency, after briefly explaining the circumstances, without including his actual words, simply asked that she reprimand him. Apparently, the kid was now frightened out of his wits. They were soon indoors, allowing me to move on. Well, as I drove off, one thing was certain, we would not be moving to Torri Di Quartesolo any time soon.

The following morning my tale was shared as office news. Eventually, it was narrated to Evelyn, a lovely Black woman from the south, for I assumed she would appreciate the narrative, and she certainly appeared to. Once it was fully delivered, she looked at me most profoundly and stated, "Julian, now you know that as soon as you drove off, those kids looked at each other and said, well, there goes the neighborhood." I believe I may have never laughed so hard in my entire life.

We would reside in the town my wife despised a bit longer. I didn't find it so bad. As a matter of fact, my neighbor Terry and I had become somewhat acquainted and occasionally went to work together either in his car or mine. One evening, he came over to watch a boxing match on TV, as he, too, was enthusiastic about the sport. We witnessed an upcoming young American boxer, Donald Curry, facing the highly overrated Italian hero Nino La Rocca.

The Italian folks in my office would be quite devastated with the result. After a couple of good rounds, their hero lost all credibility. He was outboxed and easily put away in the sixth round. It was during the match that Terry informed me about his upcoming trip to Thailand. It seemed unreal. He planned to visit Sattahip, a city well-known to me. Once the fight terminated, we continued to chat, and I eventually found the photographs of myself and the young Thai girl, my taxi driver's girlfriend.

Some explanation of our circumstances was provided. I asked Terry to attempt to locate this family, and he agreed to give it his best. So along with one of the photographs, a bit of money had been turned over to my new friend for those folks back in Thailand. It was an adequate sum, a decent gift, if you may, given simply to let them know I remembered them in the scheme of things. Of course, much depended on his being able to locate those three as I had no address to give him.

I was provided a full accounting many months later. We were no longer neighbors. During his trip to Thailand, the ex-mover in the Di Stefano household, with much help from friends in the accounting office, including Piero, had relocated to a building within walking distance to Caserma Ederle. Just how this made Francesca happier was a mystery to me. And yet the woman seemed so overjoyed and quite ready to start life anew.

My dental appointment had me in Terry's office. While browsing some magazines and finding little of interest, one of the administrative personnel, a female soldier, engaged me in a brief chat. She somehow knew I was living in Vicenza permanently, which was a bit peculiar. Anyway, her tone was polite and a tad inquisitive, especially about the local culture, but she turned a bit sour when making a reference to the "Italian slave women" we Americans living abroad were marrying.

This forced me to speak up. I stated that my Italian wife was a wonderful mother to our children, and even though we had our differences, she was also a great companion whom I cherished. It seemed only right to include how some of her interests had enriched my world both in art and literature. I concluded by stating how the lady had recently purchased a culinary encyclopedia, and she was now constantly putting it to good use. My kids and I were certainly in very good hands.

I should have stopped there. My next words created a small back-and-forth but fortunately I was called into the dental area to see my dentist. Terry looked happy to see me and sounded upbeat. He was provided a few words about our move while his assistant attended to me in the patient's chair. It was lowered, and now both dentist and assistant were looking down at me, as I heard, "Julian, just what did you do over there?"

My dentist's brief accounting, leaving out some significant details, was delivered slowly and most cautiously. None of the taxi drivers in Sattahip had recognized the girl in the photo. One informed Terry that some years back a horrible fire had devastated a large part of the town and forced many families to relocate elsewhere. One evening, in sheer desperation, my dentist showed the picture to one of the ladies in a bar. Almost immediately, all hell broke loose!

One of the women who caught a glimpse of the picture began to shout quite madly. She even started laughing and continued to speak wildly in her native tongue, while gesturing to Terry with a thumps-up expression all along saying "number one." Soon, many other bar girls were there, and upon seeing my photo, they simply went wild, which forced the confused customer to put it away in order to allow a level of normalcy to return.

Now my dentist and his assistant, a very pretty young lady, were staring at me. While looking up at them, it felt slightly odd to be reacquainted with a past so far behind and circumstances so different from my current lifestyle and character. But two sets of eyes were demanding some words of wisdom from the quiet man sitting in the chair. My voice found its tone and said, "Hey, I simply gave from the heart."

Chapter 150

Our new home was in the neighborhood called La Stanga. The three-floor building, surrounded by lots of other plain structures, was located approximately a hundred yards from the entrance to Caserma Ederle. Fortunately, on the opposite side of the road to the base was a livelier area with everything from a fruit and vegetables store to a butcher, a bakery, a newspaper kiosk, several bars, and other convenient outlets.

Francesca now worked on the base. As my dependent, and me being a veteran, she had priority over other Italian candidates applying for work. That is why the fortunate young lady landed an administrative position in a rather prestigious office. Well, perhaps my friend at the personnel office may have helped some. Anyhow, she worked with the lawyers representing SETAF, and believe me, the woman was in sheer heaven.

Our offices were close by, but we hardly ever saw each other. She was apparently super busy, but also not one prone to attend the quasi-obligatory coffee breaks both morning and afternoon. Occasionally, she arrived late at the Italian cafeteria for lunch, usually as I was just about to leave. We would exchange a few words. Fortunately, regardless of my whereabouts on the base, Bianca was long gone, having found a job on the outskirts of Vicenza.

Back at home, we shared the family chores. She drove the kids to a school downtown in the mornings, I picked them up in the afternoon. Ricky and Eric now attended the same scholastic environment, my older boy was in first grade, his brother in a Head Start program. My task was to pick up our kids and head home, but we often first stopped at the shopping area. It pretty much became a daily routine for we usually lacked something, either bread, or cheese, or fruit, or whatever was needed.

I set the dinner table around five. Then I prepared a salad or something similar, as Francesca, once among us, would take over. Apparently, my busy housewife had given some thought toward a full meal, so there were many food items ready to be tackled. An exchange of notes regarding folks we both knew or some incident worth sharing would soon follow. I can emphatically state my wife appeared slightly tired but thoroughly satisfied with the day's events. And she had much to say.

Yet one afternoon, the lady of the house was completely shocked. It was upon hearing my new mission. Folks, if I am not mistaken, it is Marlow's hierarchy laws that claim individuals demand more once all their basic needs have been met. Yes? Of course, in theory, we were certainly far from the bottom rung of quality-of-life standards. Yet something within had commanded me to now establish a career. This would never happen in Vicenza on that base even though I now had a degree in business management with enough accounting grades to qualify as a government accountant. And that is why my new mission was to return to the U.S.

Now let me include my circumstances. My one-year detail at the budget office had terminated long ago. That I was still there was a bit peculiar, but my boss would have kept me there forever, even though I had no position there and remained on a loan basis. Fortunately, the accounting branch was not demanding my return and that kept me happy. So, no possibility of advancement, no going back, it was best to move on.

My plan to establish a career elsewhere practically floored my happy wife. She immediately put on a rather sorrowful look, spoke up, and eventually shed a few tears. She proclaimed it was crazy to give up the wonderful life we enjoyed here. Plus, she highly treasured her family, friends, our lovely new home, and the beautiful things around her. Oh well, what could I possibly say?

A thought had me pondering, "Damn, we are not going to Bangladesh for heaven's sake." So, it appeared only one person would be moving. However, one evening, the lady of the house inquired about the benefits to be had once back from the U.S. I informed her it entailed a much bigger salary, a housing allowance, which meant we could rent our flat here, a great pension to retire on, and a prestigious grade way above my GS-5, which to me seemed worth pursuing.

Folks, whatever tiny progress had been made at home was eradicated on the base. At her office, some of the top-ranking civilians informed Francesca that I had no reinstatement rights. The government had not sent me to Italy, therefore my move to the U.S., and my family, if they joined me, would be at our expense, and it would certainly be costly moving us and our household goods. And if we were unhappy in America, what then? Ship everything back and return and hope to miraculously land a job back on the base?

Nevertheless, my search for work in the New World went forth. I contacted Dawn, and she quickly came to my rescue. She had left several years ago and was now working for the General Services Administration in Washington D.C. Her father had provided me with her phone number, and we two soon spoke at length. Sure enough, my resume, then known as Standard Form 171, was in her hands and almost immediately in someone else's.

Two weeks later, a Mr. Rotter called from the U.S. He sounded rather interested in me, provided some basic information about his agency and the nature of their work, and even promised to address the possibility of paying for our move. It sounded incredible, until he followed up a week later with a negative reply regarding sponsoring our move. It seemed best to not immediately share that information with anyone.

I accepted the position as an auditor with the Inspector General's Office for the Department of Defense. They hired me at the GS-7 grade and there would be an annual promotion ultimately to GS-12. This seemed incredible to me, for the highest-ranking civilian among us was a GS-12. It felt like a dream come true, but just how to bring on board my melancholic wife remained a mystery. Allow me to say it did not go over well.

My revelation almost caused her to have a complete breakdown. Which is why I then went out for a walk. My feet brought me downtown, reversing the very route which had brought me to Caserma Ederle on my first visit. Something within me strangely exalted my reality. I was a loner, and almost immediately the song "The Boxer" came to mind, specifically the part which claims that no matter how many times put down, the fighter prevails.

Well, Francesca faced pandemonium on that military base. My already distraught and unhinged wife was simply put through hell. Washington D.C.! Did I have a clue what the cost of living in that city was? And wasn't it full of crime and drugs, horrible schools, and even some prevalent old-fashioned racism? A few folks even stated they had always thought me a bright person, but something was amiss, most certainly. Someone even inquired if I was getting high.

Upon hearing all this nonsense, my heart went out to the immigrants. Those who pick themselves up and move on, never looking back and having no clue what awaits them. My folks had moved to England, spoke no English, knew no one, but they had gambled on a better future. Why, my father had even rolled up his sleeves to work in the coal mines. And what about all those uneducated, poor souls who were able to make it in our country (after passing the barriers trying to deny them entry, and access to the American dream). So, why would I fail? After all, Julian Di Stefano was just returning home, no?

My family and I visited Francesca's folks two weeks before my departure. That day our circumstances were heavily analyzed and scrutinized between mother and daughter. In the late afternoon, I had taken Ricky and Eric with me to her sister's house. There was a bit of concern over my plans, yet both husband and wife were convinced things would turn out just fine. They even insinuated a trip to the U.S. would be included in the future if this was my new home.

I have no clue who may have favored my take on things. However, a few days later, Francesca informed me that as she had accepted me as a husband, she would therefore also accept our lot and join me abroad once I settled in. It was like receiving a nicely wrapped parting gift. The news put me in sheer heaven. And I was now convinced everything coming our way would be great!

My flight was out of Malpensa Airport. My family, along with Alessandro and my mother were sending me off. Now Mr. Rossi certainly understood my predicament. He also approved of my initiative, although expressing how much we would all be missed. Then he, the ultimate optimist, convincingly stated that he looked forward to having a memorable dinner in his villa to celebrate our return to Italy one day. My overall plan was to quickly upgrade myself and then land a job on the base in Vicenza.

Perhaps, life has its own priorities. Yes, we may choose, decide, make plans, and change our minds, but too often surprises await us, providing no explanation yet allowing us to believe we master our destiny. Again, I was flying across the ocean, and who could say how many more of these trips would follow. Suddenly, a peculiar feeling creeped up, informing me that a bit of uncertainty was part of all journeys, for the uncertainty of the road ahead is usually the only path available.

Part 6

Chapter 151

My fourteen years abroad terminated in February 1989. Dawn met me in the former part of the evening at the airport now known as Ronald Reagan National. As I had departed a bit behind schedule and changed planes at JFK, it felt great to finally arrive and terminate a long trip. My friend and I hugged and kissed on the cheeks and then went off to the parking lot.

It was in a Fiat Punto, which had come over from Italy, that we loaded my baggage into. Dawn drove off, and after circling the airport grounds for a while, my good friend admitted, with a bit of frustration, that she was having trouble finding the airport exit. But exit we did, and after a fine dinner somewhere in Northern Virginia, she took me to my lodgings on the outskirts of Alexandria.

We eventually said good night in front of the motel. I made myself comfortable in a room that was extremely hot and began looking at the Washington Post which my friend had purchased for me. The ads for a room to rent pretty much had similar prices, but as to location, everything was rather foreign to me. Whether the accommodations were in Burke, Arlington, or Georgetown, I could only identify as either MD, VA, or D.C., which helped very little. However, the words nearby Metro appeared to brandish a sense of honor and required a few extra bucks in rent.

The following morning, a brief walk took me to the Metro rail station at Braddock Road. It was cold, and at the station, several women were wearing long coats, gloves, scarves, and sneakers. It seemed quite odd to me. In Italy, you would have been laughed out of town or branded as insane if you were dressed nicely and had on anything but shoes, and cheap shoes did not exist back then. But sneakers? Perhaps those working matrons, who appeared a tad gloomy, had a peculiar medical condition?

My office was located near the Pentagon in a small building on Army Navy Drive. As I entered, my eyes again confronted those gym shoes on well-dressed ladies getting in the elevators. Oh well, it was better to leave it alone. The director, Dan Rotter, appeared quite thrilled to see me. We shared a brief session about the agency and our mission, and he then slightly expounded on what to expect being new to the field of investigating, or analyzing, as he put it, what others did.

It was now time to meet my team. Everyone in the group was casually dressed. As a matter of fact, a few employees looked as if they were getting ready to clean a garage. Once again, I was baffled! But soon enough, it would be brought to my attention that Fridays are dress down days, which was a bit of a mystery to me. Just how not dressing well one day of the week made a difference was simply hard to grasp. Apparently, there was some catching up to do with modern Yankee customs, but for the moment, I simply shook hands all around and eventually sat at my desk.

My reporting date was Monday, but today, the personnel office would see me. And before we had left his office, Mr. Rotter had asked about lodgings and if I needed assistance with finding a place to stay. My intention was to rent a furnished room, preferably in a nice neighborhood, and so that gentleman gave me the name of a woman at the Pentagon's housing office and a pass to get in. I was quite impressed with how well things were proceeding and the gentleman who was helping me out.

At times, some characteristics are splattered on an individual's face. The lady who greeted me had a pleasant Southern accent, two joyful eyes, and a tad of inbred facial happiness—all this coming from someone who wore her heart on her sleeve. She soon provided me with a name and address, directions, and even showed me a map of Northern Virginia, pointing to the area of the home in question. Then she informed me that the accommodations would be more than suitable, and how the landlady was a "truly sweet gal."

I spoke to Dawn later that day, and we agreed to meet after work hours. The landlady was fine with my coming by that evening to see the room. It was now on to D.C., particularly, Georgetown, for it had registered quite clearly as the area with the most expensive rooms listed in the newspaper. My brief exploration soon left me truly impressed as there were some rather beautiful older homes in certain areas, and I even found a large bookstore on M Street which was checked out immediately.

My good friend and I met at the Rosslyn Metro station. Although Dawn gave me a sense of where we were and heading off to, it was dark. I was a tad clueless, and so we eventually parked in front of a small house. I would soon discover it had been built during the Depression era and came at the price of two thousand dollars. My soon to be landlady, Madalyn, cordial and friendly, was an older woman, not only with a strong accent, but a bit of curiosity about us two.

Now the premises within that house were immaculately clean. There were shiny wooden floors throughout, and the available room was upstairs. It was one of two bedrooms, the larger sized one was already taken, and a bathroom was shared, but not on weekends as the other lodger went home to his family in Delaware. Dawn's expression seemed to convey a sense of "this is it", which I agreed with and so took it immediately. After all, the price was incredibly cheaper than anything I had seen in the ads, and having found a most perfect environment, what was there to really think about?

My residence was on a street called North Powhatan. Dawn assisted me in moving in late Saturday morning, and everything ran smoothly. Not wanting to keep her waiting, once at the new digs, my unpacking was left for later, and we two went off to have lunch. It was not long before I was getting details about life in the big city. First of all, the person she had given my resume to months back was no longer at the IG's Office. He had found another job, which brought him a promotion, and so he, like many others, had simply moved on to earn more money.

According to my buddy, now a professional government employee, federal workers were a bit like mercenaries. That is, ready to execute their performance at the highest bid. Life here was mostly about career, promotions, and more money, because for some unexplainable reason, there is just never enough. However, one assurance was given to me quite convincingly. As my agency was a very prestigious and well-funded institution, if nothing else, an annual promotion was practically guaranteed.

On Monday morning, I met my roommate. It was over breakfast, and as luck would have it, the guy was happy to give me a ride to work. The middle-aged gentleman was employed by the U.S. Marshals, and the agency was located very close to mine. Consequently, my daily commutes became very interesting and beneficial as the lad was well-informed, having traveled around the planet, and he certainly grasped its reality. Plus, a substantial savings on Metro bus and rail fare was coming my way.

At work, my new colleagues immediately noticed me, for I always dressed impeccably well. They often complimented me throughout that first week. Dan had assigned me to the Major Acquisitions Branch, and our goal was to audit any weapons system purchased by the Pentagon which exceed 2 billion dollars. This entailed analyzing all data from inception to delivery, as our mission was to ensure the program had complied with proper technical specifications and DoD regulations.

Our team consisted of six auditors. The supervisor was a grade GS-14, and the other auditors ranged mostly from the GS-13 grade down to me at the GS-7 level. The team I joined was now conducting an audit that began a few months back, and it was still in the early stages of the investigative process. At my first meeting regarding the weapon system in question, it was apparent the auditors had some very serious concerns. Just what were they auditing?

It was called the SFW. That is, the Sensor Fused Weapon. Now the more my ears heard, the more puzzled my immediate thoughts were. And my being somewhat alarmed was justified by Dan as he later responded to someone else by stating, "We certainly should be concerned." The weapon was categorized as a bomb but did not look anything like one. Even more bizarre was its application. It was to be used against the Warsaw Pact Nations, not to destroy their weapons or vehicles, if they were advancing to combat NATO forces, but to simply slow down their movement to the front lines of battle. This just seemed so absurd!

The firearm which would maim the enemy's trucks and tanks looked like a hockey puck. It was a metal piece, and a sensor would drive it to locate heat, like that of an engine, and then the puck, once launched, would score a hit. However, according to the auditor speaking up, the sensor was unreliable, and "the metal piece" could hit just about anything. And as far as what real damage it caused, why, it was anyone's guess. Overall, the program was so behind schedule, and the reliability of the weapon was questionable, which is why a couple of the engineers working on it referred to the SFW as the Seldom Functioning Weapon.

There were also concerns over the delivery mode of the SFW. A series of these weapons were inside a box, which would be dropped out of an aircraft at a rather low altitude. Believe me, it was a well-known fact the Air Force was not so thrilled with this part. Once dropped, that box would open, and the weapons, which looked like the water pumps I and the engineer on my first ship worked on, would begin to descend. At the right altitude, an engine would start up and ultimately propel the individual weapon back upwards. Once at the correct altitude, the puck would get launched.

Now technical matters are not my forte, but this sounded ridiculous. Most of the guys around the table at my first meeting were either grinning or almost laughing. However, it was not at all amusing. The American taxpayer would ultimately spend a lot of money, and to get what? While listening to all this, my mind wandered off some. I began questioning how the hell this program had gotten this far. My goodness, Ike Eisenhower would have turned over in his grave if he could have heard it all.

It was Mr. Rotter who summarized it best. His "Well, folks, that is why we are here, to ensure our military capability means something" was so convincing that I felt right at home. About a week later, we headed off to Ft. Walton Beach to interview the military folks who ran the project and the contractors working for the firm to build the seldom functioning weapon.

Now wouldn't you know it. I, the new and lowest grade on the team, was assigned one of the most difficult tasks of the audit, the cost analysis. Upon looking over the audit manual and applicable questions, there were quite a few terms and particular phrasing which left me a bit perplexed. Fortunately, a statistician was assigned to our team to verify the authenticity of the cost models used, and this gentleman was very helpful in providing me pertinent material to familiarize myself with in grasping the overall analysis to be performed.

The audit may have begun quite well, but at times, I felt like a complete idiot. It was easy to follow the outlined form of the subject being analyzed. However, one quickly gets sidetracked after accumulating heaps of documents and too much information. It becomes nearly impossible to not lose sight of the overall initial intent. It felt like I was looking for a needle in a haystack.

Fortunately, our supervisor was a genius in stirring us all up and throwing us back into the firing line. Our motto could have been "Dig until you find something or perish trying." And so, although a tad frustrated and uncertain anything was being accomplished, finally something came my way.

In the original cost analysis done many years back, there was an amount representing a monetary risk factor associated with cost overruns due to delays in arriving at the project's established milestones. That amount had never been updated, although the SFW was many years behind schedule and facing some serious cost overruns. I had a "finding", our bread and butter, which is what our audit was out to achieve, finding many findings.

Our team spent two weeks in Florida and then returned to Arlington, our home base. On my desk there was now an overabundance of documents accumulated from various folks interviewed. My task was to continue analyzing in order to determine what other areas may have had problematic circumstances. One was already in the sack, although not too significant, but it was legitimate for inclusion in the final report.

Now, why wasn't I too thrilled with my new job? My papers outlining all the work accomplished had been given to my supervisor, not the team boss, but the auditor I reported to, a young lady at the GS-13 level. A few days went by, then a week, then a few more weeks, which is why I decided to pay her a visit. She assured me my papers would get reviewed next. It sounded promising yet returning to my desk to dig into the unknown among the many documents there being analyzed, hoping to find anything else out of whack, was strenuous and a tad boring.

Nevertheless, my mornings at work began rather well. We auditors sat in our own cubicles in a very large room and almost always gathered to enjoy a brief chat on world topics. Here was a sort of congregation near someone's area and it never ran too long, but was a very rewarding experience, even somewhat educational. Everyone was well-informed on world politics and other topics and was also very opinionated.

Those discussions helped to start a long day. Unfortunately, once through, Julian Di Stefano faced several agonizing decisions—what to read again, to ensure nothing significant had been overlooked and which area to expand on. Plus, why hadn't my supervisor gotten back to me about my work papers given to her so long ago? I had been to see her, so was an e-mail requesting info in order?

At times, it felt like my lunch break would never arrive. It was necessary, for it now included a long walk outdoors. By the way, the mystery of those sneakers had been fully resolved. They allowed both male and female feet plenty of outdoor walking, especially at lunch time, which would enrich the spirit and mind attached to them. I participated in this exercise, minus the sneakers, and later on ate a quick lunch at my desk. The afternoon consisted of reading and rereading, and if the word volunteer was ever uttered, I jumped, ready to assist anyone.

Soon enough, my phone use got slightly abused. It was there for official government business, although everyone made some exceptions. Being a tad frustrated with so much down time, that tool sometimes became attached to my ear, but never for too long. Certainly, there were no calls to Italy. Oh well, I believe the human psyche is such that one must either create or mentally perish, at least with most of us in the category of human species. I must confess to some chats with Dawn, who was never available for very long.

Chapter 152

Some great news soon came my way. Francesca had forwarded a letter from Gifford, and I discovered that he was working as a budget analyst for the U.S. Treasury in D. C. It thrilled me that we would soon catch up. But another great unexpected notice also pleased me plenty. An auditor in a different team had informed me that the IG was implementing a rule to pay all travel expenses for newly arrived personnel.

It took a few phone calls to locate Gifford. He was very happy to hear that I was living in the U.S., and he invited me to his home in Arlington. Apparently, he and his girlfriend, also from Ohio, had grown up together and were now in a serious relationship. Work had brought them to the area. She had landed a job with an important firm, and he was tagging along, ultimately taking advantage of his budget experience in Greece.

What a wonderful evening we shared! My friend was pleasant and super polite, and the couple were such great company. They appeared so right for each other. Now Gifford admitted he missed Italy and would have loved being able to work in Vicenza. I, on the other hand, had become somewhat sour with the state of affairs at the base there, where almost everyone clung to a position as if it had been created strictly for them. Perhaps this negative outlook had made me forget the beauty of the country I had lived in for so long.

The following day, I took myself to see Dan. It was to request help. I had been denied the possibility of PCS orders because I was living overseas on my own and not as a federal employee sent to work there. Now, the IG would reimburse almost anyone taking a job with them based on some new provisions it was pursuing. It seemed only right to inquire about the regulation in question which had a clause categorized as "lack of manpower." Apparently, our organization was sort of admitting they could not hang on to their employees, and finding sufficient workers was no easy task. It was therefore extending its search far and wide to bring auditors on board, and they certainly had the funds to do it. Dan guaranteed me he would look-into it.

A few days later, I shared the good news Dan had provided me with Dawn. It also included an invitation to dinner that very evening. Then on Saturday, with Madalyn's approval, I used her phone to call my wife. Although we had spoken the previous week, she was happy to hear from me again and even more so once the unexpected update came forth. She and the kids and our furniture would travel at government expense. Then the children came on, and as per our last talk, they again had a million things to ask and tell me. My goodness, how much I missed them all.

Things should have proceeded just fine. But apparently there was a small dilemma at the travel office. The employee responsible for my PCS document was up in arms and so were his colleagues. In their minds, I had pulled off the impossible. Its legitimacy was somewhat questionable. How can someone who had arrived with no PCS authorization be given one at a later date? Wasn't there some kind of irregularity here? In reality, the effective date of the new regulation was backdated to accommodate me.

Now, being treated like a criminal is not a very pleasant experience. My phone calls to that office were not returned. I visited it, and the apparent animosity toward me was beyond comprehension. So, Mr. Rotter once again heard me out. That great man gave me a name and a phone number and assured me all would be taken care of.

I called an organization known as the Travel Committee. They were the gurus of all travel regulations. The individual who heard my circumstances never uttered a word. He only asked one question, and then assured me the issue would be resolved as he sounded very professional and polite. Apparently, he was also super punctual. Two days later a very low and subdued phone message informed me my PCS orders would soon be ready.

What a welcomed relief. And why not? I had worked my butt off overseas and always given the best of myself to accomplish the task at hand. As a soldier, even when my condition was not top-of-the-line, my performance was exemplary, and it would never change. Even now I continued to be me, witnessing billions of dollars possibly being thrown away on a useless military toy which did not even work and would probably never be used.

Chapter 153

Not far from North Powhatan Street was the Pizza Pazza Parlor. It was during a late afternoon stroll on a Saturday that the owner and I met, quite by chance. The skinny worn-out looking guy standing outside the restaurant, who appeared lost also seemed a bit Italian to me. How nice it would be if he too was from the very island the two kids from Italy had left behind ages ago.

We spoke a bit then and again several days later. It was to ask if, when not traveling for my job, he would have me work in the evening as a waiter. My paisano buddy happily agreed to take me on, and the man had me start the following day. It was my first gig in this line of work and something I looked forward to doing for a brief period. Alongside me were two other new employees being shown the ropes.

All proceeded well at first. However, the final spectacle left us three new waiters quite shocked, to say the least. Perhaps stunned is the more appropriate word. For in some ways, it felt as if we had been wounded, both morally and psychologically. Our trainer was a young lady from South Carolina. Her final feat consisted of showing us how to make a cannoli. That delicious Sicilian treat was hardly known on the Italian peninsula back then, but apparently not so in Arlington.

The young lady simply placed a brown crust on a small dish. Then using a plastic filler, she began squeezing in that delicious cream which is nothing more than a lot of ricotta cheese loaded with tons of sugar. After finishing, she gently sprinkled a bit of powdered sugar on top, and voila, there is your dessert, ready to be served, which she proudly waved in front of us for a few seconds.

Well, the Ethiopian girl, the Mexican guy and I continuously stared at that mouthwatering treat. I was almost tempted to beg for it. No way Jose! That spicy Southern gal suddenly went over to a nearby trash bin and just canned it. We three very shocked employees were not certain what to make of this, but our expressions must have communicated our horror. Nevertheless, our mentor simply dismissed us and carried on with business as usual. I had to assume that those who live well, even too well, can easily forget what many others on this planet contend with. That is, if they even know.

Nevertheless, that same day, a professional waiter showed me the rounds. The following night I was taking orders and serving them. Now, mind you, customers have no clue what waiters go through. For example, I soon learned that the order you placed could easily be served to someone else. An order was given to the chefs on a small piece of paper after announcing it, but other waiters could have then served it at one of their tables, so that their clients weren't waiting too long. They would act so terribly sorry when this was pointed out to them.

Oh well, at our restaurant, our tiny boss demanded seriousness galore. We were discouraged from being too friendly or talkative with the diners, even when business was at a low peak, and there were a few evenings, not many, when we were simply dying of boredom. Unfortunately, my inability to not share an extra word with my customers put me on the bad side of my Sicilian compatriot. He spoke to me about it soon after, and from then on, he practically refused to acknowledge my presence.

The man ruled his enterprise with an iron fist. He reminded me of a certain grandmother who had never left our island. On weekends, he did back off some, especially Saturdays, as we waiters took quite a beating. Every table was taken, and lots of customers continued to arrive. There was then a long queue patiently waiting to be accommodated while we ran like mad to fill orders, serve them, check on our tables to ensure all were satisfied, bring the check, clear the table vacated and reset it, and occasionally, if possible, run to the bathroom to pee.

On a regular basis, the man some of us had nicknamed Muzzolini would constantly eye us from a distance. He never appeared happy with the affairs of the moment, lucrative though they were. As a matter of fact, that overbearing dictator was always ready to pounce if something was not right. And one Tuesday evening, he chewed me out royally.

Having just purchased a used car, I took it to work in the late afternoon. My voiture got parked in the back of the restaurant's premises. Once the man arrived, he looked at me with a rather nasty expression but chose not to attack immediately. He first carried on a brief interrogation with a couple of the waiters, and upon verifying me as the guilty idiot in question, the tiny man approached me by the kitchen area. There were not many clients nearby, and so he raised his voice a notch above his height. In Italian of course.

The staff, mostly immigrants, were frightened by his wild shenanigans. He carried on and then informed me the parking around the restaurant was for the customers. What kind of idiot was I to not understand that? Well, I simply removed my waiter's apron, obligatory there, folded it neatly, handed it to him, and told him in plain English what he could do with it.

And that is how my brief career as a waiter terminated. It was certainly too short-lived but at least somewhat instructive. For it engrained in me a deep respect and comprehension for those who bring us our food. And more importantly, since then, I have always shown my gratitude by tipping well and enjoying a few words with any individual serving me.

Chapter 154

Life at the IG was never easy for me. Too much down time will hamper any mind and dull its outlook. Dan always seemed happy to see me. He truly inspired a friendly environment, was very professional, and had established an open-door policy. The man grasped my complaint over long idle hours, but he also casually stated that our line of work was more qualitative than quantitative. This may have boosted my outlook for a while, but it would not last.

It must have been our chat which secured me a new assignment. Our branch would create an informational document on something practically no one knew much about, the SDI program. It was President Reagan who had promoted the idea of a space missile shield. That is, the U.S. would place rockets in something like an open container in space, and they could be fired to intercept enemy rockets being launched from their bases on earth. Such a fancy gig was known as the Strategic Defense Initiative, or as the few auditors acquainted with it called it, Star Wars.

And with a sliver of pertinent data, I was on my way to the Pentagon Library to, as my supervisor had told me, dig and leave no stone unturned. One of the staff members pointed out some military magazines to look over and then wished me good luck. The following day, however, by sheer coincidence, after exchanging a few pleasant words with an attractive female army officer, she informed me the program was buried in an office in the basement, which was where my happy feet and inquisitive mind took me later that afternoon.

A friendly employee appeared ready to help. However, once my mission was better defined, she insisted that almost all the individuals who could assist me were out of the office. I left her my office phone number and returned to the library. Fortunately, the next two days brought some general information my way. Again, mostly from news articles, some magazines and a few personal papers which seems best to not reveal how they came my way.

Initially, something once labeled "Smart Rocks" had now become "Brilliant Pebbles." That was the new name of the component which would harbor the missiles and use a sensor to launch them. Most of the information available about the entire project came from various studies which gave a general outline of the presumed function of the system. Many engineers believed that the necessary technology to make it work was still many years away.

In one paper, a proposed possibility was to incorporate another system to guide the rockets to their target. This was something called GPS, the Global Positioning System, and little information about it was to be found anywhere. Well, ultimately, I completed a five-page document on the SDI. My manager truly appreciated the outcome and praised me for it, but the document was soon put aside. Perhaps in the scheme of things it was not so important, or not considered as a system to eventually contend with, or maybe it was also considered a small priority because the agency had plenty of weapon systems to inspect.

Chapter 155

It was a hot day in July, and I was lingering around the airport anticipating my family's arrival. My wife had received the PCS document a while back, had recently shipped our household goods and rented our apartment in Italy to an American couple we both knew. The one car still in her possession had now been sold, and she and the kids were soon on their way. To say I was quite excited is the understatement of all times.

And there they were! We ran toward each other, hugged tightly, kissed plenty, and stayed attached for quite a while. It felt so good to finally reunite. We left the airport, no problems finding the exit, and my Mazda 626, old but in good shape, had air-conditioning, which worked perfectly. Believe me, it was somewhat of a blessing for the oppressive heat was overwhelming Northern Virginia.

Our building was located near the Seven Corners shopping center. Madalyn was happy when informed of my future move some weeks back, for she knew how much I missed my family but had even mentioned she would certainly miss our friendly evening chats. Anyhow, we had some rental furniture in the flat until ours arrived. Once home, the kids discovered the outdoor pool and wanted so much to explore it, and that was where we spent most of our first day together.

Are you ready for this? Lunch that day was pizza at the nearby shopping center. Oh well. Anyhow, what we two adults encountered at the pizza parlor was simply incomprehensible. You see, smoking cigarettes was finally recognized as hazardous, so there were initiatives to protect non-smokers. The fairly large-sized room at the pizza place was divided into smoking and non-smoking sections. Now can you guess what exactly separated the two? A cord! That is right. A cord kept the two groups of customers apart and of course, did absolutely nothing to keep smoke from invading the non-smoking area. Francesca was quite baffled by this absurdity, and I may have warned her that the best was yet to come.

If my wife was shocked on day one, a few more inconsistencies would soon make their mark. The multitude of coffee shops, bakeries, bread stores, dairy stores, and butchers which abounded in every Italian neighborhood simply did not exist. Also, cappuccino or espresso and a croissant could be had in certain parts of large cities, in Italian neighborhoods, especially New York, but absolutely no place in Virginia or D.C. All those things she had been forever accustomed to simply did not exist in our surroundings, which often felt like a bare oasis.

Luckily, Gifford lived nearby. One Saturday morning he brought me to a small retail store called Litteri. It was hidden somewhere on the outskirts of D.C. We loaded up on pasta, olive oil, ricotta, and a few more items which the supermarkets did not yet carry. Of course, for my wife and I, these provisions were far from the real thing, but they got us through. Meanwhile, my wife had requested assistance from her sister Anna. Soon enough, packages began arriving with tortellini, Nutella, cans of espresso coffee, and anything else deemed worth having. My goodness, we were still so very dependent on the Old World.

Our kids lucked out. The two foreigners, Ricky and Eric, attended a summer school program in Clarendon, near a Vietnamese restaurant, which back then was actually the only place to eat. As they could not communicate, their first few days were a bit tough. My only concern was if their daily lunch was anything like mine in 1963. Yet both guys very quickly began to fit in, and by the time regular school began, their English was incredibly good.

Things moved along fine for our family. Soon enough, the English language permeated throughout our home. I remember one Saturday morning, in particular. My wife and I were still in bed, and Eric invaded our bedroom and crawled into bed next to his mother and said, "Scoot over, mom." Our boys were most definitely getting fully acquainted with their new environment.

It was once school began that Francesca faced her first challenge. The elementary school was very close to our building, but their rules confused her. Ricky was placed at his grade level, but for Eric to be accepted in the pre-kindergarten program, she was obligated to work. And as he would only be there until noon, it was essential to find part-time employment, and more importantly, somewhere close by. So, she did. A bank near the Seven Corners shopping area needed some personnel.

Of course, this certainly puzzled us. Her being hired was somewhat bizarre. You see, in Italy, if you work in a bank, that guarantees you have been to great schools and come highly recommended, which is most important. And for sure, you probably believe you can walk on water and certainly act like you do. Whereas on American soil, at least in the late 1980s, if you could put coins into a coin wrapper, you had the job.

Soon enough, the woman was exposed to the work environment in the New World. One of her colleagues was from Bangladesh. He was often on the phone at his desk, speaking softly in his native language. Francesca believed he was running some kind of business from home, but at the bank. As he spoke, sounding like a dealer at an auction, he occasionally spit out in perfect English the words T-shirt and good colors. And, if he noticed my wife looking his way, he smiled so proudly, as if to convey "Isn't this a great country?"

I was now commuting to work by bus. It stopped right across the street from our building, on Route 7. The express bus brought me to the Pentagon quickly, and on my first morning while awaiting its arrival something a bit odd caught my attention. Several females standing by, all immigrants, were carrying sweaters. It was in the high eighties already. Once aboard, I got the full gist. It was fucking freezing! Yet every American was in summer attire and appeared very comfortable while the foreigners were now putting on their protective gear.

My goodness, had we become a nation of penguins? The following day my sweater came with me. Anyhow, while my morning ride was a bit dull, things came to life in the afternoon. Our bus driver, on the four o'clock run, was a stocky Black man, and I can state that he truly loved the human race. The older chap always wore a splendid smile and provided all a few pleasant words. It felt like you were family, and he was truly happy to see you again.

The bus driver also performed an unexpected miracle almost daily. Once he was ready to depart the Pentagon station, he made an announcement. Everyone was informed that they were on an express bus which would bypass several of the local stops, and he then specifically stated the name of the next stop. He spoke slowly, politely, and it was obvious he cared about his passengers to make sure he had been heard.

Well, not exactly. Some folks had their headphones on, a few were too busy yapping with someone else, and others had their minds wandering in another dimension. Now wouldn't you know it, as we approached the first local stop, not a required stop, someone would ring the bell and prepare to leave the bus and even appeared slightly frustrated as the bus had not immediately pulled over.

You would think the driver would become a bit angry or slightly put out. No sir! He remained true to form. He was a gentleman! He did stop, although not required to do so, to let the passenger off, and then repeated the same message given prior to our departure. Once again, in a pleasant tone, perhaps delivered with a strong dose of hope that everyone had now heard him.

This did not occur every afternoon but certainly much too often. And yet, that gentleman was never angry or lost his cool when a startled passenger wanted out. He simply went beyond the call of duty. There are probably too few souls like him on the planet. Which leads me to wonder why society does not recognize truly great human beings. Shouldn't there be a statue or a photograph and a brief narrative posted about in order to honor they who perform daily miracles? Especially when one seeks absolutely nothing for themselves but simply strives for the good of others.

Chapter 156

My brother and family came to visit after the Thanksgiving holiday. And I must inform you, they now numbered four as a girl was born the same year as Ricky. Apparently, leaving the Bronx was no problem, but they encountered snow on the New Jersey Turnpike. For a while, it seemed like they would never arrive, and we were quite clueless as to why. Public pay phones were available on the highways but could be rather hard to find.

They finally joined us that evening and later lodged at a nearby motel. It felt like ages since our last encounter. We had all met up at the villa. Theirs was an extended vacation, whereas we four had joined them for a few days. It was a time when Alessandro pulled out all the stops. He had purchased a new Jaguar the year before, so now owned a second one. Why the man needed a second car is anyone's guess, but Mr. Rossi belonged to that rare species of beings who enjoy living beyond well.

Perhaps our destination was Courmayeur. I cannot recall for sure. However, while yours truly and family drove in our fancy but far from new Lancia, my brother was at the wheel of one of the Jaguars. And believe me, the blessed man looked as if he had been handed the keys to paradise. Considering he was now a city employee, it was certainly a big step up in the scheme of things, and his huge smile confirmed it.

So, we were again reunited, only this time in Virginia. And Peter was a big hit with my kids. Of course, his children's eyes spelled out how they adored him, for you see, my brother was your true American hero. He was tall, well-built, and talkative, and he could make you laugh non-stop while also informing you very diligently on just about any topic. On our first outing, all four kids demanded pizza, so we headed off to where smoking was still cordoned off. And our entertainer surprised us all a bit, for although he indulged in plenty of pizza with the rest of us, he was not through eating, at least, not just yet. He ordered a gyro and very happily ate it while keeping the conversation going.

Our time together was so great! Yet Peter left me a dilemma to contend with. All ties with my father had been severed a few years back. It was over an incident which had occurred in Vicenza. For the first time in my life, I stood up to the man over some unnecessary foolishness he was exalting. It infuriated him. He soon began to insult me and even said something quite unforgivable. I had simply sworn he would never see me again.

My brother did not insist on a course of action. Nevertheless, the lad stated his point of view and did so most convincingly. Perhaps he was right. To err is human, and our father, as Nietzsche once said, was in that sphere of "all too human." Unfortunately, it was very apparent to me that thorny issues to contend with would always be had, whether it was a triviality, a family crisis, or whatever the man dished out, for such was his world.

That is why one Saturday morning I called the Bronx. We two spoke some, and approximately two weeks later, he and our stepmom arrived for a couple of days. Once the boys were home from school, we headed off to the hotel my folks had booked. Now, it seemed highly unusual to discover that my father was taking a nap. It was something he never did, at least as far as I knew.

Oh well, a bit of discomfort ensued. For about an hour, the man struggled to say anything, yet he never touched on any innuendoes about who did what or had said what. Neither did he inquire what exactly had brought me to the D.C. area or anything regarding my line of work. Then, he eventually got on to business as usual. It was something regarding Peter, and what could I say? He rambled on and was allowed to vent his frustration in doing what he did best.

It was after our guests departed that Francesca confronted me. She had observed something unusual. My goodness, that woman was always composed, and she missed absolutely nothing. My wife was now emphatically stating that my father did not look right. She was very convinced something was wrong with his health. Yes, I too thought his face appeared slightly thinner but saw nothing else and no longer gave it much thought.

Chapter 157

A new year was now upon us. My new year's resolution was to return to the world of accounting. I felt a need to leave behind an unsuitable profession. My wife had already changed jobs.

Francesca now worked for a firm overseeing the sale of U.S. military hardware abroad. Her tasks were mostly administrative, but they did include participating in some important phases of preparing various contracts. Now, you would assume the woman would be happy with her accomplishments. A foreigner just on board and already advancing. But after several months on the job, she informed me that her supervisor was not keen on her doing more than required or providing input into the scheme of things.

She was home from work for a few days because Eric was ill. I took over on a Wednesday, for he had not yet recovered. It was odd hearing his very severe voice. It sounded like his throat had been stuffed with wool pads. Yet the boy had no fever, was never in bed, and spent most of the day playing with his toys or with me reading to him. Later in the morning, I contacted our physician's office. He was absent that week, but his assistant spoke to me. My son's condition was fully revealed, and the doctor chose not to see him. Instead, he prescribed a medicine which he phoned in at the nearby pharmacy.

Once Francesca got home, I went out and got the boy's medicine and administered it accordingly. We four soon enjoyed dinner, and once through, the boys went off to their room to play. My wife and I continued our chat when suddenly Ricky, sounding terribly alarmed, yelled for me. I got to him quickly and found both kids on the carpet with some toys at their side. Eric was red in the face, he looked terribly frightened and had his hands around his neck. I picked him up and asked what was wrong. He replied, "I felt like I was going to blow up."

Strange words, but he seemed fine and soon resumed playing. The incident disturbed me, but after some time I fell back into the swing of my evening routine. When bedtime arrived, Eric insisted on sleeping with me. We shared my bed while my wife slept in his. Very early that morning, I woke up and the boy was jumping up and down on the bed as my wife was trying to hold him. This scene truly baffled me as my wife suddenly grabbed hold of the boy and ran off.

I was right behind her. Francesca stopped in the living room, opened the window, and with the boy in her arms, almost lifeless, began using her free hand as if to put air in his lungs. I called 911 and began describing the situation. Immediately, I was assured that they had dispatched help, and fortunately for us, the fire station was next to the Seven Corners shopping area, less than a quarter of a mile away.

While the woman on the phone continued to ask questions about the boy's condition, my wife bolted toward the entrance door. She unlocked it and ran out. I had already dropped the phone and was running after her. The woman was raving mad. She began screaming and would not let go of our son, which forced me to grab her by the throat and press while my other hand pulled Eric out of her arms.

I ran back inside. Eric was immediately placed on the floor. He was very lifeless and had turned blue. Ricky was now standing by crying and pleading for help for his brother. I pried the boy's mouth open and began mouth to mouth resuscitation. He did not respond at all, but I continued when suddenly someone said, "Keep doing that sir. Just continue doing what you're doing."

Help had arrived! And so quickly. They set up their equipment and took charge. One of the firefighters placed an oxygen mask over our son's face but nothing changed. After a few minutes, he was placed on a stretcher, and Ricky and I stood by and watched as Eric was taken away. Francesca went in the ambulance.

Ricky was accompanied to his room and instructed to return to bed. I called Gifford. It must have been 3:00 a.m., and my friend sounded super groggy. But upon hearing me out, he came right over. The man was my closest friend and someone with a huge heart. He would take care of Ricky and get him on the bus to school later, as I left the flat and took myself to Arlington Hospital.

Everything had happened so quickly. My response in trying to save the boy had come too late. He had obviously lost too much oxygen. My thoughts were totally negative and were now frightening me. I began crying like a little child—if our son was not dead, he would most certainly be brain damaged.

At the hospital, a nurse on watch directed me upstairs and gave me a room number. While approaching that room, still struggling with my inner pain, Eric's voice came to my ears. It just sounded so beautiful. A few tears rolled out of me. Miraculously, my son had come through. There were two doctors and three nurses by his bed. When asked if he recalled anything about what had occurred, he merely said, "I felt like I was floating, just like in the pool."

What occurred to Eric that night remains a mystery. He was given a series of follow-up tests at the hospital in Georgetown University, but nothing certain was ever revealed. We were informed that perhaps, he had an attack of croup, a viral disease which, in past times, killed infants by closing their windpipe. Yet according to a few physicians, and we had spoken to many, he was too old for that malady.

After this nightmarish incident was behind us, we immediately began to hear from many sources. First through mail, but soon there was a steady series of phone calls from lawyers informing us we could pursue a lawsuit. The fact was that Francesca and I liked our doctor, although we both disliked his assistant, and that is why we chose to disregard the steady stream of invitations to assist us in achieving the good old American dream.

Chapter 158

When in need of a brief chat on the phone, Gifford came first followed usually by Francesca and then Dawn. All my calls were short, and once finished, the same thought prevailed—how much longer could I continue to get through the day in a job I had no passion for? A career in this line of work was certainly out of the question.

Dawn was not only sympathetic but also helpful. Having revealed my intent to find a job in accounting, she shared it with the very person who got me to the IG, and consequently again came to my rescue. I had never met the chap, but we now spoke, and he informed me of an available accounting position in D.C. The supervisor at the agency where the position was located had informed him of wanting to find a competent individual for the vacant job which had already been advertised. Upon learning all this, my resume went out the same day.

The National Archives is located on Pennsylvania Avenue and close to the Canadian Embassy. Their administrative offices were nearby, and that was where my interview occurred. The building was old, and once the elevator arrived at my floor, some immediate concern struck me. The door continued to partly open and close rather quickly, hindering a normal exit. At some point, I simply jumped out. This was not the best commencement to a potential job.

Nevertheless, my interview went very well. It seemed incredible, but among other tasks, overseeing travel reimbursement was one and considered highly important. After a brief chat with my future supervisor, she escorted me to meet the director of the Budget and Accounting Office. Both ladies immediately threw a travel scenario my way. My answer had them both looking at each other as if to say, "Yes, he is the one."

It is amazing how sometimes life tosses you about, and occasionally with a positive grasp. A few days after the interview, my office promoted me to the grade GS-9. How incredible! Why, just a bit over a year ago my grade was GS-5, and it had remained that way for quite some time. Anyhow, it was a Friday morning and my supervisor escorted me to Mr. Rotter's office. Several people were present, for the agency wanted to highlight its positive treatment toward low-ranking personnel in the upward mobility program.

Photographs of me shaking hands with my peers were taken. Of course, I was thrilled and felt appreciated, having completely forgotten my initiative to work elsewhere. Unfortunately, or fortunately, the spell was broken a few hours later as someone in the National Archives personnel office contacted me. They offered me the position. What can I say? I simply jumped on it.

A slight feeling of guilt swam within my guts. For the joy from one accomplishment was being held in check by another one. My only consolation was to consider all my achievements as important and well deserved. Of course, the thought of facing my supervisor was nerve-wracking. There he was at his desk, banging away at his PC, and he appeared very happy to see me, even though I did not immediately get his full attention. After sitting down, my words calmly proclaimed "Mike, I am leaving." Now this got his attention. He looked at his watch and then informed me it was only eleven thirty. So, out came the facts. I was grateful for the position and sorry to leave, but a career as an auditor was just not for me.. The new position had so much more earning potential.

The National Archives hired me with promotion potential to GS-12. It would take two years to accomplish, and my performance would have to meet expectations. It was my intention to continue giving the best of myself. Plus, there was no cubicle for me. I was accommodated in an office, and this certainly furnished me with a slight sense of being elevated into a job with responsibility.

Once finished with in-processing at personnel, I was at my desk, and shortly after, greeted my first visitor. Ted was one of the technicians and the first one to come to introduce himself. Not only, but the Black gentleman felt an immediate need to add that he was gay. We shook hands and shared some casual words. Prior to returning to his cubicle, he insisted it would be his pleasure to share our office's processes and procedures and the dos and don'ts, which apparently were many.

The finance and accounting office did not do their own accounting. This task was performed by the General Service Administration, specifically the branch in Kansas City. We received financial documents from offices throughout the agency, initiated some, then sent them to the accounting office. Our task was to then ensure that they were input accordingly and that payments were ultimately rendered. We oversaw their inputs, and at times, some disputes occurred regarding how a document had been processed in Kansas City. A telephone conversation would follow, some being rather lengthy, but ultimately the matter was settled.

My main responsibilities were twofold, oversee some travel payments and manage the Imprest Fund, or what was referred to as petty cash. This required a quarterly monetary count of ours, located in the main Archives building, but also providing guidance, based on various government regulations to all the personnel, mostly in our field offices, regarding what a valid expense was. I also handled some of the agency's reimbursable accounts. For example, the Archives stored all IRS tax returns, and I would bill them quarterly.

Life at work proceeded incredibly well. I took over my new responsibilities with little supervision, and overall, things ran smoothly. But no street is paved with gold. Eventually, a few peculiar circumstances began to bug me. An unusual or complicated travel reimbursement would often require the senior accountant to become involved. The technician would await some guidance, but if the issue in question was not resolved, our manager was called on to become the judge.

At that point, things became slightly personal. The usual question, "Who is it for?" made a world of difference. If a traveler had somehow upset our office in the past, whether willingly or not, having done something which we deemed inappropriate, that individual was no longer in good standing. Therefore, a new travel problem by the same individual confirmed that they were the problem. Consequently, applying a regulation which might favor that person was not so forthcoming. Whereas those in good standing were treated very differently.

As a travel clerk, I had learned an invaluable lesson. It was totally insignificant who stood in front of me, but this had not always been so. One late afternoon, a soldier from one of the sites presented a rather thorny travel itinerary. Much too quickly, I spit out all sorts of government regulations and sounded like an annoyed teacher. The guy looking at me and declared, "Wow, you are such an asshole." And then he walked out.

Those words wounded me, but they also generated a new attitude. I tried to listen with all of me and become more sympathetic with all our customers. I now prioritized researching every applicable regulation after having scrutinized some bizarre itineraries. Our bountiful government regulations were consulted in mass to provide a more equitable payment when possible. It soon became apparent why our sergeant always spent so much time reading.

In my new office, if the accountant and manager could not agree, our director was consulted. She was an attractive elderly woman, but more importantly, she was simply brilliant and would quickly grasp the importance of any issue at stake. She easily digested legal issues and financial or accounting concepts. Yet the woman was neither a lawyer nor an accountant. Our director saw clearly, acted accordingly, and I soon found her even more attractive but never considered going beyond any reasonable work boundaries.

Although, at times, somewhat challenged, my work environment thrilled me plenty. However, a few months after my arrival, it was Ted who gave me some negative news. There were plans to build a new facility, which would be called Archives II, and it would house all the Archives material and most of us employees outside of D.C. The new state-of-the-art building was being constructed in College Park, Maryland. I did not want to commute beyond D.C. Fortunately, the move was still a few years away, leaving me quite satisfied for a bit longer.

Chapter 159

Summer arrived rather quickly. It seemed incredible that another year slipped away. Ricky had his tonsils taken out. Our son was constantly ill and home from school, and although most doctors no longer valued this practice, we parents insisted, and so out they came. It was a wise decision, for he was never ill again.

A visitor from Vicenza was now among us. The boys had their cousin, Alessio, here to spend the summer together. We enrolled the three in a day camp program called Brewster School which was less than a mile from home. And believe me, the boys were truly happy campers. At least, such was our impression from their stories and their apparent bond at school with everyone there.

Francesca took them in the morning, and I picked them up in the afternoon. It was amazing how quickly Alessio was learning the new language. Plus, the three kids got along fantastically. This was true whether it was at camp, or at the pool once home, and even more so during our frequent trips to D.C. The Air and Space Museum was constantly in demand, and we visited there quite often. Plus, what is life in the U.S. without an occasional feast of fast food? Burger King was everyone's favorite.

All was proceeding well at home, but it was not so around the planet. War was coming to the Middle East. The nation of Iraq had conquered the Emirate of Kuwait. Now, as far as I was concerned, it seemed like the news media would never get it exactly right. I am referring to the behind-the-scenes facts, which eventually one does come to terms with, and what I sometimes think of as a flicker of history partially hidden in footnotes.

The problem began over Iraqi petroleum that had been shipped out of Kuwait. This arrangement had come about due to Iran blocking the port of Basra in Iraq during the eight-year conflict between those two nations. After the war terminated, Iraq was terribly indebted to both Kuwait and the U.S. It attempted to influence OPEC by restricting oil flow so that the price would rise. Kuwait refused to cooperate, and that is when the problems began. Soon, all hell broke loose as neither side was willing to compromise or back down.

Saddam Hussein, the Iraqi dictator and never a nice guy, invaded Kuwait, his neighboring country. Iraq had never accepted this tiny nation which was created more by British diplomacy and politics than sovereign rights. Our ambassador in Baghdad had been consulted by Hussein and informed of the man's intentions, and she, in turn, immediately notified the State Department. Obviously, no one objected, for no response was provided to her, and so Iraqi tanks eventually rolled into Kuwait.

However, life is never quite that simple. Lady Margaret Thatcher came to Washington, D.C., and she informed our president that Mr. Hussein was a cold-blooded tyrant responsible for brutal atrocities and murders. It was imperative he be ousted from the now occupied country. I wonder if the prime minister mentioned that her husband's company's investments in Kuwait were now nonexistent.

And so, America was called to action. Although to some extent, the nation was still recovering from the Vietnam syndrome, the U.S. formed a world coalition to liberate Kuwait. The invasion began in January 1991, but prior to it unfolding, our news media presented some of the most ridiculous information to a nation of people who simply buy everything they are sold.

Almost every evening on TV, a school of retired U.S. generals, now Pentagon consultants, summarized and explained it all. Iraq's Republican Guard, the nation's elite troops, were even compared to the SS, and so it would be no easy task liberating Kuwait. One general even concocted an incredible tale. Mr. Hussein had placed thousands of barrels of petroleum under the desert area bordering Saudi Arabia. Once our troops came across that zone, they would be burned alive.

Such was the bullshit, in my humble opinion, being advertised. Quite by chance, one day at the Pentagon Mall, I ran into one of the auditors who was still with the IG. A truly no-nonsense person, he knew his facts, and once we discussed the war, he expressed his opinion, which was repeated word for word by a Pakistani general one month later when interviewed by the media. He said the conflict would be over quickly, and it would result in a complete victory by a powerful and better equipped coalition over a country that had no right to go to war. And so it was!

Well, another type of news, quite as horrible, soon arrived at home. This time, it came from the Bronx. Peter informed me that our father had taken ill at work and was rushed to a hospital. His malady was a brain tumor, and he would be operated on immediately. However, as the entire tumor could not be removed without risking damage to the brain, any chance of long-term survival was slim.

My brother suggested I not visit now. I agreed. A few days later, he called and informed me of the most bizarre thing in the world. Right after the operation, once our dad awoke, he could not communicate with his physicians or nurses, for he now spoke only Italian. My brother was immediately contacted to help translate, and for several days, the patient had absolutely no recollection of English whatsoever. His speaking Italian or Sicilian lasted two days, and then quite mysteriously his English returned so very naturally.

Chapter 160

Work kept me busy. All sorts of assignments came my way. The latest was to assist my supervisor in implementing a new federal regulation. It allowed government employees to perform travel sponsored by non-federal sources and accept reimbursement from those institutions. Previously, such travel was deemed risky because it could lead to a conflict of interest. Apparently, now all was well.

This new process required me to oversee these payments and document them. All federal agencies were compelled to provide biannual reports for this type of travel to the Office of Government Ethics. So, along with small initiatives to make it happen, I also created a spreadsheet format as a report to the OGE. While this kept me plenty busy, my boss invited me to her office for an additional assignment that needed to be tackled.

Our director wanted to sponsor a training class. The course, called Appropriations Law, outlined the legitimacy behind government expenditures. The training first introduced the process by which appropriations, the annual funds received by government departments and agencies to carry on their mission, are provided. It then oversaw what is considered a legitimate expense, ranging from the most minute item to some truly controversial issues.

My most challenging task was to establish a contract with the instructor. After which, I developed a memorandum of understanding, the document which described the event and requested the participating government agencies wanting to send their employees, to agree to the document by signing it. But most importantly, to provide us with their accounting data so we could bill them. This got me to speak with quite a few higher-up employees in other departments and government agencies, and eventually, I met some of them at the training.

On the day of the class, the privilege of introducing the course and the instructor was all mine. It felt good to stand in front of a crowd of federal employees who seemed pleased to participate in the event. I can truly say we all learned so much in three days. That morning, I was briefly able to toot my horn, and over the next few days I also had time to chat with a few of the managers in attendance.

Now, regardless of what task cornered me, Ted came by every morning. Sometimes for just a few minutes, other times a bit longer. He was one to speak his mind, particularly about events in the area, news making the headlines, or whatever held his interest at that moment. He was once challenged on local culture as my wife had recently related a most baffling circumstance to me.

Francesca was friends with a young lady at work, a native Virginian. She felt rather close to this extremely pretty, White, well-mannered, mid-twenties lovable girl. However, there was a peculiar bothersome detail that had occurred at work. For she was dating a young Black guy, and she was white as a ghost. It was well-known throughout the office for his photograph was on her desk, thus the setback. The Black women in her office, having seen it, were obviously not so thrilled and made sure she knew it.

My co-worker offered me his thoughts. He was born and raised in D.C. and had seen a lot of changes, but nothing fundamentally valuable. According to him, human nature is too steeped in naïveté and rotten stupidity. Those "sistas," as he labeled them, were bitter over a White woman stealing a "brotha" from the perhaps limited pool of nice Black men available. It was not necessarily just in looks, but also in manners and smarts. He then insinuated that neither of the two women in question would have lasted a day with this guy. Well, although ignorant of such matters, that lesson was casually stored away.

A few weeks later, Ted truly surprised me. No cultural diversity to dwell on here. He simply asked if I liked opera. Well, of course, my answer was negative. Having failed to appreciate Don Giovanni, even after seeing the film with Brian Sheen, this form of entertainment was far from my cup of tea. Nevertheless, I was handed a cassette with arias from different operas, all sung by Luciano Pavarotti. The man's name was familiar to me, but I knew not one iota of his line of work.

His considerate gift became an instant hit with me and the mistress. Francesca knew most of those arias rather well, and so we heard them on Saturday afternoons as she began sharing bits and pieces of scenes that the songs related to from the opera in question. My wife was taken in over this kind thought from a colleague. I, of course, considered my co-worker a good friend, and an individual full of life and love for others.

Anyhow, life was progressing well with us two folks from Italy. However, one fine morning, the unexpected occurred. It was Friday at about ten. The boys had no school that day, which had me home with them, when the phone rang. It was the missus who was insisting I go pick her up. She sounded a bit upset, deviating from her usual calm self, but her tone was slightly elevated, making it difficult to grasp her circumstances.

We three folks at home went off to Bailey's Crossroads. My lovely wife had simply walked out of the office. And there she was in front of her building. She did not appear content yet neither was she volunteering information. It seemed wise to not interrogate her. Rather than drive back home, I suggested we take in the mall at Tyson's Corner, which had the kids jumping for joy. Even my not so cheerful partner now seemed a tad relieved although still too silent.

The severity of the events that day were not questioned. Not immediately. However, once she stated she would never return to "that office," my antennas were slightly raised. They demanded facts, just the facts. Her supervisor continued to stifle her initiative to improve things, which had initially frustrated her but were now entirely unacceptable. Well, my line of thinking aligned with her returning to work once she got over her fury. It was not to be. On Monday morning she remained home having decided to seek employment elsewhere.

It was Tuesday afternoon, and I had just arrived home. While putting my coat away, the phone began ringing, and it was Francesca's office inquiring about her. The very concerned supervisor simply wanted to know if Mrs. Di Stefano was okay. In a rather diplomatic tone, yet with a slight bit of cheerfulness, I informed him she had quit. And perhaps had failed to tell anyone. The gentleman was not sure what to make of the news, however, he soon stated that Francesca was most pleasant and kind, but a woman with a rather strong character, as I too was now discovering.

A week later, I inquired about her past trip to the World Bank. She had delivered her resume to the personnel office over six months ago, yet nothing had come of it. That is why our neighbor, a middle-aged Austrian woman we both knew, who worked at the bank, was now consulted. She happily gave me the name of the personnel manager, having claimed he was a competent and likable individual.

Truth be told, my writing was still far from perfect. Yet, a letter needed to be penned. Now back at the IG, my first set of work papers were returned and had truly frightened me. There was red everywhere as annotations stated what was not so clear, what should have been expounded in greater detail, where to begin a new paragraph, and other significant writing points. A bit disheartening for sure, but a great way to learn.

My letter's introduction was more courteous than informative. But a clear purpose was stated. The body had brief details of past work experience, and a small paragraph concluded with her future aspiration, that is, a desire to join an international work environment. The conclusion included an expression from a TV ad which claimed, "A mind is a terrible thing to waste." My wife signed it and out it went.

It worked miracles. Two weeks later, Francesca was contacted and informed to present herself to the personnel office at the World Bank. The employee who greeted and accommodated her simply explained the process. To work at either the World Bank or the International Monetary Fund, at an entry level for administrative work, you had to go to a specific temp hiring agency, pay their outlandish fee, and insist you would only take a job with either of those two organizations. That is exactly what the woman did.

Perhaps I have mentioned how the Lord works in mysterious ways. A few months later, the IMF took her on to fill in for an employee on holiday for several weeks. The woman rolled up her sleeves. Between dressing like a queen and applying the manners and guile of a saint, plus, working brilliantly and quickly to perfect every task, the now temporary employee overwhelmingly impressed her supervisor.

Three months later the agency hired her in a full-time permanent position. It seemed incredible but appropriate, for she was destined to excel in any work environment she took on. Now, just so you know, most employees who had had similar circumstances had attempted for years before finally landing a permanent job with either of the two institutions.

Chapter 161

It was the mid-1990s, and huge changes were being implemented at full speed. A new type of supermarket called Fresh Fields, which sold only organic produce, had recently opened and a few more were on their way. My visit to one revealed how someone had gotten it very right, even though everything was a tad costly. Quite a few of those Italian treats we so much missed, Italian cheese, coffee, and certain wines, were now available.

Soon enough, there was also a supermarket for literature. The chain was called Borders Books, and its huge stores were overloaded with books and magazines along with a music area and a coffee shop to hang out in. One could grab something to read, buy a coffee, and make themselves at home. And their music department had it all—why, you could even listen to music via headphones, and you were not obliged to purchase it. That store became my Saturday morning ritual for after buying the Economist magazine, I enjoyed a cappuccino while reading or listening to a few songs going way back.

It was right about then when Francesca and I discovered Wolf Trap. We attended what was to be my first live opera. It happened on a fine summer evening, and this outdoor theater, surrounded by vast Virginian farmlands, was fully packed. It certainly should have been, for that evening we enjoyed great acoustic sounds under a silvery sky dotted with a few bright stars.

However, I must confess that Falstaff was not the right opera to begin this musical journey. And, if opera baffles you, that is exactly how I felt listening to the LP on three takes. Nothing sounded melodious, or harmoniously pleasurable to my amateur musical ears. And I had complied with Brian Sheen's advice shared with me when we had first met. In order to overcome the difficulty in appreciating several hours of music, first get to know it well.

The story is based on Shakespeare's Merry Wives of Windsor. It is classified, in Italian, as opera buffa, which means funny and bordering on the absurd. Brian had instructed me to listen to the first act or half of it and repeat that every day for about a week. Sort of like exercising, but in the world of operatic theater. For the pleasure of opera requires time to appreciate the music and singing. Only then would it become palpable and enjoyable.

I tried but failed miserably. Getting through the first act was no easy task, and I had thrown in the towel after my third listening. However, that performance at Wolf Trap was superb as the costumes, stage settings, and the brilliant lighting brought you back to an era where beggars and gentlemen were clearly part of two different classes. We two left feeling we had shared a wonderful experience, and one which would be repeated soon.

Hopefully, this will not confuse you. It was not a performance at an opera setting which won me over. I was driving home one Saturday afternoon listening to the classical radio station. A live broadcast performance from the Met in New York City sucked me in. My ears were treated to a beautiful aria.

It was digested by my mind and left me craving more, so once home, I ran up to our apartment and immediately turned on the radio.

When the act terminated, the broadcasters offered their insights on the production. This was Puccini's La Boheme. Although I was only acquainted with one aria from Ted's gift to us, it was now apparent that this music needed to penetrate my world of artistic sounds. The following weekend, Brian Sheen's theory was properly initiated on La Boheme, having purchased it at the Borders Books Store. I listened to it many times over several weeks and looked forward to attending my next opera. Now my father's words, obscure when initially stated, made more sense. He had asserted that opera was life on musical roller skates.

Chapter 162

We had been to the Bronx once Dad had been released from the hospital. His condition startled us. My goodness. He had previously slowed down in his physical movements, but now he was partially paralyzed and in a wheelchair. The man who had insisted he would win his fight against this devastating disease appeared quite subdued.

My brother accommodated us in his wife's large residence. We were on the main floor, had abundant room, and everyone was eager to make us feel at home. On Easter Sunday, there was quite a crowd at the dinner table. Peter's in-laws, who lived upstairs, were present, and my brother had picked up our folks and drove them home. Soon enough Aunt Mia and family along with her mother joined us. It was a gorgeous day, and somewhat enjoyable, but everyone's concern in seeing our father's condition was undeniable.

Peter had become his assistant. Our dad refused to have a nurse attend to him, which is why my brother, once home from his new shift at work, midnight-to-eight, was in Co-op City to do his part. After shaving and washing him, our dad was taken downstairs, placed in his car, wheelchair folded and put in the trunk, and off they went to the nearest park for a long stroll. It was a daily routine unless bad weather kept them indoors.

Well, our typical Italian dinner was long. And once we had enjoyed some pastry and espresso, our father insisted we three Di Stefanos take a ride. This was totally unexpected and a bit odd to me. The issue to be ironed out was over a family situation now getting rehashed. Our children had been provided with a trust fund for their college years. And our father had been super generous. He had also given equivalent amounts, as per kid, to Aunt Mia and her two children. Also, his sister in Palermo was given the same, but my brother and I had been totally disregarded.

In retrospect, that incident in Palermo, our "betrayal" for having acknowledged our mom's existence and bringing her into our lives, was the real issue. Peter was driving with our dad sitting up front. The conversation was general but much too soon came the million-dollar question. Had he done right by us? To me, it seemed preposterous to not again thank him for what had been given to the kids. My brother, however, was not forthcoming and this forced me to speak up, but I refused to ask for anything.

He was thanked wholeheartedly for the children's gift. Yet, the issue did not end there. Our father wanted to pry me open. He specifically asked if I thought he should have done anything differently. Using a most graceful tone, I closed the issue, and it did not please my brother. I gave a strong assurance to the dying man that his gesture was truly grand. So, a rather chilling silence filled that automobile and followed us home.

As we entered the premises, Peter's expression, very noticeable, said it all. He was terribly angry. It now became apparent to everyone something was amiss, and yet the issue remained firmly shut. A bit later, we four Virginian residents thanked everyone for our wonderful stay, and as I suspected, we hit much traffic on the New Jersey Turnpike.

Some weeks later, back at work, I felt quite exhausted. A few sleepless nights were now torturing me. During a coffee break one morning, Ted got my confession over that money fiasco in the Bronx. He was such a good listener, a wise counselor, and a wonderful friend. His belief, stated most diplomatically, was that my father's condition was negatively impacting me. He suggested a brief visit, on my own, just to sort things out. And that is what brought me back to the Bronx.

My train out of D.C. brought me to Manhattan where Peter picked me up. He seemed his usual self, not at all put out over what had previously occurred. Unfortunately, my brother was pressed for time and once parked in front of our folks' building, we exchanged a few more words, and he firmly stated that the old man was going fast.

I was greeted nicely by my folks. My father and I enjoyed a long talk about opera. Having recently purchased Rigoletto, one of his favorites, much was said about Verdi's first big opera. Then, he confided to me his love for Puccini. According to him, Puccini's arias were simply the best and Verdi's came second. He told me to put on "Nessun Dorma," sung by Franco Corelli, a foreign name to an amateur like me. Wow! A powerful yet smooth voice, so clear and distinguishable, won me over as Dad suggested only Corelli had a right to sing that tune.

The following morning, the man was all mine. After a tiny breakfast, he was shaven, and his wife and I dressed him. We two got to the garage, and once I had him up front, we went off to Pelham Bay Park. He complimented me on my driving and then did something quite unexpected. He wept a bit and admitted he had been too rough with us as kids. Now a bit of guilt was claimed in never having gotten to know us as men. My father looked directly at me and said, "I don't even know what kind of work you do."

It seemed only right to lessen his load. My narrative stated that I had never truly known where I was taking myself, nor did I have any inclination toward a particular profession. I still wondered if my best skills had fully manifested. And yet, my initiatives had somehow always worked out just fine—first as a sailor, then a soldier, and now, here I laughed a bit, as an accountant. Yes, the nation's capital area was treating me well, and life at home with my family in Virginia was just grand. It was what he wanted to hear.

We returned home later that morning. Dad ate very little for lunch, then took a nap. Something in me insisted I venture out, which is why I took the subway and for some unexplainable reason got off at Parkchester. Once there, I headed off to Macy's. Inside that department store, some internal questions were asking if this was a sort of inner cleansing over that irresponsible foolishness which had occurred as a young teen.

My exit from the Bronx occurred two days later. I kissed my father on the cheeks and then knelt and said, "I love you, Dad." It came out so naturally. While riding the elevator down to meet Peter who would bring me back to Port Authority, I cried a bit. We never saw each other again. My father passed away three weeks later.

Chapter 163

Spring brought some changes. We left the Seven Corners area and moved to Falls Church City, which is very nearby. Once again, an older building welcomed us, and it was just fine. More importantly, applying for jobs, so that I would not have to move to College Park, kept me busy. As luck would have it, a new one came my way having landed a position with the Equal Employment Opportunity Commission.

Francesca had fallen in love with Falls Church City. It was quaint, elegant, and small but lacked nothing. Most of all, she wanted the kids in the Catholic school there. Our new flat also had a pool, a barbecue area, and tennis courts. Plus, the farmer's market, it now being a Saturday morning stint, had fully mesmerized my wife. Seeing her favorite herbs and vegetables and claiming they were simply the best, is what regularly brought us back.

I decided it was time to buy a new car. An economic slowdown had the entire automobile industry desperately competing to outsell each other. And in my view, Japanese cars were simply the best. They were well-designed, super reliable, came at an affordable price, and, most importantly, they had manual stick-shift.

Honda was practically a golden name. So, it was time to visit the dealership on Route 50. Much to my surprise, the employee assisting me was once our neighbor. She was on our floor in the old building, but we had never actually spoken. The woman now informed me she was from Panama and had immigrated to Virginia years back along with her daughter and mom. Upon hearing this news later that evening, Francesca recalled having seen her at times. She even suspected that the man leaving her apartment on many occasions, quietly and alone, was probably her husband and in the country illegally.

Oh well, the Honda Civic immediately grabbed my attention. We looked one over, and this professional woman unquestionably knew her cars. It would have sounded naïve, perhaps foolish, to ask her if she had been a mechanic back in Panama. This salesperson was so technically inclined, but she spoke in a manner so that the facts delivered were easy to grasp. Then we took a drive, and the vehicle won me over immediately, which is why the following day I returned to retrieve my new voiture.

Isn't the scent inside a new car quite invigorating? It seems most pleasing to those senses controlling your zone of achievement. Now once driving off, the radio was turned on, and the Stones' "Satisfaction" was playing. I raised the volume and started singing with vigor. Then, for some bizarre reason, that idiot in the Bronx came to mind. The individual who had described the Japanese as little people with stupid ideas. Gee, I would have given anything to send him a photograph of me in an auto where the word big has nothing to do with size.

Folks, new car, new job, different residence, happy kids, wife in heaven at work, who could ask for more? It seemed only right to do some traveling. Which is why we decided to explore Virginia. Our first trip brought us to Williamsburg. The kids just wanted to return to Busch Gardens, having previously been there on a trip with Brewster School, whereas I wanted them to get a glimpse of what a colony once looked like. Our boys quickly rehashed much regarding the exciting rides they had fallen in love with.

We all had a wonderful weekend. Our sons appreciated the amusement park most of all. On our last day, Francesca suggested we visit something called Carter's Grove Plantation. This was a museum highlighting the old mansion on the grounds by the James River. Off we went, and once tickets were purchased, we walked down a small tunnel and then exited in front of the Carter's stately home.

The inside of that house was truly fascinating. There were many charming, expensive and attractive items from beautiful floor carpets to luxurious chinaware. One quickly sensed how the folks who had lived there were like royalty and perhaps part of a small class of well-educated people. However, upon exiting that home, our escort brought us over to see an entirely different scenario. These were replicas of the slave quarters.

How awfully crude and horribly poor those wooden shacks looked. In front of each one stood a Black person dressed in what resembled an old and worn-out pajama. Our group was given information on the living conditions of the folks who once suffered inside those tiny huts. It was an awfully depressing sight, and the description of what constituted the slaves' daily existence was horrible.

Undoubtedly, we all felt somewhat guilty. We customers were all White, and most of us had some sense of our past. The instructor concluded his narrative but also informed us that he was a history teacher. He then added that while we had just experienced a brief look at the crime of slavery, he assured us that the only people who lived better than the slaves in those huts were the people inside the mansion.

In that era, he claimed that almost everyone struggled daily with horrendous conditions. Whether you were an indentured servant, a farmer, a carpenter, or just about any individual, life was harsh and unpredictable. One worked from daylight to dark. When the weather did not cooperate, there was little or no food, and if an epidemic struck, it showed no preference. There was no doctor to call or hope to see at your doorstep. The only real freedom you had every day was to continue to endure and hope to survive.

We returned home and resumed our weekend trips to the nation's capital. My wife managed to convince our sons to bypass the Air and Space Museum for once. It was on to the White House. Now, in those days, Pennsylvania Avenue was just another street full of traffic, which ran right by the front of the president's residence. There were plenty of pedestrians walking by, no security check-points, and cars galore. The president's home was not yet sealed off like the prison it now looks like.

At times, we, too, had driven in front of the White House. Which is why I once claimed to have gotten a glimpse of our president. Ricky immediately demanded to know what he was doing. Well, he was arguing with the First Lady about who should take out the trash. It got a big laugh from the kids but nothing from the misses. Oh well, such was my humor at moments when a few extra silly words seemed acceptable.

On the day we visited "the president's palace," as it was originally known, we parked some ways off. Our walk had led us near the premises where we were first seated on bleachers. Once your turn arrived, you formed a line with others and slowly proceeded toward the objective. Believe me folks, there is nothing terribly impressive inside. Yet, as you are standing on the very premises where, to some extent, history is being made, you go through each room hoping that the most powerful person on the planet may walk in.

Maybe that is why my mind had drifted off. Suddenly, all my attention was on a huge wall carpet. It looked like velvet fabric, which is why my hand extended forward to confirm my hunch. Not so quickly! The security guard standing nearby, who was not a happy camper, said to me in a matter-of-fact tone, "I'll break your hands." That canned my curiosity as my instincts demanded I keep moving and not touch anything.

A few weeks later, it was on to Chincoteague for the weekend. The town bears the name of people who once took such pains to live life as dictated by nature's laws. Nevertheless, our trip there was to enjoy the comforts of modern life from the progress we have made. And yes, history can be terribly cruel. Hopefully, past crimes will never reoccur. By the way, I'd like to stress that my small Japanese car was a beauty and drove like a truly perfect machine.

The town is small but everything there was quite enjoyable. The wild ponies close to the main road leading to the beach were impressive. When close, they appeared to be inviting you to walk over to touch them. We had some nice walks on the beach but no swimming as it was fall. Francesca insisted we eat in a restaurant she had spotted, and although a bit expensive, the food was divine. Our tasty meals that weekend consisted of lots of fish, plenty of ice-cream, and the typical American breakfast, which although not healthy is certainly delicious.

Our visit had concluded too quickly. That morning before leaving, we visited a local diner for breakfast. It was packed! For a while, my family and I watched the help run like crazy to keep up. But eventually we sat, and at some point, a waitress took our order, however, she failed to act on it. Our chats were brief as we observed something I was somewhat acquainted with—servers running like mad. Then after the longest time, I flagged down the first waitress passing by and asked to speak to the manager.

The gentleman who came to our table offered a million apologies. He assured us we would now be fed immediately and, totally unexpected, all at no cost. The boys were speechless for a moment, and they now wore huge smiles. Of course, I, too, felt a joyous sense, and being very grateful thought it only right to look at my wife, and in my best Bangladesh accent, I simply asked, "Is this a great country, or what?"

Chapter 164

A late morning doctor's appointment kept me home from work one day. Francesca had taken the car to the IMF, where it would be parked until she returned home. Rather than later travel by bus and rail, only to arrive at the office to work perhaps two hours, I took the day off.

Soon enough, our boys were home from school. It seemed incredible. The two kids born and raised abroad were now so American. Both began their homework, and I had promised to take them out for ice-cream when they finished. Since my wife and I sometimes played tennis, the TV was on to watch the weekend weather forecast. Then, while changing channels, I froze. On the screen was a very familiar face. It seemed incredible, for the man had not aged a bit.

In front of the cameras was that truly exceptional soldier. Once a colonel, but now a general. It was him! That striking look I had been privy to for a few minutes at the office in Caserma Ederle was well-preserved. It was now being vividly displayed; intelligence, confidence, a sense of his place in society, and most of all, simply put, he was so fucking cool. Yet, rather than being celebrated, the soldier was being slightly interrogated.

He sat in front of the Senate Armed Service Committee, chaired by a Democratic Senator from Georgia. The politicians, although showing a certain amount of respect, were demanding responses to their concerns. It was absurd. Their only interest should have been his qualifications to run the Pentagon. The issue at stake did not even involve this soldier. They wanted clarifications about his father, who had fought in WWII, but not on the winning side. Much was being made about the man's association with the SS in fighting the Soviet Union.

I sat down to watch the spectacle. The general may have been slightly annoyed, but he maintained his composure. His expression insinuated the million-dollar question—this is what you want to judge me on? After a few questions, the general moved closer to the microphone in front of him and said, "I have only one memory of my father. He was the nicest man in the world."

Something deeply struck me. I would have followed that soldier into the heart of the harshest and most brutal battle quite ready to sacrifice my very existence for him.

Chapter 165

It was quite rewarding to be a part of accounting operations, and my position, which entailed a promotion to GS-13, came rather quickly once on board. Wow! Life in the world of government work was finally meeting my expectations.

The Equal Employment Opportunity Commission was located on Eighteenth and L Street. At the interview, the manager grilled me diligently but graciously and then shared information about the position, followed by me asking a few questions. Before we finished, she mentioned having attended the Appropriations Law class, and we certainly agreed the instructor was simply the best. Then, the chief of the accounting branch took me to meet her boss.

She had described the director as the king of the accounting shop. So here was an elderly Black female who had come up through the ranks, appeared serious but pleasant, and after a friendly chat regarding the organization, she immediately made it very clear how much she valued hard-working people. Once the interview terminated, some inner voice sided with the idea that all had gone truly well.

I began my new job three weeks later. On that first day, David introduced himself. He had also recently been hired and sat in a nearby cubicle. At first, the guy seemed a bit reserved, but I soon became acquainted with his quick and sharp sense of humor, plus, he played the guitar and loved most of the hard rock music I grew up with. So, there was often much more to talk about, and I cannot deny his helpful assistance in providing me various facets of accounting processes in preparing required federal accounting reports.

My main responsibility was to manage something called the Prompt Pay Act Report. Here is a brief explanation. All federal entities are required to pay their invoices in a timely manner, that is, no later than thirty days from receipt or else they would incur an interest penalty for failing to do so. In the first week of the month, after analyzing a report with the late payments made in the previous month, I interacted with the technicians who had late payment. It was to determine who was at fault, what action to take, and to resolve any outstanding discrepancies.

I then provided my supervisor with a request for a few changes, and they were approved. The technicians were happy with them, but not the employee who previously held my job. He had been promoted to a new position in our office, and apparently, was not so pleased with me performing his old tasks rather well. Thinking it wise to consult the chap before proposing another change and wanting to be certain my understanding of the process was accurate, I stood at his desk.

It seemed only right to request some information before initiating anything to ensure no unforeseen problems occurred. After speaking briefly, he looked at me most disdainfully and said things would now be perfect as I was the one handling the accounts. His sarcasm was all I got before he dismissed me. Well, things may never be perfect, but they can certainly be improved.

Anyhow, time flew away rather quickly at work. Occasionally, David and I felt like two outcasts. Mostly because we refused to be part of the unnecessary bitching and moaning, plus, we both hardly ever chatted with most of our co-workers, who had been there for ages.

We continued to bond, and one weekend, we even got out to see our very beloved idol, Johnny Winter. The musician who was playing at the State Theater in Falls Church City looked like he had aged tremendously and was slightly beaten up, mostly from self-imposed abuse via getting high too much. Nevertheless, he still mastered his craft and played incredibly well, like his guitar was simply an extra inbred sense.

Now, my intuition's main objective is to keep an eye out for the unexpected. Which is what made me feel a tad nervous when the king lady requested to see me. I quickly took myself to her office and was asked to close the door. *Oh shit, here it comes!* She, however, did not seem to have a care in the world and her smile had me slightly baffled.

First, the director complimented my work. Then came the news. I would continue my regular tasks and stay at my desk but would now also manage the Payables Section. It was a temporary assignment which would begin the following day. The branch supervisor would be working on a time-consuming project, and so yours truly would now take the bull by the horns. So, the Payables Section was mine to run as I saw fit. This even included implementing any changes deemed necessary, which, of course, she must first approve.

I inquired about my detail's expiration date. The woman assured me it was temporary. And so, I thanked my director for the extra work, and she chuckled a bit but assured me things would be just fine. That very afternoon, six technicians met with me as they had already been informed of the change. I stated my willingness to assist them with any issue, regardless of its nature or complexity.

Six set of female eyes appeared receptive and ready to give me a chance. Things got off to a great start as they individually began to bring some peculiar problems to my attention and were apparently happy with my proposals. Consequently, about a week later, the entire group did something totally unexpected. The young ladies requested to meet with the director, the king. They went into her office, closed the door, and made themselves heard.

Only one person spoke. Could the supervisor—now on loan—become permanent? That was it, and one assumes they provided adequate explanations. This was revealed to me several weeks later, and it certainly clarified some of the unhappy looks that had been coming my way from a few of the supervisors. Oh well, one of my greatest assets, which I sometimes hide so well, is that often, but not too often, I just don't give a fuck.

Chapter 166

Francesca was a member of a rather prestigious and well-known organization. Within the walls of the International Monetary Fund, Europeans, South Americans, a few Asians, along with plenty of Yanks and a mix of other people made up the overall work force. Most of those employees were well-educated, and certainly somewhat ambitious, including my wife!

As I drove us to work in the morning, her enthusiasm shone right through her impressive attire. Truth be told, the woman dressed as if she were running that institution. Along with a grand taste for fashion, she now shared something entirely different, an interest in the most critical economic situations making the headlines. I was delighted to know that she was content.

In addition to her many office duties, she was required to travel on assignments to join a team of economists, some from the IMF and others invited by the IMF. The group would provide economic advice to nations developing a modern capitalist system. This may sound exciting, but truth be told, she was practically the team's work horse in accomplishing her peculiar tasks.

Her first trip was to Azerbaijan. She worked mostly in the evenings. Once the IMF members had completed the day's meeting with the host nation's economic representatives, she took over. The IMF team would return to the hotel in late afternoon, and she was given all their work papers, which consisted of that day's back-and-forth discussions and some final agreements. It was now her turn to go to work.

First, all the data given to her was entered into a formatted file. She ensured all the contents were presented accurately and methodically. This required her presence till late hours at night or early the following morning. The completed papers became individual reports, one for each IMF team member and one for each host nation official working with them. The massive workload was given to the team leader early in the morning. The IMF folks would then regroup with their counterparts to share what she had prepared. Everyone reviewed the new workpapers, and while some issues remained as they were, others were slightly changed, a few were debated, and much extensive back-and-forth ensued.

The process continued until the two parties agreed to a final memorandum. It usually lasted approximately two weeks and ultimately resulted in a sort of contract between that nation and the IMF. After finishing her assignment, she would return to D.C, but she was free to include vacation days in her itinerary. It almost always meant a brief stopover in Italy, and my wife certainly took advantage of every opportunity to enhance each trip.

That is why my children and I were sometimes on our own. Of course, there were a few complaints. I checked homework, insisted they keep their room neat, and I tried getting them to participate in sporting events. And what about my cooking? No matter what culinary endeavor went into providing a fine meal, mom's version was so much better. Such were my shortcomings according to those fully Americanized boys who loved life in the good ole U.S. of A.

One day we stopped at Friendly's for the first time. My wife was overseas again, and I had given myself the day off. The chain-store was popular for its ice-cream but also provided fast food. We were plenty hungry. In we went, and the waitress who accompanied us to our table was apparently in a sour mood. Her eyebrows furrowed, and her mouth was set in a tight scowl. Not a word was uttered to greet us, which could have been fine, but she simply walked us to the table, threw the menus down and stomped off.

The three new clients were a bit shocked! The boys looked at me as if seeking guidance. Ricky shook his head and there was a bit of fright in Eric's eyes. I simply glanced at the menu. Just as my sons appeared ready to ask what course of action would be taken, she was back to get our orders. In a most solemn tone, using that awful nasal American female street lingo, while not even looking our way, she asked, "What'll you have?"

I had a question. My inquiry demanded the name of the establishment. She may not have caught on, for without hesitating, she replied in a low tone, "Friendly's." She continued looking at her pad, still avoiding eye contact. Believing perhaps my point had not been made, I now said, "I'm sorry, what did you say the name was?" She certainly understood now. The waitress looked at us and attempted a tiny, forced smile. Then in a more reconciliatory tone, she replied, "Friendly's." At that point we proceeded to order.

My two admirers gave me a brief thumps-up once she moved on. Yet a contentious point from my oldest son was now being aired out. Would she get a tip? It seemed only right to make sure the kids realized the whole picture. She was obviously having a bad day. This did not justify her attitude, for we were not to blame, but if we punished her by not leaving a tip, even a small one, we would undo what had just been accomplished. After all, this was an improvement, no?

I left a tip, but not a substantial one. It certainly worked. While we were leaving the table, she smiled and thanked us and appeared a little better off. And while the rest of that day proceeded fine, a completely unexpected fiasco hit that very weekend. Just so you know a bit of the circumstances, let me first inform you that my lovely wife was abroad, somewhere in Beijing, apparently bringing capitalism to more than a billion and a half communists.

It was during the time when China welcomed the Olympic Committee. The intent was to impress them and hope the games would be held there. That is precisely when my crime occurred. Back in the U.S., it was a Saturday morning around ten when I took the boys to visit their Thai friend. We had been neighbors in the old building on Route 7. The family had moved to a nearby suburban area, and my sons had kept in touch with their boy. The kids had arranged their plan on Friday evening, with my approval, to visit the following day.

My boys were left in the custody of their friend's mom. She seemed to be a most pleasant person and had assured me they would have a nice lunch and that I could pick them up in the afternoon. So, I did. It may have been around 4:00 p.m. when I drove my car on a very large street and parked it in front of our host's place. My, there were such well-trimmed lawns clutching the mild serenity lingering there, and that certainly enhanced the beauty of suburban living. For a moment, the American dream seemed to be calling out to me.

Once at their door, I rang the bell and was startled by a loud and threatening voice behind me. A man standing across the street was yelling and insisting I move my car. My car, the only one there, was parked by the side of the house I was visiting. And here was an older man, dressed in foreign attire, either from India or Pakistan or somewhere in that part of the world, and he was quite hysterical and even began cursing me out.

My inner sense was now seriously concerned. The man's ranting was not normal. I kept my finger on that doorbell silently praying someone would come to my rescue. Apparently not. The madman got more descriptive with his insults, and at some point, I simply said, "I am here to pick up my children and will leave immediately."

He started striding toward my vehicle. It was not locked. My first thought was that if he disengaged the emergency brake, my car would roll down the inclined hill it was on. That is why I moved rather quickly toward the automobile, and it may have given this lunatic the wrong impression. As he came at me, he appeared like a crazed animal foaming at the mouth.

Without even considering the consequences, I hit him with a powerful left hook. It sent his glasses flying but did not move him that much. My back was now on the hood of my car, and my adversary was over me, but I, somehow, managed to pull him off me, and we fell onto the lawn area. I was on top of the man and attempting to hold his arms while something pounded my head, back and shoulders.

It was an older woman and a teenage girl. Can you guess what sort of clothing they wore? Both were now hitting my body while attempting to assist or free the lunatic underneath me. I continued holding him down as he appeared truly enraged and even more crazy. Then the Thai family and the boys appeared at the front door having finally exited their premises.

The two females immediately stopped hitting me. The guy underneath me continued to struggle, but at least he was shouting less. I immediately yelled toward the house asking the observers to call the police and continued insisting as no one had moved. Perhaps a minute or two passed before my opponent finally began to ease up. Appearing less agitated and no longer struggling, I allowed him to get up. He then spit at me but fortunately missed his mark.

However, I was now truly flabbergasted to hear my Thai hosts defending him. He was a very nice man, so they claimed and looked at me as if I were the planet's biggest scoundrel. Well, my boys were escorted to the car, and I then returned to where the group stood. I first told those Asian folks they would never see me again, and that their neighbor was a very sick man.

Unfortunately, the police had been contacted. As I had been completely devastated by the circumstances, it never registered that they had been called. Of course, there was plenty of anger in my sails, and perhaps a powerful wind in my spirit that helped me drive away. Then a couple of hours later, a Black female police officer rang our bell. She was from Fairfax County and was not thrilled that I left the scene of a crime. The crazy bastard had filed charges against me. It seemed incredible!

She heard my version. Of course, I claimed that a scuffle ensued once approaching my car. My only objective had been to detain the madman until he calmed down. She began questioning me on specifics, appeared put out, and even indirectly summed up the event as if I had beaten up someone and simply left. I was given some form with a court date and wished the best of luck.

Sure enough, my wife called that evening to check on things. It was Eric who had answered the phone and divulged to her that I was probably going to jail. My goodness, just who was raising these kids?

Everyone at my office who heard my narrative insisted I get a lawyer. It became a concern, after all, if three foreigners testified against a helpless American, mine was surely a lost cause.

Fortunately, my very supportive wife was now back home. She assisted me in getting beyond my dramatic approach and worrisome ways. In my mind, it was a three against one summary leaving nothing positive coming my way. Now, damn, that woman was always so calm and cool as a cucumber, which was helpful, yes, but there were times I would have preferred a lioness at my side, especially when we were in bed.

The day of my court case arrived. We picked up Madalyn, who agreed to provide a character reference for me. And, Ricky, having witnessed me trying to keep things from getting worse, came along as my witness. Francesca was there to provide moral support but also very curious to see our judicial system at work. And boy what a spectacle we took in! Almost every case before mine provided outlandish situations, which sort of made our wait, my case was last, a bit easier to endure as we got a tad of entertainment.

My accuser came to court alone. He was dressed in modern attire, and the man looked quite relaxed. When our case was called, I declared myself innocent of the charges, and he was allowed to provide his story. The judge was informed that I had been parking in front of his driveway for the longest time. He often left me notes on my windshield, but it had accomplished nothing, and so, that day, he came to ask me not to park in front of his driveway.

According to this fictitious nonsense, yours truly simply went down the small hill and began to pounce on the helpless man. He told the judge he had been hurt, had sustained cuts in several areas of his face, and his glasses had been broken. So, after hearing this, I was given the floor and began by introducing Madalyn. The judge, however, was not interested in hearing anyone who was not a witness to the circumstances in question. And so that is when my son took the floor.

He looked angelic and was well-dressed in a suit and tie. Our intermediary asked him to describe what he had seen. Ricky stated that he and Eric and their Thai friend had been playing Nintendo for a while (the mom was vacuuming the basement) when suddenly they were told that there was some ruckus outside the house. Everyone exited, and Ricky claimed he felt terribly embarrassed to see me on top of this man. However, upon hearing my continuous plea for someone to call the police, he realized I was just holding him down.

Now, it was my turn to speak. My story was delivered briefly and accurately, but it did not really matter. The judge had access to the police report which showed I was parked across the street, and nowhere near the man's house. Plus, the bit about me parking in front of his driveway for the longest time was certainly a bit far-fetched. However, it was Ricky who had simply convinced the judge and won him over.

The moment that magistrate ruled not guilty, the nicely dressed coyote went wild. He began arguing, rather vividly, as to how I could possibly be not guilty. He even insisted the judge read the police report. The man ruling that court informed him he could appeal if he wanted to, but this case was closed. Our adversary, for lack of a better word, stormed out of that room, and it was apparent to all present that justice had prevailed.

Madalyn, Ricky and I walked over to join Francesca. She was ecstatic and her expression was one of sheer delight. Quite a few people who had witnessed all the cases were now coming over to shake Ricky's hand. It was he who had truly carried the day. Everyone congratulated him on his brilliant performance. He had spoken clearly and convincingly. I patted his head as he looked up at me, feeling very proud to have been helpful.

We four then celebrated with a late lunch. Madalyn was adamant that my assailant looked mad. She even said, "Ye see how he addressed de jugge?" It was now time to eat, and so I informed my troops to order to their heart's delight and put the silly case behind us. What a relief that it was over. And some months later, I was at the airport with my wife as that busy bee was off to another assignment. On her way to the check-in area she asked, with a sarcastic tone, if I would be okay or should she put Ricky in charge. At times, she was not just a cucumber, but a very cool companion.

Chapter 167

The Borders Books Store on 18th and L street was the place to get a cappuccino. Every morning at nine thirty or there about, I would head down and return to work a few minutes later. On one occasion, while preparing to leave, a middle-aged Black man, appearing slightly unkept in his attire, introduced himself and seemed very eager to get to know me.

I'm not sure what we spoke about that morning, but Joe certainly got my overall attention the following day. We sat down at a table for a minute or two. My, he was funny, but also somewhat knowledgeable of all the latest news, good and bad, and some quite hilarious. Even more interesting was him recalling a scene from a Woody Allen movie which fit quite perfectly to the very circumstances we had just shared.

That brief encounter began a long-lasting friendship. Joe loved theater and cinema, and he often discussed his take on some movies, a few familiar to me, which usually led to a quick analysis. Even quotes from Shakespeare came out, as it became apparent that he had worked in theater during his younger years. Yet, never once did he volunteer a drip of any experience on stage, and it seemed best to not pursue the issue.

We met frequently. At times, he appeared to be waiting for me. One morning, he confided that he had recently lost his father, which still weighed on him, but he believed things were better now. It became apparent, and somewhat fascinating, how easily he could strike up a conversation with just about anyone, and no subject was off-limits. Sometimes, he was a bit too loud. Some of the nearby customers waiting to be served at the coffee counter appeared annoyed, whereas others looked quite ready to join us if extended an invitation.

One Friday morning, Joe was nowhere to be found, but something entirely different caught my attention. Paintings! An abundance of them were on the walls everywhere. Each one had a blend of vivid colors applied so perfectly. Absolutely nothing appeared to be the work of an amateur. Even the frames were fantastic, reminding me of those in Uncle Antonio's shop in Salerno.

I ordered my usual drink and asked the barista about the art. He informed me that he was the artist. This truly baffled me. The idea that someone so talented was making me coffee simply shocked my inner state of affairs. The graceful artist was Justin Wiesz, a young man with a happy outlook who was now discussing a couple of the paintings with me. His style was a grand imitation of Renaissance art, very brilliantly done, but with an impeccable graceful take all his own.

One of Justin's works of art came to the office with me. This happened after visiting the nearby ATM machine. It had come at a bargain price, and my mind had already conceived the spot it would adorn back home. Of course, the very moment I was at my desk, either someone was just leaving my cubicle, or they had left me a note to see them. Every day brought plenty of contentious issues or unhappy customers overwhelming the technicians I was supervising.

And yet some problems were of our own making. Our managers had overwhelmed the agency with rules and complex processes and had lost track of what really mattered most versus trying to control everything. For example, travelers had to file for reimbursement within three days upon completion of their trip, as per our regs, but if our branch had a problem with their voucher, the document was returned to the person submitting it.

Once matters were cleared up, we made a payment. However, we continued to accrue the time the voucher was submitted from the original date, consequently penalizing the traveler as having exceeded the three-day limit. A few of the field office managers were not so thrilled as this also impacted their performance appraisal. They were right, yet it became apparent some things would not change unless a few radical ideas were adopted.

My biggest shock came once my temporary assignment terminated. I was filling in for the manager of our revolving fund for a few days. The fund was established to provide training classes to the public and federal entities in recognizing what constituted discrimination of any sort. The branch consisted of the manager and a technician, but the workload was immense. Both were under siege, and the technician was trying to do the impossible with the bountiful documents received, but also downloading tons of data daily to our field units.

A phone call had been forwarded to me. The customer wanted to know if they had been registered for a class, and as the technician was away from his desk, I inquired as to which class she was calling about. The training course in question would begin the following day in Los Angeles, so I foolishly asked the person on the phone why they did not contact the L A office.

They had already done that and had been instructed to contact us. After taking care of this matter, I sought out my boss. It seemed odd to me that a regional office could not inform a customer if they had been registered for a class they were giving. Why were we even inputting their registrations? Apparently, this was all our doing. A decision had been made by our wise leaders that all aspects of the revolving fund operations would be processed here in the headquarters office.

Once explanations came forth, I expressed that the entire process was absurd. A customer would learn of a training class in the making and would call the appropriate district office to request information. If they chose to attend, they were provided with the form to fill out and instructed to return it. That form was then sent to our office. The technician in the revolving fund branch was responsible for just about everything; inputting the registration data from the thousands of forms received, providing that data to the district offices, and processing some of the financial aspects of this training. So, I asked the million-dollar question, "Just why don't the district offices enter their own data?"

I was told more than I cared to hear and share. Also, I discovered that the technician in the branch began work at seven and left the office after seven each evening. He could barely keep up with the overwhelming amount of work but practically killed himself in trying. And, taking a healthy and necessary vacation for a few days away from his desk was almost impossible.

Chapter 168

We had been living in Northern Virginia for several years. Everything those doomsayers back in Caserma Ederle had predicted came to naught. My wife and I were in professional jobs, apparently progressing well, and we were still renting the flat in Vicenza. Once again, we lived well and had no money problems or any real worries to contend with.

Nevertheless, one must never grow too comfortable. My wonderful companion was now demanding a change. Francesca had recently been promoted and moved to another office, and apparently her new boss shared his joys of home ownership. You know, like having a monetary asset and therefore building solid credit. Things perhaps necessary in modern society but which were never really my priority.

However, my elegant wife worked with the planet's elite. Their opinions were gospel. The IMF consists of economists, managers, accountants, analysts, and administrative personnel, all basking in the glory of keeping a pulse on the world's economy, and, if possible, preventing it from getting ill. Consequently, it was now impossible to disagree with my spouse. As a matter of fact, I no longer even tried.

Now houses in Falls Church City were costly. Unless, of course, one bought an older one, which would probably bring unexpected expenses and required some skills to fix things, which was the last thing on my mind. It was David who had recently warned me, "Buy an older house, and you'll be at Home Depot every weekend." Exactly what my intuitive sense warned me to avoid.

Nevertheless, we now made plans to buy a house in the suburbs. We understood this would entail a longer drive to work, but such a minor inconvenience was deemed doable. I drove us to Fairfax City one day, and we immediately spotted some lovely town-homes right off Route 127, and one was for sale. Francesca took down the relevant information and called the realtor later that evening.

It was after dinner. I was in the living room scanning the newspaper, and after several minutes of hearing some back-and-forth, both speakers switched to Italian. The realtor was originally from Rome. Consequently, what should have been a small briefing became a long and pleasant chat. We then met Elena a few days later. She seemed most happy to engage us in Italian, and she was dressed quite sharp. A professional to the max, and that lady certainly knew her business. She took us to view a townhouse off Lee Highway in a rather secluded area in Fairfax City.

If I am not mistaken, our realtor had referred to the neighborhood in question as a hidden jewel. And the lady was absolutely on target. Our eyes encountered a green oasis off the beaten path, and the older well-built brick homes we saw looked fantastic. We entered the premises of an older townhouse, and it immediately won us over. A long corridor led to the kitchen, which was roomy and in great condition. To the right side of the entrance door was the dining area and living room, which included a lovely fireplace. Three bedrooms and two bathrooms were upstairs, and the basement looked like a new house.

The home was perfect but the price was a bit steep. Elena believed we could negotiate, however, the seller insisted on her price. Well, we were informed other homes were sometimes available in that area, though not now, and advised to be patient. Now, I must admit to feeling a tad guilty. Francesca would have given anything and everything for that townhouse. In her world, money had no value. It existed simply to be spent. And yet we lucked out, several months later, the owner met us halfway and so began our residence at Dunster Court.

On the day of our move, our neighbors came over to greet us. An amiable, retired couple introduced themselves and insisted we call on them for anything we might need. Later that evening, the ancient-looking lady who lived on the other side and admitted she smoked like a chimney, brought us a homemade pound cake baked for us that afternoon. Well, the American dream was beginning to be less of a fantasy folklore and more of a reality.

Now we certainly shocked all our neighbors! A week after moving in, we four were off to Paris on holiday. Francesca and her sister Anna from Vicenza with her family had planned every detail. Of course, I initially protested by emphasizing that my prudent ways were necessary to conserve a healthy amount of money in case of an emergency and that I disapproved of spending our hard-earned money so rashly. But my words were dust in the wind.

It seemed a bit preposterous to me. The person working for the very institution which preaches sound financial management as the key to rich living should have understood some of my sermons. But guess what? We had a fantastic week in Paris. The four kids, two Americans and two Italians, loved every minute of our trip. By the way, a most peculiar event occurred at Jim Morrison's grave.

We were leaving his tombstone when a bunch of young hippies had just arrived. They quietly invaded the area and were now lighting up some weed. While distancing ourselves, it suddenly hit me—after all, Jim would have certainly approved! From a distance, not at all visible to the singer's loving fans, my voice from the band in the Bronx came back to life.

It opened with extra force to boost. A few lyrics from one of the Doors' most extravagant tunes was properly belted out. My tenor voice thundered smoothly and so the kids laughed hysterically while we adults approved and chuckled. It felt so good letting out a bit of old steam.

Chapter 169

Once back home, a big debate led to uncertainty. The boys wanted a dog, and so did their parents. Considering we had room for one, and a backyard, it seemed doable. However, Francesca preferred a Dalmatian, as Disney's movie had had quite an effect on her. The boys, however, were all for a German Shepherd. Yet the choice was mine, and it certainly perplexed them all.

It was an impressive scene from a movie which had won me over. A pack of dogs was following the hunters who were tracking a lion deep in the African plains. Now when the king of the jungle roars, all beasts, big or small, run for safety. That was not the case. The dogs were Rhodesian Ridgebacks, great hunting dogs. These animals are quite fearless, but also very attached and overprotective of the family. Such was my choice.

Well, the lord of the manor contacted a breeder in California. Soon a little puppy was on his way to Dulles Airport. On the phone, I was cautioned about the dog we were getting, but it was something that I did not truly grasp. The lady had said, "I must warn you. He's a lively one." We four soon found out.

The new member of our family was picked up at the airport warehouse in the early evening. And so Argo, Eric's choice of name, came home with us inside a caged box. To say he was gorgeous is to totally understate the fact. Any puppy will warm your heart, but ours was just super adorable! However, once within the confines of our dwelling, the spell was quickly broken, for the little critter bit everyone but me. It was not so much a sign of meanness but rather simply who he was.

The name Argo is from the tales of Ulysses. The very son who had chosen it now renamed the dog "the ferocious beast." And for a few days, Eric kept his distance from the little animal. Yet, Argo was not only a good dog who loved us all tremendously, though he did have a slight temper, but was also true to his breed. That is, loyal to his family but also to his nature, with quite a bit of wildness still in him.

Very soon, another member joined our family, but not from California. Maria Santi was my wife's niece, her sister Viviana's only daughter. She had previously visited when we were residing near Seven Corners. The young lady had fallen in love with everything about living in the U.S. and had expressed her desire to return. She was now among us, and had purchase a one-way ticket from Venice to Dulles Airport.

Perhaps her visit was the result of a negative outcome. Maria had called off her marriage at the last moment. And while she hardly ever spoke about it, the tiny information shared made my wife and I conclude she had probably made the right choice. Well, we all loved our new guest and accepted her, and she immediately became super helpful, especially with the children and also with doing chores around the house.

She even became my personal nurse. Allow me to back up a bit to explain. You see, when I lived in Vicenza, I was cured of hay fever through a series of injections, but I also discovered a more serious illness plaguing me. An extensive bloodwork exam revealed my liver was infected with hepatitis C. My reckless ways in the past, specifically that injection which caused those troublesome boils, had made its mark.

This virus will not put you in hospital for several days, like the A type. It is a sort of dormant ailment which ultimately, after many years, destroys the liver. I had once seen my physician in Virginia, and he had brought up my liver ailment and the possibility of a cure. The logic was to heal that organ now versus risking a shorter life span as an elderly person. His reasoning seemed like a wise initiative. For my father's brother, Uncle Roberto, had died of liver cancer a few years prior. The man had gone to his dentist to complain about the excessive bleeding from his gums while brushing his teeth. This gentle soft-spoken guy was told to contact a doctor immediately. Unfortunately, various tests revealed a tumor in his liver. He was given less than a year to live. He returned to Sicily and passed away some months later.

This necessitated my initiative to improve my health. However, if one can, one should always try to be well-informed. Back then, access to information was limited or practically nonexistent, especially for a medicine called interferon. The hepatologist curing me had indifferently stated that there would be some discomfort during the treatment, but it was crucial to continue the cure till the very end to ensure eradication of the disease.

Well, being an ex-soldier and a sailor who had once experienced a bit of hell, exploring unchartered waters seemed to be no big deal. For six months, I gave myself an injection of the medicine every other day. The first shot literally shook me. After a few minutes, my body began to tremble, and both Maria and Francesca, once placing a blanket over my shoulders, attempted to hold me steady. My erratic shaking persisted until my system stopped rejecting the foreign poison it had just received.

I went through hell for six months. It was like a severe flu, rendering me totally lifeless. At times, I was so irritable and miserable. All my bodily functions began failing me. I would give myself an injection in the evening, and the following morning, it felt like mud had invaded my intestines. My bowel movements were erratic, my digestive system was in distress, my appetite decreased, and I soon lost a lot of weight. Often, a bit of mental fog would set in as I lay about feeling depressed and lifeless.

After two months, I was ready to throw in the towel. The physician talked me out of it. Such was my medical crucifixion. Good thing Maria was among us. She would encourage me to eat, make me teas and fruit juices, was overly concerned when I appeared a tad lifeless, and she even opened up about herself simply to share a few words. Whereas my wife appeared so unsympathetic to my circumstances and sometimes even slightly put out.

Now, as peculiar as this will sound, it was Francesca who dealt with a precarious situation one Saturday. She revealed having just experienced a strange incident that left her quite astounded and somewhat baffled. Perhaps life consists of only so much we can comprehend, and what follows is a shield of obscurity beyond our wildest imagination. But once again, I must first clue you in on how we got to this mysterious riddle.

When we lived in Sarmego, my dad and stepmom came to visit. My father wanted to visit my wife's folks. One morning, while I went off to work, the four travelers, Eric was not yet among us, got on the highway and drove off to the Friuli region. We now owned a different second car, a huge Alfa Romeo, the RIO model, which was made in Brazil, but I had purchased it very cheaply from a dealership in Germany.

Now, that car could run! It was once Francesca got off the highway that my father spoke up. He was sitting up front with her. He politely stated that my wife was obviously a good driver. Just the same, traveling so fast with a young child in a car was sheer madness. For if a tire blew out, she would surely lose control of the vehicle and be in serious trouble. And back then, safety belts did not exist.

Back to the future. My wife stood in front of me looking quite shocked. Maria had gone to D.C. that day, and Francesca, after leaving her at the Metro station, had taken the highway heading to the IKEA store. She was in the left lane and speeding quite a bit. Suddenly, my father's voice was in her ears as if he were sitting next to her. Her foot immediately came off the gas pedal while simultaneously the back tire blew out.

She somehow managed to control the vehicle. The car was driven into the emergency lane, and my wife stopped but never got out of it. A pickup truck was right behind her, and a young Black man exited it, walked over to the driver's side, instructed Francesca to open the back trunk, removed the spare tire, changed the damaged one, placed that tire in the trunk, and he returned to Francesca, still in the auto, and simply told her to move on. This incredibly peculiar piece of drama made absolutely no sense to her or me. Her devastated expression seemed to be asking for an explanation.

So, just what is to be made of this? We humans believe we know it all. We can add and subtract and always get the right answer. But isn't our knowledge of life and beyond and its infinite possibilities probably just a tiny speck within the immense encyclopedia governing our universe? Perhaps my father was never far from us and at that moment intervened. It is the only possible explanation. Although many would label it fictitious nonsense and simply enjoy a good laugh over it.

Oh well, my horrible interferon cure eventually terminated. Unfortunately, blood work done provided some unpleasant news. The virus had not cleared, therefore the hepatitis C remained. It seemed better to move on and disregard the physician's advice to try again the following year. I decided to let destiny run its course rather than massacre my body and mind again, not knowing if that remedy would ever work.

Chapter 170

My relationship with my wife was deteriorating. It was mostly over the kids and her lack of discipline toward anything they did or did not do. Also, the woman appeared so cold toward me. It felt like my presence was simply accepted because it entailed having a second significant salary which ensured we would continue to live well.

One afternoon, my outburst did go a bit overboard! Both boys were in front of the TV practically all day. They played no sports, hardly did any homework, and their room, well, fortunately Maria kept things rolling. My wife began arguing with me over my stifling control methods which were unacceptable to her. She informed me that she had been raised with very little discipline and had turned out fine. Therefore, our kids needed to be left to their whims and they, too, would be okay.

It seemed best to get away for a while. My flight to Milano was rather quick. Perhaps because it was the first time I slept on a plane. Mr. Rossi and my mother were so happy to see me. They certainly noticed my reserved cheerfulness and must have suspected something was amiss. Also, it was the first time I was in their presence without my family, something they were not accustomed to. Some inquiries at the dinner table over my pale pallor and thin body led to a few details about my recent liver treatment.

I left the villa a few days later. Both folks did their best to accommodate me, my mother cooked plenty of delicious food, and Alessandro brightened my outlook a tad. His insistence on a bit of wine with the meals was refused for it seemed best to abstain. My wonderful mom lent me her tiny Renault car. She had recently learned to drive and obtained her license, so Alessandro had rewarded her with a new vehicle, small but convenient. It brought me to my destination, Vicenza. And on the way there a rather perplexing thought continued to hound me.

Whenever in that city, my curiosity over Francesco never abated. Just what did the boy look like now? What kind of kid was he? Studious, a quick learner, or like me in the past, only awake when something truly made sense from a certain perspective? I always hoped to run into him and Bianca when strictly on my own. Just getting a glimpse of him would have done so much to pacify my sorrowful spirit.

That is why the following day I chanced the unthinkable. I called Bianca. She answered the phone and sounded very happy to hear my voice. I was pleasantly surprised with her welcoming tone. She even invited me to visit that morning and provided directions.

Apparently, she and her family had been living for some time in that mansion on the outskirts of Vicenza. My French voiture soon had me driving by Palladio's very popular villa, La Rotonda. What a unique and impressive façade, and those columns enriching this magnificent palace always made me think Palladio was a true genius. While admiring it, but also getting closer to my destination, I vividly recalled a scene from the movie *Don Giovanni*. Where Masetto, the peasant, feels betrayed by the woman he has just married, Zerlina, for she had accepted Don Giovanni' s invitation to spend the night with him. This was a medieval ritual where a noble could deflower a local peasant girl referred to as prima nocte, the right of the first night.

Bianca and her mother were cordial. We enjoyed an espresso in the kitchen and spoke amiably for a while. It was eventually pointed out to me that Francesco was at school, it being Saturday, something completely erased from my memory banks. What a horrible blow. He would not be home for several hours. Nevertheless, my emotions remained in check, and then quite unexpectedly, Bianca invited me to go upstairs to see the boy's paintings.

Once inside Francesco's room, my eyes were overwhelmed by sheer sadness. I almost collapsed into a fit of depression. Every painting on those walls expressed a sense of isolation, an overwhelming feeling of being lost or simply not sure of one's role in the scheme of things. It was apparent that the artist in him was expressing his need for the truth, his truth. And while excessively brooding within, a slightly wounded me heard his mother claim, "Such is the suffering of a genius who has yet to find his style."

Among the many paintings, one stood out. The concept felt somewhat familiar. Perhaps it was copied from a poster of Jim Morrison. Here was Francesco's face, but only the left side was finished, the other half was purposely left blank. My composure remained intact and no words flowed out of me. Soon enough, I was driving back to the city center. My thoughts focused on how to possibly help this young teenager. It almost felt like that drive to Arlington Hospital, not sure if Eric was still with us.

It was soon time to move on. My in-laws invited me to dinner one evening, but the following day I was on a rapid train heading to Salerno. The French car had a small engine, but the huge cost from gas and highway fees had me choose rail over driving. So, I had managed a bit of reading, but once the train stopped in Rome, several people came into my compartment.

An elderly woman and a middle-aged man, although not a couple, were engaged in an amicable conversation. They were discussing their trials and tribulations over their hep C. I threw in my lot regarding the failed cure. The information being shared bore some peculiar news. The elderly gentleman had been informed that while this drug could do some good, it left a drastic negative impact on the patient's body and mind. According to the facts revealed to him, it strongly debilitated the immune system, and it ultimately brought on depression. His doctor had strongly advised against taking it. Which is why a past incident came to mind.

It had occurred a month after finishing the interferon. Francesca had made some fritters after dinner, and I ate a bit, but not much. A half hour later, my chest was hurting me. There was a severe burning pain that slowly radiated throughout my body. It persisted and worsened, and eventually, my pleas for medical assistance were answered as my wife drove me to the emergency room.

Unfortunately, it was Friday night. The staff looked at me as if to insinuate, "Are you kidding?" There were overdoses to contend with, elderly folks with severe conditions suffering miserably, and a victim of a serious fight. We sat there forever, and hours later when inquiring about my turn, I was told to be patient. It eventually became apparent my situation was considered insignificant, so at three in the morning, as the pain began to subside, we returned home.

Oh well, my companions and a few more travelers who had just joined us were now chatting indifferently. The train had just pulled out of a station when suddenly someone opened our compartment door. A very serious looking man told one of the passengers to get out of his seat, and not so politely. He had a reservation and a right to that seat, but the person sitting there refused to budge.

A shouting match ensued and almost everyone became involved. Soon, the intruder went to get the conductor. It was a clear case of the railroad having screwed up. The sign outside the compartment notifying that a seat was reserved had not been posted. Consequently, all seats were available to anyone, which is why every person in that car insisted no one needed to move. A few minutes later, we faced the irate individual and a no-nonsense train conductor who began threatening the passenger.

Now all hell broke loose! Everyone except me was shouting. The folks in the compartment were adamant that no sign posted gave the passenger the right to sit there, but the angry conductor and his side-kick were contesting this and presenting a different conclusion. Well, I decided to intervene. My stop was coming up shortly, but I was also thinking it would bring an end to the chaos. That is why I gave up my seat and left the compartment.

Naturally, I remained in the corridor a bit. While standing there and looking out at what passed me up super quickly, the very individual who had expressed concern over my liver cure came over. He, too, now faced the large window while standing next to me, and he looked my way and simply said, "Well, you certainly betrayed us."

It was my uncle in Salerno who illuminated me. The passengers—let's just say in this case, average folks—had taken on a fight against an unjust and imperfect system. One which too often mistreats and abuses people. It was not necessarily just the railroad, although this was clearly the case here, but those passengers were standing up to the incompetence and arrogance of abusive individuals in charge of operations or processes, particularly state employees who too often feel important and believe themselves to be a notch above everyone else.

My small gesture was totally misunderstood and unappreciated. Nevertheless, soon enough, the raucous incident was far behind me as I enjoyed my aunt and her family. They always made me feel like one of them. Some days later, with a few encouraging words from my aunt, I was making my way back up north. It was then back to the villa, and I soon boarded a flight, very much looking forward to return home.

Chapter 171

Everyone on Dunster Court seemed happy to see me back. All proceeded well at home for some time. There would be no butting heads with my wife, and the boys could be who they were. Yet one day, Maria made an unusual remark regarding my attitude, or the change in me.

She had politely expressed concern over what could possibly have occurred. On her first visit, for a month, and since her arrival a year ago, she had always seen me cheerful. "You always made us all laugh," she stated most convincingly. However, for some time now, I appeared sad and indifferent with life in general. She understood it during that awful cure, but that was a bit behind us, so just what was going on?

It took some time before that tip on the train fully registered. My mind distinctively recalled hearing, "It brings on depression." Folks, I decided to get back to basics. Having recently read an article highlighting how a healthy gut brings a healthy mind, a complete change of diet would mean consuming certain foods. And, just as important if not more, I decided to start playing football, or should I say soccer.

One lovely Saturday morning I got myself to the IMF's Bretton Woods Club in Maryland. Among other folks at practice was an Italian who worked with my wife. Consequently, the Italian language was extensively utilized, as we all were playing with much gusto. This practice/game lasted more than an hour as each one of us attempted to outshine the other. We played non-stop, and it seemed incredible to be in such great shape.

All had proceeded well that day but not so the following morning. Both my legs were paralyzed due to an unbearable pain. I could not walk at all and even getting to the bathroom was a problem. Miraculously, with much help, my body was placed in the bathtub to soak in hot water for the longest time. It accomplished nothing as my entire day was passed with me lying about like a wounded athlete.

At work, my colleagues were curious about my handicap. All insisted it was a severe case of muscle cramps since I had been inactive for so long. Well, my legs were almost fully healed several days later, which is why Saturday morning yours truly rejoined the training. Although a few new faces were among us, as before, we older guys were again playing our hearts out. It was as if we wanted to defy being categorized as over thirty-five, therefore performing like the young and mighty.

Incredible! The same scenario repeated itself again at home. My body never left our bedroom the following morning, and in the afternoon, although it took forever, I was able to make it to the living room couch. Now hear this. This mysterious malady manifested itself for the next three Sundays. That is why I abandoned the game of football. Something was just not right. And having previously visited my physician for different ailments, on several occasions, my now returning with a strange new one seemed a tad ludicrous.

The following week, I attended to something entirely different. It was on to the Borders Books Store as my agenda was for a special book, or perhaps more than one. My purchase would be sent to Vicenza since I now had Francesco's address. It seemed only right to lessen his load. My theory on what I would purchase was a tad peculiar, Japanese art. You see, some years back, the works of Ohtsu Kazuyuki had roped me in. What gorgeous serenity blossomed in all this artist's craft.

Here was my take on this. Western art has a vertical lineage in its stance. In those Japanese paintings, it was horizontal, therefore making their presentation easy to grasp and inspiring a peaceful harmony overflowing so tenderly. Such were my thoughts and my fix for the young teen, along with some music. In his room, his love for the blues had stood out. So, I was now sharing my addiction to Freddie and Albert King, Johnny Winter, and a few other exceptional guitarists. A package was mailed to Bianca with a small note inside for her son.

Chapter 172

Maria had become the household maid. Every weekend, she tackled our quarters and left them spotless. She also engaged in that line of work privately during the weekdays, and was paid well, and she was now even attending English classes in the evening. The young lady was an early riser and always seemed capable of doing the impossible.

My wife instead always got up much later. After having coffee, at least in spring or summer, she would tour her garden to marvel at its beauty. And where necessary, touch up anything demanding a tiny fix. At that hour, I was usually out shopping at the supermarkets, organic food at one and everything else at another, then on to the dry cleaners, when necessary, Home Depot, occasionally, and attending to whatever else needed to be done.

The boys took up residence in the basement in front of the TV. They basically played video games the entire Saturday morning. Their main responsibility on weekdays was Argo. Once they were home from school, he needed to get out for a bit. It practically never happened. Just like doing homework or attending to some small matter I had asked them to do. And I had even attempted to introduce them to sports.

Apparently both kids were not the least interested. Which sort of confused me, for we parents had been athletically inclined as young people. Anyhow, they hated everything, football, baseball, soccer, even bicycle riding. Why, when you named a sport, it was always voted down. Nevertheless, I managed to enroll Ricky in Tae Kwando classes.

I would drive him on Wednesday evenings and Saturday mornings. His instructor had appeared sincere in proclaiming the boy had talent. This truly overjoyed me, and I hoped he would continue to improve his skills in learning to defend himself. It did not last. One Saturday morning I returned and found him sidelined. Obviously, he was beginning to experiment, just like his dad had, and may have exaggerated the night before. Soon enough, he threw in the towel.

Oh well, it was coming. Growing up in the U.S. brings teens a common fad. Parents fall to the side, as they begin to lose input into their kids' upbringing, after all, all teens simply want to be accepted by their peers in their group of friends. Of course, with inner changes come physical ones too. Ricky now had long blonde hair, wore a chain for a belt holding up loose baggy jeans, and was even demanding more freedom.

One day, the shit hit the fan. Fairfax High School had sponsored a play. Some of its students participated on stage or as a support group for the play participants. Ricky, along with a few other guys had abandoned their presence behind the stage and somehow got onto the high school roof. They spent some time drinking there. How they got caught was a mystery.

I had foolishly assumed the little rascal would be punished. No sir! My wife and a couple of other concerned mothers took on the scholastic institution over its lax standards. They insisted something needed to change immediately. The students on that roof could have fallen off and been seriously hurt. And just how did they even get up there? The fiery women persisted that the administration was to be held accountable. Such was their shared logic, and I simply bowed out. This allowed my gallant wife, along with a few other radical moms, the right to take on Fairfax High School. It sounded like she was ready to fight city hall.

Fortunately, Eric was not showing signs of rebellion. He had even, with some reluctance, accepted the idea of taking piano lessons. The boy was not overly thrilled, yet we headed off to his teacher's studio every Tuesday evening. Soon enough, my son began moaning and groaning insisting I had imposed something he had no interest in, but the lessons continued a while longer.

One evening after dropping him off, I immediately felt horrified. I had locked myself out of the car. The keys were still in the ignition ring, but the car doors were locked. My call home was to request my wife bring the spare keys. It simply required asking a lift from Terry, the elderly chap next door, and I was only four miles away. Nothing doing! She insisted I call the tow-truck company, and they would do the rest. Why, I will never know. After hearing this a second time, I simply hung up.

The annoyed receptionist on the phone informed me it was a busy night. She would not commit to giving a time a tow-truck would arrive. I waited, and eventually Eric finished his class. We sat in the nearby ice-cream parlor enjoying a banana split and making the best of things. Eventually, ousted from the ice-cream parlor, which was closing, I returned to the phone booth to call home again. The same tune was proposed which is why my Sicilian upbringing simply got the best of me. I was not very polite!

It may have been 11:00 p.m. when my wife arrived with a colleague from work. My silence and the anger plastered on my face did not help much. Perhaps it was the straw that broke the camel's back. This incident began my drifting away from a relationship already sagging, or perhaps finished but not acknowledged. And I had practically no one to bitch to. Gifford had taken a job in Italy with the Army's Department of Education. Dawn was a name of someone in my past, and as for Maria, although very neutral and hardly ever home, she at least heard me out, yet it felt like I was complaining uselessly.

It was during this timeframe that I decided to go trekking on weekends. My destination was the Shenandoah Valley, and my first hike had me ascending Old Rag. Once finished, I felt great and so the following week, an easier climb allowed me to bring Argo, who seemed truly happy throughout our well-paced walk. Not so on the way home, as our ferocious beast, at least in title, was in the back seat sound asleep and snoring like an old camel.

One day, the entire family, minus Ricky, joined me. Our dog was with us as we tackled a rather long trail which ultimately led to a small waterfall. And once by a tiny stream, I removed Argo's leash allowing him to go in and wet his paws and enjoy the cool water. We then moved on, and his leash was accidentally left behind. Further up some, my inconsistency was fully revealed once a few folks advancing in our direction, yet still some ways off, came into view.

I now began heading back to retrieve his leash. Argo immediately followed me but then stopped and looked at the trio he was leaving behind and headed back toward them. Again, he stopped, looked at me, and headed back to where I stood. His concern and indecision had him going back and forth several times until Francesca kneeled quickly and held him steady by his neck.

It was either go with the alpha animal or stay behind with the family? My wife's action allowed me to proceed and soon return to a joyful dog, seeing us all together again. Oh well, such was the nature of this immaculate creature who loved us tremendously and was totally dedicated to us all.

Chapter 173

Our commute to work was simply a routine. Every morning Route 66 brought us to D.C. We chatted briefly as I drove, and the classical music station accompanied us all the way to Eighteenth and L Street. Once at my building, my wife took the wheel and went off to the IMF to park in their underground garage.

One morning, a rather odd scene grabbed our attention. It was not yet eight o'clock, but there was an incredibly long line outside the Borders Books Store. The queue extended quite some ways on Eighteenth Street, and yet the place was still closed. Now just what was going on today? At coffee break that riddle was resolved. Joe was at my side, but it was Justin who informed me that Mikhail Gorbachev was coming at noon to sign his book.

My artistic buddy also indicated that he would enter from the side door on L Street. After a few words with both guys, my cubicle was my immediate destination. Francesca was soon informed. Now please do not judge me too harshly, but if there is a woman on this planet whose ambitions rise beyond the borders of the known universe, it is Francesca Zanin. Was she at all interested in getting a peek of the great man? YES, OF COURSE. What a ridiculous question!

Apparently, the ex-leader of the Soviet Union was more popular in the U.S. than at home. Perhaps an actual plan to direct the failing empire may not have existed as it quickly collapsed. Was it his personal belief that somehow things would ultimately improve, which led to his, indirectly, bringing down the Berlin Wall, and perhaps ultimately a few other antiquated processes? Oh well, sometimes one must simply follow their better judgement and boldly go into the unknown.

It was not yet noon, but my wife and I stood watch on L Street. And a certain sense of excitement had ignited us both, although, truth be told, we had absolutely no interest in the man's book. We simply admired his courage and tenacity and hoped his actions would somehow change old Russia into a modern state.

Suddenly, two limousines slowly advanced toward us. It had to be him! Both cars stopped a few feet away from the side entrance area. The back door of the vehicle nearest to us opened. A very natural and relaxed Mikhail exited and was looking around. The security detail in the second car apparently had not anticipated this unexpected move. The man was approximately ten yards away.

I strode toward him and was just a foot away with my hand extended to shake his. Excitement coursed through my body, but I had no clue what to say. Our two hands joined, but suddenly something lifted me up and pulled me backward. It was a huge individual wearing dark sunglasses and a dark suit, and damn if he did not resemble the guy at the White House who wanted to break my hands. Well, who knows? Maybe they were cousins.

Such was our brief encounter with history, and it will never be known. By the way, my companion never went anywhere near Mikhail, but of course, she will tell you differently. Well, that adventure was shared with Justin and Joe on the morrow, and it earned me a free espresso, which allowed me to then be generous with Joe. The man never vaunted his homeless standards but he certainly cashed in when he could.

Chapter 174

For folks not so keen on world history, the International Monetary Fund and the World Bank Group were established in 1944. Both organizations initially served in aiding countries devastated by WWII. They are located in Washington D.C. and sit close to each other on Nineteenth Street and Pennsylvania Avenue. While the latter's mission is to assist nations in reducing, and, if possible, eliminating poverty, the former basically works to promote and maintain economic growth.

It was easy to grasp Francesca's pride and joy when speaking about the IMF. After all, the woman was part of an environment she very much appreciated and admired. And my wife had some great benefits as a full-time permanent employee, not to mention some of the privileges which were shared with yours truly, like the annual Christmas party. Our first attendance to one had me in awe and to some extent still lingers within me.

We parked and entered the huge lobby. A superb feast was on display. There were countless tables full of clams, oysters, shrimp, and other delicious delicacies, and further along were so many other culinary treats accompanied by plenty of champagne, wine, and all sorts of other drinks. It was impossible not to feel part of a very elite class. As you moved up a floor or two, it then became a food fest by ethnicity.

Later in the evening, once all the impressive culinary treats had been almost totally consumed, the areas were somewhat cleared of the tables, and there was dancing. The style of dance also varied depending on which floor you were on to accommodate everyone's taste in music and dance.

Something that was also exciting, although not terribly so, were the run-ins with folks my wife was acquainted with. There was an outpouring of compliments between the two employees on their lovely attire and looks. We, the male spouses on standby, would usually struggle to get beyond an introduction but did manage a few words and the usual work-related information. After a while, a bit of silence followed. Fortunately, these casual encounters were brief. We would then head off to another area, meeting other folks and the starlight performance would be again staged most eloquently. Occasionally, a little something extra or somewhat clever would pop out, often quite by chance, yet making me feel as if a huge contribution had just been made, and at times it led to a healthy prolonged enjoyable chat.

Another one of Francesca's benefits was membership at the Bretton Woods Club. The very place where I launched myself into playing soccer for several weeks. It is in Germantown, Maryland, and offers wonderful activities, such as tennis, golf, a soccer field, swimming pools, and a huge lodge for social encounters. In summer, we sometimes went to the pool and spent most of the day outdoors. This did not please Argo, left behind at home. The young critter soon began venting his anger by chewing on and destroying some of the couches.

One day, in the parking area at that club, I spotted the perfect motorcycle. For some time now, my loner personality craved some new challenge, and it was biking which unexpectedly registered as the perfect gig to indulge in. My only experience had been riding behind someone, but apparently that feeling of freedom had never fully abandoned me.

And there it was! A Honda Nighthawk, 250 cc, and the bike was in great condition. What a joy if I could have found one exactly like it. And guess what? I did! Several months later, while browsing the wanted ads in the Washington Post, there it was. Now, who would have ever thought it was the very same machine I had previously spotted in the parking lot of a private club in Maryland.

The person on the phone had a slight accent. It sounded Italian to me, and yes, he was. And yes, he did work at the IMF, and just how did I know? Well, once we switched languages, almost immediately, my wife was on the phone, and she recognized his name. Incredible, and even more fantastic, he agreed to bring the motorcycle to our place. Having just gotten my license, and being a beginner, I was not too keen on bringing it home myself.

So that wonderful machine soon sat in front of our house. The kids arrived home in the latter part of the afternoon and were quite surprised to find it there. Both boys immediately congratulated me on the great-looking bike, and once Francesca arrived home from work, everyone stood outside to admire it. There were even a few compliments, and Maria requested viewing my riding skills, which yours truly had no intention of showing, at least not yet.

Ricky decided to get on it, so he mounted the bike. For a minute, everything was fine as he held the motorcycle steady and imagined riding while adding a few motor sounds to create a more realistic scenario. Then the lad got off the bike, but had not put back the stand, and lost control of the machine. My wonderful Nighthawk went down quickly and hit the pavement rather hard.

Such was the inauguration of my new toy. Everyone sprinted indoors, fearing I would throw a fit. Yes, I was upset, but it seemed only right to pick it up, set it up properly, and look it over. Of course, there was now a scratch or two but no serious damage. My next thought shed some concern over Ricky, my wonderful son, for something in me suspected he would perhaps be one prone to have a few peculiar scrapes in the near future.

Anyhow, my riding plan was simple. It entailed taking the motorcycle out early Sunday morning to Fairfax High School, which was very close by. It was in the school's large parking lot that I would practice in order to feel more comfortable with the machine. Soon enough, once I thought myself ready to hit the road, I would happily do so.

That Sunday morning, I boarded my motorcycle, left our residence, and decided to forgo the practice. Once on Lee Highway, I felt great and just kept going. I was heading out west, and my bike soon rewarded me with a divine and glorious feeling of being free! It must be the same for birds as they fly about and glide overhead. On a motorcycle, one no longer has a care in the world and simply abdicates all feelings to the peace of inner and outer beauty.

My new pastime afforded me time to myself on weekends. However, after becoming somewhat of a biker, Francesca proposed a sport we could both enjoy together. One of her new colleagues, a manager, had a stable behind his huge country home. It was he who convinced her to explore the great benefits of horseback riding.

We had rode horses on a trail somewhere in West Virginia once before. The terrain was a bit rough, the constant bouncing up and down not so enjoyable, and we were just two amateurs out for a ride. Therefore, I was not so keen to take lessons to learn to ride English saddle, something which, among other things, according to her experienced colleague, would do wonders for our middle body parts.

Nevertheless, one Friday morning, the Washington Post's Weekend Section was fully scrutinized. It had a sports recreation section where all indoor and outdoor activities were listed. Believe me, if not there, it simply did not exist. As luck would have it, a riding facility was not far off from our residence and arrangements were made over the phone by yours truly. So late the following morning we two arrived at that stable.

Upon leaving our house, something immediately stood out. I had on an old pair of jeans, my military boots from my soldier years, and a sweatshirt. Whereas the lady of the house had done some serious shopping. There she was, in fancy riding pants, shiny new boots, and a proper shirt under a riding jacket. I was very impressed but also slightly perplexed. What if this new pastime did not work out? Hadn't she overdone it? It seemed best to maintain my silence.

We were introduced to a horse by one of the trainers. It lasted about five minutes. Then my wife and I made it to the office and faced the administrative personnel. A young lady inquired if we wanted to sign up for lessons. I, of course, had a question. Just how long would it take before we were able to ride, and ride comfortably? Her answer came out immediately, "It depends." I then asked what it depended on. Apparently, if a person was in good shape and athletically inclined, they would probably learn faster than others. Wow, really?

I proceeded to inquire about us two. We fit that description to some extent, and so just how long before we could simply mount a horse and ride off? Once again it depended. On what? How many times a week and how long we would ride. My third question received that same singular response from an annoyed young lady who completely turned me off. That is why I stopped listening, knowing very well that we would leave and not return.

Once outside that office, it hit me. Most women about looked just like my wife. They were all in perfect riding attire, that is. Of course, once in our vehicle there was a brief interrogation as to why we had not signed up for lessons. My answer, which went to the heart of things, was given slowly and politely. I did not like the place, nor the people, and the price was a bit steep. Therefore, I would keep looking. My wife turned inward and ignored me for the rest of the day.

The following Saturday, we headed to a place in Maryland. It was quiet far from home, but it was fucking perfect! The owners were down-to-earth folks who showed us around. One of the instructors took us to see a horse and spent at least ten minutes, if not more, providing us useful information. A bit later, once my silly question came out, I was given an answer. It was the owner's wife who thought it would probably take three to four months before we were riding comfortably and perhaps even galloping.

We initiated lessons a week later. That stable had an invaluable asset, our instructor, Maureen. Perhaps every individual is meant to excel at some function in life, and lucky are those who find their true calling. When our coach had us in the ring, she would point out what was good, or not so good, by giving us a concise picture of what you were doing, therefore showing us what we looked like while riding.

Maureen would imitate the horse's posture and yours. It was so easy to grasp her point of view, and once you complied and performed accordingly, she was all compliments and bore such happy smiles. Yes, it often felt like having a video to learn from as we rode right in the very ring she managed. What a joy it became to pass our afternoons at that stable. Our Saturdays became such pleasurable days which we both very much looked forward to.

Unfortunately, one incident truly rocked the boat. It made me uncomfortable and had me questioning my fellow beings. Let me state emphatically, I love my sons and believe all kids are basically good and to be cherished with much love. That is basically it! One Saturday afternoon, as we had just arrived and were preparing to ride I noticed a small girl, fully dressed in riding gear, standing next to us. She and her mom were ready to leave.

What I saw was a cute girl dressed impeccably well in her attire. I simply said, "My, you look so beautiful." It was an innocent comment. Her mother's eyes bulged and her nostrils flared. She moved closer to me and bellowed, "Excuse me?" Her voice shook. Being no fool, I immediately clarified hoping to avoid a scene. The irate woman did back off, and then she and her daughter walked away. It seems incredible to me how some people simply yearn to fight. At times, we Americans are just too quick on the draw. My goodness, is this what we do best?

Well, I can emphatically state that Francesca and I became very good horse riders. Eventually, we rode elsewhere once a week having become very sound horse enthusiasts. What a joy to go off on a horse for an hour and cover different trails over a vast area of land. My wife's co-worker was so right. We had both fallen in love with this hobby, and I was crazy about a horse named Rocky whom I rode quite frequently. He simply wanted to run like the wind and could not be held back, and I was not about to stop him.

Chapter 175

Since our union in 1979, Francesca had contributed and expanded my outlook on things, including the joy of riding horses. Overall, she had given me a different take on life, which included a variety of interests, but most of all, she introduced me to perspectives and hobbies I would have completely overlooked.

And yet, life at home was far from optimistic. We again fought over the kids, and sometimes my anger would subside leaving me sort of isolated. My only ally, Maria, had now returned to Italy for her dad was seriously ill. And believe me, she was immensely missed all around. It was soon after her departure that my wife claimed we needed a maid. I simply replied, "I don't need one."

My refusal to take on this expense did not sit well with her. She reminded me that she was paying our mortgage. I was footing everything else, including all the expenses associated with going to Italy once a year, which required funds for a rental car for three weeks, hotel accommodations, and lots of good food. And if I purchased a new car, I paid with cash from my bank account. Nevertheless, she hired a maid who came twice a month. This, plus her super expensive wardrobe, and a recent flight on the Concorde, made me suspect that some of the money in the account in Vicenza was not being saved accordingly.

I once asked for an accounting. The woman insisted the funds were all there and growing nicely, but nothing to look at was forthcoming. Now regarding that flight. Well, she flew from Dulles Airport to Paris, as she would first visit an ex-co-worker who had married a French banker, and then proceed to her work assignment. Of course, the return trip would include a brief stop in Italy.

What a fare on the Concorde cost, I shall never know. It was certainly not cheap. She insisted the IMF had footed the bill. Now, from my experience in reimbursing travelers for their official work expenses, rule number one, which all institutions applied, is to provide employees with the lowest cost airfare available. They can purchase their own tickets and spend what they want, but they were only reimbursed the equivalent of what would have been incurred.

Money matters were not the only problematic issue. Ricky was definitely following in my footsteps. My wife and I had just arrived home from work one Friday afternoon, and our son was waiting for her in the kitchen. Once we entered, he was instantly at her side. While putting my coat away in the closet, my back was to them, but I then turned to catch her giving our son a twenty-dollar bill. In a rather bitter tone I said, "Do you realize what you are doing?" She immediately responded, "Why, what did you do when you were his age?"

This low blow truly angered me. It was then when my loyalty to her and any appreciation of her finer ways vanished. And so it happened! I found a lover. It occurred at the office, and quite by chance. My manager's birthday was being celebrated in one of our conference rooms. There was soda galore plus that awful cake covered in sugar icing which I truly hated. The employee slicing it was one of the supervisors. She had served everyone except me, as I joined them a bit late. My request for a small piece of cake was answered with, "For you, anything!"

There was no follow-up from me. Yet, the phrase had certainly registered and soon had me thinking, and thinking quite a bit. A few days later, a bit of unexpected folly guided me to her office. Without any hesitation, in a very polite manner and low tone, I proposed we meet one night. The woman removed her glasses, her face turned slightly red, and she stared at me in complete disbelief. Believing a huge blunder had just been made, I quickly apologized. Then, hoping to also avoid a scandal, I returned to my cubicle, feeling like a complete idiot. For the next few days, yours truly kept a very low profile.

It was she who eventually came to my desk. The woman asked, "Where shall we meet, and when?" And that is how it began. It happened on a Friday night in a motel in Falls Church City. To say my composure was a bit tense is to understate a solemn fact. At home, my plans had me meeting an old friend from the DoD IG's office, and we would dine at a Greek restaurant in Alexandria. No questions were asked, and so my objective proceeded nicely, but still I felt slightly nervous.

Oh well. What can I say? If the human body is starved for too long, it will seek help. In the words of a great comedian who is long gone, men will make it with anything, even mud. This was not the case with my co-worker. She was attractive, and once fully exposed, her superb body turned me on. But, more importantly, just like me, that woman was long overdue for a full night of passion. Goodness gracious, we worked out like two crazed animals for quite a long while!

Chapter 176

One morning, Justin informed me about an art exhibition at the National Gallery. The works of his favorite artist, John Singer Sargent, were on display for a month. The name was quite foreign to me. Years before, Francesca and I, along with Joe, Justin, and his girlfriend, had attended the Vincent Van Gogh exhibition. That was a mesmerizing feast for our eyes, mind and spirit. This was just as invigorating!

The Sargent exhibition was as fascinating. In his earlier works, the artist painted mostly the British aristocracy. His subjects were so vivid in both expression and pose, it felt like you were looking at a photograph and seeing the individual's unique personality. I now saw some similarity between one of Justin's paintings, we owned two, and a few in front of us. Anyway, in the latter years, Sargent touched on everything from the beauty of Mother Nature to the human existence in all its various possibilities. After our mesmerizing tour, we enjoyed a tasteful lunch and chatted about the art.

I must mention that my wife and I still shared some fine moments together. She was a good companion and an interesting individual, but also, one not so easily deceived. I had just arrived home one late Saturday night. She was in bed reading. My night out on weekends had become routine, and so it seemed a bit peculiar when she said, "Aren't you spending a bit too much time out lately?" She never took her eyes off the book or attempted to look my way.

What could I possibly have said? Upon finishing in the bathroom, my exhausted body crawled into bed. I did not want to appear rude, so a very endearing, "Good night" was uttered. It was after this incident that a general understanding of things in the human experience of what we create and face proposed the absurd. Perhaps my very existence was now traveling far from the spirit it occupied.

Now a bit of self-reflection can be healthy but sometimes regretful. Perhaps my level of stupidity knows no limits. One specific incident tortured me for years. Admittingly, its piercing wound now hurts much less, yet it is impossible to completely forget it. Occasionally a few past issues resurface, reminding me that I can be such a fool. In this case, it was my reckless decision over Argo.

That animal was a free spirit. A rather wild one. On early Saturday mornings, we were in the nearby park where soccer matches brought out a large crowd of folks from the Latino community later in the day. As there was absolutely no one around, Argo was allowed to run free. I felt pure joy watching him. He took off like a bullet, and when he cut a corner too fast, he sometimes tumbled over but would jump right back up and resume his wild sprint.

Of course, letting him off the leash was a no-no. Yet, this early morning weekend exercise was what he probably needed every single day. One morning after his wild run, the dog refused to come back to me. No matter how much I called out to him, he simply continued to move in the opposite direction, and the closer I got, the further off he ran. At some point, I simply turned around and began heading home. He was soon at my side.

We were now on the sidewalk in our beautiful community area. I was about to put his leash on him when a jogger on the street passed by us, and Argo went for her. Fortunately, I managed to grab him, and then apologized most sincerely. I didn't think much of it, but the jogger lived nearby and once approaching my residence, a dog catcher arrived. The woman insisted on giving me a fine. My attempt to explain the dog's needs, my assurance that we left our house super early when no one was anywhere nearby, and my apologies simply fell on deaf ears. That is why I walked away and told her to go fuck herself. Big mistake.

In no time at all, our front door was being pounded on. I was in the basement. Francesca opened it, and two policemen were there, quite ready to pounce on anyone not complying with their orders. I came forth, explained and apologized, but now had two strikes against me as the officers were not listening. Both officers wore grim faces. Fortunately, it was my wife's lovely accent and polite manners which saved the day. If not, they would have certainly carted me off to jail.

It was then that I decided to find Argo a better home. Our kids hardly ever walked him once they got in from school. When Francesca and I would arrive home from work, usually around six, the poor beast would immediately dart out of the front door desperately needing to pee. The neighbor was not very pleased with this. And although not often, when home alone, at times, his anger got vented on some of the furniture.

As my boss raised dogs to show in competitions, I consulted her. She was certainly knowledgeable and agreed emphatically that our dog would have been better off in a home like hers. With no one about for miles around, that dog could have happily run free there. Her advice was to contact a placing agency that would find the dog a good home and perhaps one similar to hers. Of course, my wife and kids were totally against it. However, nothing changed at home and Argo continued his solitary indoor activity every weekday.

Eventually, a dog-placing agency came through. They assured me they had found a perfect fit. The family receiving our dog actually had a Rhodesian Ridgeback. They also lived in the suburbs but in an area with lots of land all around. So, I was informed, and that is why I gave him up after being assured we could see him from time to time.

It was Ricky who handed him over late one afternoon. He watched the husband and wife lead the dog into their SUV, and as the vehicle was parked with the rear facing our house, my son saw the animal staring at him through the back window. Argo appeared to be trying to understand just what was happening. On hearing this, I felt awful and tried to convince myself to have acted in his best interest.

Several months later, we called to inquire about visiting. The news was not good. The woman asked us not to go. Argo outright refused to be put in his cage. Well, I now discovered they would cage their dogs in the basement before they went off to work in the morning. Apparently, ours refused to be jailed so easily, and he had bitten the owner twice. He had also bitten the neighbor's dog. So, a somewhat frustrated voice stated that our visit would only make matters worse.

What occurred next is both mystical and somewhat baffling. Very soon, almost all my nightly dreams included Argo. He needed to be rescued. That seemed to be the gist. My task was to seek a better home for him. This nightly message was revealed to Francesa while driving to work one morning. My wife looked at me a bit startled and informed me she was having similar dreams. I so stupidly and irresponsibly put it aside and attempted to not dwell on it.

One Saturday I was home alone. My family was in Italy attending Maria's wedding. I called to inquire about the dog hoping for better news. This time around the woman's voice was very unpleasant. When I asked if Argo had made any progress, she responded in a rather incensed tone, "We put him down." These words shocked me, and quite foolishly, I asked if that meant they had killed him. My question infuriated the moron, and she accused me of having abused the dog.

I slammed down the phone. My fury knew no limits. I cursed out the entire American race. Such uncivilized barbarians! From their extermination of the natives whose land we sit on, to making people slaves, and everything in between and after, they deserved to be punished for their fucking ignorance. My anger called on God, any God, all Gods, to punish those fuckers who had killed the dog. But almost immediately I realized, that indirectly, unknowingly, I had killed him. For, sometimes, I can be such a pathetic jerk.

Chapter 177

My daily trips to the coffee shop were still on, however, Justin was no longer with us. He was certainly missed. His girlfriend had moved to Spain to attend university, and he was there for her but also to paint away for dear life. Joe was all mine to enjoy on most days, and there was also a new guest among us.

Karen was slim and very pretty. The young Black woman in her late twenties worked at a well-known law firm nearby. It was her enthusiasm for all things which quickly captured my attention and soon most of me. Perhaps she was a tad too opinionated, yet she stated her facts so brilliantly, and the more she smiled while speaking, the more I found to like.

One weekend, we three were scheduled to meet up in Georgetown. Joe had suggested catching a popular movie, and our rendezvous was the bookstore on M Street. It was a bit early when I arrived, but Joe was already present, and he insisted we take a walk. We headed toward the Key Bridge, but not to cross it, and my friend was chatting quite lively and endlessly when suddenly, a dark sky threatening to unleash a downpour emerged.

The unexpected weather forced us to take shelter. We were now in front of a clothing store under its small triangular ridge by the entrance, and almost immediately a stranger joined us. He was wet but very happy to be there among us. We three would stay put for some time as the rain pelted the pavement. My coffee buddy was providing a bit of entertainment, and, of course, he soon extended an invitation to the new guy among us to tag along to the nearby cinema.

Eventually, there were three of us heading to the bookshop. Karen looked quite sharp, had the smarts to keep a small umbrella with her, and once she shook hands with the newcomer, off we went. Unfortunately, upon exiting the bookstore, another powerful downpour attacked us. We four dashed across the street to the nearest restaurant, sitting right next to the oldest house in D.C. It was our immediate shelter, and considering the circumstances, we chose to eat now and see a later show hoping the weather would allow it.

Our guest had little knowledge of the film we intended to watch, so Joe took over. Cinema was his personal encyclopedia. He even assessed the critics' review. And we soon touched upon the idea that films too far ahead of their time often fail to be appreciated, and yet no one could think of one. Well, our food arrived, our chat expanded, and we even splurged on dessert and an after-dinner coffee as the rain was not letting up.

All proceeded well until the check arrived. After looking it over, I passed it to our guest and asked if my calculation by four was correct. That is when Joe threw us a curve ball. He said, "No, split it by two." This brought on an innocent smile from Karen, sitting across from the speaker, but our newcomer's face frowned some and his expression appeared slightly annoyed. After all, could this have been a staged encounter?

Again, my request to divide the amount by four went out. I knew I would have to pay for Joe. At times he was a bit of a leech, but Karen would certainly pay her share. Unfortunately, the same comment followed and now, Victor, such was the newcomer's name, looked a bit concerned and very suspicious. It forced me to grab the bill and simply ask him for his share, and Karen gave me hers.

Things ultimately worked out just fine. They usually do. The bill got paid, with me paying two portions, and we finally got to the cinema for a late show and enjoyed a great flick. That unfair suggestion, stated so matter-of-factly, was registered and put aside. Yet a few weeks later it was Karen who brought it up. She and I had met on a Sunday at Dupont Circle. We shared a coffee in the late afternoon and soon enough she delicately provided a brief explanation.

Just for the record, my being with Karen was due to having gained a bit more freedom at home. After we two revisited the film we had thoroughly enjoyed, and later mentioned Joe's embarrassing gesture, she shared the unthinkable. I can be so naïve. She admitted having questioned Joe on his inappropriate act one morning when at the coffee shop. He had simply stated that there was nothing wrong with taking advantage of a rich guy like me.

Well, my generosity toward the somewhat scruffy person terminated immediately! And he certainly got the message. Whenever catching up at Borders', absolutely nothing but a bit of my time came his way. Such were our morning encounters now, and soon enough he was hardly ever present in the morning. Yet one late afternoon, the lad quite caught me off guard.

My trip to the bookstore was to make a phone call. It seemed a tad inappropriate doing it at my cubicle. Once finished using the public phone in an open area, and having hung up, I turned and stared at the old venal legionnaire himself. Joe immediately inquired about my chat. Just who was I on the phone with? I wondered how much he may have actually heard. Oh well, my reply brought on the greatest laughter ever heard coming out of a human being, for I said, "The maid."

Chapter 178

All the talk at the office was about a new accounting system. Ours was not running well due to technical problems. This created a period of downtime, as we could not accomplish our work, but we also had some concerns over its long-term use. And the only systems guru from the firm it was purchased from, who had to constantly come by to bring it back to life, was not always available.

Therefore, it was time to bring on a new system. Our manager had embarked on providing the agency the benefits from new automated systems. She was certainly well-informed and quite optimistic. Some of the new accounting systems catering to the government could supposedly provide reports required by the U.S. Treasury with just the push of a button. Such was the news shared.

Very soon, there were meetings to attend. They addressed the many challenges faced in switching systems. We knew it would not be easy, but no one had been through the process, and therefore, we were a tad naïve. One of the technicians whom I had once supervised had some serious concerns over what was being proposed. She questioned if some of our present procedures would function adequately with the new system. However, the young lady was often interrupted, then silenced in a rather brusque fashion by two supervisors who were old timers.

It was not long before the day of reckoning arrived. And in switching from old to new came a ton of problems. It is impossible to point fingers at anyone. However, it soon became apparent that some of that technicians' fears should have been taken into consideration. Most of the data being entered was continuously being rejected, and for all the fixes the new system's technical experts could provide, new and worse issues would soon surface.

The office was a mess. There were boxes full of documents lined up alongside people's cubicles and scattered about elsewhere. It was decided we would eventually enter that data once we somehow got over the complex issues being encountered and unresolved. Oh, by the way, the idea of reports being generated instantaneously was completely laid to rest. Thank goodness David had created some superb spreadsheets which kept both of us generating valuable data that were definitely not available by simply pushing a key on the PC.

After several months of pervasive headaches, I decided to bail out. And why not? For some time now, my lack of initiative bothered me, and my fine sense of accomplishment was completely gone. So, my resume was updated and sent out with the intent of finding a similar position in accounting. A promotion was not necessary, and my overall strategy was to remain with the new agency until retirement. Also, if the chance to manage a team was part of the new gig, it would be a challenge I was quite ready to take on.

Chapter 179

If you are familiar with the line "It was the best of times, it was the worst of times," I should have proclaimed it. Only the first line would have been left out. Things at home were bad. Perhaps it is best to define it as a continuous predicament over one of our sons.

Ricky was now a full blooming teenager. He had miraculously graduated from high school and had recently found work as a waiter. The restaurant which employed him was a bit far from home, and without a car, he would never get there. Oh, the glory of suburban living. Consequently, our new Honda, about a year old, was given to the young lad by yours truly, and a new one was purchased, by yours truly. Now, we three working family members could get to our jobs.

By the way, the salesperson at the dealership was shocked to receive a personal check for selling an auto. He informed me it required a disclosure to local authorities which would investigate the matter as suspicious money. Their task was to determine if drug deals or money laundering were part of my activities "on the side."

Our son's employment lasted only a few months. He was soon at home seeking another job but nothing suitable ever came his way. However, with me there was a more concerning issue, and it was his exuberant lifestyle. He was out every night. The young lad woke up at about noon, immediately lit a cigarette, took a Coke out of the fridge, and began what was the left of the day. It was a bit painful witnessing this. Apparently, things were too far gone.

I continued to keep to myself. My past concerns over our son had led to arguments with my wife. Then one day, out of the blue, I was given a direct order. It shocked me to the core. For it was delivered from the very source devoted to his excessive freedom. I was in the living room reading when Francesca approached me. Her facial expression said it all—she appeared on the verge of a nervous breakdown. The woman insisted Ricky needed to leave. That is, she was throwing him out, but his dad would do it.

It seemed wrong to me. Making him move out. Yet, all my attempts to convince her such a plan could be counter-productive were disregarded. I thought he could get himself into serious trouble or end up hurting himself. I voiced my concerns, but it did not matter. She was adamant, he had to go. Goodness gracious, we could no longer agree on anything. So, I gave our son the unpleasant news, but he took it quite well. The older teen did not object or attempt to make amends but simply phoned a friend. About an hour later, he placed a small bag full of clothes in his car and drove off.

My son's departure totally devastated me. I had absolutely no one to turn to. A constant thought began torturing me like a thorn in my head. My decision to return to the U.S. was a huge mistake! We had been so happy in Italy, and this would probably not have occurred there. Just as daunting was my lack of any concern or intimacy with the woman I had sworn to love and cherish forever. We were simply two strangers living under the same roof.

Chapter 180

I had finally found a job, or so I thought. The Drug Enforcement Agency invited me for an interview. My goodness, it had gone as well as could be expected. Two accountants questioned my work experience, both were super polite, and upon explaining my past and present accounting work, including my overall career plans, it seemed to have impressed them.

Their personnel office offered me the job. That is why I then made a second visit to their headquarters, which was, at that time, located near the DoD IG. My new trip entailed taking a drug test, but also, totally unknown to me, to fully expose any possible use of drugs in the past. And that, my friends, is where I truly fucked up.

Now allow me to express some things which baffle me. When I joined the army in Vicenza, no one asked me about any drug use. And although my four years of soldiering did encounter a few problems, once beyond them, my troubled past was completely buried. Why, even the Department of Defense Inspector General's Office had hired me without a single question regarding this issue. It was when joining the National Archives that someone grilled me. An inspector from GSA asked me a million questions. So, I came clean and had even specifically stated to the young lady, "My past is past." She, however, recommended against my being hired. Fortunately, the director, an intelligent woman, had already hired me and had no intentions of letting me go, regardless of the nonsense being advocated.

It was impossible recalling what I had told the GSA snoop. Anyhow, fingerprints and urine were taken, and then a DEA employee escorted me to a small room. He handed me a pen and a form and instructed me to fill in all information regarding any drug use in my life. Hmmm! It truly put me in a bind. That is why I simply let it all hang out.

Well, just how an ex-outcast like me in the bosom of DEA's accounting office could jeopardize the agency is a mystery. My function was not to bust anyone. Oh well, several weeks went by and no word from anyone with a reporting date. Eventually, a letter arrived at home informing me that the position had been canceled. And while taking it with a grain of salt, my curiosity had me consult a lawyer at the EEOC. She was adamant that once properly rehabilitated, an ex-addict cannot be treated like a criminal, and so it was only right to take them on, but in the end, it seemed best to avoid fighting city hall. Besides, I never go where I am not wanted.

My search for work was back on. It was the Department of the Treasury which eventually hired me. Go figure! The position was with the Departmental Office, the very institution which supports the Secretary of the Treasury and his staff. The interview had gone incredibly well, as Julian Di Stefano had verbally demonstrated his initiative to excel.

Now, something peculiar occurred on my first day at work. After being in-processed by the personnel office, I was at my desk. The office accounting guru came over and provided me a form to fill out. Once that document would get processed, I could begin to use our accounting system. It was soon filled out, and I was informed it would be forwarded to an office in West Virginia, which is why I inquired when I would be able to use the system. He told me it would take two weeks to process the form.

It seemed incredible! And a tad ridiculous. Without access to the system, my being there seemed useless. Sure, there were other things to do in familiarizing myself with the office's processes and procedures, but it was still far from what mattered most. I didn't want to upset my boss, a quiet but observant manager, but I decided to meet with him that afternoon so he could hear me out.

After stating the facts, my question came forth. Why wasn't that form faxed to me once I had accepted the position three weeks ago? It would have been returned the same day, several weeks before my arrival. I would now have access to the accounting system, it being crucial in performing most of my tasks. The man in front of me had a serene smile on his face. He replied, "I knew you were a smart person the moment we interviewed you."

Well, I did not necessarily share his affirming opinion. Need I say more? We soon touched on another subject before I returned to my desk to consider what to do for the rest of a very long day.

Chapter 181

Spring had just arrived. We had entered a new century the year before. It was always this time of the year that I purchased airline tickets for our summer trip to Italy. Also, there were the other expenses associated with traveling abroad.

This year, everything was on hold. Francesca was expecting friends from Vicenza but could not yet confirm their arrival date. Since no travel plans had been fully hatched for us three, I chose to go alone. And as strange as it may seem, her guests arrived the day before my departure. They were certainly your typical Italians, happy folks with plenty to say on just about everything. Anyhow, my wife took me to the airport and sent me on my way.

I stayed with my mother and Alessandro for two nights. My goodness, the man had aged tremendously. Yet the two seemed so good for each other, although occasionally my mother still made herself heard over any circumstance which may have annoyed her. I left for Bergamo, which is close to Milano, and it was once the home of the famous Gaetano Donizetti. His opera L'Elesir D'Amour was one of my favorites. It was not his museum that totally captured my heart, but it was more the older part of the city on a hill, called Citta Alta. There the splendid architectural might of the Venetian empire still stands out so distinctively.

My next stop included Lake Garda and my once favorite city Verona. Then it was on to Ravenna for a few days, and soon enough, Vicenza. If not mistaken, I believe my family members arrived two days later. They were staying with Francesca's sister. And Wow! When I saw wife, my mind became hazy. The woman looked super gorgeous! I mean like very sexy and vibrant. And unless my intuition was failing me, her inviting smile seemed to indicate she wanted me, like in physical passion, and right now. Just what the hell was going on?

Anyhow, my love endeavors would have to wait. The following day, my return flight out of Milano had me going home. So, my family and I would eventually see each other back at our residence. Of course, while traveling, my mind debated if that woman's vibrant attitude would still be shining so thoroughly strong once back under the same roof?

My flight was quite uneventful but not too long. However, once home and settling in, something unexpected shocked me. It was while discarding lots of junk mail, plus opening a few letters with bills to pay, that a letter from Bianca stood out. Yes, the very soul who labeled inner pain as talent par excellence. It seemed absurd receiving correspondence from this woman. Something within advised me to throw it out. Instead, it was put aside for several days.

In my mind, for all her faults or inconsistencies, my wife was the better woman. The person who had done so much for me. Once we began to live together, and she got acquainted with my past, the woman insisted my drug use needed to be truly finished. But more importantly, she had accepted me, rudderless as I was when leaving the army and not a clue as to what came next. Wasn't I a better person because of her?

On the other hand, all these thoughts could not change our present circumstances. Life at home was no life at all. For the most part, we simply lived under the same roof. And now that fucking letter made me realize I still had feelings for Bianca. But it seemed so wrong! Her mother's words dished out twenty years ago came back as if to restate the importance of keeping my distance. My goodness, an unsteady sense of doom overtook me as I opened that letter.

The writing did nothing to imply her true intentions. A few words written casually indicated her present situation. She occasionally ran into someone who knew us, and much was inquired about me which she could not answer. Apparently, she had kept my address from the package sent for Francesco some years back. Her e-mail address was included, along with the typical "Give a shout when you have time."

How was it possible to still desire this person? Wasn't it just physical? And weren't my physical pleasures outside home being cared for at an all-time high? Nevertheless, a few days later, an e-mail was sent out. A slight feeling of guilt persisted. My mind compared it to when I stole from Macy's, and how my inner being eventually grasped how sinful my actions were. Oh well. So began a new line of communication, and a week later, she called me at home, and we spoke most passionately for hours.

Chapter 182

The Treasury Building on Pennsylvania Avenue next to the White House was not where I worked. Our office was located in a building on a side road facing Lafayette Park, and being by that park was a blessing in disguise. Almost every day at lunchtime, whether sunny, cloudy, or rainy, a brief walk there had become an indispensable trip.

Upon starting my new job, I consulted a supervisor who had also just been hired. What was his opinion in summarizing things in general? His response was, "A comedy of errors." Oh well, I was now a supervisor. At the interview, the director brought to my attention that my staff would consist of contractors and federal employees. Incredible, but the circumstances were such that the contractors, who had been hired over a year ago to replace federal employees, were now on their way out.

It seems someone had proposed contractors over federal workers as a beneficial scheme. Money would be saved and output would improve, but the office soon found out quite differently. Consequently, my now managing employees, new ones who were learning their tasks and our processes, and the ones departing, some not so keen on doing much work, was quite a challenge.

The Payables Branch in Accounting for the Departmental Office was my new home. It consisted of myself, an accountant, and seven technicians. On paper that is. In reality, there were six technicians—three on their way out, two new ones, and one who had been there for ages. And if I thought the accountant would be helpful in assisting me with becoming acquainted with the office's processes and the accounting system, it was not to be.

She had applied for my position but had been rejected. It would have meant a promotion for her. So, my days were busy trying to resolve various problems, but if in need of her knowledge, she was usually on the phone or at someone else's desk chatting. It became apparent that there was also a peculiar problem within that office. We supervisors and managers were of a different color than the personnel we oversaw. It was never actually said to me, but it was indirectly brought to my attention that our office was considered a club for "White men."

Work-wise, the branch was in deep shit. A new process for our credit card payments caused confusion and frustration, and the technicians had given up trying to make it work. They outright refused to process the monthly credit card bills, which may be the reason why the previous supervisor had abandoned ship. Nevertheless, the total monthly credit card invoice was paid and timely, but the individual charges making up the whole were not posted to the pertinent accounts. They were, instead, posted to a suspense account as a total. My first task was to somehow fix this mess.

Fortunately, there was an accountant to lean on—Terry. He was the office expert and a great person to work with. Of course, my staff would never have agreed with this as he had developed that new process which drove them bonkers. He claimed that the issue was with the edit checks. Too often, the complexity of the coding created various problems that were not so easy to fix. Plus, a few new glitches and a bit more confusion had brought other concerns throughout the entire branch.

Regardless of my priorities, it seemed best to move slowly. There were plenty of problems to contend with, and my phone rang continuously all day. Vendors called to inquire why their invoice or invoices had not been paid or were paid so late. The technicians had various excuses, which sometimes required I analyze the account to assure myself that all the invoices charged to the account were correct. Also, my boss would occasionally come over to request information which was never easy to come by.

I found myself stretched to the limits. The accountant in my section refused to budge from her "no can do" attitude. She was also on a buddy-buddy basis with one of the contractors, whom I found somewhat pompous. Occasionally, however, my necessity for information had me at her desk. She would become rather solemn upon seeing me arrive, but my friendly and polite interruption generated the information needed or at least pointed me in the right direction.

Consequently, Terry became crucial for explanations on the system's functionality and our processes. He knew it all, was very willing to help, and assisted me most pleasantly whenever necessary. My workday began at seven and always ended at six. On Saturdays, I was at my desk from eight to two or three in the afternoon, attempting to put order there. Sundays were my only days free from pressure and frustration, especially seeing how little progress was being made. And yet giving up was not an option.

Soon, yours truly had the pleasure of firing one of the contractors. She was super talkative, thick as a brick, and did not convince me over an issue. It was an invoice she tried to pay. She had given it to the young lady who registered the invoices into the system. The invoices were then sent to the approving authority, that is, the office which had incurred the charge and needed to approve the payment. In this case, it was never done. When asked about it, she swore up and down the invoice had come from the office which we would bill for the payment.

Well, I took myself to see the person responsible for authorizing the invoice to be paid. She had not seen it nor had the contractor in question, and she sort of looked at me as if to insinuate, "What kind of a shop are you running." That is why, with pleasure in my eyes, perhaps not so much in my heart, the contractor was informed that her services were no longer needed. And whom do you think she immediately shared this with? Oh well, it always feels good to win without fighting.

My satisfaction was short-lived. At the contractor's desk, now gone, were a lot of outstanding invoices, quite a few for past phone bills. For all my research done on Saturdays, nothing clarified the matter at hand. Soon enough, after contacting the phone company and faxing some of the bills, they sent me the relevant information. Those invoices were not ours. They belonged to the Secret Service, which was then under the Treasury Department. So, after speaking to the responsible person at the Secret Service, off they went, and I could now attend to other crap.

Terry was truly great. He accepted and agreed on my strategy to resolve the credit card debacle. It was a simple plan, and it consisted of a two-pronged approach. First, one of the new employees hired, who joined the branch a week later, would become the credit card specialist and process all new monthly bills and nothing else. Terry agreed to train her, oversee her work, and share all pertinent information with me. After all, he had designed the new process and was rather proud of it.

The second phase was to assign a task to my accountant. She would back all credit card charges out of the suspense account and charge them to their proper ledgers. It would require quite a bit of work, plenty of research, and it would certainly keep her busy for a while and at her desk. Of course, it was necessary for Terry to also oversee the second task when necessary, and that gentleman agreed wholeheartedly!

A letter outlining the assignment and briefly describing how to proceed was completed. It was very specific as to intent, time frame allowed, and who was her point of contact if she stumbled into problems. It went out via e-mail in late afternoon after everyone had already gone home. I then headed to my abode feeling a bit certain that life at work was starting to look up.

The following morning, the accountant was at my desk. She did her best to hide her frustration, although it was still flung my way, but I saw only one face. It had surrendered to a reality. After so many years of working in this branch and wanting recognition, now was the time to prove herself. My banner imposed its request, which practically said, "Let's see how good you are." The woman was not a happy camper, but what can I say?

Well, three months later, things had certainly improved some. The new employee, Germaine, who now processed the monthly credit card bills, was doing a fantastic job, and absolutely nothing was being charged to the suspense account. The newbie had immediately grasped the process and very quickly began performing with little assistance from Terry, who was now proclaiming, "See, it really wasn't that hard."

Not only was that issue laid to rest, but there was other good news. My accountant was making great progress. One day, she happily informed me she would soon be finished. Plus, there was a rumor that she was looking for another job and perhaps had found one. How bizarre. Sometimes when it rains, it pours. And I, just like Noah, felt quite safe knowing clear skies would soon follow.

Chapter 183

I was relaxing in the living room one evening enjoying a book when I noticed Eric heading to the entrance door. He opened it and greeted his brother with a light dose of a mysterious whim about him. My reading had been interrupted upon seeing Ricky entering.

We greeted each other cordially. His expression revealed concern. Rather quickly, the two brothers headed to the basement to see their mom who was watching TV. I returned to my reading but had a tough time discarding my uneasiness.

It would be a few days later when the visit got demystified. I had just returned to my desk from another long and time-consuming managers' meeting—some seemed a tad unnecessary, especially as there was always so much to do at my desk. I found several messages on my phone. One was from Ricky. He apologized to me and seemed slow in finding words. He informed me that he was at JFK and about to board a plane to leave the country.

I had to work late that day so my wife drove home alone in late afternoon. Another baffling problem required an analysis which was extensive and kept me in the office very long. Eventually, once home, my request for an explanation as to what had occurred with Ricky fell on deaf ears. Francesca could hardly speak, refused to answer my question, and once again appeared to be on the verge of a breakdown.

It was Eric who later shared the news with me. His brother was on his way to Vicenza. He would now live at his aunt's house. Inquiring for more information led to naught. For my son now insisted this was all he knew. And as my spouse looked like she was a million light-years from home, I had no choice but to let the matter rest.

Fortunately, my motorcycle had become my new drug! The Virginia countryside always put all my worries far behind as wind and speed soothed my sail. On my ride that weekend my loneliness made itself felt very strongly. Eric and his mom had their books. My once devoted lady friend from my previous office had moved on, and Justin had recently returned from Spain but had soon vanished. Even Joe had become a person in my past. I just felt so all alone.

Chapter 184

Tuesday morning, September 11, 2001. Along with the other office employees, I was attending a meeting in a building in an area close to the White House. It was where the personnel for the Thrift Savings Plan, the government's investment program for federal employees, worked. Their large modern conference room had brought us there.

Our office difficulties and tribulations had become a problem to be reckoned with. Management had hired consultants to work with us and fix the mess. A much-needed action, at least in my opinion, for at times nothing improves if changes are not forced down people's throats. Several competent and polite consultants had worked with us for a few weeks and were now providing their solutions to change our processes and, hopefully, our output and morale.

This morning was the final phase of the task, and the lead consultant was addressing the main topics. It became a bit difficult for me to pay attention as there was some kind of chaos in the nearby streets. One siren followed another and the blaring noise continuously streamed into the building. I asked myself if everyone was driving erratically and causing an abundance of accidents. Or maybe a few employees throughout the area were getting horribly ill at their desks? It seemed odd!

Soon after, our top director came into the room. He approached the podium and interrupted the speaker, first whispering something to him but then making an announcement. The Twin Towers in New York had come under a terrorist attack, and the Pentagon had just been hit. Now the message was clear, yet it was obscure. For a moment, my mind envisioned individuals with guns blazing away at employees at those two towers. How could such a thing have possibly happened?

One of our employees began to scream and cry. Her sister worked at the Pentagon, and she was shaken to the core. We were immediately dismissed and told to go home, but most of us needed to get back to the office to retrieve our briefcases and other items. Two of us assisted the hysterical young lady and convinced her to leave with us. The conference room was now practically empty.

Outside that building was a world turned upside down. The Metro rail lines had been closed, so everyone was leaving the city any way possible. Cars, pickup trucks, vans, and taxis were overcrowded with passengers. People on motorcycles and a few bicyclists were getting around the tons of people on foot in the streets. It seemed like total chaos reigned supreme as large number of frightened folks scurried around.

Back at my desk, the phone line was dead. I sent an e-mail to my wife informing her of my departure but was uncertain she would get it. It was time to grab everything and move on. As I did not know of my wife's whereabouts, but assumed the IMF had also dismissed its employees, my now casual walk had me moving but uncertain as to my destination. My feet carried me quite some distance and soon had me heading to Rosslyn.

I was now on the I 66 Bridge and there was massive traffic. It became apparent our nation had never prepared for something like this. I once read that our main highway systems were built in the 1950s under the Eisenhower administration. It was mostly done to ensure a means of evacuating the cities in case of a nuclear strike. Well, this chaotic madness certainly outlined the overwhelming fear caused by unexpected attacks.

A taxi eventually took me home. Francesca was upstairs in our bedroom watching TV. There were scenes from one of the Twin Towers. It was simply dreadful looking at what had occurred. Some office employees were looking out from the area where windows had been, and we both immediately sensed they were doomed. Then, we again witnessed those planes flying into the buildings, and it almost brought tears to my eyes, especially recalling my dad's last job was in one of the two buildings, but that now seemed like ages ago.

Eric soon returned from school. There were three of us now watching the news covering the horrors of the day. It would be later in the evening when I managed to contact my brother. Finally, some means of communication were available, and we spoke for a while. We both found it hard to believe that this could have occurred. Then Peter said what the entire nation was probably thinking, "Oh, we'll get them. We will get them. They will pay for this."

The following morning, the classical radio station gave us some news in the car. The announcer always managed to nicely summon up world events in just a few minutes. Along with a brief review of the previous day's occurrences, a rather bizarre statement was included as if to finalize the news. According to sources reporting from Afghanistan, a spokesperson for the man responsible for the attack, Osama bin Laden, claimed he had absolutely nothing to do with it.

This made no sense whatsoever! I had to ask myself why a man who so hated us, our lifestyle, and everything we represented was not taking credit for his barbaric acts? Wouldn't he be a hero in the eyes of the many people throughout the planet who harbored nothing but contempt for the U.S.? And then it registered so quickly. Just like the assassination of JFK, we would never know the truth.

Two weeks after that horrendous attack, I flew to Venice. My original departure date was a few days after the eleventh, but the event forced a closure of all airports for several days, and so my trip was rescheduled. Perhaps it was ten days later when I made the flight.

All the passengers on board were solemn to the core. Absolutely no one seemed happy to be traveling. Silence suffocated the cabin of the plane. It was once food was served that my light sense of humor elicited some nasty looks. As dinner trays were being handed out, a baby sitting a few rows up front from my seat began to shriek uncontrollably! His pitch was loud and clear to all around. When the hostess handed me my food, I simply smiled and said,

"Come on, the food isn't all that bad." If looks could kill, I would not be informing you now.

We arrived at the airport in Brussels. Having a few hours layover before proceeding to Venice, I became comfortable on a seat next to an elderly couple. The Economist, which I read religiously, got the best of me as the world faded into the background. It may have been an hour later when I looked up to take a break. My eyes witnessed a rather peculiar scene. A large family, including a short, heavy-set African woman with five small children and a lot of suitcases all about them, settled in close by.

It is impossible to recall exactly how things occurred. At some point, the entire family moved on, but the suitcases stayed put. At first, it did not raise my antennas at all, but a bit later that scene began to stand out like a sore thumb. My inquisitive mind seemed to dwell on a few questions. Just where had they gone? And what about all that unattended luggage? I resumed my reading, however, about twenty minutes later, still seeing no one by all that luggage, yours truly grew very concerned.

My legs brought me over to the nearest bathroom. I asked the first woman exiting the lady's room if she had seen an African woman with a few children inside. One eyebrow raised as she stared at me without responding. After my brief explanation, she assured me there was no one inside fitting that description. I did not want to panic, at least, not just yet. My eyes began to look in all directions while my legs brought me a bit further to see if that motley crew was anywhere nearby. No sir. It was like they never existed.

I stopped the first airport personnel in uniform passing by. My concern became his problem as we two walked over to the area I had been occupying. The moment the employee saw the suitcases his cell phone came out and he began to speak in his native tongue. I had no idea what he was saying, but I could hear the agitation in his voice. In no time at all, three security guards and two civilians were among us, one now questioning me regarding the missing family.

I disclosed a description of the woman and her children. The area was immediately sealed off. Everyone there was forced to move very far from those suitcases. Some police officers had arrived, and yes, the place was now jumping. And Julian was at the center of attention! Folks chatted wildly as the airport personnel were relaying to others what was being done. It must have been five minutes later when the missing family made their entrance.

They were walking rather slowly and were probably curious seeing so many people to one side of the large area. Although it was apparent their suitcases were the center of attention, this may not have immediately registered with the indifferent mom. The officers who had been talking to me went over to the nonchalant hefty traveler, and let's just say they were not happy campers. However, the woman did not appear to grasp what all the fuss was about.

In no time at all, things returned to normal. Once again, my magazine was open, my nose stuck in it with me feeling a bit foolish. At some point, I stopped reading, looked up and glanced over to where the family sat. Oh well! An expression declaring coming over to smack me shot out immediately. It now seemed like a wise idea to explore the other side of the airport lounge. After all, I had brought enough excitement to that area for one day.

Chapter 185

Bianca met me at the airport. We embraced and kissed as if we had just seen each other the previous day. At first, her letter had bewildered me, but evidently my feelings for her had not changed much. However, those strong romantic sentiments of an era gone by were now quite different. That free playful attitude of mine was limited, somewhat cautious, and not rushing forward.

There was so much to catch up on. She drove us to a summer resort south of Jesolo Beach, which may have been Cavallino. The small quaint town had the beach right at the feet of the hotel. While my heart was not fully pounding, my physical addiction to this woman was still intact. Once in our room, we went at each other like two savages. My, how human bodies feast on the hunger of their suppressed mental cravings, and sex becomes that divine ritual, blessing all our inner desires.

We remained glued to each other most of the day. The following morning after breakfast and a stroll on the beach, we headed off to Venice. I was scheduled to meet Ricky in the afternoon as we had spoken on the phone the night before. It was now apparent he would again question why I dragged him out to Venice, and we were not getting together in Vicenza. And yet, he had sounded very happy to know that we would soon be together.

Venice's incredible dynamic past always pulls you in. Its history as a little empire is long behind, but its façade retains a small crown. We two newcomers enjoyed the narrow streets and hopping in and out of different souvenir shops while making our way to Piazza San Marco. Once there, we marveled at this city's prior maritime power which had ventured forth conquering quite a bit of the territory around it and even far from home, for all those splendid remnants of the past still looked so magnificent.

Eventually, we separated as I headed back to the train station to meet my son. In no time at all, we were together. Ricky looked so happy, and I was overjoyed to be there. After an exchange of pleasantries, I diplomatically delved into my concern for him and my curiosity as to what exactly prompted him to abandon the U.S.

Perhaps history does repeat itself. Not necessarily just on the world stage but even in personal family drama. Like I had many years back, my son had chosen to leave behind a most destructive lifestyle, which he now claimed was far behind him. He had no definite plans regarding anything, yet he felt certain things would work out, and even claimed he would never return to the U.S. This certainly surprised me, but I informed him that I was there to support him any way necessary.

We entered a coffee shop and enjoyed a good white wine. It was refreshing to be around him as his sense of humor, quick and clever, never ceased to entertain me. Unfortunately, when he inquired why I was not in Vicenza, I foolishly admitted to being with someone. It truly shocked him. His expression communicated a sense hurt. I later reflected on how a once dedicated family man had transformed himself into the present foolish monster.

After several wonderful hours together, Ricky and I separated. He was reassured we would talk again before my departure. I soon caught up with Bianca who was on her phone and appeared to be enjoying her chat. She was listening to Francesco who was relaying some news about his busy day with his band. Apparently, art was now second to music. The lad had formed a band and wrote all their tunes. A bit later, I also discovered he was the spitting image of me. Bianca admitted that throughout the years, whenever she looked at him, she saw me.

For the next few days, our passion never subsided once in our hotel room. Yet we now needed to part ways. She would return to Vicenza and back to work, and I would soon be heading home. It was in her car that I expressed my heartfelt desire. Could I possibly ever see our son? Hearing about Francesco was so heartwarming, and a few photographs were coming home with me, but I simply longed to see him and share a few words with him, even if only for a few minutes.

The woman's response floored me! She outright refused to ever bring us together. For it would destroy his entire world according to her. But I briefly asked myself just whose world would really be demolished. Then Bianca informed me that if I ever took the liberty to approach him and start a relationship, she would never see me again.

I could no longer talk. My spirit felt mortified. I simply sat there having finally fully grasped what a shallow selfish individual I had once been so madly in love with.

Chapter 186

Work at the office had certainly improved. New procedures I had implemented were holding steady, and my latest proposal was also in. A form to use in appraising the technicians' work received approval. The invoices sent for payment to the approving official would either pass, being free of errors, and get paid immediately, or get returned to be fixed. I now had a tool to evaluate my employees.

Anyway, an overabundance of SF 171s were inundating my workstation. Two positions needed to be filled, and it was a most tedious task reviewing the many federal resumes I had to contend with. Most of them were simply awful. The writing was atrocious, words were misspelled, some sentences made little sense, and truth be told, in my eyes, most applicants simply did not qualify to work in accounting operations. There was much to look at but little to appreciate.

One resume belonged to a certain Ray Resting. It was the best of the lot, and he was scheduled to be interviewed that afternoon. Well, the chap never showed up. Naturally, after waiting for about an hour, the personnel office was contacted to inquire of his whereabouts. The guy had not made it past the security guards at the entrance to our building. The only information shared was that he was taken away by the D.C. police. Well, you can imagine my concerns while going through some more unattractive paperwork.

Fortunately, a new CV grabbed my attention. Call me prejudiced or whatever, but it had a Japanese name. I instantly recalled the words of a sailor on my first ship as we took on cargo in Okinawa. We had been watching the longshoremen who worked non-stop when the man at my side remarked, "These people are truly amazing. They are so industrious, all of them, the whole lot." And that is why Hikari was in my office a few days later. She impressed me plenty and was hired immediately.

Two more workers were eventually taken on. Now the Payables Branch was complete. And it seems only right to share a few words about the young lady processing our credit card payments. Vanessa worked independently and all her inputs were perfect, every month. It led me to wonder just what had happened that the system had been hijacked and run to the ground. However, the young lady did occasionally get into scrapes with other Treasury employees over some work-related issues. Of course, I defended her as best as possible, and eventually the irate employee backed off some and accepted my apology over whatever had occurred.

Getting the facts was quite a challenge. My talented technician would clarify the story in a slow manner. She would then gradually pick up steam and become slightly agitated. Sometimes, she broke down and cried. Yes, as in someone who has been hurt and sheds tears to reflect their inner pain. So, my caring ways went out to her as I would immediately close my office door and begin to address her gently and listen most attentively.

It was apparent to me that the super religious single mom did not have an easy life at home. She had practically no friends in the office and kept a very low profile. Our long session would usually terminate with her expressing how much she appreciated a supervisor "who cares." And so all was fine for the day, and we would get back to our line of business until the next episode, which was always pretty much a rehash of the old one.

Aside from dealing with some minor issues at work, I would soon face major ones at home. My knowledge of modern technology is poor, and one time that got me into trouble. My wife somehow accessed my e-mail account. She immediately confronted me over the correspondence between myself and the woman in Vicenza. Confronted is incorrect. She took me on, and quite unexpectedly, the irate antagonist was not taking any prisoners.

My voice admitted my spirit had breached the unthinkable, but my mind questioned the present row. We two had sort of parted ways long ago, not officially, but almost. And never once was anything said about my lavish lifestyle. Well, except on one occasion. So why was this episode so intolerable? It was practically creating a war. For a few nights, verbal battles, pretty much all one-sided affairs, were turning ugly.

One evening the woman went completely mad. Fortunately, Eric was in the basement. Francesca and I were at the dinner table having finished eating most sparingly. She began to argue, her voice rising with each sentence, and soon started flinging dishes across the room. The woman walked out of the house, and as it was raining like mad, I followed and attempted to stop her. Her response came on like lightning as she started hitting me wildly and her face looked so vicious. After taking a few hits, she finally calmed down a bit and we returned indoors. Francesca then began to cry hysterically.

I moved out the following day. It was impossible to accept the mess I had created and felt certain she would have never forgive me. Yet, before leaving the house I was given an ultimatum, if I left, she would never take me back. It was on to Madalyn's place in late afternoon having spoken to her that morning. Explaining what brought me back was no easy pitch, but both rooms were free and the larger one became mine.

My host was an elderly woman who had never married. She had always appeared super serious and was no doubt very religious. I wondered if she had ever even been on a date. Of course, a brief and limited explanation of my return was given, and although appearing a bit suspicious, she made no comment. Oh well, it was back to a quiet and comfortable dwelling as we seemed to take up where we had left off.

I did have one concern—Eric. He was now in his mid-teens, and had always appeared mature and wise, yet something in me suspected he was terribly hurt by what had occurred and my leaving. It was all so bizarre to me. When we four had begun our stay in the U.S., never could I have imagined such a tragic fate taking us down. Life is so unpredictable, and we human creatures certainly make it so.

Chapter 187

My stay at the Treasury had begun in a slow but grand fashion. It went out like a light. After two years of giving the best of myself, I was falling apart at the seams. Not from work-related issues but rather from my personal life, which was totally out of whack. Slight bouts of depression came and went.

I couldn't blame my current predicament on that awful cure so far behind me. Yet sometime thereafter, I encountered entire days which left me feeling like I had no purpose, followed by brief periods of physical exhaustion. Such bouts were soon on and off more frequently. One day at work, for some unexplainable reason, something prompted me to throw in the towel.

My job had absolutely nothing to do with the fact that I quit. I simply went to the personnel office and gave them my resignation. The news shocked everyone. A few days later, one of the upper-level employees working for the top director came over to chat with me. We had collaborated on several projects, and she had once complimented my initiatives. She thought some of my ideas to improve office procedure were quite brilliant. Her curiosity had her at my desk.

Nothing was accomplished during our brief session. Interestingly, the charming woman insisted on having me for Thanksgiving dinner as the holiday was just a few days off. What a comforting and rewarding day that was. She and her husband were very subtle in their ways and never overstated their concern for me. Yet they did point out I was flinging away more than twenty years of government service. Was there a plan in place as to what came next?

My two saviors carried the day. It was impossible to ignore my foolishness. I still felt far from perfect, but the cheerful words and sober outlook coming from my hosts made me recognize how my inner light may occasionally dim but never darkens completely. Therefore, the following Monday, I went to the personnel office to terminate my idiotic decision.

So, just how did things get so out of hand? Well, it is far from easy to describe the agonizing internal pain, yet here are some instances which paved my way. And please stay with me. There is much to tell. My stay at Madalyn's was great, yet a small problem persisted. It was impossible to have anyone over. And this killed any chance to enjoy someone willing and very available but uncomfortable with going to a motel. A few women questioned why I did not enjoy the comforts of home in my own abode.

I eventually left Madalyn's place and again took up residence in Falls Church City. Eric had informed me that he would regularly come visit and stay a few days, so I rented a two-bedroom apartment. However, outside of one weekend visit, the young lad was hardly ever at my new digs.

Eventually, something urged me to do what others were doing—rent out the extra room. My first tenant was a young lady from Japan. It was a bit surprising to me, considering the Japanese are a very serious people, but the person inquiring about the room soon moved in. My, she was so fluent in our language and appeared so reserved. Ironically, she also worked for the same organization as my wife.

The new-bee certainly kept to herself. She would return home from work late and leave early in the morning. It was on some rare occasions that a co-worker, a middle-aged Asian woman, would come by to see her but never stayed long.

One evening, I had turned in a bit early and was awoken at three in the morning. There was some commotion going on in the flat, and as odd as it seemed, her friend was there.

My renter was upset because her co-worker's car had been towed from our parking lot. When the attractive lady had arrived was a mystery to me. But yes, her vehicle did not have the tag which mine had that would allow it to be parked on the premises of the building. That is why it was no longer where it should not have been to begin with. The two very unhappy ladies were now asking me how they would retrieve the car.

It took a few minutes to find the number to call. The issue was taken care of then and there, and who should pay was a completely straightforward matter to me. Yet the following day, it got rehashed through a series of e-mails. As my roommate did not own a car and had never asked about the parking situation, the pertinent rules were never revealed to her. So sorry!

However, she was now insinuating that I should pay, although the reason why was not forthcoming. That her friend was probably coming over frequently once I turned in at night, and that the two were enjoying each other's company as they saw fit, did not irk me at all. However, my paying for their mistake while they were having their fun was simply out of the question.

Oh well, there was a new lodger a few months after this dour incident. This time, a Chinese girl. Go figure! My curiosity attempted to grasp why Asian females were so comfortable moving in with an elderly White male lodger? Did I look harmless?

The new renter had a boyfriend. The guy was an American, Republican to the core, and on the few visits to our place, the opinionated gent shared his strong beliefs insisting there could be no other approach to problems in modern society. Oh well, at least this young lady was the opposite of the previous one for she was talkative, friendly, had no female friends stopping by, and boy could she cook!

Life at home was good. About a year later, my tenant inquired about her mom visiting. It was certainly not a problem, especially as I had assumed that as the mom was in China, she would probably arrive the following year, if at all. No sir, the woman was among us a few months later and arrived the very day prior to my leaving for Italy on holiday. As a matter of fact, I had gotten home late on a Friday night, and found it impossible to get into my apartment. The chain-lock was keeping me out. I rang the doorbell several times, and a very attractive woman, in pajamas, allowed me in. She said something in Chinese and returned to her daughter's bedroom.

I was soon off to vacation for three weeks in Italy, which flew by so quickly. As per past trips, this one had me arriving in Milano to spend a few days with my mother and Mr. Rossi. After that, I would explore some city or cities I was unfamiliar with and always revisited Vicenza, last on the list, of course. Once back home, I became somewhat acquainted with the new woman in my digs, who spoke no English.

It was now revealed to me she would stay longer than the few weeks previously proposed. This was fine with me. We three were now eating dinner together, and truth be told, it was quite a feast we sat down to. Made by that creative mom, and to me, Chinese food is so par excellence. I would have an amicable conversation with my roommate, and her mom received her daughter's translation. Now, as far as I was concerned, the mom could stay as long as she wanted! And the rent would stay the same! I am not a Christian in theory, but I certainly have the makings of one in practice.

That mom was quite a good-looking woman. Soon enough, she appeared to give me very warm smiles whenever she looked my way. Of course, there was a small problem. We could not communicate one iota, and believe me, we both certainly wanted to. Just the same, we got on with things, and soon enough her daughter began to pass most weekends at her boyfriend's place. Now what can I say? It simply happened. I am not sure it was not meant to. After all, if there was someone back home waiting for her, she certainly was in no hurry to get back to him.

My new companion and I could not converse, but we soon started going out together on weekends anyway. We learned to cope with our ongoing communication problem through body language and hand gestures. And while the friendship and warm intimacy settled in nicely, it finally came to an end for the mom returned to China. She had been with us almost a year. A few months later, the daughter moved to Florida, informing me her new job would do wonders for her career, and that her boyfriend was going with her.

What came next in my personal affairs was a series of misguided encounters. A few were pretty darn awful. I had discovered dating through the Washington Post. And yet not one single encounter led to a healthy date. My first date was with a woman a few years older than me, and although she was rather attractive, we failed to shine in each other's eyes in our take on things. When she said, "My fourth husband was so bad," it did not matter what the man failed at, I was no longer listening.

On one occasion, I found myself in the darkness of the Blackest neighborhoods in D.C. The young lady in front of me was not one bit as per the ad. She was a short and hefty Black girl, too many years my junior. Her immediate explanation of God in her life and the wonders of such a pure existence had me baffled.

What can I say? I soon ran mad. I began dating anyone and everyone from waitresses to teachers, university students, lawyers, an airline hostess, and even someone from the National Archives. Then it finally hit me. All I really wanted was sex, plain and simple. Just a body to feast on and nothing more. That carried me in a different direction, and dishing out money for it became okay, but it was soon apparent nobody would truly satisfy my unquenchable thirst for passion, even after a period of pornography galore. One day, my saga was plastered on my sad-looking face, Julian Di Stefano had truly hit rock bottom.

I decided to clean up. It would not be easy, but soon enough my life truly changed direction. Meditation took up a positive role again in guiding me forward. And it is truly odd how it came about. That mysterious word, never to be shared with anyone, flashed itself right in front of my eyes.

I had stopped at a traffic light in Arlington. There it was. It seemed incredible! A few feet ahead of me was that word. It was on a license plate, of all places. That very evening, sitting cross-legged, incense burning, silence all around, my mind relaxed for twenty minutes. Soon, a keener approach to life returned and so, less desires, less confusion, and, again, I even began to like myself.

Chapter 188

Two very significant events occurred simultaneously one week. I decided to try my hand at teaching English again, though I knew it required some preparation, plus an important phone call had come through. An ex-co-worker and friend from the National Archives, Patricia, had informed me that the agency needed an accountant. Would the job interest me at all?

Now, my lot at teaching came about quite incidentally. On early weekend evenings, it had become a habit to park my car in Rosslyn. I would walk across the Key Bridge heading to Georgetown, often to meet someone and have dinner. On a particular occasion, a sign caught my attention. It stood over a private entrance to a building on the corner near the bridge, and it read Inlingua. Something in me registered it and had me return to inquire about teaching.

One late afternoon, I stood at the counter facing a beautiful Asian female. The polite young lady greeted me with a smile. My "Are you looking for teachers?" was immediately answered with, "We are always looking for teachers." And so, I filled out a form, specified my interest in evening classes, and accepted her instructions to patiently wait for the school to contact me, which it did exactly a week later.

My first task was to observe teachers at work in two different evening classes. For the most part, it was a heaven-sent detail for those few hours with eyes wide open impressed me plenty. It most certainly laid out a roadmap as to a somewhat sound method to use in the classroom, but even more importantly, what not to do.

It feels wrong to criticize the first instructor. She certainly appeared to enjoy her work. The class was already in session when I joined it, and one of the students was reading from her textbook. Soon after, the teacher put the students in couples and had them practice asking a question and giving an answer, all at the same time. It was truly chaotic and even questionable if it accomplished anything. My immediate gut feeling voted down this method which appeared to have so little value.

The following evening, it was on to observe John. I entered as class began and immediately saw how much his students truly admired him. Watching this man teach, specifically how he made the students use the grammar in question, was like being enlightened from above. He was brilliant in creating a fun time and having the students interact wisely with each other. I now realized no note-taking was necessary as my approach in class would model itself on the methods of this truly talented person.

Inlingua gave me a class once the new semester began. My group consisted of a few students from South America, two South Koreans, a French girl, and a young guy from Italy. My Italian student approached me at break time to ask if I spoke his language, in Italian of course. My reply perhaps sounded a bit rude for I stated, in English, "To master any language, you must use it continuously and without thinking about what you are saying." He smiled, we shook hands and carried on in English, mine quite good while his had a long way to go.

Fortunately, I had found the perfect grammar book at the Borders Books Store. It cost practically nothing and came in handy for several weeks in guiding me to what soon became secondhand knowledge. The classroom books did the rest. They were fantastic, and so my evenings in class were productive and fun, for some of my wild comments brought a few witty responses, and just why I had not been able to do this back in Italy is anyone's guess.

Now, as far as that phone call regarding a new job. Years back, Patricia had arrived at the Archives a couple of months after me. She was in the office next to mine, and we soon became quite inseparable at work. She was friendly, laidback, and had such a positive attitude. It was her and Ted who were closest to me, and my interacting with them was very endearing.

I decided to return to the National Archives. After an intense interview, I was later hired. Unfortunately, a nasty flu prohibited me from starting work in late December. I was at my desk on the second day of the year 2003, still feeling ill but somewhat guilty for having been absent. Anyhow, Patricia was at my cubicle when our manager came by holding a letter. He was uncertain who in the section should get it, process it, and follow up on the gist of things. That is when my buddy simply said, "Give it to the new guy." Wouldn't you know it!

Once they left, the letter's contents were carefully read. It was from the Department of the Treasury requesting to see the Archives' plan to implement financial statements. It not only shocked me, but now had me feeling even more sick than I was. It was apparent that our manager, who should have understood what it entailed, had no clue. Oh well, a new year, a new task due in a year, and plenty of time to prepare. That is, if you know what you are doing.

It seems necessary to present some information regarding government budgetary accounting. The fiscal year begins on October 1 and ends the following year on the last day of September. Government organizations, from the departments to all the big and minuscule agencies, record the funds they need to spend in that time frame. For example, a contract for $100,000.00 is recorded in the accounting system and is called an obligation, and the government is obligated to pay that much to the merchant in question.

If with the final invoice, all expenses billed total $92,000.00, then things change. The budget office in question gets back $8,000.00 of funds, which can be used again if that amount is recovered in the fiscal year it was obligated. Once the fiscal year terminates, if the $8,000.00 was not recovered, then it is just a number in the accounting books, and it has no fiscal validity. Such was the scenario which got a politician thinking that money, real money, was to be had.

According to hearsay, it was in the halls of some military institution that said events came about. Someone in the political hierarchy discovered this and thought that these sums (the difference between what was obligated and expensed) over various past fiscal years and still recorded in the accounting system was money available to be spent, and it was quite a bit at that. Consequently, when explanations brought out the true picture, our so-called budgetary accounting system was deemed rather inadequate and certainly in need of improvement.

So, the federal government initiated its task to produce financial statements. It was in the 1990s when the Chief Financial Officers Act became a reality. Then the Federal Accounting Standards Advisory Board was established to develop the accounting standards that would guide the preparation of financial statements. It must have been recognized that implementing it across the entire federal government would have led to chaos, so fourteen departments and ten agencies were to go first, and everyone else would follow at a later date.

That infamous date was not too far off. After digesting the letter with the Treasury's request, I paid a visit to my manager. The following day we both met with the director, the office top dog, and we briefly discussed the issue. A few days after that, we three paid a visit to two accounting managers from across the hall, as they oversaw different systems. At some point, the whole lot of us went to see the Archivist. Now, that gentleman's observant look is still vividly implanted in my mind. From time to time, he simply stared at us most carefully as if to insure himself we were not exaggerating in laying out the new mission and its level of difficulty.

Our office certainly needed assistance in preparing its first financial statements. Therefore, the overall approach was to immediately bring in federal consultants to help us prepare the data required, while a new section would come on board with experienced federal employees to take on the new responsibility permanently. This is what we had accomplished in the first month of the new year.

Life back at the National Archives was good, but this time around I was in a cubicle. My first task was to prepare a statement of work (SOW) which would spell out exactly what the consultants needed to do in analyzing, proposing adjustments where necessary, and ensuring the agency met requirements in order to issue its first financial statements.

The SOW was finished in a month and went to our procurement shop. Hopefully, they would find the most qualified folks to assist us. It was time for me to breathe a bit easier, and a rather attractive accountant was assigned to work on other tasks with me. But, as no one there had been through this process, yours truly included, at times, exactly what needed to be done was anyone's guess, and although my assistant was sharp and helpful, she may have occasionally felt like she had been sent on a wild goose chase.

One of my first tasks was to review the various financial accounts the agency had. Wow, a bizarre problem presented itself immediately. One of the accounts which should have only held a couple of hundred thousand dollars in financial resources had a huge cash asset totaling in the millions. My inquiry led me to discover what a few employees referred to as, "Archives II money." For some time, that was all I heard. Occasionally, it almost sounded threatening. The more information that came my way, the more apparent it became that something was way off track.

It took quite a bit of digging to figure it all out. When I had first joined the Archives in D.C., plans for the construction of a new building in College Park, Maryland (Archives II) already existed. What came with it was an innovative and brilliant idea. The National Archives was granted authority to get a loan from a bank and use the funds to pay for the construction of the Archives II Building. Such a venture had never been done before.

The loan, like a mortgage, would be paid back by NARA (National Archives and Records Administration) through funds received in its annual appropriation. That is, the amount of money authorized by Congress for the agency's yearly expenses. The money borrowed was in a bank account and was continuously reinvested. That money was used to pay the invoices to the construction firm.

The final invoice had been paid years back. Whatever funds were left, continued to be invested and had now accumulated into millions of dollars. The investment authority we had received was solely to pay for the construction of the building we now occupied, so we should have stopped the investing process at this point. My opinion was stated in a meeting, but without barking too loudly for everyone in the room outranked me. Someone insisted the agency lawyer had reviewed the facts. And here we go again, it was "Archives II money."

What was being misinterpreted was a statement in the original authority. The legal jargon stated that using what remained in the bank account, once the building was completely paid for, could be for items to decorate the new building. Apparently, it was assumed that having a zero balance upon paying the last invoice was not possible. Therefore, what was left in the bank account could have been spent on Archives II then, but not now. The investing process should have been terminated once the last invoice was paid. Oh well, such were the circumstances creating much disagreement with the management authorities.

Chapter 189

A long and grueling work year finally came to an end. Plus, we had lost our manager since he found a promotion elsewhere. My old friend Dawn, now someone from my past, had stated it so brilliantly, "We are like mercenaries—ready to swear loyalty to the highest bidder." Well, he was replaced by one of the accountants on board, and she was both competent and gracious.

In the new year, everything moved so quickly. The consultants eventually finished their gig and were gone, and just what they did remained a mystery to me, but their input was given to our director. The National Archives had a new branch, completely independent of our office, with three experienced and highly skilled ladies to handle our agency's financial statements. They issued the agency's first statements and we got a "qualified opinion," which is big stuff in the world of accounting.

Oh, by the way, the new branch manager had met with me upon arriving. For what it is worth, we two reviewed the agency's accounts to make her aware of any particular issues. We, of course, tackled the suspicious money for Archives II. Obviously, she had more say than me, for the investing was stopped immediately and the millions of dollars associated with it were transferred to the Department of the Treasury to use as they saw fit.

Now being less in demand with regard to work, my travel plans had me going to the other side of the planet. Perhaps it is best to explain why. Some years back, I had visited my cousin in Switzerland for a week. We had not seen each other in ages but kept in touch, and she had pleaded with me to come to Geneva. She was now married, had two lovely daughters, and they were all practically strangers to me. What a wonderful time we spent together.

On my last day, I visited Saint Peter's Cathedral. Upon exiting, I noticed an Asian woman eyeing me and so I approached her and introduced myself. After a long chat, we promised to keep in touch via e-mail, and we certainly did. Li Na was from Malaysia and was traveling throughout Europe for several months. She finally did contact me many months later and began to write quite frequently. Her tone always reflected a sense of calm and warmth by someone who was in no rush toward anything. My e-mails said little but did so rather eloquently.

Our line of communication then changed. Writing was replaced by phone calls, and at times, quite long ones. Li Na lived alone, was very independent, and she soon filled me in about her past life, including a few of her ups and downs. She understood my need to travel, ride my motorcycle, enjoy my operas, and letting into my life they who were pleasant and willing to participate. So, it was time to head off to a part of the world left behind almost thirty years ago.

An unforeseen event sprang up. I had purchased my plane ticket when my son Ricky called me. He now lived in Sweden, but once my travel plans were revealed, the young man insisted he would happily join me in Kuala Lumpur, for as he put it, "It's been a while since we met up in Venice." He was so right. And so I gave him my blessing to join me in Malaysia.

My son had made a few important changes in his life and was now quite independent. He had lived in Vicenza for some time, yet he always felt as if he were in transit, sort of waiting for something unique to come along. Sure enough, he ventured into a new gig one day and pulled off an amazing feat.

His love for rap had always baffled me. Not only was the lad well acquainted with that music, but he kept in touch with some of the artists in the D.C. area. Sometimes I questioned myself for having purchased him a double turn-table machine, if that is what it was, so he could practice being a DJ. Anyhow, in 2002 he decided to sponsor a tour in Europe and try his hand at being a manager.

Strangely, it was his mother who made me aware of his plans. I became involved and prepared a contract plus dished out quite a few bucks to make the tour happen. Ricky had first ensured the artists he knew where available, and then he contacted various clubs in different countries to confirm their interest in this gig. He even created a brilliant poster for advertising purposes and sent them to the pertinent establishments where the rappers would perform. He did this in addition to procuring transportation and hotel accommodations in each city, and it is my understanding that he and a friend rented a couple of vans in Milano and drove off to Stockholm. They met the rappers and began the first show.

Apparently, destiny did the rest. It was in the capital of Sweden where he met someone whom he fell madly in love with. However, a few days later, the group was on the road to visit different capital cities in Europe and had some success. Now, the young manager had his share of interesting experiences, good and bad, in keeping things and people together throughout the tour. And as all that glitters is not gold, once the gig terminated, he decided to move on and forget managing anyone or anything.

However, once back in Vicenza, Ricky felt quite restless. Something was missing, and that something was the girl he had met in Stockholm. They had kept in touch, and she soon came to visit. The couple spent a week together, and once she returned home it became practically impossible for him not to think about her. That is why he moved to Stockholm, found work, established himself in the country and mastered a new language to settle in for the long haul.

Chapter 190

Li Na greeted me at the airport most enthusiastically. Ricky had arrived a few days prior but chose not to make the trip with her. He was staying in a hotel, whereas I was Li Na's guest for she had previously insisted on it.

We met Ricky the following morning. It was apparent that my son was not a happy camper. I now fully understood that neither of my sons would ever accept seeing me with a woman who was not their mother. Nevertheless, our first day together brought us to a huge mall. Not so much to shop but simply because it was close to the Petronus Towers, which we happily explored. And although heights have always been a problem for me, on top of that one, the world about me looked grand.

For the next few days, my son and I toured the area, exploring a very modern city center. It was interesting to see a mix of architectural elegance consisting of mosques, older Southern European facades, and everything in between. A few days later, we two headed off to Pangkor Laut Island. Ricky was cheerful and as always had much to say. We are so different. My inclination is to revert inward rather quickly, after stating the obvious, whereas his warm jovial personality was on display until late at night when we turned in.

Our days were full of laughter. All my son's doing, but one morning he stunned me. After joining them for breakfast and was informed that the waiter serving our table was quite startled to learn I was his dad. Assumptions by the staff had us, in modern terminology, "together." Wow, it was a big slug to swallow so early in the day. And if such news had slightly dampened my spirit, what awaited us once back in Kuala Lumpur pulverized all of me.

I had rejoined Li Na. We were both clueless regarding the outside world for I had not brought my PC, and she never turned on the TV. Modern phones did not yet exist. It was Ricky who informed me that CNN had reported a very drastic scenario regarding a tsunami, a new word to us two. Apparently, he had seen some devastating scenes where the immense rogue waves had struck. Fortunately, we had been spared, but the northern part of Malaysia was hit rather hard. My mom had just contacted him at the hotel. Apparently, upon seeing the news on TV and knowing my whereabouts, but not where to get a hold of me, it was my brother who had spoken to our mom, who then spoke to Ricky's mom, who spoke to him, for everyone was terribly concerned over us two family members.

Well, we three were soon looking at the latest news on a huge screen. It was midday, and we were at a bar in a restaurant waiting to get a table. The pictures of some beach areas appeared totally devastated, and the death estimate, initially predicted in the thousands, was now over fifty thousand and would increase daily. Everyone watching with us appeared totally shattered and horrified, almost as if they had lost someone very close to them.

Once back at Li Na's place, I used her phone. My brother was quite upset with me. He had worried himself to death and now made himself heard, loudly, but soon insisted he was happy to hear my voice. He agreed to inform our mom for me, even though my son had assured her all was well. After that call, my wonderful guest let me use her PC. Dear me! Many were the e-mails asking for news. Apparently, my co-workers, teachers and students at the school, and a few close friends were all pleading to hear from me. What can I say? When I strike out, I fully swing with gusto.

Ricky returned to Sweden a few days later. Then Li Na drove us to a seaside resort quite far from her city. However, my peace of mind was in tatters. Especially as our lodging was right on the shores, and my mind refused to relax that night, convinced the tsunami had not yet terminated its visits. After some desperate pleading, I managed to convince my wonderful mate to bring us back to Kuala Lumpur.

The year concluded on a quiet note. There were no celebrations anywhere in Kuala Lumpur. The Malaysian government canceled all festivities, leading to clubs closing and no fireworks permitted anywhere, so it felt only right to have a quite night out, and, after dinner, just go home.

Overall, it was a good vacation despite that awful disaster. My last day before departing consisted of meeting Li Na's family members. Of course, she being Chinese, and having once cooked in the family restaurant, that wonderful gal prepared a meal fit for a king. It was only the smell of the durian, which is so popular there, that had me slightly concerned.

We were a nice-size family at the table enjoying a delicious dinner. Then, once we were finished eating, the environment felt a bit like a third degree. Her aunts and uncles, super concerned but meaning well, were politely grilling me about my status, my future-plans, any alimonies, and so on. Now, you know me, all smiles and polite to the max. A few days later, once back in Virginia, I was enjoying a long motorcycle ride.

Chapter 191

If my office kept me busy, so did my evening classes. It was never my intention to overdose on work, so teaching was strictly off-limits once warm weather set in. But mid-autumn through winter saw me happily engaging my students. Almost from the beginning, the class environment filled me with joy, and the students' happy faces made me feel that something very positive was being accomplished.

To grasp my frame of mind as a teacher, it is important to first delve into the halls of English as a language. In class, everyone would familiarize themselves with grammar and its usage, but it was crucial they also master the arsenal which constitutes everyday speech. For upon arriving in the Bronx as a kid, one day, my mind grappled with something strange. Someone on television had said, "It's raining cats and dogs." So not only were idioms on our agenda, but it was essential that my students got to know all possible aspects of our peculiar means of communication.

One of my initiatives included plenty of reading at home. I purchased numerous books, including classics for young readers, which were distributed in class, and the students needed to finish the story and exchange books every week. At the end of a course, they had read at least five or six stories, often discovering the complexity of words and phrases. For once class terminated, students always came over to inquire about the mysteries of the English language. For yes, one can be poor—it was a poor show—if in hospital, perhaps in poor condition—why, one can even be a poor soul. Such were the oddities which often stunned most folks in my class.

Perhaps I can use an expansion to better bring home the point. Yes? When President Kennedy proclaimed that the U.S. would put a "man" on the moon, he was not being sexist, arrogant, or ignorant, but just using the language of his times. The word man once represented us humans. And another famous American by the name of Roy Rogers made himself very popular in expressing his love for all people. He said, and I quote, "I never met a man I didn't like," which, by today's standards, equates to something entirely different and should be used with extreme caution no matter what your fancies.

Well, I sort of prescribe to Roy's concept, only the word man gets substituted by student. My classes never had the feeling of simply doing exercises, verbal or written, as our time together was just a pleasant interaction, sort of like coming home from work to relax and enjoy the people you love being with. Inlingua was my home away from home, and the one which afforded me what the real one lacked.

Soon enough, some of the teachers working alongside me became friends. We began chatting, mostly during our evening breaks and there was much to share. Only one married couple appeared a bit high-strung. Both were into martial arts and obviously brought their fighting spirit into the classroom. Consequently, during break time, we were soon hearing about a problem with a different student, and this became their evening fodder, and believe me, their telling said it all.

Fortunately, there was Roger. He was previously teaching but had become the evening administrator. The man was cool to the max, friendly, funny, and could always be relied on if you needed a helping hand. He made sure classes remained user-friendly, led by teachers who acted professionally and that students and teachers would never be at odds. We two became rather close, and I soon considered him a good friend.

Chapter 192

It seemed like the years were slipping away too quickly. Another decade was now coming to a close, and my overall attitude with life, in general, was great. At work one day, all sorts of wonderful circumstances came my way. It included a morning surprise, and a couple of other flings which brightened up my afternoon so gingerly.

At times, I often had to abandon my desk. It was because something important kept me there until finishing, and so my needs were put on hold till it was impossible to defer them any longer, or perhaps my kidneys were beginning to fail me. I had just stepped out of the office and was making my way down the huge corridor to get to my much-needed destination. Suddenly, a familiar person was heading toward me. It was Hikari! What a pleasant surprise, and even more satisfying was learning she was being interviewed by my supervisor.

We shared a few words before she proceeded to see my boss. I ran off to the john. A few hours later, having finished my assignment, it seemed only right to visit my supervisor. She immediately told me that Hikari had mentioned having worked for me. All good stuff, but hearing she was the most qualified candidate on paper and the best interviewer so far with only one more person interested in the position certainly made my day. It seemed only right to state the facts, according to Julian, that is if she was hired, we would gain an incredibly competent graceful woman.

Once back from a quick lunch, I found several e-mails to contend with. One was from my wife. And just so it is common knowledge, we had not yet divorced and now managed a respectful relationship from afar, which served us both quite well. She informed me she had found Francesco's website, which was attached. The news was truly odd. His name had never been mentioned to her. Oh well, that woman was rather keen on the art of surprising me. And while the unexpected news certainly thrilled me, I soon discovered how clueless I was on finding an opening line to get us acquainted.

My workday then ended with one last surprise. While exiting the main entrance, I noticed a beautiful, elegant Asian girl nearby. She was apparently waiting for the shuttle bus which brought guests to our location from the Archive building in D.C., and also back to the city. Something stirred within me, and it brought me closer to her.

Was she waiting for the shuttle bus? Such was the million-dollar question believing she would answer in the affirmative. My revelation to her stated that the bus drivers had just gone on strike, but she could ride to the city with me because it was my destination. Her look was that of someone observing and thinking, and yet she quickly approved as we now began to converse while walking to the parking lot.

Like many of the visitors who take themselves to Archives II, she was doing research. Takako was Japanese and a professional photographer presently reviewing photographs from WWII. She was with a colleague from her country who had decided to stay behind to finish up. The laidback person sitting next to me was many years younger than yours truly. And although that meant little in my desperate need for the right one, something instinctively warned me our ride together was all there would be.

We soon began sharing some interesting notes on art. My little bit of knowledge did make its mark for she intended to visit the National Gallery of Art. There, she could see John Singer Sargent's Street in Venice, which to me was a perfect scene of Venice in 1882. It shows a narrow street whose façade probably still clings to modern times. Of course, similar folks to the ones in that painting are nowhere to be found in Venice today, but someone a tad similar in expression of character, more so than dress, may not be out of the question.

The soft-spoken princess then said something magical. Her exact words were "When I stand in front of a painting I like, I just feel so happy." My heart filled with a fiery joy plus a reassuring feeling that I was not totally alone on this huge planet. It was either the context or expression or both, but her words were like feasting on a delicious meal with a great wine for everything within me was totally satisfied. Well, the girl's serenity, peaceful attributes, and gorgeous smile were all I digested. Suddenly, she somehow fulfilled my lifelong dream of someone to love.

For a few seconds, it felt like my desperate search was over. How foolish I can be! Once we arrived in D.C., after parking near my old stomping grounds, the Borders Books Store on Eighteenth and L, reality struck. She very politely thanked me. And though she was poised, gracious, and beautiful as ever, my now ex-passenger informed me she needed to move on. Oh well, the ride being over, so was our encounter.

Such is reality. The princess accepted my e-mail address, and so I asked her to send a few words after she visited the Metropolitan Museum of Art in NYC. For a few moments, something in me since a small boy came to fore. Stand your grounds and accept your fate, for yours is a long and secluded journey, and one which will never be measured by the road not taken.

Chapter 193

News regarding my son Eric has not been forthcoming. My apology! The lad got through high school with no problems, and one of his teachers, who had strongly influenced him, convinced the student to follow a career as an architect.

He had even found Eric a client to experiment on. A family wanting their kitchen redesigned took him on, and for a newbie, the teen took to his computer and did a splendid job. At least, such was the news that he shared with us parents. He soon headed off to Boston to expand on this subject, but a year later, he discovered that this line of study was of little interest and not at all what he had anticipated. He returned home to live with Francesca.

Quite unexpectedly, he then moved to Rome to attend the American University and study linguistics. This puzzled me a bit. Not his love for literature, which was very evident from a young age, but that he chose Rome to do something which could have been accomplished in his backyard. Yet it eventually struck home. My two sons, like their father, were born to move.

I soon visited him. At the airport in Rome, a rental car got me on my way and although I had consulted a paper map and thought it would be easy to find the hotel, somewhere on the outskirts of the city, I got lost, and then even more lost. At some point, I parked my vehicle near a coffee shop, and I stopped a customer exiting to ask if he knew the proximity of my destination. The older man first looked a bit perplexed, thought it through in a few seconds, and then happily said, "Well, just follow me."

It is truly endearing how friendly Italians are. My experiences have always been such that they appear polite, very willing to chat, and can be extremely helpful. Here was someone going out of his way to assist with my brief but disoriented journey, and after following the chap a bit, that blessed soul indicated a side street for I had practically arrived at my destination. Soon enough, father and son hooked up at the hotel that had been booked for me.

Once my things were put away, we headed out to eat. And of all the places to go, Eric chose a Thai restaurant, which was quite good, and surprisingly, very packed. Father and son ate like true connoisseurs and compared our food to what was usually served back home, and we both agreed it was no easy call to make. Of course, the meal was finalized with an espresso, it being a must, even though it was close to midnight, and we soon parted ways.

Since Eric had the summer free, we were able to roam the city. Whereas Ricky conquers me with charm, Eric's knowledge of the world around us simply pulls me in. He shared information so discreetly, almost like a tour guide. My son sounded professional and very sure of himself. Plus, he took me to see things off the beaten path, like the San Clemente Basilica. Perhaps it is not quite impressive from the outside, but it leaves you flabbergasted once you step in, as from the entrance to the altar a strong touch of divinity never abandons you. And later on, he clued me on his favorite artist, Caravaggio—a man, whom according to him, was slightly furious, perhaps also a bit mad, but a true genius in the world of art.

Our last evening in Rome became my day of infamy. It is due to me not always being fully awake, even in the middle of the most interesting days. Anyhow, two of my Sicilian cousins worked and lived in Rome, and we had met on a previous occasion. My son knew both, but he avoided them. One was simply too critical of Americans, and the other always exaggerated in highlighting his latest romantic encounters. I had wanted to see my Casanova cousin, and not having his phone number, I assumed Eric understood which Massimo was being sought out.

The person on the phone sounded a bit different. Yet he was terribly excited to hear my voice, and he immediately insisted on having us for dinner that very evening. Eric had assured me he had his address, which is why we were there as per the agreed time. However, my cousin's name was nowhere on the building register, which appeared a bit odd, and so my son then phoned him and Massimo said he would come right down.

The person who approached the glass doors made me burst out in laughter. It was simply impossible to contain myself! This stopped Massimo in his tracks, looking quite confused, even a bit hurt, almost as if my gesture was a big slap in the face. It was not my cousin. This Massimo was the gentleman who had married Sara, Francesca's neighbor, the maid of honor at our wedding.

We were both well acquainted but had not seen each other in ages. Yet his unexpected appearance had exalted my sense of far-fetched craziness. Our host opened the door, and I was still grinning like an idiot but provided an apology and an immediate explanation. He understood, and even suggested that the ridiculously funny sometimes stems from a sheer mishap—mine being rather huge. He and my son were already acquainted, having seen each other when Eric and his mom had visited him the year before.

Dinner was fantastic. Sara and Massimo occasionally chuckled a bit whenever recalling how the night had begun. Well, there was so much to catch up on, and we certainly did. Later that evening, someone proposed a call to the U.S. to share our evening's folly with Francesca. So we sort of got briefly reunited, verbally that is, and once my ex got the full gist of the arrival scene, she suggested to all that the night was still young.

Eric and I drove to Naples the following afternoon. Once there, we boarded a ferryboat heading to Palermo. Our plan was to first visit my aunt for a few days, and we would eventually head south to the city of Sciacca. Eric would remain there for the summer. He was a guest of an Italian family which hired him to simply speak English to their kids so they could improve theirs. Such were our plans, as his mom had recruited him for this out-of-the-blue adventure.

Our vessel soon pulled out, and we were taking in the large crowd on the pier waving good-by to us passengers. Unexpectedly, my son spotted his soon to be hosts on our ferryboat. It seemed incredible, yet there were the husband, wife, and their two boys. Eric was certain it was them, having been interviewed some months back. They were surprised but happy to see Eric, and we were informed we would be accommodated in a small flat in the city center. They lived on the outskirts of the city but were in the process of moving into a bigger home.

We docked in Palermo the following morning. It was on to Carini, an area near the airport, where my aunt now lived. After much hugging and kissing, I was surprised to see my grandmother joining us. She had recently moved in as my aunt had strongly insisted on it. And just so you know, my grandfather had passed away years back, and according to legend, half the city had attended his funeral. After all, that gentle soul had always been adored by all who knew him.

Accommodations at my aunt's place were great. However, my stomach suffered one day as my thoughtful uncle constantly came home with a variety of delicious Sicilian street food, which can be a killer for an unhealthy liver. I, of course, could not resist anything, leading to an upset stomach, nausea, and weakness. I even found it difficult to stand up. Miraculously, my aunt prescribed a cure and injected me with something which put me back on my feet.

Well, it was exciting to converse with my grandmother. Although she was in her nineties, she was sharp as a whistle. She revisited a few incidents, specifically pointing out how my brother and I had occasionally worried her to death. In her retelling of some episodes, we all enjoyed a few good laughs. And I felt no anger, resentment, feelings of abuse, or an uncertain take on what the past had been. For the woman had raised us according to long-standing traditions, her personal whims, and the ideas of her times. One evening, she even declared, "I prepared you for life." Sometimes that notion still rings in my ears and seems very true.

Before our departure, this woman of steel spoke from her heart. She looked at me with a rather serious air and gently stated, "When you see your wife, give her my apology for how she was treated that time." This shocked me to the core! More than a quarter of a century had passed, yet she had come to terms with her overwhelming silence and stern eyes, which had offended us, especially the newcomer in town. Well, I laughed inwardly, but I appreciated her gesture in recognizing and admitting a past fault, and the fact that she had waited forever to right a wrong. I gave her a strong hug and such heartfelt kisses when saying good-by.

We two American tourists, if you may, headed south and soon bypassed Corleone. As Eric pointed out, if not for the Godfather movies, hardly anyone on the planet would know it existed. We arrived at our destination a few hours later and found a small but charming city. It faces the Mediterranean Sea and looks out toward Tunis. According to history, everyone from the Greeks to the Arabs had occupied it. Legend has it that the town's name comes from an Arabic word meaning crevice.

Once in our digs, we gathered our things, put them away, and took a walk. Like other Italian cities, it offered a charming center and much movement of folks. Of course, I was avoiding the street snacks, but Eric was definitely not. We observed how most of the houses were of small height but offered a myriad of colors. Practically every terrace was loaded with gorgeous flowers in rather quaint pots. Plus, on several streets, hanging from similar terraces hung the family's laundry, like personal flags hailing tourists to see how much care house chores are given. We eventually found ourselves on Roma Street and were right by the sea. There, lots of folks were sitting around on benches undoubtedly rehashing the same old stories.

My son's hosts called that evening to inform Eric that he would join them a few days later. We drove to Agrigento the next morning. At the Temple of the Concordia, one gets a true feel for who the Greeks were. Its stunning sturdy columns intensify the entire edifice, and my mind wondered how such brilliant architectural work could have been accomplished so perfectly by a people who lacked modern tools and machinery. It undoubtedly symbolizes the greatness of early cultural growth by a truly great race whose uniqueness was years ahead of everyone else.

The following afternoon, I returned to Palermo and began visiting my relatives. With the exception of Uncle Luca, who appeared immune to the passing of time, almost everyone else had grown old. Nevertheless, their sacred traditions held fast for we dined like kings and chatted voraciously regarding everything good and bad about Italy. Their once young children were all married and on their own, and when dropping by, they showered me with too much generosity. At times, it was almost impossible to turn down anything and not cause a scene.

A few days later, I discovered my grandmother had returned to her apartment. Uncle Nicola informed me she was back for good. Apparently, the woman needed her personal space, her time to herself, plus the joy of passing her mornings with her flowers and those lovely birds on her terrace. I was even informed she declared she simply could not just live in a room. I dropped by and once again we parted via a few hugs and kisses.

A flight eventually took me back up north. My agenda included an important event. For a while back, I had taken the initiative to contact Francesco and eventually did. I had posted a few friendly words on his website wishing him a happy birthday, as it was a few days off. Yet no response ever arrived. Then, many months later, I found an e-mail from him apologizing for having failed to see my greetings.

We now began to correspond via e-mail. Soon enough, after some extensive writing, the young man requested a photograph. Not just any picture. He wanted to see me in my early twenties. I, of course, sort of feared him coming to terms with the truth, and that it could perhaps cause some negative issues at home. No photo was sent until a second request was made some time later. So, a picture was included in my e-mail, and the immediate reply was, "This is how I have always seen you in my dreams." We eventually chatted on the phone and had agreed to meet on my next visit to Vicenza.

We never met. Once in Vicenza, our phone conversations terminated with his being tied up. It became apparent our encounter would not occur yet. So, I allowed myself a few days at Mr. Rossi's villa, and eventually he and mom brought me to the airport. I had even mentioned my tale about Francesco one evening, as neither of them were aware of his story, and they assured me one day things would simply fall into place.

Chapter 194

My health insurance did not have a dental plan. And my teeth presented me with nothing but problems. The damage in my mouth had begun while eating in a restaurant. Suddenly, it felt like I was chewing on a stone, but it was a piece of a tooth, my tooth. The front bottom one had slightly broken off. A few months later, one began wobbling, not excessively, but enough to worry me.

Over a short period of time, the bizarre circumstances in my mouth became a consistent headache. It brought to mind what my army captain had referred to upon my return from Nuremberg. Ex-heroin addicts were prone to serious dental issues once aging. Sure enough, my front bottom teeth were replaced, as they had begun to simply break off. And one look in my mouth, between abundant receding gums, two slightly broken back teeth and the false ones just recently gained, this certainly resembled Custer's Last Stand.

I was forced to change insurance carriers for one that had a dental plan. A new insurance carrier also meant a new physician. Like my brother and I, my new doctor had arrived in the U.S. at an early age but from India. This middle-aged lady was quiet in her demeanor and always seemed happy to see me. After addressing the health issue which had brought me to her, she would engage me in a brief chat. On my first visit, she even suggested doing blood work once a year to monitor my liver. According to her, hepatitis C wreaks havoc on that organ as one ages.

I visited her again—this time for a urinary problem. It felt like my constant runs to the bathroom were occurring way too often. She referred me to a urologist, he also Indian, super polite, and a tad silent but very observant. He suggested a small procedure to check the inside of my urinary sack. Yes, a super small pin-sized tube would enter the tiny hole in the middle of my penis, and once fully inserted, it would reveal just what was going on there.

A few weeks later, I was at a large clinic. While laying comfortably on a gurney, a young and rather mellow nurse carted me off to the surgery room. The scene inside that room truly shocked me! As the machine being used for my intervention was brand-new, the firm responsible for it had sent several technicians to witness its functionality. What can I say! The heavens above have not blessed me with much in my lower arena. Fortunately, it works well and consistently. Yet, eyeing all these strangers who would observe what little there was to see, well, I simply wanted to die.

Fortunately, the lovely nurse at my side came to my rescue. She said, "Mr. Di Stefano, I am going to drop this into your IV, and we shall see you later." She offered me a huge smile, and although I have no clue what was in that liquid, I certainly know something about drugs. Which is why I immediately looked at her and said, "Wow, is that heroin?" Folks, I woke up much later feeling pretty darn good!

The urologist informed me that I had a rare disease. It was mostly common in females, but something for which there was no cure. I was told that he could inject some liquid into the sack, bi-annually, and it would offer slight relief from the discomfort, but it would not fix the problem. Well, it felt like I had provided enough exposure in showboating my penis so freely, and therefore I chose to keep my pecker out of the limelight.

Chapter 195

Undoubtedly, I find most Asian women so attractive. Almost all women are somewhat desirable, of course, but something strongly tickles my insides when an Asian female smiles. Is it because my coming of age was with a Korean girl? The many others, all like gracious companions, friendly and graceful, had always brought me where the spirit soars rather high. Such is my outlook, yet I wonder if my simple mind sees things which do not exist.

I met Meili in a bookstore at Du Pont Circle. She was teaching Chinese for a private school in Bethesda, where she lived. Our chat delved into life in the U.S. and how it can take the individual to almost any heights, both work-wise and personal. We shared much about teaching, and we soon discovered we both had only a few friends, but we kept them close. Our first date got us into D.C., and all went rather well. My only serious mishap occurred a month later when taking her to an opera. She neither understood nor appreciated it but faked it so well.

We soon hiked the Dumbarton Oaks Park on a sunny but chilly Saturday afternoon. That evening, although a tad exhausted yet feeling great, we made plans for the upcoming holidays. It was mid-December, and we would soon spend Christmas and New Year's Eve together. We eventually sat down to a great meal, and I spent the night. For breakfast the following morning, it was on to Le Pain Quotidian, where I devoured an omelet and enjoyed a salad, plus regular coffee, while my lady friend stuck to cappuccino and a croissant. And as she then insisted on needing to be alone to prepare a test and grade some homework, I returned to Virginia.

Once my car was parked, I proceeded toward the nearby CVS to get the New York Times. At the intersection of Lee Highway and Route 7, there were police and a lot of people around, as the area had been completely sealed off. This prevented me from achieving my objective. I asked one of the officers standing by what had occurred. He replied, "Keep moving." Those words and the tone of his voice truly hurt. It was the first time someone in uniform, representing law enforcement, treated me in such a rude fashion.

While this response irked me some, my walk now carried me in another direction. There, too, a few people were standing by chatting quietly. My inquiry as to what had occurred went out to someone. Apparently, earlier that morning, police were chasing a speeding auto driven by young criminals. The villain driving went right through the intersection against a red traffic light, and the police car, some distance behind him, did so too. Unfortunately, the police vehicle hit an oncoming automobile which was then at the intersection. An entire family died. They were returning home from church services.

The news created a small pilfering pain in me. Anytime anyone's life is so drastically and unexpectedly taken from them, it always sags my weary soul. Rather than proceed ahead with my plans, I shuffled home in a daze. I dressed warmly and then mounted my motorcycle with the Virginian countryside as my destination. There is no room in my world for drugs or a need to get high, and my drinking is so limited, but my solitude still soothes my soul. Perhaps, just like my Sicilian grandmother, a bit of personal seclusion constitutes the real me, and it was certainly a perfect day to ride as the chilly wind dusted off my cloudy spirit.

Later that evening, I returned home, and my mother called. She began to speak slowly, sounding somewhat irked, and was soon crying a bit. Alessandro was in the hospital. She informed me that she had been driving and had lost control of their SUV and crashed. Apparently, mom and Alessandro had visited Udine for a few weeks and were returning home when the incident occurred.

Years back, they had sold their apartment on the outskirts of Udine and purchased a new one closer to the city. They intended to spend their golden years there. That morning, they were on the highway in the Veneto region when my mother hit the metal rail separating the lanes, and their car spun out of control and overturned. Fortunately, they were out of the vehicle when it caught fire. Mom was slightly bruised, but Mr. Rossi was hurt badly. He was unconscious and was rushed to the hospital in the city of Verona.

I did my best to console her. We spoke at length, and she promised to keep me updated, as she again expressed her sorrow over the current situation. She was presently staying at a hotel in Verona but intended to return home once a decision was made as to when Alessandro would be released. A week later we spoke again. Mr. Rossi was doing fine and would soon be going home. The hospital would transfer him to the clinic close to his town, and he would then be discharged.

Well, it seemed only right to visit them. Of course, another trip overseas would lead to plenty of idle talk from some of my co-workers; that is why my trip was booked for only six days. I would travel toward the end of January over a weekend so that only a few workdays would be involved. However, it was not meant to be. My mom called again in the latter part of December. She was hysterical. Alessandro had passed away at the hospital near their town.

How was that possible? In our last chat, she swore he looked well and had recovered fantastically. He was coming home soon, and she had happily stated how anxious she was to see him back at the villa. My goodness, such is the irony of life in the inconsistency of the morrow.

Two days later, Ricky met me at the airport in Milano. We then awaited my brother, coming in from JFK, who soon joined us. Peter was not a happy camper over my rental car, but it seemed unnecessary to get a large vehicle as the car only served in getting us to the villa and a few days later back to the airport. Nevertheless, we arrived at our destination and found our mother terribly distraught. She was barely able to speak.

We accommodated ourselves upstairs, and eventually there was a full house. My cousin Angela arrived from Switzerland, and Aunt Maria's son, Alessio, had joined us earlier that afternoon. Mom's youngest brother was also among us. My son Eric could not make it. He was living in Greece, and I had no clue as to why. It was Alessio, who after getting himself settled, wanted to see Mr. Rossi, whose body lay in the villa's chapel. Peter, Ricky and I soon took ourselves there also.

Alessio and Mr. Rossi had formed a very strong bond. As children, he and his sister had often stayed at the villa for the summer. Both Alessandro and my mother found him a curious, intelligent, and adventurous boy with a fun-loving spirit. As the years progressed, Mr. Rossi and Alessio's relationship blossomed. He was practically an uncle to the boy and many years later helped him choose a profession once he was of age in school. That is how Alessio went on to become a notary—by applying much studying and dedication to joining what in Italy is a stable and very lucrative occupation.

A fairly-medium size crowd attended the funeral. Most of Alessandro's family members had passed away, so it was our side of the family and some local friends who constituted the bulk of those in attendance. After the church ceremony, Mr. Rossi's body was brought to the family mausoleum in the nearby cemetery. It was then revealed to us by the only family member of Alessandro present, that there was room for our mother if she chose to lie there one day.

Perhaps the evening should have been a mournful event, but not exactly. We all agreed that Alessandro Rossi had lived well, allowed himself most of what he desired, and his lavish lifestyle suited his personality and character. The man was king of his personal realm, and he had enjoyed the wealth created through his investments. But more importantly, he was remembered as a kind, lovable, and generous person when necessary. He had certainly given our mom a world she could never have been a part of, and to Alessio and me, he was a role model.

That evening, Peter took over. It was once dinner had ended and the table had been cleared that my wonderful brother revisited past situations and funny circumstances. All done through hilarious anecdotes and charming detailed stories as he brought out the best of himself, reminding us, although never mentioning it, that laughter is the best medicine.

A few days later, Villa Rossi was practically empty. Peter had flown home, my cousin and uncle had returned to Switzerland, Alessio was back in Salerno, and Ricky had gone off to Vicenza to visit some friends before flying back to Stockholm. I was preparing to return to Virginia.

My mom was terribly withdrawn. A few of the town folks and friends who had always been close to her and Alessandro, came to pay brief visits, but upon leaving, the woman seemed so alone. She exclaimed how unreal it felt that Alessandro was not there. They had been together for forty-five years. After helping a bit that day by just being there, it was now time for me to depart.

On that occasion, I promised to move to Italy upon retiring. That is how the year 2008 began, and those memories of a few sad days are now long gone. However, my summer vacation that year had me improvise and return to Asia where a rather unique and exciting experience, including a couple of scrapes, has never fully left my memory banks.

It was my Honda Civic which occasionally had me at the mechanic for an oil change. The man was from Vietnam, and we had probed the country he had left behind. I had narrated a bit about life in Saigon during that awful war, whereas he always insisted that things were now truly changing even though his contribution was rather slim. On one occasion he encouraged me to go see for myself. I decided to follow his orders.

My flight to Tokyo was super long. I then dealt with a four-hour stopover before reaching Ho Chi Minh City, so my mind was exhausted upon arriving. A friend of my mechanic greeted me at the airport, and we rode a taxi to my abode, a hotel which was apparently built when the French occupied the country. It had been fully renovated and came at a very decent price. My chaperon insisted we go out. It was nine in the evening, and although somewhat drained of energy, once my things were in my room, I hopped on the back of his motorcycle with no clue as to where he was taking me.

I must state that I never drink much. Yet on this trip, my exaggerated sense of things became loyally displayed. Our destination was a lavish bar which was practically empty. The owner was a gorgeous middle-aged woman, and a couple of pretty young ladies appeared to be on standby. We two clients enjoyed some Vietnamese music, not too intrusive, and I soon realized how English was a foreign concept, even with my tour guide, who knew a few words, but very few.

We guzzled a lot of Vietnamese beer. I expressed myself slowly rehashing my past in that city, but my recipient only nodded while contributing very little. Around midnight, after I paid our tab, which was practically nothing considering the exchange rate, my driver went home. The young ladies had previously been dismissed, and the gorgeous owner closed-up the place. Another ride, on the back of a scooter would bring me to my place, and my beautiful host occasionally glanced my way showing a warm smile which had me foolishly hoping. However, as much as she appreciated my hand gestures and incomprehensible words, it was apparent she would drop me off and go home to her family.

I arrived at the Hotel Majestic Saigon. It is in the heart of the city and by the Saigon River, and it accommodated me just fine. The following morning, I walked to Notre Dame Cathedral, mostly because the name sounded worth a visit, and the pleasant hike offered me a unique perspective of my surroundings. And let's just say people living there had very little in terms of modern things. At the church, one senses the huge contrast between the shops and homes encountered and this attractive work of art which seems to utter, *I am a European church.*

Just as eye-catching was the nearby post office. Soon enough, I moved on but stopped a street vendor, a woman carrying her goods on a shoulder pole, and purchased a few of the snacks she was peddling. It seemed incredible, she outright refused to keep the change. It was a bit startling, considering her attire which spelled out her apparent poor circumstances, and yet, although her gesture shocked me, it was quite admirable. Oh well, so much for my good deed for that day.

I returned to the hotel that afternoon. And just who was there waiting for me? The mechanic's buddy, my tour guide, if you may, and I had to assume that perhaps he did not work. We stepped out to lunch, maybe it is more appropriate to say, we drank our lunch, for once again an awful lot of beer was devoured. The chap brought me back to my hotel much later and happily stated he would return the following day.

My state of mind was good, although I was a bit tipsy. It was my intention to read a bit, but I fell asleep fully clothed, and at four in the morning a rooster, apparently in the vicinity, loudly welcomed me to a new day. The plan later that morning was to get to Chinatown. After all, there is probably one worth visiting in every major city on the planet. I distinctively recalled what one of my Chinese students had once remarked in class. When North Vietnam took control of the south in 1975, a lot of well-off Chinese families were forced to flee, leaving everything behind. Yet according to him, Chinese resilience is a long-standing virtue.

Oh well, Chinatown did not impress me much. However, lunch was in a nearby outdoor restaurant and only possible because someone there spoke a few words of English, and so I simply allowed him to feed me a wonderful and totally inexpensive meal.

My tour buddy made his entrance the following afternoon. He took me to a hair salon for women, apparently everyone there knew him well, and the guy appeared to be entertaining the ladies who worked there. I was in a chair bearing the brunt of sitting idly, and about an hour later, we went off to a fancy outdoors restaurant.

After settling in, all sorts of Vietnamese food came our way. Once again, we drank plenty, and it surprised me just how well I could bear all that I consumed. Karaoke was soon the house fad forcing me to hear lots of Vietnamese songs, and even my escort participated. He was quite popular with most of the folks there. I eventually gave a perfect rendition of *Light My Fire*, acapella, and for sure no one had ever heard it. Nevertheless, the song was received well as a decent round of applause came my way.

The following morning presented me my first entanglement. The hotel personnel were startled with my questions. No one spoke English, and the confused faces made me fully grasp how very challenging my stay would be. Somehow, through much gesturing and pointing to my map, the message penetrated. I simply wanted to go to Vung Tau, which is not that far away from their city. A few of the American soldiers I had briefly known almost thirty years ago had spoken so well of it. It was where they went for R&R.

They got me a taxi and it brought me to a bus station. It felt like we would never arrive. The traffic was chaotic, our vehicle competed with thousands of scooters and motorcycles, plenty of bicycles and a few automobiles, and perhaps we were not taking the most direct route. Now once at that station, I realized how naïve I am. The super old buses concerned me. Oh well, life is both a journey and an experience, the latter being a must.

Those vehicles were probably already ancient during the war. How they stood the test of time was a mystery. I boarded one of those old relics, sat down, and did not need to open the windows for they were all open. A few elderly raggedy-dressed men and women sitting close to me reminded me of that experience on my ship when I attempted to give out a few donuts as a snack. The men had smiled at me once moving past them, almost as if to show their appreciation over my being there with them.

Suddenly, one came over and gave me a chilled bottle of mineral water, completely sealed. What a grateful gesture, and yet, it somewhat confused me. To be treated with such respect and kindness by a people who, on perhaps too many occasions, had seen a rather nasty side of us, seemed unfair. Offering him money felt unwise, so I stood up and shook his hand, and then slightly bowing to the others sitting nearby, using the only Vietnamese words I knew, I simply said "cam on."

It is incredible how we humans adapt. At the bus station in Vung Tau, a young lady caught my attention through much hand gesturing. We soon climbed on her scooter and off we went. The city did not appear to have much to offer at first. She took me to a beach, having shown her my bathing suit, and we found it rather empty. There were just a couple of guys, who may have been foreigners but Asians, and they were sitting about chatting. That blue ocean water looked so inviting.

I assume you know that the ancient Greeks believed in several gods. Those gods played with humans according to favoritism, the individual's status, and outlook. Perhaps such were my circumstances that day. It is the only possible explanation. None of the waters in the oceans on our coastlines nor the mild ones in the Mediterranean have ever plunged me into such deep fear and a sense of a doomed ending.

Initially, once inside that warm water all proceeded well. However, it became quite impossible to return to shore. A powerful current was taking me further and further out. My mind began to panic, and my spirit believed the end was near. I kept getting pulled further out, and the shore appeared further and further away. Truth be told, I was petrified. But then something simply took hold of me. Using all strength within, mental and physical, I began to swim like a mad contestant at the Olympics who was applying all he had and more. It felt like nothing could stop me. Miraculously, my fully exhausted body had made it back to shore.

My enthusiasm for swimming ceased that day. The young lady later found me a cozy hotel. And, incredible as it was, for the improbability of possibilities is certainly mysterious, the older Vietnamese hotel owner had lived in San Francisco. He had worked for the city's cable car system. How refreshing it felt to speak freely in English and have many references to share. I even discovered that there was a ferry/hydrofoil connecting his city to Ho Chi Minh City, which allowed me a most pleasant ride back the following afternoon.

Now don't ask why I was off to Da Nang a few days later. A private driver who only spoke Vietnamese set me out on a rather long, silent, and lonely trip. The following afternoon we explored the city, and we sat outdoors for lunch. While eating, we spotted a most unusual scene. A three-wheel bicycle, used as a taxi, had the passenger pedaling, and the older Vietnamese owner sitting in the back enjoying the ride. I am certain the young guy happily working as if it was a privilege, was an American. He certainly looked like a Yankee. Besides, who else would do such a thing? And why not?

During my last few days, I chose to see a couple of museums. The first one was the War Crime Museum. And while walking, I felt the need to verify that my destination was close at hand. A small park by the road came into view, and there on a bench sat a young girl and a middle-aged man who was reading a newspaper. Gambling on the chance the man perhaps knew a bit of English, I approached them. My inquiry was happily delivered, and it was the pretty girl, perhaps no more than nine years old, who replied, "I speak English." She sounded great, her pronunciation being very good, and her reply delivered with a huge smile. The man simply looked on.

She then addressed who I assumed was her father, in their language. Her response to what he had said was delivered in such a concise manner that I felt quite impressed. It then seemed only right to celebrate the occasion with a photograph or two. They happily complied, and yes, I now finally had a couple of truly lovely pictures of a different breed of Vietnamese folks that up until now had hardly been seen anywhere.

The museum was further up ahead. I should not have gone. If my spirits were soaring upon entering, they immediately cascaded. My cousin Angela had made me aware of some of the atrocious acts committed by our military in Vietnam. We had first applied WWII tactics, and therefore a bombing campaign that showed no mercy. This much I knew. However, once entering and facing the first huge photograph, I was stunned. An American soldier, helmet on his head, bare chested, and looking into the camera while smiling, was holding up the head of, I assume, a Viet Cong soldier.

It became impossible to remain neutral. Then came the sight of villages before and after our bombing them, not to mention the massacre at My Lai which was well exposed. I opted out without looking at anything else. Unfortunately, the following day, at the Reunification Palace, the full wrath of the employee giving us a tour was on display. She stated, through gritted teeth, that our bombing, first with conventional bombs, then napalm bombs, and even a chemical called Agent Orange, had killed more than a million civilians.

That night, I was off to a club after enjoying a quite meal. My escort, who was no longer coming by but had previously suggested visiting this place as a few Americans hung out there. I met someone from Tennessee, an ex-soldier, who was too young to have served in the war, but whose curiosity about it had recently taken him to visit the tunnels at Cu Chi. He was very impressed. The guy adamantly claimed our enemy had taken the war more seriously than us, something debatable in my line of thinking, but just not with him.

My preference was for chats about things which were visible. Like the great inexpensive street food, copious amounts of people on scooters navigating so easily, some carrying their families on one, and even the fact that the soldiers scattered about the city on duty were from the north. Oh well, the love the South Vietnamese once had for the music of Creedence Clearwater Revival just came out and startled my listener. And yet, this tidbit seemed a bit insignificant now, for even the Vietnamese knew nothing about it; apparently, once the war ended, all foreign influence was completely eradicated.

It was soon midnight. I was making my way back to the hotel when I spotted two very attractive girls in traditional Vietnamese dress. My feet carried me over to them. They were standing outside the club they worked in, and of course, we could not communicate. Next to them was a short fellow who seemed to be just hanging around, and for some stupid reason I asked him for a cigarette. I had not smoked since 1980, but the last few nights, in different clubs, I began indulging again. After stepping inside the club, he returned a few minutes later and handed me one.

I lit it and began smoking. I almost passed out. My brain automatically kicked in with instructions to keep moving and not stop, but my vision began to fail me as my surroundings soon vanished, yet my legs kept going. I'm not sure when, but my consciousness slowly prevailed, for I was now looking at a fancy brand-new building. I turned to look back and the two girls and their buddy were no longer outside that club.

A crowd of people were now exiting the very lavish façade. It was a wedding party walking down the steps of its entrance. Everyone looked so happy, and these folks were dressed quite elegantly in modern attire, and I sensed a few were wondering just who was the foreign fool looking somewhat lost and quite confused.

No doubt, that cigarette was loaded. It almost took me out. I assume the intent was that once down, the guy would have taken my wallet and disappeared into the night. Of course, the girls would resume their workstations inside, which I am sure is what happened anyway. Fortunately, all ended exceptionally well. Have I already mentioned that at times the gods seem to favor me?

I left Vietnam the following evening. A taxi brought me to the airport. Upon arriving, I paid the driver the equivalent of five dollars in Vietnamese Dong. The guy then jumped out of the vehicle, grabbed my suitcase, and accompanied me to the airline counter. All along, he practically pushed folks in front of us out of the way. It seemed a bit strange that he was treating me like royalty. And once finished, the jovial middle-aged man almost bowed before he left.

Could he simply have been an enthusiastic worker beaming with joy? It left me feeling a bit strange, and during my layover in Tokyo it struck me. I had accidentally given him the equivalent of $50. Which made me wonder if he ran home to tell his wife he had almost a month's wages in one evening or if he kept his good luck all to himself.

Chapter 196

I had lost contact with my stepmother and her family. Then Aunt Mia called one day. She gave me some truly awful news regarding her sister. My stepmom had been hospitalized and had had both her legs amputated. This made me feel terrible, but also slightly guilty for not having kept in touch with either woman for quite some time.

My thoughts over our past were sporadic. They even included how she had made a complete transformation from one who loved joking and being the center of attention to a rather morose and super negative person. Undoubtedly, Ricky's illness and his death had totally devastated her, and then dad's passing contributed a further downfall. At times, I wondered if she had ever fully accepted having Peter and I in her life, but she had given it her best.

A bit of guilt engulfed me. Nevertheless, upon arriving at my aunt's place, her good spirit brought me back to a more natural level. My aunt spoke kindly, always sharing her propensity to be upbeat, and it was only while riding to the hospital that she expressed a bit of sorrow over her sister's agonies. I heard some of the more distressing circumstances, like her sister being rejected and abandoned by a man she had lived with, and my aunt divulged that her sister would often question the meaning of life. On some occasions, she claimed to outright detest it and longed for it to be over.

Such was a bit of what escorted me to the hospital. Upon entering her room and by her side, I had reached out to take my stepmother's hands in mine. She looked up at me with a most bewildering glare and said, "I hate you—because you are having a good time in life." Her sister intervened and slightly reprimanded her. Apparently, the surly patient had expressed a pent-up loathing ready to be aimed at anyone. So, a few words were offered in a peaceful tone to simply get beyond the one-way hostility which had just been flung my way.

When we left, I experienced deja-vu. Just as with my father, I knew this would be our last encounter. My stronger side accepted this fate versus her continuing to suffer. A slight reflection of our past as a family, and the present, queried why we were destined to such piercing tragedy? Oh well, who could say. On my drive back home, I played one CD after another. All music by the Rolling Stones, which had me singing along loudly, and so my wounded inner bruise coming with me to Virginia began to slowly dissipate.

I returned to New York City to attend her funeral a few months later. Seeing all her relatives and family members in attendance was little consolation considering our reality. This was the third burial bringing us together, and practically the only time we saw each other. But even more painful was watching the coffin being lowered in the same grave where Ricky and my father were. For all my attempts to stay strong, a few tears flowed out once we began to move on.

Chapter 197

My Honda Nighthawk had always served me well. Eventually, I replaced it with a 750. For many years, I rode only on weekends, but eventually it became part of my commute to work from spring to fall, and my need to reach higher speeds soon followed. However, riding that motorcycle remained a personal affair for I never joined anyone else or a group of bikers.

One day, two things stood out. There were now more females riding motorcycles. Whereas on Memorial Day, thousands of male veterans overran our region. What had begun as a small gathering of bikers coming to the D.C. area for the weekend to commemorate a holiday had become a massive gathering, earning the name Rolling Thunder. Both events were just fine with me. The former had seemed long overdue, while the latter had its place for those who wanted to visit the Vietnam Veterans Memorial, but also be seen and not forgotten.

I occasionally recall the very first bikers gathering at the Harley Davidson in Fairfax City. Initially, it was mostly single riders, only a few had their girlfriends with them. However, that ritual picked up pace very quickly, becoming an annual event which could no longer be contained in our small city. Rolling Thunder, a name not yet known, went from hundreds to thousands, and eventually, hundreds of thousands became its size. Consequently, Fairfax City and the adjacent counties would close Route 66 on the morning of the holiday, allowing only the bikers into the city.

During one of these celebrations, I had gone to Front Royal for the weekend. On Sunday morning, my motorcycle cruised leisurely bringing me home while allowing me to absorb the beautiful greenery all around. I eventually got to my place around noon, but rather than go do my weekly food shopping in my car, something inside me voted to just keep riding. I was soon approaching D.C., and then my bike took me over the Key Bridge heading into Georgetown.

It was once on M Street that it happened. At some point, the many cars in front of me had slowed down. My eyes took in a massive number of motorcycles parked on both sides of that street. Yet the immense difference stood out. On my left were over a hundred bikes, while on my right, perhaps a dozen or so were parked there. Suddenly, it registered! All the bikers standing by their motorcycles on the left were White, but all the ones on the right were Black. My Uncle Roberto's words of wisdom, which had completely perplexed me back then, had now taken center stage and brought home its meaning, "The more things change, the more they stay the same."

Chapter 198

On December 7, 2008, I turned fifty-five. The greatness of the day was not only associated with celebrating it, for I certainly did, but knowing that having thirty-five years of service with the federal government, I could now retire. But truth be told, my early rising and routine commute to work provided me with a satisfying way to start and pass my days. Should getting a pension and terminating my employment wait some?

It was Peter who enlightened me. He had been collecting a pension for some years. The happy camper had me on the phone and insisted there was never a dull moment, plus, he almost immediately delved into a sullen but important subject, our family genes. My brother recalled the summer I had spent at Aunt Mia's as the time our father and our Uncle Robert enjoyed a long chat at the dinner table one evening. We rarely saw the man back then, but he did occasionally drop by.

Both men had taken on an interesting conversation. They discussed how many years Mother Nature had left in store for them. The two began analyzing the family history, pointing out that their grandmothers had lived into their mid-nineties, and their mother was solid as steel. On and on they went, both men assuring themselves that their future looked promising. Well, my brother's woeful anecdote made me grasp a possible negative reality, therefore, retiring was certainly on, and soon.

And why not! My office routine was not so challenging, and missing were those occasional analytical tasks which brought out some brilliant energy. That is why I soon terminated my career knowing there was a grand retirement salary to live on. However, teaching English was still my cup of tea, and Inlingua was one of my favorite places to meet people. Not necessarily to date students, although some were impossible to avoid, but simply to continue enjoying the friendly human relationships persisting in my classes.

Now, you know about my quest to acquaint the students with more than English grammar. We also read from handouts I prepared, which covered everything from cultural topics to tragic events, especially any that had somehow sparked a new outlook on life or impacted society. My students truly appreciated this initiative, and while the books provided to them indulged their fantasies to grasp the essence of known tales in our language, some of the handouts shocked them to the core. Such a narrative was about Nicholas Green.

The boy was with his family touring Southern Italy. His dad was driving, mom sat up front, while Nicholas and his sister were in the back seat. Suddenly, two local criminals attempted to force them to stop the car to rob them. Rather than succumb to their threatening gestures, Nicholas' dad began to speed away. One of the thieves shot into the car, wanting to frighten the driver but accidentally killing Nicholas. The boy was seven years old.

A national outrage permeated the entire country. However, it was the American family which completely shocked everyone. Nicholas' parents chose to donate his organs. This was a practice hardly known back then. Five people received his major organs, and two received a cornea transplant. The generosity from a devastated family wanting to help others via their personal tragedy was simply unheard of in a nation of devout Christians. After this, donation rates in Italy, then the lowest in all of Europe, increased dramatically and continued doing so year after year. The family was awarded a medal of honor and personally thanked by Italy's president receiving them in Rome.

My students loved to hear interesting stories like these. They were discussed and digested, and all were challenged to familiarize the class with something of interest from their country. They could work as a group or individually, then gather the facts, write a brief essay to hand in, and provide their narrative in class. This, along with popular songs, brief videos, once internet was available in the classrooms, and conversations which covered everything under the sun, made for some unique fun classes.

It seems only right to mention a few of my most fond memories. One of my classes had the usual mix of students, but two stood out. There was an extremely beautiful South Korean woman who was in the country because her husband worked at their embassy. She would always express herself in a low tone. She was poised and charming, and her English was pretty decent. To state she had captured my heart is to not share the full picture.

Yong always wore dresses, rather short ones, and she looked fantastic. However, once she sat, she would cover her knees and legs with her sweater, as she felt a need to not stand out or be seen as audacious. This gesture, plus her telling us about her country's traditional ways and values and why they mattered, had me under her spell. I love learning the cultural aspects of life, plus, her gesture in class seemed both respectful and appropriate, and in my world a little consideration always goes a long way.

Next to her sat Lucille. She was from Brazil and possessed a laidback attitude. Most things about American life captivated her. And yet, in one of our class chats, she stated that too often, girls from her country were sometimes seen as easy to have by us Yanks. The young lady politely insisted that was certainly not the case. And, as she had recently informed us her birthday was coming up, we had made plans for that Friday evening.

We left class early that night to go to a club on the outskirts of Northern Virginia. As the students and I approached our vehicles in the parking lot adjacent to our school, something very odd occurred! Lucille and three other students were by her car looking at a large piece of paper under the windshield wiper. As she reached out for it, a set of headlights from an auto directly across shone on her. This baffled us all. I, along with the other students standing by my vehicle were a bit concerned. But the staged scene was the work of her old boyfriend. It was his vehicle's headlights shining on Lucille, and the message on the large card read "Happy Birthday."

Her ex then came over. The two embraced and chatted briefly, and we all proceeded with our plans for a night out. The club was not too far away and had only recently opened. We found the music a bit loud but good, and soon enough, plenty of food and drinks came our way. I could not help but notice how the birthday girl did not appear overly thrilled with her unexpected guest. It was put aside as I then provided a bit of verbal entertainment to all my students. It was after one in the morning when I headed home.

Our night out was briefly touched on in class that Monday evening. It was during the break when Lucille shared a few facts with me. The handsome guy who had so lovingly surprised her was an actor. They had met last year, after which he soon found work in Hollywood and had returned that day hoping she would follow him to L.A. My student informed me that her uncertainty over their relationship was based on a gut feeling. She was not convinced he was the right person to spend the rest of her life with. I certainly could relate to this. Someone, somewhere, someday, somehow would make me happy, challenge me, brighten my outlook, and become a companion for the duration of life. However, it did seem like the one was nowhere near my parking lot either.

It was the following month when an upper-level business management course came my way. There were a few older students, but the mix still consisted mostly of younger folks and all from various countries. Some of the issues we tackled certainly had them perking up and taking notice. Like the incident of the Tylenol capsule poisoning in Chicago in 1982, where seven people died within a few days after taking the medicine someone had laced with potassium cyanide. This tragic event had totally shocked a concerned nation, but fortunately it was resolved very quickly.

The students admired the company chairman. It was James Burke. In their eyes, he was more than a hero. The man had immediately acted by recalling one million bottles of the product, going against the advice of the FBI personnel involved, and the company's top brass, who believed the value of the company's stock would plummet and never recover. As one student put it, "Sometimes a great leader simply follows his heart and defies all odds." I could not have said it better myself, especially when saving human lives is the only prize.

Our class then tackled the movie, *Bowling for Columbine*. After discussing the horror of the crime and the pain associated with the victims, everyone expressed their inability to grasp why Americans believe in this right to own weapons. One student stated it may have made sense when the nation was founded, for most people lived in sheer wilderness, but not today. Almost all were fine with a weapon to use at a firing range to practice a sport, but never for other reasons. A girl from Poland informed us, and everyone concurred, that in her country, the only people who possessed guns were the police and the criminals.

Oh well, the night of their verbal presentations had arrived. Each student would now speak on a topic I had previously been informed of. They had researched it, wrote a brief essay and its narrative would now be shared with the rest of the class. We had taken a break before commencing the presentations. Now, you should know that our classroom was on the opposite side of the school entrance. We were isolated from everyone else in the school and would use the exit door right next to our classroom when leaving the building. Never in a million years would I have guessed what came through that door.

The student from Peru did his paper on Peruvian beer. When I reentered class, a large box full of beer bottles was the first thing my eyes saw, and guess what, folks? Not only would we learn about the product, but we would also judge its quality, though I certainly had some concerns and began rattling my head as bottles were being handed out by the speaker. Oh well, what can I say?

A sense of caution led me to the door, shielding the small rectangular window which allowed anyone to look in. While listening to the jovial speaker and now savoring the product, the door began to open as someone tried to come in. All the students were at their desks. My heart jumped into my mouth, but thank heavens, it was Roger. I immediately gave him a bottle and sent him on his merry old way. I loved that guy; he was just so cool! Then after the presentation terminated, it seemed only right to share my opinion, which gets to the core of who we Yankees are as a people. I said, "Only in America can something like this happen."

Chapter 199

It was time to move to Italy. My plan was to return to Vicenza to live there permanently. I loved that city, and besides, it was only a two-hour drive to my mom's place whether I headed north to Udine or west to the villa. If she needed me for anything, I would be there to help out in any way possible. Both my sons blessed my initiative, especially Ricky who was very close to his grandmother.

Francesca had come to my rescue. She would take care of shipping all my household goods. As an IMF employee, she was authorized a huge amount of weight to be transported at the agency's expense once returning to Italy upon retiring. And, if any of her dependents moved before her, we were still married, the same rules applied. I was extremely grateful because her gesture would save me a lot of money.

I had chosen to arrive in Milano and spend a few weeks with my mother. During our chats on the phone, she sounded like herself again and seemed happy to host me for a while. My arrival date, which was drawing closer, was provided to her, along with me landing at Malpensa Airport and coming in on a Lufthansa flight via Frankfurt.

So once again, the skies over the Atlantic escorted me to Italy. Peter and I had spoken before my departure, he being reassured of my occasionally returning to visit him and family but also to travel some. There was much of the country I was not yet acquainted with and would return to explore. Once up in the skies, it felt a bit peculiar returning to live permanently in the very nation that had a long while back been completely erased from our lives. The very one which had also rehabilitated us both, and it had nurtured me most rewardingly for fourteen years. Oh well, so much was yet to come, and I was quite ready to bring it on.

Part 7

Chapter 200

Information regarding my trip had been provided not only to my mom but also to a close friend of hers. She was given a complete itinerary and time of arrival, and I had been assured she and my mother would be at the airport waiting for me.

I left the check point at customs loaded down like a mule. Upon exiting, and seeing neither of the two ladies anywhere, I moved myself and all my gear to a secluded area to sit and wait. Then after some minutes slipped away, a plan of action was formulated. However, not having a phone meant not communicating with my host, so I now kept an eye out for someone who could help me. Luckily, a very courteous employee at a nearby stand allowed me to use her phone.

No one answered at the villa. Could the ladies be on their way, or maybe they were stuck in traffic? Then for some strange reason, a tiny notion asserted my return to Italy was a big mistake. I sat again, hoping to see someone, but approximately fifteen minutes later, my new initiative forced me to move on. I walked through the airport hoping for a positive result and sure enough, there they were. Like docile children, the two elderly women were sitting quietly awaiting my arrival.

My mother, of course, insisted this was where I had exited last year. To explain that this area serviced only direct flights coming from overseas would have been futile. Her friend, someone who worked for the city authorities, should have understood something was not right. The fact that neither of the two had considered checking the arrival screen, which is huge, seemed a tad incredible. Oh well, need I say more?

After this tiny fiasco concluded, we went home. My mom appeared in good spirits and began to inform me about the villa, which had been on the market for over a year but with very few interested parties. She moved on to other issues, including the fact that the following evening we three, and someone else, would go out to dinner. Not many facts were given. Yet, I would come to learn that the individual joining us was somewhat interested in my mother. She had simply labeled him a friend.

Once back at the villa, I settled in upstairs. After putting everything away, I returned to my hosts, and mom's friend soon moved on. Almost immediately, there was an outpouring of concern over money matters. It seemed rather strange. Mr. Rossi had left the woman a large inheritance. Oh well, apparently, the once partially deflated soul had resurrected herself to the tee, found life worth living again, and was certainly a busy bee.

In the afternoon, we visited a friend of hers in a nearby town. The woman sold fruit and vegetables. After being introduced, the two began exchanging some boring gossip which had me wondering why such nonsense could not have been accomplished over the phone. Then, quite unexpectedly, something was mentioned about my mother's date. I made no contribution as if I hadn't heard a word.

My take on this was most conservative. My mom certainly had a right to a companion, but the word date had a sinister tone. Not only, but Alessandro had given her a world beyond all her possibilities, and while the man was not my father, it felt inappropriate to listen to this gossip. Why, a woman nearing eighty should certainly be free to enjoy what comes natural at that age. But not so much being with someone who perhaps wanted more than to share a dinner.

It was the very next day when out came some serious news. For some unexplainable reason, my mother had purchased a small apartment in the center of town. It was now being built, that is, the building's structure was slowly going up but not much else was visible. Apparently, what was worrying her was how little work progress had been made, and that she had given a ton of money to the firm. It seemed best to keep my thoughts to myself, perhaps more facts would come out before my departure.

Then, a more contentious issue was aired out. Most negatively by the speaker. It involved me. As Alessandro had left my mother quite a bit of money, she was almost a millionaire, and once the villa sold, it would bring her and the nephew who inherited it with her, much more money. My simplistic thoughts had favored her making a small gift to her four grandchildren. That is why yours truly made a bold move.

Peter's youngest daughter, Silvia, had married the previous year. I had convinced my mother to be quite generous. That is, I would give the couple a nice wedding gift (money-wise) from us two. She would pay me back once we were together. The generous amount was most certainly appreciated by my niece and her husband, and even my brother and his wife were very thankful and stated so to us both for quite some time.

My real plan was to now convince her to give an equal amount to her other grandchildren. I truly believed neither of the three would marry. At least not any time soon. Therefore, it seemed fair to provide them the same as what had been given to the marrying couple. The total amount was truly insignificant compared to what she had inherited. She would then inform them that the gift was their wedding money, and if no marriage occurred, it was just a gift. I had foolishly assumed my mom would agree once informed.

What was I thinking? She now berated me for having advised her to be, "so foolishly super generous." Not only did she show regret having given the lavish sum, but the irate woman insisted that I needed to wait to get the amount I had advanced on her behalf. And that very evening, my infuriated mother began to list her expenses at the villa and even showed me the exuberant gas bill from the previous year. Which is why I suggested she move to the apartment in Udine. She could return to the villa in spring and stay until the beginning of fall and not have such outlandish expenses to contend with.

The answer practically floored me. The villa needed her constant presence. For if some interested party wanted to see it and found it unkept, they may not vote in favor of purchasing it. I remained silent. The following day, the banker who had worked with Mr. Rossi managing his investments came calling. It was not said, but I sensed he was insinuating mother was making withdrawals faster than he could fill them. Perhaps I would not see my money for some time.

Such were my first few days back at Villa Rossi. I wished that the man of the house, now departed, was still among us. He was pleasant, calm to the max, and never faced any financial struggles. Anyhow, please do not judge me too harshly, it seemed to me that the lady of the house who had cleaned and cooked her life away was just not well-informed on these matters, and she was apparently struggling to manage her affairs and new responsibilities. Eventually, a few changes came about, but most of her problems endured for some time.

It was soon time for me to move on. I still lacked my money but was reassured it would come my way shortly. On my departure day, once again, as more than a year ago, my mother appeared sad, lonely, insecure, and a tad worried about everything. Yet she remained plain stubborn and feisty as ever and appeared so indifferent to the idea of changing anything.

Well, it hit me on the train ride to Vicenza. My mom's strong attachment to the villa was now understood yet not fully agreed with. Over the past forty-five years, she had been the live-in companion of the town's most well-known person. The name Rossi was practically a household word there. And she was his signora, which surely branded her with a sliver of high stature among the locals. Apparently, it was her intention to continue to enjoy her status, whereas my advice to live in Udine, even if part-time, did not much enthuse her. In that city, she was just another face, hardly known by anyone, and with few friends to be had.

Chapter 201

Life back in Vicenza was off to a good start. My in-laws had invited me to stay with them until my furniture arrived, and so the same room which had once accommodated Ricky was given to me. Their son and daughter, now young adults, lived elsewhere. One was studying in England, while the other was employed by an Italian firm in Santa Barbara.

My brother-in-law was his charming old self. He conversed about anything, nicely tackling the most amusing part of it all, while his wife made herself heard but only if necessary. It was grand being in their company, and I immediately attended to my first objectives, establishing residence, and then getting a driver's license. Finding a place to live was put aside as someone they knew had an empty flat not far from theirs.

Once again, my British passport legally established my presence in that city. At city hall, I was given an ID card, which is sort of the national passport which must be on you at all times. Upon leaving the premises, the sign Inlingua, right across the street, grabbed my attention. Which is what brought me there, and the administrative person was very certain a class could come my way the following week. She received lots of information, work experience, address, phone number at home, all after happily displaying my new identification.

And finally, Francesco and I met. My inclination regarding the reality of our relationship was sidelined. It seemed wise to let things play out on their own. We met up for lunch at Righetti, a place he knew and liked very much. So, there we were! We embraced and shared a few kind words and felt quite at ease. He was rather tall, just like Ricky and Eric, all three slightly towering over me, but he was very slim and certainly a handsome devil. Soon enough, my curiosity over his interests allowed him to speak plenty.

Music was the topic which had us both making long contributions. I discovered that he wrote for the local paper about music, but his true love was his band. Their tunes required long practice sessions, he getting the best out of everyone, and then the group perfecting both lyrics and sounds to everyone's approval. We may have spent three to four hours chatting, and upon separating, we both agreed to stay in touch and meet again.

Things were proceeding rather well but slowly. One day an unexpected e-mail from Roger came my way. He and his wife, whom I had met on previous occasions, would be vacationing the following week in Asti, which is in the Piedmont region. The two were joining Roger's wife's folks coming in from Scandinavia. Any interest in catching up? Well, as my brother in-law allowed me to borrow his old Fiat, I replied, "Sure!"

I first headed out to my mother's place and found her quite upbeat. Incredible but true, she now accepted the temporary move to Udine. It seemed only right. She had a truly elegant flat in that city, and her expenses would be minimal compared to those here, which would now be minimized plenty. That is why a few days later, I headed out west, while the following morning she proceeded to the region where she was born and had grown up until her move to the U.K.

My drive took me to where Asti Spumante is harvested and brought to divine perfection. Roger and the others were already lodged at a bed and breakfast. The following day, we cruised the small city, and the day after, we were off on an arduous hike. Sunday morning saw us going for a walk near the B&B, but we again managed to overdo it. Our legs carried us much further than anticipated, so we decided to have a light meal in the first town we encountered. Eventually, we coasted a small rural area, and while the ladies were all for eating something light just about anywhere, everything was closed.

While strolling on and yapping away, something caught my attention. Behind an open curtain were some elderly folks sitting around a table enjoying a meal. Me, being me, without the slightest hesitation, simply walked into the premises via a large door, and Roger followed me in. Goodness gracious, we were inside a nursing home. Luckily, two very pleasant employees accepted our apology and one even inquired about my accent.

Once my identity and our intent was solidified, the head administrator recommended a local trattoria. She was informed we were on foot, and so the woman happily proposed giving us a ride. Of course, once exiting and seeing three folks outside on standby with us, that gentle person frowned slightly as her petite car would not do. She stopped a person leaving the premises, they certainly knew each other, and enrolled him in assisting us. A fleeting thought, which perhaps Roger grasped, questioned if a similar incident could ever occur back home?

Our driver spoke some English. She had appeared happy to discover that Roger and I were Yanks and informed us about her trip to New York City, even insisting she would return. My enthusiasm for that city, having fully matured over time, was shared with her after admitting it had not always been so. We chatted some more, and I suspected our three mates may not have been faring so well. Their chauffer, recruited by ours, appeared to be a local townsperson, the type who probably only spoke their dialect, which is like a different language, and English was certainly not on his agenda.

A long winding road brough us to our destination. We all offered our saviors a million thanks. Once inside the trattoria, our idea of a light meal was immediately canned. The place had a rustic touch, and we were seated next to a young couple. On the other side of the large dining room were two huge tables where a group of about thirty people sat. Our host informed us there was no menu, but she would tell us what dishes were available while assuring us everything had been made from scratch that day. She then took our wine order.

All was fine with me. Perhaps less so with my companions over the idea of ordering without knowing the price. We soon drank a Barbera wine which was heaven-sent. Even my liver seemed fine with indulging a tad. The food which followed arrived at decent intervals and was truly appetizing. First, we were served several platters of various local cheeses along with salami and other delicious cold meats. This kept us busy for a while.

Now, my curiosity got the best of me. That large group was certainly carrying on in a grand fashion. We could hear laughter galore and praises and sometimes a bit of hand clapping. Everyone appeared so playful and super happy. I inquired with our waitress, and she informed us they were friends and co-workers from different firms who always holidayed together. Today's reunion was simply to decide on their next trip. Now, for sure, something pleasant and reassuring hinted nicely that life in Italy would do me plenty good.

Soon enough, we were served an assortment of scrumptious roasted meats complemented with tasty grilled vegetables. This caused us to talk less and eat more, but at some point, my move to Italy was invoked. My reason? There were several. My sons were all in Europe, and my mother was getting older and would soon need a bit of assistance, plus, there were relatives in country to visit, and besides, a flight to the U.S. was inexpensive and always worth catching.

Suddenly, out came the million-dollar question. Living here permanently would entail a new and different lifestyle, plus, unknown customs and traditions. Perhaps all would seem fine at first, but once one was fully incorporated into the scheme of things, was I certain I would fit in? It was a valid concern. After all, my years in Vicenza were mostly under the army tutelage as a soldier and civilian. I wondered if my take on life abroad, based mostly on my previous fourteen-year overseas stint, may have been fashioned with too much optimism.

Well, we eventually finished our fantastic meal. It was crowned with a dessert, spumante, and espresso, and we five then continued chatting a bit longer. The price of the bill was decent, and we even visited the owner's cantina afterwards. A few bottles of homemade wine went to Finland. I, however, was through drinking for a while. My return to Vicenza would have me start a class the following day. Nevertheless, Roger and his wife were reassured that I would see them next year, and so we certainly parted on a good note.

Chapter 202

In Italy, a tourist can drive with an International Driver's License. Or with a valid license from your country if you remain a year. My circumstances were a bit odd. I was driving with a license from Virginia, but I had an Italian ID card which labeled me a Brit. It would have been challenging to explain my unusual circumstances to the police, if ever stopped. If there is a way to complicate life, at times, I fully excel at it.

I prepared to get a license. My nose was stuck in a rather huge driver's manual. It became apparent that remembering tons of information would not be easy, and if you think practicing for a written test for a license is rather demanding, you have no clue how much useful and useless knowledge one must fully memorize in Italy. It makes the holy Bible seem elementary, and certainly heaven-sent. After reading, rereading, and realizing my memory banks could only do so much, it was on to motor vehicle.

My visit that day was simply to pass the written test. Fortunately, that Fiat, which may have looked ancient but ran like a beauty, brought me there quickly. There were a dozen or so waiting to test, and as everyone looked eighteen, or there about, I certainly stood out. A couple of expressions coming my way seemed to be inquiring, "What's with the old man?" Nevertheless, I failed the stupid test, and although upset with myself, I returned to my aged vehicle and drove home.

A few days later, my furniture and household goods arrived. Everything was in tip-top shape. My only complaint was with my wife's sister. She had found my lodgings but had the landlord hike up the rent price some. Perhaps being a Yankee, and well-off, may have legitimized her reasoning, but just what was she thinking? I was a bit disappointed, especially seeing the flat was not so great. Why, it even needed a sink in the kitchen, which an old American friend living in Vicenza brought over, and we quickly installed it.

Oh well, my in-laws had done their part. They lived nearby, and often had me over to eat with them, and my surroundings in the immediate outskirts of the city suited me just fine. Plus, getting to the city center via a brief walk was divine. By the way, I had already left Inlingua over a contentious teaching method they had insisted on and a few days later began work at another school.

It was run by an Italian woman and her English husband. Several Brits also worked at the school. They even employed an American, who was ex-military and had remained in Vicenza for quite some time. Everyone appeared super friendly, helpful, and no strange teaching method was imposed on anyone. The schoolbooks and our ability to create a pleasant scholastic environment allowing all to participate and learn was the only requirement.

An evening class immediately came my way. It was back to what I loved most, and all my students were so enthusiastic. Then came another group to teach, which required that I travel to a private clinic in the outskirts of the small city, and that class consisted of two female doctors and quite a few good-looking nurses. I met both groups twice a week, the latter in the late afternoon, and all were simply great folks that enjoyed expanding their knowledge of a language much in demand.

Chapter 203

The year ended rather nicely. I lived well and was again participating in something which kept me cheerful. A few Italian friends from Caserma Ederle had joined me at a restaurant one evening to reacquaint and chat plenty. Christmas had me at my in-laws, whereas New Year's Eve was shared with a young lady from the school. Settling down overseas had certainly started off well.

And yet, the year 2010 soon steered off course. My excellent state of health went south very quickly and seemed to remain in dire condition. Well, please allow me to narrate everything accordingly. One Saturday morning, I left my flat around ten thirty. Up at five, once an espresso was consumed, my complete dedication was given to the mid-term exams for my evening class. All the students had performed satisfactorily, and I soon placed their tests in a large folder on the dining room table. The very place where they had been worked on for several hours.

I drove to my friend Rachel's place. She was also a teacher and a Brit. Once there, we set off for Bassano Del Grappa, mostly to explore the small town, but also to purchase a wine jug not found elsewhere. Inside the bottom of the jug was what looked like—are you ready for this—POOP. Yes, like in what comes out of a butt. It was considered funny by some folks, especially the locals, and my mate assured me the person receiving it would love it.

We accomplished her task and then had lunch. I got us back to Vicenza in the latter part of the afternoon, and we took ourselves to the city center. The bar where we sat was packed with the usual crowd enjoying a glass of wine and small talk. Rachel soon gave me an exemplary lesson on everyday common phrases used in London. Some sounded very foreign, or perhaps her pronunciation exalted them to a sort of more unknown and mystical catch phrase. But I certainly got the point.

A few hours later, before separating, we agreed to meet at eight that evening. I went home and upon entering the flat, something immediately stood out. The folder with the graded exams was no longer on the table. It seemed absurd and rather strange to digest. Apparently, someone had entered the apartment. But why take something which could not possibly serve anyone any purpose? Nevertheless, I foolishly searched the premises hoping the folder was elsewhere.

Nothing was accomplished. My sister-in-law heard me out over the phone, and she assured me she would inquire with the landlord. The following day I was informed, as per the landlord's middle-aged daughter, that her dad was taking a new medication and had been acting strange lately. It seemed absurd to me that this man had entered the premises and left with a folder full of exams. Enough said. My real dilemma was facing a dozen students and pleading with them to take the exam again, which, believe me, did not sit well with anyone. They certainly complied, but only after making themselves heard.

A few days later, I was just not myself. Suddenly, the man who was always out of bed by five a.m. could no longer accomplish that feat. It was just impossible to get up. I felt totally exhausted, and usually around ten thirty I would make my way to the bathroom to shower, hoping to revive myself a bit. Not only was my body sagging, but there was a bizarre feeling of confusion, and it soon began to manifest itself in class.

It was a truly strange situation plaguing me while teaching. Teachers learn all their students' names in the first week of class. This is so whether there are five or twenty-five faces looking at you, every name remains well catalogued. No longer true. It now became imperative to keep the school register open. Whenever a student addressed me or participated in the ongoing exercise, I needed to look at the names to confirm who was speaking. So just what was happening? I was definitely puzzled and somewhat concerned.

Soon enough, a most embarrassing mishap occurred. The students had reentered the classroom after taking a break, and I asked them to do the exercise at the end of the chapter. Quite a few faces looked at each other as if confounded, then someone informed me it had already been completed before going on break. I wanted to find a hole and crawl in. That very incident, plus my daily mental struggle, and the morning exhaustion drove me to see a physician.

It was one of my students, a doctor, who had suggested it. She claimed she was certain something had happened to me, for according to her, I was no longer the same person who had initiated the class months back. Plus, my sister-in-law had recently insisted I did not look right. My face was super thin, slightly green, and my eyes had a strange haze about them. All this was enough to get me to take advantage of my health care card and find a physician.

Now, of all the people to run into! Piero was sitting patiently, waiting his turn to see the doctor. We had previously been together some months back. A few folks from the accounting shop had organized a dinner and karaoke afterwards and had extended an invitation to me. My singing was sort of well-known. Years back, before returning to the U.S., at a Christmas dinner party, a microphone came out, and someone had brought his guitar. My voice simply took over.

My old boss heard a brief description of my malady. He soon went in to see the physician, and upon exiting we said goodbye. I had with me a complete set of blood work exams. My doctor in Virginia had suggested it. Upon informing her of moving to Italy permanently, she insisted I come by before leaving so she could do my blood work. According to her, the results were fantastic as everything looked perfect, except my liver. Yet she assured me the hep C viral load was not excessive, and she was convinced a cure would be available within a few years, as so much new medicine to fight AIDS and infectious diseases was now available.

A middle-aged doctor serviced me. He heard my accent and inquired about my origins. As no one else was waiting to see him, he was given some historical information from my soldier years at Caserma Ederle to present. The chap was quite amused, and upon hearing my health concerns, he ordered all sorts of bloodwork and asked me to return with them and bring the old ones which I had mentioned to him.

My brother in-law had advised me to arrive at the hospital early. At about six thirty, my bicycle, which had recently been purchased, got locked up near the hospital entrance. I encountered a huge waiting room full of patients, and no one looked too thrilled waiting for eight o'clock to roll around. At the exact hour, two doors on opposite sides opened, and everyone appeared to know which one to take, whereas I had to ask, and then proceed onward to get in-processed.

After finally registering and a brief wait, I went into the room where blood was taken. Once in, four nurses dividing the room in half accommodated their individual patients to a stretched out long chair and began the process. The very nurse which would assist me was having a wonderful chat with the patient at her cot, and it appeared they knew each other and had much to say.

That nurse was jovial and full of mirth, until I sat down. Not sure what happened, but her tone had a crude edge. Now just what gives? It could not be my accent, for I had not yet opened my mouth. And she was having some difficulty hitting a vein. It even looked like she was considering slapping me a bit, which almost tempted me to speak up and say, "Here dear, let me show you how it's done."

The exam results left the doctor baffled. He compared the new tests to the old ones, and every single test result had changed. Each blood count had gone from perfect to way beyond acceptable limits. He could not determine the cause, but he asked me if I had perhaps come into contact with something toxic. Like what happened at Chernobyl. His words baffled me, but my answer was negative. He then informed me to have an endoscopy done, which eventually forced me to return to the hospital.

On this occasion, I was in a different ward. The procedure was about to begin. From my memory of this incident, I dare state that I saved my own ass! Two nurses instructed me to lay down on a stretcher/bed and then turned me over on my left side. A tube was inserted down my throat, but now everything was a problem. My previous attempt to tell them that being on my left side created a chest pain was ignored. My heart now ached, my breathing became difficult, and very soon I sensed I was in trouble, serious trouble.

Moving my hands and making noises to signal my difficulty was disregarded. The two held me down, forcing me to stay still, while my inability to breathe properly caused my heart rate to rise. My attempt to move forced the nurses to shout a bit, and they tightened their hold on me. At that moment, my Sicilian anger made its grand entrance. I shoved the two off me, which certainly frightened the hell out of the doctor. Then, I stood on my knees on the bed, looking quite crazed, and pulled the tube out of my chest.

It must have looked like some frantic scene out of a horror movie. The two nurses disappeared immediately, while the doctor continued to stare in disbelief. Another nurse nearby watched with wide eyes and mouth open.

Fortunately, my clothes were on a chair nearby, and rather quickly, Giuliano Di Stefano was fully dressed and leaving a place that had probably shown him the worst of Italy.

Back home that evening, I was in crisis. It would be impossible to continue to work. However, leaving the school meant losing my health care card, but getting to the bottom of this strange ailment was a priority, that is, if it would ever be properly diagnosed. I now fully understood that my best solution was to return to the U.S.

I spoke to my mom on the phone a few days later. She certainly understood, but her voice sounded a bit concerned, and I was informed she would soon visit. She agreed that my furniture and other belongings could get stored in the huge garage she had in Udine. That is why the following day I returned to the mover's warehouse, Roiatti, and the new manager was very helpful and allowed me to take plenty of boxes and wrapping paper.

Everything was properly packed, and there were plenty of boxes. It was Ricky and Eric who performed the actual move. Both arrived in Vicenza and worked with my brother-in-law to obtain a rental truck and move everything to mom's place. I had paid the rent until the end of the month, yet left mid-month, and the landlord was now complaining to my in-laws about the shower no longer working properly. He wanted to be compensated. Oh well, it had always worked fine for me.

My wife and I had spoken on the phone. Remember we were still married. She had happily agreed, much to my surprise, to get me at the port of entry, JFK. She even insisted I could remain at her place until my health improved. Oh well, things were looking slightly better, now. Hopefully, I would get to the bottom of it all.

Part 8

Chapter 204

I now lived in Washington D.C. Francesca had abandoned life in the suburbs and purchased a tiny flat on Thirteenth and M Street. She loved everything about the apartment, which was on the top floor of an older building, but the place was tiny. My living space consisted of a studio room, which was the size of a bathroom, reminding me of my first years as a sailor. But why complain?

It felt reassuring to have someone to share myself with. My biggest concern, however, was being able to get to a doctor quickly. And as neither of us had a car, rather than spend hours on mass transportation to get to my physician in the suburbs of Northern Virginia, someone in D.C. saw me. Blood work was done and so was an endoscopy and colonoscopy. The results were bizarre. At least to me. Outside of several polyps, which were removed, and my hep C, nothing else was out of place—my blood was back to normal.

Although confused a bit, my take on this was to simply move on. However, according to my host, she categorically stated that my breath was just disgusting and claimed so every morning. Now, mind you, we were not sharing a bed or kissing to start our mornings, and so this comment seemed pointless as once again, my diet had me eating like a monk, minus the wine. What can I say? Not only was my mouth out of whack, but I lacked energy and felt too exhausted. Nevertheless, having been given a green light, it seemed imperative to just get on with life.

Francesca and I walked to the IMF on workdays. Once my ex entered that building, I then stopped to purchase the Washington Post and made it home. Fortunately, as I never left the flat, the World Cup, as in soccer, was in full swing in South Africa, and a few matches were worth watching. Now allow me to share an opinion without giving offense. Although the game was now being executed far from its home of origin, it made me wonder why White folks are continuously being accused of all the world's modern ills. Perhaps, just maybe, occasionally, we have also given the planet a few things to enjoy and celebrate.

Anyway, some reading got done. And in late afternoon, if no game interested me, then an opera would put me in a relaxing mood. Soon, a bit of research was done online, computers had come a long way, and I now believed my health problems may have stemmed from my sick liver. I even found a promising product, so I contacted an old friend now teaching English in Tokyo. That is how Shosaiko-to, an herbal medicine which was used in a clinic in New York City for hep C patients, came my way. No one was cured but everyone felt a lot better. And sure enough, my fatigue and weariness slowly began to dissipate.

It seemed only right to now visit Roger. After a friendly talk, out came his request to consider doing a morning class. I did not feel ready to tackle my old passion and refused his offer. On my way out, a weird incident occurred. An ex-student who had attended several of my classes ran into me. Junwei appeared startled. Why, her expression almost conveyed taking in the Rocky Horror Picture Show. It was as if she were judging the strange creature who stood in front of her. Yet her polite words inquired about life in Italy and nothing regarding what may have frightened her so. Could I have possibly looked that awful?

If that peculiar incident startled me some, a much bigger surprise shocked me that evening. My host, still wife by law, gave me the monthly amount due for my lodgings. It was not cheap. While making this contribution was no problem, although truly steep, the gest irked me, especially considering what I had left her in the bank account in Vicenza upon separating. For a moment, I felt like a fool, but one who finally grasped that this woman was certainly one calculating bitch.

Should I have left? There was someone in the suburbs I had once enjoyed a relationship with. Unfortunately, her home was in one of those peripheral oases in Virginia where without a car there is no life. Not only that, but our time together had always been a bit rocky; for I (so pathetic and stuck up then) just wanted to live off her body, while she, the better person, wanted me to appreciate all of her. Plus, my intuition always suspected we would have never lasted long. And so, my super expensive cubbyhole would simply have to do for now.

Chapter 205

Another year slipped away. And if you believe a man and woman under the same roof cannot have a non-sexual relationship, you are wrong. There is an old cliché which says that a relationship without sex is called a marriage. Apparently, we were still happily married, for that most exotic and healthy of all human acts, which is impossible to survive without, was never even considered nor ever came to fore.

It was time to finally move on. I had found an apartment to buy near my old stomping grounds in Arlington. It was Francesca's real estate agent, who had brought her to D.C. and sold the house in Fairfax City, who met with us. We entered Stoneridge Knoll Condominium to see a flat on the top floor which was going at a low price. It seemed only right to jump on it, after all, this was Cherrydale, an area I was acquainted with and truly cherished.

The selling price made sense as the apartment needed a complete makeover, however, if the amount held, it still came at quite a bargain. After a thorough check, my approval to proceed with a bid was given. The realtor asked me to state the highest sum I was willing to offer in competing with other bidders. Easy! Frugal me simply added an extra twenty-five grand to the going price and stood firm, yet I suspected the process would lead to a higher sum.

Now guess who immediately frowned on this? Yes, the capitalist entrepreneur from the IMF appeared upset with my proposal. She strongly asserted I raise the amount. It almost tempted me to ask, "Excuse me, but whose side are you on?" It then dawned on me that in some ways, the woman was still a bit of a foreigner. My original total was repeated which led the agent into his monologue. Other offers would be coming in and probably higher than mine. Therefore, my amount needed to rise in order to secure the apartment. I begrudgingly complied and considered the offer still somewhat fine, just more costly.

The realtor notified me the following morning that the apartment was mine. I was not so surprised and felt it was time to concentrate on my new gig. I needed to return to Italy as my mother was fiercely demanding her garage in Udine return to being a garage. Having been away almost a year it seemed only right. That is why a few weeks later I was on my way to the airport. While proceeding to leave D.C., a most bizarre incident occurred, and it certainly speaks volumes on some of our negative law-abiding trivialities.

My wife was now in a car sharing program. We had walked to a nearby parking lot to take over the reserved automobile. It was a brief stroll, and the delightful spring weather made us both feel quite good. However, she could not get into the vehicle she thought she had reserved. After several tries, and no one around to check with, we returned home so she could use her computer to resolve the matter.

I remained below and enjoyed that glorious sunshine. Francesca soon returned to informed me the reservation had been mistakenly made for the following day. I felt like valuable time was waning.

Finally, she was able to procure a different vehicle—a rather fancy one, of course. We quickly made it to Constitution Avenue heading west. The south lawn of the White House was to our right, and unfortunately our car was in the left lane. Once stopped at the traffic light, we discovered it was left turn only. I, the passenger, lowered my window and signaled to the car to our right behind us to let us in. The serious looking lady most politely did, and this led to a—BIG GAFFE!

Time-out. Is it possible that in the greatest country in the world, the average citizen cannot make a fucking mistake? There is always someone at the helm ready to deal out a just punishment. Perhaps it is this fanatical pressure to uphold every rule and regulation which leads some folks to lose it and go on a rampage, and consequently do some awful shit.

Our vehicle did not get very far. We were immediately pulled over. It was not the D.C. police but some local White House Security detail with lights flashing galore. Once parked on Virginia Avenue, I was thinking, or maybe not, of informing the guy we were heading to Dulles Airport and were late. Big mistake! Exiting the car and walking toward the one behind us led to a person in uniform jumping out and reaching for his gun. He placed his left hand up in the air, as if stopping traffic, and the guy screamed like a lunatic.

I simply froze! He continued to shout, sounding like a drill sergeant ready to kick ass. I was ordered to get back in the car, but apparently, I did not move fast enough, so out came the pistol, which, fortunately, was not aimed at anyone. Now, believe me, Julian Di Stefano, who if anything, looks like an accountant or a flute player in an orchestra, was wondering what the fuss was all about? My physical image is the furthest thing from that of a criminal. Why, I could not even frighten a fly.

Two D.C. motorcycle cops and a patrol unit arrived immediately. It promptly became apparent that there was no issue to be had. Our frantic encounter turned into a bullshit session, and an apology from me was given while getting a fine for the illegal maneuver. We two resumed our journey with me feeling nervous over more wasted time, quite stupid about the incident, and my companion was now questioning my lack of know-how in the very land I grew up in. Suddenly, it dawned on me that maybe I was still the foreigner, and perhaps would always be one.

Chapter 206

My arrival in Udine coincided with my mom's return to the villa. We spent a few days together, and she appeared relaxed and happy to have me. Naturally, she reminded me to clean up after myself, open all the windows in the morning to air out the flat, and she also gave me a few other candid orders. The garage needed to return to its previous condition, yes?

The very next day her accountant came by. We had met years back in one of my brief visits to Udine. As we had kept in touch, the very attractive but a tad morose young lady paid me a visit. She had arrived at JFK, and we had spent a week touring Manhattan. She fell in love with the city, and what apparently thrilled her most was seeing West Side Story on Broadway. A few days later, she even got a taste of bagels and could not get enough of them.

Well, as the garage sits below the building, that is where I took her. She had recently purchased an apartment and needed furniture, so she was given several things including the kitchen table and chairs. The following morning, I took myself to a nearby Chinese store for they sold everything under the sun. The owner agreed to come over and check out a few items. She certainly did, and that afternoon she and her husband left with practically everything.

It was now time to head to Vicenza. Francesco and Gianna, his girlfriend, met me at a restaurant on the outskirts of the city. I immediately took a liking to this young lady. She appeared very mellow, spoke with much enthusiasm about art and music, and the couple were apparently in love, which led me to believe they would soon marry. Anyhow, the issue regarding my true relationship to Francesco had been filed appropriately as it seemed best to let sleeping dogs lie.

I was soon back in the U.S., but not in D.C. A friend from the school was going abroad and allowed me to use his home. The fully furnished basement was sufficiently nice and all at no cost. A week later, work on my apartment began as it would have new bathrooms, a new kitchen, and expensive wooden floors throughout, for being frugal was apparently put aside. After about a month, Peter joined me having insisted he would help me paint the place.

My brother and I were in a townhouse in Clarendon. The family was off to Scotland for several weeks, and so we had the place to ourselves. Why hadn't I returned to my wife's minute residence in D.C.? Well, once back from Italy, it seemed best to pass up the expensive cubbyhole, but also begin to distance myself a bit from the landlord.

On our first morning together, Peter and I had a hearty American breakfast at a diner near my condo. We made it to the flat, now in excellent shape, and it received my brother's full approval. He absolutely loved it. Our mission was to paint the entire place, and I soon discovered just how efficient and organized my brother was having done this work on a part-time basis a few years back. He also tended to give orders, and I simply complied and thanked my lucky stars for his presence.

If you include his constant bantering ways, we two spent three cheerful days together. However, I immediately became concerned over his health. On that first morning, I was awoken by this loud continuous coughing. It sounded truly awful. The man in the bathroom was struggling with his lungs for the longest time. That day, it became apparent Peter smoked entirely too much for he simply lit one cigarette after the other.

I was quite alarmed again the next morning. Later, during a break when he was again smoking, my concern was laid out rather seriously, and yet my brother insisted he was fine and instructed me not to exaggerate. However, that same dreadful event evidenced itself each morning, and that is why before his departure, I pleaded with him to consult a doctor once home. Peter informed me he had never been to one and would not go now. What can I say? In any event, we remained proud over the work accomplished, and he soon departed and appeared most happy to return to the Bronx.

Well, it was time to return to my old love, teaching. Roger happily gave me a class the following semester, and all proceeded well, but unfortunately, my friend soon abandoned us. He moved to a linguistic school in the suburbs, and after a brief visit, I decided to join him. Having a car now meant a brief fifteen-minute commute, and classes there ran Monday through Thursday, from nine a.m. to one p.m. This allowed me to enjoy both work and a three-day weekend, which in opinion, was something the entire American work force should have been given long ago.

New school, different students. At Inlingua there was always a mix of Europeans, Asians, South Americans, and an occasional person from North Africa, and prior to my departure an avalanche of Mongolians had begun to arrive. At my new gig, the cadre was mostly Asians, with the biggest group being Thais, then Koreans, a few Vietnamese, and some Chinese, and occasionally even a Turk or two would join us. Of course, nothing changed regarding how I interacted with my students as my course of action maintained a cheerful, scholastic environment.

Chapter 207

It was spring 2013 and time again to have a real vacation. My suggestion to Ricky to tag along was accepted. Mind you, there are no favorites in my book, yet Ricky had certain peculiarities in that he, too, wanted to explore areas which sort of complemented mine.

My son had actually grabbed my attention years back. It was over Napster. A few of his high school friends were with him in the basement listening to music and arguing. I was heading to the backyard when someone said, "Napster's stealing music," and the guy suggested the firm needed to be ousted and buried. Ricky disagreed. He was convinced the future had arrived, and Napster was simply ahead of everyone else. He boldly stated that soon enough, getting music online would be a way of life, it being properly managed and distributed.

His incredible vision of things caught my attention again years later. He had called from Stockholm, and we had talked plenty. Before hanging up, some advice came my way as my son suggested I invest in a fairly new company, which according to him was run by a genius and went by the name of Apple. He felt certain it was here to stay and would grow into a small empire. Now, as I have no knowledge of modern technology or any interest in stocks, I simply left it at that.

We spoke again some months later. His mantra was repeated which is why I bought some stocks. The price of the shares was truly low. For the next seven months, the stocks' price continued to rise making me feel quite happy. Suddenly, however, they began to fall and continued doing so as if they had no intention of ever leveling off. On the day they were still a few dollars above the purchase price, I sold everything.

Ricky eventually discovered my insubordination. He attempted to bring me back on board, yet my personal make-up has no investing domain in it. And so, due to my inability to see beyond my nose, and endure some tough going, I simply let it go and missed out on quite a deal. Which is why I thought a bit of compensation was due as he had attempted to make me wealthy and perhaps a tad better off. Our plan was to meet in Tokyo, and he would be my guest once there.

We reserved a hotel near the Toyosu Fish Market. It was tiny, the price not so, and breakfast was unheard of. However, it was close to something which very much interested Ricky. He wanted to photograph the morning auction at that market, and we needed to be there super early. My son was now a professional photographer. He worked mostly sporting events, especially but not only football, and he also photographed all sorts of festive occasions throughout Sweden. The lad had found a profession he loved and excelled at, and he was quite anxious to now capture a bit of Japanese tradition.

Unfortunately, we arrived a bit late to see the auction, but we took in the premises, and the photographer at my side shot everything. I enjoyed watching him record the interchange of fish and how the human spirit acts when engaged in commerce, especially if the prize is the food we devour daily. Soon enough, I discovered his passion for sushi right there at the outdoor market. He ate like one starved fisherman, and while it was exciting to see his love for this traditional delicacy, a few days later, another sushi meal seemed like too much.

Now, Tokyo is a modern city that has it all. The guidebook I had consulted did not speak so highly of it, yet, when considering it was razed to the ground during WWII, it is impossible to not admire how quickly the Japanese bounced back. Their industrious, creative, and smart planning is so evident, and they can be very considerate when helping someone out. The city has an excellent rail system which got us about, just don't ride it during rush hours. And we both walked a lot. Being influenced by my son, I also began photographing everything in sight and got some compliments from the professional at my side.

The cherry blossoms were in full bloom and looked gorgeous. Most tourist sites we visited, especially the temples, were captivating, and one morning we discovered something unusual but rather unique. There were outdoor smoking sites, that is, areas designated as places to light up and not disturb others. While enjoying a cigarette or two, one had access to ashtrays which served as wi-fi connections, and it seemed like a very clever idea, at least back then. Since Ricky smoked, we stopped at several of these smoking sites but not too often.

Next, it was on to Kyoto. The bullet train had just arrived. Several workers in uniform were on standby, portable vacuum cleaners strapped to their backs, while they waited for the cars to stop. All the passengers exited and the cleaning crew entered, doors were closed, and in a few minutes, those carriages were spotless. Ricky looked at me and said, "Just like in Italy." I must have laughed like a madman for a few minutes.

Our accommodation in Kyoto were a big improvement. We had a much larger room, a friendlier staff, and even an abundant breakfast awaited us each morning. However, at that meal, father and son briefly separated as Japanese food was served on the left side of the room and American on the right. Of course, once our plates were quite full, we reunited at a table and began to plan our day accordingly.

Unlike Tokyo, this city makes you feel the spirit of Japan. It has an old-fashioned charm, slightly palpable and somewhat visible. It simply grabs you. Upon visiting the Kinkakuji temple, a few thoughts from one of Yukio Mishima's books made their mark; particularly one which states that the old are eternally ugly, while the young eternally beautiful. This monument remains forever young. Even more interesting was coming to terms with Wabi-sabi later in the day. If something brings about a sense of accepting the imperfections within and without, then you have arrived. No further search in life is needed.

Oh well, the following day I began to feel terribly ill. In the late afternoon, we had just bought some ice-cream from a Japanese girl who spoke perfect Swedish. It was while listening to the Scandinavian lingo, which sounded a tad musical, that my body became overtaken with flu-like symptoms. I had to abandon my son because my energy level had plummeted. Once back at the hotel, I laid in bed and soon enough went through hell.

I was so weak that I could not move. My lungs were full of phlegm, and it was almost impossible to clear them out. That evening, I began using the steam from the bathroom shower, as it allowed me to spit out what continuously accumulated in my lungs. But a few minutes after exiting the bathroom, my persistent coughing would resume, forcing my return to that room to rehash the cure. I sounded truly awful, and Ricky was terribly concerned.

The next morning, my son insisted on getting me medical attention. My situation was slightly better and not wanting to ruin our plans for the day, I held fast to the scheduled program. We got about, and although still feeling ill, I was able to somehow survive. Yet, the very same horrific ordeal prevailed later that evening and was perhaps more severe than the previous bout. It became a night of hell for us both, especially for my super concerned son who was witnessing something truly worrisome.

We took a taxi to the local hospital after a light breakfast. Of course, English was as foreign as we two, and my attempt to communicate with the staff members accomplished absolutely nothing. Thankfully, a young Japanese girl came to our rescue. It almost sounded like music from heaven when in good English she asked, "Can I help you?" My slow but cheery reply stated, "Yes! I always need all the help I can get." She heard about my ailment and then translated, and she even remained with us as someone eventually brought us to an isolated area.

A nurse would soon attend to me, and then a doctor was to examine me. We were informed of this as the young lady prepared to leave, and she even showered us with a few kind words. I thanked her profusely. Truth be told, I wanted to say, "God, we owe you people an apology." For the barbarity of two atom bombs killing over hundreds of thousands of helpless people in a few seconds, and we justifying it as a necessary evil has never sat well with me.

Apparently, my illness was a bit odd. During the day, once outdoors, my condition was not so precarious. The female doctor, who spoke some English, gave me a thorough physical exam but could not determine exactly what was debilitating me. She suspected it was a very severe flu that was beginning to pass. I received a prescription consisting of several herbal medicines, which were purchased there at the hospital. The cost for being seen by a physician and the items bought was less than $50. Also, I now possessed a medical card which could be used again if I ever returned. Need I say more.

My night of living hell slightly abated but not much. Ricky was again just as worried, yet we somehow got through it. After two more days in Kyoto, a train had us heading up north to a rather secluded tiny town in the mountains. Our lodging was at a bed and breakfast, and upon coming to terms with my condition, the owner was kind enough to insist on providing us an evening meal. We were served a delicious soup, lots of vegetables and some meat and rice, and all at a super cheap price.

We returned to Tokyo but now resided elsewhere. And before Ricky's departure for Stockholm, it felt imperative to get to a sumo wrestling event. Although those bouts usually lasted only a few minutes, or even seconds in some cases, the preparation by the two contestants was a rather solemn affair. Ample movements and gestures were made and salt was tossed over the wrestlers' shoulders to purify the ring, all before the two huge men finally went at each other. It is certainly not the greatest of sports, but it seemed most appropriate before exiting Japan.

Ricky flew to Sweden, and I caught a flight to Hanoi. One of my neighbors at the condo was from that city, and she had convinced me to visit there. My plan was to explore northern Vietnam, but my health conspired against me. The same horrible Kyoto disease returned, not as devastating, but it convinced me to fly home, and so I soon boarded a Japanese flight for the long haul back to the U.S.

Chapter 208

My next-door neighbors at Stoneridge Knoll were a gracious elderly couple. There was something slightly peculiar about the lady, for in our first encounter, my intuitive sense flung me some hints which did not necessarily confirm anything. So, it was quickly put aside.

Several months later it finally hit me! The couple and I ran into each other in the parking lot. We spoke a bit, then proceeded to enter the building while sharing news about our exuberant condo fees. When the rather talkative woman mentioned having worked as a realtor, I instantly remembered she had been the one we worked with to purchase the townhouse in Fairfax City. Goodness gracious, it is not just a small world; it is truly tiny.

She and her husband informed me that they were enjoying their retirement in that wonderful building. I, too, was quite happy there, for my lifestyle was most serene and pleasant. The school granted fulfillment and the pleasure of making young people feel like they were learning more than a language. I also frequented various concerts and operas at the Met in NYC, whereas Washington D.C. had a few good theaters worth going to. And some occasional weekend trips to Chincoteague in summer were still on.

I was also able to see Eric on various instances. The lad was again living with his mother, only now in that tiny apartment, hopefully he was not being charged rent. To summarize his adventures, upon my route from Vicenza due to illness, he eventually left Greece heading to Estonia. It was to pursue a master's degree in the field of Semiotics, which sounded very Greek to me. He moved to Vicenza for a few years and then returned to the U.S.

Eric now lived and worked in D.C. He was a manager at an Italian restaurant, and I discovered that he occasionally did more than manage. At times, he was also the host or filled in for a missing waiter. Often, he would even lend a hand in the kitchen when asked to do so. It seemed like the young man never shied away from rolling up his sleeves and taking charge.

One evening, we met and had dinner in D.C. After, we headed to the Studio Theater to catch, *A Clockwork Orange*. It was all Eric's doing, as I was not certain that such a story could possibly work on stage. Kubrick's movie had somewhat captivated me and convinced me of its futuristic outlook on violence in society, but the idea of it being presented to an audience looking up at its production simply failed to convince me as very being effective.

Once inside the theater lobby, we were informed that the show would be performed elsewhere. We followed an employee who led us across the street. He headed onto a tiny avenue which appeared semi-deserted and then entered what looked like a warehouse. This was our destination, and upon approaching it, we encountered a narrow alley. There, some gang members were fighting each other. My son and I and the others were somewhat apprehensive but also questioning if this was real or just a performance?

Oh well, we all entered what may have once been a repository. Our seating arrangements stood out immediately as they had been cleverly organized. There was a round stage and the seats surrounding it went up like in a stadium, making the center area below us our theater. It was not only well assembled, but the dim lights added a bit of suspense. Eventually, those folks brawling outdoors, the Droogs, came rushing in to bask in the limelight.

So began a well-executed and intriguing tale. Our attention never left the stage below us as we enjoyed a mapped-out violent journey where Alex ultimately becomes a victim to modern medicine, and through religion, also gains spiritual salvation. To say my son and I were totally pleased is to not properly state the facts. It was a truly fantastic show!

Once the play terminated, we began to leave but noticed a young lady behind us holding a pen and a notebook. I asked if she was somehow involved with the play. Yes indeed! Her task was to record any particulars which could be improved upon or even propose changes deemed necessary. Eric suggested a Tom Wait's tune in the background for a particular scene, not sung but harmonized, and her look said it all. It not only expressed a huge appreciation for a clever idea but may have gotten approved right then and there.

After leaving the improvised theater behind, we two chatterboxes, which is not always the case with us, could not contain ourselves. My initial inclination had been to go see a musical, but I was so thrilled with the performance we had just devoured. And it being my son's suggestion suddenly made me fully grasp how fatherhood never terminates. Yes, we raise our kids with the idea of preparing them for life, but then it is only right they complement our efforts by simply being there, participating with a life quite full of everyday brilliance, whether running a corporation or simply giving their best in a restaurant.

Chapter 209

I never completely turn my back on anyone. Unless someone has really hurt me, and as far as my memory banks tell me, no one truly had. My inability to close a door and keep it shut has always prevailed as a stable set of ground rules. Good or bad, well, who can say? It is just an inherited trait from my mom.

Joe had sent me a Christmas card every year. Included were a few well written words praising my greatness, something which would slightly baffle me, for if I am great, it has yet to manifest itself. Such is my theory on this. We had lost track of each other prior to my move to Italy, and I was not keen on seeing him once back, but quite by chance I ran into him. He was at the park in Dupont Circle on a late Sunday morning, and he spotted me leaving the farmer's market while returning to my car.

It was my new Mazda 3 which we both boarded. Joe had requested a ride home, and so after small talk, and having no immediate event to attend to, I complied. More discussion regarding D.C. came forth, and I briefly narrated my failed adventure abroad. Before separating, the happy camper insisted I occasionally join him on Sunday mornings at a coffee shop called Tryst in Adams Morgan. Well, eventually I did. There, I found a most casual and comfortable ambiance shared by some interesting and well-informed people.

Joe always managed to bring together a small group. We were usually about five, and he engaged us all about every imaginable topic worth sharing. Yet one Sunday morning, we had the floor to ourselves. It was he who began to chat with three airline hostesses from Lufthansa. They had spent the night in D.C. and would be flying home in the afternoon. Joe delved into a fun chat, executed both cleverly and jovially, and soon had all of us conversing. Those three ladies were not just beautiful, but smart, opinionated, friendly, and perhaps gifted with huge hearts. Their demeanor reminded me of Christian values without the religious tag to go with it.

I began to love my Sunday mornings in Adams Morgan. My buddy was always present and entertaining someone. Quite by chance, I even met an Italian couple and was surprised to learn the gentleman worked at the IMF. He claimed to barely know my wife and professed his love for his job. He was an editor, and surprisingly, willing to help out with my new endeavor. Back to Japan for a second.

It was in Tokyo that Ricky had suggested I pen my life story. An interesting challenge, but I feared I would fail to connect all the dots. Yet it seemed best to give it a go. The endeavor would allow me to revisit my past, good and bad, and if uncertain or lacking details, I could at times verify some things with Peter. Now, just why I chose to write in Italian is a mystery. Was my intent to narrate according to the whims and customs where it all, almost all, began?

My guest from Italy answered positively. A few days later, I send a file via an e-mail. I soon began to suspect it was lost, for it was only fifty pages, and no response arrived until many months later. According to him, the story was written badly, lacked structure and was a bit too rambling. So, that file was deleted and a new one was penned in English, hoping to converse properly and perhaps even win a few hearts.

Chapter 210

Another lovely Thanksgiving was spent in the Bronx. Our delicious and plentiful meal had me full and quite ready to not move a muscle. What happened next, however, surprised and fascinated me. One of Peter's hidden talents came to fore. He had never demonstrated certain traits but apparently possessed more than I was aware of.

First, allow me to dwell on a peculiarity. Peter had seemed so greatly overjoyed at his daughter's wedding some years back. His eyes sparkled as if something priceless glittered before him. The youngest daughter had done fantastically well in school, was now a pharmacist, and on her wedding-day appeared super happy. Such were the facts boosting this man's ecstasy. He also admired and spoke highly of his new son-in-law, had even branded him as true blue. Well, his most joyous feelings were certainly running wild that day.

Now, on the last Thursday of November, something entirely different made him stand out. Once through eating, someone suggested we all play a game of Password, quite unheard of during previous occasions. Everyone began to provide words to compliment others in a quick and fun take. My brother was simply incredible. Here was someone who had hardly gone to school, plus books, newspapers or magazines were simply not his cup of tea. Yet Peter competed like a champ. Not only that, but with each word provided came a punchline, which made me feel a tad plain, even boring, but certainly happy to participate.

Later, everyone had moved on. The now not-so-newlyweds drove home to Long Island. My sister-in-law and her oldest daughter took themselves to the apartment above, and Peter sat nearby in the living room watching a basketball game. Quite by chance, his father-in-law and I began talking about WWII. My love for history will never abate. I had simply mentioned that Mr. Rossi had once shared a bit of his past regarding the defense of Sicily.

Alessandro had been a lieutenant in the Italian armed forces. His troops were assigned the task of protecting a chunk of the southern Sicilian coastline, which was an impossible mission. His company was equipped with two machine guns to accomplish their task with, but more disturbing, many of the local soldiers had already deserted and returned home. I was told that on the morning our Navy and merchant fleet made its presence felt, Mr. Rossi insisted they could hardly see the sea in front of them. A white flag was raised immediately. However, that evening, he cried, having fully realized all his dreams of glory and staunch patriotism had been crushed.

The gentleman in front of me now spoke. He had witnessed no combat of any sort and was rather grateful his native town of Corleone had been spared the brutal bombing Palermo took. However, he claimed once U.S. troops arrived in his town, things became very troublesome. Most of our soldiers were usually drunk and often went on a rampage. They tore bars apart and ransacked some of the local shops, and on a few occasions, a couple of soldiers had even become violent with the women. Obviously, war is hell, and to the victors belong the spoils.

Our talk eventually terminated, and the man took himself to his apartment on the top floor. All my conversations with him had always engaged me plenty. He was very well-composed, informed, and a good to the core chap. Years back, his wife had passed away from illness, yet he still visited her tomb religiously. Plus, although up there in age, the man enjoyed his daily walks in the neighborhood. And when I visited in the summertime, he would take me to his garden and had me return home with lots of vegetables, for he insisted natural foods were healthiest, and his garden was the perfect proof.

I left the Bronx the following morning. Once about to exit the New Jersey Turnpike, it suddenly came on. That vicious Japanese illness was again plaguing me. My physical weakness was accompanied by an abundance of phlegm, and both symptoms had no intention of subsiding. Then upon crossing into Maryland, a different problem tackled me, and perhaps I was somewhat to blame, but not entirely.

My vehicle was in the right lane. A traffic jam had subdued us, so everyone was driving at a snail's pace. Eventually, I noticed a long stretch of road further up ahead, practically void of vehicles. It was my intention to simply get out of this impasse and move there. Arriving at my dwelling as soon as possible was my only objective. It took a while, but eventually my car was in the left lane, and I accelerated to a very high speed.

Where this police car came out of, I just don't know. Yet he was right behind me. Once in the emergency lane, my sneezing and spitting up crap onto my handkerchief kept me from stopping my car quickly enough for the officer. Using his microphone, he instructed me to stop the vehicle immediately. Eventually I did. Unfortunately, the order had been repeated. Then a new one instructed me to shut off the engine and drop the keys outside the car, something I did not do.

Anyhow, one angry cop appeared at my driver's side window. He demanded to know why my car had failed to stop immediately. I am certain my response meant nothing to him as he took my documents and returned to his vehicle. The good law man certainly took his time. He eventually returned and handed me four traffic violations totaling $975. Believe me, that prick got a silent but long list of unpleasantries and expletives, also better left unsaid. As I drove off, my Japanese killer flu was still getting the best of me. It was certainly not a good day.

Sometime before midnight, an overdose of phlegm almost choked me to death. That is why I called Eric and pleaded for his assistance. He arrived quickly and insisted we go to the hospital. Now, it is impossible for me to explain why years back when living in Fairfax City, I was taken to Arlington Hospital, and now that I lived in Arlington, we went to the hospital in Fairfax County.

Nevertheless, it was a rerun of the old visit. When asked by the nurse what brought me there, I began to speak but immediately covered my mouth to keep from spitting on her, which may have made a point with her, but apparently no one else. We two sat and waited, and waited, and at some point, Eric inquired if someone would eventually see me. He was reassured it would happen. At about 4:00 a.m. we headed home. So ended another dreary visit to a hospital.

My physician saw me the following afternoon and prescribed a bunch of different medications. It took several weeks before my lungs fully recovered. I had previously spoken to Peter about the outlandish traffic ordeal, and although he sympathized with my situation, he advised me to pay the fines, for in his words, "You can't fight city hall."

It seemed best to comply with my brother's counsel. However, a couple of close friends completely disagreed and insisted I hire a lawyer. It was actually a wise move. Having been ticketed several times in Virginia the year before and receiving another fine in Manhattan before arriving at my brother's, my driving record was rather dire. Paying these four new fines would have most certainly have caused me to lose my license.

Now, the ticket in New York City truly pissed me off! I had simply made a right turn, not having seen the sign prohibiting it as it stood quite a-ways before the intersection. And of course, someone just happened to be hiding nearby waiting for a sucker like me to pounce on. There was no greeting, no clarifying the dirty deed, just a firm request for my documents from one truly sad-looking mug. Yet I gave it my best. For here was a police officer with an Italian last name. Hoping to perhaps lighten the load, I informed him on the meaning of his family name and its importance throughout Italy. Well, from his looks, I am surprised he didn't spit at me. So, a fine came my way, which would not be a problem financially, but it certainly meant accumulating more negative points.

An attorney was contacted. The lawyer on the phone heard my story, quoted a price, and believed we could win. I was instructed to be in his office two hours before my court case began, and that is what I did. After entering and introducing myself, the gentleman sat me down, and he took a chair and placed it in front of me and sat down. We were face to face when he asked me to again brief him on what had occurred. A great way to evaluate any person. As before, I offered the truth.

At the courthouse, I was the only one contesting a fine. Well, more than one fine. Therefore, I would be dealt with last. And what a show! America certainly is a great nation, but a few of its institutionalized systems can be overwhelming and perhaps, at times, even unfair. I witnessed all the traffic violations being processed, and there were many. Everyone entailed a guilty plea, and then the judge's gavel came down hard once the amount to be collected was given. Please forgive my take on this. Perhaps, to some extent, upholding the law had become a bit of a racket, for I noticed that the man who had me in court was the one with the most, and quite a few, violations issued.

According to his narrative, I arrived like Speedy Gonzalez where traffic was moving slowly. I failed to maintain a safe distance from the car in front of me, his exact words indicated me being, "Two inches away from that vehicle." No turn signal was used to access the center and left lane, while also driving recklessly in making my way into the left lane, and once there, my vehicle sped away like a rocket. This is what led to the four fines he was now defending rather proudly.

It was not only my version of things which highlighted the truth. My talented lawyer blew him away. His first question asked where exactly was the officer's vehicle while I was practically on top of the car before me? The policeman thought for a few seconds, then replied he could not recall for sure. Then, how much time had lapsed between my arrival to that crowded area and taking off in the left lane. He again claimed he could not say exactly, and this led the female judge, who was wearing glasses, to lower them while looking directly at him as if to make eye contact in expressing some incredulity.

He even bungled the next question. The judge found me guilty only on what I had already confessed to, speeding. Justice had prevailed! The officer now stated he had not made up anything, but that rather attractive and serious female arbiter, although replying positively, was not buying it. My fine was $250, and my lawyer cost me about the same. But being proven innocent, when you are, has no price. Julian Di Stefano was certainly a happy person, and he even swore to drive more cautiously, especially on my way back home.

Chapter 211

Francesca had retired, and she, along with Eric moved to Italy. And we had finally divorced. This did not change anything, but our union had certainly instilled a most basic principle in me, never again. After all, living as a lone wolf was just fine, and my social life, whether dating, getting out, or seeking some sexual gratification, demanded a bit of effort but was certainly proceeding well.

Life should have continued fine, but unfortunately, it did not. Not sure when it first occurred, but whatever had happened in Vicenza was plaguing me once again, only this time more intensely.

One morning, after settling in my classroom, I was forced to excuse myself with my students and seek help. The teacher in the classroom next to ours noticed that I did not look right, and she immediately took charge of my students. Roger brought me home in my car, while his assistant followed us in hers.

The following afternoon my physician saw me. She prescribed something, which was not taken, for the idea of clouding my mind did not sit well with me. Approximately a week later, I still did not feel right. My entire day was spent home alone, lying in bed watching some boring TV shows. I was unable to read anything or concentrate, and later that day recalled I had a date with an ex-student, a very lovely Mongolian woman. We had previously gone out and had shared a wonderful time together. Not wanting to concern her over my circumstances, it seemed best to get a bit of fresh air and revive myself.

Soon enough, my car was on the outskirts of Rosslyn. Once near her residence, a parking space was available, although a bit tight, and I had almost parked when someone a bit further up the road left a larger gap available and so I began to pull out. Now, just what occurred next remains a mystery. Suddenly, my vehicle was on the sidewalk, and the back of it had smashed into the fire hydrant. I exited my car but could not make sense of what happened.

I took in the ghastly scene. It was apparent that folks passing by appeared to be asking themselves, "What the hell is he on?" I somehow managed to park the car, and then walked to my friend's place. My accounting of the incident had her in total disbelief, and we took ourselves to view the damage. Upon seeing the back of my car, she looked at me and appeared slightly bewildered.

We headed toward Rosslyn. The plan was to get to Georgetown for dinner, but that didn't happen. While strolling at a leisurely pace, I began to bump into my friend and did so several times. My balance was slightly off. At some point, she stopped walking, took hold of my hands, and insisted I see a doctor first thing Monday morning.

My physician heard me out and ordered a CAT scan. The doctor at the hospital who provided the results of the test could not explain what he found. There was some white matter in the front part of my brain. As to just what it was and how it got there, no one had a clue. The diagnosis created some difficulty for my physician to prescribe anything. Perhaps she did, I do not recall. Then, as bizarre as it was, whatever had been pestering me for some time, simply vanished.

Fortunately, something positive occurred a month later. The virus in my liver was fully eradicated. And it is a bit strange that it all came about by chance. My physician had sent me to see a specialist for an entirely different problem. Once there, I was required to fill out a form outlining all my health ailments, present and past. Naturally, the hep C was included, and it caught the nurse's attention.

Truth be told, my ailment was something I kept in check. I ate healthy and well-balanced meals, avoided strong medicines when prescribed, no longer indulged in that Vietnam embellishment with beer, and still exercised a little. It was the nurse tending to me who mentioned that a new miracle drug was curing patients of their hep C. Of course, my mind relived that six-month crucifixion and opted to not be saved. Then the doctor entered, and he and the nurse were staring at me most triumphantly.

He spoke, and it sounded like we finally got it right. The good doctor, like a cheerful salesman, delivered a perfect monologue as his verbal range was dispensed most convincingly to win me over. After rambling on, once given my cue, I informed him what had brought me there. The physician apologized and told me there had been some kind of mistake. His area of expertise was not for the problem I was confronting. Very soon, the nurse escorted me to the office exit area.

Well, it happened in my building. I had met a Greek girl over the Fourth of July holiday. Our condo allowed us access to the roof, and there were many residents witnessing the evening fireworks in D.C. She had inquired about my abstinence, and so my malady was revealed. Apparently, she worked in a clinic and now informed me about a liver specialist at the Howard University Hospital. That medic was supposedly curing everyone. Was I at all interested?

The physician who greeted me was an Indian woman. She never attempted to persuade me to do anything. I was properly informed about the success of a new drug called Harvoni. A few weeks later, I began the treatment. It seemed incredible. My first blood work showed my liver was free of the hep C. I stayed on that medicine for three months, for such was the cure, never had any problems, and once terminating it, I was free at last.

Chapter 212

Peter's wife called one day. The news from the Bronx totally devastated me! My brother had been hospitalized. He was out on his morning walk with a friend. Suddenly Peter could not continue. He sat on the sidewalk quite helpless, awaiting an ambulance which would get him to a hospital. He was diagnosed with lung cancer.

Within two weeks, Peter would begin chemotherapy. His wife and I were both optimistic and convinced he would pull through. I promised to visit very soon. Later that day, my mother was informed of the circumstances, and her response truly upset me. We argued but not too drastically nor too condescending either. The call, however, accomplished nothing as she refused to reach out to Peter. The two were not talking due to some minor incident.

I simply hung up. We would never talk again if she continued with this nonsense. It was a few months later, after a brief visit to the Bronx and seeing Peter a bit under but somewhat optimistic, that I flew out of JFK and landed in Milano. The villa was completely bypassed as I stayed true to course in keeping my distance from my mother.

My rental car took me to Vicenza. That city always pulled me in as if I still belonged there. I met with a few old friends the first day, and soon enjoyed a wonderful afternoon with Francesco and Gianna, who were now happily married. Our long discussion covered the world of music, and we shared much about various artists we liked plus how they had influenced the world by singing and giving something of themselves in a field of harmonious lingo.

I then drove a rental car to Salerno. Everyone was happy to have me among them, but my aunt felt a tad disappointed in learning my visit would be brief, having already planned to explore two cities further up north. I feel a need to include my opinion on some differences regarding north vs south. The south of Italy is, in many ways, quite divine; however it does possess some unique challenges. Once you are south of Rome, you encounter a completely different world. One apparent difference is the lack of modern trends, especially in small towns. What does exist is barely adequate; at least such is my take on things. And yet, those tolerable inconveniences are quickly discarded as the richness of antiquity, a laidback lifestyle, plus all that delicious food do bear their own rewards.

I was now with my cousin Stefania driving to Ercolano. On the Amalfi coastline, the splendor of sturdy, old cities sitting above a still azure water enriches the spirit and elevates the spell of the tourist sites to be explored. However, once we were at our destination, that enchantment disappeared. The town had us in its clutches, as parking anywhere was impossible. It annoyed me as we struggled for quite a while trying to find a place to leave the vehicle.

My cousin remained optimistic, and sure enough, a young teen suddenly got our attention. I stopped the car, and he inquired if we needed to park. I, of course, was reluctant to engage him, but Stefania spoke in a most casual tone.

The lad insisted we follow him and took us to a nearby school. It was summer, so it was closed, yet cars were parked all around the premises, and they probably belonged to folks like us. Well, that young critter earned himself a pretty good tip. But such is life in the big city, of a small town, in a minute country, which miraculously manages to survive.

We approached the ancient ruins. My cousin began narrating a bit of history. The town's Latin name was Herculaneum, supposedly named after Hercules. And like Pompei, it was buried under the volcanic ashes of Mount Vesuvius in A.D. 79. In the early eighteenth century, it was rediscovered by chance, but soon, some of the artifacts found began to disappear. That is why a better managed excavation process was established which ultimately provided the incredible archaeological site we see today.

The remnants of small streets, perfectly laid out, built almost two thousand years ago, were now in front of us. It seemed incredible. And, even more amazing, was the idea that the city center had water flowing in from a nearby aqueduct. Then came the marvelous frescoes on walls in various homes showing scenes of everyday life. Apparently, the richer patrons had more to show off, and a few were obviously enjoying their sex life. It triggered a contemplative state of mind. I pondered civilization's enduring traits. I even asked myself if religion played any role in the conduct of personal human affairs. After all, matters of the heart or the body should remain a private issue to the individual.

The following morning, I visited my uncle's shop. It was soon time for an espresso, and once in the nearby coffee shop, he received details regarding my incredible flight on United Emirates Airlines. For I had flown on a new Airbus plane from JFK to Milano in a spacious seat and hardly ever hit turbulence, which seemed like a sheer miracle to me.

Once back in his store, my uncle insisted I use the PC. For many years, he and his wife had enthusiastically declared their desire to see the U.S. It was time to purchase tickets and make that trip happen. He decided on traveling next year in the spring, and so two tickets were purchased with UEA, and then a bit of work was done in clearing my relatives through the customs' website to register them to enter the U.S. It was soon a done deal.

Chapter 213

My brother and I were at JFK awaiting our aunt and uncle. He did not look good. Peter had lost too much weight, and his once joyous mood was practically nonexistent. Although the person we all knew was simply not there, he swore he would beat the illness. He owed it to his beautiful grandson, his youngest daughter's little boy, whom he loved so immensely, and the boy reciprocated wholeheartedly.

As we waited in the lounge, we rehashed our years as kids in Barazzetto. Our aunt had become like an older sister for she played a huge role in always being there for us. Peter still recalled the day of our departure, a memory that had been lost deep in the recesses of my brain. Our Sicilian grandfather, a stranger to us two, took possession of us and brought us home to Sicily. The townsfolks must have been devastated once informed, and not only had we simply disappeared, but nothing was ever heard about us again until his reappearance in 1974. Peter informed me he had a photograph somewhere at home of us two after our arrival in Palermo. He swore we both looked shell-shocked.

Oh well. There they were! The long embrace Peter shared with our aunt was very touching. There was an exchange of greetings and kisses, a bit of pleasant talk, and we soon headed back to the Bronx where my brother's entire family was present to greet us. We later sat to a hearty meal, lots of talk about life in Italy, but Peter soon abandoned us as he felt exhausted. We three guests eventually moved on to the Rosehill Bed and Breakfast in Mount Vernon.

The hotel was great. The next morning, we joined an Italian couple for breakfast. They were vacationing and preparing to return to Manhattan, being down to their last few days. Our conversation in Italian allowed our host, the owner, to run some errands, knowing we were all in good hands. The young cheerful couple compared some social practices they had witnessed since their arrival and favored them over their own back home. They insisted Italy lived too much in the past. We three soon got going on our drive to Virginia.

D.C. had us visiting for a few days. Our outings started early, and as my guests refused to eat out, we were home by late afternoon. My aunt insisted on home-cooked meals, which required that we shop for fresh food at the nearby Whole Foods Market. Eventually, we ate like kings. Wanting to give them a taste of something entirely different, in terms of our country, I took them to see the Grand Canyon. Unfortunately, they were in country for only two weeks, therefore, too soon, it was back to New York and the B&B.

It felt like we explored the Big Apple rather quickly. My relatives were impressed with the immensity of the city but not so much with the walking required. My uncle fell in love with the MoMA. He was simply mesmerized seeing the vast amount of different art and how cleverly it was laid out, plus, he made a peculiar comment on the exterior of the Guggenheim Museum.

According to him, it was simply a perfect unique design for where that edifice sat.

We spent our last two evenings at Peter's place for dinner. My brother's wife and her father were so incredibly hospitable, but it was soon time to leave. At JFK, my aunt assured me our mom would be informed of Peter's condition. It seemed sad to me that someone needed to force the issue. But such were my family trials and tribulations then, and they did not change for quite a while.

Chapter 214

Eric did not remain in Italy very long. He returned to the U.S. on a merchant ship. I am certain his fear of flying comes from me. During my very first excursion in the skies, I did not have a tranquil state of mind. Anyhow, my son arrived on the east coast and then rode a train across country. It was to settle in with his cousin, now working and living in San Francisco. However, once there, he discovered the chap had just lost his job and would soon return home to Vicenza.

It may have been a month later when Eric moved in. He was more than welcome, and he soon replaced me at the school in Annandale. Roger was happy to have him but sad to lose me. Eric took his new initiative quite responsibly and was soon working entirely too much. He taught a morning and evening class, and then began waiting tables on weekends at a restaurant in Arlington. I hardly ever saw him, but occasionally, we managed to dine at an Indian restaurant we both loved.

After Eric began teaching, and I stopped, Inlingua called me. One must assume a grapevine system engulfs the entire planet, and we humans are the leaves left out to dry. The school needed teachers, particularly ones who make a difference. I decided to visit and see if it still appealed to me. The school was almost unrecognizable. The administrative staff was all new, so were the teachers, and those fantastic books we had used were unheard of. The new owner, whom I briefly met with, was keen on improving the establishment, but one change he had brought about truly shocked me. It was the new cadre of students flocking there.

Allow me to clue you in. They were all Saudi Arabians. And just what had brought such a large number of Arabs to our shores? It seems that the Saudi king had wanted his people to make a difference. Therefore, Saudi citizens, who perhaps knew little about the world outside their confines, would come to any English-speaking nation to learn the language. Not only that, but they could also pursue any other studies they desired. The overall intent was for them to make a more positive contribution to any profession or work environment once back home.

And if you think the students on board were the elite, that is not the case. The program was for all Saudis, and the overall package, funded by their government, paid everything. This included transportation, school fees for the linguistic schools and universities if applicable, money for food, entertainment and lodging, and if parents were concerned over their daughter being in a foreign land, why, they too could go abroad to accompany her and even learn a language. It was this kind of generosity which had me sometimes claim, "Gee, I certainly wish we had a king!"

All my classes were full of Saudis. Of course, Arabic people, including their customs and traditions were quite foreign to me. Nevertheless, I quickly came to terms with what a wonderful bunch of students attended my sessions.

They were friendly, courteous, eager to learn and improve, and, to a large extent, they had good hearts. Yet, there was one issue which confused me, the attire of the females. In the same classroom, it was quite common to see women in a different facial garb.

Some ladies wore the Abaya, which only allowed their eyes and foreheads to be visible. Whereas others donned something called, the Burqa. They were so concealed, you saw only a tad of their eyes, but absolutely nothing else. And yet occasionally, there were young ladies in modern clothes, that is, they dressed in jeans and fancy blouses, and most of them looked so good.

One day I inquired about the different attire. The answer they gave me did not clarify anything. It depended on the person's interpretation of the Koran. Well, I had no more questions as this was a bit beyond me.

All proceeded well in the scheme of things. It seemed incredible it could happen again, yet it did. One of my students came to class after being absent for several weeks. He had been present for a few days the first week but had then simply disappeared. Feeling happy to see him, it seemed legitimate to inquire if he had been on holiday. The young student appeared a bit irate upon hearing me, and quickly informed me he had been ill. Perhaps he looked a bit run-down, but certainly nothing to be concerned about.

Not so the following morning! The class had just resumed after a fifteen-minute break. The students were tackling a written exercise on using the present perfect tense. Once finished, upon a student providing an answer to a specific question from the exercise, I would intervene with a pertinent question to reinforce the use of that form of speech. All was proceeding fine. Suddenly, my ill-looking student was on the floor and shaking violently. There was a verbal explosion as some women began wailing and crying, and all the students stood up, most looking quite shocked, some praying, and others loudly expressing their anguish in Arabic.

I shouted for everyone to leave the classroom and then immediately attended to the victim on the floor. There was vomit in his mouth, and the student was totally unresponsive. His body had stopped trembling. I cleared his mouth as best as possible and realized he was not breathing. While my intervention was more spontaneous this time, it did not immediately accomplish anything, but still, I persisted. Suddenly, the student's eyes opened. He kept staring at me, and now two men by my side joyfully expressed themselves in Arabic. Well, it certainly sounded Arabic to me, but also quite joyful at that moment.

The ambulance response was immediate. The crew took over and began questioning the somewhat startled and baffled young man still sitting on the floor. The few queries addressed to him, in English, appeared to slightly confuse the student, and he answered in Arabic, which of course led to someone now translating for him. How bizarre! It was decided that he be taken to the hospital for observation, and we saw him again several days later.

The school chose to terminate our class for the day. Once I exited the classroom and faced a few staff members, they all smiled at me most graciously while proclaiming me a hero. Apparently, there was much talk about what had occurred. Yet the real glory shone so brightly the following day. My students looked at me with so much admiration and personal esteem. It was like I was one of them. A young lady gave me a box of fresh dates her cousin had just brought from Saudi Arabia. A small gift reminding me of one of life's most valuable lessons, we are all one.

Chapter 215

Eric simply shocked me one day. After being with me for almost a year, the young man informed me he had taken a teaching job in China. It was not only surprising news but an odd choice. Whenever I proposed we go out for Chinese food, which I love, he would decline. It was his least favorite cuisine. And yet the lad was moving to Guangzhou for a two-year stint. I certainly hoped he would enjoy his new quest, not starve, and perhaps even get to explore some of Asia.

While my son headed to China, I became involved with a Chinese woman. I had not been dating anyone for a while. This was due to my somewhat non-committal stance. Forgive me if you find this odd. I had begun to enjoy being on my own, plus, whenever someone was with me and we bonded nicely, a question was soon pitched out as, "So, am I your girlfriend?" It sounded like a requirement in the realm of relationships which had either been overlooked or simply left out. Yet it now needed to be included or reinstated.

So why was I now with a Chinese lady? We really had nothing in common. And in instances when the conversation turned slightly serious, she sometimes appeared confused, which immediately led me to sprinkle our chat with a small dose of humor but also accept her slim contribution regardless of good, bad, or indifferent. Oh well, I was giving it my best.

At times, however, Lisha, brought her Christian faith to fore. Her personal belief regarding me, of course, constituted my need for God, which made me click my heels, she having truly lost me. I believe my biggest sin occurred when I once proclaimed, "I thought people in China had no religion, what happened to you?" The small, angry, spicy, foxy lady did not speak to me for a while.

Anyhow, as far as our love life went, it was simply superb. We seemed to go for the longest time and most passionately, and it was incredible how much energy we both had. All this is being presented simply in affirming that, although occasionally my time alone was lengthy with no dating of any sort, I would eventually come up for air and certainly breathe quite naturally.

Perhaps my life had begun taking in a healthy dose of fresh air. However, one issue constantly troubling me was Peter's condition. We had last reunited at the baptism of his daughter's second child. He looked terribly gaunt and sickly, hardly spoke, and it was very disheartening to see him so debilitated. Nevertheless, we continuously chatted over the phone, especially in instances when an important football match was on. By the time the game terminated, we had spoken plenty.

Peter loved Chelsea, whereas my preference was for Manchester City. Regardless of which team was on the pitch that day, our dialogue, sometimes before and after the game concluded, was interesting. And it was not unusual for him to call me right after some incredible play, either a goal or some well-executed move, for his excitement and praise of the footballers was profound. I would quickly forget his circumstance while hearing his excited tone.

It was very devastating seeing him one last time. Peter was home alone. His father-in-law was now in a nursing home, while his wife and oldest daughter were in Florida. He looked awful. His whole demeanor sagged just like the clothes he wore. As he outright refused to have me cook for us, we went out to eat, and he ordered some of his favorite dishes, then sent down a morsel or two but nothing more. It was so apparent he would not make it.

One afternoon, my truly ill brother fell asleep in front of a match. It was an exciting game, moving at a fast pace, but suddenly Peter was out like a light. I simply lowered the volume, allowed him to rest, and as the match terminated, he awoke and then looked at me and said, "I can't believe mommy doesn't call."

I felt slightly devastated. Yet it was only right to speak up. First, I reminded him I was there, and that we had been together since his birth. His eyes wanted to smile. Perhaps my words may have slightly lessened his load, yet they hardened me and truly sunk any positive thoughts for our mother. I would never forgive that she refused to call her dying son.

So, it finally occurred! Peter's wife destroyed me completely! What can I say? We all practice the art of survival and learn to believe in a meaningful existence. Therefore, we deceive ourselves and forget that often the brutality of things never conforms to our expectations. When she told me my brother had passed, although I was expecting this news, it hurt me deeply. It just seemed so unreal. All he wanted was to be there for his grandchildren.

Once the facts were shared, I hung up and cried uncontrollably. I loved my brother so much. At times, my recollections of our growing up in Palermo would come to fore, and I suffered a bit. We had been brutalized, but he much more than me. In the Bronx, we had sort of parted ways, found different friends, but then finally reunited in Italy. As adults, we had bonded strongly, no matter the distance nor the circumstances. Now I truly felt the weight of being alone!

Chapter 216

In September 2017, British Airways flew me from Dulles Airport to Venice, my ultimate destination. Yet our plane had to circle around London for some time as heavy winds kept it from landing. But land it did. I had now missed my connecting flight and therefore had to retrieve my luggage and go through customs before making another flight. A rather unusual thing occurred leaving me frowning a bit.

I have always traveled with my U.S. passport. It is the one which gets me in and out of my country and around the world. That document represents my nationality, upbringing, traditions, way of thinking (to some extent), and a bit of vision of the world. The British one, last renewed some years back, was somewhere in a drawer and had probably expired. Oh well, it was the customs agent who baffled me. The gentleman looked at my passport, then checked me out on his computer. Once he handed the document back to me, he said, "Mr. Di Stefano, the next time you come to the U.K., please use your British passport." Strange! I concurred by nodding.

My immediate thought was, *Welcome to the twenty-first century*. If back in the 1970s, a mere sailor at the airport in Chicago discovered how the FBI, in a few minutes, knew even when he farted, today with the untouchable reach of modern technology, it is a piece of cake for certain institutions to see more than what is necessary about anyone. Anyhow, that a customs officer knew how many passports I possessed made me uneasy.

Eventually, I arrived in Venice, and drove to Vicenza in a rental car. Whereas my past stays were with my ex-in-laws, I now decided to maintain a bit of distance. For my ex-wife seemed to embellish how she had been the driving force behind our accomplishments, and yours truly was simply the loser whose good luck had brought me to her. Her sister apparently agreed and would regurgitate her take religiously. So, it seemed best to just pay a small visit but continue to lodge elsewhere.

I certainly visited Francesco and Gianna. They were now parents to a gorgeous little girl, who was growing so exquisitely. After seeing them, it was difficult for me to move on, even though my schedule was quite full. Our relationship was blooming, which is why all my trips to Vicenza included a fine day with them. I always left feeling soulfully nourished, and my spirit remained quite elevated throughout my entire stay in country. Plus, we three adults had finally come to terms with the facts regarding Francesco's paternity.

It got ironed out one evening. After dinner, the seven-month-old baby was put to bed, and Gianna then joined Francesco and me in the living room. The woman looked at me and asked if I had any news to share with them. After inquiring just what subject was of interest to her, she said, "Well, my daughter looks exactly like you, and so does my husband." Accordingly, a bit of my past was fully revealed, nicely explained, and it was fully accepted.

It was the following year when the truth was confirmed. Francesco's mother was not very pleased with my revelation. She classified it as fiction. Perhaps it was part of my desperate need to fit in. So, my son and I took ourselves to the hospital in Padova for a paternity test. The four categories analyzed concluded that 99.9 percent favored me being his father. Now, without sounding too vain, I believe we both knew what we had long suspected. At times, the erratic may be your best remedy.

Chapter 217

A few days later, I made my way to Livorno to visit my Sicilian cousin. Following in his older brother's footsteps, he too had become a carabiniere. And perhaps his new territory may have made him feel quite far from home. For he now incurred a new dialect, totally different food, an unknown background, and few friends. Eventually, he began to fit in, married, and was now father to two boys. He came to terms with a straightforward fact; life anywhere is simply what you bring to it.

Our talks were quite long, and we sometimes covered unknown territory. Our grandmother would occasionally take center stage even though she had passed away a few years back. That woman had certainly left a strong impact on most of us cousins, and I felt a need to state my gratefulness with what had occurred after her departure. My aunt and uncles had gifted the unexpected to Peter and myself. Once the woman's apartment was sold, a portion of the funds, which would have gone to our dad, were provided to us two. It was totally unexpected and so very highly appreciated!

One day, I took in the well-known sights in Pisa for it sits next to Livorno. Soon enough, it was on to Palermo to visit my Sicilian clan. The short flight was a breeze, a quick bus ride had me downtown, and I walked to my B&B in ten minutes. What a grand resort, and though far from new, I found it to be an attractive place. It was super clean, nicely decorated, and managed by some very professional individuals. One even shared the best affordable restaurants in the vicinity.

All my relatives were shocked to hear from me, as I had not announced my arrival. Of course, I promised to visit everyone, but informed them all that my mornings and afternoons were strictly dedicated to exploring Palermo. As a child, it was simply the territory I occupied, whereas now it displayed its eloquent historical cultural and artistic richness to me. Its street food was still to die for, as long as I did not eat too excessively.

My family visits always began in late afternoon. They consisted of much hugging and kissing, and long discussions followed while devouring scrumptious food. Italian food is certainly great, but Sicilian food is even better. Uncle Luca and family had me first. My goodness, the man never aged. And yet, a few years back, his oldest son perished in a plane crash. The horror of such a loss never ceases to linger. Both he and his wife, lovable and kind, still bore the pain on their faces. His wife's silence was a personal grave she partially hid in.

My uncle's family members joined us that evening. They all rendered remarks regarding my uncanny resemblance to my father. I am him, although he is long gone. Of course, I was spared the Sicilian dialect, even though I could grasp bits and pieces when it accidentally came out.

Someone mentioned wanting to see the U.S., which delighted me, as I welcomed them to come visit me. Then we tackled Italy's thriving tourist industry, and that morning I had witnessed a group of Chinese tourists getting on their bus. It was rather odd to me, having never seen a large group of Chinese people in Italy before. Tourism had become a booming trade, yet one which required constant expansion on all fronts to keep it going. It spelled out how globalization knows no limits and is here to stay.

I visited Termini Imerese the following afternoon. Uncle Andrea's daughter Anna picked me up at the train station. She reminded me so much of her mother. That very angelic woman who had plied the child in me with a mysterious gift from a passing bus. Unfortunately, years ago, my aunt had lost her fight with cancer.

My cousin brought me to her brother's coffee shop. It was grand seeing him, and a pleasant surprise meeting his wife. The woman kept the place going full speed ahead. She even introduced me to a bit of novelty. For the place served such foreign and unknown treats like cupcakes and pancakes. I say foreign, as southern Italians never indulged in any non-native grub a while back. I was informed they were even considering introducing the idea of brunch. Well, I shook the couple's hands and considered promising to revisit once it was up and running.

Eventually, Anna drove us to her place, while my uncle was waiting at her home. Although a bit enthusiastic to see me, the man appeared quite reserved all evening, even though plenty of his grandchildren were there. To be exact, his daughter had six daughters. The girls were mostly teenagers, and all were well-mannered. They were quite curious to know a bit about life in America. I shared mostly positive news, a few personal tales, and those sisters contributed most happily after their dad or mom had spoken first. I had to ask myself if such manners get instilled via a love-oriented upbringing or the severity of imposing mom and dad's ways, or perhaps a bit of both.

Anyhow, they were all devout Christians. Strange as it may sound, I, at some point, felt like I was revisiting the Harrison Ford movie where he finds himself among the Amish community in Pennsylvania. For my hosts' gentle expressions and thoughtful ways brought that flick to mind. It was soon very late, and my cousin and her husband insisted on driving me to Palermo even though it was a long ride. It strongly reinforced my appreciation of their considerate kind ways after having witnessed it all night.

I finally visited Aunt Felicia's place. It always felt like she laid out the royal carpet to welcome me. My uncle had picked me up from the city center and brought me home. My aunt was so thrilled to see me and super happy to receive all the news accumulated over the years.

The following day, two of my cousins got together with me. It was Uncle Nicola's third son and his sister. Their dad had recently passed away but was mentioned a bit throughout the evening. They had picked me up at my B&B and brought me to Mondello. We dined on a fancy dinner which included every imaginable aquatic species available, and I do believe I ate entirely too much but loved every minute of it.

It was time to return home. Soon enough, I was back in the beautiful state of Virginia and began to fully dedicate myself entirely to finishing my life story. For rather than occasionally penning a bit of my past life, something within urged me to make it become my new mission.

Chapter 218

One early afternoon, Ricky got a hold of me. He informed me that my mother was having some health issues. Although listening attentively and expressing some concern, my heart simply refused to fully participate. My son had always been very close to his grandmother, and whenever with her, he made her laugh, and she reciprocated with warm gestures and a few pleasant words. As we terminated our conversation, I did promise to call her but it never happened.

My son contacted me a month later. Some very specific news was slowly broadcast. It involved some of the past and latest mishaps. A few months back, my mother was at home and had apparently done something truly reckless. The local pigeons would always congregate on the roof of the inside of the villa, in the latter part of the afternoon. She decided to take immediate action and fired a pistol, not to hit them, but to chase them off. Apparently, it worked. However, she held the gun much too close to her face and damaged her eardrums.

She now lived with an intermittent ringing in her head. And sometimes, a few bouts of serious pain lingered for a while. Plus, another peculiar adventure had occurred, and it seemed more concerning. She had recently left the villa heading to Udine to remain until spring. Somehow, the woman completely bypassed her exit, and left the highway at Trieste, which is approximately fifty miles away. Ricky was certainly worried and began pleading for me to get involved. He even mentioned that she often stated feeling a strong sense of guilt in not having contacted Peter. Apparently, she also now suffered some from a feeling of uselessness. So, could I not simply look in on my mother for a while and be of some help?

I decided to comply with my son's appeals. Francesca met me at the airport in Venice. She then drove to Udine where she now lived. My ex-wife had grown up in a small town outside that city and had become somewhat acquainted with it when she attended university. Upon retiring, it was back to a city she was quite familiar with and had felt comfortable in. My mother and her had remained in good standing and met occasionally.

Once home, my mom greeted me as if we had separated in ancient times. She could not contain her joy and would even repeat herself continuously. Once my ex-wife left, the lady of the house spoke a bit about her present circumstances, and she even agreed it was time to leave the villa behind permanently. She would now live in her flat and occasionally return to see her old house and some of her friends in that town. It finally appeared to be a done deal.

Of course, some things never change. In late afternoon the following day, my Aunt Maria had called and kept my mother on the phone a bit. She then asked to speak to me, and so I put down the newspaper I was reading and went over to where the line phone was located. We talked quite a bit and before finishing, she sort of insinuated that I could perhaps reside in Italy, yes? I promised to consider it, and after signing off, returned to my reading. The open newspaper I had left on the couch had been neatly folded and put way.

My mother's problems soon began to manifest themselves. She would occasionally stop whatever she was doing, and her facial expression conveyed pain. It never lasted long, but it was very noticeable and repeated itself more often. On other occasions, the woman simply spoke about whatever issue had caught her attention. At times, she would overly amplify her tune. We then paid a visit to her physician but that accomplished little.

A trip to the villa came about so she could retrieve some of her clothes left behind. I had just entered the highway, and something strange stood out. Trucks dominated the entire right lane, and used the middle lane to surpass each other, leaving only the left lane for automobiles. My mom stated that trucks should be prohibited from using the highway. I may have agreed, but she soon began repeating it for the longest time. I was eventually forced to pull into a gas station, just to take a break and perhaps drown her overwhelming chorus. Of course, I informed her I needed to use the restroom, and I did.

Once back in Udine, life resumed its daily routine. Every morning at eight-thirty, the lady of the house opened all the windows and began to clean the premises. It was accomplished six days a week and nothing could impede her dedication to this compulsion. On one occasion, I was smitten with flu, nevertheless, I had to evacuate the flat for nothing was going to curtail her commitment to her work schedule. Thankfully, she always concluded her performance before noon.

I would then arrive home to consult with her. My main responsibility was lunch and a small dinner later in the evening. Once we had agreed on the food for that day, I took myself to the nearby supermarket, purchased all the necessary food items, and returned home to do my part. It was amazing how much she complimented me on whatever donned our plates, always displaying her gratitude by devouring everything and thanking me most kindly.

After lunch, while the Italian newspaper was my afternoon endeavor, mom would eventually fall asleep in the living room in front of the TV. It was turned off, allowing me to return to my task of seeing the world through an Italian lens. Later in the afternoon, we took in the city center and went to the same coffee shop where I had my last espresso for the day, and she usually enjoyed a hot chocolate.

It was soon time to return to the U.S. For those of you not acquainted with Europe, there is something called the Schengen Agreement. Among other things, it allows us Yanks to stay in any of the twenty-six European member countries for three months without a visa. Then exit and stay out for three months before returning. I was not overly concerned leaving my mother alone as my ex-wife promised to look in on her more often.

Life back in Virginia was proceeding well. Then suddenly matters began to decline. I had been back more than three months when Francesca called me. There was a recent issue to contend with, and it had become problematic. My mother had begun requesting she be taken to the emergency room. She believed herself to be ill. Yet nothing was found out of place. My ex had complied willingly in assisting her, but it soon became routine. The hospital kept her under observation most of the day but always concluded there was no illness.

Too many such visits brought a drastic change. The hospital sent my mom to a state-run nursing home, on a temporary basis and all at no expense. Apparently, this was part of the process, especially as she had no relatives to assist her. My ex visited her on several occasions, kept me informed, and eventually brought her home. She appeared to have improved and was happy to be back in her flat. She was now in the hands of a caregiver who spent the entire day with her. Francesca had kept me informed and received my approval to proceed in taking care of all the necessary arrangements.

Unfortunately, once again, the unexpected occurred. For some unexplainable reason, my mother resumed making trips to the hospital, with assistant in tow. It was immediately terminated as she was sent away, but this time to a different institution. My ex pleaded with me to return, mostly to decide on the woman's future, as she believed a permanent nursing home was the best solution.

Chapter 219

It was May 2019 when I settled in at my mother's apartment. At first, it felt strange being there in her absence and knowing she was somewhat ill. The woman had always been so lively and full of vigor. On the following day, Francesca took me to visit a nursing home which she believed would be a perfect place for my mom to ultimately reside in. My approval was necessary and some paperwork needed to be signed.

Apparently, the place was new. It lacked patients. Nevertheless, it was not the emptiness which made me change my mind. I suddenly felt as if I were putting the woman aside too quickly. Of course, the director was stunned and made little attempt to hide her sense of being appalled with my request to bring the documents home to review and then sign them. It certainly did not sit well with her or her assistant.

Such was my course of action. Now believe me, my ex-wife was also quite displeased. She had done a bit of research on my behalf and had contacted these folks. Our ride back to Udine was a solemn and gloomy affair. The woman hardly spoke. The following day, it seemed best to visit my mother, and although uncertain as to what sort of situation I would confront, my initiative needed to be blessed off by the physician who cared for her.

The institution was located outside the city limits. I was greeted by a very friendly staff, and a nurse escorted me to the second floor. She then turned me over to someone else. Suddenly, my mother appeared from a distance. She was assisting a much older woman to a nearby table where a snack had been set. Upon finishing her course of action, she started walking toward us but did not immediately recognize me. Then she froze. The woman appeared slightly confused, but once her uncertainty vanished, she happily advanced forward as if in sheer heaven.

We embraced and held each other for some time. She had lost quite a bit of weight but appeared pleasant and looked fine. Once we sat, our conversation delved into her circumstances, and she spoke convincingly of feeling good. Almost immediately, I sensed her signaling a bit of relief believing she was coming home. After mentioning having just arrived in Udine and being at her place, she soon inquired about the cleanliness of the flat. What could I say!

A bit later, her physician spoke to me. The woman assured me my mother could come home. Her only concern was that she take her medication religiously. Mom was afflicted by a strong case of dementia, some confusion, and at times a sense of worthlessness. It was a few days later, once the flat had been thoroughly cleaned, that my mother returned to her residence. And while driving home, she hardly spoke, this coming from a person who always had something to say.

She settled in nicely that day. The following morning, there was a request to go to Barazzetto. It was not to visit anyone there. She simply wanted to bring flowers to her sister who had passed away the previous year. The two had never been close years back, but they had forged a strong bond once my mother visited Udine more often. Apparently, my mom would drive to her small town 2 to 3 times a week, and the sisters spent entire days together with much to chat about. So, it was now on to the cemetery.

Once our mission concluded, I suggested visiting the lovely town of San Daniele. It was not accepted. Mother wanted to go to the nearby coffee shop by the entrance road to Barazzetto. Which is where we enjoyed cappuccino and croissants, and she soon mentioned the owner, the son of old farmers who had gone abroad, worked his butt off, and returned to open the now popular establishment. And quite by chance, the gentleman in question passed by and immediately recognized her. What a spectacle, for the two enjoyed a long happy conversation over family matters, relationships, and even the joy of a successful business.

Whereas all had proceeded very nicely that day, it was not so the following morning. My mother was simply not herself. She appeared terribly frightened, almost slightly paralyzed, and it was apparent something was wrong. I asked her to explain exactly what she felt, and she replied, "I am not right." Her head tilted to the side and her eyes peered intently into the space in front of her. She was not one bit the woman form the previous day. An ambulance arrived rather quickly, and the crew obviously knew her, having been there a few times in the past.

I drove to the hospital in her car. About two hours later, they allowed me to see her. She now appeared quite normal and had regained her old fiery spirit, as she was happily carrying on with me and soon insisted that I demand she be discharged. However, it was early evening before this occurred, and I was reassured by a physician that she was fine. He insinuated that perhaps her illness stemmed from anxiety.

This bizarre situation lasted almost four weeks. It seemed like almost every other day, I brought her to the hospital. The entire day, and often most of the evening, was passed there simply awaiting her discharge. It finally came to an end. My mother was kept overnight, and the following morning transferred to a different building to be visited by a psychiatrist. Upon my arrival, the personnel at the desk informed me of her move, but also that I needed to consult their medical group regarding her situation.

Two very polite doctors spoke to me. They provided what they thought was a possible malady but appeared uncertain. Nevertheless, both strongly advised me to consider placing my mom in a nursing home. She would be under constant care from professionals, enjoy some of the daily activities to keep her busy, and if such accommodations did not work out, she could always return home.

My mother was discharged a week later. In the meantime, I had visited various nursing homes to ensure that the place she might go to provided more than a bedroom for her, and I did hope she would fit in. She soon came home. I eventually mentioned the doctor's proposal, now also mine, and she accepted it without hesitation. There were no questions or concerns as she seemed ready to move on. A few days later, she entered a nursing residence which was only fifteen miles outside Udine.

Our last evening together was not easy for me. It became impossible to fall asleep. Then while twisting and turning in bed for the longest time, my mind was slightly baffled with all that had occurred. A woman so full of life, who had always appeared indestructible, had transformed so quickly into a helpless child-like senior who either had a fine day or a scary one. Just what had happened?

Something entirely different soon began perplexing me. I would have to return to the U.S. once the three months expired. My mother would not see me for some time. Would she feel abandoned, and even wonder about my long absence. Such thoughts were impeding my sleep and agitating me endlessly. Now, who knows exactly when both my mind and body finally collapsed. And it felt as if my resistance to temporarily perish was suddenly pushed off a cliff.

While darkness entails silence, the spirit wanders aimlessly

Gifford was no longer with me. Where could he possibly be? Our hike up the trail had proceeded fine, plus our long walk under those shady trees had been pure bliss. And we had both been talking for the longest time. But he was no longer anywhere, and I was quite lost and had absolutely no clue of my friend's whereabouts.

My feet continued to carry me forward. Suddenly, the sound of rushing water began to manifest itself as I proceeded in its direction. It was a constant swishing of a stream hitting up against rocks now getting louder. It then drummed in me the idea that once near it, my problems would be solved. My friend would be there waiting for me. Then a large path simply came into view.

My eyes took in this long distance stretching far ahead. There was a large stream nearby and something by it. It did not appear to be a person but there was some slight movement about it. And upon getting closer and closer, an image of an animal moving by that water came into view. Its colors were somewhat familiar. As a matter of fact, why there could be no denying it. It was Argo!

Our beautiful dog was there! Yes, that wonderful spirit who had offered us all so much love and spiritual warmth. Seeing him so close had me moving faster and even calling out his name. His superior masculine body stood out. It was our warrior dog, who just like the ultimate fighter fears nothing and believes death just another stage in our passage of time. I was just a few feet away when his head began to turn toward me. It completely shocked me! My father's face now stared at me while the animal's body was no longer visible.

Ted was in a room at a bed and breakfast in Chincoteague. He appeared to be battling some physical ailment, and his expression bore not only pain but a serious look of some incomprehensible puzzle. Just what was taking him down? Soon enough, it became clear his only concern was mostly for me. Then a few abstract messages left his head to enter mine. They spelled out how some evil forces intended to destroy me and nothing could deter them from their mission. Mine was a lost cause.

As these scenes got registered, my eyes adjusted to the darkness in my room. I was now in the apartment in Vicenza which my in-laws had found for me. Although in bed sleeping, all my senses stood on watch and began taking in a vision, a very mysterious one. Someone's shadow was in the flat. His mission was to poison it and consequently me. It was absurd. For strangely enough, he was someone familiar to me from my military years in Caserma Ederle.

He, too, once wore a uniform, that of a carabiniere. We had gotten to know each other some and had shared a few good conversations at his mess hall. At times, our chats were about growing up in the south. He was very proud to be a carabiniere, and his family even more than he. He was now moving toward the entrance door to leave. Mission accomplished. He then took the exams in the folder on the table with him. It would be a clue. One I could not possibly miss—someone had been there. Hopefully, I would grasp my reality.

My father is driving on the right side of the vehicle. I am up front and holding back tears. He is so angry. BUT WHY? For not having challenged him in Peter's car. He wanted me to plead for money and show "a bit of balls." My inability to desire certain things strongly enough to want to fight was deemed disgusting. He would no longer protect me. And yes, my destiny was doomed. For an evil institution, considered patriotic by the masses, would terminate my existence. I began pleading for him to not abandon my cause. It fell on deaf ears. Dad simply put his head down on the steering wheel and fell asleep. The automobile was exiting the highway we were on indicating our journey was finally over.

An immense clear sky engulfs the area around my plane. I am truly alone. But my family's prayer is guiding this suicidal ritual which will give them the honor they deserve. The plane, although hit, continues to descend at great speed. It is almost as if the target is strongly pulling my aircraft toward it. It is inviting me to complete the mission. My body has been grasped by powerful forces keeping me locked in my seat, like a victim, but in truth, I have chosen this mission. It is time to die for the greater good. My eyes now see only the immense object, straight in front of me and only a few yards away. The impact is eminent—my voice pounds out: "BANZAAAIIIIIIIIIIIIII!"

Goodness gracious! What an awful fucking nightmare! And it seemed to drag on forever! Wow, it is still thundering outdoors and pouring down heavily. It is almost as if to make a statement, perhaps there will be no letup for quite some time. Now, had I not previously awoken to a rather puzzling scene where two images resembling me were at odds with each other? It was so bizarre!

Oh well, it is 5:30 a.m. Quite early for sure. I am usually up a bit later, but this is going to be one busy day. My morning walk, which is now a daily ritual, starts at eight. Hopefully, the rain will have ceased by then. And the accountant is coming by later. She has some information regarding the taxes on the villa, as per my request. This afternoon I shall get to the pool, and afterwards I am meeting my friend Roberto.

It seems incredible. Here is someone I encountered by chance. Not only is his English truly perfect, but it seems amazing what a few years in England can accomplish in mastering both language and customs. He encompasses a more expansive and impartial view of the world. One where the possibilities to enhance changes are endless. We plan to meet at a pub called, The Black Stuff, just to watch a football match, and his girlfriend will not join us tonight.

Sometimes during the games, Peter comes to mind. I still miss him tremendously! Especially when recalling some of his craziness, for his playful ways simply filled my world with so much joy. Roberto thinks some mourning pain still lingers in me. My healing has yet to fully process according to him. Oh, I almost forgot to mention it. Gifford recently called. He is coming to visit Italy. I cannot wait to see him. It will be grand getting about with him.

Now, tomorrow is totally dedicated to my mother. She is doing fine and appears happy in the nursing residence outside of Udine. And as soon as she sees me, she always repeats the same mantra, "Giuliano, you are so elegant!" But something in me suspects she sees my father. He being someone who has perhaps never entirely left her mind and heart.

My Aunt Maria once expressed an interesting thought. She felt a sense of pity toward her sister. Knowing she and my father could not get along, therefore, they never enjoyed the nurturing bliss from a healthy and happy family lifestyle. Oh well, I usually share pictures on my phone of her great grandchildren. Ricky has two kids who are Swedish but have Italian names, and Francesco's beautiful daughter is very charming. She finds them all so adorable. By the way, Eric is still single, and we both suspect he will remain so.

Our hour together slips away too quickly. It was not so before the COVID-19 outbreak. My visits were much longer, but we have had to adapt. What can I say? It still seems incredible that my once fiery mother has transformed into a senior sedated by her many years. She mentioned to hopefully making it to 94, just like her mother. I suspect she may go a bit further.

What about me? Life is treating me well. All my past struggles and concerns have vanished as I convince myself a positive turnout is always nearby. My days are serene and at times pass not so brilliantly but very harmoniously. Even my prudish ways have disappeared. It is best to put little value in money, so spending it becomes quite insignificant.

My spirit remains at the center of my existence. It walks alone rather proudly. It knows life is an illusion, but one which we master unknowingly and rather well. A woman once introduced me to Shakespeare. Please allow me to quote:

Our revels are now ended. These our actors,
As I foretold you, were all spirits and
Are melted into air, into thin air:
And, like the baseless fabric of this vision,
The cloud-capp'd towers, the gorgeous palaces,
The solemn temples, the great globe itself,
Yea, all which it inherit, shall dissolve
And, like this insubstantial pageant faded
Leave not a rack behind. We are such stuff
As dreams are made on, and our little life
Is rounded with a sleep.

Last month, Francesco and I spent a most enchanting day together. He knows so little about my past. My growing up in Italy, the streets of the Bronx, those vast oceans whose spirit guided mine, and he was shocked to hear me happily admit that I was born by accident. But isn't it true that sometimes mistakes can be the best things that happen to us? And to the notion of chance, it is imperative to accept the self.

I believe in the art of love. Love who you are, love what you have, love everyone, even those less deserving, for in the long run, a happy heart is better than no heart at all.

Sometimes my personal whims insist that life owes us nothing. It simply guarantees to test us. For all humans struggle in their search for personal validity. Recently, some of my thoughts brought back the memory of a young Japanese woman I was once so madly in love with. During a rather long night in bed, she shared a particular phrase when we took a break. It was Taiki Bansei. I understood it to mean as you age, you get wiser. But someone recently informed me that it means great talents mature late. What can I say? Perhaps I have finally truly arrived!

Well, as you know, I was born by chance. And I am still here to talk about it. And I do hope my words will never reveal the depth of my scars, for it is so easy to wear them well.